EXPLORING
A CHANGING
WORLD

Cover Photo: *Two different ways of showing our world:
an antique map of the Americas made in 1570 and photos of
earth from outer space taken by NASA astronauts.*

Teacher Reviewers

John Paul Bianchi, District Office 8, Bronx, New York

Adrianne Snair-Cantor, Social Studies Chairperson, Weaver High School, Hartford, Connecticut

John Flathmann, Supervisor of Social Studies, West Chester Area School District, West Chester, Pennsylvania

Michael Kohler, Boyton Middle School, Detroit, Michigan

Russell Maruna, Social Studies Supervisor, Cleveland Public Schools, Cleveland, Ohio

Judy Parsons,Coordinator, Social Studies, Columbia Public Schools, Columbia, Missouri

Nicholas Sferrazza, Assistant Supervisor Curriculum/(Retired), Gloucester Township Public Schools, Blackwood, New Jersey

Mark Stewart, Shepard Center, Columbus, Ohio

Jack Bridner, Social Studies Supervisor, Howard County, Maryland

Consultants

Northern America

Glenda Redden, Department of Education for Nova Scotia, Halifax, Nova Scotia

Latin America

Doyle Casteel, Center for Latin American Studies, University of Florida, Gainesville, Florida

The Heart of Eurasia

Elizabeth Talbot, Outreach Coordinator, Russian and East European Center, University of Illinois at Urbana-Champaign, Urbana, Illinois

North Africa and the Middle East

Herbert L. Bodman, Professor of History, University of North Carolina at Chapel Hill, North Carolina

Laurence O. Michalak, Vice Chairman, Center for Middle East Studies, University of California at Berkeley, Berkeley, California

Africa

Louise Crane, Outreach Coordinator, Center for African Studies, University of Illinois at Urbana-Champaign, Urbana, Illinois

The Asian Region

The Asia Society, 725 Park Avenue, New York, New York

Program

Nancy Winters, Graduate School of Geography, Clark University, Worcester, Massachusetts

Chandrika Kaul, Ph.D., Gulliver Academy, Miami, Florida

EXPLORING
A CHANGING
WORLD

Melvin Schwartz • John O'Connor

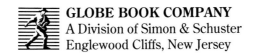

GLOBE BOOK COMPANY
A Division of Simon & Schuster
Englewood Cliffs, New Jersey

Melvin Schwartz

B.S.S. and M.S., The City College of the City University of New York, Ed.D., Teachers College, Columbia University

Dr. Schwartz taught social studies in the New York City school system for many years before being a school principal. Schwartz has authored several other well-known Globe social studies textbooks, including *Exploring American History* and *Exploring the Non-Western World.*

John O'Connor

B.A., St. Francis College M.A., University of Pittsburgh

Mr. O'Connor taught social studies for many years before becoming a principal in the New York City school system. He is widely known for his lectures and articles on reading skills in social studies. Mr. O'Connor coauthored the textbooks *Exploring World History, Exploring American Citizenship,* and *Unlocking Social Studies Skills.* In addition to this book, he has edited *Exploring American History, Exploring the Non-Western World,* and *Exploring United States History.*

Executive Editor: Stephen Lewin
Project Editor: Francie Holder
Editor: Kirsten Richert
Art Director: Nancy Sharkey
Production Manager: Winston Sukhnanand
Marketing Manager: Elmer Ildefonso
Photo Researcher: Jenifer Hixson
Maps: Mapping Specialists, Ltd.
Graphs, Diagrams, and Charts: Keithley Associates Inc.

Printed in the United States of America.
1 2 3 4 5 6 7 8 9 10   96   95   94   93   92

ISBN: 0-835-90479-2

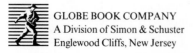

GLOBE BOOK COMPANY
A Division of Simon & Schuster
Englewood Cliffs, New Jersey

Contents

Unit 6 The Heart of Eurasia   316

Unit 7 North Africa and the Middle East   368

Unit 8 Africa   426

Unit 9 The Asian Region   480

World Charts

List of Maps

List of Graphs, Charts, and Diagrams

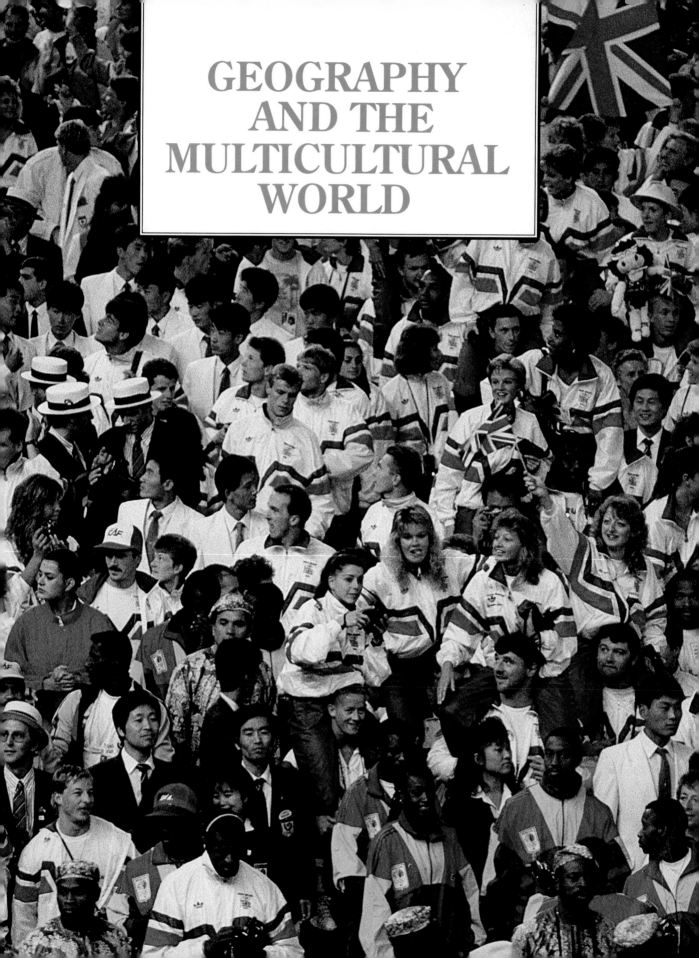

GEOGRAPHY AND THE MULTICULTURAL WORLD

KEY IDEAS

- An understanding of geography is essential for living in a multicultural world.

- Geography is the study of the earth and how people live on the earth.

- The five themes of geography—location, place, human-environment interactions, movement, regions—provide the framework for geographic inquiry.

- Geographers use these themes to learn about relationships on the earth.

- Information collected by geographers is often present on globes and maps.

- Interpreting this information helps geographers learn more about human beings and their environments.

The massing of athletes to celebrate the end of the 1988 Olympic Games is evidence of the great diversity of peoples in our multicultural world.

Chapter 1

Diversity in Our Multicultural World

How does geography help us understand our world?

READING FOR A PURPOSE:
1. What is culture?
2. How do differences in culture enrich our lives?
3. How and why are people of the world interdependent?

1. In the United States, people greet one another by shaking hands. In Thailand, people bow low, their palms pressed together. Some people eat meat, fruits, grains, and vegetables. Some people believe it is wrong to eat the flesh of animals. Some people eat with their hands. Some eat with chopsticks. Some eat with pronged instruments called forks. In some places, people measure wealth by the size of their homes. In other places, wealth is measured by the number of pigs a person owns.

2. All these differences are differences in *culture*. Culture is what people add to the natural world. Everyone has a culture. Culture is learned, but it is not like learning algebra or biology. You begin learning your culture from your family members the minute you are born. You learn to eat certain foods, wear certain clothes, and speak a certain language. You learn appropriate ways to behave. You learn certain beliefs and customs. You learn your culture from family and friends, and perhaps from religious teachers.

3. The study of different cultures is an important part of *geography*. Geographers study places—how they differ from one another and why. Places have distinct natural and human features. Some have cold climates; some have warm or hot climates. Some are mountainous; some are flat. Some have many people crowded together; some have only a few people living far from one another. Geographers study the relationship between people and their environment. They study the human drama played out on earth's natural stage. How do people build their houses? How do they build their cities? How do they farm the land? How do their cultures affect the way they change the land?

4. Geography helps us understand our *multicultural* world, a world made up of many, many cultures. You know that you have a set of unique fingerprints, different from those of any other human being. Different cultures leave different "prints" on the land. Muslim *mosques,* or places of worship, are the unique "prints" of the Islamic world. Each mosque usually has several minarets, or towers. From those towers, *muezzins,* or criers, call Muslims to prayer five times a day. Their melodic calls over loudspeakers fill the air. Some churches in regions with large Christian populations have steeples that pierce the sky. They were originally designed to be the highest structure in any city or town. They were intended to be the structures nearest to God, and to be seen far and wide. These mosques, minarets, churches, and steeples are marks of their cultures.

5. Cultural values, or the beliefs and principles of a culture, affect the way people live. For example, in many cultures in Asia,

In Austria, a church steeple dominates the landscape. What other marks of Western European culture do you see in this picture?

people believe that it is a son's responsibility to care for his parents in later life. Therefore, families tend to be large to guarantee that there will be many sons. Many generations of a family often live together in a single home or compound. Food is shared equally by all, regardless of the earning power of any one person. If the family owns land, family members often work together to make it produce food. Geography helps us examine these differences among cultures and understand why they exist.

6. Different cultures have changed the land in different ways to meet their needs. For

The St. Sophia mosque in Istanbul, Turkey, is a unique mark of Muslim culture.

Nomad yak herders in Lhasa, Tibet, live in portable tents. How is this an example of ways people adapt to their environment?

example, people living in dry climates developed different technologies to adapt to their surroundings. In ancient times, people in what is present-day Iran constructed underground tunnels to channel water from the mountains to drier areas. People in ancient Egypt learned to build dams to control the floodwater of the Nile River and use it for irrigation.

7. Different cultures use resources in different ways. In countries with modern technology, many different kinds of materials

This water carrier in Kassala, Sudan, is returning to a home built with materials that are plentiful and practical in the region. What building materials have people in your community used to build houses?

are available to use in construction. Houses can be made out of any material—wood, brick, or stone. But in countries without many industries or good transportation, people must make their homes out of local materials. In the South Pacific, where the climate is warm, homes are thatched with branches and palm fronds (leaves). In some dry parts of the world—in India or Africa, for example—people use mud mixed with other ingredients to make homes. In western China, people move about often in search of greener pasture land. There they build *yurts,* round homes made of felt wrapped around poles. Yurts can be collapsed and hauled easily.

8. The world is like a great crown filled with countless gems of many colors and shapes. The gems are the many cultures of the world. Each is unique, and adds to the richness of our world. Some countries of the world, such as Japan, are made up of mostly one culture. Other countries mirror the diversity, or variety, of the world's people. They have many cultures within their own borders. The United States is such a country.

9. In the United States, we have great cultural diversity. Many, many culture groups make their home in our country. They came from countries all over the world—Great Britain, Germany, Ireland, Ghana, Poland, Cuba, Korea, China, India, Nigeria, Mexico, Guatemala—to name a few. People from some culture groups traveled or were brought to our country long ago. Others are newcomers. Many people have kept some parts of their original culture. A walk through the neighborhoods of any one of our large cities shows the richness of culture. A Mexican restaurant stands next to a Swedish bakery. Arabic signs appear just down the street from Vietnamese and Spanish signs. Chinese neighborhoods celebrate the Chinese New Year with fantastic parades.

10. The cultural diversity of our own country is a good reason to study geography. In learning about different cultures of the

The neighborhood of Little Haiti in Miami, Florida, is an example of cultural diversity in the United States. The top line of the sign says "Welcome to Little Haiti."

world, we learn a little more about ourselves. We learn to appreciate the richness of our multicultural heritage.

11. Despite the fact that we are a country and a world of great diversity, no culture exists in isolation. Cultures borrow items or ideas from other cultures. Blue jeans are a perfect example. They were originally developed in San Francisco, California, in the mid-1800s. They were worn by miners first. Less than 100 years later, blue jeans are popular all over the globe. They are worn by children and adults, regardless of their occupation. What caused this *cultural diffusion*—the spread of culture from one society to others? Newspapers, television, and magazines showed people in jeans. Travelers wore jeans. Clothing manufacturers used modern transportation systems to sell jeans to people in other countries.

12. Since ancient times, people have borrowed ideas from one another. As the following quotation reveals, our life in the United States today is the result of a long history of cultural diffusion. A man getting dressed in the morning

> "puts on shoes made from skins tanned by a process invented in ancient Egypt.... If it is raining [he] puts on overshoes made of rubber discovered by the Central American Indians and takes an umbrella, invented in southeastern Asia. Upon his head he puts a hat made of felt, a material invented in [Asia]. On his way to breakfast he stops to buy a paper, paying for it with coins, an ancient Lydian invention. At the restaurant... his plate is made of a form of pottery invented in China. His knife is of steel, an alloy [mixture of metals] first made in southern India, his fork a medieval Italian invention.... He begins breakfast with an orange from the eastern Mediterranean...or perhaps a piece of African watermelon.... He goes on to waffles, cakes made by a Scandinavian technique from wheat domesticated in

An offshore oil rig in Malaysia in Southeast Asia. Why do people in one region need to trade with people in other regions?

> Asia Minor. Over these he pours maple syrup, invented by the [Native Americans] of the Eastern woodlands.... While [eating] he reads the news of the day, imprinted in characters invented by the ancient Semites upon a [paper] invented in China by a [printing] process invented in Germany. As he absorbs the [news] of foreign troubles he will...thank a Hebrew [god] in an Indo-European language that he is 100 percent American."

13. With improvements in our transportation and communication systems, these exchanges take place faster and faster.

Products and ideas reach people in the most remote places of the world.

14. Our economy today is a global system. Resources, such as oil and iron, are distributed unevenly. One place might be rich in many resources. Another might be rich in only one. Therefore, the people of the world must trade with one another to meet their needs.

15. Sometimes natural events can dramatize our connections to others. In 1988, a tremendous earthquake reduced northern Armenia to rubble. Whole cities crumbled. Thousands of people were buried alive. Within hours of receiving the news, volunteers from nearly 70 countries came to the rescue. Doctors came, as well as planes loaded with food and medical supplies. The efforts of people from around the world saved lives and helped hundreds of people. Our global systems of economics, transportation, and communication showed we are a planet of one people.

16. Human events, such as wars, can upset global systems. The Persian Gulf War of 1991 is a good example. Iraq and Kuwait were major suppliers of oil to many of the industrialized countries of the world—Japan, the United States, Germany, and Great Britain, for example. When the war started, their oil production stopped. That resulted in fears that there would be shortages of oil.

Drivers in many parts of the world found the price of gasoline had gone up. Then Iraqis set fire to the oil wells in Kuwait. Feeding on vast supplies of oil, the fires burned for many months. They polluted the air and land, puffing out plumes of black, greasy smoke. Economic systems were affected by the war. So were environmental systems, such as the global circulation of air and water.

17. We live in a world where everything and everybody are *interconnected.* No one culture lives in isolation. Our grandparents may have been able to survive knowing very little about the world. But now with information circling the globe in seconds, it is vital that we understand other cultures. It is vital that we understand how the world works—its economic, political, and environmental systems. We are all dependent on one another. An event on one side of the globe can affect lives on the other side.

18. With this interdependence comes responsibility. Understanding how small the world is should help us avoid conflict. We have seen how conflict in faraway cultures affects our lives. By understanding other cultures, we are better able to bridge the gulfs that separate us. Only through cooperation and peace are we able to keep global systems in balance. Studying geography is the first step.

UNDERSTANDING WHAT YOU HAVE READ

1. The main idea of paragraph 1 is
a. that customs in the United States are unique
b. that customs in Thailand are unique
c. that the world is made up of different cultures, each with its unique customs

2. Geography is the study of
a. rocks and minerals
b. people and places, where they are located, and why
c. economics

3. Culture affects the way people live by
a. affecting the number of children people have
b. affecting the kinds of foods people eat and clothes they wear
c. both a. and b.

4. The United States
a. is made up of mainly one culture, English
b. has a two-culture society, English and Spanish
c. is a multicultural society

5. Which of the following is NOT an example of how different cultures have changed the land?

a. Blue jeans are worn around the world.

b. People in ancient Iran constructed tunnels to transport water.

c. Egyptians built dams to control flood water.

6. To make bicycles, the United States uses bauxite from Jamaica and chromite from Turkey. This is an example of

a. cultural diversity

b. cultural diffusion

c. interdependence

DEVELOPING CRITICAL THINKING SKILLS

Drawing Conclusions

1. Which are examples of culture?
   a. a turban
   b. the spicy food of India
   c. a belief in many gods
   d. Pawnee earth lodges
   e. the Polish language
   f. the color of your pencil

2. Which are examples of interdependence?
   a. A volcanic eruption in Mexico affects fishing in Peru.
   b. People from the United States provide Ethiopians with food during a drought.
   c. A family in Brazil grows the food they will need.
   d. Gear shifts made in Japan are added to bicycles in Taiwan.
   e. Mosques are found in Southeast Asia.

WRITING

In this chapter, you learned about culture. You discovered that cultures vary with different groups of people. You also learned that people all over the world are influenced by cultures other than their own. Think about your own life and your own culture. Then, in a paragraph describe three ways you have been affected by cultural diffusion.

Chapter 2

Geography and Its Themes

What is the focus of geography?

READING FOR A PURPOSE:
1. What are two basic questions geographers ask?
2. What are the five basic themes of geography?
3. How are the themes of geography used by geographers?

1. Have you ever had this kind of conversation? You and your friends have decided to get together. Now you have to decide where to meet. "Let's meet at the corner near my building," someone says. You think that's not fair because then you'll have the farthest to go. You offer an alternative nearer to where you live. Your friends reject that idea because then they'll have farther to go. So you suggest meeting in the middle, a central location for everyone, and it's decided.

2. If you have had that kind of conversation, then you have used geography. Geographers use location as the basis of their study. They examine how location affects nature and people. As they look at the world around them, geographers ask two questions: "Where are certain things located?" and "Why are they located where they are?"

3. Once geographers are able to answer these two questions, they are able to solve certain riddles about the earth's surface. For example, have you ever noticed that in summer it's hotter in a city than outside the city? It is not just your imagination. When geographers looked at detailed temperature maps, they realized that air temperatures are higher in cities. "Why?" they wondered. As they began to answer the question, they discovered a number of reasons.

4. In cities, the land is covered. Streets and parking lots are paved, and buildings cover much of the rest of the land. Concrete and pavement hold in heat at night; soil does not hold the heat as long. In cities when it rains, water runs off into sewers. Outside the cities when it rains, water does not run off. It has a chance to *evaporate,* or dry. Evaporation cools the air. Also, cities make heat. Heat comes from the heating systems of buildings and factories, and from cars. Even human bodies generate heat. All these factors make cities warmer than other areas. Geographers call cities "urban heat islands." By answering the "where" and "why" questions, geographers were able to make this discovery.

5. Geographers are curious about places. As a science writer once wrote, "Who has not spread out a map on the table and felt its promise of places to go and things to see and do? Look at these names, will you—Oodnadatta, Ilbunga, Rumbalara, Bundooma, Rodinga, Alice Springs—you can almost see the lonely cattle stations, the dingoes and kangaroos...here they are on the map, inviting dreams, speculations, perhaps exploration."

6. All places on earth are unique. They vary in their *natural features,* the things nature provides, such as lakes and mountains. They vary in their *cultural features,* the things people add to the land, such as cities and irrigation systems. Geographers study these differences and draw conclusions about why they exist. Why are some places mountainous and others flat? Why do some places have many people and others only a few?

The location of the house shown in this photograph is Bamiyan Valley in Afghanistan. Can you consult a map and give the absolute location of Afghanistan using a global grid system?

7. Geographers answer the "where" and "why" questions using five basic themes. Just as a doctor uses certain instruments to analyze the human body, geographers use the five themes as tools to analyze particular places. Short words and phrases have been developed to identify the five themes. They are *location, place, interaction (between people and their environment), movement,* and *regions.* Generally, the first two themes—location and place—answer the "where" question. The other themes—interaction, movement, and regions—answer the "why" question.

8. Location To study a place, geographers begin by finding out where it is located. Every place on earth has its own location. A place's location can be expressed in two ways, absolute and relative. *Absolute location* is an exact, precise spot on the earth. The absolute location of your home might be expressed as your address.

9. Another way to express the absolute location of your home is by using a *global grid system.* This system is a set of imaginary lines that circles the globe. Lines of *latitude,* called *parallels,* circle the globe east and west. Parallels do not intersect, but instead stay the same distance apart as they circle the earth. The parallel that circles the middle of the globe halfway between the North and South Poles is called the *Equator.* Parallels are used to measure distance north and south of the Equator. The Equator is 0 degrees latitude. North America is located roughly between 10 and 70 degrees north latitude.

10. Lines of *longitude,* called *meridians,* circle the globe north and south. Unlike parallels, these lines intersect at the North and South poles. Meridians are used to measure distance east and west of the *Prime Meridian.* The Prime Meridian is 0 degrees and is located at Greenwich, England. Like the left end of a ruler, it is the place where measurement begins.

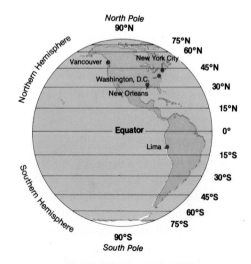

Latitude Lines (Parallels)

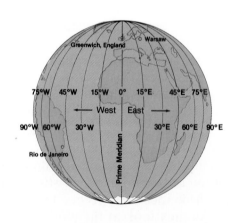

Longitude Lines (Meridians)

11. The absolute location of any place on earth can be expressed using measurements of latitude and longitude. For example, the absolute location of New York City is 40° N, 74° W. It is 40 degrees north of the Equator and 74 degrees west of the Prime Meridian. Navigators on ships and planes use this grid system to mark their locations. Knowing the absolute location of a place can tell you something about it. For example, places with low latitudes, near the Equator, tend to be hot. Places with high latitudes, near the poles, are cold.

12. Geographers use the global system to refer to location in another way. Notice how the Equator divides the earth into two halves. These are called *hemispheres*. The hemisphere north of the Equator is called the *Northern Hemisphere*. The hemisphere south of the Equator is called the *Southern Hemisphere*. The Prime Meridian divides the earth into an *Eastern Hemisphere* and a *Western Hemisphere*. Geographers often use these terms when referring to different parts of the world.

13. A place can also be described in terms of its relative location. *Relative location* is the location of a place in relation to other places. If a man said, "I live in Coral Gables," you wouldn't have much information about the place. But if he said, "I live near Miami, Florida," you would know a great deal more. You would know it is on the southeastern coast of Florida and near the Atlantic Ocean. You might even guess that shipping is a big industry there.

14. Place The theme of place is used to describe a location's natural and cultural features. When you visit a place, you might describe its snow-capped mountains, its white-sand beaches, or its crystal-clear lakes. These are its *natural features*. You might also describe its *cultural features*. These are the parts of the landscape that were added by people. You might describe Chinese or Puerto Rican neighborhoods in terms of the foods for sale, the languages on signs, the architecture of

The Hemispheres

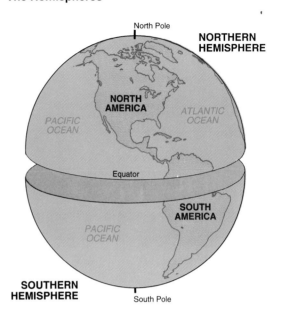

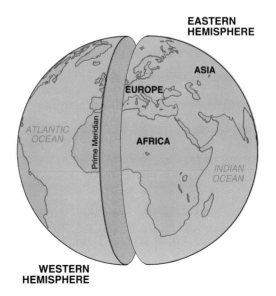

the buildings. When you know something about the natural and cultural features of a place, you know a little about what makes that place unique.

In Indonesia, Bali, farmers work in the rice terraces. What are the advantages and disadvantages of growing crops in terraced fields? What changes were made in the environment to create terraces?

15. Interaction The theme of *interaction* is used to understand the relationship between people and their environment. Each place on earth may be described in terms of its advantages or disadvantages for the people who live there. Usually those places that have advantages have large populations. These places may be near sources of water, because people need water to survive. They may be relatively flat, because it is easier to grow food and build homes on flat land. Usually, few people live where it is more difficult to survive. Few people live in deserts where water is scarce, but if they do live in desert areas, they tend to live near sources of water—along rivers, for example.

16. However, people are problem-solvers. Even if the environment is not ideal for survival, people are sometimes able to change it. They build dams across rivers to trap much-needed water. That is one of the changes people made in the southwestern part of the United States. Los Angeles is located in a desert. If water were not brought in from faraway rivers and lakes, the population of Los Angeles could never have grown as large as it is today.

17. As you study a place, you can ask various questions related to the theme of interaction: "What are its advantages for people?," "What are its disadvantages?," "How have people changed the environment?" You also must ask, "What are the consequences of these changes?" Sometimes the changes people make harm the environment. As Los Angeles draws water from the surrounding areas, farms are sometimes left without water for irrigation. Los Angeles's growing population is sandwiched between mountains. This has created air pollution because winds cannot blow away the smog. Using the theme of interaction will help you understand the relationship between people and their environment at a particular place.

18. Movement The theme of *movement* is used to understand the relationship between places. As you study a particular place, you might ask the following question: "How do people, products, and ideas move from this place to that place?" Use the theme of movement as you think about your own country. Our population is made up largely of people whose roots are in other countries. People came to the United States from all over the world. Some were brought by force. Sometimes wars and hardships caused them to leave their homelands. Others were drawn to the United States because of the freedoms and opportunities it offered. It was not only people that moved. Ideas moved, too. When people move from one country to another, they take their cultural "baggage" along with them. As people came, different beliefs and customs came with them.

19. Products move, too. Remember the blue jeans example we discussed on page 6. Products move because people in one place want something they don't have. When Chinese people began moving to the United States, they still wanted many of the foods they liked in China or Hong Kong. So, food manufacturers in Asia began sending certain Chinese food products to the United States. They found that they had a market in the United States because of the large Chinese population here. Soon other people discovered and enjoyed Chinese foods.

20. When people, ideas, and products move from one place to other places, the cultural landscape changes. The theme of movement helps you understand those changes. You would use the theme of movement when studying a place like Singapore. It is a very small country. However, it has a fine harbor and good location on shipping routes and near other ports in Asia. It was once a place with a traditional way of life. Homes there were modest, single-storied structures. Now skyscrapers mark the skyline. Singapore has become one of the world's busiest trading cities.

21. **Regions** The theme of *regions* is used as a base for making comparisons. A region is a part of the world that has cultural or natural characteristics different from other places. Maps are the best way to show regions. A land form map could show mountainous regions or regions of low plains (relatively flat land). An agricultural map could show cotton-growing regions or dairy farm regions. A religions map could show Christian regions or Buddhist regions. A single place might be part of many

Boats crowd Hong Kong harbor. Using the theme of movement as a guide, what can you guess about Hong Kong?

different regions. For example, Florida might be part of a plains region. It also might be called a beef cattle region, a tourist region, and a hot climate region.

22. When you think about the "where" and "why" questions, the theme of regions can help organize your thinking. For example, you know that the United States is made up of many culture groups. If you were to look at a culture regions map of the United States, you would see that specific culture groups tend to live in certain places. The majority of Spanish-speaking people lives in the southern part of the United States. Why? Most moved here from Latin America, a region to the south. If you studied a large country like the United States, all the places and facts would blend together in your mind. If you studied its regions, you would have mental "categories" in which to store the facts you learned.

23. The five themes of geography are tools for you to use to analyze information about the world. You need not think about each

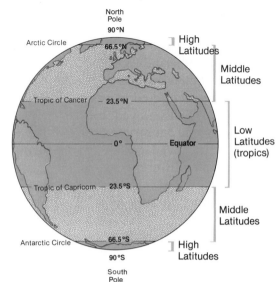

The Low, Middle, and High Latitudes

theme every time you read about a new country. Simply consider those themes that will help you organize your thinking. How do we know which ones apply? Apply the ones that help you discover answers.

UNDERSTANDING WHAT YOU HAVE READ

Finding the Main Idea

1. The two questions geographers ask when studying a place are

a. who and when
b. what and where
c. where and why

2. To find out the distance of a place from the equator, you would use

a. parallels
b. meridians
c. the prime meridian

3. To find the relative location of a place, you would

a. measure from the prime meridian
b. look at the place in terms of other places near it
c. find out what regions it is a part of

4. You would use the theme of place when you want to

a. describe its population
b. list its latitude and longitude
c. find out its trading partners

5. Building the Panama Canal is an example of

a. interaction

b. a region

c. absolute location

6. You would probably use the theme of regions when you study

a. a tiny country

b. a trade between countries

c. a large country

DEVELOPING CRITICAL THINKING SKILLS

Drawing Conclusions

In your notebook, tell which of the five themes you would use to study the following countries. Explain your reasoning. You may choose more than one theme per country.

1. Egypt: a dry desert country where people have used the Nile River to irrigate the land
2. Netherlands: a small country, busy in shipping, where people have added land by draining parts of the North Sea
3. Brazil: a country rich in resources, where people are cutting acres of rain forest per day
4. Hong Kong: a tiny country, famous for its harbor, worldwide trade, and relationship to China
5. India: a country with different culture groups and environments
6. Canada: a country of vast resources where most people tend to live within 100 miles of the U.S. border
7. Israel: a small Jewish country surrounded by Arab countries, which has succeeded in making the desert bloom
8. Indonesia: a heavily populated island country, where people farm the fertile volcanic soil and earn income from the export of oil
9. China: a large country with many different culture groups, climates, and land forms
10. Japan: a country off the east coast of Asia, small in area but noted for the export of manufactured goods, made up mostly of one culture group

Chapter 3

The Tools of Geography

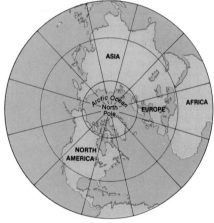

How do maps represent the earth?

READING FOR A PURPOSE:
1. How do geographers collect information about the earth?
2. How is information about the earth shown on globes and maps?
3. What are the necessary parts of a map and how are they used?

1. A journalist who accompanied a group of mapmakers on a mapping trip wrote: "One hot afternoon in a June not long ago, our helicopter circled the stark pinnacle [peak] of Dana Butte. We found a landing place below the pinnacle and eased down.... We stepped out.... Bending forward, under the burden of our gear, we felt the slope steepen.... Rocks gave way,...falling out of sight into the chasm [canyon] below...so much sky below. A shuddering sight. Better not to think about it. We anchored our feet and hefted [lifted] the gear over the top. Then, we reached the high ground where we had a job to do, the establishment of a mapping station. For we had come to measure and to map the Grand Canyon of the Colorado.... We could see and

be seen from all directions.... Here we could make more measurements needed to give the map its basic frame of reference, its mathematical skeleton...."

2. This adventure helped geographers gain information about the Grand Canyon. Geographers use information from many sources. Some information is gathered by observing the earth itself. The mapping expedition described here took place in the 1970s. The goal was to map an area that had never been mapped in exact detail. At that time, mapping was changing. Before, it had been done mostly in the field. Mapmakers had to scramble down ledges and up cliffs to get to the best viewing points. They had to survey points on the land using star sightings and measurements of latitude and longitude.

3. Today much of the field work has been replaced. Now cameras in airplanes and computers on satellites are the "observers" of earth. Satellites send electronic data, which is used to make pictures of the earth's surface. The pictures can be color-coded to highlight features such as cropland or forestland, cities, forest fires, even pollution. This method of gathering data by satellite is called *remote sensing*. It is the most accurate method for observing earth. Satellite pictures of the Amazon River in Brazil, for example, revealed that the branches of the river are very different from those shown on the most recent maps. Islands exist that do not appear on maps. Small villages and towns were located in the wrong places on some maps. As remote sensing becomes even more refined, mapmakers may not need to climb high and dangerous canyon walls ever again.

4. Much of the information that geographers use is information about people. Most countries conduct a *census* every ten years. A census is a population count. In our country, questionnaires are sent to every household. The census takes a count of people in the country, in cities, and in towns. The questionnaire asks what languages people speak, their occupations, their religions, their incomes, their types of homes, and how many children they have, among other information.

5. Once all the information—whether it is from observations of the land, from photographs taken in space, or from people—has been gathered, geographers must make use of it. They must organize it into a form they can understand and study. The geographer's best tools for organizing data about the earth are maps. By using maps, people can see information about the earth in a simple, visual way.

6. A globe is the best "map" of the earth. A globe is round, so it shows the earth almost as it is. (The earth really is slightly pear-shaped). It is the only map that shows the correct distances and sizes and shapes of the land and water areas on earth. But a globe has some disadvantages. You can't fold it up and put it in your pocket. You can't keep it in the glove compartment of your car. You also can't see the whole earth at one time.

7. Therefore, mapmakers had to represent the earth on flat, paper maps. But flat maps are tricky. The next time you eat an orange, cut the peel off carefully and try flattening it out. You will find that it can't be done without ripping the peel in several places. Mapmakers

have wrestled with the same problem as they tried to show the round earth on flat paper. The earth cannot be shown on a flat surface without some *distortion,* or change in the accuracy of its shapes and distances. In making any flat map, the mapmaker decides the purpose of the map, then designs the most accurate map to fit the purpose. Different versions of maps are referred to as *map projections.*

8. Some maps show the true shapes of land masses. But these maps do not show true distances and sizes. These are called *conformal* maps because the shapes of the land conform to those on a globe. The Mercator projection below is an example of this kind of map. Compare the Mercator map to a globe. You can see that the land masses look reasonably accurate near the Equator. Now look at Greenland on both the map and the globe. Greenland looks huge on the Mercator projection. You could conclude that on these kinds of maps, distortion is greatest nearest the North and South Poles.

9. Some maps show the land and water areas in true size. But land shapes are inaccurate. These are called *equal-area* maps. Look at the maps in the Atlas at the back of

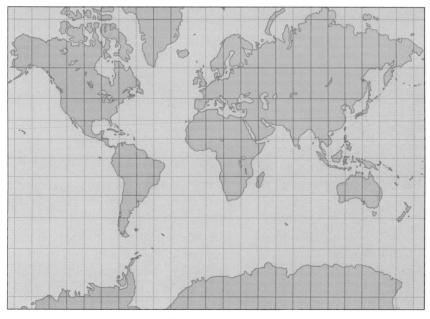

Mercator Projection

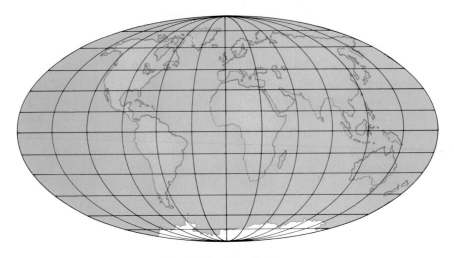

Equal-Area Projection

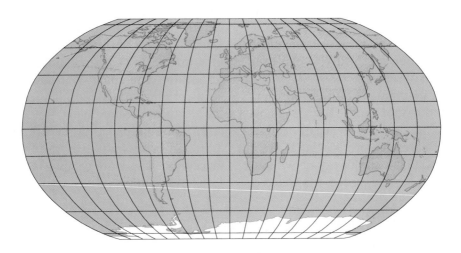

Robinson Projection

this book. They are all equal-area maps. Compare the land masses to those on a globe. You will notice that the southern "tail" of South America seems to be twisted. Australia looks like it's going to fall off the page. North America appears to be leaning toward Europe. These are the distortions that occur on an equal-area map.

10. One way to help correct the distortion of an equal-area map is to interrupt the oceans. See the map with the broken edges. Now the land masses are shown correctly, but the oceans are distorted.

11. You can now understand the challenges that mapmakers must meet as they try to represent the round earth on flat maps. It is not necessary to memorize all the different map projections shown on these pages. It is important, though, to realize that any flat map you use will have some distortion. The distortion may be in sizes, shapes, or distances. Maps of the world will have more

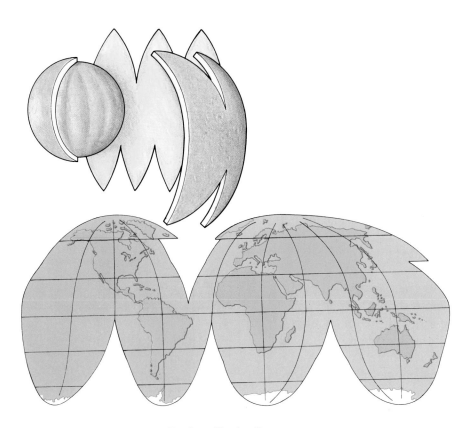

Broken Projection

distortion than maps of smaller areas, such as the state of Illinois.

12. Geographers use maps to show different kinds of information. Each one usually shows a single topic. Suppose geographers wanted to show the major culture groups of the world. All other information about the surface of the earth would be omitted. The maps would show no land forms, no symbols for population, and no climate regions. This is what makes maps so simple and easy to use.

13. *Physical maps* show only the shape of the earth's natural surface. There are many kinds of physical maps. They may be elevation maps that show the height of the land above sea level. They may be landform maps that show mountains, hills, plains, and plateaus in different colors. Precipitation maps show the amount of rain or snow that falls in different places. Climate maps show the *climates*—the

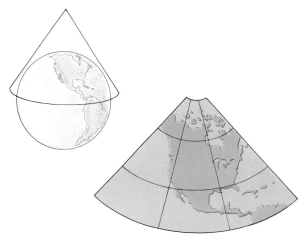

Lambert Projection

weather over long periods of time—of different places. Product maps show the major products made in different places. Population maps show where people live. Political maps

19

show the boundaries between different countries. Often political maps also show major cities.

14. No matter what the topic is, all the features on a map are shown as *symbols.* Symbols are colors, marks, or pictures that stand for real things. For example, on most maps the symbol for water is the color blue. Sometimes deserts are shown as tan with black dots scattered throughout. Cities are shown as dots. The symbol for a capital city might be a circle with a star in it. Boundaries between countries are shown with lines. Many countries are divided into smaller areas called states or provinces. These boundaries are shown differently, perhaps as broken lines.

15. Good maps should have four elements: a title, a map key, a direction symbol, and a scale of distance. The title tells you what the map is about. The map key is the key for unlocking the meaning of the symbols used on the map. It tells you what the symbols mean. The direction symbol shows where the directions "north, south, east, and west" are located. North means toward the North Pole. South means toward the South Pole. As you face north, south is always behind you. East is always to your right. West is always to your left. On most maps, north is at the top of the map, though there is no rule that north must be at the top. It depends on the type of map. On a polar projection for example, north is in the middle. Sometimes the direction symbol will be no more than an arrow pointing toward the North Pole. Often it "rides" a line of longitude. Once you know where north is, you know where all the other directions are located. The scale of distance in a legend helps to convert the space on a map to actual distance.

16. Obviously, maps cannot show the actual size of a place on earth. It would be impossible to bring such a map into your home or classroom. Even a map that is made to be 1/100 of the size of a country would be far too large to handle. It would cover as much room as a large city. For a map to be small enough to

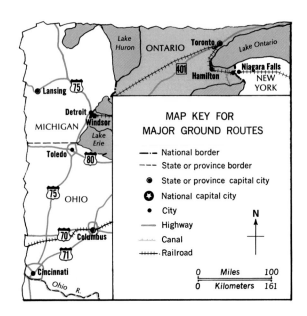

use, it must be drawn to *scale.* That means that a section of the earth is copied exactly, but the copy is much, much smaller.

17. To understand how scale works, try this activity. On a separate sheet of paper, draw a square, the sides of which are six inches long. On another sheet of paper, draw a square with each side only one inch long. You have just demonstrated scale. The small square is the scale drawing of the large square. One inch on the small square equals six inches on the big square. Now look at the two maps on page 21. They both show the city of Miami. One map shows only Miami. The other map shows the state of Florida, with the city of Miami marked on it. These maps are drawn at different scales. On the map of Florida, one inch stands for 100 miles. On the map where only Miami is shown, one inch equals five miles.

18. You can use the scale to measure distance on the map. Try it using the map of Miami. Lay the edge of a piece of paper along the scale. Make two marks where the scale begins and ends. Now line up one of the marks on your paper with any point on the map. From the first mark to the second mark shows five miles on the map. You can calculate longer distances by marking the distance on your sheet of paper, then marking off five-mile

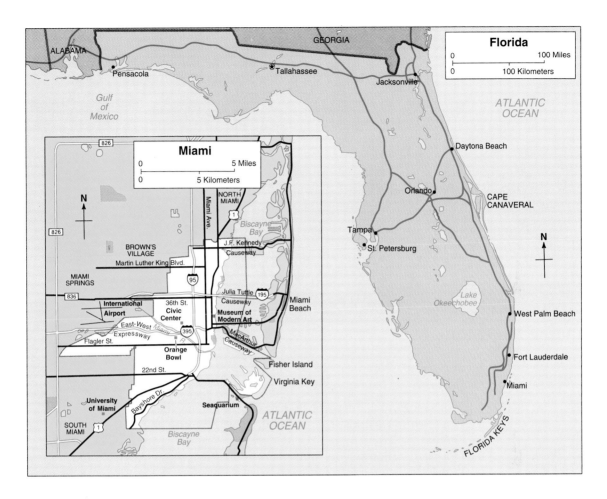

sections. Multiply the number of lengths of the scale times the miles on the scale.

19. As you can see, each type of map has its good and bad points. However, people will always need maps, because we cannot study or travel without them. When you travel by car, you need a road map. You may gave a large map showing a section of North America. Or you may have a state or city map. In the subways of our large cities, you must look at maps to find your stations. At sea, a ship's captain must use a map to plot the ship's course. Maps are used on planes and in the armed forces. They are a necessary part of our lives. By simplifying information about the earth, maps make the job of exploring our changing world much easier.

UNDERSTANDING WHAT YOU HAVE READ

1. Today, the information used for maps is gathered by
a. surveying the land and star sightings
b. star sightings and census taking
c. remote sensing and census taking

2. Flat maps of the world are always inaccurate because
a. they are so small compared to earth
b. parts of the earth are very mountainous
c. the earth is round

3. Globes are the best "maps" of earth, but their disadvantage in mapping is that

a. all parts of the earth are not shown at the same time
b. they distort land shapes
c. they do not show distance accurately

4. The maps that have the greatest distortion are

a. world maps
b. city maps
c. physical maps

5. The four elements of a good map are

a. symbols, title, colors, direction symbol
b. title, map key, direction symbol, scale of distance
c. symbols, map key, scale of distance, map projection

6. Maps are always drawn to scale because

a. they cannot be as big as the area they are representing
b. the continents are different sizes
c. we use both miles and kilometers

DEVELOPING IDEAS AND SKILLS

Building Map Skills

Study the map of the United States and Canada. Then write your answers on a separate sheet of paper.

1. Write a map title and design a map key for the map below.
2. What two states are not shown on this map? Why do you think they are omitted?
3. Draw a direction symbol. Tell where you think it should be placed on the map.
4. Which city is farther from Los Angeles, Chicago or Atlanta?

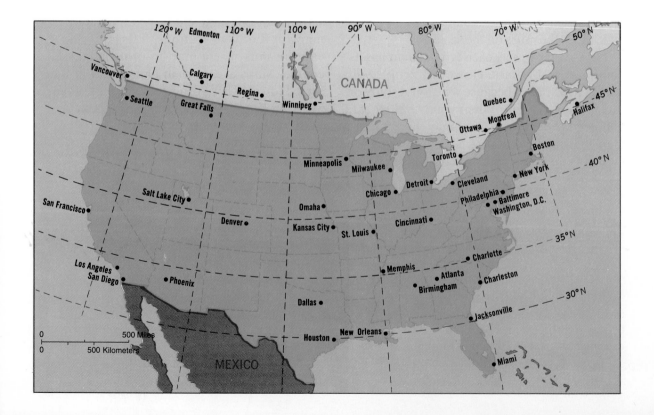

Reading a Tourist Map

People need different kinds of information about places. As a result, there are different kinds of maps: land form, climate, political, land-use, and so on. Another type of information people may need is tourist information. A tourist map would be helpful to someone visiting a new place. This type of map would show all of the historic places and camping sites, parks, beaches, mountains, lakes, resorts, and other places to visit. It would help people to locate places of special interest.

Below is a tourist map of New Zealand. Look at the map key. The map key helps you to read the map. The symbols stand for certain things. If you want to find a place to hike, what symbol would you look for? What symbol would you look for if you wanted to go skiing? Now find this symbol on the map.

1. In what city in New Zealand would you probably arrive by plane?
2. What symbol on the map shows scenic areas?
3. What tourist attraction is located near Rotorua on North Island?
4. What city would you visit to see New Zealand's Parliament?
5. Where would you go to both fish and ski?

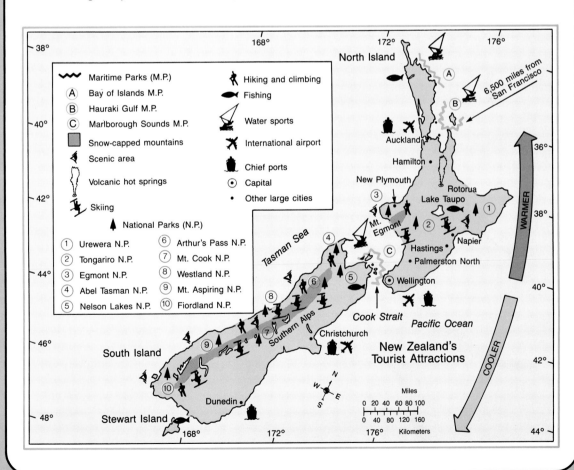

UNIT▾ONE

THE
EARTH

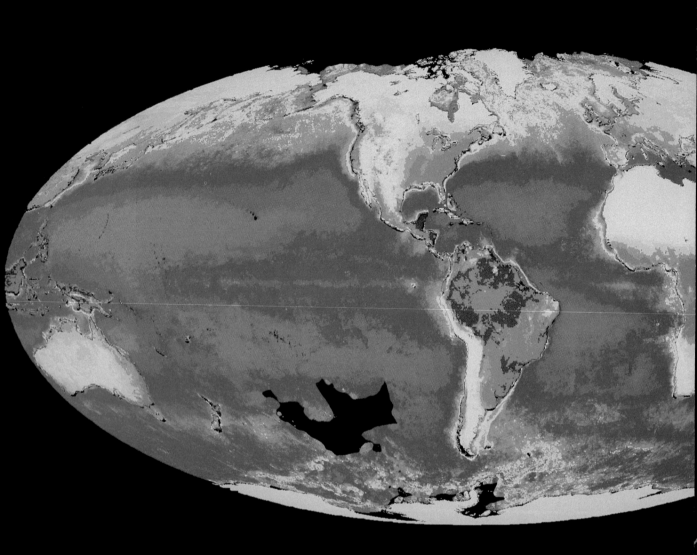

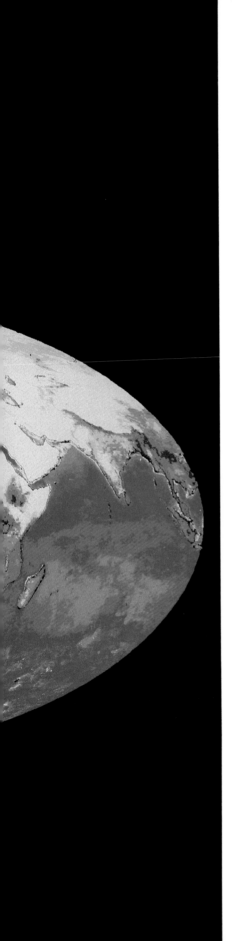

KEY IDEAS

- Life on earth is ruled by three great convection systems: plate tectonics, wind and precipitation, and ocean currents.

- Earth's land forms are shaped by these three systems that build up and wear down the earth's crust.

- Temperature, winds, and precipitation are elements of climate.

- Ocean currents also affect climate.

- Climates and vegetation vary, and human beings have adapted to different climates.

- Two types of energy are important to human beings: renewable and limited.

Hundreds of satellite pictures create this image of earth's vegetation. The dark greens are areas of densest land vegetation. The red areas show plankton growth in oceans.

Chapter 1

Earth's Land and Water

How is the land continually changing?

READING FOR A PURPOSE:
1. What are the earth's four main kinds of land forms?
2. How are land forms affected by the forces that build up the earth?
3. How are land forms affected by the forces that wear down the earth?

1. "It all started," Maria Rivera said, "with a shower of ash about 6:00 last night. Around 11:00 at night, the ash rain increased and the whole world began to scream. I woke my husband, grabbed my baby daughter, and raced into the street with them." That was the night of November 13, 1985, when a snow-covered volcano near Bogotá (boh-guh-TAH), Colombia, exploded. It shot fire and ash into the air. Floods of water and mud swept through the surrounding valleys of the Andes Mountains. Mud buried most of the town of Armero. Government officials said that 23,000 people were killed. Maria Rivera and her husband Edeliberto were spared. "I saw many of my neighbors buried under a wall of

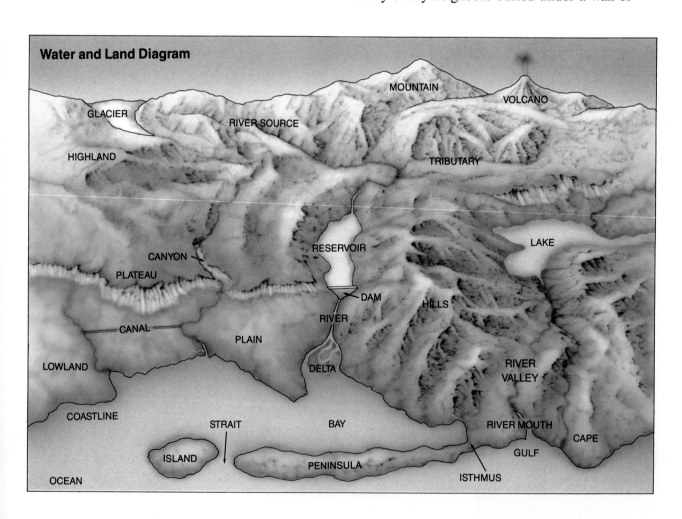

Water and Land Diagram

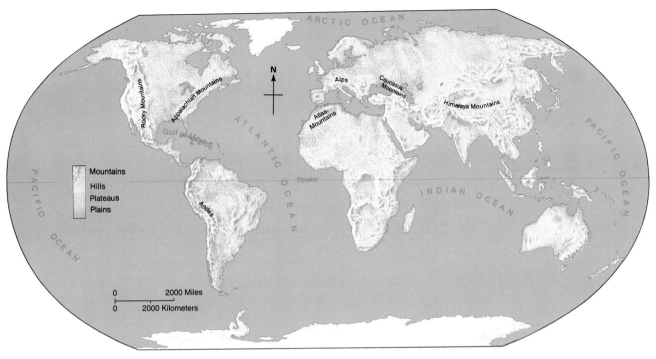

The Lands and Waters of the Earth

mud. It dragged houses, cattle, tree stumps, and giant rocks. There was no time to do anything," Edeliberto said sadly. "The church, the school, the theatre—all were buried."

2. Although such a destructive eruption is rare, volcanic eruptions give us quick looks into the interior of the earth. They show us that powerful forces are shaping and reshaping the earth. They help us discover what the earth is made of. They also teach us how the surface of the earth is continually changing.

3. About 75 percent of the earth's surface is covered by water. Only 25 percent of the earth's surface is land. There are four main kinds of land forms on earth—mountains, hills, plateaus, and plains. *Mountains* are highest, some of them soaring as high as six miles above sea level. *Hills* are lower and more rounded. *Plateaus* rise sharply above the land that surrounds them. Because they tend to be level on top, they are also called tablelands. *Plains* are areas of low, flat land. They are sometimes called lowlands. As you read in the Introduction, plains support most of the world's people. These four kinds of land forms

have been created by the forces that build up and wear down the earth. As the centuries creep by, the land continues to be affected by these forces.

4. As geographers studied world maps of land form regions, they asked the "where" and "why" questions that you read about in the introductory unit. They realized some land forms that are located great distances apart seemed to be related. For example, if you look at the physical map above, you can see that a great chain of mountains seems to run almost continuously along the Pacific coast of North and South America. Another chain seems to extend from southern Europe eastward through Asia. Geographers wondered why.

5. The answer is a fascinating one. A century ago, a German scientist named Alfred Wegener announced a new idea. He believed evidence suggested that about 200 million years ago all the continents were once joined together in a great continent he named Pangaea (pan-JEE-uh). (The name is Greek in origin. *Pan* means "all" and *gaea* means "earth.") He observed that the eastern coast-

27

Pangaea 200 Million Years Ago

135 Million Years Ago

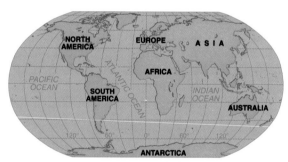

The World Today

oceans. By drilling samples of rock from the ocean floor, scientists realized there was a pattern. Rock at the center of the ridges was much younger than that at the edges. In fact, samples that were taken on either side of the ridge grew progressively older. This led scientists to reason that new rock was being created at the center of the ridge. As new rock formed, it pushed older rock out to either side.

7. Geographers realized that the crust of the earth is broken into huge pieces they called *plates.* We now know that the plates are not anchored, but instead move slowly. Wegener was correct: the continents ride on the giant plates like packages on a conveyor belt. What causes this movement? The answer lies in the center of the earth. The outer "skin" of the earth is called the *crust.* It is very thin. Under continents, it is about 25 miles (40 kilometers) thick. Under oceans, it is only about 5 miles (8 kilometers) thick. Beneath the crust is the *mantle,* a thick layer of very hot rock. It is so hot that it is in a liquid state. *Convection* currents deep within the mantle fuel the movement of plates. Convection is the transfer of heat from one place to another. As you may know, hot air rises. As it rises, it cools. As it cools, it begins to sink, and the process begins again. The hot liquid rock in the mantle also moves in a circular motion. As the currents move beneath the plates, the plates move too. You can see this on the chart on page 29.

8. Look at the map of plate boundaries. As you can see from the arrows, some plates are moving away from each other. If you live in New York City, your home is an inch or two farther from Europe than it was last year. As the plates move apart, hot liquid rock seeps out through cracks in the crust. This material cools and builds up over time, forming ridges in the ocean floor. Find these ocean ridges on the map. They mark the boundaries between plates. The country of Iceland was formed by such a process.

9. In some places, the plates are pushing against one another. As this happens, one

line of Africa seemed to fit together. Studying South America and Africa, Wegener found that the *fossils,* the hardened remains of plants and animals from prehistoric periods, of each continent matched the other. Wegener reasoned some tremendous force caused Pangaea to break apart into the continents we know today. Since that time, the continents have continued to move. He called his bold new idea the *continental drift theory.*

6. It was not until 100 years later that proof finally came. In the 1960s, scientists began to map the sea floor. They discovered there were mid-ocean ridges in the Atlantic and Pacific

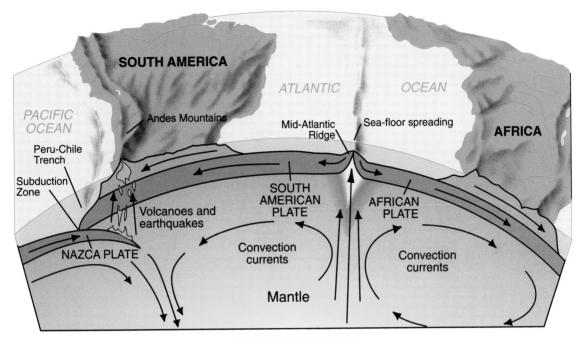

PLATE MOVEMENT

plate is forced under the edge of the other. As the plate sinks into the mantle, a deep trench forms. Tremendous pressure builds up, generating great heat. The heat melts the crust. When the hot melted rock breaks through the surface, a volcano is born. Locate the trenches on the map. You will notice that these are where most volcanoes and volcanic mountains form. Earthquakes occur at plate boundaries too. They are the result of energy released as the giant plates push and scrape one another.

10. Many mountains are not volcanic, but are formed by the movements of plates. Take a sheet of paper. Place your hands on either side of the paper. Your hands represent two different plates. Slowly push your hands toward each other. What happens? A large bulge is created in your paper. That is what happens to the earth's crust as two plates push against one another. The Himalayas, the highest mountains in the world, the Andes, Alps, and Rockies, all were created by this process called *folding*.

11. Now compare the physical map showing land forms of the world with the plate boundary map. What do you notice about the location of mountains in relation to the location of plate boundaries? They align. In fact, because the plates continue to move, mountains continue to grow. The Himalayas are pushed up an inch or two every year. As geographers discovered, the movement of plates is the force that builds six-mile mountains and fire-spewing volcanoes.

12. While the forces that build up the earth continue, other forces are at work that wear the earth down. These forces are called weathering and erosion. *Weathering* is the breaking down of rock into pieces. Wind and rain are two agents of weathering. Like a sandblaster, they bombard land forms, breaking off tiny bits and pieces. Hills and low, rounded mountains are evidence of their handiwork. The Appalachian Mountains used to be as lofty as the Rockies. But wind and rain blasted away at their sharp peaks for thousands of years. Now they are rounded and much lower than their younger cousins to the west.

13. Ice can do similar damage. When water freezes, it expands. So as rain trickles into tiny

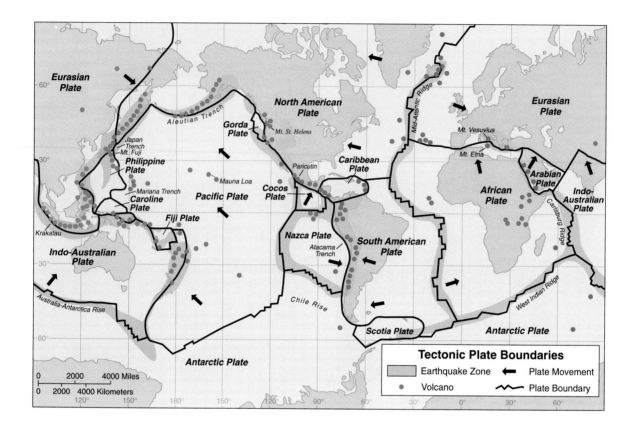

Tectonic Plate Boundaries

| | Earthquake Zone | ← | Plate Movement |
| • | Volcano | ∿ | Plate Boundary |

cracks in rock and freezes, it splits the rock. New cracks form, and new pieces of rock break off. If you've ever visited a cemetery, you have seen evidence of weathering. The names chiseled in older gravestones are smooth and difficult to read. Their sharp edges have been gradually worn away by the elements.

14. Once the tiny grains of rock have been loosened from land forms, they are carried away to new locations. This process of moving the pieces is called *erosion.* The agents of erosion are the same as weathering: wind, water, and ice.

15. As weathering chips away at earth's mountains and erosion rearranges the pieces, new land forms are created in the process. As the wind howls, it picks up tiny grains of sand that once were rock. Only when the wind dies down or hits a solid surface are the grains *deposited*, or laid down, in a new location. Blown up against the Rocky Mountains, a

huge collection of sand dunes was created in this way in southern Colorado.

16. Water is like a highway system for transporting *sediment* (fine grains of sand and soil). Streams begin their journeys high in the snow fields of mountain peaks. As they pick their way down slopes, they join other streams to make rivers. As water flows, it picks up sediment from the stream bed. The faster the water, the more sediment it carries.

17. Water creates new land forms. In the spring when snow melts in the mountains, streams swell. Where the slope gets less steep, rivers flow over their beds. The waters begin to slow. Much of their sediment is deposited, or dropped outside the river's banks. Over time, this causes the formation of a *floodplain.* As you know, a plain is a broad expanse of flat land. If you look at the physical map showing land forms of the world on page 27, you will see that the largest plains in the world lie in the paths of major rivers. Find the Mississippi

River. It, and the rivers flowing into it, created a great fertile floodplain. Floodplains contain the world's richest soil, and are the world's richest agricultural regions.

18. Rivers form another kind of land form. At the mouth of rivers, the place where they enter large bodies of water, rivers drop their loads of sediment. Eventually the sediment builds up until it forms a *delta,* a fan-shaped section of new land. There is so much sediment dropped at the mouth of the Amazon that it can be seen for miles out in the Atlantic Ocean. The delta at the mouth of the

The result of thousands of years of erosion and weathering are these giant sand dunes located in southern Colorado.

The floodplain of the Ganges River frequently overflows in the rainy season, with terrible loss of life in one of the world's most densely populated regions.

Mississippi is so vast that it has changed the river's course.

19. Ice is a sculptor of new land forms, too. Thousands of years ago, much of the earth's surface was covered by ice. Then the temperature warmed, and the ice retreated. Scientists believe there were as many as four ice ages. As the ice advanced and retreated, it moved rocks and soil along with it. Today, many low hills in the Midwest and New England, called *moraines,* are the piles of rock and soil deposited when the ice melted. The ice ages also created new bodies of water. The weight of the ice, as much as two miles thick in places, made great depressions in the land. When the ice melted, the depressions filled with water. Depressions like these became the five Great Lakes, as well as many of the beautiful lakes of New England, New York, Michigan, Wisconsin, and Minnesota.

20. Today, a different kind of ice erosion takes place. It occurs on mountain slopes.

31

The giant Portage Glacier in Alaska has flowed down the mountain, carving out valleys as it moved.

"Rivers" of ice called *glaciers* begin as unmelted snow fields. As more snow accumulates and packs down year after year, the snow field gets heavier. Finally, gravity wins, and the glacier begins to inch down the slope. As it moves, rocks freeze onto the glacier's belly. The rocks scrape the slope, changing its shape. Whole valleys have been gouged out by the erosion of glaciers. Where glaciers finally melt, at lower elevations, they leave the rocks.

21. Weathering and erosion have changed the shape of the land. We owe them many of our land forms and fantastic landscapes. These agents that wear the earth down have given us such marvels as the Grand Canyon in Arizona and Niagara Falls on the U.S.-Canadian border. But if mountain building ever stopped, weathering and erosion over thousands of years would make the surface of the earth as smooth as a billiard ball.

UNDERSTANDING WHAT YOU HAVE READ

1. The surface of the earth is covered mostly by

a. water
b. mountains
c. land

2. Plateaus and plains differ in that

a. plains are at lower elevations
b. plateaus are not flat on top
c. plateaus have no rivers running through them

32

3. The theory that the earth's crust is divided into plates that move is the
   a. plate tectonics theory
   b. continental drift theory
   c. mid-ocean ridge theory

4. When plates push against one another, this causes
   a. mid-ocean ridges
   b. earthquakes and volcanoes
   c. convection currents

5. The force that transformed the Appalachians into low, rounded hills is
   a. erosion
   b. convection
   c. weathering

6. The difference between weathering and erosion is
   a. only in degree of severity
   b. one breaks rock down; the other carries it away
   c. one builds mountains

7. Flood plains are created by
   a. rivers that drop their sediment when they flood
   b. rivers that dump their sediment into oceans
   c. glaciers when they melt

8. When glaciers melt (both now and in the past), they drop their rocks and soil, creating land forms called
   a. deltas
   b. terrain
   c. moraines

DEVELOPING CRITICAL THINKING SKILLS

Agree or Disagree?

Decide whether or not each of the following agrees with what you have read. If the answer is disagree, explain why.

1. Mountains are only affected by the forces that build up the land.
2. The continental drift theory and plate tectonics theory are two theories very much in agreement.
3. The discovery of the mid-ocean ridges proved the theory of continental drift because it meant that the ocean floor was moving.
4. The location of earthquakes where plates spread apart proves they are unrelated to volcanoes.
5. Without weathering, erosion could not occur.
6. The creation of sand dunes in Colorado was the work of erosion alone.
7. If weathering did not occur, mountains would grow higher and higher.
8. As agents of erosion, glaciers perform exactly the same actions as rivers.

Chapter 2

Why Climates Differ

What factors affect climates all over the world?

READING FOR A PURPOSE:
1. How does the earth-sun relationship affect climate?
2. How does the global circulation of air and water affect climate?
3. How does the shape of the land affect climate?

1. Have you ever noticed if your mood is affected by the weather outdoors? Do days and days of cloudy skies and rain leave you feeling a little depressed or bored? After periods of gray sky, does a sunny day seem to lift your spirits?

2. People all over the world are affected by the weather. But it is not just their moods that are affected. In some countries, the weather means the difference between life and death. In some parts of India, for example, rain falls only one month a year. As people lower their buckets into rapidly drying wells, they hope for the clouds that will bring life-giving rain.

3. *Weather* refers to the day-to-day changes in the air. Weather is measured by two elements: precipitation and temperature. *Precipitation* is the water that falls to the ground. You know plenty of words that are used to describe precipitation: rain, snow, sleet, hail, drizzle. *Temperature* is the amount of heat or cold in the atmosphere at a certain time.

4. *Climate* and weather are different. Climate is the average weather over a long period of time. Climate refers to averages. What are the average temperatures of a place in winter and summer? If a place has temperatures in January that vary from 10° to 20° (-12°C to -7°C) degrees Fahrenheit, the average temperature in January is 15° (-10°C). If a place has cold temperatures in the winter and cool temperatures in the summer, geographers would say it has a cold climate. Many different climate regions exist in the world and even in

These mountains are part of the Canadian Rockies. What kinds of precipitation would you expect to find in the Rockies?

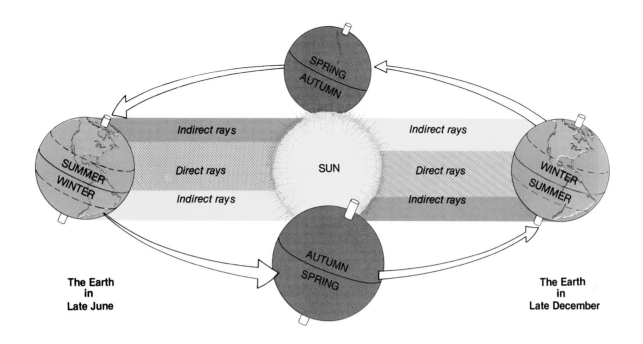

Labels within the diagram:

SPRING / AUTUMN

Indirect rays

Indirect rays

SUMMER / WINTER

Direct rays

SUN

Direct rays

WINTER / SUMMER

Indirect rays

Indirect rays

AUTUMN / SPRING

The Earth in Late June

The Earth in Late December

Revolution and the Earth's Tilt Cause the Seasons

our own country. There are hot climates, places where people have no need for overcoats. There are cold climates, where snow blankets the earth for much of the year. There are dry places, where all the rain that falls may be collected in a single tea cup. There are places where 30 to 40 feet (9 to 12 meters) of rain fall in one year.

5. Geographers ask the "where" and "why" questions you read about in the Introduction as they study climates. In the next chapter, you will read about the different climate regions that exist all around the world. In this chapter, you will learn the "whys"—how certain factors affect climate. Climate is affected by latitude, by water, and by the shape of the land.

6. Most of all, climate is affected by the sun. The source of all life on earth is the sun. Without it, nothing could grow. Ours would be a lifeless, barren planet. The relationship between the earth and the sun has a great deal to do with determining seasons and differences in climates.

7. You know that the earth *revolves,* or circles, the sun. Once every year, in about 365¹/₄

days, the earth makes a complete trip around the sun. This revolution causes changes in seasons. If you could travel in space, you would see that the North and South poles are not straight up and down from each other. Instead, the earth is tilted at an angle. Through the course of a year, the angle of tilt always stays the same, but the earth's relationship to the sun changes. Look at the diagram above. In June, the Northern Hemisphere of earth is tilted toward the sun. During that time, the Northern Hemisphere catches the direct, hotter rays of the sun. It is summer north of the equator. The Southern Hemisphere, however, is tilted away from the sun. The sun's rays hit it at an indirect angle. It is winter south of the equator. If you take a flashlight and shine it straight down on a piece of paper, the light appears very bright and intense. But if you shine the flashlight at an angle to the paper, the light is indirect and seems less bright. The same thing happens to the sun's warmth as its rays strike the earth.

8. By December, the earth has moved halfway around the sun. The Northern

Hemisphere is now tilted away from the sun. It catches the indirect rays. The Southern Hemisphere is tilted toward the sun. The hotter, direct rays strike the Southern Hemisphere now. At this time, it is winter north of the equator. It is summer south of the equator. If you are a sports fan, you may have noticed that tennis championships are played outdoors in Australia in January.

9. In March and September, the rays of the sun strike the earth directly at the equator. Both hemispheres experience similar temperatures. But when it is spring in the Northern Hemisphere, it is autumn in the Southern Hemisphere. The Northern Hemisphere awaits the warmth of summer. The Southern Hemisphere prepares for winter.

10. Climates are established by earth's relationship to the sun, just as seasons are. No matter the season, the sun's rays always strike directly at or near the equator. Places at the equator tend to have the hottest climates. These are known as tropical regions. The far-

ther from the equator, the sun's rays are less direct, and the climate is cooler. Polar regions exist at the highest latitudes, near the North and South poles. Consequently, latitude is a major factor in influencing climate. If two places in the world are located at the same latitude and are similar in their physical features, they will have the same climate.

11. Have you ever been inside a greenhouse? A greenhouse is a glass enclosure that traps the sun's warmth. It creates a perfect atmosphere for growing plants. Our earth is surrounded by blankets of gases called an atmosphere. The atmosphere temporarily traps much of the heat that the sun provides. In this way, the atmosphere provides a "greenhouse effect." Without it, the earth would be too cold to support life.

12. You know that it is hottest at the equator. But heat also moves around the earth. Our atmosphere plays a role in this. *Prevailing winds,* winds that blow in certain directions, move the air. Convection currents circulate

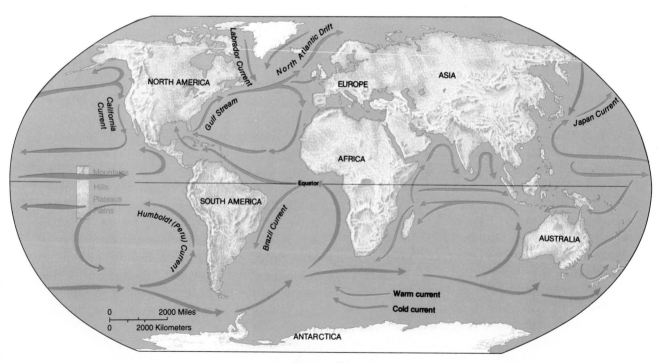

Ocean Currents

36

heat around the planet. Hot air from the equator blows toward the poles. Cold air from the poles circulates back toward the equator.

13. Currents in the oceans behave in much the same way. Currents are like fast-flowing streams of water within a larger body of water. Some currents are warm, and others are cold. Together, they follow circular motions in the oceans. Warm currents from the equator move toward the poles along the east coasts of continents. Cold currents move cold water away from the poles toward the equator. Cold currents travel along the west coasts of continents.

14. These currents can have a great effect on climates in many parts of the world. For example, the Gulf Stream is a warm current. As you can see on the map, it flows northward along the eastern coast of the United States, then turns and flows across the Atlantic Ocean to the British Isles. The winds blowing over the Gulf Stream are warmed. These warm winds blow across the British Isles and Western Europe. As a result, the people of Ireland, Great Britain, and Western Europe enjoy a warmer climate than that of Hudson Bay, Canada. Yet these regions are located about the same distance from the equator. In this way, air and water currents distort the influence of latitude.

15. Water affects climate in another way. Land warms up and cools off fairly quickly. Water, however, takes a longer time to heat and to cool. The air takes on the temperature of the earth's surface below it. So, in the winter, after the land has cooled, the water still feels the glow of summer. The air near the water stays warmer than air over the land. Consequently, in the winter, a place near the ocean will be warmer than a place in the center of a continent. In the summer, the ocean still carries the chill of winter. So in summer, a place near the ocean will be cooler than a place in the center of a continent.

16. Thus, water has a moderating effect on climate. This means places located near oceans are neither very hot, nor very cold. San Francisco, located on the Pacific coast, has such a climate. Temperatures average between 50° and 60°F (10°C to 16°C) all year around. However, St. Louis, a city located at the same latitude but in the center of the continent, far from an ocean, has a much more extreme climate. In the winter, temperatures might average 20°F (-7°C) degrees. But in the summer, the average temperature might be as high as 80°F (27°C). As you will read in the next chapter, places in the center of continents, far from the moderating effects of oceans, have a different kind of climate.

17. Land forms can affect climate too. Mountains create their own climates. How can snow fall at the equator where it is always hot? It can fall if there are mountains. *Elevation* is the height of land above sea level. The higher the elevation, the lower the temperature of the air. The temperature drops about three degrees Fahrenheit for every 1,000 feet above sea level. Consequently, up the slopes of mountains you find several different climate layers. The lower elevations have warmer climates. The higher elevations have cooler climates. If the mountains are very high, snow crowns them all year long. The plants growing there, called *vegetation,* change as the climate

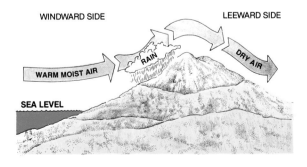

Winds, Mountains, and Rain or Snow

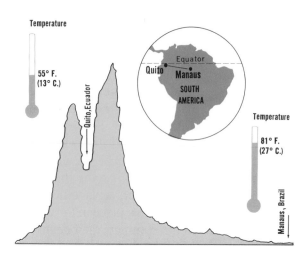

Temperature

55° F.
(13° C.)

Quito, Ecuador

Equator

Quito
Manaus
SOUTH
AMERICA

Temperature

81° F.
(27° C.)

Manaus, Brazil

Altitude and Temperature Differences

changes. These climates are called *vertical climates*. They occur on mountain slopes whether the mountains are located at the equator or at higher latitudes.

18. Mountains also affect the flow of air on the earth. Air carries moisture with it. Warm air can hold more moisture than cool air. As air blows against mountains, the mountains act as walls, forcing the air upwards. As the air floats higher, it cools. Unable to carry its mois-

ture any longer, the air drops its weight. Moisture drops to earth in the form of rain or snow. The precipitation falls on the *windward* side of the mountain, the side struck by the wind. The other side of the mountain is the *leeward,* or sheltered, side. That side receives very little rain. Geographers say that it exists in a *rain shadow.* The windward side of the mountain is wet. There the vegetation is thick and lush. The leeward side is dry with desert-like conditions. Vegetation is sparse. If the land is farmed, it must be irrigated. Two climates exist only a few miles apart, one on one side of the mountain, one on the other.

19. These differences in climate conditions are even more obvious if the mountains are located near an ocean. In that instance, air blowing off the ocean is loaded with water, and abundant rain falls on the western slope. That is the case in Washington State and Oregon.

20. You have learned about the causes of climate. You now are equipped with the right tools for analyzing the various climate regions discussed in the next chapter. You are ready to answer the geographers' "why" questions.

The thick Carillo Rainforest of Costa Rica

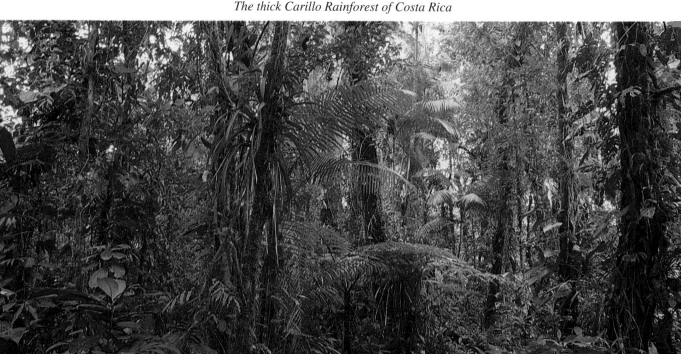

1. Climate is different from weather in that it is
   a. the average temperature of a certain month
   b. the average precipitation during a year's time
   c. the average weather over a long period of time

2. When it is summer in Australia,
   a. the sun is shining more directly at the Southern Hemisphere
   b. it is spring in Africa
   c. the sun is shining more directly north of the equator

3. The hottest climates are at the equator because
   a. no matter the season, the sun's rays always shine directly at or near the equator
   b. the equator has the highest latitude
   c. the sun's rays shine indirectly there

4. The fact that our atmosphere traps heat is called the
   a. rain shadow effect
   b. continental effect
   c. greenhouse effect

5. When wet winds blow toward mountains, the side that gets the most rain is the
   a. northern side
   b. windward side
   c. leeward side

6. Midwestern United States has hot summers and cold winters because
   a. the land is far from oceans
   b. the land is high above sea level
   c. cold ocean currents bring cold winds

7. Great Britain is warmer than other places that are the same distance from the equator because of
   a. its nearness to mountains
   b. its elevation
   c. the warming effects of the Gulf Stream

8. The western side of the mountains along the Pacific coast receives more rain than the eastern side because
   a. the Gulf Stream brings warm winds
   b. the western side is nearer the equator
   c. winds from the Pacific bring rain

9. If two places are located at the same latitude in the center of a continent, but one is on the leeward side of mountains,
   a. they will both have the same climate
   b. one will have a drier climate
   c. one will have a colder climate

10. If you want to visit several kinds of climates, all you have to do is
    a. travel around the world
    b. climb a high mountain
    c. either a. or b.

REVIEWING AND WRITING

Making an Outline

Using the following headings, write at least two topics under each heading for your outline of the factors that affect climate.

A. Latitude   C. Mountains   E. Ocean Currents
B. Elevation   D. Nearness to Oceans

DEVELOPING CRITICAL THINKING SKILLS

Fact or Opinion?

Which of these statements are facts and which are someone's opinions?

1. The climate of Oregon is better than the climate of South Carolina.
2. Mountains make climates more interesting.
3. Ocean currents have an effect on the climates of many places in the world.
4. As the population of the world grows, more people will move to the tropics.
5. People who live in hot climates are harder workers than those in cool climates.
6. There are many different climates in North America.
7. It would be a good idea to play the Superbowl in Australia because it is summer there in January.
8. No country having a cold climate will ever be a leading nation of the world.
9. Lower elevations have warmer climates.
10. Larger countries have more climates.

Chapter 3

Climate and Vegetation

What are the world's climate and vegetation regions, and where are they located?

READING FOR A PURPOSE:
1. How is vegetation related to climate?
2. How are people's lives affected by different climate regions?
3. What climates occur in low, middle, and high latitudes?

1. People are ingenious. They have learned how to adapt to extreme climates. In Minneapolis, Minnesota, winters can be very severe. As much as four or five feet of snow can fall in winter. Temperatures can sink as low as 10°F (-12°C) and stay there for days. To adapt to these severe winter conditions, people who live in Minneapolis have changed the landscape of their city. They have built skyways between buildings. Skyways are glassed-in, heated corridors that connect buildings, often at the second-story level. From the street you can see them overhead. The city has become like a space station. People can go to work, go to the bank, eat lunch at a restaurant, and go to the grocery store and a museum without ever having to put on a coat.

2. All over the world people have learned to adapt to their climates. People in Siberia (in eastern Russia) have invented new ways for building on permafrost. *Permafrost* is permanently frozen water in the soil. It makes building very difficult and very unstable. The type of climate often determines the kinds of materials available for building. Timber is often used in heavily forested areas, such as Alaska. In northern China, every available acre is used for growing crops. Thus, many people have built cave homes in nearby cliffs. The cliffs are made of *loess,* a soil that can be formed to make vertical walls. The cave homes are cool in summer and warm in winter.

3. Climate also affects the clothes people wear. Some desert people of the Middle East wear loose-fitting cotton clothing to keep cool while they travel in the hot desert. In the mountains, shepherds wear clothing made of wool or leather to keep warm. In the Amazon rain forest, people wear little clothing because it is always hot.

4. The type of climate determines the kinds of plants that can grow in certain regions. For example, some plants are suited for life in hot, dry climates. The cactus plant stores abundant amounts of moisture within its thick stalks. It is covered with needles that prevent animals from eating its flesh. (Any bites would drain its moisture.) Some cactuses are covered with tiny hairs that reflect the sun's hot rays and keep them cool. They have shallow roots to soak up any rain that falls before it evaporates.

5. It is important to understand the different climate regions of the world. Climates can affect the types of human activities that take place. For example, farmers cannot always grow the same crops in both wet and dry regions. Rice needs a hot, wet climate. It

The valleys and mountains of the Dolomite chain in Italy show how altitude affects the natural vegetation of a region.

41

grows well in Southeast Asia, but it could never be grown in Minnesota. If a country is located near the equator, it would be safe to say that it might export bananas, but not blueberries.

6. *Trade,* the exchange of goods among nations, is often the result of differences in climate. The United States (except for Hawaii) does not have the right climate for growing rubber, coffee, or bananas. So, it buys coffee from Brazil and Colombia. It buys rubber from Indonesia and Malaysia. Parts of the United States have an excellent climate for growing corn and wheat. So the United States exports these crops to other countries of the world. Generally, each region grows what suits the climate best.

7. In this chapter, you will read about the different kinds of climate regions of the world. There are several different ways to present climate regions. In this book, climate regions are grouped in the following way: *tropical, dry, mild, continental,* and *polar.* As you read, study the climate graphs representing each climate. They will help you understand the differences in temperature and precipitation of each region. You should realize that there are no sharp boundaries between climates. On the earth's surface, the changes between climates are gradual. We will discuss low, middle, and high latitudes in this chapter. Low latitudes range from the Tropic of Capricorn to the Tropic of Cancer, $23\frac{1}{2}°$ north and south of the equator. Middle latitudes stretch from there to the Arctic and Antarctic circles, or $66\frac{1}{2}°$ north and south of the equator. High latitudes extend from $66\frac{1}{2}°$ to the poles.

8. When you think "tropical," you should think hot. That is the one thing that the two tropical climates have in common. The two are the tropical rain forest and the savanna. Both occur in the tropics, the low latitudes. The tropical rain forest is hot and wet. The savanna is hot, with wet and dry seasons.

9. Rain forests thrive in tropical climates. Large rain forests are located in parts of Central and South America, central Africa, and Southeast Asia. The rain forest is lush because of showers that fall almost every day of the year. The rain forest forms an

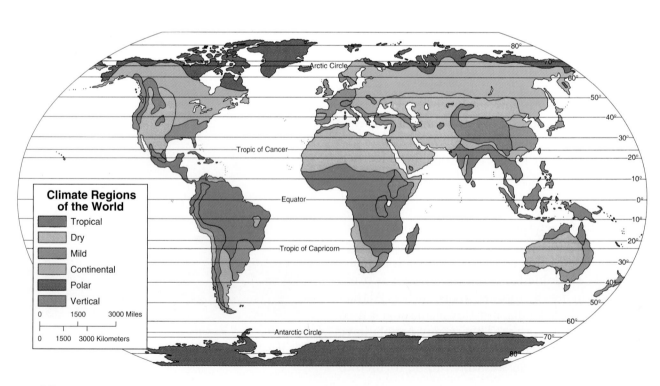

42

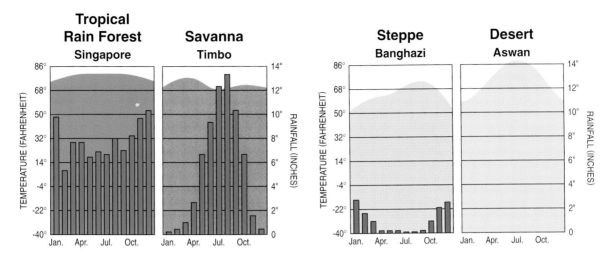

A climate graph shows rainfall and temperature for a particular place. Rainfall is shown by the bars, while temperature is shown by the curved line across the top of the graph. The months of the year are shown at the bottom of the graph. During which month is rainfall highest in Singapore? Which month has the highest temperature in Banghazi?

"umbrella" overhead that is so thick it blocks sunlight from reaching the ground. Temperatures rarely fall below 80°F (27°C). The rain forest thrives in the hot, damp, sticky heat. You can see why this climate was named after the vegetation that makes it unique.

10. North and south of the rain forests are the tropical *savannas*. A savanna is a tropical grassland with scattered trees. This is the "land of two seasons." There is a winter dry season and a summer wet season. During the dry season, the grasses turn brown as the hot sun burns the earth. Streams shrivel and bake into empty, brown gullies. Finally, in the summer, the rains come bringing relief. Showers pour down day after day. Rivers swell with swirling muddy water. Soon, water floods the land. The ground becomes soft and muddy. Green shoots appear. People celebrate. Herds are able to nibble contentedly.

11. *Deserts* and *steppes* are the two types of dry climates found on earth. Unlike the tropical climates, their location is not as related to latitude as it is to wind currents and mountains. Deserts are dry. Steppes are semi-dry.

12. Deserts are the driest regions on earth. In parts of some deserts like the great Sahara, sand dunes stretch hundreds of miles, as far as

the eye can see. Like brown waves, the dunes span the horizon. Not a tree, not a bush, grows. As little as 5 to 10 inches (13 to 25 centimeters) of rain may fall in one year. In the lower latitudes, deserts are hot with searing temperatures over 100°F (38°C) during the day. At night the land cools quickly. The temperature may drop as much as 50 degrees. Although little grows in deserts, the soil is not poor. As Israel has shown, crops can be grown in the desert if the soil is *irrigated,* or watered. Middle latitude deserts are cold and dry. The Gobi in northwestern China is such a place.

13. *Steppe* climates are semi-dry regions. They are the transition zones between deserts and other climate regions. Like deserts, they occur in both low and middle latitudes. They are shown by the gold color. They tend to loop around deserts. Rain falls, but in short supply. It is enough to support scattered trees and short, scruffy grasses. You know the steppe climate by a more familiar name. Steppes are called prairies or the Great Plains in the United States and Canada.

14. Several variations of mild climates exist. They are found mainly in the middle latitudes. They fall under the "mild" category because their temperatures are not extreme.

43

They are the Mediterranean, the marine, and the humid-subtropical climates.

15. The *Mediterranean* climate is the driest of the three mild climates. Very little rain falls in the summer. Bright blue skies and warm summer temperatures draw tourists to Mediterranean climates. Winters are cooler and wetter.

16. The *marine* climate is the coolest of the three mild climates. The marine climate gets its name from its location. Marine refers to water. Find the regions on the map that have a marine climate. You will see that all these regions are near water or are surrounded by water. Winds that have blown over warm ocean currents float over the land and leave a wet, cool climate in their wake. On the Pacific coast of North America, the marine climate is quite narrow. That is because mountains block the flow of air. However, in western Europe there are no mountain ranges running north and south. Thus, much of Europe has a marine climate. The warming effect of the water keeps temperatures from falling below freezing much of the year.

17. The *humid-subtropical* climate is the warmest of the three mild climates. It is warmer than the other two because it is nearer to the equator. Find these regions on the map on page 42. They tend to be located on eastern coasts of continents. Warm ocean currents flow along these coasts. Consequently, warm,

moist air bathes the land during all seasons. Summers are hot and wet. Winters are short and mild.

18. *Continental climates* tend to be located in the center of continents, far from the moderating effect of oceans. In this book, we discuss two groups of continental climates: humid-continental and taiga. *Humid-continental* is a middle latitude climate. *Taiga* regions straddle middle and high latitudes. Extreme temperatures characterize continental climates: hot or warm in the summer, cold in the winter.

19. Humid-continental simply means that precipitation falls year-around. People who live in continental climates have closets to suit the extremes. They might have shorts and sandals for summer and heavy coats and boots for winter. Winter temperatures often drop way below freezing.

20. Taiga regions are also known as the subarctic. The biggest difference between the taiga and the humid-continental climates is the length of summer. Winter in the taiga can endure for as long as eight months. Remember the description of Siberia and the difficulty of building on permafrost? Permafrost is a common problem in the taiga. Taiga is a Russian word meaning "forest." Few people live in the taiga because it is so cold, but forests thrive. Taiga regions are home to the world's largest forest lands.

21. *Polar* climates are those located in the

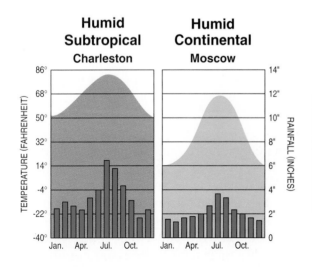

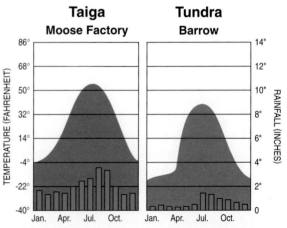

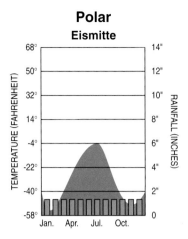

Polar
Eismitte

highest latitudes. They are called polar, referring to the North and South poles. There are two types of polar climates: tundra regions and regions covered by ice caps.

22. *Tundra* is another Russian word. It means "marshy plain." It is an apt description of the region. The ground is frozen for most of the year. The short glimpse of summer thaws the surface. It becomes mushy and soupy. Flowers and mosses spring to life, as though they are hurrying to take advantage of the warmth. No trees are able to grow here. No crops can be raised. The region is almost empty of human life.

23. Ice cap regions "cap" the land near the Poles. There is no landmass at the North Pole. But ice and snow do permanently cover much of Greenland and almost all of the continent of Antarctica. Ice cap regions are the coldest regions on earth. Temperatures remain below freezing all year long. As we said before, ice cap regions may also be considered deserts. Because the air is so cold, it can hold very little moisture. Thus, very little precipitation falls to earth.

24. One other type of climate exists. You read about it in the last chapter when we discussed mountains' effect on climate. It is called a vertical climate. If you think of all the other climates as being represented each by a different color, then a vertical climate region is like a rainbow. It is layered with many "colors." Up mountain slopes, the climate changes sharply and different activities take place. Corn might be raised at lower elevations. Sheep might graze on higher ground.

Cooking yams in Tanzania, Africa. What can you guess about the climate from the clothing, sun-dried bricks, and the field?

UNDERSTANDING WHAT YOU HAVE READ

1. Different climates are often described in terms of the plants that grow there. This is because
   a. vegetation determines climate
   b. climate determines vegetation
   c. climate and vegetation are both determined by soil types

2. One way climate affects human activities is by
   a. affecting the kinds of agricultural products that can be grown
   b. determining the type of technology available
   c. determining soil types

3. Low latitudes refer to
   a. tropical regions
   b. the region between $23^1/_2°$ to $66^1/_2°$ north and south of the equator
   c. polar regions

4. Deserts and steppes occur in
   a. high latitudes
   b. low latitudes
   c. low and middle latitudes

5. The single characteristic that identifies the tropical rain forest and the savanna is
   a. the abundance of rain
   b. high temperatures all year
   c. seasonal changes in temperature

6. In general, grasses, rather than forests, tend to grow in
   a. wetter regions
   b. colder regions
   c. drier regions

7. Continental climates differ from mild climates in that they
   a. have extreme temperatures in winter and summer
   b. have wet and dry seasons
   c. are located on the coasts of continents

8. Marine, Mediterranean, and humid-subtropical are all types of a
   a. hot climate
   b. low latitude climate
   c. mild climate

WRITING

Now that you have read about the different climates and how people adapt their lifestyles to them, choose one climate from the five groups in this book and plan a recreation area that people in your climate zone would enjoy.

First draw a diagram that shows the recreation area. Then write a paragraph that explains where your recreation area is located and how the area makes use of the climate zone.

SUMMING UP

I. Matching

Match the items in Column B with the climatic regions in Column A. There is one extra item in Column B.

COLUMN A
1. marine
2. humid-subtropical
3. taiga
4. rain forest
5. savanna
6. humid-continental
7. steppe
8. desert
9. tundra

COLUMN B
a. high-latitude forest region
b. grasslands near rain forests with hot and dry seasons
c. wet, cool lands of Western Europe
d. less than 10 inches (25 centimeters) of rain a year
e. climate with cold winters and hot summers
f. always hot and wet
g. mild all year with warm temperatures
h. scruffy grasslands encircling deserts
i. cold polar region without trees
j. also known as Mediterranean climate

II. Using Graphs

Use the four graphs below to answer the questions that follow.

1. If you wanted to visit Kinshasa, Zaire, in what season would you go and why?
2. How is the weather in Asunción, Paraguay, affected by its location?
3. Suppose you wanted to take a vacation. You prefer bright sunshine, blue skies, warm temperatures, and no chance of rain. Which city would you choose and why?
4. Suppose you want to travel south of the equator. Where would you go and in what month? Why?
5. Which city gets the most rain all year, Perth or Mocamedes? Which has the driest summer?

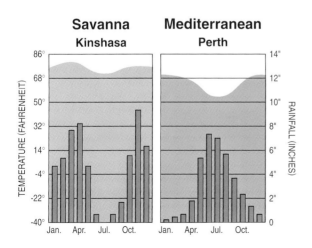

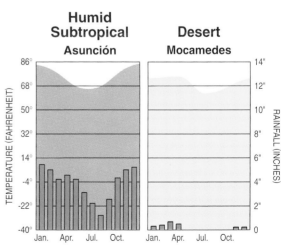

DEVELOPING IDEAS AND SKILLS

Getting Information From Maps

There are many ideas and much information that we can find out from maps. It is not even necessary to know the name of the map we are studying. If we know about land forms, latitude, longitude, the factors that affect climate, and the ways in which climate influences people, we can gather a great deal of information.

On p. 49 is a map of a land we will call "Solaria." Solaria does not really exist. It is imaginary. Yet we are going to study this map and see how much we can learn about this land.

See if you can answer each question about the map. If you cannot, the answer is explained after the question. Check yourself. See how much you can learn from the map without reading the answers.

1. Is the land north or south of the equator? *Answer:* It is north of the equator. The degrees of latitude grow higher as we go north. We know that 0°, the equator, is south of 10°. Therefore, the land must be north of the equator.

2. Is Solaria in the low, high, or middle latitudes? *Answer:* The southern part—the smallest part—is in the low latitudes. North of $23^1/_2$° are the middle latitudes. Most of the land lies in the region of the middle latitudes. None of Solaria is in the high latitudes.

3. Is Solaria east or west of the prime meridian? *Answer:* It is west of the prime meridian. Zero degrees (0°) longitude must lie to the east of Solaria because the degrees of longitude increase as we go west.

4. Where will most of the seaports be? *Answer:* On the west coast, probably. The western coastline is rough—it has many inlets and harbors. The other coastlines are smooth and probably have few harbors.

5. Where will the largest city be? *Answer:* Probably at C. This city is located a small distance below the place where the rivers have joined to

empty into the sea, a good location for trade. The harbor looks as though it will have a wide mouth, and it is sheltered from the ocean.

6. What kind of land form is shown by letter A? *Answer:* An isthmus, a narrow piece of land connecting two larger bodies of land.

7. What land form is shown by letter B? *Answer:* A peninsula—a body of land almost completely surrounded by water.

8. What are the latitude and longitude of city D? *Answer:* About 55° north latitude and 43° west longitude.

9. What city is located at 47° north latitude and 59° west longitude? *Answer:* E.

10. In which direction does River 2 flow? *Answer:* It flows almost directly west. It rises in the mountains and flows to the ocean—to the west.

11. Which side of the mountains will have the most rain? *Answer:* The western side. The winds blow from the west in the middle latitudes, and they have come from the ocean. Therefore, they bring moisture with them.

12. What is the difference in climate between cities R and L? *Answer:* City L will probably be hotter in the summer and colder in the winter since it is not near the ocean. Remember that water has the effect of keeping temperatures even.

13. What might keep city F from being a large city? *Answer:* It does not have a good harbor. Also, it lies in the low latitudes in a lowland. It no doubt has a very warm and wet climate.

14. If you flew in an airplane from E to F, in what direction would you fly? *Answer:* Southeast.

15. If you traveled by air from D to F, how far would you have traveled? *Answer:* About 4,000 miles (6,400 kilometers). Measure 2,000 miles (3,200 kilometers) on the scale. From D to F is about twice that distance.

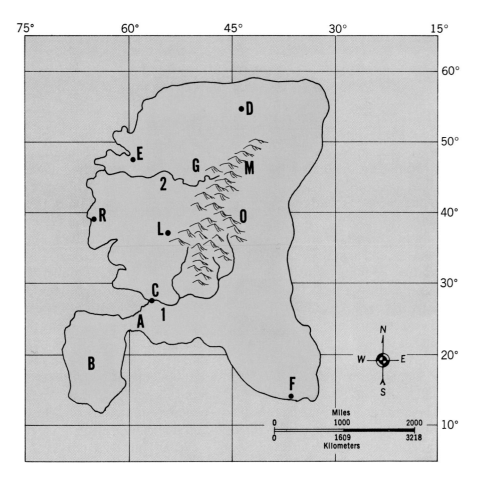

Solaria

I. Matching

Match the items in Column B with the climatic regions in Column A. There is one EXTRA item in Column B.

COLUMN A

1. marine
2. humid-subtropical
3. taiga
4. rain forest
5. savanna
6. humid-continental
7. Mediterranean

COLUMN B

a. High-latitude forests
b. Sunny lands with dry summers
c. Grasslands north of the rain forest
d. Wet, cool lands of Western Europe
e. Less than 10″ (25 cm) of rain a year
f. Good farmlands on the east coast of continents in the middle latitudes
g. Climate of the four seasons—cold winters and hot summers
h. Always hot and wet

49

Fragile Ozone Layer

In 1985, scientists who study the environment received some surprising news. Word had come from the British Antarctic Survey that an ozone "hole" existed over Halley Bay in Antarctica.

The Role of Ozone. What exactly is ozone? Ozone is a form of oxygen. Most of it is located 10 to 25 miles (15 to 40 kilometers) above the earth's surface. There, in the stratosphere, the ozone layer absorbs the ultraviolet energy in the sun's rays. As a result, it shields life on earth from the sun's harmful effects.

Why is ozone important? Without the ozone shield, ultraviolet rays can cause skin cancers. The rays can also cause changes in the genes of plants, trees, and food crops. Life in the oceans may also be affected. So, the cause for concern is real.

Scientists hurried to Antarctica to see if they could find out what was happening. Studies showed that there was 40 percent less ozone overhead during Antarctica's springtime. Satellites confirmed the findings. They found that the spring ozone drop had been taking place for ten years!

The scientists also discovered that the ozone hole varies in size from year to year. It is usually largest in cold years and smallest in warm years. In some years the ozone hole expands to cover 10 million square miles (26 million kilometers) or roughly three times the area of the entire United States!

CFCs and the Ozone Layer. The main culprits are chemicals known as CFCs. By the 1950s, CFCs were widely used to provide the coolants for refrigerators and air conditioners. Their popularity grew. In the 1970s, CFCs were being used in aerosol spray cans containing everything from deodorant to cooking oil. Insulating foams, packaging, plastic foam cups, and industrial cleaners were soon added to the list of CFCs' many uses. World use of CFCs rose from 400 million pounds a year in 1960 to 2,500 million pounds in 1990!

In 1974, two scientists, Sherwood Rowland and Mario Molina, discovered that CFCs do not break down when released into air near the earth's surface. They rise up unchanged until ultraviolet light in the stratosphere begins to break them down and release their chlorine. The released chlorine then reacts with ozone in the stratosphere and converts it to ordinary oxygen. Why has this happened in Antarctica? The process requires very cold temperatures and sunlight.

What Can Be Done? United action is needed to stop the release of ozone-destroying CFCs into the air. A few countries, including the United States, banned CFC aerosol use in 1979. Stronger control soon proved necessary since aerosols are only one CFC use.

In 1985, the United Nations Environment Program (UNEP) held the Vienna Convention for the Protection of the Ozone Layer. The meeting led to the Montreal Protocol on Substances that Deplete the Ozone Layer. Countries signing the Montreal Protocol agree to end or severely restrict use of ozone-destroying chemicals by 2000. The Montreal Protocol, signed by the United States and 23 other countries, went into effect in 1989.

How might destruction of the ozone affect you? Why do you think it has taken so long for countries to restrict the use of ozone-destroying chemicals? What can you do to make the Montreal Protocol work?

Chapter 4

Energy: A Gift From the Earth

How can we use our supplies of energy wisely?

READING FOR A PURPOSE:
1. What are renewable sources of energy?
2. What are nonrenewable sources of energy?
3. How can we tap alternative sources of energy?

1. Imagine you are in your kitchen at home as you read this. Look around. See if you can name all the things that use energy. The toaster, the refrigerator, the stove—these need electricity to work. Electricity is a form of energy. Do you have other appliances? They use energy, too. As you look around your kitchen, remember that everything that was manufactured in a factory was made with energy. Now, count the things made of plastic: maybe the dishes, a coffee pot, salt and pepper shakers.

Giant Hoover Dam supplies water and electric power to much of the U.S. Southwest.

Petroleum, or oil, is used to make plastic. Oil is a source of energy. Do you have anything made of steel in your kitchen? How about the knives and forks? Chances are they are stainless steel. Coal is used to make steel. Coal is a source of energy. Some form of energy is used to heat your kitchen and the rest of your home. You can see from this one example that without energy your life would be very difficult.

2. We need energy for fueling our cars, for heating our homes, for manufacturing the products we buy. The energy required to fulfill all these needs falls into two categories: renewable and nonrenewable. Renewable resources are those that are constantly being replaced by nature. Water is a renewable resource, for example. Power plants near rivers and waterfalls use water to turn machines called turbines that produce electricity. Electricity produced by waterpower is called hydroelectricity.

3. Nonrenewable resources are those that cannot be replaced once they are used. Much of our energy comes from fossil fuels, which are nonrenewable. Fossil fuels are coal, oil, and natural gas. They were formed deep in the earth from the remains of plants and animals that died millions of years ago. Not only are they used to provide power. They are also widely used to make things from plastics and steel.

4. Energy resources are distributed unevenly around the world. Some countries, such as those in the Middle East, have abundant supplies of petroleum, or oil. Some countries, like China and the United States, have vast deposits of coal. Other countries, like Japan, have very few of these sources of energy.

5. Those countries that possess abundant energy resources are not always the heavy users of energy. The United States, China, and Commonwealth of Independent States outrank all others. Japan consumes more than twice as much energy as the entire continent of Africa. The biggest users of energy are those countries that are the most industrialized. They include the United States, Japan, and

Off the coast of Mexico, an oil rig extracts oil from beneath the sea floor 24 hours a day.

Western Europe. Thus, countries of the world that do not have adequate supplies of energy resources must trade with others to meet their needs.

6. But trade can sometimes be disrupted, as the Gulf War in Iraq showed us. War can slow oil production and cause temporary energy shortages all over the world. When an energy shortage occurs, you probably end up feeling its effects. Your parents might have to wait in long lines at gas stations. They might complain about the jump in the price of gasoline. Or, the price of a bus ride might go up.

7. The shortages just described are temporary. Can you imagine what life would be like if they were permanent? One day, certain energy resources will run out. Let's take fossil fuels as an example. The Middle East possesses about 60 percent of the world's known oil reserves. But their reserves will only last another fifty years or so, at best. Smaller reserves are found in the United States, Venezuela, and the for-

mer Soviet Union. But their lifetimes are equally as short. Reserves of natural gas and coal will last another 150 to 200 years. Then it will be millions of years before the supply of fossil fuels is built back up.

8. Scientists are searching for new places to tap. Two places that hold promise are the oceans and Antarctica. Fossil fuels, such as oil and natural gas, have been discovered in the rocks of the sea floor. For years, offshore rigs have been pumping substantial amounts of oil and gas. These rigs are located in the shallow waters above the continental shelf. A continental shelf is the extension of the continent beneath the ocean. While as much as 20 percent of the world's oil comes from offshore oil fields, there may be much more waiting to be tapped. The problem is getting to it. Also, laws governing the ocean are not yet established. Several countries have supported international treaties governing fishing, mining, and exploration. However, only a few have signed.

9. Antarctica might be called earth's last frontier. Beneath all that ice, Antarctica is believed to be a treasure trove of minerals. Fossil fuels might be the "gems" of the treasure. In 1972, scientists discovered traces of certain gases when they were drilling on the continental shelf surrounding Antarctica. The gases suggest the presence of oil. If this assumption is correct, then scientists estimate the oil reserves to be enormous.

10. Finding the reserves is quite different from actually tapping them. Antarctica has a forbidding climate. Finding ways to mine the reserves is quite a problem. Transporting the oil from the frozen polar waters is another problem

11. These geographical problems cannot be solved until the political problems concerning Antarctica are solved. Early in the 1900s, several nations made claims on Antarctica. Many were the results of explorations on the continent. Look at the map on page 53. Antarctica has been divided like a pie. The South Pole is the center of the pie, and each country's claim is a piece. In the 1950s, those nations claiming parts of Antarctica recognized the need for international cooperation. They and other nations signed the Antarctic Treaty, which was in effect from 1961 until 1991. The treaty called for cooperation in scientific research and banned military activities. Although the treaty expired in 1991, international cooperation in Antarctica remains an important issue.

12. Many scientists believe that instead of looking for new sources of fossil fuels, we should be thinking of other possible sources of energy. They believe there are serious problems with our present forms of energy. For example, we know that burning fossil fuels causes a terrible pollution problem. Many industrialized countries have issued laws regulating pollution emissions. But developing countries are just in the process of building

their factories. Pollution seems to be the least of their worries.

13. Nuclear energy is an inexpensive way to generate electricity. The source of energy for nuclear power is a mineral called uranium that is found in the earth. Uranium is a nonrenewable resource. But nuclear materials are very dangerous. They cannot be handled except by robot arms. The process of generating nuclear energy results in the production of waste materials. These materials remain dangerous for thousands of years. Scientists have yet to solve the problem of how to store nuclear waste.

14. For several decades scientists have been experimenting with new sources of energy. For hundreds of years, water has been a reliable resource. It is clean. Because it uses a force of nature, it is relatively inexpensive. It is

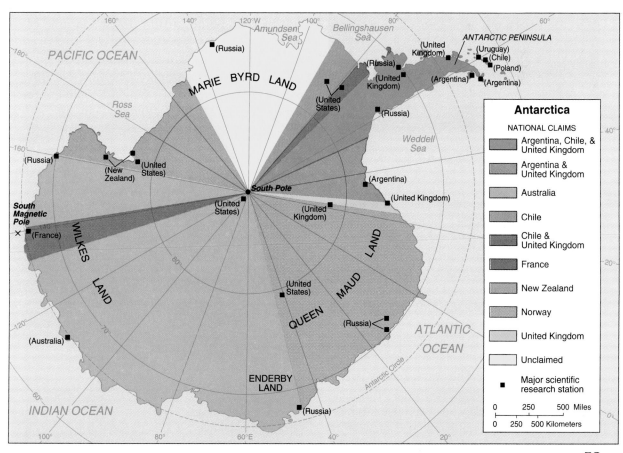

An Indian nuclear reactor. What are advantages of nuclear power?

16. Scientists are also experimenting with wind energy. Windmills turn as the wind blows, generating electricity. Reliability is a problem, because the wind does not blow at a consistent level all the time.

17. In places like Iceland, people generate energy by taking advantage of their location—on a boundary between tectonic plates! They use geothermal energy, energy that comes from heat within the earth. Hot liquid rock is very close to the surface at plate boundaries. It heats underground water that in turn produces steam. The steam is used to heat homes and generate electricity. However, use of this resource is limited. You must live on a boundary between plates in order to tap it.

18. There is no one right answer as we face the coming energy crisis. But there is something that you can do. It will make a difference. Learn to conserve our energy resources. Use them sparingly. Turn the lights off when you are not using them. If you have a thermostat in your home, turn it down a couple of degrees. Just that little change will save precious fuel. Conservation is an important part of everyone's responsibility. The valuable gifts of nature must be used wisely if people are to keep and improve their standard of living.

renewable. Water on the planet continues to recycle itself. Just as they tapped the energy from waterfalls, scientists are trying to do the same with ocean tides and waves. As tides surge up against the coast twice a day, the rushing waters turn engines that make electricity. So far, generating electricity in this way is still in the experimental stage.

15. Solar energy is being used on a small scale fairly effectively. Solar energy is energy provided by the sun. The sun's energy is collected on solar panels on rooftops of homes. In this way, solar energy has been used to heat homes but so far has not been used successfully to generate electricity.

The power of wind, used by this New Mexico windmill, may someday a reliable source of renewable energy.

UNDERSTANDING WHAT YOU HAVE READ

1. Water and coal are examples of
a. nonrenewable resources
b. renewable resources
c. energy resources

2. Nonrenewable resources are those that
a. cannot be replaced once they are used
b. are replaced by nature
c. we can live without

3. The heaviest users of energy tend to be
a. entire continents
b. those in polar regions
c. highly industrialized countries

4. If a country possesses no supplies of energy resources, the quickest way to fulfill its energy needs is to
a. trade
b. survey the oceans
c. send scientists to Antarctica

5. Mining of Antarctica cannot go ahead until
a. additional mapping takes place
b. political problems of who governs Antarctica are solved
c. ships are designed to withstand frigid temperatures

6. The major obstacle to tapping resources of the ocean is
a. finding supplies to tap
b. designing the technology to get at the reserves
c. persuading other countries to allow it

7. Scientists believe Antarctica to have abundant oil reserves because of the discovery of
a. minerals
b. a continental shelf
c. the presence of certain gases

8. The world's oil reserves will run out in about
a. 50 years
b. 100 years
c. 150 years

9. A serious problem resulting from burning fossil fuels is
a. pollution
b. disposing of waste
c. harm to crops

10. The limitation of geothermal energy is its
a. location
b. expense
c. pollution of the atmosphere

DEVELOPING CRITICAL THINKING SKILLS

Making Inferences

Whatever you read, you gain ideas not only from the words you read, but also from what is not said. You read "between the lines." This is true in your study of the world, too. You know some things even though they are not stated. You are able to understand because you can infer some things. One of the skills in reading social studies is to be able to infer meanings from what you have read. Here is an example:

"They loved walking with their fishing rods to the edge of the cool stream. The wet grass brushed against their bare feet, making them wet but not uncomfortable. And to think that they didn't have to go back until lunch."

What do we infer from these few sentences? We have gained some ideas without those ideas being put into words. We know that it is morning—the grass is wet, and lunchtime has not yet come. We know that it is problably a summer day—the people are going fishing in their bare feet. Another example:

"The five o'clock whistle meant that the rush of workers had begun. Off many went in their shiny cars. Others poured into the subways nearby. The bright street lights were already lit."

What can we infer from these sentences? First, this is probably a city. There are subways and street lights. It is probably winter, too, for the lights are already on at 5 o'clock, the end of the working day. We also know that the people probably have a high standard of living, since many workers have their own cars. In this exercise, see if you can infer from each sentence whether it is written about a renewable or a nonrenewable resource. Some of the resources are not related to energy. Name the resource(s) and tell whether it is renewable or nonrenewable.

1. Many people of the world live near volcanoes. They endure the threat of eruptions because they are able to grow crops so well with the natural fertilizer.
2. Deserts can be made to produce if they are irrigated.
3. If a country wants to generate electricity, all it has to do is build a dam.
4. Lumber companies take an active role in helping nature along.
5. Using plastic instead of paper plates is not the best way to conserve resources.
6. Nuclear power plants are probably not the best answer to our energy needs because their wastes pose a risk to people for centuries.
7. Iron is used in the steel-making process as well.
8. Because of acid rain, wildlife in lakes is dying out.

Pioneers of Geography

Most people remember **Ptolemy** (TAHL-uh-mee) for his mistaken idea that the sun revolves around the earth. However, this Egyptian of the 300s B.C. should be remembered as the father of modern geography. The grid system he used for mapping the earth is the basis for all modern mapmaking. In fact, Ptolemy began the practice of drawing maps with the north at the top and the east on the right. Many historians believe that Ptolemy also invented the terms "latitude" and "longitude."

A traveler's comment caused one famous geographer to "think big." **Eratosthenes** lived in Alexandria, Egypt, in the 400s B.C. When someone told him about a certain well at Syrene (now Aswan), he became very interested. It seems that at noon every June 21, there was no shadow to be seen in this well. This meant that the sun was directly over the well. Yet to the north in Alexandria, there was always a shadow at noon. Using this knowledge and a rough idea of the distance between Alexandria and Syrene, Eratosthenes calculated the circumference, or distance around the earth at the equator. His estimate that the earth was 28,700 miles (45,920 kilometers) around was only about 15 percent too high. If he had known the exact distance between Syrene and Alexandria, he would have calculated the exact circumference of the earth.

People often describe a shrewd person as someone who "knows which way the wind is blowing." In the 300s B.C., a Greek ship's pilot named **Hippalus** changed history because he knew which way the wind blew. Hippalus noticed that year after year the wind blew east toward India in the summer. It blew in the opposite direction in winter. The discovery of this wind called the monsoon led to the opening of a sea route between Europe and Asia. Merchants used the monsoon winds to travel to India for spices and silks. The trade in Eastern luxury goods drained the treasury of Rome. This love of luxury eventually contributed to the fall of the Roman Empire.

In the early A.D. 1000s, an Arab scholar wrote that "the habitable [fit to be lived in] part of the world has been placed in the center of a vast area, environed [surrounded] on all sides by the sea." At the time, saying that the earth's land was surrounded by oceans created quite a controversy. Many people did not believe this was true. However, others realized that if the ideas of **Al-Biruni** were correct, the oceans would provide good routes for trading. Soon, Arab traders ventured from home and discovered the vastness of the oceans.

When European explorers sailed on voyages of discovery, they wanted wealth, fame, and converts to the Christian faith. The Chinese explorer of the 1300s **Cheng Ho** had different reasons for his voyages. Emperor Yung Lo wanted the world to know of the power of China and of his great Ming dynasty. So, he sent Cheng Ho on a series of voyages. Cheng Ho sailed across the Indian Ocean. He sailed to Java, Ceylon (now Sri Lanka), and the Persian Gulf and up and down the coast of Africa. To each new country Cheng Ho visited, he brought treasures from his emperor. When he returned to China, he brought back knowledge of the lands he had visited and the oceans on which he had sailed.

PEOPLE IN A CHANGING WORLD

KEY IDEAS

- The culture of a place describes its human environment or the way of life of the people living there.

- A culture depends on how the people have adapted to the natural physical environment.

- Movement of people, ideas, and goods changes a culture.

- People must learn the beliefs, language, and customs of their culture.

- Use of machinery in industrialized countries has given the people a high standard of living.

- Most countries are striving to make fuller use of their natural resources.

- Eight major culture regions formed through common physical and human characteristics make up the world.

Humans adapt to, and change, their environment. Every inch of this rice field on the Indonesian island of Bali is used by carefully building terraces into the sides of hills.

Chapter 1

People and Their Cultures

What is culture?

1. There are more than 5.4 billion people living today on the planet earth. They live all over the earth's surface—on plains, on hillsides, in jungles, and in deserts. Some even make their homes on the waters of the earth. There are places where as many as 13,000 people live crowded together on one square mile of land. In others, there is not a person for miles. In some places, people make thousands of dollars a year from their work. In others, they barely earn $100 a year. There are places where houses have heat in the winter and air-conditioning in the summer. In other places, mud walls are the only protection against the weather.

2. Wherever people live, they have developed ways of working, playing, and governing themselves. How people live day by day, how they work, the songs they sing, the god or gods they worship, the sports they enjoy—all these things make up their *culture.* The culture of a people is passed on to their children and to their children's children. Culture is learned. It may change greatly or very little over the years. Ours is a fast-changing culture. Among the San people of Africa's Kalahari Desert, ways of living have changed little in the past few hundred years. They still use simple tools in gathering wild plants and hunting for animals.

All people need protection from the weather, but the kinds of shelters they build vary from place to place and from culture to culture. These photos show the typical shelters of three different cultures. Which is likely to be the home of farmers? of office workers? of herders?

3. Culture depends in part on a people's surroundings, their *environment*. Soil, climate, minerals, the kind of land surface, power resources—all of these make up a people's natural environment. Ways of living may vary greatly among different environments. On the other hand, people in similar environments may have very different ways of living. No matter where people live, they have a great deal to say about *how* they live. Our culture depends less on the natural environment than does that of many of the Inuit (Eskimos). Through science we have changed our surroundings to make life more comfortable for ourselves.

4. Let us look at some things that are part of the culture of Europe. (In this book we shall be studying the countries of Europe as one *culture region*—an area throughout which the way of life is much the same.) In most of Europe, soccer is the most popular sport. It is part of the culture of the region. Most people of Europe are Christians. Religion is part of their culture, too. Careful farming on small plots is also important. In Europe there are many fine churches, forts, and palaces hundreds of years old. They have been saved and cared for because respect for the past is part of European culture.

5. In the United States and Canada, some people play soccer. Most Northern Americans belong to one of the Christian religions. Some Northern Americans like caring for small gardens. Some do not want to see old, historic buildings torn down. This does not mean that the culture of the people of Northern America is the same as that of the people of Europe. It does mean that there is a kinship. It also means that Northern Americans have borrowed from Europeans. On the other hand, Europeans have borrowed from Northern Americans. People may take things from another culture and use them as their own. Spaghetti is a favorite dish of many Northern Americans, yet it began as a part of the culture of Italy, where it was brought from China. Automobiles, computers, photocopiers—to name a few items—were first used heavily by North Americans. Today they are part of the culture of many countries.

6. Cultures of one place are often a mixture of the cultures of many places. This borrowing occurs in a number of ways. Sometimes borrowing happens when people *migrate*, or move from one place to another to live. They bring much of their culture with them. That is what happened when people migrated to what is now the United States. The first people in the

Soccer players in England. Why are sports considered part of a people's culture?

61

area were Native Americans (American Indians). Later, millions of people came from Germany, Italy, Great Britain, Ireland, Canada, and Africa. Many also came from Austria, Hungary, Russia, Mexico, and Norway. Still others came from France, the West Indies, Greece, China, Cuba, and Poland. The list runs even longer. All these people brought much of their culture with them to the United States.

7. Another example is Canada. The first people in Canada were Native Americans and Inuit (Eskimos). Some of the largest groups that came to Canada were from Great Britain, France, Ireland, Germany, Ukraine (a newly independent republic west of Russia), China, and Portugal. Many people from the United States also moved to Canada. In Canada today, the English and the French cultures can easily be noticed. Within the same country, some areas are chiefly English in their culture. Others are chiefly French.

8. Ideas, beliefs, and learned ways of behaving can spread even without migration. People learn about other ways of living from newspapers, books, and magazines. TVs, radios, movies, telephones, and electronic equipment also help to spread culture.

9. Once the culture of a people did not spread as rapidly as it can today. Mountains, deserts, and oceans kept people apart. People

Folk dancing in Norway. Name some forms of play and recreation that you take part in and that are borrowed from another culture.

developed their own ways of living, their own language, and often their own religion. They developed a culture that was separate from others. Now, however, ideas spread quickly. TVs, cars, airplanes, computers, and satellite communication have had much to do with breaking down the "walls" between people. Rapid communication and transportation help bring people and ideas together.

UNDERSTANDING WHAT YOU HAVE READ

1. **Which of the following questions are answered in this chapter?**
a. Why have people moved to Canada to live?
b. What is culture?
c. How do farmers in warm climates teach their children to raise crops?

2. **The main idea of paragraph 9 is that**
a. Television, cars, and computers are modern inventions

b. mountains, deserts, and oceans keep people apart
c. rapid communication and transportation bring people and ideas together

3. **To *migrate* means to**
a. move from one place to another to live
b. learn ways to work, play, and govern
c. influence the ways people live by means of changing the environment

4. The cultures of the United States and Canada are

a. just like the culture of Europe
b. very different from each other because the Great Lakes keep people apart
c. a mixture of the cultures of people from many places

5. People can learn about other people's cultures by

a. traveling
b. reading books
c. both *a* and *b*

6. Ways of living

a. are the same everywhere
b. may vary greatly among different environments
c. are always the same in similar environments

7. How people live, work, and play

a. depends in part on their environment
b. has nothing to do with their environment
c. is based entirely on their environment

8. The foods people eat have

a. nothing to do with their environment
b. little to do with their environment
c. a great deal to do with their environment

DEVELOPING CRITICAL THINKING SKILLS

Make two headings on a page of your notebook. Head one column CULTURE and the other NATURAL ENVIRONMENT. Then place each of the following items in the correct column.

1. The soil of an area
2. The language a person speaks
3. The climate of a country
4. The religion a family has
5. The natural resources of a region
6. The games a person plays
7. The job a person holds
8. The minerals in a region
9. The government a person chooses
10. The clothing a person wears

Conclusions: What makes a person what he or she is—culture or environment, or both? Which is more important in your opinion? Why do you think so?

Cultural Borrowing

Takuo Nakamura is a 37-year-old vice-president of a design and marketing company in Yokohama, Japan. He lives with his wife and three children in his parents' home. Now that Takuo is doing much better, the Nakamuras have decided to buy a home of their own. However, they do not want a traditional Japanese home. The Nakamuras' dream house is a Western-style house with dormers, bay windows, French doors, a white picket fence, and a wrought iron lamp at the entrance. This type of home is now becoming very popular with Japanese couples in their 30s. They pay an average price of $226,000 for the home, which is slightly higher than that for a comparable Japanese home. Because of the high cost of real estate in Japan, however, the lots for these homes are not as large as those in the United States.

The Nakamuras are very pleased with the house they have chosen. "We were living the tatami life style," Mrs. Nakamura said, "and now we are living the chair life style. I like it much better now." What she means is that the Nakamuras enjoy the comforts of living Western style—with chairs rather than tatami straw mats, and with beds rather than the futon mattresses that the Japanese have slept on for centuries. There have been other changes as well: there is now thick wall–to–wall carpeting instead of mats. One thing has not changed, however. There is a genkan, or recessed entrance hall, for people to leave their shoes before stepping inside. This is one custom that Mr. Nakamura believes will continue to resist westernization.

Kenzo Yamashita is also pleased. He is the head of the company that is building these new Western-style houses. His new Western-style houses are called "two-by-fours" because they use lumber that is pre-cut to the familiar 2 × 4 size. Most of the lumber comes from Canada and the United States. Mr. Yamashita's catalogue features different styles of homes. One is made with a brick veneer finish and a brick chimney jutting up from the roof. One calls for a "family room" and a den or "hobby room." The designs are prepared by Japanese and American architects. Although only a small number of Western-style homes are being built presently, Mr. Yamashita predicts a bright future for his company. He believes that the Japanese will be increasingly drawn to homes with Western designs and Western construction methods.

1. What are the Nakamuras planning to buy?
2. Why have they decided on this type of house?
3. What is Mr. Yamashita's role?
4. In what ways does this story show how one culture borrows from another? What is Japan borrowing from the United States?
5. Sometimes cultural changes happen quickly, in the span of a generation. What does this mean?
6. Sometimes it is easier for young people to deal with cultural change than older people. Would this be the case in this selection?
7. What have Americans recently borrowed from the Japanese?
8. What is the tatami life style?

Chapter 2

Understanding Culture

How is race different from culture?

1. As we study the regions of the world, we will learn about people of different cultures and races. We learned in Chapter 1 of this unit that *culture* refers to the way a group of people live, work, and play. What is meant then by the term *race*?

2. There is much disagreement and confusion over the meaning of race. Many people think a person's race is the same thing as the color of his or her skin. These people say that everyone belongs to one of three races—the black, the white, or the yellow race. If race is the same as skin color, however, in which racial group would we include Native Americans (American Indians) or people from India? Native Americans have brown skin, but their facial features are quite different from those of brown-skinned people from Africa. People from India have brown skin, yet they do not look like people from Africa nor like Native Americans. Skin color, then, is not enough to tell us what race is.

3. Some people confuse race with other characteristics—religion or language, for example. But people are not born with any particular religion or language. Usually, people learn to share their parents' religious beliefs. They generally speak the language of their parents and of the country in which they are raised. But they can also learn other languages and religious beliefs. For example, a Christian or Muslim might be a member of any race. He or she might speak English, Portuguese, Bantu, or some other language.

4. People sometimes confuse race with nationality. Yet people of many different races may be citizens of a particular country. Therefore, one cannot make race mean the same thing as nationality.

5. What then is race? Race is a set of bodily traits shared by a group of people. Skin color is just one of these traits. People in the same racial group generally share many other bodily features. These include such features as shape of eyelids, texture of hair, length of legs, and kinds of blood types. Another trait is the ability of the body to protect itself from certain diseases. These characteristics are passed down from parents to their children by way of *genes*. Genes are tiny units in the cells of the body. Because races have been mixing since human life began, there is no completely "pure" race. A member of a racial group may not have all the traits of other members of that group.

6. Racial groups share inherited characteristics. On the other hand, language, religion, nationality, customs, and dress are not passed on at birth from parents in the same way as race is. People learn these things from their parents and surroundings. They do not inherit them through their genes. Language, religion,

A Japanese family. What cultural differences can you see among the three generations of this Asian family?

What are some of the differences between race and culture? List three items in these photos that are part of people's culture.

and customs are part of culture. They are learned.

7. Scientists use body chemistry and bodily features to compare groups. However, experts cannot agree on how many races there actually are. Some say there are as many as 30. Many experts speak of 9 different major groups of races: African, Native American (American Indian), Asian, Australian Aborigine, European, Indian, Melanesian, Micronesian, and Polynesian. The major races, also known as geographical races, are collections of similar races who lived near one another long ago. Today, many of these groups have members who live in other areas. For example,

many Europeans moved to North and South America to settle. Many Africans were brought by force to the Americas where they were used as slaves.

8. Some people say that one race is superior to another. Even some who do not say it, act as if they believe it. People who believe or act as if one race is superior to another are *racists.* Racists usually claim that people of their own race are smarter, stronger, more artistic, or morally better. Experts have found no acceptable scientific proof for these claims. There are bright people of all races. All groups of people can point to their brilliant thinkers, builders, and artists.

UNDERSTANDING WHAT YOU HAVE READ

1. People's language generally depends upon
a. the natural environment
b. their race
c. the language of their parents and of the country in which they were raised

2. *Genes* are
a. tiny parts of the cells of the body that pass bodily traits from parents to their children
b. traits influenced by a person's nationality
c. traits learned from parents

3. A member of a racial group has
a. all the bodily traits of other members of that group
b. many of the bodily traits of other members of that group
c. very few of the bodily traits of other members of that group

4. A member of any race can learn
a. any culture
b. any religion
c. both *a* and *b*

In the World Today

Evaristo Nugkuag, an Aguarunan Native American from Peru, became very concerned about the misuse of the rain forest in Peru. He decided to become a spokesman for more than a million of his fellow Native Americans. He has been campaigning for the rights of the Native Americans to serve as the caretakers of the Amazon rain forests. He has gained support to pass laws against trespassing on Native American land by loggers, miners, and drug traffickers. In 1990, he received an award of $60,000 from the Golden Environment Foundation for his work in preserving the environment.

How could cakes and cookies in Scandinavia help save the rain forest in Central America? **Eha Kern,** a teacher in Sweden, encouraged students to start a small fund. With profits from a bake sale in their village, students raised enough money to buy 10 acres (4 hectares) of rain forest in Costa Rica. From this simple idea came the beginning of The Children's Rain Forest—a nonprofit organization to save the rain forest. The group has already bought some 17,300 acres (7,000 hectares). Now, the idea of The Children's Rain Forest has spread to such countries as Germany, Japan, and the United States.

It is not easy to fight against big businesses that are economically powerful. But **Yoichi Kuroda** of Japan has done just that. He has opposed such practices as importing illegal African ivory, cutting down endangered tropical trees, and ways of fishing that threaten sea life. He founded the Japan Tropical Action Network in 1987 and campaigns tirelessly against the Japanese trade in tropical wood.

Ranger **Steve Domm** of Queensland National Parks and Wildlife Service guards one of nature's marvels. Australia's Great Barrier Reef is the largest structure in the world made by living things. The 1,260-mile (2,016-kilometer) reef contains thousands of species of fish and 400 kinds of coral. The reef also provides a safe haven for such endangered species as the humpback whale. Steve Domm has many worries. Pesticide runoff from the mainland is a growing danger to life in the reef. Another threat comes from the crown of thorns starfish, which feeds on coral and has severely damaged some of the reef. The biggest problem is human visitors. Domm is willing to compromise with the tourists, though. "If we can enjoy a reasonable amount of privacy, a reasonable catch of fish, and still keep the reef for future generations to enjoy, then I figure we've done our job," he says.

Chapter 3

Machines Have Changed Our Way of Living

How have machines changed some nations of the world?

1. An important part of culture is the way people have learned to deal with their environment. The greatest change in the way people use the resources of the earth took place in the 18th and 19th centuries. This change is called the Industrial Revolution. (A revolution is the kind of change that brings about a new way of life for many people.) At that time machines were invented to turn out goods. Many goods were no longer made by hand in the home. They were made by machines in factories. New kinds of power were found to run these machines. Steam, made by burning coal, began to do some of the work once done by people and animals. This revolution changed the face of the earth. It divided the world into those countries that have many industries and those that do not.

2. With the use of machines it became possible to produce large amounts of goods of many kinds. These factory-made goods were cheaper than handmade goods because they cost less to make. As more and more people found work in the factories, they earned more money. They used this money to buy things they never had before. They became a market for the products of the factory. (Factories will not make goods unless people buy them.)

3. The factories needed more and more raw materials from which to make the goods. Coal and iron ore were used to make steel. New uses for oil were discovered. As factories grew, there were jobs for more and more workers. Thousands of men and women left their farms and moved near the factories. Cities grew around the great industrial centers. Their growth created still more jobs for people. For every person who worked in the factory, there were two others in *service occupations.* (These include grocers, teachers, doctors, and police.)

4. How could all these city people be fed? New machines began to be used on farms. With improved methods of farming and machinery, it was possible for farmers to grow more food with fewer workers. Farmers not only grew food for themselves, but they were able to feed people throughout the nation and the world as well. They grew *money crops—*crops they could sell at a profit. The farmer was now in business just as much as the factory owner was.

5. Coal became the chief source of power for travel over land and water. Railroads took the place of horse-drawn coaches. The great sailing ships were replaced by steamships. In time, there were other sources of power such as oil and atomic energy. The automobile and airplane were invented. Goods were carried swiftly and cheaply almost anywhere in the world. With the invention of the telephone, telegraph, and radio, people in all corners of the world were able to communicate.

6. Today, countries like the United States, the United Kingdom (Great Britain), Canada, Japan, Germany, France, Italy, Russia, and

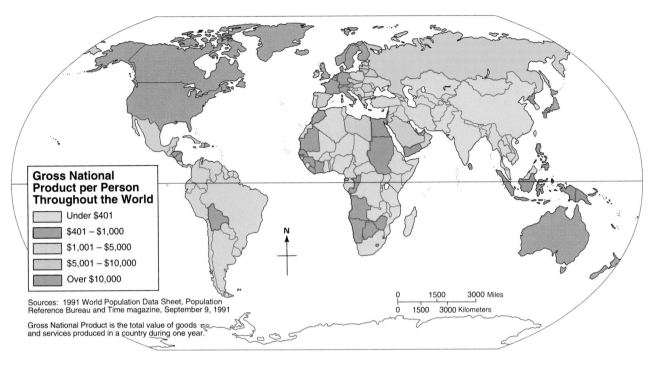

Gross National Product per Person Throughout the World

Ukraine are industrial societies. The peoples of these and other countries like them make up about one-quarter of our world. Their way of life is different from those of the rest of the world.

7. Here is how people live in industrial nations. First, most of the people use goods made in factories. They have power-driven machinery and make great use of the raw materials of the earth. They also use computers to design and make many products. Their factories produce goods for sale not only to their own people but also to people in other nations. They are able to ship goods from one place to another.

8. Most of the people live in towns and cities. Many live and work in buildings made of stone, brick, and steel. Their homes have doors and windows, electricity and running water—conveniences that most of the world's people do not have.

9. Most people in industrial countries have a high standard of living. They have jobs in which the pay is high and the hours of work are short. Machines do much of their work. They have enough food and water for their needs. Their medical care is good and they live longer. Nearly all adults can read and write. They learn much about the world through newspapers, radio, television, books, and films. They have money to spend for new clothes, trips, and cars. They are able to give support to theaters, museums, and libraries.

10. In general, these people live in democracies. They can choose their own leaders and make their own laws. These countries have several political parties. Each citizen can vote for the candidate of his or her choice. Those chosen to make the laws are expected to serve the people. In return, the people are willing to pay taxes to support government services. Most of these industrialized countries operate under the system of capitalism, in which the government plays a limited role in controlling businesses. Decisions about what to produce and how much to charge are made by individuals.

Workers using modern tools. List three ways that machines affect the way you live.

11. The peoples of industrial countries are highly dependent on each other. They need goods and services not only from each other but also from other parts of the world. The farmers rely on the cities for the goods and services they need. In turn the townspeople depend on the farmer for their food. Everyone depends on the flow of raw materials and goods from nation to nation. Anything that stops the goods from moving—a flood, a power failure, a strike, or a war—can make life hard for everyone.

12. Industrialized nations have some serious problems that must still be solved. In the United States, for example one-eighth of the people live in poverty. Families in many in-dustrialized nations still go to bed hungry. Some workers cannot get jobs. They cannot earn enough money to support their families. Unemployment continues to be a serious problem for most industrialized countries.

13. Industrialization has also threatened the environment. The air in many cities is heavy with smoke from factories and cars. Harmful chemicals have been dumped into streams and lakes. In addition, industrialized nations use large amounts of the earth's natural resources, such as oil and natural gas. In recent years, there have been shortages of these vital sources of energy. It is important to the entire world that the industrialized nations solve these problems.

UNDERSTANDING WHAT YOU HAVE READ

1. The main idea of paragraphs 1 through 5 is to decide

a. the countries where most people make a living through farming
b. the changes brought about by the Industrial Revolution
c. the world's natural resources

2. A high standard of living can be found in

a. most of the countries of the Middle East region
b. Canada
c. all of the countries within the area of southern Africa

3. In which of these ways was farming changed by the Industrial Revolution?

a. Fewer machines were used on farms.
b. Farmers raised food only for their families.
c. Fewer workers were needed on farms.

4. The Industrial Revolution is the name given to the

a. use of machines to do work once done by many people
b. discovery of oil
c. rise of independent countries

5. When there are people who will buy a product in places where it can be sold, we say that the product has

a. an industrial center
b. a market
c. been advertised

6. In general, the people of an industrial society

a. have a high standard of living
b. trade little with their neighbors
c. know little about the world

DEVELOPING IDEAS AND SKILLS

Using Pie Graphs

One of the most important kinds of graphs is the circle graph. A circle graph shows the relationship between a whole thing and its parts. Because the parts of a circle graph look like pieces of a pie, a circle graph is often called a *pie graph*. The circle stands for the whole pie, or 100 percent. Pieces of the pie stand for parts of the whole. Each piece of the pie is less than 100 percent. All the pieces of one pie added together should equal 100 percent. By comparing two pie graphs, we can see patterns such as changes with time. As you read about the different regions of the world, you will see graphs that help to give you information.

Study the two pie graphs. Then answer the questions that follow them.

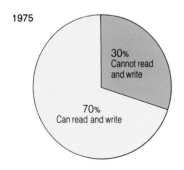
1975

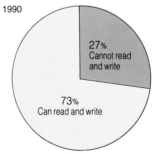
1990

Source: Central Intelligence Agency

**Percentage of the World's People Over 15 Years of Age
Who Can Read and Write**

1. The percentage of the world's people over 15 years old who could read and write in 1975 was
   a. 70%   b. 30%   c. 73%

2. The percentage of the world's people over 15 years of age who could not read and write in 1975 was
   a. 70%   b. 30%   c. 27%

3. The percentage of the world's people over 15 years of age who could read and write in 1990 was
   a. 70%   b. 27%   c. 73%

4. One pattern shown is that the percentage of people who could read and write
   a. went down from 1975 to 1990
   b. went up from 1975 to 1990
   c. remained the same from 1975 to 1990

The Greenhouse Effect

 The summer of 1988 was unusually hot and dry in the Northern Hemisphere. City dwellers suffered as temperatures stayed in the upper 90's for several weeks. With the heat came a long dry spell and calls to conserve water. Farmers watched helplessly as their crops withered in the sun. People began to talk about what some scientists had been predicting for years: the start of a global warming trend—an increase in the earth's yearly temperature.

While it is unlikely to happen, scientists have created a worst case scenario—a prediction about the most severe results possible. Global warming would cause ice in polar regions to melt. The melting would raise sea levels and flood coastal areas. Some of today's farmlands would grow too hot for crops and livestock. Farmers would have to move to new lands that are now too cold for farming. Dry regions and deserts would probably get larger, and rainfall patterns would also change. Rivers might dry up, become a trickle, and then disappear.

The "greenhouse effect." To find the cause for the global warming trend, you need to examine the actions of humans. Cutting forests and burning fuel—two main human actions—have been blamed for the global warming trend.

Burning fossil fuels like coal, oil, and natural gas account for most of the world's carbon dioxide buildup. When burned, these fuels release carbon dioxide into the air. Carbon dioxide traps warmth in the atmosphere.

In what has become known as the "greenhouse effect," heat-trapping gases, like carbon dioxide, keep the earth warm like glass keeps a greenhouse warm. An increase in greenhouse gases means that the earth—our greenhouse—will get warmer. Studies show that air today contains 25 percent more carbon dioxide than it did 200 years ago.

Major producers of carbon dioxide. Industrial countries are responsible for some 75 percent of the greenhouse gases released into the air. The United States, the European Community, and the republics of the Commonwealth of Independent States are leading sources.

Developing countries use less fossil fuels than industrial countries. Most of them, however, still burn wood for fuel and set fire to forests to clear trees for land needed for farms. This deforestation contributes to carbon dioxide buildup. Trees need carbon dioxide to grow. They help regulate world carbon dioxide levels. When trees are destroyed, an increased amount of carbon dioxide occurs in the atmosphere.

What to do? The question of global warming is one of today's most widely discussed topics. Many people are calling for actions to reduce the risk. Scientists are not certain that an actual global warming trend is happening. But if it is, nations will have to get together to reduce the supply of greenhouse gases. Replacing fossil fuels with other types of energy is one method. Although it will be expensive, developing alternate energy sources is one way to reduce greenhouse gases. People are working to make hydroelectricity, solar energy, wind energy, and tidal energy economical enough for daily use. Meanwhile, scientists are exploring new possibilities.

What do you think should be done about global warming?

What can individuals do right now?

Chapter 4

Developing Countries

What are the problems of the poorer nations?

1. There are many countries in the world where the Industrial Revolution has not really reached most of the people. Most of the world's people live in these countries. People in industrial countries must have a better understanding of their way of life. Unless they do, they cannot expect to know much of what the world is really like.

2. These poor countries have many things in common. First, they have not made full use of their natural resources. They still depend on hand labor to do their work in the fields and at home. They do not manufacture goods in great amounts, so they must buy them from other nations at high cost. Many of the people are farmers who work all day just to provide their families with food, clothing, and a place to live. They have nothing left over to sell to other peoples. (Farming that provides only the bare necessities of life is called subsistence farming.) Such countries are often referred to as agricultural, nonindustrial, less developed, or developing countries.

3. Most of the people are poor. Their average yearly income per person, or the amount they earn for one year's work, is very low. In Africa south of the Sahara, the average income is less than $500; in Asia, outside of the developed countries, it is about $600. There are millions who do not have enough to eat. Their poorly furnished homes often lack running water and electricity. Most live in crowded villages and small towns. Many of them do not own the lands they work.

4. The population, or number of people, in some of these developing countries is growing fast. Even with their problems, the people are healthier and live longer than ever before. Yet the average person in Africa, for example, can expect to live only about 49 years. It is important that the resources of the developing world be used to help the people get better health care, diet, homes, and schooling so they can improve their lives and have an active role in their future.

5. Many of these people cannot read or write. For example, in Afghanistan and Chad, about eight out of ten adults cannot read or write any language. People in some developing nations do not believe that everyone should go to school. Many cannot afford to go. In some of these nations only rich or very bright students go to school. Many of the new, independent nations have a population in which only one person in 1,000 has gone to college.

6. Most of the people in the developing world are members of one of several non-European groups. As you learned in Chapter 2, in past centuries, many people thought there were three races based on skin color: black, white, and yellow. Scientists now use body chemistry and body features to compare groups. Most of the people in the developing world are members of one of the following groups: African, Native American, Asian, Australian Aborigine, Indian, Melanesian, Micronesian, or Polynesian.

A health care worker in Sierra Leone, Africa (left). Workers in the People's Republic of China (above). How are these people working to improve life in their countries?

7. In the developing world, many of the people are not Christians. In the Middle East and large parts of Africa and Asia, Islam is the chief religion. In India, the major religion is Hinduism. In China, Buddhism is very strong. There are native religions in Africa and on the islands of the Pacific. As a result, the ideas these people have of what is right and what is wrong may not be the same as ours. For example, in North America we raise cattle and eat meat and drink milk. In India, Hindus believe the cow is sacred and should not be killed or used for meat.

8. The developing countries do not trade much with other nations of the world. In fact, this three-fourths of the world carries on only one-fourth of the trade among the world's nations. The people work hard just to keep themselves alive. They have little left over to sell to others. As a result, many have no money with which to buy machine-made goods from other nations.

9. Many developing nations grow only one kind of crop, such as coffee or sugar. They must then sell this crop at prices that are set on the world market. In many cases, the crop and the land it is grown on belong to large companies owned by people in richer countries. The profits, if any, are taken out of the developing nations. But if the crop fails, or if the world price for it is low, the people who work the land suffer most.

10. Since the 1940s, many of these developing nations have won their freedom from stronger countries in Europe. Although they supply large amounts of food crops and minerals to the industrialized nations, they need more help in the form of money, food, and experts. But they do not want to give up their freedom in exchange for this help. They want to learn how to use the help and to rule their own countries—even if it means rule by one-party states or military leaders.

11. As you read about the different nations of the world, you should keep the following in mind. Problems vary from one developing country to another. Some developing countries have much higher standards of living than others. Even within these countries, conditions are different from one area to another.

Even within the same developing country there may be great differences in the way people live. Both of these photos show life in present-day Colombia, South America. As you study the different regions of the world, you will discover both similarities and differences in the way people live within regions and countries.

12. There are some countries and peoples who would like to turn their backs on the Industrial Revolution. They want to avoid some of the problems of industrial societies, such as pollution, overcrowded cities, increase in crime, and the loss of traditional values. However, most people in the developing nations do not want to be poor. They want to bring the Industrial Revolution to their own lands. They feel that machines can bring about progress. They want more schools and hospitals, electricity, radios and television sets, refrigerators and washing machines. In addition, their populations are growing fast. They have to be fed. Their leaders believe that only more factories can offer enough jobs and money to buy food. Indeed, the factory has brought great changes to many countries in eastern Asia. Oil too has changed the lives of millions in the Middle East.

UNDERSTANDING WHAT YOU HAVE READ

1. The main idea of this chapter is to describe
a. the different religions of people in the world
b. how people have become closer to each other
c. how people live in the poorer areas of the world

2. A large share of the people cannot read or write in
a. Afghanistan
b. Canada
c. France

3. Two great Asian religions are
a. Catholicism and Judaism
b. Protestantism and Islam
c. Hinduism and Buddhism

4. Which of these is closely related to the standard of living of any country?
a. The size and shape of the land
b. The number of people
c. How resources have been used

5. Poverty of people in the world is a problem because

a. poor people will not be able to buy U.S. goods
b. poor people may suffer from hunger
c. education cannot help poor people

6. Most developing nations of the world are ruled by

a. leaders chosen in free elections
b. military leaders and dictators
c. officers chosen by industrial nations

7. A developing country is one in which

a. there are few water resources
b. most of the people are poor and there has not yet been full use made of natural resources within the country
c. most of the people work in factories

8. All of these are problems of developing countries EXCEPT

a. little money to buy goods
b. few people
c. lack of schooling for most people

9. All of the following statements are true of developing nations EXCEPT

a. most were colonies of other nations
b. they lack food crops
c. they want to make their own mistakes

10. All of the following statements about the Industrial Revolution are true EXCEPT

a. television made the revolution global
b. it has been welcomed by most developing nations
c. it has brought about few changes in people's way of life

DEVELOPING CRITICAL THINKING SKILLS

Can you tell whether these statements are facts or someone's opinion?

1. The United States has about 2 million people of the Islamic religion.
2. Many nations of the world do not have money to provide schools for all children.
3. It is important that we buy as much as we can from poorer nations.
4. Not all people have the same kinds of laws.
5. The needs of poor people in the world are as big a danger to world peace as is global warming.
6. Education is the answer to the problems that face the people of the world.
7. Within ten years, there will be an end to poverty in most countries.
8. People all over the world are interested in how the United States treats all its people.
9. The United States depends upon other people for many raw materials.
10. The United States has areas where there is great poverty.

Understanding Pictographs

A pictograph is a type of graph. It uses pictures or symbols to give information. For example, a small picture of a person could stand for one person. Two pictures of a person could stand for two people, and so on.

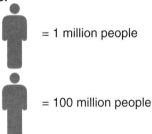

= 1 person

= 2 people

A symbol may not always stand for the same number of people. It could stand for one person, one million people, or 100 million people.

= 1 million people

= 100 million people

The symbol must be simple and countable. It must show clearly what it stands for, or represents. It must be explained or shown in a *key*. The key tells you what the symbols represent.

Key

= 25 million people

Sometimes, the pictograph will show you a quarter or half of a symbol:

= a quarter   = a half

For example, if a key shows that each symbol stands for 100 people, then a quarter of that symbol would equal 25 people or a quarter of 100 people. A half of a symbol would equal 50 people.

Once you know what each symbol stands for, you can figure out the number that is shown on a graph. Say, for example, that each symbol stands for 10 people. Then five symbols on a graph would stand for 50 people. Seven symbols would stand for 70 people, and so on.

Now look at the pictograph below. Then answer the questions.

1. What information is given in this graph?
2. How many people does each picture symbol stand for?
3. What is the source of this information?
4. What was the population of the United States in 1960? 1980? 1991?
5. Has the population been increasing, decreasing, or remaining the same?

U.S. Population Growth, 1960–1991

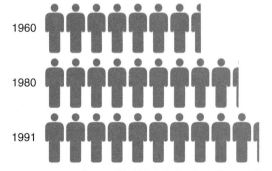

Source: World Population Data Sheet of the Population Reference Bureau, 1991.

Chapter 5

World Regions

What are the world regions into which this book is divided?

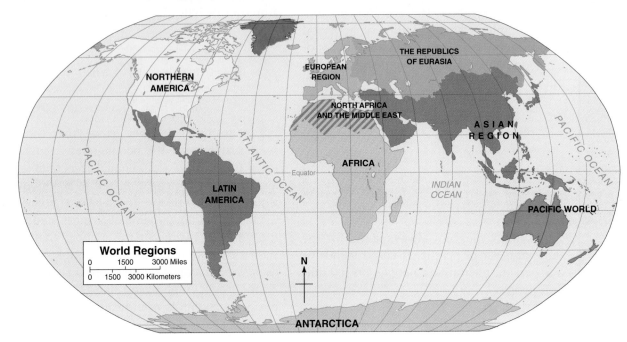

1. Each of the next eight units of this book tells about one of the eight regions of the world. Each region has features that make it a single region. The people and countries may be tied together through climate, land features, history, religion, or ways of making a living. Until 1991, the region called the Republics of Eurasia was in one country, the Soviet Union. It is now made up of twelve independent nations. Here are a number of questions to guide you as you prepare to study each of the eight world regions:

1. Why are we interested in this region?
2. How do the land and climate of the region explain, in part, the way the people live?
3. How has the geography of the region influence the history of the people?
4. Who are the people of the region? How are they trying to solve their problems?
5. What are the resources of the region? How do the people make use of these resources?

2. The first region we will study is *Northern America*. This includes the countries of the United States and Canada, two of the largest nations of the world. Only Russia is larger than Canada. The United States ranks fourth in land size after China. Both the United States and Canada are located in the middle and high latitudes of the Northern Hemisphere. They have many things in common. English is spoken by a majority of people in both countries. People in the United States and Canada have similar ideas of government. They have great industries and a high standard of living. Both countries have been friendly and have cooperated with each other for more than 150 years. They are one of the richest regions of all in natural resources.

3. *Latin America* is the next region of study. Most of the countries in Latin America were colonies of Spain, Portugal, or France. They are studied together because most of them are Catholic in religion and Spanish or Portuguese in the language their people use. This is largely a region of tropical rain forest,

Canals, such as this one in the Netherlands, have been built by people. What are some other ways people have used their surroundings to make transportation or trade easier?

or humid-subtropical or savanna climate. Mountains provide a cooler home for many people. Most of the people are descendants of Europeans, Native Americans, and Africans. About two-thirds of the people live in towns and cities. In the countryside, farming on estates and small farms is the chief kind of work. The countries of Latin America export many raw materials to other parts of the world.

4. The countries of the *European region* (other than Russia and the Commonwealth) are our next area of study. Europe is the smallest region we will explore, but there are a large number of countries within this region. These countries have a variety of climates. These climates include the taiga in the north and the marine climate in the west. The humid-continental climate is in the east, and the Mediterranean in the south. The leading countries are thickly populated. Many of the countries have made good use of their resources—the fertile lands, the iron and coal from the earth, the lumber from forests, and the fish from nearby seas. Their factories make iron and steel goods. They now also export much grain and meat to the rest of the world.

5. The fourth region we will study is the *Republics of Eurasia.* Most of the nations in

this region belong to the *Commonwealth of Independent States.* This region extends across parts of Europe and Asia. Its land has many resources and large areas in which few people live. From 1922 to 1991, the land was called the Soviet Union and governed by the communist party. In 1991, the Soviet Union collapsed as each of the individual republics declared independence.

6. The lands of *North Africa and the Middle East* are combined into one region in this book for several reasons. This area, stretching across northern Africa and southwest Asia, is almost all desert region. Most of the people live near sources of water. It is a region of both farmers (who work on irrigated land near the few rivers and oases) and city people. In some areas there are herders who travel with their flocks from place to place. Most people are Muslims. Many are poor and unable to read. However, in the oil-rich countries, the standard of living is rising rapidly. Modern hospitals, schools, and factories are being built.

7. *Africa* is studied as a whole, although in Africa south of the Sahara most people have ways of life that are very different from those peoples in North Africa. Africa is a region of great variety with vast rain forests, grasslands, and desert. The region is

Clearing the land for planting in Tanzania in Africa south of the Sahara.

rich in natural resources that people are now beginning to develop. Most people are either farmers or herders. Their ways of life are very different from those of the people who live in the region's cities and towns. Since 1945, most of the region has gained its freedom from European nations.

8. The Asian region is such a large area that it has been divided into three smaller regions for purposes of study. These smaller regions are the subcontinent of India, the countries of eastern Asia, and the countries of Southeast Asia. Over half the world's people live in Asia. Most of these people live on small farms. Yet some of the world's largest cities are also in Asia. As in Africa, many of the countries gained their freedom after World War II. The countries of Asia are trying to make better use of their resources. Japan has become a leading industrial nation. The people of Hong Kong (a British colony until 1997), South Korea, Taiwan, and Singapore have become much richer as their factories produce goods for sale throughout the world. China, a communist-controlled nation since 1949, is just starting to become a competitive world producer of goods.

9. To complete our study, we will look at the land areas of the *Pacific*. This region contains the continent of Australia and islands scattered throughout the Pacific Ocean. This is the region smallest in population. Australia and New Zealand have long been independent from the United Kingdom. People live in industrialized societies with a high standard of living. Since 1970, many but not all of the smaller islands and island groups in the Pacific region have gained self-government. The people of most of the Pacific Islands fish or farm for a living.

10. The war in Vietnam, the holding of American hostages in Iran, and the overthrow of President Marcos in the Philippine Islands were all reported on American television and in our newspapers. Because of these and other world events, many Americans became interested in what happened in these faraway places. This book will reinforce what you may have read or seen on television and help you to understand these foreign places. It can begin to tell you where these regions are and where these events took place. It will help you to understand what is happening there now. You will learn how events in one region can affect how people live in other regions. You will gain an understanding of the changing world. Moreover, the book will teach you about different ways of life and about your own place in the human community. We do indeed live in a global village!

UNDERSTANDING WHAT YOU HAVE READ

I. Matching

Match the items in Column B with the regions listed in Column A. There is one extra item in Column B.

COLUMN A
1. Northern America
2. Latin America
3. The European region
4. The Republics of Eurasia
5. North Africa and the Middle East
6. Africa
7. The Asian region
8. The Pacific world

COLUMN B
a. Many islands—farming and fishing
b. Region in the Northern Hemisphere made up of two countries—most of its people speak English
c. Large region in which most nations gained independence after 1945—farming and herding
d. World's smallest region—high standard of living
e. Region in Eastern Hemisphere—contains over half the world's people
f. Region in Southern Hemisphere—mainly taiga and tundra
g. Largely desert—major oil supplies
h. Most nations belong to the Commonwealth—used to be ruled by the Communist party
i. Western Hemisphere region—most people speak Spanish or Portuguese

II. Choosing the Best Answer

1. The main idea of this chapter is to describe
a. the land forms of the world
b. the world's largest cities
c. the regions explored in this book

2. The two main countries of the region of North America are
a. Spain and Italy
b. the United States and Canada
c. Japan and China

3. All of the following statements about the lands of North Africa and the Middle East are true EXCEPT
a. they are largely a desert region
b. the people are largely Christians
c. oil plays an important part in this region

4. All of the following statements about Russia are true EXCEPT
a. it is ruled by a communist government
b. it is the largest country in the world
c. it is a major industrial nation

5. All of the following statements about the Asian region are true EXCEPT
a. three of the major countries in this region are India, China, and Japan
b. many of the world's people live in this region
c. there are no democratic governments in this region

6. Africa is made up of
a. rain forests, grasslands, and desert
b. colonies of other nations
c. largely industrialized countries

DEVELOPING IDEAS AND SKILLS

Understanding Bar Graphs

Usually, information that can be shown on a pictograph can also be shown on a bar graph. For example, the following graphs show the same information:

Population of the United States

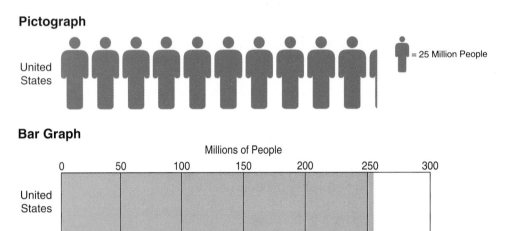

Source: 1991 World Population Data Sheet to the Population Reference Bureau.

Often bar graphs are used to show a relationship between two ideas or to compare two related things. Study the following bar graphs. Then answer the questions.

Length of the Average Life in Switzerland and Columbia, 1975 and 1991

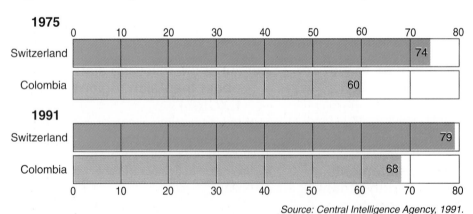

Source: Central Intelligence Agency, 1991.

Length of the Average Life in Switzerland and Columbia, 1975 and 1991

1. How long was the average life of a person in Switzerland in 1975?
2. How long was the average life of a person in Colombia in 1975?
3. How long was the average life of a person in Switzerland in 1991?
4. What happened to the average lifetime a person could expect to live in both countries between 1975 and 1991? Was there an increase in people's lives? a decrease? or did life expectancy remain about the same?

Some Material Goods for Selected Countries

COUNTRY	Number of automobiles	Number of telephones	Number of television sets	Number of radios
Afghanistan	34,900	32,000	12,600	823,000
Argentina	5,080,000	3,250,000	5,915,000	20,500,000
Australia	7,243,000	8,727,000	7,800,000	20,500,000
Austria	2,902,949	3,102,814	3,100,00	4,000,000
Belgium	3,864,296	5,138,000	3,274,236	4,608,000
Brazil	9,527,296	13,905,290	34,000,000	75,000,000
Bulgaria	815,549	2,386,462	1,692,711	1,982,929
Canada	12,086,001	16,200,000	12,400,000	21,800,000
China	152,899	10,000,000	10,500,000	150,000,000
Commonwealth of Independent States	14,343,900	40,100,000	92,400,000	84,800,000
Egypt	580,000	600,000	4,000,000	12,000,000
France	4,373,675	24,635,000	17,950,000	20,000,000
Germany	38,447,854	40,669,000	29,069,623	31,585,997
India	2,284,000	4,408,000	12,500,000	63,500,000
Indonesia	1,073,106	864,372	5,814,262	6,800,000
Iran	2,246,143	1,305,000	2,100,000	10,000,000
Israel	753,450	1,940,000	936,000	1,120,000
Italy	24,360,167	26,873,730	14,851,310	15,009,268
Japan	32,621,000	49,900,000	72,000,000	105,500,000
Libya	415,000	102,000	171,000	166,000
Mexico	5,817,169	7,329,416	9,500,000	21,000,000
Nigeria	215,436	708,340	650,000	15,700,000
Philippines	454,554	931,742	2,220,000	8,000,000
Poland	4,850,000	2,630,000	10,050,000	11,112,000
Saudi Arabia	2,250,000	1,049,000	3,600,000	3,200,000
South Africa	3,316,706	4,744,000	1,982,000	10,900,000
South Korea	1,117,999	10,306,000	8,643,000	42,070,000
The Sudan	99,400	68,838	1,000,000	5,000,000
United Kingdom	19,248,000	29,518,000	19,300,000	65,100,000
United States	143,081,000	176,391,000	199,000,000	519,450,000

Source: 1991 Europa World Yearbook.

UNIT·THREE

NORTHERN
AMERICA

KEY IDEAS

- The physical setting and rich natural resources of Northern America have helped Canada and the United States achieve high standards of living and world leadership.

- Northern America is a multicultural region. The cultures result from a blend of European, African, Asian, Native American, and Latin American Heritage.

- Although both Canada and the United States are democracies, their systems of government differ.

- Northern America is the world's largest and most productive manufacturing region.

- Agriculture in Northern America employs only a small percentage of the labor force, but produces a huge surplus of crops to sell to other regions.

- Although the population of Northern America is not large by global standards, it is the most urbanized in the world.

Tucked under beautiful Mount Rainier, the harbor at Seattle, Washington, is a great hub for the huge trade between the United States and the nations of East Asia.

Chapter 1

Northern Giants

Why do we study the United States and Canada together?

READING FOR A PURPOSE:
1. What makes up the region of Northern America?
2. How are the United States and Canada similar in land forms?
3. How are the United States and Canada similar in ways of life?

1. Stretching north of Mexico as far as the Arctic Ocean is a vast region that covers about four-fifths of the continent of North America. This region is called Northern America. It is shared by two countries, the United States and Canada. These two countries contain a variety of land forms, climates, and people.

2. Canada takes up most of the northern half of the North American continent. It covers an area of almost 3,850,000 square miles (9,970,000 square kilometers). As such, it is the second largest country in the world. South of Canada is the United States. It covers about 3,620,000 square miles (9,370,000 square kilometers), including the Hawaiian Islands in the Pacific Ocean and Alaska west of Canada. It is the fourth largest country in the world. Both nations border the two largest oceans, the Pacific Ocean on the west and the Atlantic Ocean on the east.

3. The United States and Canada share two long common borders. There are no guns or active forts along these borders. The longer of these two borders stretches more than 3,000 miles (4,800 kilometers) from the Atlantic to the Pacific Ocean. The eastern part of this border is made up of two great waterways—the Great Lakes and, for a few miles, the St. Lawrence River. Farther west, this border stretches along the 49th parallel until it reaches the Pacific Ocean. The second border

is about 1,250 miles (2,000 kilometers) long. It divides western Canada from the state of Alaska. For over 150 years, Americans and Canadians have crossed their common borders without difficulty.

4. In many ways the Canadian and American ways of life are alike. Often it is as if there were no borders between the two countries. For example, the Canadian farming lands near the St. Lawrence River are very much like the farming region of the New England states. Along the St. Lawrence River and the Great Lakes, factories on both sides of the border turn out machinery and manufactured goods.

5. The coastal areas of New England and the Atlantic provinces are also similar. There are many good harbors. Fishing is important. Parts of this region are rich in forests, coal, and minerals.

6. Suppose you were to visit the Canadian cities of Vancouver or Toronto and the American cities of Seattle or Chicago. You would see much that is similar. Most of the people speak English. They use many of the

Toronto, Canada, is similar in many ways to American cities. What are three ways in which most Canadian and American cities are similar? What are some differences?

An automobile factory. Industries in both the United States and Canada produce high-quality goods sold around the world.

same products. They eat many of the same foods. The children go to school and play such games as hockey and baseball. Both peoples, Canadian and American, have a high standard of living. Of course there are differences. A visitor would notice one right away. English is the major language of the United States. Both English and French are the official languages of Canada. French is the official language of the province of Quebec. Montreal is the world's second largest French-speaking city.

7. In the Central and Great Plains region, there are large wheat farms on both sides of the border. The farmers of both nations use large machinery to plant and harvest their wheat. Farther west, on the drier prairies, ranchers raise large herds of cattle and sheep.

8. The Rocky Mountains extend north and south through both countries. In both countries miners dig for gold, silver, lead, and zinc. Farther west, on the Pacific coast, Canadians and Americans fish for salmon. Lumberjacks cut down trees in the western forests of both the United States and Canada.

9. The relationship between the United States and Canada was described very well by President John F. Kennedy. On a state visit to

Wheat farming on the plains of Northern America. You cannot tell from this photograph whether this farm is in the United States or Canada. What does this fact tell you about this region of Northern America?

Canada over 25 years ago, he said, "Geography has made us neighbors. History has made us friends. Economics has made us partners; and necessity has made us allies." In the next chapters, we will explore how this statement applies today. We will learn how the two nations are using their great resources for the benefit of both their peoples.

UNDERSTANDING WHAT YOU HAVE READ

1. **Which questions are answered in this chapter?**
   a. What kinds of work do many people in the United States and Canada do?
   b. What does *Northern America* mean?
   c. What are Canada's two official languages?

2. **The main idea of *paragraph 3* is that**
   a. people of the United States and Canada trust each other
   b. two great waterways form the boundary between the United States and Canada
   c. the United States and Canada share common borders

3. **The United States is the**
   a. largest country in the world
   b. smallest country in the world
   c. fourth largest country in the world

4. **On both sides of the St. Lawrence River you are likely to find**
   a. forests
   b. farms and factories
   c. fisheries

5. **We are studying the United States and Canada as one region because**
   a. both countries lack natural resources
   b. most people in both countries are farmers
   c. both countries are similar in many ways

6. **People in both countries do much the same kinds of work because**
   a. both have similar land forms, climates, and ways of life
   b. both are located in the high latitudes
   c. both lands are surrounded by water

DEVELOPING IDEAS AND SKILLS

Building Map Skills — Northern America

Study the map on page 89. Then answer these questions.

1. Is the Northern American region north or south of the equator?
2. Is the region east or west of the prime meridian?
3. Which country is directly west of the region?
4. What are the chief bodies of water that border the region?
5. What are some of the important rivers in the region?
6. Which waterways form part of the boundary between the United States and Canada? The United States and Mexico?
7. What is the capital city of each country in the region? How do you know they are the capitals?

Northern America

DEVELOPING CRITICAL THINKING SKILLS

Understanding Charts

Study the chart. Then answer the questions that follow it. Use the map on page 89 to help you answer the questions.

Largest Canadian Cities

CITY	PROVINCE	POPULATION OF METRO AREA (the city and its suburbs)
Toronto	Ontario	3,427,168
Montreal	Quebec	2,921,357
Vancouver	British Columbia	1,380,729
Ottawa	Ontario	819,263 (includes the nearby city of Hull in Quebec)
Edmonton	Alberta	785,465
Calgary	Alberta	671,326
Winnipeg	Manitoba	625,304
Quebec	Quebec	603,267
North York	Ontario	602,109
Hamilton	Ontario	557,029
Mississauga	Ontario	311,195
St. Catherines	Ontario	343,258
Kitchener	Ontario	311,195
London	Ontario	342,302
Halifax	Nova Scotia	295,940
Laval	Quebec	255,547
Windsor	Ontario	253,988

Source: Europa World Yearbook.

1. Which province has the most large cities? How many?
2. How many of these large cities are within 100 miles of Canada's border with the United States? Why do you think this is so?
3. In which provinces of Canada are none of the largest cities located? Why might this be so?
4. What information on the map on page 89 might help to show you why Quebec, Montreal, and Halifax became such large cities?
5. In the United States, there are over 150 metropolitan areas with populations larger than Windsor's Metro area. How do you account for this difference in the number of large cities?
6. How many of Canada's large cities are in provinces west of Ontario?

90

Chapter 2

Geography Has Made Us Neighbors

How are the land forms of Canada and the United States alike?

READING FOR A PURPOSE:

1. What are the main land forms of Northern America?
2. Which land forms do Canada and the United States share?
3. Where are the major land forms located in Northern America?

1. In many ways, the United States and Canada share the same topography, or land features. Look at the map on this page. You will see that a large coastal plain stretches north and south along the Atlantic Coast and around the Gulf of Mexico into Texas. It is narrow in the north but widens in the south. The Atlantic Coastal Plain is bordered along its western side by the Appalachian Mountains. The Appalachians are low mountains whose peaks were smoothed by the ice of the glaciers. The Appalachians extend northward over much of southeastern Canada. These mountains are a great source of wood, coal, and water power.

2. Most of the continent between the Appalachians in the east and the Rockies in the west is covered by a vast lowland, called the inner plains. This area is one of the world's richest farming regions. Here the soil is very fertile. The inner plains are made up of two parts. The eastern part of these gently rolling lands was once covered with forests. The eastern part is called the Central Plains. The western part is called the Great Plains. West of the 100° meridian, the inner plains become the prairies, or dry grasslands. These grasslands rise slowly toward the Rocky Mountains. The

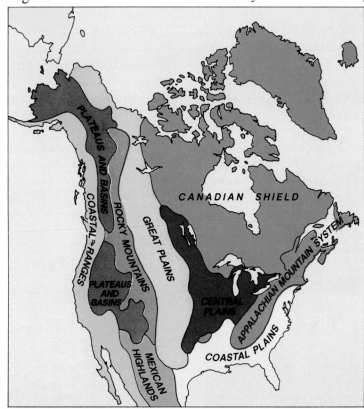

Major Land Forms of Northern America

inner plains spread north through Canada to the Arctic Ocean. They also include the St. Lawrence River Valley and the lowlands around the Great Lakes.

3. The inner plains of the United States are drained by the Mississippi River and its tributaries, or branches. The Mississippi River begins near the border of the United States and Canada. As it flows southward, the Mississippi is joined by other rivers. Two of these are almost as large as the Mississippi—the Ohio River from the east and the Missouri River from the west. The Mississippi flows southward through Louisiana and empties into the Gulf of Mexico. The Mississippi River and its tributaries form the longest river system in Northern America. The lowlands drained by these rivers of the plains form the greatest farming and grazing region of Northern America. Parts of this region also contain large deposits of oil, gas, and coal. In Canada, the Mackenzie River flows northward across the inner plains to the Arctic Ocean.

4. The snowy peaks of the Rocky Mountains mark the end of the Great Plains and the beginning of the western highlands. The Rocky Mountains are higher than the eastern Appalachians. They begin in Alaska and run southeast through Canada. Then they run south through the United States into New Mexico.

5. West of the Rockies is a dry, rough area of plateaus and basins. (A basin is a low area in the middle of the mountains.) Great rivers like the Colorado and the Columbia cut across the plateaus, making deep canyons. Many of the streams in this area flow into lakes that have no outlet to the sea. The streams bring salt and other minerals with them. When the water evaporates, or dries up, the salt is left in the lakes. The largest and most famous of these lakes is the Great Salt Lake in Utah. Many rivers rise in the highlands of the Canadian and American Rockies. In Canada, some flow into the Arctic Ocean or Hudson Bay. In the United States, some of the rivers flow eastward. (They join the Missouri or Mississippi rivers.) Other rivers flow westward to the Pacific Ocean. The ridge that divides the flow of rivers is called the Continental Divide. Near the southwestern edge of the Rockies' Great Basin lies Death Valley, California. This is the driest and hottest desert in Northern America.

6. Farther west are the coastal ranges, or mountains, which border the Pacific Ocean. They extend southward from Alaska into Mexico. These ranges change names from place to place. Between the coastal ranges are

This snakelike river is the Colorado River. As it cuts across the plateau, the river makes deep canyons. The Grand Canyon, which is a few miles from here, is one of the world's most famous canyons.

Death Valley, California. During the summer months, temperatures can rise as high as 125°F (52°C). It is part of the area of plateaus and basins west of the Rockies. Why is its name well chosen?

valleys, some of which are very wide. The great Central Valley of California is the largest of these. There is no great coastal plain along the Pacific Ocean as there is along the Atlantic.

7. Canada has one topographical region that is different from most places in the United States. It is called the Canadian Shield. The Canadian Shield is an upland that encircles Hudson Bay like a giant horseshoe. It covers more than half of Canada and extends into the United States in only two places. One is near Lake Superior. The other is the Adirondack Mountains in New York. This vast area of hard, old rocks was once scraped by glaciers. As these large masses of ice moved southward from the Arctic Ocean, they created valleys, hills, and thousands of lakes and rivers. The Canadian Shield is rich in waterpower, forests, minerals, and fur-bearing animals. However, only a few people live in this cold northern region. They earn their living mainly by trapping, fishing, mining, and cutting timber.

Far back in time, glaciers ground the area called the Canadian Shield into gently rolling hills and plains with many valleys and lakes. What are the land forms of your area?

UNDERSTANDING WHAT YOU HAVE READ

1. Which questions are answered in this chapter?
a. How did the glaciers affect the lands of the United States and Canada?
b. How do the people of Northern America use these lands?
c. What large land form is found in Canada but in only two places in the United States?

2. The main idea of this chapter describes the
a. land surface of Northern America
b. effects of the glaciers
c. Canadian Shield

3. The longest river system in Northern America is the
a. St. Lawrence   b. Mississippi   c. Colorado

4. The highest mountains in Northern America are the
a. Rockies   b. Appalachians   c. Ozarks

5. Few people live in the Canadian Shield because
a. the land is filled with streams and lakes
b. there is a lack of wood and minerals
c. the climate is too cold

6. The inner plains of the United States are valuable because
a. they have a wonderful climate for tropical fruits
b. the soil is easy to plow
c. the land is good for farming and grazing

7. A *glacier* is a large mass of
a. ice   b. land   c. hardened minerals

8. A branch is to a tree as a *tributary* is to a
a. person   b. river   c. mountain

9. In paragraph 5, the word *evaporates* means
a. "carries salt" b. "cuts deeply" c. "dries up"

10. The word *topography* refers to
a. climate   b. crops   c. land features

Reading a Land Form Map

The map on page 95 is a land form map of Northern America. There are several maps of this kind throughout the book. Land form maps try to give you an overall picture of the *surface of the earth*. The earth is not even. It is flat in some places. In other places it rises. How high a place rises, or goes up, is called its height, its *elevation,* or its *altitude.* The starting point for measuring the height of any place is the level of the sea. A land form map shows you where the high and the low places are.

Geographer's divide the earth's land forms into four groups: mountains, hills, plateaus, and plains. They look like this.

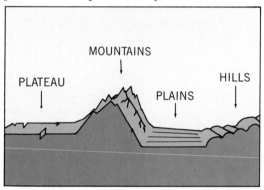

The plains are flat areas of land or slightly rolling hills. They are usually less than 500 feet (152 meters) above sea level. They are also called lowlands. Coastal plains are plains that border the sea. Interior plains are plains located in the inside of continents.

Plateaus are level areas of land that rise above surrounding plains. They are bordered by steep cliffs or bluffs. They are about 2,000 feet above sea level.

Hills are higher than 500 feet and less than 2,000 feet. In many places, people have been able to use hills successfully for farming, lumbering, raising animals, and vacation areas. Mountains rise at least

2,000 feet. They are bigger and more rugged than hills. Of the four land forms, they contain the least number of people. These are also called highlands.

Look at the map and its key. Its main purpose is to show you the four land forms. If you are to understand the map, you must have a clear picture of these land forms in your mind. When you see green, you must picture a plain or lowland, and all the activities it suggests. When you see light green, you must see those small, gentle hills. When you see yellow, the land is flat, but high up. When you see brown, you must picture snow-capped, rugged mountains. The map shows you other things, of course. It shows you coastlines (where the land meets the sea), rivers, political boundaries, and inland bodies of water.

When you look at a land form map, you must form certain "impressions" or general pictures, of it. You must be prepared to read the map and get some knowledge from it. Answer the following questions by reading the map.

1. What seems to be the main land form of this region?
2. How do you think the lowland can be used?
3. Where is the chief mountain chain?
4. Where are the major rivers located?
5. Where are hilly areas located?
6. How does human life differ in each of the land form areas?
7. On which kind of land form do you live?
8. What kind of land form do the green areas represent?
9. What color is used to show mountains?
10. Into which 4 land forms do geographers divide the earth?

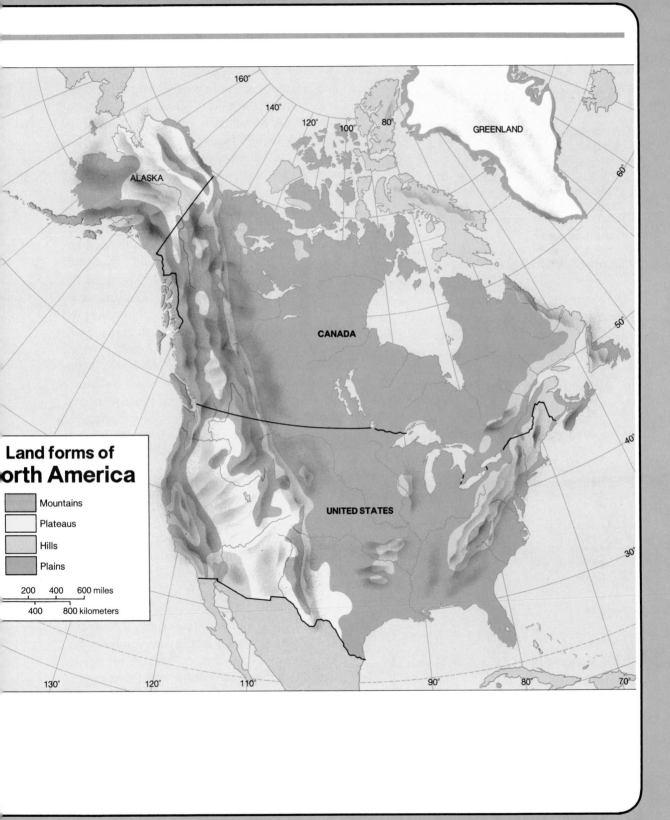

Land forms of North America

- Mountains
- Plateaus
- Hills
- Plains

200   400   600 miles

400   800 kilometers

GREENLAND

ALASKA

CANADA

UNITED STATES

160° 140° 120° 100° 80° 60° 50° 40° 30°

130° 120° 110° 90° 80° 70°

Chapter 3

The Cold and the Warm Regions

What are the many climates of Northern America?

READING FOR A PURPOSE:
1. What are the main climates of Northern America?
2. Which climates do the United States and Canada share?
3. Where are the major climates located in Northern America?

1. Northern America covers a vast area on the earth's surface. Because of its great size it has many different climates. There are a number of reasons for this. The most important reason is latitude, or distance from the equator. All of Northern America lies in the middle and high latitudes.

The Canadian tundra in summer.

2. In the far north of the continent is the cold, treeless area called the *tundra.* Because of its climate, this region of Northern America is not a desirable place to settle. The tundra stretches from the Bering Sea across Alaska and northern Canada to the Atlantic Ocean. It includes the island of Greenland. (Most of Greenland, however, is covered by a thick ice cap.) The winds from the Arctic Ocean blow far southward across the tundra. They bring cold air to much of Canada and the United States.

3. South of the tundra is the *taiga,* or northern forest climate. Forests cover most of northern Canada. The climate of the northern forestland is also harsh. The cold, icy winter lasts from six to seven months a year. In the spring, the snow and ice melt. The surface of the ground thaws, or unfreezes. However, the soil underneath remains frozen so that the water stays on the surface. As a result, swamps and marshes form, making land travel in the taiga almost impossible. When summer arrives the weather becomes warmer and many insects appear. The few people who live in this climate depend upon logging, mining, hunting, fishing, and trapping for their living.

4. Much of the middle eastern part of Northern America has a *humid-continental* climate. The northeastern part of the United States and the southeastern part of Canada have this climate. So does much of the Central Plains of both countries. The humid-continental climate is mainly the result of two things: distance from the equator and wet winds that blow from the Atlantic Ocean and the Great Lakes. Farther north in this region the winters are cold. As you go south, the summers become warmer and longer. Westward, or inland, the winters are colder and the summers are hotter because there are no large bodies of water nearby to even out the temperature. In the central part of the United States, farthest from the effects of the ocean, temperatures may be as low as $-30°F$ ($-34°C$) in winter and as high as $110°F$ ($43°C$) in summer. There is plenty of rainfall in the humid-conti-

Some regions of Northern America have cold, snowy winters that create excellent conditions for skiing. What types of climate do these regions have? Where are they located?

nental climate. Most Canadians and many Americans live in this climate area. They live and work mostly in large cities. However, there are also rich farmlands devoted to dairying and to growing corn and wheat.

5. The southeastern part of the United States has a *humid-subtropical* climate. There is a long, hot summer and a mild winter. Plenty of rain falls throughout the year. The Gulf Coast plains have much rainfall because of winds that blow from the Gulf of Mexico. The growing season is at least seven months long. No part of Canada has a climate like the humid-subtropical section of the United States. About 32 percent of Americans live here. The area has rich farmland with fields of cotton, tobacco, peanuts, soybeans, citrus fruits, and rice. Fast-growing forests make parts of this area important for wood and paper products. Most people here live and work in cities and towns. The oil, space, and aircraft industries provide jobs for many people in this area.

6. There is enough rainfall for farming westward as far as the 100° meridian. At this point the climate gradually becomes drier and the prairies, or dry grasslands, begin. This is the *steppe* zone of the North American continent. If you travel westward, you will find that there is less and less rainfall until you reach the deserts of the southwest. There you will find almost no rain. The lands west of the 100° meridian are drier because of the coastal mountains that border the Pacific Ocean. These mountains stop the rain-filled winds as they blow inland from the Pacific Ocean. The rain falls on the western side of the mountains, but the eastern slopes are dry. The dry air then passes over the Great Basin region. The Rocky Mountains stop most remaining rain-filled winds from reaching the prairies.

7. These dry lands of the western prairies and the western mountains and basins make up about one-third of the United States. Yet they contain only about 5 percent of the American people. In Canada, too, the area for the most part is thinly settled. However, Edmonton and Calgary are two large Canadian cities in the area. At one time, great herds of buffalo roamed these plains. Now they are shared by cattle ranchers, sheep herders, and dry farmers. The few who live in the highlands work chiefly at mining and raising sheep.

8. Some western parts of Canada and the United States have a vertical climate. This climate occurs in the mountains of the region. The climate at the foot of the mountain is the same as that of the nearby area. As you go higher up the mountain, the climate changes, becoming cooler. The top of the mountain usually has a tundra climate.

9. The wettest part of Northern America is a section along the Pacific coast stretching from northern California across the western coast of Canada to the southern tip of Alaska. This is the *marine* climate area of Northern America. This strip of coastal land gets plenty of rain throughout the year, and its winters are cool. A warm current flows along the coast causing warm winds to blow over the land. The coastal mountain ranges force these winds upward, where they cool and drop their moisture as rain. Because of the heavy rainfall, this land is rich with forests. The many inlets and rivers along its coast are good fishing grounds.

10. While northern California has a marine climate, southern California enjoys the warm, sunny *Mediterranean* climate. In southern California the summers are hot and dry and the winters are mild. Nearly all rainfall takes place in the winter months. The population of California is growing rapidly, partly because the climate is so pleasant. While this climate area covers only 2 percent of the United States, it has 9 percent of the people. In its irrigated valleys, all kinds of crops can be grown.

11. Hawaii is actually located in the Pacific world region, which you will study in Unit 10. Hawaii is famous for its climate. Because it is surrounded by the warm waters of the Pacific Ocean, it is always warm. Summer temperatures are always near 80°F (27°C), and it is never cold in the winter. Like the people of Miami, Florida, Hawaiians rarely if ever need to heat their homes. In their fertile fields the farmers of Hawaii raise sugarcane, pineapples, and other tropical fruits.

A desert region in Arizona. Why does this area have so little rain?

UNDERSTANDING WHAT YOU HAVE READ

1. Which questions are answered in this chapter?
a. Why is the climate on the Pacific coast so wet?
b. What is the tundra?
c. Where does the Gulf Stream begin?

2. The main idea of *paragraph 6* is that
a. the Rockies extend a great distance from north to south
b. the coastal mountains and the Rockies affect rainfall in western states
c. wet winds blow from the Gulf of Mexico

3. Part of the Pacific coast has a
a. marine climate
b. humid-subtropical climate
c. humid-continental climate

4. A large part of northern Canada is
a. taiga   b. steppe   c. desert

5. The western inner plains have cold winters and hot summers because they are
a. close to the equator
b. open to the winds from the Arctic and are far from the effects of the oceans
c. open to the winds from the snow-covered Appalachian Mountains

6. The western part of the Great Plains is dry because
a. it lies too far north
b. it lies near the cold Pacific currents
c. rain-bearing winds are blocked by mountains

7. In *paragraph 2*, the expression "the cold, treeless area called the *tundra*" refers to
a. northern Canada
b. the top of the Rocky Mountains
c. the winds from the Gulf of Mexico

Building Map Skills—Climates of Northern America

Study the map carefully. Then decide whether or not each of the following statements agrees or disagrees with the information on the map. If the statement does not agree, explain why.

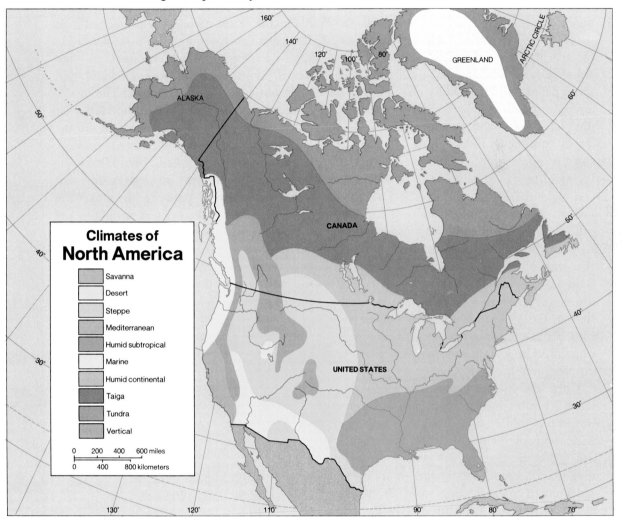

Climates of Northern America

1. Both the United States and Canada have an area of vertical climate.
2. The marine climate is located on the western coast of Northern America.
3. Large water areas of Canada are found in the tundra climate.
4. The humid-continental climate is found only in Canada.
5. The steppe is found largely west of 100° west longitude.
6. The smallest climate area in Northern America is the Mediterranean climate.
7. The southeastern coast of the United States has a humid-subtropical climate.
8. The marine climate is found only in the high latitudes.
9. The humid-subtropical climate is found mainly north of 50° north latitude.

— Life in the Canadian Northwest —

Much of Canada is covered by the taiga or tundra climates. If you look at the map of Canada on page 89, you will see that much of this land is organized as the "Northwest Territories." About 50,000 people live in these territories, mainly Native Americans, or Indians, and Inuit. Most of these people depend mainly on fur-bearing animals for their livelihood. As a result, they have made Canada one of the world's largest producers of fine furs. Here is the story of a few people who live and work in this cold land.

Corporal Jack Stoughton is feeling good today. He is a Mountie, one of 235 police officers who enforce law and order across the Northwest Territories, an area one-third the size of the United States. Corporal Stoughton's post is in Rae, a little village at the north end of Great Slave Lake. Although the Mounties no longer deliver babies, pull teeth, or carry the mail, they still remain an important link between the government and the Inuit.

Corporal Stoughton has just received a letter from his brother, Bob, also a Mountie. Bob is stationed at Broughton Island, a windswept settlement of rocky, treeless tundra across the ice-clogged Davis Strait from Greenland. Broughton Island is about 60 miles north of the Arctic Circle. Things are much worse on Broughton Island. The Inuit who live there are no longer allowed to hunt seal. Unable to earn a living many live on welfare. Because of the lack of work and extra spare time, many people were hard to control. It is not an easy job for the one Mountie there.

Even the children in the north are challenging the Mounties' authority. Many feel the violence on TV is causing this problem. Teachers are having a hard time motivating the children to learn. With 80 percent unemployment they feel they have nothing to look forward to unless they leave the area.

On the other hand, things are better at Rae. Just this morning, Philip Husky, a 61-year-old Dogib Indian, brought six fine martin skins into the Rae cafe and laid them out carefully on the floor. The owner of the cafe, Martin Cole, paid him $215 for the furs. He plans to send them to the fur auction in Vancouver. "What will you do," Corporal Stoughton asked Philip Husky, "if the government will no longer let you trap?" Mr. Husky paused. "I think," he said, "they forget we exist as people in the far north. We have to feed our families. We've always been in tune with the land. I hate to think of what would happen if they stop us. As it is, there isn't enough work to go around. But I have to hurry, there are only a few hours of daylight to do the job." Corporal Stoughton looked at Philip Husky as he rushed out and thought, "Rae could become a difficult place if . . . ." Cafe owner Martin Cole, as if reading his thoughts said, "Yes, it won't be easy, especially if you're on your own."

1. What is the tundra climate?
2. What is the taiga climate?
3. Why do you think so few people live in Canada's far north?
4. How does Philip Husky make a living?
5. Which groups, do you think, are against the killing of seal and other fur-bearing animals?
6. What does Philip Husky mean when he says, "We've always been in tune with the land"?
7. What would the Native Americans do if they could not trap for a living?

Chapter 4

History Has Made Us Friends

How have we grown from colonies to free nations?

READING FOR A PURPOSE:
1. Who were the early peoples who lived in Northern America?
2. Where were the British and French colonies in Northern America?
3. How did the young nations of the United States and Canada grow?

1. Groups of Native Americans and Inuit (Eskimos) came to Northern America long before Europeans did. The Native Americans lived along the rivers, on the plains, and in the woodlands. There were many Native American peoples, each with its own language and ways of life. Some were mainly hunters. Others gathered wild plants, farmed, or fished. Many Inuit lived far to the north along the shores of the Arctic Ocean. They fished and hunted seals, walrus, polar bears, and whales. Other Inuit peoples lived in the far north, but inland. They depended on caribou meat and on fish caught in the many lakes.

2. About 1,000 years ago, Vikings from northern Europe built permanent settlements in Greenland. Shortly after that their ships reached Newfoundland. There they built several settlements. They met the Native Americans, whom they called Skraelings. The Vikings did not remain permanently in Newfoundland. Other Europeans failed to learn about the Vikings' voyages.

3. When Columbus reached the New World, in 1492, the news led other explorers to come to North America. One of the first European powers to explore the region was Spain. In 1539, the Spanish explorer Ferdinand de Soto marched across the southeastern part of what is now the United States. He reached the Mississippi River. Francisco de Coronado explored the mountains, deserts, and plains of what is now the American Southwest in 1540. The city of St. Augustine, Florida, was founded in 1565. Soon after that

Native Americans of southeastern Canada in the 18th century. In what ways did they use plants and animals to provide food, clothing, and transportation?

Mission built by the Spanish in San Antonio, Texas. List three American cities, lakes, or rivers that have Spanish names.

they built other settlements in what is now South Carolina and Georgia. Santa Fe, New Mexico, was settled in 1609. The Spanish left their ways of living in these and other parts of what is now the United States.

4. French interest in the New World began in the 16th century. In 1524, Giovanni da Verrazano sailed under the flag of France, exploring the coast of North America. He was looking for a short route to Asia. In 1534, Jacques Cartier claimed for France the land around the Gulf of St. Lawrence. The next year he sailed up the St. Lawrence River, finding land that was rich in fur-bearing animals. In 1605, the first permanent French settlement in North America was founded at Port Royal, Nova Scotia. In 1608, Samuel de Champlain founded Quebec. The colony was known as New France. The French explored the nearby waterways in search of furs and claimed all the lands surrounding them. In 1682, La Salle reached the mouth of the Mississippi and claimed the river valley for France.

5. Only five years after Columbus's first voyage, John Cabot sailed from England and explored the eastern coast of North America. British settlers came to stay in America in the early 1600s. The first settlement was made farther south along the Atlantic Coast in the present state of Virginia. The British gradually established 13 colonies along the eastern coast of what is now the United States. Most people in these colonies were farmers. The farms were small in the northern part of the colonies, but they were much larger in the southern part, where tobacco was grown. In order to help work the tobacco fields, the first Africans were brought to the South in 1619. A few years later, a system of slavery was set up in the southern colonies. In 1670, the English claimed trading rights to all the land around Hudson Bay in northern Canada. They set up trading posts. They wanted a share of the fur business as well.

6. The French built forts and trading posts along the Great Lakes and in the Ohio and Mississippi river valleys. The English colonists also wanted to settle the fertile farmlands of the Ohio Valley. Before long, there was a war between England and France over the Ohio Valley. After several years of fighting, the French were forced to give up their claim to New France, or Canada, and all the territory east of the Mississippi River. Although the lands of New France became British colonies, the French settlers were allowed to keep their own language and religion and the laws they brought from France. The British colonies were known as British North America.

7. As new settlers came from Europe in greater and greater numbers, they pushed the Native Americans off their land. Many of them now live on reservations. The original peoples could not hold their hunting and farming grounds against the guns and machines of the newcomers. They did, however, make many contributions to farming in Northern America. They showed the Europeans how to live in the wilderness. They gave the settlers corn or maize, the white potato, tobacco, beans, pumpkins, tomatoes, and other foods.

8. In 1775, the 13 American colonies began their fight for freedom from Great Britain. A

new nation was formed, the United States of America. The Americans thought that colonists in British North America would also fight against Britain for its freedom. An American army invaded Canada for this reason but was not successful. At this time, those American colonists who remained loyal to England left for parts of British North America, mainly Nova Scotia, New Brunswick, and Upper and Lower Canada.

9. There was peace between the United States and British North America until 1812. At that time, some United States lawmakers accused the British in Canada of giving guns to the Native Americans. They said that the British urged the Native Americans to attack the United States frontier in the West. In the war that followed, the United States forces again invaded Canada, and again they were turned back. Shortly after the war ended, the United States and Great Britain signed a treaty. They agreed not to build any more forts along the Great Lakes. Later this agreement was extended to include the entire length of the 4,250-mile (6,800-kilometer) borders between the United States and Canada. Such trust and friendship between neighboring nations cannot be found in most parts of the world.

10. From 1803 to 1853, the American frontier moved westward until it reached the Pacific coast. In 1803, the United States bought the Louisiana Territory from France. In 1819, Florida was acquired from Spain. In 1845, the Republic of Texas became part of the United States. Great Britain and the United States agreed in 1846 to divide the Oregon Territory at the 49th parallel. Two years later, the United States gained a large area of land from Mexico as a result of a war. This included what is now a large part of the American Southwest. In 1853, the government bought from Mexico a strip of land in southern New Mexico and Arizona. This was called the

The Growth of the United States

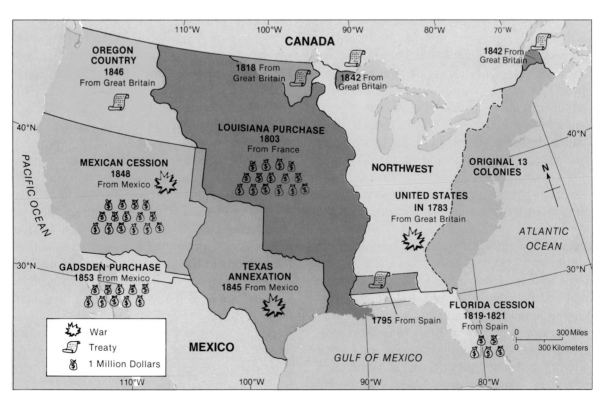

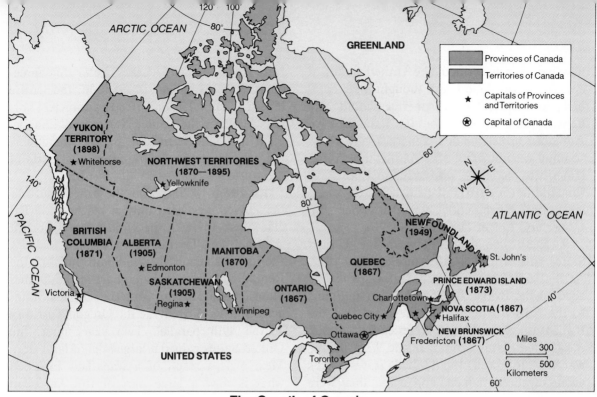

The Growth of Canada

Gadsden Purchase. At that point, the westward movement was slowed by the Civil War.

11. After the Civil War, the growth of the United States continued. People were busy building factories, railroads, and bridges. Steel mills were busy trying to keep up with the demand for steel. The mills were worked by people who had come to this country from other lands. Cities grew larger as people moved to homes near their work. Factories turned out more goods. Alaska was bought from Russia in 1867. In 1898, as a result of war with Spain, the United States obtained colonies in the Atlantic and Pacific oceans.

12. During the 19th century, British North America gained more freedom from Great Britain. In 1867, the British Parliament passed the British North America Act. This act created the Dominion of Canada. The colonies of Upper and Lower Canada, Nova Scotia, and New Brunswick joined to form a new nation that had the right to govern itself. These colonies became the provinces of Quebec, Ontario, Nova Scotia, and New Brunswick. A central government was set up in Ottawa, the capital city of the new nation of Canada. The eastern provinces wanted Canada to reach to the Pa-

cific coast. (The United States already did.) Laws were passed giving homesteads to settlers taking up land on the prairies. After a transcontinental railroad was completed in 1885, more settlers began to move westward. Six other provinces joined Canada, the last being Newfoundland in 1949. In recent years, Canadians began to object to having to ask Great Britain to approve their constitutional amendments. So Canada ended its legal tie to Great Britain with the Constitutional Act of 1982. This act gave Canada complete self-government.

13. The United States and Canada have many ties. They share a border thousands of miles long. Millions of people cross the border each year, without passport or visa. There is more two-way trade between the United States and Canada than between any other two nations in the world. The armed forces of the two countries have served side by side in various wars. The two countries also have close political ties. Like the United States, Canada is a member of the North Atlantic Treaty Organization (NATO). The heads of each country meet often to discuss common interests and problems.

UNDERSTANDING WHAT YOU HAVE READ

1. Which questions are answered in this chapter?

a. Where were most early French settlements in Northern America?

b. Who was John A. Macdonald?

c. Why did the Europeans come to Northern America?

2. The main idea of *paragraph 11* describes

a. the growing demand for steel

b. how the United States reached the Pacific coast

c. the growth of the United States after the Civil War

3. The French came to Northern America in search of

a. furs

b. religious freedom

c. a place to build a canal from the St. Lawrence River

4. The French lost Canada as a result of

a. the American Revolution

b. a war with England

c. the War of 1812

5. During the American war for freedom from Great Britain,

a. Canada tried to annex the United States

b. the United States gained complete possession of the St. Lawrence River

c. the United States invaded Canada

6. Canada became completely self-governing

a. about the same time the United States became independent

b. in 1982

c. shortly after the American Civil War

7. Another word for *maize* as used in paragraph 7 is

a. corn

b. guns

c. vegetables

8. In paragraph 12, the word *transcontinental* means

a. long and difficult

b. across Canada from coast to coast

c. modern and western

DEVELOPING IDEAS AND SKILLS

I. Making Charts — Growth of the United States

Complete this chart in your notebook. You may use the map on page 103 to help you.

TERRITORY	DATE ADDED TO THE U.S.	HOW
1. Louisiana		
2. Florida		
3. Oregon		
4. Texas		
5. California		
6. Gadsden Purchase		
7. Alaska		

Reading Time Lines

Time lines are useful for teaching many aspects of history. They help students understand when and in what order certain events took place. They can help students learn a few key dates and relate other events to them. To begin your understanding of time, review some of the words you have learned that deal with time.

minute	week	decade	last	period
hour	month	century	next	generation
day	year	ago	late	ages ago

Do you know the meaning of all these words? Can you tell clearly the differences between events that happened in the past, the present, and the future? Do you know how long ago 1950 was? 1900? 1850? It may be easy to give the answer mathematically. But how long does it *seem* to you?

Perhaps you can find out how long ago 10 years was, or 50 years, by drawing a simple time line. It can be drawn in two ways:

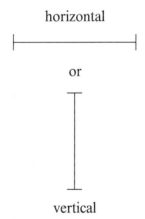

horizontal

or

vertical

Each line on a time line represents an equal number of years. For example, the space between each line could stand for one year, five years, ten years, or even one hundred years. The spacing between each line must be the same.

Draw one of the time lines in column 1 in your notebook. On the time line place dates that are important to you: (a) the year of your birth; (b) the year you entered elementary school; (c) the year you entered junior high school; (d) the year of a relative's birth; (e) the year a great event in your life took place. First, you should decide how many years you want to show on the time line. Then, add lines to show the years, and label the years. Finally, write the events below the proper dates.

As a next step, interpret a time line with one key date on it.

1865

Using the time line above, indicate if the following events came before or after the key date. Place the events on the time line, using a B for events that came before the key date and an A for events that came after.

- the Louisiana Purchase
- World War I
- The Mexican Cession
- the presidency of Ronald Reagan

Time lines can be used to review and recall events described in the chapter. Put your knowledge of time into practice by completing the following.

1. Reread the paragraphs on Canadian history in your text, looking carefully at the map on page 104.
2. Draw a time line (either horizontal or vertical) and divide it into equal segments of 25 years each.
3. Select important dates in Canada's history and place them on your time line in the correct time frame and in the correct order.

Chapter 5

The People of the United States and Canada

Who are the people of Northern America?

READING FOR A PURPOSE:
1. From what parts of the world did the people of the United States and Canada come?
2. How are the ways of life of Americans and Canadians similar?
3. Where in the United States and Canada do the people live?

1. Over a quarter of a billion people live in the United States and Canada. About 253 million of them live in the 50 states of the United States. The United States ranks fourth in world population. The map on this page shows where most Americans live. Millions of them live in the huge cities and towns on the northeast coast, near the Great Lakes, and in parts of Texas, Florida, and California.

2. People have come to the United States from all over the world. During the past 200 years, over 38 million Europeans settled in the cities and on the farmlands. The greatest numbers of people have come from Germany, Italy, Great Britain, Ireland, Austria, Hungary, Russia, Sweden, Norway, Poland, France, and Greece. Over 4 million Canadians have moved to the United States. Many Africans were forced to come as slaves in the 17th, 18th, and early 19th centuries. Spanish-speaking people lived in the area that the United States gained from Mexico and in Puerto Rico, which was gained from Spain. Millions of other people have come from Mexico, Puerto Rico, the West Indies, Colombia, and Cuba. Many Asians from China, the Philip-

Population Density of the United States and Canada

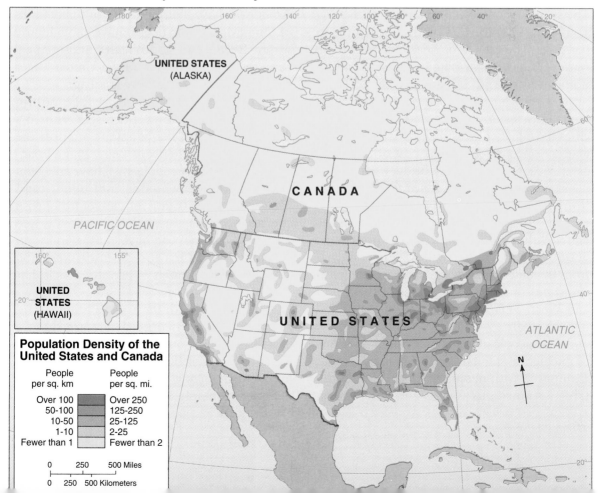

Population Density of the United States and Canada

People per sq. km	People per sq. mi.
Over 100	Over 250
50-100	125-250
10-50	25-125
1-10	2-25
Fewer than 1	Fewer than 2

pines, the Japanese islands, Korea, and Vietnam have also settled in the United States.

3. Members of almost all the world's races and religions live in the Unites States. Those with European backgrounds make up the largest group. About 84 percent of Americans identify themselves as white. About one American in eight identifies himself or herself as black. Asians, Native Americans, and others make up the rest of the population. Most Americans belong to either Protestant or Roman Catholic religious groups. Several million Americans are Jews or Muslims or are members of Eastern Christian churches. English is the official language. However, many Americans do speak other languages. Spanish is the most widely spoken non-English language.

4. Until the early 20th century most Americans lived on farms. By 1990, 2.4 percent of America's population lived on a farm. Today most of the nation's people live in towns and cities. Why did people move to the cities? Most of the new jobs in offices, stores, and factories were located in or near cities. The schools, colleges, hospitals, theaters, museums, and libraries also attracted people to the cities. The growth of cities is called *urbanization*. Besides providing benefits, urbanization can bring with it many problems. These include poor housing, polluted air from autos and factories, and increased crime. Many cities have higher taxes than rural places. The taxes are needed to pay the cost of fire fighters, police, teachers, roads, bridges, water supplies, and sewer systems. Since the 1940s, millions of Americans moved from the old central cities to new nearby communities called suburbs. By 1970, more Americans lived in suburbs than in cities. Others moved from the older cities of the northern and eastern states to the growing cities of the South and West. This suburban growth continued into the 1990s.

5. The people of the United States have one of the highest standards of living in the world. Compared with people in most other countries, Americans work shorter hours,

From what parts of the world have people in your community (or their ancestors) come?

receive higher pay, and have better working conditions. The United States has more radios, TV sets, refrigerators, automobiles, washing machines, telephones, and other labor-saving machines than any other nation. Americans have a large supply of many kinds of food. Most of the people have enough pure water. Because of good health and medical care, the average person in the United States can expect to live to be 75 years of age.

6. The United States has free public schools for all children. Local governments collect taxes from the people to support the public schools. Americans know that a country governed by its people must have educated citizens. Anyone who does not understand what he or she is voting for cannot make wise choices. Schooling through high school is free so that all children can have equal opportunities to get an education. Some Americans attend religious schools or private schools that are not tax supported.

7. Compared with the United States, Canada has very few people. There are slightly more than 26 million people in Canada. This is about the same as the number of people living in California alone. Compare this, too, with the approximately 253 million people living

108

in the United States, which is smaller in size than Canada.

8. About 80 percent of all Canadians live within 100 miles (160 kilometers) of the southern border it shares with the United States. Here the soil is fertile and the climate is warmer than in the rest of Canada. Aside from the land near the United States, Canada is largely a cold wilderness. Many of the people in northern Canada log, drill for oil, mine, trap animals, or fish. About half the people live in the southeastern part of the country near the Great Lakes and the St. Lawrence River. That region has many large cities, including Montreal, Toronto, Ottawa, Hamilton, and Quebec. Vancouver, Calgary, Winnipeg, and Edmonton are among the large cities in western Canada.

9. A little less than half of Canada's people are of British descent. Almost one-fourth of the people are of French descent. Most French-speaking people live in the province of Quebec. In this province, French is the official language and French culture is the main way of life. Most people in Quebec are Roman Catholic. In Canada as a whole, most people belong to either Roman Catholic or Protestant religious groups. Several hundred thousand Canadians are Jews or members of Eastern Christian churches. Many Canadians have families that came from Europe over the past 100 years. They came mainly from the United Kingdom, Ireland, France, Italy, Germany, Ukraine (now part of the Commonwealth), and Portugal. Canada has also had many immigrants from the United States, China, and the West Indies. In recent years, immigrants have come from Asia and Latin America. The Native Americans live on lands set aside for them by the government. In the far north is the land of the Inuit.

10. Most Canadians work in offices, stores, factories, and mines. Only 1 out of 24 people works on a farm. The major industries are making cars and trucks, refining oil, producing wood pulp and paper, and processing meat. Many work in iron and steel mills, mines, forests, or on fishing boats. Like most Americans, most Canadians enjoy a high standard of living.

11. Canadian boys and girls must go to school, as do children in the United States. All children can enjoy the benefits of free public education. Towns and cities have large modern *public schools.* The subjects taught are like those that students in the United States might study. In some provinces, there are publicly supported religious schools called *separate schools.* This is different from the United States, where religious schools are not tax supported. About 1 in 20 children goes to a private school. *Private schools* are not supported by the government. With the exception of the province of Quebec, most students are taught in English. In areas with a large French-speaking population, children may be taught in French or English or both. In Quebec, however, most students are taught in French.

A pastry shop in the Montreal metro, *or subway. How does the shop show mingling of cultures in Canada?*

UNDERSTANDING WHAT YOU HAVE READ

1. Which questions are answered in this chapter?

a. How did the French and English come to settle Canada?

b. What religions are practiced by the people of Northern America?

c. Why is free education important to the people of Northern America?

2. The main idea of *paragraphs 8 through 10* describes

a. where Canadian people live and work

b. the religions of the Canadian people

c. the workers of northern Canada

3. The United States and Canada are different in that there is a much larger

a. French-speaking population in the United States

b. black population in the United States

c. Spanish-speaking population in Canada

4. The United States has

a. a larger population than Canada

b. a smaller population than Canada

c. about the same population as Canada

5. The majority of the people of Canada live near the United States border because

a. few large cities are located there

b. the climate is milder and most jobs are there

c. the northern part of Canada has few resources

6. Education is important to the people of the United States and Canada because

a. people who have come from other countries have had no education

b. in the past, only the rich have had education

c. it is necessary if the people are to run their governments wisely

7. *Immigrants* are people who

a. come from other lands

b. work in factories

c. work in the government

8. In *paragraph 4,* the word *urbanization* means

a. joining together

b. treated differently

c. growth of cities

9. All of the following statements are true of United States population EXCEPT

a. The number of people living in the United States is growing larger

b. the farm population in the United States is getting smaller

c. most new people coming to the United States are moving to the Rocky Mountains

10. Most Americans are members of which race?

a. white

b. black

c. Asian

11. Growing numbers of Americans live in the cities and suburbs because

a. they can find jobs there

b. they can make use of libraries, museums, and schools

c. both of these statements

12. Canada's major industries include all of the following EXCEPT

a. oil refining

b. meat processing

c. farming

13. Which statement about Canada's population is not true?

a. Many Canadians are of British descent.

b. Many Canadians live near the border of the United States.

c. There are no native Canadian peoples as in the United States.

14. The United States and Canada both have

a. a large French-speaking population

b. a high standard of living

c. an even population distribution

DEVELOPING IDEAS AND SKILLS

Understanding Graphs — Population, Area, and Standard of Living in Northern America

Study the pictograph below. Then answer the following questions.

1. Is the standard of living in Canada high, low, or about the same when compared with that of the United States?
2. Is Canada more or less crowded than the United States?
3. Are the people of this region literate?
4. How long can the average Canadian expect to live?
5. Which facts tell you the standard of living of the people of Canada and the United States?
6. How does Canada compare with the United States in size?
7. How long can the average American expect to live?
8. What is the population of the United States?
9. Who owns more passenger cars, Canadians or Americans?
10. What is the average income per person in Canada?

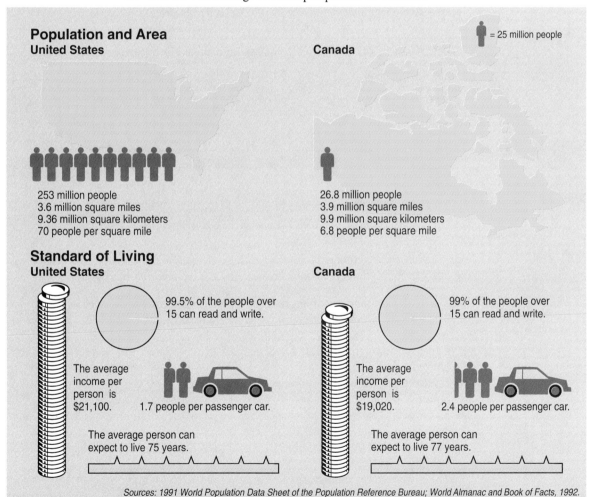

Population and Area
United States

Canada

= 25 million people

253 million people
3.6 million square miles
9.36 million square kilometers
70 people per square mile

26.8 million people
3.9 million square miles
9.9 million square kilometers
6.8 people per square mile

Standard of Living
United States

Canada

99.5% of the people over 15 can read and write.

99% of the people over 15 can read and write.

The average income per person is $21,100.

1.7 people per passenger car.

The average income per person is $19,020.

2.4 people per passenger car.

The average person can expect to live 75 years.

The average person can expect to live 77 years.

Sources: 1991 World Population Data Sheet of the Population Reference Bureau; World Almanac and Book of Facts, 1992.

Population, Area, and Standard of Living in Northern America

DEVELOPING CRITICAL THINKING SKILLS

Understanding Charts — Immigrants to the United States and Canada

We don't discover new ideas only by reading. Often ideas are to be found through maps, photographs, charts, and graphs. Here is a chart. It tells us something about immigration to the United States and Canada. See what ideas you can discover from the chart.

Immigrants to the United States and Canada, 1989

UNITED STATES		CANADA	
Country or Region	*Number*	*Country or Region*	*Number*
Mexico, Latin America	95,000	Asian region	95,487
Vietnam, Asian region	25,800	United Kingdom-Ireland, European region	8,417
Philippines, Asian region	50,700	West Indies, Latin America	16,769
Korea, Asian region	34,700	United States, Northern America	6,924
China, Asian region	38,400	Portugal, European region	8,155
India, Asian region	26,300	Italy, European region	1,036
West Indies, Latin America	67,600	France, European region	2,882
Dominican Republic, Latin America	27,200	Netherlands, European region	824
United Kingdom, European region	13,200	Australia, Pacific region	626
Cuba, Latin America	17,600	Germany, European region	2,933

Sources: Canada Yearbook, Statistical Abstract of the U.S. 1990

Tell whether these statements are *true* or *false*. If there is not enough information on the chart to help you decide your answer, say *not enough information.*

1. The largest number of immigrants to Canada came from countries in Asia.
2. The largest number of immigrants to the United States came from countries in Asia.
3. European immigrants form a greater part of newcomers to Canada than to the United States.
4. France provided a large number of immigrants to both Canada and the United States.
5. More people came to the United States from the Philippines than from any country in Latin America.
6. The number of Asians coming to the United States and Canada has increased steadily since 1970.
7. There were fewer immigrants to Canada than to the United States.
8. Twice as many people migrated from the United Kingdom to Canada than from the United Kingdom to the United States.

New Americans

By the time the 13 American colonies won their independence, their population was already made up of different immigrant groups (people who came from other countries). After the Revolution, immigrants continued to come to the United States. They contributed their knowledge and skills to the growth of this country. Over time, each of these immigrant groups were drawn into the mainstream of American life. That this process is still going on today can be seen in this brief story.

LaSalle Junior High School is located in mid-Manhattan in New York City. It is an old red brick building surrounded by tenements, rooming houses, and businesses. Recently, the school counted 34 different languages and dialects spoken by the students—Persian, Hindi, Spanish, Portuguese, Greek, Cantonese, Japanese, Korean, and Russian—to name a few. How many countries are represented here, you ask?

"Don't ask," says the principal, Mr. Donald Shaw. "We really have no time for counting. We've got every kind of group here. I imagine the school was easier to run when the neighborhood was made up largely of only two groups. It didn't take long for immigrants from all over the world to begin to settle in the neighborhood. New students walk in every day. Many are from war-torn or troubled countries. New York City is once again a home for immigrants."

Ms. Deborah Gold, a physical education teacher at the school, agrees. "There is never a dull moment," she says, "especially at roll call—Ho Suh, Ping He, Zorba Chakires. . . . But I'm amazed at how quickly they learn English and adjust to our ways. There is not a sari or sarong among them. They wear designer sweatshirts and jeans. They have electronic pocket translators. They are in a rush to be completely American. The students are eager to learn, and you can see their progress."

Junior high school students in a science class.

Choose the correct answer.

1. This story takes place in a
   a. factory
   b. junior high school
   c. department store
2. Immigrants are people who came from
   a. other countries
   b. other states in the United States
   c. only Communist countries
3. The students in this school
   a. recently came from foreign countries
   b. are native-born Americans
   c. are largely of Irish or Italian descent
4. The students in the school
   a. speak only their native languages
   b. do not like American ways
   c. are eager to learn American ways
5. The staff of the school finds the new students
   a. both exciting and confusing
   b. noisy in the halls
   c. unwilling to learn

Chapter 6

Two Democratic Governments

How are Canada and the United States governed?

READING FOR A PURPOSE:
1. What is the system of government in Canada?
2. What is the system of government in the United States?
3. In what ways are the governments of Canada and the United States similar?

1. Canada has a *federal* system of government that divides power between the provinces and the national government. Canada has 10 provinces and two territories, the Northwest and the Yukon. Each province has its own government. The national government is located in the capital city of Ottawa. While the United States government is based on the Constitution and its amendments, the Canadian government is based on the Constitution Act of 1982. Until 1982, it was the British government that had the power to make changes in Canada's government. Now, by the act of 1982, Canada's government is free from British regulation. The 1982 act also has a Charter of Rights and Freedoms. The Charter is very much like the Bill of Rights of the United States. It describes the legal or civil rights all Canadian citizens have. Only the province of Quebec refused to agree to the new act.

2. The Canadian Parliament makes the laws for the people of Canada. Parliament is made up of two lawmaking houses. One of these is called the House of Commons and the other one is called the Senate. The House of Commons is the more powerful body. Its members are elected. They serve for five years unless an election is called sooner. Their chief duty is to make laws. Members of the Senate are named by the prime minister. Senators can serve until 75 years of age. They have little power in making laws.

3. The chief officer of the Canadian government is the prime minister. The prime minister is a member of Parliament. This person is the leader of the political party that has the most members in the House of Commons. The prime minister selects members of that

Canada's Parliament Building in Ottawa. How are members of Canada's Senate and House of Commons chosen?

party to be the advisers, or ministers. This group is called the cabinet. The cabinet carries out and enforces the laws. It directs the armed forces, makes treaties, declares war, and makes peace. Unlike an American president's cabinet, this cabinet plans most of the bills that are brought before Parliament. Only the cabinet can introduce bills for raising or spending money.

4. The prime minister and the cabinet stay in office only as long as most of the members of the House of Commons are supportive. If a majority of the House vote against them, then the cabinet and the prime minister must either resign or call a new election. Then the Canadian people may vote for different representatives in the House of Commons or reelect the same members. Most of the time the prime minister can depend on the support of Parliament. (A president of the United States cannot always count on the support of Congress to pass the preferred laws.)

5. The courts of Canada explain and uphold the laws and protect the rights of the people. The highest court in Canada is the Supreme Court. It meets in Ottawa.

6. Each of nine of the provinces is governed by a premier. The province of Quebec has a prime minister. Each province has a one-house lawmaking body. The provinces have more power than do the states of the United States.

7. Canada is a monarchy. The queen or king of Canada is also the queen or king of the United Kingdom. In theory, the queen or king has great power. In fact, she or he does not. Although called the head of state, the queen or king does not govern. She or he appoints a governor-general who represents the Crown in Parliament. This person has little power.

8. Whereas Canada is a monarchy, the United States is a republic. The United States has no queen or king. The basis for the government is the Constitution and its amendments. The Constitution was written in 1787. It set up a *federal* system that divided power between the national government and the states. Each of the 50 states has its own government. The capital of the national government is Washington, D.C. (District of Columbia). The powers of the national government are divided among three separate branches: the legislative, the executive, and the judiciary. Each branch has certain powers.

9. The president is the head of the *executive,* or law-enforcing, branch of the U.S. government. The president is elected for a term of four years, and may be elected only twice. The executive branch enforces the laws passed by Congress. The president is commander in chief of the army, navy, and air force, and may either sign or *veto* (disapprove) bills passed by Congress. The chief executive is helped by a cabinet. The members of the cabinet do not have to be members of Congress.

10. Congress is the *legislative,* or lawmaking, branch of the government. As in the Canadian Parliament, there are two houses of

The U.S. Capitol in Washington, D.C. How are members of the U.S. Senate and House of Representatives chosen?

Congress. But unlike the Canadian Parliament, both houses—the Senate and the House of Representatives—have power. There are two senators from each state. They hold office for six years. Every two years, one-third of the Senate is elected. The House of Representatives has many more members. They are elected for two-year terms. Congress has some very important powers, such as the power to tax, the power to borrow money, and the power to declare war.

11. A third branch of U.S. national government is the *judiciary*. This branch is made up of the Supreme Court and the lower courts. They help explain the laws passed by Congress and protect the rights of the people.

12. Each state also has three branches of government. The executive branch is run by a governor. Each state has its own lawmaking bodies and courts.

13. Both peoples, American and Canadian, believe in democracy. Citizens have the right to vote in free and fair elections. They can choose the officials who make the countries' laws. Citizens have the right to speak out without fear. People have the right to a fair trial. There is freedom of religion. Children can go to free schools. People can choose their own jobs and own their own homes. This is the opposite of a *totalitarian* government. A totalitarian government is run by a few people who control the activities of others. Under such a government, individuals are important only as they serve the state. They do not have the rights and freedoms that Northern Americans have.

UNDERSTANDING WHAT YOU HAVE READ

1. Which questions are answered in this chapter?
a. How can the United States Constitution be changed?
b. How does the Canadian government work?
c. What are the powers of the president of the United States?

2. The main idea of this chapter describes
a. the powers of the prime minister
b. how power is divided among different branches of government
c. how the United States and Canada are both governed

3. The working chief officer of the Canadian government is the
a. queen of Canada
b. governor general
c. prime minister

4. The lawmaking branch of the Canadian government is called the
a. Congress   b. Parliament   c. Supreme Court

5. How are the powers of the prime minister of Canada different from the powers of the president of the United States?
a. The prime minister is the chief executive of the country.
b. The prime minister is a member of the lawmaking body of the country.
c. The prime minister appoints the cabinet.

6. Why are both the United States and Canada called democratic countries?
a. In neither country can the national government tax the people.
b. In both countries the national government has little power.
c. In both countries, in free and fair elections, the people vote for the officials who make their laws.

7. Canada is divided into *provinces.* These are somewhat like American

a. states
b. cities
c. counties

8. *Parliament* is the branch of government that

a. makes the laws
b. explains the laws
c. enforces the laws

DEVELOPING CRITICAL THINKING SKILLS

Understanding Diagrams
A. The Government of the United States

Study the pictograph. Then tell whether these statements are true or false.

1. The national government is divided into three parts.
2. The president is the head of the branch that enforces the laws.
3. Helping the president are 9 departments of government.
4. The Senate has more members than the House of Representatives.
5. The Supreme Court is the highest United States court.
6. The Senate and the House of Representatives make the laws.
7. The powers of the government come from the people.
8. Matters concerning war and preparations for war are handled by the Department of Defense.

The Government of the United States
The U.S. Constitution
We the People

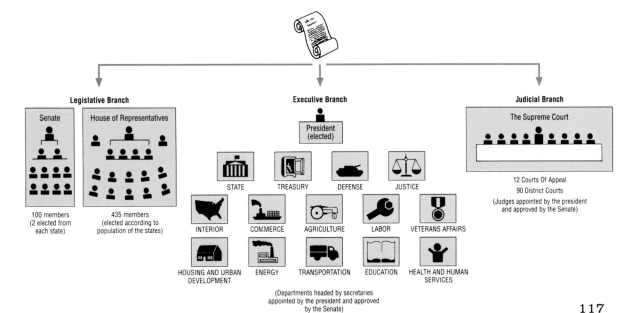

117

B. The Government of Canada

Study the pictograph. Then tell whether these statements are true or false.

1. The working head of the Canadian government is the prime minister.
2. Canada's Supreme Court has more members than the Supreme Court of the United States.
3. Both the Senate and the House of Commons share in making laws.
4. Members of the prime minister's cabinet cannot be members of Parliament.
5. Members of the Senate are probably closer to the people and their needs than members of the House of Commons are.
6. The cabinet of the prime minister has fewer departments than the cabinet of the president of the United States.
7. Members of the House of Commons may serve terms of less than five years.
8. The Crown (the queen or king of Canada) is the head of state but does not really govern.

The Government of Canada

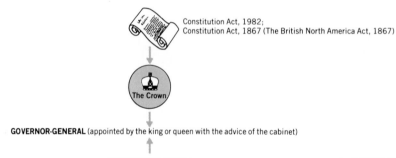

Constitution Act, 1982;
Constitution Act, 1867 (The British North America Act, 1867)

The Crown

GOVERNOR-GENERAL (appointed by the king or queen with the advice of the cabinet)

LEGISLATIVE BRANCH
PARLIAMENT
EXECUTIVE BRANCH
JUDICIAL BRANCH

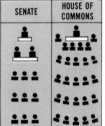

SENATE	HOUSE OF COMMONS

104 members (appointed by the governor general with advice of the cabinet; can serve until 75 years old)

282 members (elected at least every 5 years on basis of population)

PRIME MINISTER (leader of the party able to hold the support of a majority of the members of the House of Commons)

Cabinet
MINISTERS (appointed by the prime minister, almost always from among members of the prime minister's party holding seats in the House of Commons)

MINISTER OF STATE FOR FINANCE
TRANSPORT
JUSTICE, ATTORNEY GENERAL OF CANADA
INDIAN AFFAIRS AND NORTHERN DEVELOPMENT
ECONOMIC DEVELOPMENT AND SCIENCE AND TECHNOLOGY;
INDUSTRY, TRADE, AND COMMERCE; REGIONAL ECONOMIC
EXPANSION
AGRICULTURE
CONSUMER AND CORPORATE AFFAIRS
ENERGY, MINES, AND RESOURCES
LEADER OF THE GOVERNMENT IN THE SENATE
FISHERIES AND OCEANS
ENVIRONMENT
NATIONAL HEALTH AND WELFARE
SUPPLY AND SERVICES
COMMUNICATIONS
NATIONAL DEFENSE
EXTERNAL RELATIONS

CANADIAN WHEAT BOARD
SECRETARY OF STATE OF CANADA
FITNESS AND AMATEUR SPORTS
DEPUTY PRIME MINISTER AND SECRETARY OF STATE FOR
EXTERNAL AFFAIRS
SOLICITOR GENERAL OF CANADA
MULTICULTURALISM
NATIONAL REVENUE
FINANCE
SMALL BUSINESSES AND TOURISM
INTERNATIONAL TRADE
PRESIDENT OF THE QUEEN'S PRIVY COUNCIL FOR CANADA
PRESIDENT OF THE TREASURY BOARD
EMPLOYMENT AND IMMIGRATION
PUBLIC WORKS
SOCIAL DEVELOPMENT
LABOUR
VETERANS AFFAIRS

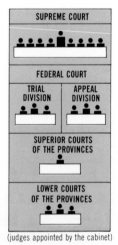

SUPREME COURT

FEDERAL COURT	
TRIAL DIVISION	APPEAL DIVISION

SUPERIOR COURTS OF THE PROVINCES

LOWER COURTS OF THE PROVINCES

(judges appointed by the cabinet)

118

In Northern America

Maria Verala is a community organizer. Her special talent is finding ways to improve people's lives without making them give up their rural way of life. "What I do is to unlock people's hopes and abilities," she says. What she did in the remote Chama Valley of New Mexico was to show the local ranchers how to save money by combining their small herds of sheep and raising them in one larger herd. Verala then helped the people plan other small businesses. A weaving cooperative and a shop that sells organically grown meat are among the successful new businesses. Maria Verala is particularly proud of a new general store she helped establish. Before the store opened, people had to travel hundreds of miles to buy their food. Now they can walk to the new store.

Lois Gibbs was raising her family in an upstate New York neighborhood known as Love Canal when she noticed something strange. Her children—and her neighbors' children—were getting sick too often. She believed that the illnesses were caused by poisonous gas that leaked from a chemical-waste dump three blocks from her home. She wrote letters to try to get business and government officials to pay attention to the problem, but they would not. Then Mrs. Gibbs got tough. She knocked on doors, gave speeches, pestered politicians, and finally got the attention of then-President Jimmy Carter. After a careful investigation, the government moved all the people who lived in the Love Canal neighborhood and paid them for their houses. Today, Gibbs is the head of the Citizens Clearinghouse for Hazardous Wastes. This organization helps communities with problems like those of Love Canal.

Each fall, thousands of Texans turn out for the Texas Coastal Cleanup. Dressed in old clothes and carrying trash bags, they gather up more than 150 tons of garbage from the beaches. All this activity began because **Linda Maraniss** visited the Texas Gulf Coast six years ago. She was disgusted at the sight of rotting garbage and litter on the once-beautiful beaches. Maraniss got her fellow Texans organized to clean up this mess. But she did not stop there. She urged Texas lawmakers to help protect the beaches for the sake of marine life in the gulf, and she got results. New laws in Texas now make it easier to recycle plastic bottles. Linda Maraniss has even persuaded an oil company to ban plastic foam cups on its gulf oil rigs.

Native American Chippewas in Minnesota are preserving an ancient tradition. They are hand-harvesting wild rice. Chippewas **Winona LaDuke** and **Margaret Smith** of the White Earth Reservation founded the Ikwe Wild Rice Program. "Wild rice is indigenous [native] to North America, and we want to protect it," says LaDuke. Their method of harvesting rice by hand is hard work, but it protects the water and the surrounding plant life. The Chippewas use no insecticides or chemical fertilizers. "Instead of trying to tame the wild, we're showing people how to respect it," says LaDuke. "This helps both the Chippewa and the environment."

Chapter 7

The United States—Its Vast Resources

What resources have contributed to the industrial strength of the United States?

READING FOR A PURPOSE:
1. What are the raw materials and fuels needed for industry in the United States?
2. Where can these raw materials and fuels be found in the United States?
3. How have the American people contributed to the industrial strength of the United States?

1. In 1776, the United States was a country of farms, villages, and towns. Most Americans were farmers living in small cabins. The whole family worked hard all day to provide the things that were needed. Today most Americans live in cities and towns. The United States is the leading industrial nation of the world. The American people have one of the highest standards of living in the world. Let us look at some of the reasons for this change.

2. First the United States has many raw materials for industry, such as minerals and forests. The United States is one of the world leaders in the production of copper, phosphates, lead, sulphur, and iron ore. (On pages 52 through 54, you learned about the importance of these nonfuel minerals.) Of course, the United States does not mine all the minerals it needs. But it has the wealth to buy and import them.

3. The United States is one of the greatest iron-ore mining countries. Other countries may have greater iron-ore reserves, or supplies in the ground, but in most years, only the Commonwealth, China, Brazil, and Australia mine more of it. Open-pit mines of the Mesabi Range, near Lake Superior in Minnesota, have been the greatest source of iron ore. Michigan is the nation's other major iron-producing state. But the nation uses so much iron that more is imported from Canada, Venezuela, and Brazil.

4. The United States produces about one-seventh of the world's copper. The major copper mines are located in Arizona. There are also copper mines in Utah, New Mexico, and Montana. Lead is mined in Missouri. Zinc is mined in Tennessee, Missouri, New York, Colorado, and Idaho. Gold is found in Nevada, Utah, and South Dakota. Silver is found in Idaho, Utah, Arizona, and Colorado. Sulphur comes chiefly from Texas and Louisiana. The United States is the world's leading manufacturer of aluminum. This modern metal is made from an ore called bauxite. Some bauxite is mined in Alabama and Georgia. However, most of it is imported from the Caribbean nation of Jamaica, the African country of Guinea, and the South American countries of Brazil and Suriname.

5. When Northern America was first settled by Europeans, it was a land of great for-

Oil field near Wilmington, California. What is crude oil used to make besides gasoline?

ests. Wood was useful in building ships and homes, in providing furniture, and in burning as fuel. Some forest land was cleared as the need for farmland grew. Despite this removal, forests still cover almost one-third of the United States. Great forests are found in the Pacific Northwest, the South, and New England. Most of the timber is cut in two areas. One is in Oregon, Washington, and California. The other is in Georgia, Alabama, and Mississippi. Wood is used mainly in making paper, plastics, homes, and furniture. So much wood is used in these industries that more wood products must be imported, chiefly from Canada.

6. A second reason for industrial strength is that the United States is rich in energy resources: coal, oil, gas, and falling water. The United States has larger coal reserves than any other nation. Most coal is mined in the Appalachian Mountains of Kentucky, West Virginia, and Pennsylvania. Coal is also mined in Illinois and Ohio. Montana and Wyoming have rich coal reserves. Coal provides fuel to heat homes and to make power for factories. It is used to smelt ore in the manufacture of steel. The leading industrial nations of the world are those that are able to make large quantities of steel products.

7. Oil is the chief energy resource of the United States. (See graph, page 125.) About one-fifth of the world's supply of oil comes from the United States. The largest oil-producing fields are found in Alaska, Texas, Louisiana, California, Oklahoma, and Wyoming. Oil is *refined*, or treated after it comes from the ground, to remove the impurities in it. One of the products of refining is gasoline.

Major U.S. Nonfuel Natural Resource Production

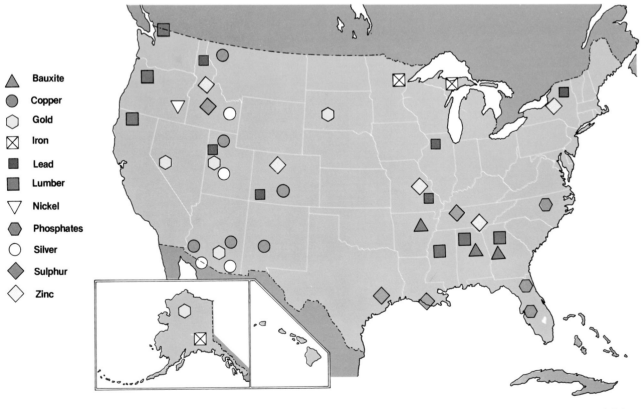

Huge amounts of gasoline are used to power cars, trucks, trains, and planes. Oil is also the greatest source of heat for American homes. As a result, to fill the nation's needs, oil must also be imported. The people of the United States depend on foreign oil to meet their energy needs. Most of it comes from Mexico, Saudi Arabia, Nigeria, and Canada. Since the late 1970s, the United States has reduced its use of oil and depends less on foreign oil for its needs.

8. Natural gas is a resource of the oil fields. When it first appeared along with oil, it was wasted. Now, however, giant pipelines bring gas from Texas, Louisiana, Oklahoma, and New Mexico to the northern and eastern parts of the country. Thousands of miles from the gas fields, people in Chicago and New York use the gas to heat their homes and to fuel their stoves.

9. Almost 200 years ago, waterfalls in New England began to power the country's first

The gigantic wall of the Hoover Dam holds back the waters of the fast-flowing Colorado River. The United States has built many dams to produce electricity, to stop flood waters, and to provide water for farming.

factories. The water turned large water wheels that ran the machinery. Starting in the 1880s, dams were built on rivers to turn the power of falling water into electricity. The national government runs many hydroelectric power projects. For example, the largest American hydroelectric plant is at the Grand Coulee Dam. It was built on the Columbia River in Washington. Other huge hydroelectric projects are at the John Day Dam in Oregon, the Chief Joseph Dam in Washington, the Ludington plant in Michigan, and the Robert Moses-Niagara power project in New York. The TVA (Tennessee Valley Authority) has built a series of dams on the Tennessee River and nearby rivers. The TVA provides electricity for people in seven states.

10. Since World War II, another source of power has been developed. This is the atom. Atomic (nuclear) energy comes from the mineral uranium. The United States and Canada are among the largest producers of uranium. The United States has ships and submarines that use nuclear power. These ships can travel for months without coming into port to refuel. However, only a small part of the nation's industries use electricity made in nuclear plants. The nuclear power plants that produce the most electricity are in Tennessee, North Carolina, Oregon, Washington, Illinois, Pennsylvania, Alabama, and New York. There are many who believe that nuclear energy is the energy of the future. Others believe that nuclear plants are dangerous. There have been protests against the building of new nuclear power units. The wastes from nuclear plants are a problem in providing nuclear energy. These wastes can give off radioactive material that is harmful to living things. The future of nuclear power in the United States is uncertain.

11. The United States is looking for new sources of power to reduce its dependency on foreign oil. *Solar energy,* the use of heat from the sun, is growing in popularity. There are experiments to make liquid gasoline from coal and from a kind of rock called shale. Tar sands in the United States and Canada can provide oil. Often these resources are in regions far from the places that need the fuel. The cost of extracting and transporting the oil would be high. Because of this, in New England alone, over 100 plants now use wood instead of oil as fuel.

12. A third reason for the industrial strength of the United States is its people. The United States has the fourth largest population in the world. It has a huge work force of almost 127 million people. Many of them have been educated and trained for work in modern industries. Not only are their skills important, but so is their willingness to work, and their health. One measure of the American people's health is the long life span. (See the graph on page 111.)

13. Americans have found the resources and invented the machines to run the nation's industries. They have provided the money to build factories, buy machinery, and start new businesses in America. They are the skilled men and women who work in the mines, in the factories, and on the farms to turn out the goods. They have built railroads, airlines, pipelines, and highway transportation systems. They are the ones who make it possible to distribute raw materials and finished goods from America to markets all over the nation and the world.

UNDERSTANDING WHAT YOU HAVE READ

1. Which questions are answered in this chapter?
a. How is iron made into steel?
b. Where are there great power projects?
c. What are some possible new sources of energy?

2. The main idea of *paragraphs 6 through 10* is that
a. waterpower is the greatest source of energy in the United States
b. oil and oil products are widely used
c. the United States has a variety of power resources

3. The United States leads the world in the production of
a. tin   b. iron   c. aluminum

4. *One country* from which the United States imports some of its iron, lumber, and oil is
a. Argentina
b. Saudi Arabia
c. Canada

5. Great oil fields of the United States are located in
a. Ohio and Pennsylvania   b. Alaska and Texas
c. Florida and Georgia

6. An energy resource usually found near oil fields is
a. natural gas   b. bauxite   c. uranium

7. A reason for the search for new sources of power is that
a. forest reserves are being used at an alarming rate
b. the American way of life depends on foreign oil
c. nuclear power cannot do what people expected of it

8. When oil is *refined,*
a. it is made into plastics
b. impurities are removed
c. it is used as fuel

9. *Nuclear* energy refers to
a. steam power
b. hydroelectric power
c. atomic power

DEVELOPING IDEAS AND SKILLS

Building Map Skills—Iron, Coal, and Oil Production in the United States

Study the map. Then tell whether these statements are *true* or *false*.

1. The largest producers of iron ore are found near the Great Lakes.
2. There are large coal production areas east and west of the Mississippi River.
3. Large oil-producing fields are in the northeastern states.
4. There are no oil fields on the West Coast.
5. Coal is mined in almost every state in the United States.
6. Texas produces both iron and oil.
7. Many coal fields are found in mountain regions.
8. Most of the large cities are near iron, coal, or oil resources.

Iron, Coal, and Oil Production in the United States

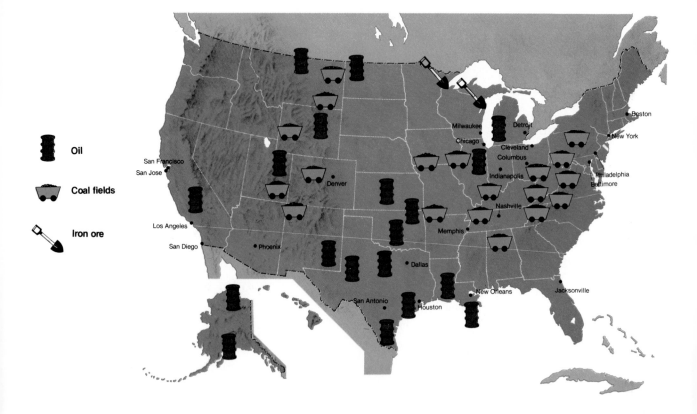

REVIEWING AND WRITING

Making an Outline

Complete the outline on page 125 in your notebook. Enter *three* topics under each of the headings.

How the United States Became a Leading Industrial Nation
A. The United States has great natural resources.
B. Its sources of power are highly developed.
C. Human resources are the great strength of the nation.

DEVELOPING CRITICAL THINKING SKILLS

Using Graphs——Energy Sources and Users in the United States

Tell whether these statements about the information on the graphs is *true, false,* or there is *no information* on the graphs.

1. Almost half the energy used in the United States comes from oil.
2. Most of the oil used in the United States is consumed in heating homes and businesses.
3. Coal provides more energy than either water or nuclear power.
4. Most natural gas is used on farms and in industry.
5. The use of nuclear power will increase in the next 10 years.
6. Autos, trucks, and other kinds of transportation use more of the United States' supply of oil than all the homes and businesses combined.
7. Solar and wood heating make up about 5 percent of Americans' heating needs.
8. More oil is used by industry than by homes and businesses.

Energy Sources and Users in the United States

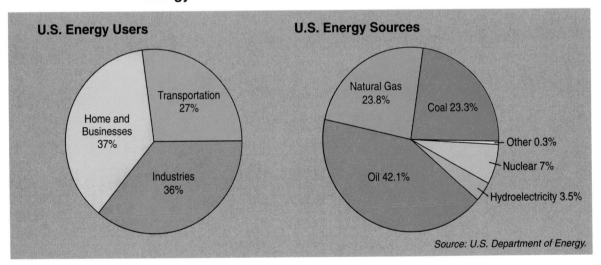

Source: U.S. Department of Energy.

Chapter 8

The Free Enterprise System

How do Americans satisfy their needs and wants?

READING FOR A PURPOSE:
1. How is American economic life organized?
2. How does capitalism work in the United States?
3. What are the benefits of mass production?

1. Raw materials, much power, and skilled workers are needed for manufacturing. But these alone would not make the United States the leading industrial nation of the world. With only 5 percent of the world's people, Americans produce more goods and make greater use of their resources than any other people in the world. In fact, the United States produces about 25 percent of the entire world's goods and services. The American way of making and selling goods is called *capitalism* or *free enterprise*.

2. Under capitalism, the land, mines, factories, and resources of the nation are owned by individuals or groups—not by the government. They are *private property*. Persons who own property use it as they see fit, provided they do not interfere with the rights of others. They may buy almost any goods they want. They may sell almost any goods they produce. The prices people pay for goods and the prices at which they sell goods are decided by agreement with other persons. The government does not tell people how much to pay for the goods they use.

3. The American people have a *freedom of choice* in the kinds of work they want to do. People may run their own businesses or work for others. They may try to become doctors, lawyers, plumbers, or carpenters. The choice is each person's to make. They can quit their jobs and can do so without giving a reason. The freedom to choose one's life work is not found everywhere in the world. Workers can also join labor unions to seek higher wages and better working conditions. Under a system of capitalism, labor unions are not run by the government.

4. Capitalism is a way of life in which people run their businesses or shops with the idea of making a *profit*. Workers in a capitalist system try to get the most money for their labor. Owners of land and buildings try to get the

In what ways does the American economic system of free enterprise support the political values that most Americans hold?

highest rentals. Business people try to sell their goods for more than the cost of producing or obtaining them. Americans believe that the desire to make a profit encourages people to work hard, to find better methods of working, and to invent new products.

5. When many people are working to make the same goods, *competition* is the result. For example, many factories make the same kind of product. All manufacturers want to sell their products. Their factories are in competition with each other. Americans believe that competition results in high-quality goods at a low price. (The manufacturer who makes tools and sells them at higher prices than other tool manufacturers will not sell many of them. Such manufacturers must take less profit or they must learn to make their product at a lower cost. This helps the people who buy that product.) Manufacturers *advertise* their goods because they want people to buy them. Commercials or advertisements on billboards and in newspapers are all attempts by manufacturers to sell their products. Advertising is necessary to the capitalist system.

6. Capitalism also depends upon *mass production.* This is a method that makes use of the *assembly line, division of labor,* and *standardized parts.* The modern automobile factory is a good example of how mass production works. A line or belt runs from one end of the building to the other. Frames of cars move along the line. As each car passes by a section of the plant, new parts are added to it by workers. By the time the car reaches the end of the line, it has been *assembled,* or put together. Each worker along the assembly line has a job to do. This is called *division of labor,* since the work is divided up among workers. In mass production, the parts for a particular car model are exactly alike. They will fit into the same place in other cars of the same model. These are *standardized parts.*

7. Today, most factories use the methods of mass production to make all kinds of goods. It is the fastest and cheapest way to make many things. In recent years, special

An American auto assembly line. What are some of the problems American industries have faced in recent years?

machines have been used to replace workers on the assembly line. The use of machines to produce goods, and to run and regulate other machines that make goods, is called *automation.* At the present time, auto manufacturers and others are using *robots* along the assembly line. Robots are machines that can do many of the jobs that used to be done by humans. The same robot can also be readjusted to do other jobs when new products are needed.

8. In the past, American workers and businesses have turned out more goods at a cheaper price because of their skill and their greater use of machines. In recent years, the owners of factories in countries in Westen Europe and East Asia have adopted the American way of making goods. They are training their people to be skilled workers. Moreover, they are able to pay them less money. As a result, they are able to turn out well-made goods at lower prices. The United States is losing markets at home and abroad because of this. For example, the United States was once the leading carmaker of the world. Today, because of strong competition from Japan and Germany, the United States now sells fewer cars. This, of course, has also meant a loss of jobs for American workers. This is happening not only in the car industry, but in other industries as well.

9. Capitalism has also succeeded because of government help to different groups. From its beginning, the United States government

placed a *tariff,* or tax, on goods brought into the country. This made Americans prefer to buy the less costly American products. There are no taxes, however, on goods moving from one state to another. As a result there is a free flow of goods from one part of the nation to another. In the 19th century, the government encouraged railroad building. It has allowed mining and lumber companies to make use of the resources on some public lands. The government has also built dams and water projects. These provide energy and water that benefit farmers and the workers and owners of industries. The interstate highway system helps businesses move goods to their markets. The government makes sure that all agreements or contracts are kept. Farmers have been paid to control their crop production. The reduced amount of crops helps keep up the price of the farmers' crops. The government protects the rights of workers to join labor unions in which they can work to get better wages and working conditions.

10. At the same time, the government has passed laws that affect the practices of industry. These laws protect the American people from unsafe foods and medicines. The government has passed laws to end children's working in factories and to establish a basic level of wages. It has rules for safe and healthful work places. The communications industries such as radio, movies, and television are carefully watched for fairness and decency. In this sense, free enterprise is not as "free" as one might think. It is not free to harm the people living under it.

11. As you can see, there are many reasons for the United States' becoming the greatest manufacturing country in the world. The United States has a rich store of natural resources and fuels, skillful and inventive people, and a vast system of transportation. All of these are brought together through capitalism. Americans believe this system to be the best in the world. Other peoples may not think so. They may think their system is better. Each nation's system grows out of its geography and its history.

UNDERSTANDING WHAT YOU HAVE READ

1. Which questions are answered in this chapter?
a. What is mass production?
b. How is planning carried out in the United States?
c. What is meant by *freedom of choice?*

2. The main idea of this chapter describes
a. how capitalism works
b. how resources have made the United States strong
c. the political freedoms that Americans have

3. Workers are able to turn out many goods because of the greater use of
a. machinery
b. atomic energy
c. hand labor

4. Goods flow freely from one state to another because of
a. government planning
b. lack of tariffs between states
c. airlines

5. Workers receive high wages because they
a. are highly skilled
b. have private property
c. hope to make a profit

6. Mass production is important because
a. more goods are now made at home
b. new minerals have been discovered
c. more goods are produced at lower prices

7. Another example of *competition* as described in paragraph 5 would be

a. actors preparing to put on a play
b. two basketball teams playing against each other
c. assembly-line workers doing different jobs

8. Under the system of *capitalism* there is

a. private profit and competition
b. government control over the prices of all goods
c. control over most manufactured products by the government

DEVELOPING IDEAS AND SKILLS

Understanding Diagrams——The Flow of Goods, Services, and Money Through Free Enterprise

Study the pictograph. Then answer the following questions.

1. In this pictograph, people are receiving money as wages from government and business. The people must then give part of the money to the government. What is this paying of money to the government called?
2. Where do businesses obtain the materials for the goods they make?
3. What do people receive in exchange for their labor?
4. Businesses make goods that people want. How do the people obtain these goods?
5. What part do banks play in helping businesses and stores?
6. Where do banks get their money?

The Flow of Goods, Services, and Money Through Free Enterprise

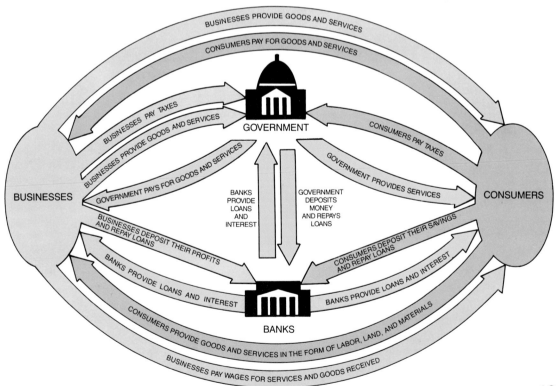

Understanding Graphs——The United States Compared to the Rest of the World

Study the pictograph. Then tell whether these statements are true or false.

1. The United States has about half of the world's land area.
2. The United States has less than 10 percent of the world's people.
3. The United States produces more automobiles than the rest of the world.
4. The United States produces twice the amount of oil that the rest of the world does.
5. The United States produces as much corn as all other countries in the world combined.
6. The United States produces less than half of the electric power in the world.

The United States and the Rest of the World

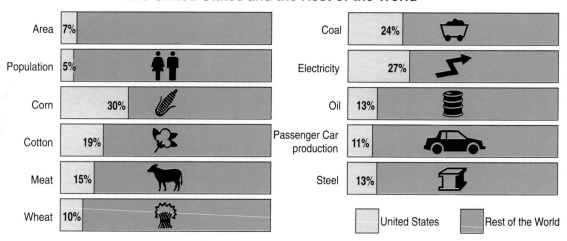

	United States	Rest of the World
Area	7%	
Population	5%	
Corn	30%	
Cotton	19%	
Meat	15%	
Wheat	10%	
Coal	24%	
Electricity	27%	
Oil	13%	
Passenger Car production	11%	
Steel	13%	

Sources: Central Intelligence Agency, 1991; World Almanac and Book of Facts, 1992.

DEVELOPING CRITICAL THINKING SKILLS

Making Inferences

In our reading, many facts are given to us. From these facts we can draw conclusions. The following are some conclusions or inferences that you might make after reading this chapter. Tell whether these conclusions are correct or incorrect. Give reasons for your answers.

1. A storekeeper may keep workers from joining a union.
2. There is one chief reason why the United States has the greatest factory system in the world.
3. Any person may start a factory on personal property if he or she wants to do so.
4. Nearly all of our soap products are made by one large company.
5. The United States has a small share of the world's resources, but it has made greater use of its resources than any other nation.
6. The government cannot keep people from becoming doctors if they want to become doctors and receive the proper training.

Chapter 9

The Cities— Centers of Trade and Manufacturing

Where are the great manufacturing and trading cities of the United States?

READING FOR A PURPOSE:

1. Why did the Northeast and Great Lakes region become such an important industrial area?
2. Where are the major manufacturing and trading cities located in the United States?
3. What are some of the most important industries in the United States?

1. As you have learned, an industrial region is an area in which many people make their living by manufacturing or turning raw materials into useful goods. There are important industrial regions in the United States. The largest and most important manufacturing area in the United States is in the Northeast and the Great Lakes region. This area reaches from southeastern Wisconsin and Illinois to the Atlantic coast. Near it are some of the largest coal mines in the world. About 90 percent of the iron ore mined in the United States comes from nearby Minnesota and from Michigan. Throughout this area are supplies of coal and falling water for power. In addition, oil and natural gas are easily obtained from the Southwest.

2. The manufacturing region of the Northeast and Great Lakes area has excellent transportation facilities. The area is crisscrossed by highways, railroads, rivers, canals, and lakes. (The Great Lakes–St. Lawrence Seaway and the Ohio and Mississippi rivers are heavily used water highways.) Boats, barges, and freight trains carry raw materials from mines

to factories. Trucks, trains, and riverboats carry the products of farms and factories to the cities and towns.

3. For all these reasons, there are both *heavy industries* and *light industries* in this area. (Iron and steel mills, and auto and other factories that turn out goods made from heavy materials, are known as heavy industries. Industries in which the products are made from light materials and are not bulky are known as light industries.) The products of the factories in this region are almost endless: farm machinery and children's toys, railroad cars and finished clothing, ocean-going ships and

A steel mill. Is steel making a heavy industry or a light industry? What kinds of industries are located in or near your community?

pocket-sized cameras, chemical products, and electronic equipment.

4. Eleven of the 25 largest cities in the United States are located in the Northeast and Great Lakes region. There are always reasons why a city grows up in a certain place; it does not happen by accident. There are different kinds of cities in the Northeast and Great Lakes region. Some are mining towns. Some are factory cities or trading cities. Some are capital cities, and some are so large that they have many purposes. A few of the great industrial cities in this region are New York, Chicago, Philadelphia, Detroit, Cleveland, and Pittsburgh. Farther south is Baltimore, while to the west is Indianapolis.

5. New York is the largest city in the nation. It has one of the busiest harbors in the world. Because of its location on the Atlantic Ocean, it has long been the best place to bring in goods from many parts of the world. From New York the products are carried to all parts of the nation by river, railroad, truck, or airplane. In addition to its being a trading and banking center, New York is a leading factory center. The chief industries in New York are printing, publishing, and the manufacture of clothing.

6. In the Northeast, Pittsburgh, Chicago, and Cleveland are leaders in the making of steel. Pittsburgh, where the Ohio River begins, is the greatest iron and steel center in Northern America. Most of its iron ore comes from Minnesota by huge ore boats and rail. Coal is mined close by in the Appalachian highlands and is brought by river barges to the mills of Pittsburgh. The Chicago-Gary area, located on the shores of Lake Michigan, is another great iron and steel center. Iron ore and coal are brought to these cities over the Great Lakes. Other important Chicago industries include producing machinery and electrical equipment. Because it is near the corn, wheat, and cattle regions, Chicago is also a leader in flour milling and food processing. Because of its location, Chicago is a railroad and trucking center. Its airport is the busiest in the nation.

7. Cleveland, on Lake Erie, has been a heavy steel producer. Iron ore is brought over the Great Lakes. Its coal comes from the Ap-

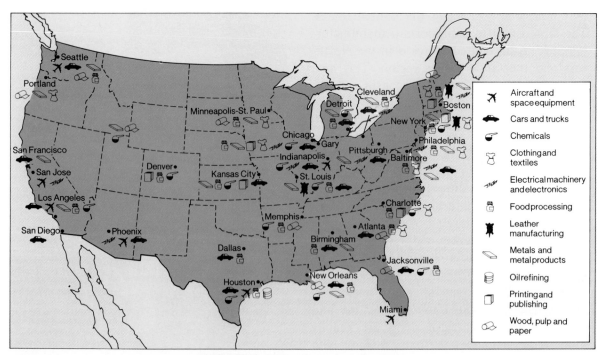

Major U.S. Manufacturing Centers

palachians. Detroit, located on the Great Lakes waterway, is the "auto city." Heavy materials like coal, iron, and steel can be moved cheaply to Detroit by water. Baltimore, on Chesapeake Bay, has one of the finest harbors in the nation. It is also a leader in iron and steel manufacture, electronic equipment, and chemical products.

8. The United States has other important manufacturing and trading cities. St. Louis and Kansas City are located in Missouri. St. Louis has very important auto, truck, and aircraft industries. It is second only to Chicago as a railroad and trucking center. Kansas City is sometimes called "the world's food capital." Billions of dollars from the sale of farm products flow through the city's businesses. Flour production and grain storage are important. Huge caves are under the city. They are used as warehouses for such products as frozen foods.

9. The South has some important advantages for industry. It has waterpower, useful minerals, and a large supply of workers. Birmingham, Alabama, has long been a steel-making city because coal, iron, and limestone are found nearby. The South has many textile factories that turn raw cotton into ready-to-wear clothing. Memphis, Tennessee, is a leading cotton marketing and storage center. Factories process cotton seed into vegetable oil. Memphis also has important chemical, paper, wood, and machinery industries. Charlotte, North Carolina, and Atlanta, Georgia, are cities in the hills at the western side of the coastal plain. Charlotte is a large manufacturing city. Atlanta developed as a transportation center and remains so today, both for travel by road and air. It is also a leading center for the manufacture of textiles, chemicals, and metal goods. In addition, it is a major banking center.

10. New Orleans, at the mouth of the Mississippi River, is one of the nation's busiest ports. Grain, cotton, oil, rice, and sugar are among the many products shipped from New Orleans. Along its docks are banana and cof-

fee boats from Latin America and oil tankers from the Middle East. New Orleans is one of the major tourist centers in the United States. Miami, Florida, is also a leading tourist center. It has become a banking and trade center for many Latin American businesses.

11. The 1970s and early 1980s saw a great movement of people and businesses to cities of the South and West. Older cities in the North and East lost population. Houston, Dallas, and San Antonio in Texas, and Los Angeles and San Diego in California are now among the 10 largest cities in the country. The region from southern California through Texas to Georgia and Florida has been termed "the Sunbelt." Houston is an oil-refining center, the headquarters of the national space program, and a major seaport. It is a leading center for medical research. Los Angeles has been the home of much of the movie and TV industries. It is also the home of aircraft and electronics manufacture and oil refineries. Although the Northeast–Great Lakes region is the biggest manufacturing region, California has the most industry of any single state. Phoenix, Arizona, is also an aircraft and electronics center.

12. Denver, Colorado, at the foot of the

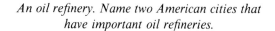

An oil refinery. Name two American cities that have important oil refineries.

133

Rocky Mountains, is the largest city of the drier western mountain states. Since mining and sheep raising are the chief occupations of this region, there are few cities of great size. Denver's industries include flour milling and meat packing. Denver is also noted for the manufacture of electronic and mining equipment and tools. It has large military and space-age equipment industries. Many people work for the state and federal government agencies located in the city.

13. Along the northern Pacific coast are the cities of San Francisco and San Jose in California, Seattle in Washington, and Anchorage in Alaska. San Francisco is an important banking and trading center. Its major industry is food processing. South of San Francisco is San Jose, one of the centers of the United States's computer and electronics industries. Seattle is closer to Asia and Alaska than any other large American city. As a seaport, Seattle carries on a large trade with Asian countries. Its aircraft industry employs thousands of workers. The forests of the Northwest provide the raw materials for the manufacture of paper. Fish canneries are located in Washington, Oregon, and the cities of northern California. The city and port of Anchorage, Alaska, serves as the business center for most of Alaska.

UNDERSTANDING WHAT YOU HAVE READ

1. Which questions are answered in this chapter?
a. Where are there manufacturing cities along the Great Lakes?
b. How have mineral resources been wasted?
c. What causes an industry to develop in a particular area?

2. The main ideas of *paragraphs 1 through 3* are that
a. large cities of the Northeast and Great Lakes area are capital cities
b. the Northeast and Great Lakes area has many advantages that make it a manufacturing region
c. factories in the Northeast and Great Lakes area make few kinds of products

3. An important resource of the northeastern region of the United States is
a. oil   b. coal   c. climate

4. Cities that greatly increased their population in the 1970s and early 1980s were
a. Cleveland and Chicago
b. Baltimore and St. Louis
c. Houston and San Diego

5. Centers of the aircraft industry are located in
a. Los Angeles and Seattle
b. Atlanta and New Orleans
c. Philadelphia and New York

6. The Ohio River and the Great Lakes transport much
a. meat and fruit
b. oil and lumber
c. coal and iron ore

7. Which city is farthest removed from a large body of water?
a. Denver, Colorado
b. New Orleans, Louisiana
c. Houston, Texas

8. The city on the western side of the coastal plain that serves as a transportation and banking center and as a manufacturer of textiles, chemicals, and metal goods is
a. St. Louis, Missouri
b. Atlanta, Georgia
c. San Antonio, Texas

DEVELOPING IDEAS AND SKILLS

Building Map Skills——The Northeast and Great Lakes Area: The Leading Industrial Region of the United States

Study the map on this page. Then tell whether these statements are true or false.

1. Almost every northeastern state has an important industrial area.
2. One area extends from Massachusetts all the way to Baltimore.
3. Pittsburgh and Wheeling are both steel cities.
4. The auto industry is centered around Philadelphia and Baltimore.
5. Waterways are close to the big industrial areas.
6. Textile manufacturing is most important near Chicago.
7. People no longer have to depend on neighbors. They can get goods from all over the region.
8. The goods made in this region are sold throughout the world.
9. The northeast region provides people with few choices for goods.
10. For the most part, cities are places where goods are made and jobs are available.

The Northeast and Great Lakes Area:
The Leading Industrial Region of the United States

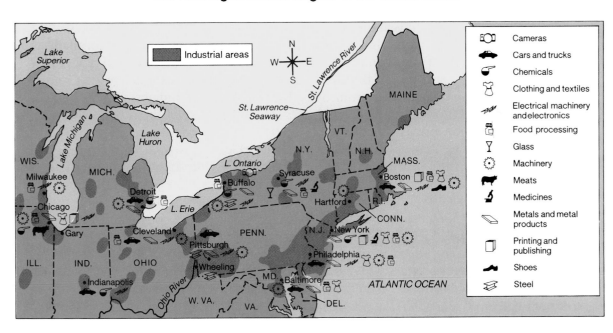

La Grande Complex:
Powerhouse of the North

Where does electric power come from? It comes largely from nearby power plants that burn oil or gas, or possibly from a nuclear reactor. In some parts of our country, however, the power companies cannot provide all the electricity the people need. This is true of the northeastern United States. As a result, the power companies import much of their electricity from Ontario and Quebec provinces in Canada. One such source of electricity is Canada's *La Grande complex,* or the James Bay project. It is the largest hydroelectric power project in North America.

The Canadian Shield lies in northeastern Canada, curving around Hudson Bay like a giant horseshoe. Many rivers wind across this hilly land. Many of the rivers empty into James Bay, the lower part of the Hudson Bay. In 1971, the Canadian government decided to harness, or tame, these wild waters to produce electricity. The Société d'Énergie de la Baie James (SEBJ) was formed to manage the construction of the La Grande complex. The project has two phases. In phase one, the SEBJ built three huge dams and three reservoirs. Six smaller power stations will be added in phase two.

Work began on the complex in 1972. Planes from Montreal brought workers to and from the isolated complex. Some workers built roads. Others built channels that diverted, or steered, the water toward the La Grande River. Surveyors roamed the land nearby looking for places to build dams. They needed places that would offer the best water flow and fall. The force of the falling water is very important in producing electricity. Countless truckloads of materials came in daily to build each dam.

At its peak, there were about 18,000 people working at the complex. A new town, Radisson, was built where the work first began. The workers, or "rough necks," were happy to be on the job. They made about $800 to $1,000 a week while on the job. They usually worked six days a week. Free food, housing, and recreation were given to the workers, so they were able to save a good part of their earnings.

At first, the Native Americans, or Indians, and Inuit who lived in the area were very unhappy. They made a living by trapping wild animals in this area. They felt that the new reservoirs would endanger the animals. By 1975, a compromise was worked out. The trapping area for the Indians and Inuit was greatly enlarged. A new town, Chisasibi, was built on La Grande River to house the Indians.

The first phase of the project was completed in 1985 under budget. Three massive dams, called LG (for La Grande) 2, 3, and 4 have been built. At the base of each dam is a powerhouse. The water fills up in the reservoir waiting for the gates to open. The water then rushes through the waterwheels that turn the turbines producing electricity. Other phases will add more power stations and provide more power for customers in Canada and the United States.

1. Where is the Canadian Shield? What valuable resource does it have?
2. How did the Canadian government decide to make use of this resource?
3. Why did some people object to this plan? What agreement was worked out?

Chapter 10

Farmlands of the United States

Where are the farmlands that provide an abundance of food for the people of the United States and the world?

READING FOR A PURPOSE:
1. Where are the four main farming regions in the United States?
2. What are the main crops grown and livestock raised in the United States?
3. What important changes have taken place in American farming?

1. The United States is so large that climate and land are not the same in all parts of the country. Thus, there are different farming regions. A farming region does not have a boundary line like a state. The change from one kind of farming to another is gradual. Differences in climate and soil mean there are different farm products in each region. In the United States, there are four main farming regions: the Central Plains and the eastern part of the Great Plains, the Atlantic and Gulf Coastal Plains, the western part of the Great Plains, and the valleys of the Pacific coast. In this chapter, you will learn about these and several other farming regions.

2. The Central Plains are among the finest farmlands in the world. The chief crop is corn. The growing season is hot and moist. The soil is fertile. The land is flat, making it easy for farmers to use machines to plant, cultivate, and harvest their crops. Ninety percent of the corn is used to feed hogs and cattle. Cattle from Texas, Oklahoma, Kansas, and other states are shipped to the corn belt for fattening. (Nebraska and Iowa are among the leading cattle-raising states.) The leading corn belt states are Iowa, Illinois, Nebraska, Minnesota, Indiana, Wisconsin, and Ohio. Wheat, oats, and soybeans are often grown along with or rotated with corn.

3. The western part of the Central Plains and the eastern part of the Great Plains is the wheat belt. Here there is less rainfall. In the southern part of the wheat belt, where winters are not as cold as they are farther north, wheat is planted in the fall. It stays in the ground during the winter and is harvested in July. This is winter wheat. Kansas, Texas, and Oklahoma are among the important producers of winter wheat. In the northern part, wheat is planted in the spring and harvested in the fall. This is the spring wheat belt. The farmers of North Dakota, Montana, western Minnesota, and the wheat farms of Canada form the greatest spring wheat area in the world. Wheat farms are larger than farms in the corn belt. Farm machinery can be used on a large scale.

4. Across the northern states, from Minnesota through Ohio and Pennsylvania to New England, is a belt of dairy farms. The growing season here is short and cool. The climate is good for growing hay used as feed for cattle. Milk, cheese, cream, and butter are the major

Dairy cattle. The United States leads the world in beef production. Are dairy cattle or beef cattle raised in your state or province?

dairy products. Wisconsin has been the leading producer of cheese for many years.

5. The second of the great farming regions is located along the Atlantic and Gulf Coastal Plains. In the northern part of the plains, soils are rocky and sandy. Here fruit growing and dairy farming are important. Tobacco is a leading product of North Carolina, Virginia, South Carolina, and Georgia. (It is also grown west of the Appalachians in Kentucky and Tennessee.) Peanuts are often rotated with tobacco. In the southern part of these plains, there is a warmer climate and a longer growing season. It is ideal for growing tobacco, cotton, fruit, and soybeans.

6. At one time, the cotton belt reached from the Carolinas to the coastal lowlands of Texas. Over the years, the place for most cotton producing has changed. Arizona, Louisiana, Arkansas, and Alabama still produce cotton. However, the leading cotton-growing state, by far is Texas. Next in cotton growing after Texas are California and Mississippi. Their warm climate and irrigated lands are excellent for growing cotton. At one time, the large cotton plantations of the South were worked by *tenant farmers* and *sharecroppers.* A tenant farmer paid rent for use of the land. Sharecroppers, however, gave a share of their crops, as rent, to the owner of the land. Today, cotton farms are worked by people who receive wages, as in a factory. Cotton is rarely picked by hand. Large machinery does that work. In addition to cotton, other crops such as corn, soybeans, and peanuts may be planted. These crops tend to replace minerals taken from the soil during repeated planting of cotton. Cattle raising is becoming more important in the South.

7. Along the hot, rainy coast of Texas and Louisiana, rice and sugarcane are raised. In Florida and southern Texas, citrus fruits—oranges, grapefruits, and lemons—are raised.

8. West of the 100th meridian (100° west longitude) are the dry grasslands, or steppes. This is the third great farming region. Most of this area receives 10 to 20 inches (25 to 51 centimeters) of rain a year. This region is the western part of the Great Plains. It extends north and south through the United States into Canada. Part of the wheat belt extends west of the 100th meridian. This is especially true for much of the Canadian spring wheat belt. But in many places, the dry western Great Plains is better suited for cattle grazing. Much of the grazing land is owned by the federal government and rented to the ranchers. Huge herds of beef cattle roam the fenced-

Irrigated fields in a western state. Eighty-seven out of every 100 gallons of water used in the United States are used to grow food crops for people and livestock.

in plains. Texas is the leading cattle-raising state.

9. In the past 40 years, a new cattle-raising practice has become widespread. Most beef cattle now spend only the first part of their life grazing in pastures. Then they are moved to feedlots on farms in the Central Plains or Great Plains. There they are fed grain and soybeans to increase their weight. Rich pasture lands and farms that grow the cattlefeed are scattered throughout the Great Plains. Some water comes from rivers and streams that flow east from the Rocky Mountains—for example, the Platte and Arkansas rivers. Even more irrigated acres depend on water pumped from a huge underground lake in Texas, Oklahoma, Kansas, and Nebraska.

10. Sheep-raising country is in the western Great Plains and in the even drier land of the Rocky Mountain states. Texas, Wyoming, Colorado, South Dakota, Montana, and Utah have millions of sheep. Sheep can get along with less water than cattle can. They can eat shorter grass and shrubs. Sheep ranches in the highlands are big because the animals must roam over a large area in order to find enough to eat. Parts of this region are irrigated. In parts of the dry western states, dams form reservoirs along rivers such as the Colorado River. Canals carry water from the reservoirs to the fields. Wheat, alfalfa, sugar beets, vegetables, and fruits are the crops of irrigated lands. The Idaho potato is also grown on irrigated land.

11. The fourth great farming region is the coastal area of the Pacific. Differences in climate have created two main farming areas—the valleys of California and the rainy lands of Oregon and Washington. First, let us look at California's most important farming areas: the Great or Central Valley, and the Imperial Valley.

12. The Great or Central Valley, at least 400 miles long, is one of the richest farming areas in the world. Water comes from streams in mountains known as the Sierra Nevada. The two main rivers in the valley are the Sac-

Harvesting vegetables. Both machinery and hand labor are used to pick the crops. What are some of the kinds of crops that migrant workers help harvest?

ramento and the San Joaquin rivers. Almost every crop grown in the United States is raised here—citrus fruits, nuts, grapes, vegetables, wheat, and cotton. Water projects supply water to over a million of the valley's acres. The Imperial Valley in southern California was once a desert. It gets practically no rain. However, irrigation from the Colorado River has made it a rich farming land. A large part of the oranges and lemons eaten in the United States comes from the valleys near Los Angeles. Cotton, dates, lettuce, and grapes are also grown. California is among the leading states in raising dairy cattle and sheep. It is also one of the leaders in producing cotton, wheat, and tomatoes.

13. There are many small farms in the California valleys, but most fruit and vegetables are grown on large farms, like "factories in the field." Workers come from other parts of the country and Mexico to help during the harvesting season. In the winter, they may pick lettuce in the Imperial Valley. In the summer, they move northward to pick oranges near Los Angeles. Then, they move farther north, and later return for the cotton harvest in the Central Valley. These people are *migrant workers.* Usually, they take their families with them. They often live in a camp near the farm where they are working. Because the family is always on the move, their children have little chance to attend school. Most likely they will work in the fields along with their parents.

14. Farther north are the marine lands of Oregon and Washington. While much of the land is covered with forests and mountains, there are also fertile farming areas. The cool, rainy climate is good for dairy farming and growing apples, berries, and flower bulbs. The central valleys are drier. There, apples and vegetables such as sweet corn, green peas, and beans are grown on irrigated land. In eastern Washington, wheat is the most valuable crop grown on lands irrigated from the Columbia River.

15. Some 2,000 miles (3,200 kilometers) across the Pacific, the farmers of Hawaii produce two main crops: sugarcane and pineapples. The climate is warm throughout the year, and there is plenty of rainfall. It is almost the only part of the United States where tropical foods can be grown.

16. In 1900, about two out of every five Americans lived on a farm. Now, only about 1 American in 41 lives on a farm. The reason for the change is a simple one. Fewer farmers are needed to grow the food Americans need. One farmer in the United States can raise enough food to feed 65 people. In addition, American farmers grow so much food that they can feed people in many parts of the world. As a result of these large harvests, the price of food to the American people is often low. The farmer must then rely on government aid to earn enough money to continue to farm. The farmers receive two types of aid. The government can approve the sale of grain to other countries or it can pay the farmers

An apple harvest. Why are Michigan, Pennsylvania, Virginia, and Washington particularly well suited for apple growing?

when the prices of their crops are very low.

17. Finally, American farms are big and getting bigger. Many small farmers are selling their farms to bigger landowners or corporations. It is easier to use scientific farming methods on these big farms than on the small ones. The big farms can use large amounts of fertilizer and pest killers, and many kinds of machinery. Therefore, the owners of these large farms grow many different crops, including various kinds of fruits and vegetables. They make a bigger profit than the small farmer. The small farmer leaves the land, moves to the city, and finds another type of job.

UNDERSTANDING WHAT YOU HAVE READ

1. Which of the following questions are answered in this chapter?

a. What are the differences between the wheat belt and the corn belt?

b. How is farming carried on in the Great Plains?

c. How is corn used by farmers of the corn belt?

2. The main idea of *paragraph 16* is that

a. fewer farmers are needed to produce large crops

b. the United States is a leading importer of grain

c. Americans are living on larger, more scientifically run farms

3. Different kinds of wheat are grown on the Great Plains because

a. land is more fertile in the north than in the south

b. most flour-milling cities are in states farther south

c. there are differences in climate

4. Most large farms in the United States today

a. are dairy cattle farms

b. raise one special cash crop

c. are in the corn belt

5. The Central Valley of California is important because

a. desert soils are made fertile by irrigation

b. a large part of the country's fruits, vegetables, grapes, wheat, and cotton are raised there

c. potato fields have given work to thousands of people

6. A belt of dairy farms would most likely be found in Wisconsin, Minnesota, and

a. Arkansas   b. Idaho   c. New York

7. Deserts of California have been made fertile through irrigation from the

a. Colorado River

b. Arkansas River

c. Columbia River

8. A corn belt would need a growing season that is

a. short and dry

b. dry and cool

c. hot and moist

9. Special crops raised along the warm, moist lands of the coast of the Gulf of Mexico are

a. cotton and tobacco

b. rice and sugarcane

c. potatoes and sugar beets

10. *Migrant workers*

a. move from farm to farm to harvest crops

b. work the land for a share of the crop raised

c. own their own citrus fruit farms

WRITING

In Chapter 10, you read about farming in various regions of the United States. Imagine that you had an opportunity to visit a farm in one of those regions. Write a letter to a friend telling what you saw on your visit. Include information about the land, the climate, and the crops. Also mention any special advantages or problems farmers in the region you "visited" have experienced.

DEVELOPING IDEAS AND SKILLS

Building Map Skills—Agricultural Regions of the United States

Study the map on this page. Then tell whether these statements are true or false.

1. Irrigation is an important part of farming chiefly in the western part of the United States.
2. The New England states are shown to be a great farming region.
3. Grazing is found in the drier areas of the United States.
4. Most of the land in the United States is suited for growing corn.
5. Spring wheat is grown in a cooler climate than winter wheat is.
6. Beef cattle are raised chiefly in the western part of the country.
7. Cotton is the only important crop of the southern states.
8. Fruits are important only in the western states.
9. Dairy farming is located near the area of large eastern cities.
10. Corn and wheat cannot be grown in the same climate.

Corn

Cotton

Dairy farming and hay

Fruit and vegetable, and mixed farming

Grazing or ranching

Wheat

Nonfarming area

Agricultural Regions of the United States

An American Farm

Mr. Kenneth Miller is a corn farmer in western Ohio, about 150 miles (241 kilometers) southwest of Detroit. He lives on his 400-acre farm with his wife and 15-year-old son, Jimmy. His other two children have grown up and left home. Mr. Miller took over the land from his father more than 30 years ago. While Mr. Miller's main interest is corn, he also has a small herd of dairy cows, a few chickens, and pigs. The Millers live in a large modern house. There is a small town three miles away and a new shopping mall 17 miles away.

Mr. Miller does most of the farm work himself. His son helps to milk the cows in the early morning and evening. His wife cares for the chickens and the small vegetable garden. Mr. Miller also grows oats, wheat, soybeans, and clover. By rotating his crops, he keeps the land in good shape.

In March and April, Mr. Miller plows and prepares his fields. In May he plants the corn. Mr. Miller drives a tractor-drawn machine that can plant four or more rows at once. The same machine can be used to spray fertilizers and *pesticides* (weed and bug killers).

Before long, the young corn plants push through the soil. By August, the corn stalks have grown very tall. In September, the corn is ready to harvest. Again, a huge machine, called a combine, mows down the rows. It pulls the ears of corn from the stalks. It husks the corn and removes the kernels from the cobs. The shelled corn and stalks are ground into silage, fodder preserved in a silo.

Machines, seed, and chemicals enable Mr. Miller to turn out huge crops. For many years he was well paid for them. The government even paid him at times to let some of his field remain unplanted. About 10 years ago, he thought he would increase the size of his farm. Today, he is glad he did not because the prices of farm goods have gone down sharply and it is hard to earn a living farming. The government has even told him he is producing too much milk. He has agreed, therefore, to decrease his dairy herd. He doesn't mind, because he wants to increase the number of his chickens. "I must keep up," he says, "with the changing food tastes of Americans, if I am to stay in business."

A gleaning machine clearing old corn stalks. The corn has already been harvested.

1. Where is Mr. Miller's farm located?
2. What is his chief crop?
3. What animals does he raise?
4. Why does Mr. Miller rotate his corn with other crops?
5. Why is Mr. Miller able to work his fields by himself?
6. What jobs are done by his wife and son?
7. When is the corn harvested?
8. What is the harvested corn used for?
9. What are some of the problems facing Mr. Miller as a farmer?

Chapter 11

The Resources of Canada

What are Canada's resources?

READING FOR A PURPOSE:
1. What are Canada's major natural resources?
2. What are Canada's leading industries?
3. Where are Canada's large cities located?

1. Like the United States, Canada is rich in natural resources. Minerals are the most valuable of its gifts from nature. Canada supplies much of the world's nickel, asbestos, and potash. Iron ore, cobalt, lead, zinc, copper, gold, silver, and platinum are other riches of Canadian mines. The discovery of large deposits of uranium has made Canada a leading producer of this valuable ore. Coal, oil, and natural gas are also plentiful. Many of these minerals have been found in the Canadian Shield, once thought to be a wasteland. Ontario and Quebec are the main mineral-producing prov-inces. Yet rich deposits of over 60 different minerals are found across Canada.

2. Canada leads the world in the production of asbestos. This is a mineral that is made up of fibers. These fibers can be woven into many materials. Asbestos has one important quality—it is fireproof. Therefore, it is used in fire fighters' suits, in shingles for homes, and in cement building materials. Although asbestos is useful, it has been found to be dangerous. It has been linked to lung cancer.

3. Before World War II, Canada produced little iron ore. Afterward, valuable iron ore deposits were found near the Quebec-Labrador (Newfoundland) border. The ore there is easy to mine, but at first it was not easy to bring to the cities. Then a railroad was cut through the wilderness. The ore can now be taken to distant industrial centers. Other rich sources of iron are located in central Quebec and near the northern shore of Lake Superior. Canada is among the world's top six iron-producing countries. Rich supplies of this mineral are exported to the United States.

4. Canada has many power resources. The most important source of power is falling water. Most of its industries (such as aluminum and paper) are run by hydroelectric power.

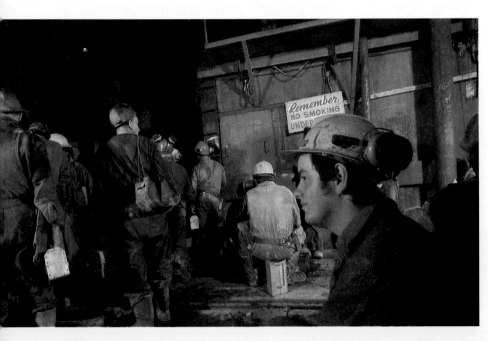

Miners at a uranium mine in the province of Ontario.

One of the world's largest hydroelectric projects is located at Churchill Falls in Labrador, Newfoundland. The province of Quebec produces electricity from its waterpower. Huge power projects are being built on Quebec's rivers flowing into James Bay. Waterpower projects on the St. Lawrence River supply electricity to the nearby parts of Canada and the United States. In western Canada, dams on the Columbia River provide electricity for homes and factories in British Columbia, Washington, Montana, and Oregon.

5. Two other important sources of power are petroleum and natural gas. Canada once had to import oil. Now the nation exports more than it imports. Discoveries of oil and natural gas in the province of Alberta have made the oil industry in Canada important. Calgary, at the foot of the Rocky Mountains, is the home of many large oil companies. It has become known as Canada's oil capital. Edmonton is also a refining center. North of Edmonton are new plants to extract oil from tar sands. Saskatchewan also produces oil and natural gas. Pipelines now carry gas and oil to many parts of the country. New finds of oil and natural gas continue to be made in the prairies, British Columbia, the Northwest Territory, and off the Arctic and Atlantic coasts.

6. Although there are large coal fields in Canada, only a few of the nation's factories use coal. Much of the coal is not very good. Then, too, the coal mines are located far from Canada's mills and factories. Because many of Canada's industries are near the coal fields of the United States, it is often cheaper for Canada to import coal than to mine it.

7. Canada's other resources include fish, forests, and furs. Canada's Atlantic and Pacific coastal waters are among the world's best fishing grounds. The Grand Banks, off the coast of Newfoundland, are the world's richest source of fish. Fishing boats from European nations also use these waters. Cod, lobster, scallops, and herring are the chief catches of these Atlantic waters. On the west coast, salmon fishing is most important. Canada's

A wood pulp and paper mill in the province of New Brunswick. Why is this industry located near water?

many lakes and streams provide a large supply of freshwater fish. Fisheries provide food for Canadians, as well as for people of other countries through export.

8. A great belt of forestland stretches across Canada from the Atlantic to the Pacific. Over one-third of Canada is covered with forests. All 10 provinces have forest regions. The most valuable product of the forests is wood pulp, from which paper is made. Nearly all the wood pulp is exported, and the largest buyer is the United States. The western province of British Columbia is the home of the tall Douglas fir. Vancouver, at the mouth of the Fraser River on the Pacific Ocean, is the major seaport for shipping lumber, as well as grain and minerals. British Columbia ranks first in Canada's lumber industry. However, the province of Quebec produces the most wood pulp and paper.

9. Canada was first settled as a fur-trading colony. Fur-bearing animals are still a valuable resource. But fur trapping is not as important as it was 200 years ago. There have been disputes over the killing of seals. Mink, fox, beaver, ermine, and other fur-bearing animals are still plentiful in the northern woods. However, many of these animals are now raised more easily on fur farms.

145

An aluminum production plant in the province of Quebec. Canada is one of the world's leading aluminum producers.

10. Canada's leading industries are refining oil, building cars and trucks, processing food, and manufacturing pulp and paper. The pulp and paper industry depends upon rivers and streams to carry the logs to mills and to furnish power to run the factory machines. It uses about a third of all the electrical power produced in Canada. Another of Canada's major industries is aluminum production. Only the United States manufactures more aluminum products. One reason for Canada's importance in aluminum is its large supply of waterpower. Canada imports bauxite ore from Latin America and manufactures the aluminum near the sources of waterpower.

11. Canada is now one of the world's most industrialized countries, even though it has a small population. Its industries draw materials from the nation's mines, forests, and fisheries. The greatest industrial region is in the provinces of Quebec and Ontario, along the Great Lakes and the St. Lawrence River. Minerals are brought from the Canadian Shield, waterpower is available, and there is a large

market for selling goods. Transportation is also available in this lowland region. It has been easy to build roads and railroads here. Also, the St. Lawrence River and the Great Lakes form a water highway. The St. Lawrence Seaway was completed in 1959. Ocean-going ships can travel all the way from the Atlantic to ports along the Great Lakes. Power stations of the seaway provide electric power to the homes and industries around it.

12. Many of Canada's largest cities lie along the St. Lawrence–Great Lakes lowland. Montreal, Quebec, is the world's second largest French-speaking city. (Paris, the capital of France, is first.) It is one of the centers of Canada's industrial life and a major port. Toronto, Ontario, has a metropolitan population of over 3 million. Its location on the shores of Lake Ontario make it a leading center for trade and industry. Quebec is Canada's oldest city. It is located nearer than Montreal to the mouth of the St. Lawrence River. In its fine harbor can be seen ships from almost every country of the world.

Toronto skyline. Name three of the large cities in the western provinces.

UNDERSTANDING WHAT YOU HAVE READ

1. Which questions are answered in this chapter?
a. Why are Canada's forests important?
b. Where are Canada's oil fields?
c. What fishing agreements does Canada have with other countries?

2. The main idea of *paragraph 11* is that
a. mines and forests feed Canadian industries
b. the Great Lakes–St. Lawrence region has the conditions needed for a great industrial region
c. oceangoing ships use the Seaway to travel to the Great Lakes

3. Canada has a storehouse of minerals in
a. Baffin Island
b. western deserts
c. the Canadian Shield

4. Canada's forests have been most useful in providing
a. wood pulp   b. potash   c. asbestos

5. Canada's most important source of power for industry is
a. coal   b. water   c. wood

6. Large cities near Canadian oil fields are
a. Calgary and Edmonton
b. Toronto and Montreal
c. Regina and Winnipeg

7. Cod and herring are two of the fish caught in great numbers off the coast of
a. British Columbia b. Ontario c. Newfoundland

8. Canada is one of the world leaders in the production of
a. nickel   b. tin   c. diamonds

9. Bauxite ore is important in which Canadian industry?
a. Lumber   b. Aluminum   c. Oil

DEVELOPING IDEAS AND SKILLS

Building Map Skills—The Resources of Canada

Study the map. Then tell whether these statements are true or false.

1. Canada has few mineral resources, except for oil and iron ore.
2. Much of Canada's industry is located in the northern part of the country.
3. Large cities are grouped together in the St. Lawrence River valley and near the Great Lakes.
4. Canada has many forest resources.
5. Coal production is important in Nova Scotia.
6. Asbestos is found chiefly near Quebec.
7. The Yukon is a major oil-producing area.

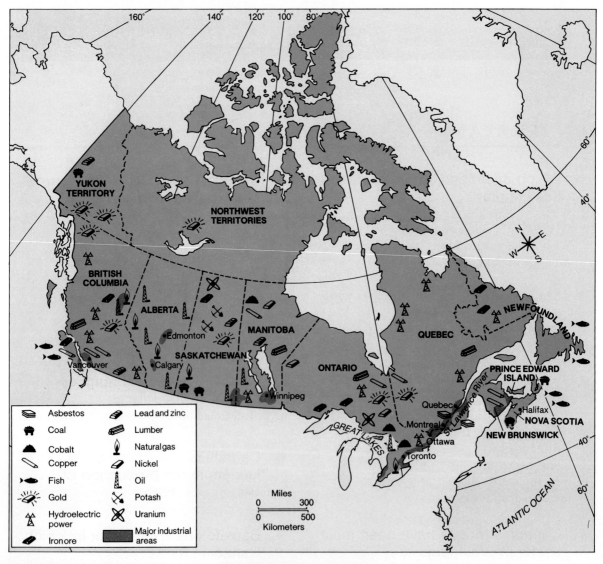

The Resources of Canada

DEVELOPING CRITICAL THINKING SKILLS

I. Do You Agree or Disagree?

Give reasons for your answers.

1. Refining oil and building cars and trucks are among Canada's most important industries.
2. One of Canada's problems is that there are few places where it can sell its manufactured goods.
3. Canada sells some of its mineral resources to the United States.
4. Furs are Canada's most important forest product.
5. The publishing industry in the United States would suffer if it could not get material from Canada.

II. Making Comparisons

Tell whether the following items refer to the United States, Canada, or both countries. If the item applies to the United States only, use the letters **US.** If the item applies to Canada only, use the letter **C.** If the item applies to both the United States and Canada, use the letter **B.** Write the answers in your notebook.

1. Large area and large population
2. Great use of coal as power for industry
3. Large aluminum industry
4. Fur-bearing animals plentiful in the northern forest
5. Leading producer of asbestos
6. Imports large amounts of wood pulp
7. Resources of oil and iron ore
8. One of the world's largest producers of nickel
9. Industrial area near the Great Lakes–St. Lawrence River
10. Power projects along the St. Lawrence and Columbia rivers

From Forest to Newspaper:
Canada's Important Wood Pulp Industry

One of Canada's largest industries is making wood pulp and paper. Canada is the second largest producer of wood pulp in the world, after the United States. It is the largest producer of newsprint. (Newsprint is used in printing newspapers.) Here is a brief story of how Canadians use this valuable resource from the forest.

Mr. Dudley is the manager of a large pulp mill in Arnprior, a city in the province of Ontario, Canada. He is talking to Mr. Wilkens, an advertising man. "Our company," says Mr. Dudley, "would like to put out a booklet showing how the wood pulp and paper industry works, from A to Z, as you would say. Do you think your firm can do it?" "I think so," replied Mr. Wilkens; "however, I could use more information." "That can easily be arranged," said Mr Dudley; "this is the month of September. . . . A good time to begin . . . In a few days, we can fly you to our northern forests where it all begins." Before long, Mr. Wilkens arrived at the company's camp among the fir, pine, and spruce trees, ready to begin his report.

The loggers start working in September. They have to get out as many trees as possible before the snow gets too deep. Much of the work is done by machines. Power saws are used to cut the trees and trim them of limbs. Bulldozers are used to cut roads through the forest and to drag the logs to trucks. Cranes are used to lift the logs onto the huge trucks, which take the logs to the mill. Some logs are floated on the nearest waterway. Here the logs are held together loosely and towed downstream to the mills by small tugboats.

At the mill, the bark is removed from the logs, which are then cut into short peices and stacked into piles. The pieces are ground into fine chips and mixed with water until they form wood pulp. The wood pulp is carried slowly on a belt through a series of rollers. The rollers squeeze out the water. The wood pulp slowly becomes newsprint. A great deal of power is needed to run all the machinery. The newsprint is put into rolls and shipped, largely to the United States. Mr Wilkens was fascinated by everthing he had seen: men cutting trees, loading them on huge trucks, guiding them down the river, or grinding them at the mill. It was more exciting than he had thought! Now he has the information needed to write the booklet on the wood pulp and paper industry.

1. What kinds of trees are found in the province of Ontario?
2. How are the trees taken out of the forest?
3. How are the trees brought to the pulp mill?
4. How does the climate affect the lumber work season?
5. What happens to the trees at the pulp mill?
6. What is the chief use of wood pulp? Why is this valuable?
7. How do you think lumber companies replace the trees that are cut down?
8. Which parts of this job do you think might be dangerous?

Chapter 12

Comparing Farming in Canada and the United States

In what ways are the farms of Northern America alike and different?

READING FOR A PURPOSE:
1. Where are the major farming areas in Canada?
2. What are Canada's most important crops and livestock?
3. Why do both countries export food?

1. Only a small part of Canada is useful for farming or grazing. In the north, forest and tundra cover more than half the land. Along the western coast is a chain of high mountains and plateaus as in the United States. Most of the Canadian Shield is too rocky or hilly to be farmed. (As the glaciers moved southward, they scraped away the fertile topsoil. They deposited the soil in the northeastern states of the United States.) In many parts of Canada the growing season is too short for raising most crops. Except for the Pacific coast, the farming land of Canada is within a few hundred miles of the United States border.

2. The inner plains are Canada's richest farming region. These plains are an extension of the Great Plains of the western United States. The good soil, summer rains, and dry harvest season are good for spring wheat. The farmers of the plains use machines to cut and thresh their crops. Canada is the world's sixth largest producer of wheat. Farther west, Canadians also graze cattle and sheep on the dry prairies.

3. The other major farming area of Canada is the lowland of the Great Lakes in southern Ontario. The winds from the lakes make it warm enough to grow hay, corn, oats, potatoes, and various fruits. The southernmost area is noted for peaches, cherries, grapes, and vegetables. The crops are used in the area's important canning industry. Dairy farms provide milk, cream, and cheese here and along the St. Lawrence River. Since this is the region of the greatest population in Canada, the dairy products find a good market in the cities of the lowlands.

4. The apple is Canada's most important

Harvesting wheat in Saskatchewan. The province's rich prairie soil produces over half of Canada's wheat. Saskatchewan farmers are also major producers of barley, oats, flax, and beef cattle.

151

A dairy farm in the province of Quebec. The province is also noted for its livestock, vegetables, apples, and maple syrup. This farm is probably in what river valley?

fruit crop. Orchards are found in Nova Scotia, New Brunswick, southern Quebec, and Ontario. Apples are also grown in the Okanagan Valley of British Columbia. This valley is also known for its grapes. Potatoes are the most important vegetable grown in Canada. Prince Edward Island and New Brunswick are major potato-growing areas.

5. Although only a small part of Canada is useful for farming, Canada is one of the world's great food-producing countries. As you remember, Canada's population is small. Canadian farmers grow much more food than the people need. Therefore, they export the surplus to other parts of the world. For example, Canada is the world's second-largest exporter of wheat.

6. What are some of the conclusions we can reach regarding farming in both countries of Northern America? In the United States, there are vast areas of fertile farmland. The farming area is much smaller in Canada. Nevertheless, both countries raise more than their people need. Both countries are large exporters of food.

7. The farms in both countries vary in size

from very small to very large. About half of all American farmland is rented. Some farmers rent all their land. Others own part of their land and rent the rest. In Canada, fewer than one-third of the farmers rent land, and most of those who do rent also own land. Most farms in both countries are run by farm families. However, many of the biggest farms in the United States are businesses owned by groups of people. In both the United States and Canada, most farmers live in farmhouses surrounded by their fields. They do not live in houses in small villages, as farmers do in many other parts of the world.

8. In both countries the farmers make great use of machinery, fertilizer, good seed, and the latest farming methods. This great use of machinery has made it possible for fewer workers to turn out larger crops. Science has helped farmers to grow larger and better crops. Without adding to the amount of their land, the farmers of Northern America since 1960 have more than doubled the amount of food they are able to produce. Because there is a lesser need for farmworkers now, many have left the farms to work in the cities.

9. Most farms in the United States and Canada are *commercial* farms, or farms that raise a *cash* crop—a crop for sale. This means that the farmers produce enough for their own needs and still more to be sold in markets in Northern America and throughout the world. Many farms *specialize*—that is, they depend upon one main cash crop. Others raise a variety of cash crops such as vegetables, fruits, and grains.

10. In some places where land was too dry for farming, as on the dry plains, rivers have been dammed to provide water for irrigation. These dams form a reservoir and store water until it is needed. To get the stored water to the farms, many miles of canals have been built. In other places, farmers pump water from underground lakes and water supplies. The sheep and cattle industry is carried on in both nations on the drier lands of the West.

11. Because of the great size of the United States and Canada, a variety of crops are grown. Yet there are a number of crops that cannot be grown in Northern America because of its northerly location. These are the tropical crops such as bananas, coffee, cocoa, rubber, spices, and tropical vegetable oils. Such crops are imported by the United States and Canada from other parts of the world such as Latin America.

UNDERSTANDING WHAT YOU HAVE READ

1. Which questions are answered in this chapter?
a. Why is only a small part of Canada used for farming?
b. How are Northern American farms alike?
c. Where are apricots grown in Canada?

2. The main idea of *paragraphs 1 through 4* describes
a. the farming regions of Canada
b. wheat farming on the plains
c. the growing seasons of Canada

3. Canada's chief farm crops are
a. lettuce, beans, and pears
b. rice, cotton, and sugarcane
c. wheat, potatoes, and apples

4. Canada's chief farming areas are located
a. in the western highlands
b. on the plains of the Pacific coast
c. on the inner plains near the southern border

5. Only a small part of Canada can be used for farming because
a. much of the land is forest and tundra
b. mining is a more important industry
c. the government controls the use of land

6. Canada is a leading exporter of food because
a. its people have a low standard of living
b. much of the land is used for farming
c. Canadian farms grow more food than its people need

7. When we say that farmers *specialize,* we mean that they
a. raise one or a few main crops to sell
b. divide their land among several crops for their own use
c. use machinery at harvest time

8. A *reservoir* is used for storing
a. food for farm animals
b. water
c. wheat once it has been cut

9. A *commercial* farm, as mentioned in paragraph 9, is one that
a. is probably a wheat farm
b. raises a crop for sale
c. raises what is needed by the farm family

153

DEVELOPING IDEAS AND SKILLS

Building Map Skills — Agriculture in Canada

Study the map on this page. Then tell whether these statements are true or false.

1. Saskatchewan is the number one wheat-growing province.
2. Prince Edward Island is noted for its potato farms.
3. Corn is the major crop of British Columbia.
4. The leading beef cattle region is located near Hudson Bay.
5. Dairy farms are located in the St. Lawrence River–Great Lakes region.
6. Apples are an important crop in Nova Scotia.
7. The Okanagan Valley is an important agricultural area in southern Quebec.

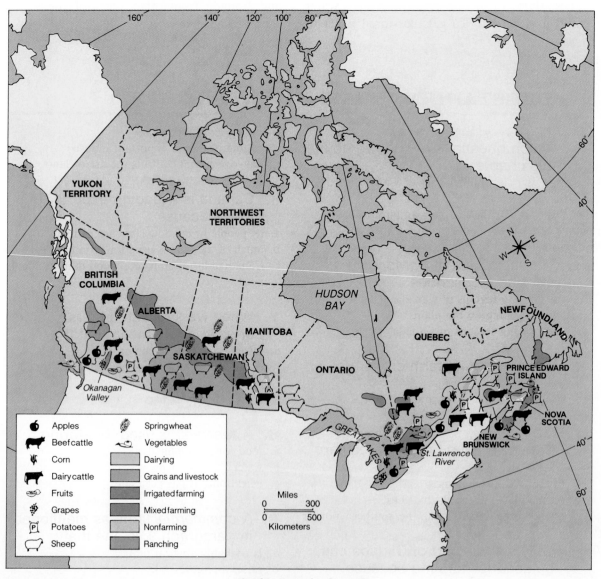

Agriculture in Canada

DEVELOPING CRITICAL THINKING SKILLS

Identifying Facts That Support Generalizations

Read the statements in the chart below. Then check the correct column in your notebook:

WHY NORTHERN AMERICAN FARMERS ARE SO PRODUCTIVE	YES	NO
1. Extensive use is made of machinery.		
2. Farm plots are very small.		
3. Great use is made of fertilizer.		
4. Most farmlands belong to a few people.		
5. There are large areas of level, fertile soil.		
6. There are no areas of desert.		
7. Rivers are dammed to provide irrigation.		
8. Everything is planned by the government.		
9. Farmers make use of scientific discoveries.		
10. All kinds of fruits can be raised.		

Chapter 13

Trade, At Home and Abroad

Why is trade important to the people of industrial nations?

READING FOR A PURPOSE:
1. Why do people carry on trade within a country?
2. Why do the United States and Canada trade with the rest of the world?
3. Why are nations of the world interdependent?

Coal mined in the Appalachian Mountains of West Virginia goes across the nation to people and industries that need it. How is this an example of interdependence?

1. In the United States and Canada, people do not live by their own work alone. Farmers in North Dakota harvest their wheat with a reaper made in Chicago, Illinois. Ranchers in Texas wear shirts made from Alabama cotton and perhaps manufactured in New York City. Miners in Quebec take their families for drives in automobiles from Windsor, Ontario. We all depend on others in different parts of our own country for things we need and want.

2. For example, in the United States most of the oil is found in Texas, Alaska, Louisiana, and California. Coal is mined chiefly in Kentucky, West Virginia, Wyoming, and Pennsylvania. Iron is taken from the open pits of Minnesota and copper from the mines of Arizona. Yet all of these products—in fact, all products—go to people across the nation who need them. In the same way, products made in one part of Canada are used by people in another part of Canada.

3. Each section of the United States or Canada exchanges its riches with another. Millions of people live in cities. They work in factories or stores or provide needed services for other people living there. These people turn the raw materials of the farms, mines, and forests into thousands of useful products. The materials for these products are supplied by those who work close to the natural resources—farmers, miners, foresters, ranchers, and fishers. Likewise, those people who make their living far from the city depend on the products and services of city workers. This is called *interdependence.* The large and quick system of transportation makes this exchange of goods possible.

4. The exchange of goods is called *trade.* Trade takes place when people produce more goods than they need and have some left over to sell. Other people buy the goods that they need from those who have them to sell. People who use the goods that are grown or are made are called *consumers.* (You are a consumer. So are your parents, your friends, and everyone else who has ever bought and used anything.) The process by which goods are sent from producer to consumer is not a simple one. When you buy a cotton shirt, many people are involved. The product passes from the cotton grower and picker to the baler, shipper, designer, manufacturer, salesperson, wholesaler, and retail store. And these are only a few of the stops on its journey from raw material to consumer product.

5. Not only is there trade within a country, but there is also trade among different countries. Trade with other nations—foreign trade—has several causes. First of all, no nation—not even the United States or Japan—has all the goods it needs. (The United States has little tin, for example. It must get this important mineral from countries that mine it.) Second, some countries have the right climate or soil to raise one kind of crop: coffee in Brazil, pepper in Malaysia, and so on. It is cheaper for some countries to import these products than it is for them to try to grow them.

6. Third, people of different countries have developed different skills. The people of Switzerland are famous for making fine watches. They sell their valuable product for money to buy goods they cannot get in their own country. Japan, famous for its cameras, autos, computers, and instruments, does the same. Fourth, some countries are able to produce more than they need. For example, American farmers grow more wheat than the people can

use. What is left over is sold abroad. Selling *surplus* (extra) cotton and wheat brings in money to buy the goods that people need and want. (When we say that *we* are buying and selling goods, we mean that individual persons or companies are trading, not the national government. Only in countries where there is little or no free enterprise does the government do almost all the actual buying and selling.)

7. The foreign trade of a country is measured by the amount of its *imports* (goods bought from other countries) and *exports* (goods sold to other countries). The United States is the largest trading nation in the world. Other large trading nations include Germany, the United Kingdom, France, and Japan. Canada is sixth in world trade. The United States and Canada trade mostly with each other and with Japan and the nations of Western Europe. These nations use machines to turn out more food and goods than they can use. Their people also have money to buy goods.

8. On the other hand, the industrialized nations do not carry on a large trade with underdeveloped or developing nations. These are countries that either have few resources or they are not yet using their resources to turn

The United States and Canada are among the world's leading trading nations. How does international trade demonstrate how nations throughout the world depend on one another?

157

out large amounts of goods and services. Trade is not ruled out entirely, for many developing countries may have certain raw materials that the industrial countries need. For example, the United States buys tin from Malaysia, oil from Nigeria, and cacao from Ghana. In turn, the developing countries buy products they need from the industrial countries. For example, China buys wheat from Canada and machinery from the United States.

9. The endless flow of materials and finished goods from one part of the world to another is one of the striking features of our modern world. The needs of any one group in the nation can set in motion businesses, mines, and plantations in far corners of the earth. And, as advances in science increase, the needs of people change. The discovery of how to make nylon almost ended the purchase of silk from Japan. As we have found greater uses for oil, gas, and electricity in our daily lives, the coal industry has suffered.

10. Since trade affects our lives in so many ways, it is important that the flow of goods continues without difficulty. A revolution or change in the government in a foreign country can affect business there. The United States is the world's largest seller of goods. Canada is also a leading seller of goods. Both nations must have places to sell their goods. The more people who want to buy these goods, the better. This is another reason why aid is given to developing nations. If living conditions in developing nations improve they will be able to buy foreign goods. Through trade, people work together to achieve a better way of living.

UNDERSTANDING WHAT YOU HAVE READ

1. Which questions are answered in this chapter?
a. How do different parts of the United States or Canada depend on other parts of each nation?
b. How does transportation affect trade?
c. What will stop trade among peoples?

2. The main idea of *paragraph 5* is that
a. the United States must get tin from other countries
b. coffee cannot be grown in Canada
c. nations trade with each other because they cannot produce all the things they need

3. Most of American and Canadian trade is carried on with
a. developing nations
b. other industrial countries
c. people who make a living by hunting and fishing

4. Goods that are sent out of the country are called
a. exports   b. imports   c. free-trade articles

5. People trade with each other because they
a. like to travel to different places
b. have more of some goods than they need and not enough of others
c. help to develop new products

6. Trade is important to a nation because it
a. helps poor people to receive goods from richer people
b. provides the nation with goods that it cannot always produce
c. makes wars and revolutions less likely to happen

7. Which of the following gives the best meaning of *interdependence?*
a. depending only on oneself
b. depending on each other
c. depending only on others

8. *Consumers* are people who
a. produce goods
b. use goods
c. transport goods

DEVELOPING IDEAS AND SKILLS

I. Understanding Circle Graphs——Foreign Trade of the United States

Study the two circle graphs and the list of statements about them. In your notebook, write the numerals 1 through 10. Beside each numeral, write **T** if the statement bearing that numeral is true. Write **F** if it is false. Write **N** if no information is given for that statement.

Foreign Trade of the United States

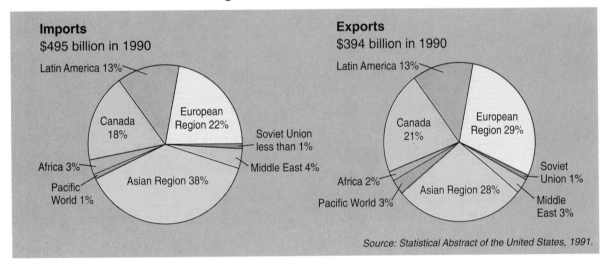

Source: Statistical Abstract of the United States, 1991.

1. Exports of the United States are greater than its imports.
2. The Soviet Union ranks lowest of all regions in trade with the United States.
3. The United States sells more goods to the countries in Western Europe than it buys from those countries.
4. People of the Middle East and North Africa have little money to buy United States products.
5. The United States has a larger trade with Canada than with all of Latin America.
6. More than half the imports of the United States come from Canada and the European region.
7. Trade with Australia, New Zealand, and the rest of the Pacific region is a small part of the total trade of the United States.
8. The large amount of goods imported from the Asian region is caused only by a growing trade with Japan.
9. The United States' trade with Canada is more than $70 billion a year.
10. The United States imports more from countries in Africa south of the Sahara than it exports to them.

II. Building Map Skills — The St. Lawrence Seaway

Study the map below. Then answer the questions that follow.

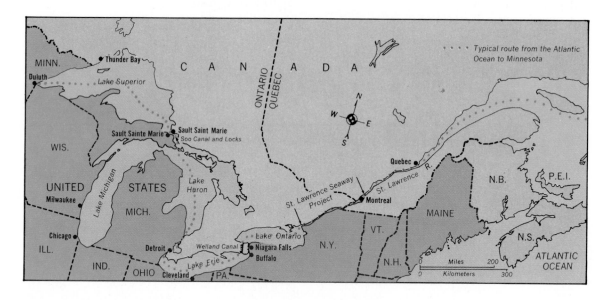

The St. Lawrence Seaway

1. The St. Lawrence River is connected by locks and canals to
   a. the Atlantic Ocean
   b. the Great Lakes
   c. Montreal

2. The canal that connects Lake Huron to Lake Superior is the
   a. Welland Canal
   b. Erie Canal
   c. Soo Canal

3. There is no canal between
   a. Lake Ontario and Lake Erie
   b. Lake Erie and Lake Huron
   c. Lake Huron and Lake Superior

4. The typical route from the Atlantic Ocean to Minnesota shown on the map ends in
   a. Duluth
   b. Sault Sainte Marie
   c. Thunder Bay

5. Ships enter Lake Erie from Lake Ontario through the
   a. Niagara Falls
   b. Soo Canal
   c. Welland Canal

6. The St. Lawrence Seaway Project is located between Montreal and
   a. Quebec
   b. Niagara Falls
   c. Lake Ontario

7. Which state is bordered by four of the Great Lakes?
   a. Minnesota
   b. Michigan
   c. New York

8. Downstream on the St. Lawrence River is
   a. southwest
   b. northwest
   c. northeast

9. A ship sailing from Europe to Chicago would pass these places in which order?
   a. Welland Canal, Lake Ontario, Lake Michigan
   b. Montreal, Welland Canal, Lake Erie
   c. Lake Erie, Lake Huron, Lake Superior

Chapter 14

Northern American Partners

How do the United States and Canada work together and help each other?

READING FOR A PURPOSE:
1. How do the United States and Canada benefit by working together?
2. In what ways do the United States and Canada cooperate?
3. What are some of the disagreements between the United States and Canada?

1. You have studied many things about the two giant nations of Northern America. To make sure that we understand the many ways in which the United States and Canada are similar, let us review the things they have in common.

2. Both nations were once colonies of the United Kingdom. As a result, English is spoken throughout the United States and in most of Canada. About one-fourth of the people of Canada speak French. Most of them live in the province of Quebec.

3. Both peoples believe in a democratic government. The citizens of each country have the right to elect representatives to make the laws that govern each country. Both believe in such rights as freedom of speech, assembly, and religion.

4. Both countries are rich in natural resources. Among the most important are oil, iron ore, coal, and hydroelectric power. These have been used to make the two nations of Northern America leading industrial nations. Much of the work in factories, farms, and homes is done by machines. Both peoples, American and Canadian, have a high standard of living. Their food, clothing, shelter, and general way of life are very much alike.

5. The two countries are tied together by great transportation systems. Autos, trains, ships, trucks, and planes travel back and forth freely between Canada and the United States. This transportation system makes it possible to exchange many products. The United States imports cars and auto parts, iron ore, lumber, natural gas, paper, oil, wood pulp, nickel, uranium, asbestos, and fish from Canada. Canada imports cars and auto parts, chemicals, coal, computers, farm machinery, fertilizers, textiles, and household machinery from the United States. More than two-thirds of Canada's imports come from the United States. About 73 percent of its exports go to the United States.

6. The people of the United States and Canada use their resources to help each other. In 1959, the two countries opened the St. Lawrence Seaway. This made it possible for ocean-going ships to reach ports on the Great Lakes. The St. Lawrence Power Dam provides both countries with electric power. In 1964, both countries signed an agreement to use the Columbia River for flood control and electric power. In 1965, the two countries signed the

The St. Lawrence Seaway is about 450 miles (724 kilometers) long. But the whole system includes not just the canals and locks but the Great Lakes. Using the whole system, ships can travel 2,400 miles from Montreal to Duluth.

161

Auto Pact. This allows free trade in cars, trucks, and auto parts. There is no tariff, or tax, on the billions of dollars of trade in these products between the two countries. In the 1970s, both countries agreed to work together to prevent water pollution in the Great Lakes.

7. Both the United States and Canada are interested in the Arctic region. A polar map will show you that the shortest route from northern Europe and Asia lies across the frozen north. With modern planes it is no longer necessary to travel around the North Pole. Now we can fly over it. As a result, the two nations have cooperated in building strings of radar stations across Canada. These stations will give the Northern American nations an early warning in the event of an air or missile attack from across the Arctic.

8. Politically, Canada shares some common interests with the United States. As several eastern European states came under Soviet control, Canada moved with the United States to form NATO (North Atlantic Treaty Organization). Since 1940, it has sent a large part of its armed forces to serve in NATO. In 1945, Canada joined the United Nations. On various occasions, Canada agreed to supply troops for "peace-keeping" operations in various countries.

9. While there are many things that the United States and Canada have in common, there are also some things that are different. For example, Canada is a large country, but it does not have many people. Therefore, Canadians have often been helped in developing their industries and resources. Many of its industries were started with the help of American money. Because of these *investments*, Americans now own large parts of Canadian industry. Canadians are not pleased that so much of their industry is owned by Americans rather than by Canadians. The Canadian government has taken steps to limit American ownership of oil and gas companies in Canada. On the other hand, Canadians have invested a great deal of their money in businesses in the United States. Many Canadians do not like to see this money leave Canada.

10. In recent years, there have been other differences. Some Canadian leaders have complained that much of the air pollution in Canada is caused by factories and power plants in the United States. They say that this pollution falls as acid rain and harms crops, trees, and lakes. They believe that the fish that live in their lakes and streams are dying because of the acid rain. Canadians were also concerned about the rich fishing grounds close to the Atlantic and Pacific coasts. Both countries claimed to have certain fishing rights in these areas. In 1984, both nations accepted a ruling of the World Court setting the boundaries on the fishing grounds near the Gulf of Maine. In 1985, the United States and Canada signed an agreement to control the fishing of salmon on the west coast. Because of their close relationships, it is only natural that there will always be many issues and problems between the two nations. Because we are friends, we have always been able to work out our problems.

Both the United States and Canada are members of the North Atlantic Treaty Organization. Many democratic countries in Europe are also members. The NATO treaty states, "An armed attack against one . . . shall be considered an attack against all."

11. On another matter, many Canadians want to keep their culture different from American culture. They are concerned because Canadians watch so many American TV shows and movies. Canadians also listen mainly to American records and read mainly American books and magazines.

12. There is no doubt about the United States–Canadian friendship. There are many examples of their help to each other. Yet there have been some disagreements, too, over foreign policies. The United States and Canada do not always agree on ways to deal with other nations. When the United Kingdom declared war on Germany in 1914 and in 1939, Canada also declared war right away. At first, many Americans thought that the wars were European problems and did not want to get involved. The United States stayed out of the World Wars until 1917 and 1941. However, in the 1960s and 1970s, Americans fought in the Vietnam War. Many Canadians were against that war. Canada began selling food to Communist China some years before the United States opened up such trade. Canada, too, has taken the lead among North American nations in urging more trade between the peoples of North and South America.

UNDERSTANDING WHAT YOU HAVE READ

1. Which questions are answered in this chapter?
a. Why are both Northern American nations interested in the Arctic?
b. What products do both countries lack?
c. How are both countries sharing their resources?

2. The main idea of *paragraphs 1 through 7* describes
a. ways in which Canada and the United States are very much alike.
b. what makes an industrial nation
c. the standard of living in Northern America

3. Many Canadians want to keep their culture
a. as much like Spanish culture as possible
b. different from American culture
c. the way it was 100 years ago

4. In 1959, Canada and the United States opened the
a. Missouri River Valley Project
b. World's Fair
c. St. Lawrence Seaway

5. Both Canada and the United States have
a. always agreed on foreign policies
b. sometimes disagreed on foreign policies
c. never agreed on foreign policies

6. Canada and the United States are important to each other because
a. Canada trades with Communist countries
b. the two nations share many resources
c. the two nations share the Panama Canal

7. In paragraph 9, the word *investments* refers to
a. industries in Canada
b. discoveries of Canadian minerals
c. money used to begin industry

REVIEWING AND WRITING

Making an Outline — The United States and Canada

Below are some headings for your *outline*. Following them are topics to be placed under these headings. In your notebook, make the correct outline.

A. Ways in Which the United States and Canada Are Alike
B. Common Interests of the United States and Canada
C. Where Canada and the United States May Disagree

1. Radar warning stations
2. NATO
3. American investments in Canada
4. Belief in democracy
5. Standard of living
6. Building of power projects
7. Air pollution and acid rain
8. Trade of raw materials for manufactured goods
9. Use of machinery to do people's work
10. Use of the English language

DEVELOPING CRITICAL THINKING SKILLS

Making Comparisons

Tell whether the following items refer to the United States, Canada, or both countries. If the item applies to the United States only, use the letters **US**. If the item applies to Canada only, use the letter **C**. If the item applies to both the United States and Canada, use the letter **B**.

1. Two official languages
2. Members of NATO
3. Vast Arctic region
4. Large black population
5. Many pulp and paper mills
6. Divided into provinces
7. Industrial region near the Great Lakes
8. Once a colony of the United Kingdom
9. Great Lakes are an important waterway
10. Great railroad system
11. Exports cars and auto parts

164

Acid Rain

Vacationers who return year after year to New York State's Adirondack region have noticed changes in the environment. Although located far from any pollution, this wild area seems to be changing. Spruce trees have brown needles instead of green. Many birch trees have no leaves. Fish, once plentiful in the region's lakes, have been disappearing. Gone with them are flies, frogs, and some species of birds.

Many scientists now believe the changes in the Adirondacks can be traced to a specific cause: acid rain.

Role of Air Pollution. Acid rain is caused by air pollution. The two leading pollutants in air are sulfur dioxide and nitrogen oxide.

Tons of sulfur dioxide rise into the skies above North America every day. Leading sources are electric power plants, metal smelters, and factory smokestacks. The biggest polluters are power plants making electricity from coal. Most power plants burn a cheap type of coal with a high sulfur content. Burning these high-sulfur coals sends huge amounts of sulfur and sulfur dioxide into the air.

Very tall smokestacks—some over 800 feet tall—shoot the sulfur dioxide and other wastes high into the air. There prevailing winds in the jet stream pick up the pollutants and carry them northward and eastward across the continent. Eventually the sulfur dioxide mixes with moisture in the air and becomes a form of sulfuric acid. Sulfuric acid is one of the acids falling back to earth in acid rain.

Tons of polluting nitrogen oxides also rise into the air of North America every day.

Most nitrogen oxide pollution is produced when oil and gasoline are burned. Motor vehicle exhausts and oil-fired electric power plants are the leading sources of nitrogen oxides in the air. The nitrogen oxides combine with the moisture in clouds and fog to form a nitric acid. Nitric acid is one of the acids falling back to earth as acid rain.

A Killing Rain. Acid rain disrupts the life cycles of many living things. Trees and lake-dwelling animals are the first living things to show signs of damage by acid rain.

Lakes, too, "die" as their waters become too acid for the animals living in them. Trout and fish eggs suffer first from rising lake acidity. More acidity kills off other fish as well as lake clams, snails, frogs, and insects.

What to Do? The acid rain problem can be solved. Canada and the United States have both passed laws to end acid rain and air pollution. The Clean Air Act of 1990 is an ambitious plan to reduce acid rain and air pollution in the United States. The Clean Air Act calls for many changes in the way Americans will live.

Coal-burning electricity plants will have to cut sulfur dioxide and nitrogen oxide pollution by half between 1995 and 2000. They can do this by placing scrubbers in smokestacks. The scrubbers remove the sulphur dioxide before it enters the atmosphere. Car makers will have to cut tailpipe exhausts by 60 percent in 1994 models. Car makers must also build pollution controls able to last for 10 years. **How are acid rain and its control likely to affect your future? What can individuals do to help stop the damage caused by acid rain?**

Northern America

Country	Area (Square Miles)	Capital	Population (1991 estimates)	Number of Years to Double Population	Life Expectancy	Per Capita Income
Canada	3,851,792	Ottawa	26,800,000	96	77	$19,020
United States	3,618,770	Washington, D.C.	252,800,000	89	75	$21,100

Canadian Provinces and Territories

Province or Territory	Area (Square Miles)	Capital	Population (1990)	Per Capita Income (1990)
Alberta	255,285	Edmonton	2,472,500	$21,075
British Columbia	366,255	Victoria	3,138,900	$21,101
Manitoba	251,000	Winnipeg	1,090,700	$18,329
New Brunswick	28,354	Fredericton	724,300	$16,087
Newfoundland	156,185	St. John's	573,000	$14,996
Northwest Territories	1,304,903	Yellowknife	54,000	$23,584
Nova Scotia	21,425	Halifax	892,000	$17,155
Ontario	412,582	Toronto	9,187,400	$24,700
Prince Edward Island	2,184	Charlottetown	130,400	$15,300
Quebec	594,860	Quebec	6,770,800	$19,613
Saskatchewan	251,700	Regina	1,000,300	$17,114
Yukon Territory	207,076	Whitehorse	26,000	$24,840

States of the United States

State	Area (Square Miles)	Capital	Population (1990)	Per Capita Income (1990)
Alabama	51,705	Montgomery	4,040,587	$14,826
Alaska	591,000	Juneau	550,043	$21,761
Arizona	114,000	Phoenix	3,665,228	$16,297
Arkansas	53,187	Little Rock	2,350,725	$14,218
California	158,706	Sacramento	29,760,021	$20,795
Colorado	104,091	Denver	3,294,394	$18,794
Connecticut	5,018	Hartford	3,287,116	$25,358
Delaware	2,045	Dover	666,168	$20,039
Florida	58,664	Tallahassee	12,937,926	$18,586

State	Area (Square Miles)	Capital	Population (1990)	Per Capita Income (1990)
Georgia	58,910	Atlanta	6,478,216	$16,944
Hawaii	6,471	Honolulu	1,108,229	$31,220
Idaho	83,564	Boise	1,006,749	$15,160
Illinois	56,345	Springfield	11,430,602	$20,303
Indiana	36,185	Indianapolis	5,554,159	$16,866
Iowa	56,275	Des Moines	2,776,755	$17,249
Kansas	82,277	Topeka	2,477,574	$17,986
Kentucky	40,410	Frankfort	3,685,296	$14,929
Louisiana	47,752	Baton Rouge	4,219,973	$14,391
Maine	33,265	Augusta	1,227,928	$17,200
Maryland	10,460	Annapolis	4,781,468	$21,864
Massachusetts	8,284	Boston	6,016,425	$22,642
Michigan	58,527	Lansing	9,295,297	$18,346
Minnesota	84,402	St. Paul	4,375,099	$18,731
Mississippi	47,689	Jackson	2,573,216	$12,735
Missouri	69,697	Jefferson City	5,117,073	$17,497
Montana	147,046	Helena	799,065	$15,110
Nebraska	77,355	Lincoln	1,578,385	$17,221
Nevada	110,561	Carson City	1,201,833	$19,416
New Hampshire	9,279	Concord	1,109,252	$20,789
New Jersey	7,787	Trenton	7,730,188	$24,968
New Mexico	121,593	Santa Fe	1,515,069	$14,228
New York	49,108	Albany	17,990,455	$21,975
North Carolina	52,669	Raleigh	6,628,637	$16,203
North Dakota	70,702	Bismarck	638,800	$15,255
Ohio	41,330	Columbus	10,847,115	$17,473
Oklahoma	69,919	Oklahoma City	3,145,585	$15,444
Oregon	97,073	Salem	2,842,321	$17,156
Pennsylvania	45,308	Harrisburg	11,881,643	$18,682
Rhode Island	1,212	Providence	1,003,464	$18,841
South Carolina	31,113	Columbia	3,486,703	$15,099
South Dakota	77,116	Pierre	696,004	$15,872
Tennessee	42,144	Nashville	4,877,185	$15,798
Texas	266,807	Austin	16,986,510	$16,759
Utah	84,899	Salt Lake City	1,722,850	$14,083
Vermont	9,614	Montpelier	562,758	$17,436
Virginia	40,767	Richmond	6,187,358	$19,746
Washington	68,139	Olympia	4,866,692	$18,858
West Virginia	24,232	Charleston	1,793,477	$13,747
Wisconsin	56,153	Madison	4,891,769	$17,503
Wyoming	97,908	Cheyenne	453,588	$16,398

UNIT FOUR

LATIN AMERICA

KEY IDEAS

- Latin America's location covers the huge continent of South America and two parts of North America—the long isthmus of Panama and many Caribbean islands.

- The physical characteristics of Latin America include high mountains, tropical rain forest, and deserts. These hinder transportation and communication and limit lands for farming.

- Although a mixture of many ethnic groups, Latin Americans are bound together by the Spanish and Portuguese languages and their Roman Catholic religion.

- Many Latin American countries depend on cash crops such as coffee, cotton, sugar, or wheat, but profits from these farm products change as world prices for them go up and down.

- A few Latin American countries are very rich in oil, but new energy sources, capital, and better education are needed throughout Latin America for industries to grow.

- Latin America exports raw farm and mine materials and imports machinery, which results in the movement of people, ideas, and goods.

- Latin America is the most urbanized of all the developing regions of the world.

- As one of the world's fastest growing regions, Latin America faces problems of debt, low standard of living, city slums, and destruction of valuable rainforests.

La Paz is Bolivia's largest city. Yet it is dwarfed by the immense splendor of the Andes Mountains.

Chapter 1

Our Southern Neighbors

Why are we interested in Latin America?

READING FOR A PURPOSE:
1. How is Latin America important to the safety of the United States?
2. What are the ties that bring Latin American nations together?
3. Why is the Panama Canal important to all American nations?

A street scene in one of Brazil's large cities. Brazil has nine cities with over a million people. Most people in Latin America live in cities and towns.

1. Many of us have used the words *America* or *Americans* when speaking of the United States. This is not completely accurate. There are others who are not from the United States and who are Americans, too. These are the people of Latin America. Latin Americans sometimes resent it when people of the United States call themselves Americans as though the title belonged to them alone. It is common in Latin America to refer to people of the United States and Canada as *North Americans*. People in Latin America usually do not call themselves Latin Americans. The people in each country are nationalistic. They say, "I am Colombian," or "I am Peruvian."

2. Latin America is made up of several parts. South of the United States is the country of Mexico. From Mexico a "bridge" of land extends to the southeast. This land, sometimes called Central America, contains seven small countries. East of Central America is the Caribbean Sea and its many islands. Cuba, Haiti, the Dominican Republic, Puerto Rico, Trinidad, and Jamaica are among the largest and most important lands of the Caribbean island region. Stretching southeast from Central America is the continent called South America. This continent is connected to Central America by a narrow strip of land, the Isthmus of Panama. All of these parts to-gether—Mexico, Central America, the Caribbean Islands, and South America—make up Latin America.

3. This region has 33 independent nations. There are also small areas that are colonies of nations of Europe. Some countries, like Brazil, are very large. It is almost as big as the United States. Others, like Grenada and Barbados, two island nations in the Caribbean Sea, are quite small. Some of the countries, like Mexico and Cuba, are close neighbors of the United States. Others are a great distance away. Buenos Aires, the capital of Argentina, is farther from Washington, D.C., than any capital of Europe is. It is even farther from Washington, D.C., than Moscow in the Commonwealth of Independent States is.

4. We call this large region south of us Latin America because the people who first settled there—the Spanish, Portuguese, and French—spoke languages that came from Latin. (Latin was the language of the ancient Romans.) Most of the 33 republics were once colonies of Spain. Brazil was a colony of Portugal. Others, mostly small, were colonies of the United Kingdom, France, or the Netherlands. In former Spanish colonies, the usual language is Spanish. In Brazil, the language is Portuguese. However, large numbers of Native Americans who live together in mountain or tropical rain-forest communities speak their own languages.

5. The United States is interested in Latin America for many reasons. *First,* a friendly Latin America is important to the safety of the United States. If an enemy country had bases in Mexico, Central America, or the Caribbean Sea, the United States would be in danger of attack. Likewise, the nations of Latin America know that an attack upon any one of them would be dangerous to the freedom of the others. That is one of the reasons why the United States joined with many Latin American countries in 1948 to form the *Organization of American States* (OAS). Besides working for peace, the OAS works for justice and economic development.

6. *Second,* the United States and Latin American nations carry on a great deal of trade. The people of the United States need many of the products of Latin American countries. For example, the United States imports oil from Mexico and Venezuela, tin from Bolivia, copper from Chile and Peru, gold and silver from Mexico, and bauxite from Jamaica and Suriname. Coffee, bananas, and chocolate (made from cacao beans) are some United States favorites. These farm products cannot be grown in the climates of the United States. On the other hand, the United States sells cars, trucks, machinery, food, chemicals, and

A market in Peru. What are some of the food products that Latin American countries sell to the United States and other parts of the world?

electronic equipment to Latin American countries. Many American businesses have branches in Latin America. Most Latin American countries buy more from the United States than from any other country. Most of them also sell more to the United States than to any other country. Trade between the United States and Latin America has increased from about $7 billion 30 years ago, to about $72 billion in 1990.

7. *Third,* like countries in other parts of the world, the governments of Latin America are trying to raise the standards of living of their people. They want to make their farms and factories as modern as possible. They want to improve housing, schools, and health services. The United States has tried to help them in this effort. Young people of the Peace Corps work and teach in Latin America. In 1961, the Alliance for Progress was started by President Kennedy for this purpose. Under this plan, Congress provided money to help the Latin American people. In the 1980s, the U.S. government continued to supply Latin America with billions of dollars in aid and loans. Private American banks also provided Latin American countries with loans. This, combined with amounts saved and invested by Latin Americans themselves, has helped build factories, modern farms, and better schools.

8. *Fourth,* the Panama Canal is an important waterway. The canal is located on the Isthmus of Panama, in an area, or zone, rented from Panama. The canal was completed in 1914 by the United States. In 1978, the U.S. Congress approved a treaty with Panama. The United States agreed to turn over operation of the canal to the government of Panama by the year 2000. The canal is open to all nations in times of peace. The United States considers the canal important to the national defense. Warships can use the canal to pass from the Atlantic to the Pacific Ocean in a short time. Some of today's larger ships cannot use the canal. A second canal may be built. Naval and air bases on some of the Caribbean islands protect the canal from attack.

171

UNDERSTANDING WHAT YOU HAVE READ

1. Which questions are answered in this chapter?

a. Why are we interested in Latin America?
b. What is the Alliance for Progress?
c. What is the average income in the countries of Central America?

2. Which of the following questions describe the main idea of the chapter?

a. How did the United States build the Panama Canal?
b. Why does the United States trade with Latin America?
c. Why do the American nations need each other?

3. The nearest neighbor to the United States in Latin America is:

a. Mexico   b. Brazil   c. Argentina

4. All of these Latin American nations are Spanish-speaking countries EXCEPT:

a. Mexico   b. Brazil   c. Argentina

5. This region is called Latin America because

a. the first settlers were Latins
b. the people speak Latin languages
c. Rome once conquered this part of the world

6. The Panama Canal is important because it

a. shortens the distance between two great oceans
b. is a sea-level canal
c. is the center of trade between Latin America and the United States

7. A narrow strip of land connecting two larger bodies of land is a(n):

a. island   b. strait   c. isthmus

8. In paragraph 2, a sentence reads, "From Mexico a *'bridge' of land* extends to the southeast." The best meaning for the words in italics is

a. a chain of islands
b. land that connects larger areas of land
c. wet, swampy land reaching into the ocean

DEVELOPING IDEAS AND SKILLS

A. Building Map Skills —Latin America

Study the map on page 173. Then answer these questions.

1. Which parts of the region are north of the equator? Which are south?
2. Is the region east of west of the prime meridian?
3. How far north and south does the region extend?
4. What is the largest country?
5. What are the chief bodies of water that border the region?
6. Which countries have no outlets to the sea?
7. What are some of the important rivers in the region?
8. What are the capital cities of each country? How do you know they are the capitals?
9. Which countries are island nations?
10. Which countries are located on a peninsula?
11. Which lands are colonies of other nations?

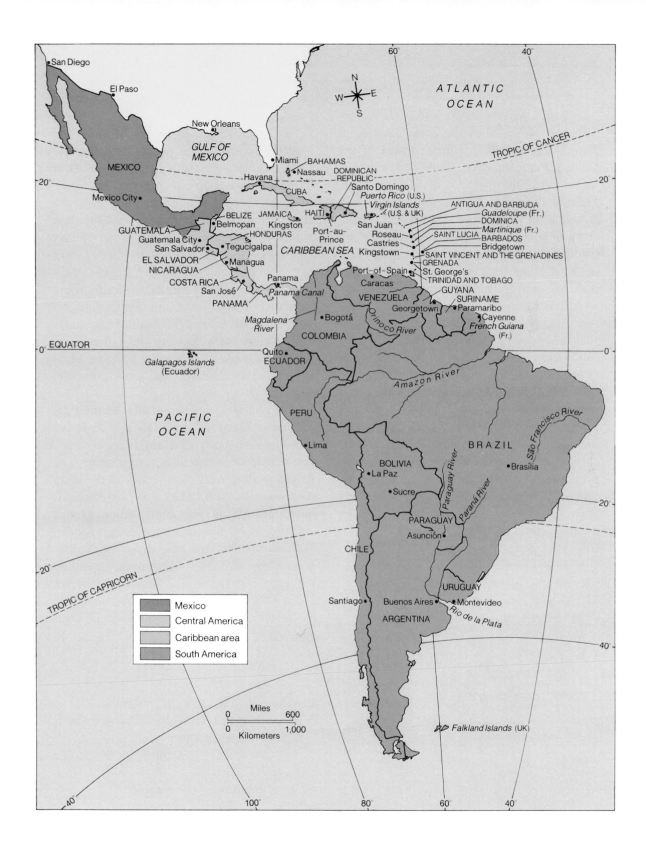

Latin America

Otavalo

North of Peru lies the small country of Ecuador. Like Peru, it formed part of the vast Inca empire. Most of the people in Ecuador are either mestizos or Indians. Most Indians are farmers, working mainly with simple tools and equipment. Here is a brief story of a small group of Indians who are leading a different way of life. They are holding on to their traditional ways while making room for modern business.

Alfonso Morales wears the white trousers, blue poncho, braided hair, and felt hat that is typical of Otavalo Indians. He lives in Otavalo, a small town 50 miles north of Quito, Ecuador's capital city. There are about 45,000 Indians in Otavalo. Mr. Morales owns a small textile factory. He has put in six electric looms. His 15 employees, including some non-Indians, make ponchos, shawls, and other woven items for export to the United States, Panama, and Spain. Other Otavalo Indians sell their weavings in Otavalo's Saturday market or in small stores in town.

Mr. Morales's neighbors, Marina and Jose Farinango, have opened a small workshop in their two-story brick home. They have hired six people to run wooden Spanish-style looms. The Farinangos now use acrylic materials rather than wool for their ponchos and carpets. Wool is too heavy and bulky for the tourists to carry home. Acrylics are much lighter. Like Mr. Morales, they are doing well. Their living room is furnished with sofas and chairs, a television, and a stereo set. "We are always looking for new markets," say the Farinangos. "We have traveled to Miami, Florida, Mexico City, Puerto Rico, and the Dominican Republic."

The selling of weavings and handicrafts to markets abroad has raised the living standards of many Otavalo Indians. They are proud of what they are doing. The Ecuadorean government now treats them with more respect. They are not discriminated against as are some Indian groups elsewhere. Despite their success in business, the Otavalo Indians still wear their traditional dress and speak Quechuan, an Indian language. Unlike many Indian groups in Latin America, the Otavalos have been able to continue to follow the customs of their people.

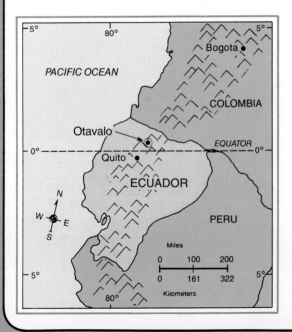

1. Where do the Otavalo Indians live?
2. How do some Otavalo Indians make a living?
3. How have they managed to save their culture?
4. What have been the results?
5. What might be another title for this story?

Chapter 2

The Hollow Continent

What are the important features of the topography of South America?

READING FOR A PURPOSE:
1. How are the continents of North and South America alike?
2. Why is South America sometimes called the "Hollow Continent?"
3. What are the major river systems of South America?

1. The region of Latin America is about 8,800,000 square miles (22,800,000 square kilometers) in area, slightly larger than the United States and Canada together. The continent of South America makes up about 80 percent of this land mass. A look at the map on page 173 will show you that nearly all of South America lies southeast of the United States. The eastern bulge of the continent that is part of Brazil brings South America closer to Europe and Africa than to the northeastern states of the United States. During World War II, the United States sent planes to Africa by flying them south to Brazil. Then they were flown across the Atlantic to Africa. Making two shorter flights was a safer way of delivering them to the battle areas.

2. The northern part of South America is crossed by the equator. (This is also the widest part of South America.) Therefore, Latin America lies partly in the Northern Hemisphere and partly in the Southern Hemisphere. As a result, the seasons in most of Latin America are the opposite of the seasons in the United States and Canada. When we have winter, the people of Latin America (south of the equator) have summer. When we have summer, they will have winter. Furthermore, a large part of Latin America is in the low latitudes. In general, this means that much of Latin America has a hot climate. Most of the people of this hot region live along the seacoast or in the mountains where it is cooler.

3. Latin America has many mountains. The western highlands stretch from the southern border of the United States to the very tip of South America. In South America, these mountains are called the Andes Mountains. The Andes are the second highest mountain range in the world. Some of the peaks are more than 20,000 feet (6,100 meters) high. These mountains are very hard to cross. To the west of the Andes is a narrow coastal plain, in some places only 5 miles (8 kilometers) wide. On the east coast of South America there are lower mountains or hills known as the Guiana and Brazilian highlands. The islands of the Caribbean Sea are really the tops of underwater mountain peaks of these highlands. The Patagonian Plateau is the flat rocky highland area in southern Argentina. Because of the mountains, travel by land from one part of South America to another has been a serious problem.

The Andes Mountains are among the highest in the world. Are they near the east coast or the west coast of South America?

Patagonia is a plateau in southern Argentina. It's landscape is largely dry but there are wooded areas as well.

4. Between the eastern and western highlands are the great inner plains or lowlands of South America. In Venezuela and Colombia the plains are called the *llanos.* In eastern Argentina the rich grassy plains are known as the *pampas.*

5. The plains are drained by great rivers. The largest and longest is the Amazon River of Brazil. The Amazon rises in the Andes Mountains of the west. It flows eastward across the continent to the Atlantic Ocean. The Amazon flows through the hot, thick tropical rain forest like a mighty inland sea. The river and its branches are so vast that they drain nearly half of South America. Along its path, the Amazon's shores may be as much as 60 miles (97 kilometers) apart. Its mouth is 200 miles (322 kilometers) wide. The Amazon is so powerful that the mud that it carries along with it colors the water for 50 miles (80 kilometers) out into the ocean.

6. The Orinoco and the Plata are two other great rivers of South America. The Orinoco flows through northern South America. It

The Amazon River. The Amazon River plains make up the largest river basin in the world. In what direction does the Amazon flow?

drains the lowlands of Venezuela. The Rio de la Plata (River of Silver) is in the southeastern part of the continent. The two branches of the Plata begin in Brazil and flow southward through the pampas. The river empties into the Atlantic Ocean near the city of Buenos Aires, Argentina. For the most part, the rivers of South America are *navigable.* (Large ships can sail upstream from the ocean for long distances.)

7. In many ways, the land forms of North and South America are very much alike. Both continents have high mountains along their western coasts—the coastal ranges—the Pacific coastal ranges and the Andes. Both have an inner plain drained by mighty rivers. Both have highlands in the east—the Appalachians and the Guiana Highlands and Brazilian Highlands. Both have great seaports along the eastern and western coasts.

8. There are also differences between the two continents. First, Northern America's largest river, the Mississippi, flows from north to south. The Amazon flows from west to east. The Mississippi flows through the most fertile part of the United States. The Amazon flows through a tropical rain forest where few people live. (We might call the Plata the "Mississippi" of South America. It flows in a north-south direction, through the rich grasslands of the pampas. It is also a great highway for trade like the Mississippi.) Second, the Rocky Mountains are not as high as the Andes. It has been easier to build roads and railways through the Rockies. Third, Northern America is lucky to have a great inland waterway system, the Great Lakes. There is no such water highway in South America.

9. Because of its geography, South America is called the "Hollow Continent." The mountains of South America border the coasts, while the plains are found inland. Therefore, the surface of South America makes it "high on the outside, low on the inside," like a saucer. Much of the inland plains is also hot, and part of it is tropical jungle. As a result, most of the people of South America live along the rim, or coastline. Brazil, in particular, has tried to encourage settlements farther inland. Thus far, the hardships met by frontier settlers have held back the success of many such efforts.

UNDERSTANDING WHAT YOU HAVE READ

1. Which questions are answered in this chapter?
a. Where does the Amazon River begin?
b. How do the mountains affect Latin America?
c. When was South America discovered?

2. The best title for paragraph 5 is
a. Mighty River of the Rain Forest
b. Lowland River of South America
c. The "Mississippi" of South America

3. A river of South America that flows through fertile land is the
a. Amazon   b. Plata   c. Madeira

4. The highest mountains in Latin America are the
a. Rockies   b. Andes   c. Guiana Highlands

5. How have the mountains affected Latin America?
a. Most of Latin America is dry.
b. Most of Latin America is cold.
c. Travel is difficult from one part to another.

6. The large rivers of Latin America are useful because they
a. provide waterpower
b. all drain fertile farmlands
c. are used by ships for long distances

7. The *llanos* and the *pampas* are both
a. mountains   b. deserts   c. lowlands

8. A river that is *navigable* is one that
a. is used to supply waterpower
b. can be used by large ships
c. carries with it a large amount of oil

DEVELOPING IDEAS AND SKILLS

Building Map Skills——Land Forms of Latin America

Study the map on page 179. Then tell whether these statements are *true* or *false*. Be able to explain your answers.

1. A high mountain area extends almost the length of South America, from north to south.
2. Hills occupy only a small part of South America.
3. Most of the central part of the continent is mountainous.
4. All of the land at the southern tip of South America is at sea level.
5. The western coast of South America is a very broad lowland.
6. Plateaus are located near the northeastern coast.

REVIEWING AND WRITING

Complete the following outline in your notebooks.

Land Forms of North and South America

A. How They Are Alike
   1.
   2.
   3.

B. How They Are Different
   1.
   2.
   3.

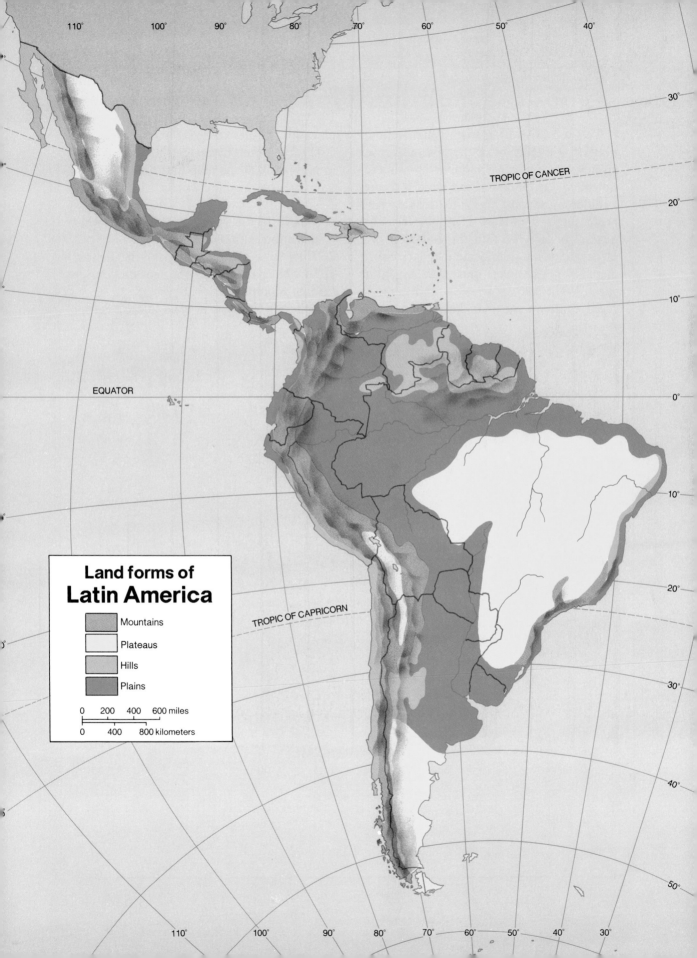

Land forms of
Latin America

Mountains

Plateaus

Hills

Plains

0   200   400   600 miles

0   400   800 kilometers

TROPIC OF CANCER

EQUATOR

TROPIC OF CAPRICORN

110°   100°   90°   80°   70°   60°   50°   40°

30°

20°

10°

0°

10°

20°

30°

40°

50°

110°   100°   90°   80°   70°   60°   50°   40°   30°

Reading an Elevation Map

This is an elevation map. What is elevation? It is the height of the land above sea level. Color is used on a map to show elevation. Look at the key. Each color indicates a different elevation. For example, dark green shows areas that are 1,000 feet (305 meters) or less. To find the elevation of a place you would first locate the place on the map. For example, find the Argentine coast. What color is it? Now find the dark green color on the map key. What is the elevation of the Argentine coast? It is 0 to 1,000 feet (0 to 305 meters).

Now look at the map and the key to answer the following questions.

1. Where is the Amazon Basin? At what elevation is the basin?
2. How high are the pampas? the llanos?
3. In what part of the continent do you see high mountains?
4. Where would you be able to raise cattle?

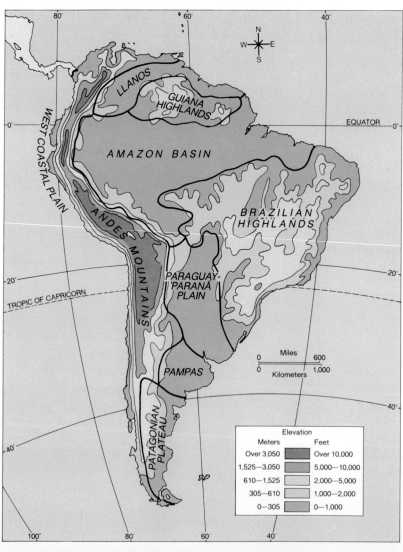

Elevation	
Meters	**Feet**
Over 3,050	Over 10,000
1,525—3,050	5,000—10,000
610—1,525	2,000—5,000
305—610	1,000—2,000
0—305	0—1,000

A Region of Many Climates

Why are there differences in climate in Latin America?

READING FOR A PURPOSE:
1. Why are there differences in climate even in the tropics?
2. What parts of Latin America have climates like those in the United States?
3. How do winds and ocean currents affect climates in Latin America?

1. If you were asked to plan a trip to Latin America, what clothing would you take with you? For several reasons, this would not be easy to decide. First, Latin America extends over a great distance from north to south. This means there is a great range in latitude. Second, Latin America is mountainous. It may be cold in one place, while only a few miles away in another place it is very hot. Third, because of the differences in wind direction, it may be very rainy or very dry. Fourth, in parts of Latin America the seasons are opposite from those in Northern America, so you would have to know whether it is winter or summer at the time you wish to travel.

2. A large part of Latin America is near the equator. This area is hot and wet throughout the year. It is a tropical rain forest. The rainforest climate is found in the Amazon River Valley, along the Caribbean coast of South and Central America, and along the Pacific coast from Ecuador to Panama. The average temperature throughout the year is 80°F (27°C). It is never as hot, though, as the hottest summer days in the midwestern United States. (In Kansas, Nebraska, and South Dakota, temperatures of more than 100°F (38°C) are sometimes recorded in the summer months.) At night in this tropical part of Latin America, one sleeps under a light blanket. But

In the hot, damp lowlands of Central America, there are banana plantations.

some rain falls almost every day. There is no dry season, and every day is sticky and damp.

3. Knowing that so much of Latin America is in the tropics, you might think that the entire region is hot. This is only partly true. There are differences in temperature between places only a few miles apart, even in the tropics. There are parts of Colombia, Ecuador, Peru, and Bolivia that are very cold, although they are located near the equator. How is this possible? These places are high in the Andes Mountains. Therefore, they have a *vertical* climate. This means that the climate grows cooler as you travel higher up into the mountains, away from the lowlands.

4. At sea level the climate is tropical, or hot. The people of Latin America call this the *tierra caliente,* or hot country. As you go higher, the climate becomes somewhat cooler. This is the *tierra templada,* or cool country. Near the peaks of the mountains, you are in the *tierra fria,* or cold country. Because mountains are found in many Latin American countries, the vertical climate is common.

181

These women are spinning and weaving cloth near Lake Titicaca in Bolivia. They are high up in the Andes Mountains, over 2 miles (3.2 kilometers) above sea level. What can you tell about the climate from these workers' summer clothing?

5. North and south of the tropical rain forest are the tropical grasslands, or savannas. (In Venezuela and Colombia the savannas are called the *llanos*.) There are two seasons in the savannas—wet and dry. The wet, or rainy season brings floods, and the dry season bakes the land. The soil and grasses of the savannas are tough. There are also many insects that carry diseases. Because of these conditions, few people live in the savannas.

6. South of the savannas in the middle of South America is the humid-subtropical climate. Many Latin Americans live in this kind of climate. Here winters are mild and summers are warm. The pampas of Uruguay and Argentina lie in the humid subtropics. Buenos Aires, Argentina, is about as far south of the equator as Charleston, South Carolina, is north of it. Therefore, you can see that the southeastern part of both the United States and South America have the same kind of climate—although the seasons are opposite.

7. The winds and ocean currents affect the climate of South America as they do that of the United States and Canada. In Northern America, the coastal mountains and the Rocky Mountains shut off the wet winds moving *eastward* from the Pacific Ocean. The eastern side of the Rockies is dry. In much of South America the rain-carrying winds blow from the Atlantic Ocean. These winds are

warm and wet. The West Indies and the northern part of South America get much rain. These winds move *westward* across South America until they reach the Andes Mountains. There the winds rise. The air is cooled, and the rain falls on the eastern side of the mountains. When the air passes to the western side of the mountains, it is dry. Therefore, the narrow coastal area on the west has little rain. The result of this is the Atacama Desert of Peru and northern Chile. The winds from the Pacific Ocean are of little help. They blow from the cold Peru Current (Humboldt) and bring little rain.

8. Much farther south, the winds over South America come from the southwest. These winds travel until they reach the Andes Mountains. The mountains force the winds to rise and rain falls along the coast. East of the mountains it is dry. This causes a dry plain in western Argentina.

9. Chile is a long, narrow country in the southwestern part of South America. Since it is 2,650 miles (4,264 kilometers) long, it has several kinds of climate. Northern Chile is a desert, the Atacama Desert. South of the desert is a 600-mile (966-kilometer) strip of Mediterranean climate. Summers are hot and dry, and winters are mild and rainy. Most of Chile's people live here. Farther south, the climate is marine, usually cool and damp.

The Atacama Desert is one of the driest places on the planet. The climate is dry and cool all year round. The land is rich in copper, nitrates, and gold.

UNDERSTANDING WHAT YOU HAVE READ

1. Which questions are answered in this chapter?

a. Why is it cold in some places near the equator?
b. What animals live in the rain forest?
c. Why are parts of South America's west coast a desert?

2. The main idea of this chapter describes

a. how the winds affect Latin America
b. the vertical climate of Latin America
c. the different climates of Latin America

3. The largest part of Latin America is in the

a. low latitudes
b. middle latitudes
c. high latitudes

4. The mountains of Latin America cause a climate that is called

a. rain forest   b. vertical   c. subtropical

5. The reason for the desert of northern Chile is that

a. lowland areas in a vertical climate have little rain
b. the Andes Mountains cut off rain from the east
c. the seasons are opposite from those in the United States and Canada

6. Some of the large cities of Latin America are located in the highlands because

a. disease-carrying insects are found in all the low-land areas
b. all of Latin America is near the equator
c. the climate is more pleasant there

7. The best meaning for *subtropical* is

a. near the tropics
b. grassland
c. rain-carrying

DEVELOPING IDEAS AND SKILLS

Building Map Skills — Climates of Latin America

Study the map on page 185. Then tell whether these statements are true or false.

1. There is no marine climate north of the equator in Latin America.
2. Only the tropical rain forest is found along the equator.
3. An area of vertical climate stretches the length of South America.
4. The largest region of little rainfall is found along the north and eastern coasts.
5. South America has a Mediterranean climate in areas both north and south of the equator.
6. Latin America has a marine climate along the western coast.
7. The savannas lie both north and south of the tropical rain forest.
8. Nearly all of Brazil lies in a region of heavy rainfall.
9. The subtropical climate of Latin America is found much farther from the equator than it is in Northern America.
10. Although Mexico has some dry areas, none of it can be called a desert.

DEVELOPING CRITICAL THINKING SKILLS

I. Agree or Disagree

Decide whether or not each of the following statements agrees with what you have read. If the answer is *disagree,* explain why.

1. All of Latin America is hot and wet.
2. It is always hot near the equator.
3. Dry grasslands are found north and south of the rain forest.
4. South America has no deserts.
5. Temperatures along the equator are the hottest on the earth.
6. Chile is a land of different climates.
7. Most people live in the tropical lowlands.
8. The Caribbean and Atlantic coasts are dry.

II. Making Inferences

In our reading, many facts are given to us. From these facts we can draw conclusions. The following are some conclusions or inferences that you might make after reading this chapter. Tell whether these conclusions are correct or incorrect. Give reasons for your answers.

1. Mexico City, the largest city in Latin America, is probably located on a lowland near the sea.
2. In flying from New York to Rio de Janeiro, Brazil, your plane would fly almost directly south.
3. Latin Americans grow some crops that we do not have and some that are the same as ours.
4. Latin American countries trade more with Europe than they do with Australia.
5. There are few cities in the valley of the Amazon.
6. Buenos Aires, Argentina, would have the same climate as Seattle, Washington.
7. The airplane has become an important means of travel in Latin America.

Climates of
Latin America

	Tropical rain forest
	Savanna
	Desert
	Steppe
	Mediterranean
	Humid subtropical
	Marine
	Vertical

0   200   400   600 miles

0   400   800 kilometers

110°   100°   90°   80°   70°   60°   50°   40°

BAHAMAS

TROPIC OF CANCER

CUBA

DOMINICAN
REPUBLIC
HAITI

MEXICO

BELIZE
GUATEMALA
HONDURAS
EL SALVADOR
NICARAGUA

JAMAICA

ANTIGUA AND
BARBUDA
DOMINICA
ST. VINCENT   ST. LUCIA
AND THE   BARBADOS
GRENADINES   GRENADA
TRINIDAD AND TOBAGO

COSTA RICA   PANAMA

VENEZUELA

GUYANA
COLOMBIA   SURINAME   FR. GUIANA

EQUATOR

ECUADOR

PERU

BRAZIL

BOLIVIA

TROPIC OF CAPRICORN

PARAGUAY

URUGUAY

ARGENTINA

CHILE

30°

20°

10°

0°

10°

20°

30°

40°

50°

110°   100°   90°   80°   70°   60°   50°   40°   30°

From Empires and Colonies to Free Nations

How has Latin America changed in nearly five hundred years?

READING FOR A PURPOSE:
1. What were the leading civilizations in Latin America before the Europeans arrived?
2. How did Spain and Portugal spread their influence in Latin America?
3. How has independence affected the Latin American people?

Mayan ruins in Mexico. Ancient Mayans used the round building to observe the sun, moon, and stars.

1. Long before Columbus came to the New World, there were people living on the American continents. The first Americans probably came from Asia. They crossed the Bering Strait into Alaska. Then they moved southward, exploring the land and settling it. Three of the most famous Native American peoples in Latin America were the Maya, the Aztecs, and the Incas.

2. The Maya lived in southern Mexico and Guatemala. They built many beautiful cities in Central America before the arrival of Columbus. They studied the skies and learned about the movements of the sun, the moon, and the stars. The Maya learned to keep time and also made a calendar. They built huge pyramids and other buildings of stone. They painted pictures and wove cotton cloth. Around 1300, for some unknown reason, the ancient Mayan empire disappeared. Their language survived, however. Many of their villages were overgrown by the tropical forest. About one and a half million present-day Mayans live in southern Mexico, Belize, Guatemala, and Honduras.

3. The Aztecs lived in a valley in the central highlands of Mexico. Their capital city was Tenochtitlán. It was built on islands in the middle of a lake. The Aztecs conquered the other tribes living around them. They forced these tribes to work for them and to pay taxes in gold and silver. Their temples were built on the tops of great stone pyramids. The Aztecs wove cotton cloth, made beautiful pottery and jewelry, and wrote poetry. For food, they planted corn, beans, and potatoes.

4. The Inca empire was in the Andes Mountains, from Ecuador to Chile. The ruler was called the Inca. We call the people he ruled Incas. The leaders lived in stone palaces, or fortresses, on the tops of mountains. The empire's capital was at Cuzco, in Peru. The people lived on the hillsides or in the valleys below. They lived chiefly by raising corn, beans, and potatoes, or by herding llamas and alpacas. The Inca farmers learned to terrace—that is, to build steps on the mountainsides for farming. They irrigated their farmland with water from the highlands. The Incas were sun worshipers and made many objects in the form of round golden disks. They were also excellent road builders and had a fine communications system.

5. While Columbus was sailing westward from Spain, he reached some of the lands of Latin America. During his second voyage to the New World, he began the first European settlement there. Before long, both Spain and Portugal claimed lands in America. These countries asked the Pope—the head of the Roman Catholic Church—to divide the New World between them. In 1493, the Pope drew an imaginary line running north and south on the map. This was called the *Line of Demarcation*. All lands west of this line would belong to Spain. All lands east of this line would belong to Portugal. Because of this settlement, Portugal later claimed the land that is now Brazil.

6. By 1500, there were a number of Spanish settlements in the islands of the West Indies. The Spanish brought horses, cattle, sheep, citrus fruits, and sugarcane to the New World. They carried the potato, corn, and tobacco to Europe. From their island forts, soldiers were sent to explore the nearby coasts in search of riches. In 1519, Hernando Cortez landed with a small force on the coast of Mexico. With the help of guns and horses, he was able to conquer the Aztecs. In 1532, Francisco Pizarro sailed southward along the west coast of South America and discovered the Inca empire. He captured the Inca chief and killed him. The Incas were soon defeated. The Spanish were now masters of two treasure houses in Latin America—Mexico and Peru.

7. By 1600, the Spanish had explored and conquered most of Latin America. They divided their conquered lands into two kingdoms. The kingdoms were ruled by *viceroys,* or governors, who were appointed by the king of Spain. The viceroys divided the best lands into huge estates, or *latifundios.* These were given to friends of the king. The Native Americans had to work for the Europeans in the mines or on the farms and ranches. Missionaries also traveled to the New World. They brought the Roman Catholic religion, set up schools and missions, and taught.

8. In 1500, Pedro Cabral, who was sailing for the Portuguese, reached Brazil. The lands along the coast were divided into large farms or plantations. Sugar was the chief crop. The planters found there were not enough Native Americans to work in the sugar fields, so they brought people from Africa. The Africans were forced to become slaves on the plantations. As time went on, the Portuguese kept moving westward until they had conquered nearly half the continent.

9. For 300 years Spain ruled its colonies with a firm hand. The colonies could not make their own laws. After the success of the American and French revolutions, though, the colonists wanted their freedom. The first revolt in Latin America, however, was not in a Spanish colony. It took place in Haiti, which was ruled by the French. Many Africans had been brought to Haiti by the French to work in the sugar fields. Toussaint L'Ouverture, a former slave, led them in their fight against French rule. In 1803, after his death, the colony gained its freedom. It is the second oldest republic in the Western Hemisphere (after the United States).

10. The ideas of freedom spread

Terraces at Machu Picchu in Peru. The Indians and later, the Incas built terraces on the mountainsides to increase the amount of farmland. The terraces also stopped the rain from washing away the soil.

throughout Latin America. In 1810, Father Hidalgo, a Mexican priest, led the Mexican people in the first revolt against Spain. The Mexicans finally won their freedom from Spain in 1821. Before long, other people in Latin America began to rebel against Spain. Simón Bolívar, the "George Washington of South America," led the fight for freedom in Venezuela, Colombia, Ecuador, and Bolivia. José de San Martín helped to win freedom in Chile and Peru. In 1822, Brazil became free from the control of Portugal. By 1824, most parts of Central and South America were no longer colonies of Spain and Portugal.

11. For a time, it seemed that the independence of the new nations might be lost. Some rulers of Europe wanted to give back the nations of Latin America to Spain. The people of the United States were glad to see the Spanish colonies win their independence. They did not want the powerful nations of Europe helping Spain. In 1823, President James Monroe made a statement concerning the new nations that became known as the Monroe Doctrine. He said that Europe was to keep "hands off" the new governments in the Americas. Any attempt to help Spain to regain its colonies would be thought of as an unfriendly act against the Unites States.

12. When the people of Latin America became free, they did not unite like the people of the United States. Separate nations were formed. In the beginning, many of the new

Simón Bolívar, one of South America's greatest heroes in the struggle for independence. Why did the colonies want independence from Spain?

countries tried to draw up constitutions, or plans of government, like that of the United States. However, most of the people were poor. They could not read or write. They had not had a long history of being active citizens. The new nations came to be ruled by military dictatorships. The people still had only a few rights even though they were free from their European rulers. However, in the late 1980s and early 1990s, many Latin American dictators realized that they must allow free elections if they were to avoid complete collapse of their countries. By the early 1990s, many of the military governments in Latin America had crumbled and civilian governments replaced the military ones. Democracy has made great headway in Latin America.

UNDERSTANDING WHAT YOU HAVE READ

1. **Which questions are answered in this chapter?**

a. Who was Simón Bolívar?

b. How did Spain govern its colonies?

c. What new crops did the Spanish bring from the Americas to Europe?

2. **The main idea of *paragraphs 9 through 11* is to describe**

a. how the United States treated the countries of Latin America

b. the Latin American struggle for freedom

c. the European rule of Latin American colonies

3. **Brazil was settled by the**

a. Spanish   b. French   c. Portuguese

4. **The Inca empire was destroyed by**

a. Cortez   b. Pizarro   c. Columbus

5. The Spanish came to the New World for all of these reasons EXCEPT:

a. the desire for silver and gold
b. to convert the Indians to the Roman Catholic religion
c. to get furs from the animals in the forests

6. A viceroy is much the same as

a. a governor   b. an explorer   c. a missionary

7. Africans were brought as slaves to Latin America chiefly to

a. work in the factories
b. work in the sugar fields
c. settle the inland plain of Brazil

8. In a country ruled by a dictator, the people

a. enjoy freedom of speech
b. choose their own leaders
c. have little voice in their government

DEVELOPING IDEAS AND SKILLS

Reading a Time Line

Look at the time line. Write the letter of the period of time in which you would place each of the following events.

A	B	C	D	E	F
1300	1400	1500	1600	1700	1800	1900

1. Francisco Pizarro discovers the Inca empire.
2. Monroe Doctrine issued.
3. Line of Demarcation declared by the pope.
4. Mexico wins freedom from Spain.
5. Mayan empire disappears.
6. Hernando Cortez conquers the Aztecs.

SUMMING UP

Reviewing Chapters 1 Through 4

Choose the item that does not belong with the others in each group.

1. Reasons for Northern American interest in Latin America.
   a. Panama Canal
   b. trading for each other's goods
   c. source of machinery
   d. source of tropical foods
2. Climates of Latin America
   a. tundra   b. rain forest   c. vertical   d. desert
3. Land forms of Latin America
   a. mountains   b. plains   c. plateaus   d. large inland lakes
4. Native American peoples who controlled empires
   a. Incas   b. Seminoles   c. the Maya   d. Aztecs
5. Settlers in Latin America
   a. Swedes   b. Spanish   c. Portuguese   d. French

DEVELOPING CRITICAL THINKING SKILLS

Making Generalizations

Study the following chart and list. Then answer the questions at the bottom of page 191.

Latin American Nations That Became Independent Since 1973

New Nation	Year of Independence	New Nation Used to Be a Colony of the Following	Area
Bahamas	1973	United Kingdom	5,380 sq mi (13,934 sq km)
Grenada	1974	United Kingdom	133 sq mi (344 sq km)
Suriname	1975	Netherlands	63,251 sq mi (163,820 sq km)
Dominica	1978	United Kingdom	290 sq mi (751 sq km)
Saint Lucia	1979	United Kingdom	238 sq mi (616 sq km)
Saint Vincent and the Grenadines	1979	United Kingdom	150 sq mi (389 sq km)
Belize	1981	United Kingdom	8,866 sq mi (22,963 sq km)
Antigua and Barbuda	1981	United Kingdom	171 sq mi (442 sq km)
St. Christopher and Nevis	1983	United Kingdom	101 sq mi (261 sq km)

Some Northern American Comparisons:

1. Rhode Island, the smallest U.S. state in size, is 1,055 square miles (2,732 square kilometers) in area.
2. Prince Edward Island, the smallest Canadian province in size, is 2,184 square miles (5,657 square kilometers) in area.
3. Alaska, the smallest U.S. state in population, has about 500,000 people.
4. Prince Edward Island, the smallest Canadian province in population, has 130,400 people.
5. Average income per person in the United States is $21,100.
6. Average income per person in Canada is $19,020.

Sources: Population Reference Bureau, Inc., 1991; Europa World Yearbook, 1990.

Population	Food Products	Mining/ Industry/ Natural Resources	Average Income Per Person
300,000	fruits, vegetables, fish	tourism, oil products, medicines, salt, timber	$11,370
100,000	spices, cocoa, bananas	tourism	$ 1,900
400,000	rice, sugarcane, bananas coffee, fish, shrimp	bauxite, aluminum, processed food, timber and wood products	$ 3,020
100,000	bananas, citrus fruits, coconuts,	tourism, soap, timber	$ 1,670
200,000	bananas, cocoa, coconuts, citrus fruits, livestock	tourism, clothing, electronic parts	$ 1,810
100,000	bananas, arrowroot	tourism, processed food	$ 1,200
200,000	sugarcane, citrus fruits, rice, beans, corn, cattle, bananas, honey, fish	clothing, building materials, cigarettes, timber, furniture, soap	$ 1,600
100,000	cotton, rum, lobsters	tourism, clothing, lobsters	$ 3,880
40,000	sugarcane	sugar processing, tourism, cotton, salt, copra	$ 2,860

Write a one-sentence generalization about each of the following topics. Begin each of your generalizations with one of the following: *All, Most, Some, A few.*

1. Food products
2. Population
3. Area
4. Industries and resources
5. Nation that controlled each country when it was a colony
6. Average income per person

Chapter 5

The People

Who are the people of Latin America?

READING FOR A PURPOSE:
1. Why are Latin Americans not greatly concerned with a person's race or skin color?
2. What ties hold Latin Americans together?
3. Where are the population centers in Latin America?

1. The population of Latin America is growing at a fast rate. Latin America is one of the fastest growing regions of the world. Mexico and Central America are two parts of Latin America that have had a rapid increase in population. There is a slower increase in other parts such as Argentina, Uruguay, and Jamaica. About 452 million people live in the lands south of the United States. There are four main groups of people. One group is made up of Native Americans. Those with African backgrounds make up a second group. Those with European ancestors are a third, and the people of mixed background are a fourth.

2. Native Americans were the first people in this region. They were conquered by the Spanish and forced to work in mines and on farms. Today there are about 30 million Native Americans in Latin America. They are the largest population group in Bolivia and Peru. Many Native Americans live in Ecuador, Mexico, and the Amazon valley of Brazil.

3. In the 16th century, African slaves were brought to Latin America from Africa. They were the chief source of labor on the large sugar plantations. The black population of Latin America is found mainly on the Caribbean islands and the west coastal lowlands of Brazil. Most of the people of the Bahamas, Barbados, Dominica, Grenada, Haiti, Jamaica, Saint Lucia, Saint Vincent and the Grenadines are of African descent. Many blacks live in Belize, Cuba, and the Dominican Republic.

4. Most whites in Latin America are European descendants of the early Spanish and Portuguese settlers and other immigrants from Europe. In the 19th and early 20th centuries, many people came to Latin America from Italy, France, and Germany. They settled chiefly in the milder climates of Argentina, Uruguay, Chile, and Brazil. Today, many of the people of Argentina, Uruguay, Costa

A street scene in Port-au-Prince, the capital of Haiti. This city is also Haiti's main seaport and trading center.

While much of Latin America is heavily populated, areas of South America, such as the village of this farm family in Paraguay, have few people.

Rica, Brazil, and Cuba are of various European backgrounds.

5. Since the Spanish explorers came to Latin America, there has been much mixing among Native Americans, Europeans, and Africans. As a result, a large number of people are of mixed background. Many are *mestizos,* people who are part Native American and part European. Mestizos make up the largest group in Paraguay, Honduras, El Salvador, Nicaragua, Panama, Venezuela, Chile, Colombia, Ecuador, and Mexico. *Mulattos* are of mixed African and European background. Many of the people in the Dominican Republic, Cuba, Brazil, and other countries are mulattos. Other people are of mixed Native American and African descent. Because of this great mixing of races, the people in many parts of Latin America have not been greatly concerned with a person's race or skin color.

6. Spanish is the official language in 17 Latin American nations. In Brazil, the people speak Portuguese; in Haiti, French; in Suriname, Dutch. English is the official language in the Bahamas, Belize, and most of the island nations of the Caribbean. Native Americans in many parts of Latin America speak their own languages. In fact, in both Peru and Paraguay, Native-American languages are the official languages along with Spanish. More people speak Spanish than any other language in Latin America. But all languages have been changed slightly. Native-American words have been added to the Spanish. In the south, Spanish may also be spoken with Native-American words or accents.

7. Religion is another tie that brings Latin Americans together. More than 90 percent of the people are Roman Catholic. The Spanish and Portuguese brought Catholic missionaries with them to the New World. They converted many of the people to the Roman Catholic religion. The Roman Catholic Church is important in the everyday life of the people. Even in tiny Indian villages in the mountains there are churches. While there are Protestants, Jews, Muslims, and Hindus in Latin America, they are small in number compared with Roman Catholics.

8. Until the 1950s, most Latin Americans were farmers who lived on large farms. (Throughout the 1970s and early 1980s, there has been a great movement of people from rural areas to cities.) In the Caribbean region, large farms are called *plantations.* In Mexico, they are called *haciendas,* in Argentina and Uruguay, *estancias,* and in Brazil, *fazendas.* Many of the large farms are owned by one

Many of Peru's Native Americans live in the highlands, where they farm and raise livestock. Their sheep and llamas graze in the mountain valleys.

family. Farmers work on the plantation owners' land. This system of land ownership has caused problems in Latin America. Most people living on farms do not own their own land. They are poor. A few people, the landowners, profit from their labor. These wealthy landowners live most of the year in large cities.

9. There are small farmers who do own their own land. Most often, the soil is very poor. The small farmer is too poor to buy fertilizer and good seed. In remote areas, some farmers use the same methods used by their ancestors years ago. Other farmers raise llamas or sheep on the grassy mountain slopes. Some leave their farms to work in mines for wages. The poverty of Latin America's small farmers is a reason for their migration to cities. For many, the city is the only hope for a better life.

10. While Latin America is big in size and is growing in population, it does not have a large share of the world's people. Large areas of South America, such as the tropical rain forests, the mountains, and the dry plains and deserts, cannot support many people and are not pleasant to live in. Except for the Caribbean islands, most Latin Americans live in the eastern and western highlands where it is cooler than in the hot lowlands.

11. About two-thirds of the people of Latin America now live in cities and in the densely populated areas around cities. Latin America is the most *urbanized* of all the developing regions of the world. In many ways, the cities are like those in North America and Europe. They have wide streets, tall buildings, and beautiful shops and homes. There are restaurants, theaters, and heavy automobile traffic. (To help stop traffic jams, in Caracas, Venezuela, drivers are allowed to use their cars only every other day.) Large landowners, business people, office workers, factory workers, and government leaders live in the cities. Here, the children have the best chance for an education. But most of the city people are very poor. Rio de Janeiro, Lima, Bogotá, and other large cities are surrounded by shantytowns. A home in a Latin American shantytown is often made of scrap metal or packing crates. The people who live in shantytowns came from rural areas looking for a better life. Many believe that no matter how bad it is in the cities, it is better than the places they left behind.

12. Many of the cities in Latin America have more than a million people. The urban areas of Mexico City (the largest), São Paulo, Rio de Janeiro, and Lima, all have more than 15 million people. Buenos Aires is the largest seaport and railroad center of the southeast. São Paulo, Brazil, is one of the fastest-growing cities in the world. It is located near a coffee-growing region and is a leading industrial city as well. Its modern factories produce cars, electrical equipment, machinery, chemicals, medicines, clothing, and many other products.

13. Today, most of the governments in Latin America are democratic. Nicaragua held free elections after nine years of civil war. In Argentina, Brazil, and Uruguay, military governments were overthrown in favor of civilian governments. Both Paraguay, which had had the same ruler since 1954, and Chile, which had had the same ruler since 1973, installed democratic governments in the late 1980s and early 1990s. Not all governments in Latin America are democratic. Although the future of communism in Cuba was in doubt when the Soviet Union fell, the Cuban government vowed never to accept either democracy or capitalism. But the people of Latin America now have greater hope for freedom than ever before.

Workers checking electric pacemakers, health equipment used by people with heart problems. Millions of factory workers, office workers, and business people live in the modern cities of Latin America.

UNDERSTANDING WHAT YOU HAVE READ

1. Which of the following questions are answered in this chapter?
a. Who are the mestizos?
b. Where do most Latin American people live?
c. What do the city people of Latin America wear?

2. The main idea of *paragraphs 1 through 6* describes
a. the mixture of people in Latin America
b. people who have come from other lands
c. the small population of Latin America

3. A country with a large population of African background is
a. Argentina   b. Haiti   c. Costa Rica

4. The great seaport of southeast South America is
a. Buenos Aires   b. São Paulo   c. Bogotá

5. Many people of Latin America live in the highlands because
a. there are many winter sports
b. gold and silver are mined there
c. they are cooler

6. Latin America does not support more people because
a. there is a lack of machinery
b. much of the land is rain forest or mountains
c. cows and other farm animals cannot live there

7. Most of the good farmland in Latin America is owned by
a. a few large landowners
b. millions of small-farm owners
c. the governments

8. The official language of most of the Caribbean island nations is
a. Dutch   b. English   c. Spanish

DEVELOPING IDEAS AND SKILLS

Study the pictograph. Then answer the questions below.

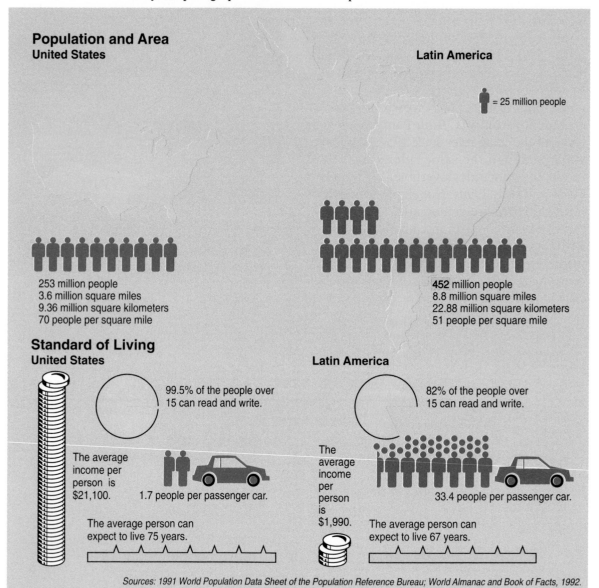

Population and Area
United States

Latin America

= 25 million people

253 million people
3.6 million square miles
9.36 million square kilometers
70 people per square mile

452 million people
8.8 million square miles
22.88 million square kilometers
51 people per square mile

Standard of Living
United States

Latin America

99.5% of the people over
15 can read and write.

82% of the people over
15 can read and write.

The average
income per
person is
$21,100.   1.7 people per passenger car.

The
average
income
per
person
is
$1,990.   33.4 people per passenger car.

The average person can
expect to live 75 years.

The average person can
expect to live 67 years.

Sources: 1991 World Population Data Sheet of the Population Reference Bureau; World Almanac and Book of Facts, 1992.

Population, Area, and Standard of Living in Latin America

1. Is the standard of living of this region high or low compared with that of the United States?
2. Is this region as a whole more or less crowded than the United States?
3. Are the people of this region literate compared with the people of the United States?
4. How long may the average person in this region expect to live?
5. What facts tell you the standard of living of the people of this region?
6. How does this region compare with the United States in size?

Argentina's Beef Industry

Night after night in Buenos Aires, *porteño* society partakes of its most important ritual: the beef break. But in Argentina beef is much more than just the preferred main course for dinner. It is a way of life.

Argentina consumes more beef each year (2.5 million tons) than the rest of South America combined, excluding Brazil. On a per capita basis Argentines are the world's biggest beef eaters; the average Argentine eats 190 pounds per year, or almost two-and-a-half times more beef than the average North American, who eats a mere 78 pounds.

Beef is and always has been the staple and the primary protein source of the Argentine diet. But this wouldn't be possible without the Argentine cattle industry, which began in the 16th century. When explorer Juan de Garay struck out from the Spanish stronghold of Asunción (now in Paraguay) in 1572 and founded present-day Buenos Aires in 1580, he allowed several head of cattle to escape from his expedition somewhere along the way. The handful of original runaways had multiplied into hundreds of thousands of animals by the early 1600s, and Argentina's cattle industry was started.

The region's 17th-century population was so small and transportation so slow, that all that beef had very little value. But leather did, and the sales of hides established the region's economic base. It was both an economy and a society based on leather. Furniture, hammocks, and every type of container were fashioned from hides. Leather was used in the construction of roofs, walls, and carts.

Beef finally became a marketable product in the late 1700s with the establishment of the first *saladeros* (meat salting plants) along the banks of the Río de la Plata. But it took the French to start a real Argentine beef stampede. In 1876 the French steamship "La Frigorifique," fitted with a refrigeration system, arrived in Buenos Aires with a load of chilled French beef. The experimental voyage proved economically important for Argentine cattle owners and traders.

By the early 1900s, millions of chilled and frozen Argentine steaks were crossing the Atlantic to Europe and Great Britain each year. Supplying 40 percent of the beef on the international market, Argentina became the 11th-ranked country among the major trading nations of the world. It was considered one of the world's most developed nations.

The Golden Age of Argentina and its beef industry came to a halt with the Great Depression. In addition, such post-1930 trends as a growing emphasis on industrialization, a drying up of the trans-Atlantic beef pipeline, and an increase in grain cultivation led to a diminished role for beef.

Despite those developments, the beef industry today remains a large part of the Argentine economy. From a national herd of about 60 million head (two for every citizen), the country produces about 3 million tons of beef a year. Until a recent downturn in foreign sales, Argentina had been exporting about 500,000 tons of its beef annually, ranking it behind only Australia among beef-exporting nations.

Economic planners would like to see more beef reach Buenos Aires shipping wharves, and perhaps a little less in neighborhood butcher shops and restaurants. Beef exports provide the country with as much as 20 percent of its foreign exchange earnings, or $2 billion per year. Yet before it can get anywhere near the port of Buenos Aires, Argentines eat about 85 percent or more of the country's beef. Thus, for Argentine governments, the task of carving up the nation's beef between refrigerator ships and family iceboxes is one of the most persistent problems.

1. What is the staple in the Argentine diet? Why?
2. How were cows introduced to Argentina?
3. How did the beef industry develop?
4. Why was leather a more important product than beef in Argentina in the 17th century?
5. What problem does the Argentine beef industry have today?

Herding cattle on the pampas in Argentina.

Chapter 6

Village Life

How do people live in the villages of Latin America?

READING FOR A PURPOSE:
1. What kinds of farming are carried on by Latin American villages?
2. How do villages add to the income they get from the fields?
3. What are the serious problems faced by villages in Latin America?

1. In Latin America, most farmers do not live on their own farms, but in small villages. The center of the village is usually a small square or *plaza*. Around the plaza may stand the church, the school, and a few small stores. The plaza is also the market place.

2. Near the plaza are the homes of the villagers. These homes are built differently throughout Latin America. In the dry climates they may be made of *adobe* (bricks made of sun-dried mud). The roofs of the houses may be covered with tile or straw thatch. In the

A village in the southern highlands of Mexico. What is the largest building in the village? What kinds of material are the homes and other buildings made of?

rainy areas, the houses or huts are often made of reeds with thatched roofs. Corrugated iron roofs are also used. In the colder areas of the highlands, there are few trees and bushes, so houses are made of stone.

3. Most of the houses are small and simple, and have only one room. The furniture may be only a bed, some sleeping mats, a table, and a few chairs. There may also be no windows. The family spends a lot of time outside, the father working in the fields and the mother cooking, sewing, and taking care of the children. In countries like Bolivia and Haiti, there is probably no electricity or plumbing.

4. The whole family works hard each day to raise the things it needs in order to live. The chief crops are corn and beans. Most of the work is done by hand. The grains of corn are planted by hand. The field is cultivated with a hoe or a digging stick. When the corn is full grown, the ears are gathered by hand. The cornstalks are then cut down with large knives called *machetes*. For several reasons, it is very hard for farmers to raise more than their families need. The plot is small. Sometimes the soil is dry. The farmer has no fertilizer, so the soil wears out. There is no machinery. Many of the farmers have poor seeds. Little is done to stop erosion (the washing away of the soil).

5. Some families may have a vegetable garden and a few fruit trees of their own. These and the corn and beans from the fields provide nearly all that the villagers get to eat. They eat little meat because very few can afford to have large meat animals. In some places the corn flour is often made into flat cakes called *tortillas*. On the islands of the West Indies and in the Amazon Basin, *manioc*, or starch from the root of the cassava plant, is eaten. Coffee and tea are favorite drinks. Villagers seldom drink milk, for they do not keep dairy cows.

6. Since the family has little money, almost everything the people need is made at home. In most parts of Latin America, the farmers and their families wear plain clothes that are homemade. The men wear shirts and trousers

South American villagers making straw hats. What other things do farm families make to add to their income?

of coarse white cotton, and the women wear simple cotton dresses. The women also weave a *rebozo,* or shawl, that serves as a head covering or baby sling. The men have *serapes.* A serape is a hand-woven blanket with a slit in the center for the head. The farmer uses the serape as both a blanket and a coat.

7. To add to their income, many farmers make other things. They make and sell clay pots and bowls, jewelry of silver and turquoise, colorful wool blankets, sandals, and straw hats. Many villages may have a shoemaker, a basket weaver, a hat maker, and a brick maker to fill the needs of the people.

8. Once a week the people take their handiwork, some pigs and chickens, and some fruits and vegetables to the nearest market place. They may sell these goods or trade them for other things they need. Several times a year there are village *fiestas,* where there is plenty of drink, food, and dancing.

9. The farmers just described are subsistence farmers. Such farmers probably cannot read or write because many of the poor villages or farm areas cannot afford to build

A village market place in Ecuador.

200

schools. Many of the children do not attend what schools there are because they are needed at home to help with the work in the fields. Finally, the members of the farm family are probably not well. In many villages there are no sewers, and the drinking water is unhealthful. The water for cooking or washing clothes may come from a ditch alongside the road.

10. Despite these hardships, the villagers find many joys in their way of life. There is a strong sense of family life. Each person in the family has his or her own task. They go to the fields with their neighbors and work together. Once a week, they meet at the village community house to hold dances or recall the traditions of their ancestors. (Although they hold on to the beliefs of their ancestors, they are Christians. The priest usually comes to their village once a month.) They look to each other for help when someone is ill or has problems. Many, however, are forced to leave for the plantations or the cities, because their small pieces of land do not produce much.

More and more villages, such as this one in Bolivia, are being visited by doctors and health-care workers. One result is that Latin Americans can expect to live 5 years longer than they could have during the 1970s.

UNDERSTANDING WHAT YOU HAVE READ

1. **Which questions are answered in this chapter?**
a. How do Latin American farmers live?
b. Why are many farmers in poor health?
c. What games do the children play?

2. **The main idea of this chapter is to describe**
a. how village farmers meet their daily needs
b. goods manufactured in the home
c. the meals of the small farmers

3. **The chief crop of the village farmer is**
a. corn
b. wheat
c. rice

4. **Village people sell their handiwork**
a. to the large department stores
b. to buyers in the cities
c. in the nearby market

5. Many farm families have poor health for all of these reasons EXCEPT:

a. lack of sunshine
b. lack of pure water
c. poor diet

6. In most countries of Latin America,

a. land is owned by a few people
b. the Native Americans farm large plots in the highlands
c. most people wear colorful clothing and speak Native-American languages

7. In many Latin American villages

a. there is a need for better health care and education
b. people live without running water
c. both of these statements

8. In recent years, people from rural areas

a. have moved to the cities looking for work
b. are raising "cash crops" on their land
c. are buying television sets for their homes

SUMMING UP

Making Charts

Complete the following chart in your notebook.

	SMALL VILLAGE FARMER OF LATIN AMERICA	CORN-BELT FARMER OF THE UNITED STATES
1. HOMES		
2. MACHINERY		
3. CROPS AND ANIMALS		
4. STANDARD OF LIVING		
5. MARKETS FOR THEIR PRODUCTS		

FOLLOW UP

In your notebook, match each item in Column A with one of the items in Column B.

COLUMN A	COLUMN B
1. machete	a. blanket
2. fiesta	b. festival
3. adobe	c. village square
4. mestizo	d. flat cakes of corn bread
5. plaza	e. large knife
6. tortilla	f. part Native American, part European background
7. hacienda	g. large estate
8. serape	h. sun-dried brick

Chapter 7

Using the Land

How do the people of Latin America make use of the land?

READING FOR A PURPOSE:
1. How do the people make a living in the rain forests?
2. What are the features of farming in a vertical climate?
3. What Latin American farming regions are like those in the United States?

1. In the great region of Latin America, only a very small part of the land can be used. Much of the land is covered by mountains, jungle, and desert. The Andes Mountains are too high and too cold for large-scale farming. The soils of the rain forest and dry grasslands are poor. The deserts cannot support life. Yet, for hundreds of years, most people have made their living from the land. Let us see how the people of Latin America meet the challenge of these difficult conditions.

2. A large part of Latin America is tropical rain forest. In the forest, a few Native American tribes live in villages near the rivers. These villages are always crowded by trees and plants that grow fast in the hot and wet climate. There are many insects, here, that carry diseases such as malaria. People cannot travel far because there are few paths through the thick jungle. Growing food is a problem because the soil is poor. Keeping the food from spoiling is also difficult in this hot climate.

3. The people in the rain forest live simple lives. They grow most of their food in small forest clearings. The men clear the land by chopping down trees or burning away the thick brush. Once the land has been cleared, the women start planting. The men go into the forest to get more food by hunting and fishing.

4. The chief foods in the rain forest are ba-nanas, yams, and cassava (manioc). Flour is made by cutting up and crushing the roots of the manioc plant. Flat cakes are then made from the flour. Every two or three years, the people have to move and make a new clearing because the soil in the old one has worn out. Heavy rains leach, or wash out, the minerals in the soil that food crops need in order to grow. Most travel is by canoe, along the rivers and streams, because the forest is so thick.

5. The rain-forest people make nearly everything they use from the products of the forest. They make their houses out of thatch—straw, grass, and leaves. These are cone-shaped so as to shed water. The men make fish traps, bows and arrows, and blowguns from which they blow or shoot small poisoned darts. They also make canoes or dugouts by hollowing out the trunks of large trees. The women weave clothing, mats, and baskets out of grasses and leaves. Some of these are sold.

6. The rain forest has many products that are useful to people in other parts of the world. These products include mahogany and other hardwoods, chicle for chewing gum, and cinchona bark from which a medicine called quinine is made. The products are gathered by the Native Americans and brought to trading posts at Belém or Manaus, Brazil. (These port

What kinds of livestock does this farm in Ecuador have? What are the people doing?

A farmer in Colombia. Farm families raise corn, beans, and cassava.

cities also supply the people of the rain forest with the things they need from the outside world.) Only a small part of its riches is brought out of the rain forest. Few people live there and it is hard to ship goods through the thick forest.

7. As you remember, grasslands are found north and south of the Amazon rain forest. Thus, the south-central part of Brazil, and the *llanos* of Venezuela and Colombia in the north, have a tropical savanna climate. This means there are two seasons, one rainy and one dry. How do the people make a living in this climate? Cattle raising is important in the grasslands of Brazil and the *llanos* of Venezuela and Colombia. The land is divided into large cattle ranches, or *haciendas*. The cattle are always on the move. The herds are guarded by cowboys called *llaneros*. These cattle are raised for their hides and for their meat.

8. In the dry season the rivers become little more than streams. Cattle graze near the streams where the grass is still moist and green. In the rainy season the rivers flood their banks. Then the cowboys drive the cattle to higher lands, or mesas, between the swollen rivers. After eating all the grass on one mesa, they wade through the waters to another.

9. The savannas are not the best land for growing crops. The soil is poor because the minerals have been washed out by the heavy rains. However, a number of cash crops are grown in this climate. Sugarcane is the chief crop of the tropical grasslands. The hot weather, the rainy growing season, and the dry harvest time are good for growing sugarcane. Sugarcane is also grown on large plantations on many of the islands of the West Indies, particularly Cuba, and also in Mexico. Another wet-and-dry crop is *henequen,* or sisal, from which rope is made. Henequen is raised on the Yucatan Peninsula in Mexico.

10. As you have learned, an important feature of the Latin American climate is that it is vertical. That is, the climate changes as you travel upward in the mountains. Farming is also vertical. In the hot and damp lowlands of Central America there are plantations of bananas and cacao beans. (Cacao is the bean from which chocolate is made.) These crops need the wet, rainy weather and long growing season of the tropics. Bananas need more than a year to ripen. Most of the workers are blacks and mestizos. They live on land owned by the plantation or in villages near the plantations. Many Central American countries raise beef cattle. Much of the meat is exported. The poor

do not have enough money to buy beef. In the lowlands of Venezuela, rice is a major crop.

11. As you travel higher into a cooler climate *(tierra templada),* the most common crop is coffee. Coffee is grown in the highlands of Brazil and Colombia. In Brazil, coffee is grown on large estates, the *fazendas.* At first the coffee beans are green. During the hot, rainy summers, the little beans turn red and open. During the dry, cooler winters, the beans turn brown and are picked. Brazil is the world's leading coffee grower. Colombia is the second largest.

12. Many people live in the higher altitudes *(tierra fria).* They farm on the steep mountainsides. They raise the crops that fill their needs—wheat, barley, beans, potatoes, and corn (maize). They graze herds of sheep, llamas, and burros. The llamas and burros are used for riding and for carrying heavy loads. The temperature may be from 40°F (4°C) to 50°F (10°C) all year round. Some also work in the tin, copper, lead, and zinc mines found at this height.

13. In South America, the humid-subtropical area is also found along the southeastern coast. In southern Brazil, farmers began planting soybeans in the 1960s. By the late 1970s, only the United States produced more of this protein-rich crop. Soybeans are used to make vegetable oil, soy flour, and animal feed. Soybeans are now one of Brazil's chief crops. The humid-subtropical area includes part of Bra-

Soybeans are one of Brazil's main exports.

zil, Paraguay, and Argentina, and all of Uruguay. Because of the climate and soil, the best cattle-grazing lands are found there. There is a long, hot summer and a short, mild winter. The most famous grazing lands are the *pampas,* or plains, of Argentina.

14. The pampas are divided into large ranches, or *estancias.* The wealthy owners live mainly in Buenos Aires. The cattle are cared for by colorful cowboys called *gauchos.* Most of them are Native Americans. The cattle are raised chiefly for their meat. Large amounts of alfalfa are grown on the pampas as food for the cattle. Corn and wheat are grains grown on the rich, black earth. Argentina exports the riches of the pampas—beef, corn, and wheat—to other parts of the world. Only the United States, Canada, France, and Australia export more wheat.

15. Two other important crops of Latin America are corn and cotton. Corn is a basic food in the diet of millions of Latin Americans. It had been raised by the Native Americans long before Columbus's voyages. In Mexico, corn is largely eaten by the people, although about one-third of it is fed to the livestock. In Brazil, it is an even more important food for animals. In Argentina, corn is an

A sugarcane field being cleared by burning. Brazil, Cuba, and Mexico are the leading Latin American producers of sugarcane.

export (You will note that Argentina's major farm products are much the same as the farm products of the United States. This is because the climates of the two countries are similar.) The United States grows large amounts of corn and wheat and raises millions of beef cattle. It is therefore not a good customer for Argentina's farm products. Argentina looks to other regions (Western Europe, Russia and other Eurasian Republics, Japan) for trading partners for its farm products.

16. Cotton has become an important product of the dry lands of Mexico. Brazil grows even more cotton on its irrigated lands. Brazil is the world's fifth-largest grower of cotton, but Mexico exports more of its cotton. In addition, irrigated Mexican farmlands now provide the United States with many vegetables and fruits. These include tomatoes, strawberries, grapes, asparagus, cucumbers, and cantaloupe. In the desert of Peru, cotton is also grown. The water is brought from the mountains near the coast. All over the world, it has been found that the finest cotton can be grown in dry areas through water supplied by irrigation.

UNDERSTANDING WHAT YOU HAVE READ

1. Which questions are answered in this chapter?
a. What are the chief crops of Latin America?
b. Why are the pampas good for grazing cattle?
c. How does the banana tree grow?

2. The main idea of this chapter describes
a. the many farming areas of Latin America
b. how people live in the rain forest
c. the crops of the vertical climate

3. The chief products of the lowland plantations of Central America are
a. wheat and pineapples
b. bananas, cacao beans, and beef cattle
c. palm oil and corn

4. The chief products of the pampas are
a. cotton and coffee
b. wheat and beef cattle
c. sugarcane and bananas

5. A country of Latin America that produces much the same kind of crops as the United States is
a. Cuba   b. Venezuela   c. Argentina

6. Life in the *tierra fria* is difficult because
a. it is too far above sea level to grow any crops
b. the forests must be cleared before planting
c. the steep hillsides must be terraced before planting

7. A *mesa* is the same as a
a. lowland plain
b. small high plateau
c. mountainside

8. *Cacao* is a small tree whose beans are used in making
a. medicine   b. rope   c. chocolate

9. *Gauchos* are the famous cowboys of
a. Mexico   b. Argentina   c. Brazil

10. The cattle-raising grasslands of Venezuela and Colombia are called the
a. pampas   b. llanos   c. henequen

Building Map Skills——Major Producers of Food and Forest Products in Latin America

Study the map. Then complete the statements next to it.

1. The largest crop zone in Latin America is the
   a. rice zone   b. corn zone   c. wheat zone
2. The leading wheat-producing country in Latin America is
   a. Venezuela   b. Mexico   c. Argentina
3. Fish are a major food product of
   a. Mexico and Haiti
   b. Peru and Chile
   c. Uruguay and Paraguay
4. Potatoes are an important crop in
   a. Argentina, Bolivia, and Chile
   b. Suriname, Venezuela, and Panama
   c. Guatemala, Honduras, and Costa Rica
5. Bananas are a leading crop in
   a. Barbados, the Bahamas, and Haiti
   b. Costa Rica, Honduras, and Panama
   c. Chile, Peru, and Uruguay
6. The leading cattle-raising countries are
   a. Dominica, the Dominican Republic, and Puerto Rico
   b. Brazil, Argentina, Mexico, and Colombia
   c. Suriname, French Guiana, and Guyana
7. Latin American countries that produce valuable timber include
   a. El Salvador, Grenada, and the Bahamas
   b. Chile, Bolivia, and Colombia
   c. Brazil, Guyana, and Paraguay
8. The nation that is one of the world's leading producers of *both* cacao and soybeans is
   a. Mexico   b. Uruguay   c. Brazil

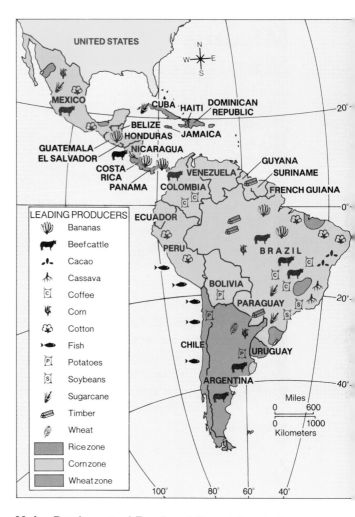

Major Producers of Food and Forest Products in Latin America

SUMMING UP

Match each item in Column B with one of the farming regions in Column A. One item in Column A is used twice.

COLUMN A	COLUMN B
A. Rain-forest farming	a. Mahogany and chicle
B. Savannas	b. Coffee plantations
C. Highlands	c. Sugar plantations
D. Pampas	d. Bananas and cacao
E. Hot, damp lowlands	e. Cattle, wheat, and corn
	f. Sheep, llamas, and potatoes

Chapter 8

Mining and Manufacturing

Why have industries grown slowly in Latin America?

READING FOR A PURPOSE:
1. Where are important raw materials for industry located?
2. How do the United States and Canada depend on Latin America's mineral resources?
3. What does Latin America need for greater development of its industries?

1. Compared with the number of people who work on farms in Latin America, there are not many people working in the mines. Yet minerals are an important resource for Latin America. The earliest Spanish explorers found riches in silver and gold. Silver is still mined in Mexico, Peru, and Bolivia. Mexico mines more silver than any other country in the world. Gold is mined in Brazil, Colombia, and Mexico.

2. Even more important than silver and gold are other minerals that play a great part in all our lives. Bolivia has rich tin mines. The tin is located high in the plateaus, more than 10,000 feet (3,048 meters) above sea level. Working in the tin mines is very difficult. Workers constantly breathe in the dust from the ore. Because of this the life of a tin miner is a short one. The Atacama Desert in northern Chile is rich in copper and nitrates. Nitrates are used for fertilizers. The people who work in the desert also lead a hard life. Everything they need must be brought in from outside of the desert—food, clothing, and even water. These important minerals—tin, copper, and nitrates—are found in areas that are hard to reach.

3. The entire industrialized world depends on oil. Some of the richest oil reserves in the world are found in Mexico, Venezuela, and the coastal plains of Ecuador and Peru. Some experts believe Mexico is "sitting on a sea of oil." It is one of the world's leading producers of oil. Most of its oil is shipped to the United States. In Venezuela, wells have been sunk into Lake Maracaibo. Some of the oil from its

Tin mining in Bolivia. Bolivia also produces natural gas, oil, lead, zinc, and copper.

rich deposits is exported to the United States. The sale of oil has brought much wealth to Venezuela. As a result, the average income of Venezuelans is one of the highest of any people in Latin America. (Many experts believe that Venezuela has become too dependent upon selling its oil. They say that the country should spend more money on improving its farms.)

4. Since World War II, Venezuela has also become a leading producer of iron ore. In Peru, iron-ore production has also grown. But by the 1980s, Brazil had become the greatest iron-ore producer in Latin America and the third greatest in the world. (China and the Commonwealth of Independent States produced more.) Ore deposits are not easy to reach. But the world needs iron for building and machinery. As a result, foreign countries and banks have supplied Latin America with money to find this valuable mineral and bring it to factories where it can be used. In Latin America, steel mills produce twice as much as they did only 15 years ago.

5. Aluminum is much in demand for making airplanes, buildings, and hundreds of other products. Aluminum is made from an ore called bauxite. A great share of the world's bauxite is found in Jamaica, Brazil, Suriname, and Guyana. Much of it is shipped to the aluminum mills of the United States and Canada.

6. Most of Latin America's factories do not make use of the region's mineral wealth. Many of them still depend on the products of the farm. For example, there are meat-packing plants near the grazing areas of Argentina and Brazil. There are textile mills in Mexico, Peru, and Brazil turning out cloth from raw materials nearby. However, Latin America still exports much of the raw materials of its farms and mines to other parts of the world. The United States, Japan, and the nations of Western Europe are its best customers. In turn, the United States, Europe, and Japan sell all kinds of machinery to Latin America.

7. Industry has not grown as rapidly as it might have for various reason. First, there is

Oil towers in Lake Maracaibo, Venezuela. Besides oil, Venezuela produces natural gas and iron ore.

a lack of coal. Coal is important as a source of power for mills and factories. It is needed as fuel in the making of steel. There are great possibilities, however, in the use of falling water for power. The heavy rainfall and snows in the mountains provide plenty of water. Less than 10 percent of the possible waterpower is used, however. Sometimes this is because the sources of waterpower are far from the centers of population and industry.

8. Second, transportation and communication in Latin America have been poor. Transportation is necessary to bring raw materials to factories. Because of the mountains and rain forests, it has been easier to ship raw materials by water or air than to send them overland, from one port of Latin America to another. (This meant, of course, that before the coming of the airplane, industry in Latin America was held back even more.)

9. Skilled workers are needed for factory work. In some countries, great efforts have been made to educate people. For example, literacy is high in Argentina, Chile, Colombia, Costa Rica, Cuba, Trinidad and Tobago, and Uruguay. But in Haiti and Guatemala the

Mexican oil-drilling rig. Jobs in modern industries require skilled workers.

America has lacked capital. In 1961, the United States began the Alliance for Progress. (This was started because the United States was worried that like Cuba, Latin American countries would become Communist.) Between 1961 and 1975, the United States sent large amounts of aid to the nations of Latin America. Although some of it was misused, much of it was used to build roads, set up telephone lines, and build small factories and power plants. Life began to improve in the cities and on the farms. Jobs were created. People had money to spend. In the 1970s, however, this changed. The OPEC nations raised the price of oil. While this helped oil-rich Mexico and Venezuela, it badly hurt the rest of the region's countries. To make matters worse, the price for their "cash crops"—coffee, cotton, and sugar—began to fall. Unable to pay their bills, many Latin American governments turned to American banks for loans. Today, many Latin American countries are deep in debt. They hope that as in the past, their resources will carry them through this difficult period.

situation is still bad, especially among village families and Native Americans. Yet, improvement is taking place. Latin American leaders know that education is important in producing goods skillfully.

10. Money is also needed. Money that is used to build factories and power plants is called *capital.* Throughout the years, Latin

UNDERSTANDING WHAT YOU HAVE READ

1. Which questions are answered in this chapter?

a. Why are there fewer factories in Latin America than in some other parts of the world?

b. What power resources does Latin America need?

c. How is tin mined?

2. The main idea of *paragraphs 1 through 7* describes

a. the mineral resources of Latin America

b. the hard work in the mines of Latin America

c. Latin American trade with other lands

3. Latin America has some minerals, but it lacks

a. coal   b. oil   c. tin

4. Brazil is one of the leading producers of

a. gold and silver

b. copper and nitrates

c. iron ore and bauxite

5. The desert of Chile is valuable because it is a source of

a. irrigation   b. minerals   c. oil

6. Many Latin American countries are now having hard times because

a. there is a lack of foreign aid

b. their cash crops are too expensive

c. they had to borrow money when oil prices rose and prices of cash crops dropped

DEVELOPING IDEAS AND SKILLS

Building Map Skills——Natural Resources and Industries in Latin America

Study the map. Then choose the item that best completes each of the following sentences.

1. The nation that leads Latin America in iron production is
   a. Argentina   b. Brazil   c. Cuba
2. Leading oil producers in Latin America include
   a. Mexico, Venezuela, Ecuador, and Peru
   b. Bolivia, Chile, and Paraguay
   c. El Salvador, Grenada, and the Bahamas
3. Valuable emerald gemstones are found in
   a. Mexico   b. Colombia   c. Cuba
4. Bolivia is a major producer of
   a. gold   b. tin   c. bauxite
5. The leading car maker in Latin America is
   a. Argentina   b. Brazil   c. Mexico
6. The country that makes the most steel in Latin America is
   a. Cuba   b. Mexico   c. Brazil
7. Important meat-packing plants are in
   a. Belize   b. Brazil   c. Saint Lucia
8. Mills that produce textiles are important in
   a. Mexico   b. Chile   c. Barbados
9. A country noted for its huge shipbuilding and aircraft industries is
   a. Brazil   b. Cuba   c. Mexico

Natural Resources and Industries in Latin America

DEVELOPING CRITICAL THINKING SKILLS

Fact or Opinion

Read each statement carefully. If the statement is a fact, write F in your notebook. If it is an opinion, write O.

1. A change in the system of land ownership should be the most important goal in Latin America.
2. Oil is an important mineral resource in Mexico.
3. Latin America has many minerals that the United States can use.
4. Many valuable products cannot easily be brought out of the tropical rain forest.
5. Without oil and iron ore, Venezuela would be a poor country.
6. The land system in Latin America will be very slow to change.
7. If it is used, Latin America could have a large amount of electricity from water power.
8. Latin America will never industrialize because it lacks coal.
9. Control over the mines of Latin America is necessary for the safety of the United States.
10. American and Canadian trade with Argentina will double in the next 10 years.

Chapter 9

The Needs of Latin America

What are the problems of Latin America?

READING FOR A PURPOSE:
1. Why is there a problem of food supply in Latin America?
2. What problems have resulted from population growth?
3. Why is there little democracy in many Latin American countries?

1. The poverty of many people in Latin America is the biggest problem of the region. There are thousands of farmers who live on tiny plots of the poorest land. They are barely able to grow enough food for their families. The money they make from farming each year is very small. Many make less than $1,000 per year. Their health is also poor. They do not eat enough healthful foods. Many cannot read and write. Their basic needs are simple, but everywhere they are the same: more and better land, pure water, better roads, electricity, public schools, and health services.

2. The number of people in Latin America is growing so fast that the population may double in 30 years. Most of this growth in population is taking place among the poorer families. Thus, there will be more mouths to feed where there is the least ability to feed them. There is already a problem of raising enough food for the present population.

3. Much of the fertile land is occupied by huge plantations. Many of these plantations are owned by foreign business people or by a few wealthy families of Latin America. The plantations have become like factories. Workers are housed and fed like armies in large buildings. Crops raised on the plantations—coffee, sugar, and bananas—are raised for export to other countries. They are not an important part of the diet of most Latin Americans. Therefore, a large amount of food must be imported by these countries for their own people.

4. As you learned in Unit 2, the kind of farming that causes a country to depend upon one chief crop may cause problems. Latin America has sometimes been called a region of "one-crop countries." For example, Colombia has long depended on one crop—coffee—for most of its income earned from foreign trade. The countries of Central America de-

A plantation worker picking coffee beans in Honduras.

212

Homes outside Rio de Janeiro, Brazil. The families may pay no rent since they built their houses on empty plots of land. Many such homes have no running water. How can you tell that some of these houses have electricity?

pend a great deal upon their sale of bananas. El Salvador gets more than half its export sales from coffee. Cuba depends upon sugarcane for over three-fourths of its export sales. This kind of farming is called *monoculture.* If the crop is a poor one, or if there is a drop in its market price, the whole country suffers greatly.

5. Latin American countries are facing the need for more land for the small farmer in several ways. Governments are opening new lands for the people. For example, Brasilia, the capital city of Brazil, has been built inland to attract people to a new area. There is a growing demand that the large estates be broken up and given to small farmers. People like to own their own land. The chance to have a farm of one's own is the dream of many people all over the world.

6. Economic growth in Latin America has caused problems. These problems are shared by developing nations everywhere—urban crowding, pollution, poverty, poor housing, and a large number of unemployed. In Latin America, the population of cities and suburbs rises sharply each year. Latin American cities do not have enough factories to provide jobs for the newcomers. Many job seekers are unskilled people from the countryside. Some Latin American countries have begun to use the money from mineral exports to develop industry.

7. Education and jobs may help Latin America rid itself of social and economic in-

equality. In many places, there are two major classes of people: the wealthy and the poor. The wealthy own much of the land, the mineral deposits, and the factories. The poor people farm small plots of land, work on the large estates of the wealthy, or live in the shanty towns that surround cities. There are few people in the middle class. (In most of Latin American countries this small middle class is made up of skilled workers in businesses, stores, offices, and government.) The demands of the poor are being heard more often now. They want land, training in different skills, and jobs.

8. The 1980s were a poor economic decade for Latin America. At the beginning of the 1990s, however, the economic picture was brighter. The three largest Latin American

A private home in São Paulo, Brazil.

countries, Brazil, Argentina, and Mexico, have many large industries and are important exporters of industrial goods. Chile and Colombia also export large amounts of industrial goods. Latin America has more land that could be used to grow crops than any other part of the developing world. After the Middle East, Latin America has the world's largest reserves of petroleum. There are also huge mineral reserves in much of the region. Brazil and Chile have just begun to scratch the surface of their copper, iron ore, and tin supplies. Hydroelectric power, already in wide use, has potential to become even more widespread. Although Latin America still has huge debts and domestic problems, it may be able to develop its exports and become economically powerful.

The National University of Mexico's library. Why is education so important for the people of Latin America?

UNDERSTANDING WHAT YOU HAVE READ

1. **Which questions are answered in this chapter?**
a. How are some Latin Americans governed?
b. What are the problems of Latin America?
c. How does the United Nations help Latin America?

2. **The main idea of *paragraph 8* describes**
a. reasons for the new economic outlook
b. the three largest Latin American countries
c. social and economic problems

3. **Most Latin American nations obtain money by**
a. manufacturing goods
b. selling raw materials abroad
c. dairy farming

4. **In Latin America, most of the best farmland is owned by**
a. a few wealthy families

b. many small-farm families
c. the armies

5. **More factories will help Latin Americans because**
a. they will provide more raw materials
b. education will be improved
c. Latin Americans will be able to use their own raw materials to make products

6. **In a *monoculture,* a country depends upon**
a. exports of machinery
b. one crop
c. many farm products

7. **The *middle class* refers to**
a. the very rich
b. those who are neither rich nor poor
c. the very poor

Building Map Skills——The Standard of Living in Latin America

Study these two maps. Map A shows the number of years of life that a newborn baby will, on average, live in each country. Map B shows the percentage of people over 15 years old who can read and write in each country. After studying the maps, answer the following questions.

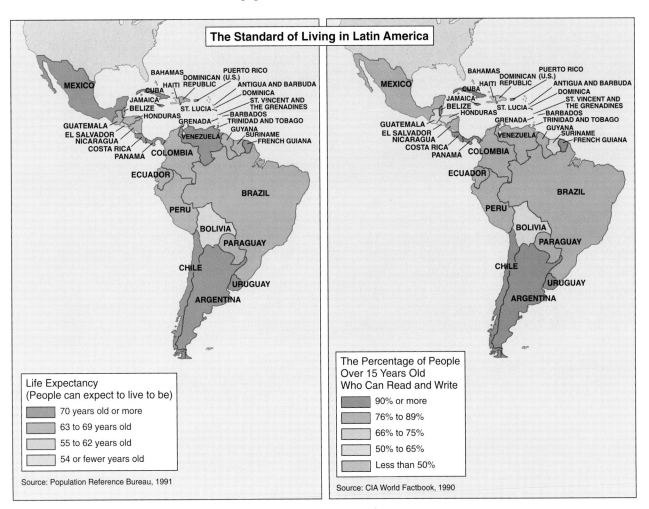

The Standard of Living in Latin America

Life Expectancy
(People can expect to live to be)
- 70 years old or more
- 63 to 69 years old
- 55 to 62 years old
- 54 or fewer years old

Source: Population Reference Bureau, 1991

The Percentage of People Over 15 Years Old Who Can Read and Write
- 90% or more
- 76% to 89%
- 66% to 75%
- 50% to 65%
- Less than 50%

Source: CIA World Factbook, 1990

The Standard of Living in Latin America

1. In which countries is the average life 70 or more years?
2. In which countries is the average life under 55 years?
3. In which countries can 90 percent or more of those over 15 years old read and write?
4. In which countries, if any, can less than half of the people over 15 years old read and write?
5. In which countries does the average person live to be 70 or more and over 90 percent of the people read and write? What might you infer about the peoples' health and education in these countries?
6. What can you learn from these maps about the standard of living in Venezuela?

Chapter 10

Latin America and the United States

What have been the relations between Latin American countries and the United States?

READING FOR A PURPOSE:
1. What actions by the United States have caused resentments among Latin Americans?
2. How has the United States tried to improve relations with Latin American countries?
3. Why has the United States been concerned with events in Central America?

1. In 1823, President Monroe stated that the United States would defend the freedom of the new countries of Latin America. His statement was greeted with approval by the countries south of the United States. However, this friendly feeling toward the United States has changed from time to time.

2. In 1836, Texas became an independent country free of Mexican control. In 1845,

A small section of the U.S. naval base at Guantánamo Bay in Cuba. Treaties signed in 1903 and 1934 give the United States the right to have this base. But since the early 1960s, Cuba has refused to accept U.S. rent payments.

Texas joined the United States. The next year, the United States went to war with Mexico over the boundary between Texas and Mexico. In 1848, as a result of the war, the United States gained a large area of land extending from Texas to the Pacific Ocean. Many Latin Americans thought that the United States had "picked on" its smaller neighbor. This bad feeling caused by the war lasted for many years.

3. Fifty years later, the United States went to war with Spain. People in the United States were aroused by newspaper stories of Spanish cruelty toward Cubans. Americans sympathized with the Cubans. After the war, the United States gained possession of the island of Puerto Rico from Spain. The United States also became Cuba's "protector." Until 1934, the United States watched over Cuba's affairs. That year, Cuba was finally given complete freedom. To this day, however, the United States has a large naval base at Guantánamo Bay, though the leaders of the island are no longer friends of the United States.

4. In 1903, the United States encouraged Panamanians to free themselves from Colombia. Shortly after Panama became free, the United States got permission and land from Panama to build the famous Panama Canal. The canal was important to the United States. It provided a quicker way for ships to go from the Atlantic to the Pacific. There were those in Latin America who felt the United States had used its power to help Panama revolt against Colombia.

5. In 1902, President Theodore Roosevelt sent warships to Venezuela to stop European nations from occupying that country. Venezuela owed money to these countries. President Roosevelt did not want any European nation landing troops in Latin America. Three years later, he sent Americans to Santo Domingo (the Dominican Republic) to make sure that that nation paid its debts. At other times, the United States Marines were sent to Haiti and Nicaragua to keep order and to protect American property there. The people of

Latin America did not want this kind of help. They resented the power of the United States. They felt they could take care of themselves.

6. But as early as 1889, an effort was being made to improve relations between the United States and the Latin American nations. The group, later called the Pan American Union, was formed. Twenty-one nations were members. They agreed to settle their disputes peaceably. In 1948, this Union grew into the Organization of American States (OAS).

7. President Franklin Roosevelt helped to bring about a better understanding between Latin American countries and the United States. In 1933, he announced the Good Neighbor Policy. United States troops were brought home from the Caribbean. The United States agreed that it had no right to interfere in the affairs of other countries. Latin America and the United States set up programs to exchange teachers, students, and cultural leaders. American experts on farming, industry, and health services traveled to Latin America. During World War II, a spirit of cooperation grew. The nations of all the Americas worked together to defeat their enemies. In 1947, at Rio de Janeiro, the American nations agreed to the Rio Treaty. Each country would help the others in case of attack.

8. At the present time, the Organization of American States is trying to find ways of improving the lives of all Latin Americans. In addition, the United States has offered to help many Latin American nations. In 1961, President Kennedy announced the Alliance for Progress. Through it, the United States and most Latin American countries agreed to improve conditions in Latin America. As part of the agreement, the United States gave and loaned billions of dollars to Latin American countries. The money was used to provide more land, schools, health services, and jobs for the people. The program ended in the 1970s. The Peace Corps, also started by President Kennedy, has continued to help farmers in Latin America. In the 1980s, the United States continued to give and loan billions of dollars to Latin America. In 1984, President Reagan started the Caribbean Basin Initiative. This plan encourages U.S. investment in the area and allows many Caribbean products into the United States duty free.

9. Latin American countries have sometimes worked among themselves to solve some of their problems. One problem was the high tariffs, or taxes, on goods traded among Latin American countries. In 1960, Mexico and many South American countries set up an or-

The Panama Canal. Ships are lifted above sea level by several locks. Panama will gain control of the canal by the year 2000. The United States will still have the right to use military force to protect the canal.

ganization to reduce these tariffs. In 1963, several Central American nations set up the Central American Common Market. Both these groups have helped increase trade and therefore industries within Latin America.

10. In 1978, the United States took a major step in solving one of the big problems between itself and Latin America. It agreed to give up control of the Panama Canal by the year 2000. The people of Panama were pleased about this decision. They felt very strongly that a foreign nation should not control the territory within their country. The canal is already too narrow for use by the largest U.S. ships. Travel through it is slow, since it is not a sea-level canal but must use a system of locks. Many feel that the canal cannot be defended in case of an atomic war. Therefore, new routes for another canal are now being studied.

11. The United States had always been concerned about Cuba, a Communist country only 90 miles (144 kilometers) from the United States. In late 1991, however, the Soviet Union was crumbling and was in desperate need of economic aid from the United States. In order to help ensure that aid, President Mikhail Gorbachev announced that he would withdraw all Soviet troops from Cuba and end all economic subsidies to Cuba. The Soviet Union's withdrawal of support created terrible economic trouble for Cuba. The withdrawal, together with the fall of communism in Eastern Europe and the collapse of the Soviet Union, put pressure on Fidel Castro to move toward a capitalist system in Cuba. But Castro vowed never to embrace capitalism.

12. There have been many wars and border disputes in Latin America. In October 1983, a small force of American and Caribbean troops overran the Caribbean island of Grenada. The United States had been called by Grenada's governor-general and its neighbors to get rid of a "leftist" government. Claiming a need to protect U.S. medical students, the United States sent troops to Grenada. Some Latin American nations assisted the United States. The island was soon returned to a democratic form of government.

Fidel Castro. Why has his control of Cuba meant increased influence of the Soviet Union in the region?

13. The United States also invaded Panama in 1989. General Manuel Antonio Noriega was a dictator who had prevented a legally elected president from taking office. Noriega was also said to be involved in drug trafficking. In December 1989, President Bush sent 12,000 troops into Panama. Noriega's government was replaced by one led by the legally elected president. United States troops captured Noriega and brought him to the United States to stand trial for drug trafficking.

14. In September 1991, the first democratically elected president of Haiti, Jean-Bertrand Aristide, was overthrown by the Haitian military. Aristide was a Roman Catholic priest who was popular with Haiti's poor. Despite a strict United States ban on trade with Haiti, the military government remained in place.

15. Parts of Central America have greatly concerned the United States. Nicaragua and El Salvador have been particularly worrisome. In 1979, rebels in Nicaragua overthrew the Nicaraguan dictatorship and took over the government. These rebels called themselves Sandanistas. The United States did not have friendly ties with the Sandanista government. The United States sent economic aid to opposition groups fighting a guerrilla war against the Sandanista government and prohibited all trade between the United States and Nicaragua. The loss of money from exports and the cost of the war brought Nicaragua close to collapse. To end the war and resume exports, the Sandanistas realized that they needed to allow a free election. In early 1990, Violeta Chamorro, an anti-Sandanista candidate, was elected president.

16. El Salvador was torn by civil war from 1980 to 1991. The war had a devastating effect on El Salvador's economy. As a result, El Salvador was dependent on aid from the United States, which provided $4 billion in assistance between 1980 and 1990. A peace treaty was finally signed in 1992, but Salvadorans face a period of adjustment to peace after a long period of civil war.

UNDERSTANDING WHAT YOU HAVE READ

1. Which questions are answered in this chapter?
a. Who is Fidel Castro?
b. How did the United States help Mexico in 1864?
c. Why was the Pan American Union formed?

2. The main idea of paragraphs 6 through 8 describes
a. why some Latin American people did not trust the United States
b. how the United States has helped Latin America to solve its problems
c. efforts of the United States to cooperate with Latin America

3. After the Spanish-American War, the United States obtained
a. Jamaica b. the Virgin Islands c. Puerto Rico

4. A plan suggested by President Kennedy was the
a. Pan American Union
b. Alliance for Progress
c. Good Neighbor Policy

5. Latin American nations
a. sent troops to help Argentina hold the Falkland Islands
b. were often ruled by dictators, protected by the army
c. have fought no wars among themselves in over 100 years

6. Which was *not* a reason that the United States invaded Panama in 1989?
a. There was a civil war in Panama.
b. Manuel Noriega had prevented an elected president from taking office.
c. Manuel Noriega was believed to be involved in drug trafficking.

7. Which statement is most accurate about relations between the United States and Cuba today?
a. The United States has helped Cuba overcome most of its problems by increasing trade with the island nation.
b. The United States regards Cuba as a threat to its interests in Latin America.
c. The United States has threatened to invade Cuba to stop the spread of Communist influence in Latin America.

8. Jean-Bertrand Aristide, the president of Haiti, is
a. a Roman Catholic priest
b. a general in the army
c. a communist dictator

9. The OAS was formed to
a. find ways of improving the lives of Latin Americans
b. build a strong Latin American army
c. control the price of Latin American oil

DEVELOPING IDEAS AND SKILLS

Building Map Skills — Latin American Imports and Exports

Study the map. Then answer the questions below.

Latin American Imports and Exports

1. Which Latin American countries export meats?
2. What are two major exports of Brazil?
3. What products does Latin America import from Europe?
4. From which part of Latin America are most bananas exported?
5. Which countries export wheat?
6. What products does Latin America import from the United States?
7. Which Caribbean Island nations export cash crops such as sugar?
8. What kinds of products are the main exports of Central America?
9. Which countries are major oil exporters?
10. What products does Latin America import from Asia that it does *not* import from any other region?

REVIEWING AND WRITING

I. Outlining

Below are three headings for your outline. Subtopics follow the list of headings. In your notebook, make the outline, placing the subtopics under the correct headings.

HEADINGS:

A. Why Latin America Distrusted the United States
B. Cooperation Between Latin America and the United States
C. Problems in Latin America Today

SUBTOPICS

1. Civil wars in Central America
2. Panama becomes free from Colombia
3. Good Neighbor Policy
4. Poverty in Latin America
5. The Panama Canal today
6. The Organization of American States (OAS)
7. Mexican War of 1846–1848
8. Work of the Peace Corps
9. United States Marines in Nicaragua
10. Rise of Fidel Castro to power in Cuba

II. Special Reports

Now that you have completed your overall study of Latin America, you should be prepared to make a special report. Select one of the countries of Latin America for special study. In your report, try to answer some of these questions:

1. What do the farmers want in the country you have chosen? What is their day like?
2. What stands in the way of farmers' getting what they want?
3. What might be the goals of children of farm families?
4. What do they know of their country? Of ours?
5. What does the farm family do in its spare time?
6. What part does religion play in its life?

Try to answer the same questions for a factory worker, a store or an office worker, or a large landowner in the country you have chosen.

Chapter 11

Mexico—Our Southern Neighbor

How has Mexico become a leading nation in Latin America?

READING FOR A PURPOSE:
1. How has Mexico tried to solve the problems of land ownership?
2. How has Mexico benefited from its mineral wealth?
3. What problems trouble Mexico despite its industrial growth?

1. Much of what we have been learning about Latin America is also true of Mexico, the country south of the Rio Grande. Mexico is a mixture of old and new, part Native American and part Spanish. There are villages where the people live and work much as their ancestors did. Here, there are the remains of Aztec and Mayan pyramids and temples. One can buy pottery and jewelry made from designs hundreds of years old. The Spanish part of Mexico can be seen in the language, churches, homes, and family life in the growing cities. Most Mexicans are mestizos, people with both Native American and Spanish ancestors.

2. Mexico is of interest to Americans for many reasons. Until 1848, much of the Southwest belonged to Mexico. Today, there are more than 13 million Americans of Mexican descent. The United States and Mexico share a 2,000 mile border. People and goods cross that border in great numbers, many illegally. More than four million Americans travel to Mexico each year. The United States is Mexico's most important trading partner and Mexico is the United States' third most important trading partner after Canada and Japan.

3. Mexico is one of the larger countries of Latin America. It is about one-fifth the size of the United States. The country is partly in the low latitudes and partly in the middle latitudes. Most of Mexico is covered by a broad central plateau or highland. Mountain ranges are on the east and west sides of the plateau. Mexico has narrow coastal plains that border the Pacific on the west and the Gulf of Mexico on the east. The westernmost part of Mexico is a long, narrow peninsula. It is called the Peninsula of Lower California or Baja California. The Yucatán Peninsula is in southeastern Mexico. It separates the Gulf of Mexico and the Caribbean Sea.

4. Because of the highlands, much of Mexico has a vertical climate. Northern Mexico is very dry. As you travel southward the land rises; the climate is cooler and there is more rain. This is the *tierra templada*. Still higher, it is colder—the *tierra fria*. The lowlands on the gulf coast are hot and rainy. These lowlands are covered with a thick jungle. This is the *tierra caliente*. The Pacific coast is hot, but drier.

Mexico City is one of the largest cities in the world. It is the center for Mexico's industry, government, the arts, and education. Mexico City has many parks, gardens, museums, universities, and sports centers.

5. The central and eastern parts of Mexico were once ruled by the Aztec peoples. In 1519, the Aztecs were conquered by the Spanish under Cortes. They were put to work in the gold and silver mines by the Spanish conquerors. Spain ruled Mexico for 300 years.

6. In 1810, Father Miguel Hidalgo led the first revolt against Spain. In 1821, Mexico finally became free. The new government, however, was run by only a few people. The land was made up of large estates called haciendas. The poor workers who raised the crops on these farms were called *peons*. In 1848, Mexico lost a large part of its northern lands in a war with the United States. Then, in 1910, the workers revolted. They wanted a better government that would treat them more fairly. In 1917, a new constitution or plan of government was adopted in Mexico. Some haciendas were divided up and the land was given to the small farmers. The people could now vote for their own leaders. Since then, Mexican governments have gradually been giving more land to the small farmers and farming communities.

7. About three-fourths of Mexico's 88 million people live in cities and towns. There are only a few very large cities in Mexico, though. Mexico City is the largest with about 20 million people in its metropolitan area. It is also the oldest city in the Americas. Some experts predict Mexico City will soon become the largest city in the world. Mexico City is located on a plateau over 7,000 feet (2,133 meters) above sea level. The city is surrounded by higher mountains. Modern boulevards, beautiful apartment houses, museums, fine hotels, and restaurants attract many foreign tourists. Monterrey and Guadalajara are Mexico's other big cities. These cities are growing bigger each year. Thousands of poor people flock to the cities daily in search of jobs and a better life.

8. Life is very hard for most people in Mexico City. About one person in eight has no job. Many others work at unskilled, part-time jobs that pay too little to support them and their families. Many live in shantytowns built on the edges of the city. These are homes of cinder block or wood and cardboard shacks. Many of these homes have neither running water nor electricity. Many of the young people quit school. Luckily, the prices for many things are low: food, housing, and transportation. Mexico City is also one of the most polluted cities in the world. Fumes from cars, buses, and factories create a blanket of smog over the city. The high mountains trap the dirty air over the city. Despite all of this, many Mexicans are still moving to the city. In the villages, many earn barely enough to stay alive. They feel that the city is their only hope for the future.

9. About one-fourth of the people are farmers. Most Mexican farmers live in small villages. Most do not own the land they farm. A system called *ejido* allows people to farm the land without owning it. However, the farmers cannot sell this land or pass it on to their children. Some Mexicans own their own farms. Others work lands belonging to the village. Their plots of land are small. Most often the soil is poor, and large areas have little rainfall. Only one-eighth of the land in Mexico is good enough to raise crops. Most of the food raised is used only by the farm family. It has been difficult for Mexico to raise enough food to feed its growing population. As a result, corn and wheat have been imported from the United States. Because of a growing lack of jobs, thousands of people are leaving Mexican villages daily. Some head for the United States border. Most head for Mexico's big cities.

10. Corn is the most important crop of the highlands. A favorite food is *tortillas,* flat pancakes made from corn meal. Corn and beans are the basic foods for most Mexicans. Wheat and coffee are grown where the climate allows. Cotton, strawberries, tomatoes, and vegetables are grown on irrigated lands in the north. Most of these farm products are exported. So are the bananas, sugarcane, and *henequen* (a fiber used in making twine and rope). They are grown in the tropical lowlands. Cattle, sheep, and goats are raised in the drier northern region.

11. The highlands of Mexico are rich in minerals. Mexico is the world's largest producer of silver. Gold, sulfur, lead, zinc, and manganese are other minerals in good supply. Today, the most valuable mineral resource in Mexico is oil. Mexico's leaders hoped that income from oil and natural gas would improve the way of life of both the city people and farmers. When oil prices rose in the 1970s, Mexicans were happy. They earned more money from oil than any other export. With this new money, the government began to spend freely on new roads, dams, power projects, and aid for the poor.

12. In the early 1980s, the oil boom came to an end. Suddenly the world had more oil than it could use. Prices began to fall. The government did not have enough money to pay for the things it needed. It began to borrow heavily from foreign banks. To pay back the banks, it began to cut back government spending on programs for the people such as health and education programs. Factories had to lay off workers. To add to its problems, an earthquake shook Mexico City and parts of the west coast in September 1985. It killed 10,000 people and left about 100,000 homeless. Today, Mexico is struggling to pay its debts and overcome the effects of the earthquake.

13. In the past 15 years, Mexico's population has jumped from 58 million to 88 million. Each year, thousands of young people leave the farms for the cities. Each year, a million young Mexicans enter the job market. Unfortunately, there are not enough jobs for these people. Many try to cross the border into the United States. The United States wants Mexico to take stronger measures to control this illegal immigration. Slowing population growth, providing more jobs, controlling illegal immigration, and reducing foreign debt are not easy tasks. However, Mexico has overcome hardships before.

UNDERSTANDING WHAT YOU HAVE READ

1. Which questions are answered in this chapter?
a. Who was Juárez?
b. What are the kinds of foods eaten by most Mexican people?
c. What problems face Mexico today?

2. The main idea of *paragraphs 7 and 8* describes
a. farming in Mexico
b. life in Mexico City
c. the meals of a Mexican family

3. Mexico carries on most of its trade with
a. Brazil   b. the United States   c. Spain

4. Mexico leads the world in the production of
a. silver   b. lead   c. tin

5. Which statement is most accurate?
a. Mexico has few schools.
b. Mexico is a leading producer of oil.
c. Mexico exports food to the United States.

6. Only a small part of Mexico's land is used for farming because
a. it is located in the middle latitudes
b. most people work in mines
c. much of the land is mountains or desert

DEVELOPING IDEAS AND SKILLS

Building Map Skills——Mexico and the United States

Study the maps. Then answer the questions at the top of page 226.

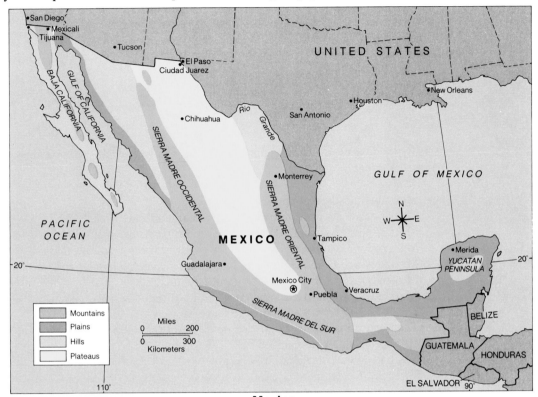

Mexico

UNITED STATES
POPULATION: 253 MILLION
LAND AREA: 3.6 MILLION SQUARE MILES
9.36 MILLION SQUARE KILOMETERS
70 PEOPLE PER SQUARE MILE

MEXICO
POPULATION: 88 MILLION
LAND AREA: 761,604 SQUARE MILES
1.97 MILLION SQUARE KILOMETERS
115 PEOPLE PER SQUARE MILE

Mexico and the United States

1. Does Mexico lie in the high, middle, or low latitudes?
2. Does Mexico extend farther from north to south or east to west?
3. What bodies of water border Mexico?
4. What is the approximate longitude and latitude of Mexico City?
5. Is Mexico more or less crowded than the United States?
6. What are Mexico's major seaports?
7. Why do you think there are few large seaports in Mexico?
8. How would you describe the topography of Mexico?
9. How far is Mexico City from Houston?

DEVELOPING CRITICAL THINKING SKILLS

Agree or Disagree

Decide whether or not each of the following agrees with what you have read. If the answer is *disagree*, explain why.

1. Mexico is mostly a mountainous country.
2. Mexico has a civilization that is part Indian and part French.
3. Most Mexicans are small farmers who work land near their villages.
4. Mexico does not have a climate suitable for growing tropical plants.
5. Mexico is rich in mineral resources; the chief minerals are oil and silver.
6. Mexico has little trade with the United States.
7. Mexico City is similar to other large cities in the Americas.
8. Lack of jobs has caused people to leave Mexico.
9. The Mexican government divided up many of the haciendas among small farmers and farming communities.
10. Much of Mexico's climate is vertical.

FOLLOW UP

Tell whether these statements are true or false. The underlined words make the statements true or false. If a statement is false, what words would you place in it to make it true?

1. The border between Mexico and the United States is the Rocky Mountains.
2. The United States imports minerals from Mexico.
3. Irrigation provides water for crops in northern Mexico.
4. Early Native Americans in Mexico were the Incas.
5. An important part of life in modern Mexico is an increase in industry.
6. Much of Mexico's power for industry comes from coal.

Chapter 12

Puerto Rico—The Caribbean Commonwealth

Why is Puerto Rico important to the United States?

READING FOR A PURPOSE:
1. What is the relationship between Puerto Rico and the United States?
2. How has the climate affected the kinds of crops grown in Puerto Rico?
3. How has Puerto Rico developed its industries?

1. Puerto Rico is an island 885 miles (1,416 kilometers) southeast of Florida. Even though it belongs to the United States, the United States is not the only country interested in this beautiful island. Tourists from the United States, and also from other parts of the world, pour into Puerto Rico for their vacations. The growth of industry has changed it from a land of poor farmers to a modern one of small factories and towns.

2. Puerto Rico is only about 100 miles (160 kilometers) long and 35 miles (56 kilometers) wide. It is smaller than any of the U.S. states, except Delaware and Rhode Island. It is located between the Caribbean Sea and the Atlantic Ocean. A visitor coming by air to Puerto Rico first notices the green, hilly land. It has a warm, rainy climate throughout the year. The rain-bearing winds blow from the northeast. When the winds hit the mountains, they rise and drop their moisture on the northern half of the island. The southern coastal plain—the leeward side—is drier.

3. In 1493, Columbus reached Puerto Rico on his second voyage to the New World. In 1508, the Spanish began to settle the island. They divided the land into large sugar farms, which were first worked by Native Americans and then by African slaves. Puerto Rico was not rich in gold and silver, but it was still valuable to the Spanish. Because of its location, it helped to guard Spanish treasure houses in the New World.

4. In 1898, the United States went to war with Spain. Spain was defeated and gave up the island of Puerto Rico to the United States. Since that time, the Puerto Rican people have won many rights. In 1900, they gained the right of free trade with the United States. In 1917, Puerto Ricans became American citizens. By 1947, the people were electing their own governor and making their own laws. Luis Muñoz Marin was the first Puerto Rican governor elected by the Puerto Ricans. In 1952, the people adopted their own constitution and set up a *commonwealth* with ties to the United States. Under this form of government, the Puerto Rican people have remained Americans. People of the island have almost the same powers as any of the 50 states. They elect their own local government. Puerto Ricans living in Puerto Rico cannot vote in national elections, however. The representative of Puerto Rico in the U.S. Congress may speak, but is not allowed to vote.

A farm worker uses modern equipment in this sugarcane field in Puerto Rico. What are some of the other kinds of crops grown on the island?

5. Puerto Rico is a crowded island. There are over 3,335,000 people in Puerto Rico. There are nearly 944 people for each square mile of land—one of the most crowded lands in the world. For hundreds of years, most of the people were small farmers. Now many are moving to the cities for jobs in the new factories. In the 1950s and 1960s, many left the island for the mainland of the United States in order to find better jobs. While most of the people are Roman Catholics, there is also a large number of Protestants. Most Puerto Ricans are of Spanish, African, or mixed descent.

6. The Puerto Rican people are proud of their Spanish culture. Spanish is the language used in schools. But all Puerto Rican children are taught English as a second language. It is not surprising, therefore, to find that so many Puerto Ricans speak two languages. Puerto Ricans are proud of their families too. The family is very important in the life of the people. The family is expected to take care of all its members.

7. Under Spanish rule, most of the land in Puerto Rico was owned by a few persons who raised sugarcane, tobacco, and coffee. Today, more people own their own small farms. Although these crops are still being grown, land is now being used for beef cattle and dairy farming. As the people move to cities like San Juan and Ponce, the demand for meat and fresh milk for the city people grows. Citrus fruits, bananas, plantains (a fruit similar to bananas), and pineapples are also grown. Nevertheless, Puerto Ricans must still import much food from the mainland of the United States.

8. Puerto Rico has no oil, coal, or iron ore, but this has not stopped it from becoming a land of small factories. Puerto Ricans have used what they have: their hardworking people and waterpower for electricity. Because of low taxes, factories have been encouraged to come to the island. These factories turn out medicines, chemicals made from imported oil, and electronic products. Puerto Rican indus-

Workers in a San Juan plant producing medicines. What other products are made in the factories of Puerto Rico?

try also makes machinery, cigars, cement, clothing, and other products. Puerto Ricans advertise their wonderful climate, beaches, and modern hotels and have a successful tourist trade.

9. Their next most important resource, besides themselves, has been their relationship with the United States. Puerto Ricans, as U.S. citizens, can move to the mainland if jobs are scarce on the island. U.S. armies protect the island. U.S. business people have invested money to help develop industry. The people of the island do not have to pay taxes to the United States government. They can trade with the United States without paying tariffs on their imports.

10. Today, many Puerto Ricans are healthy, go to school, and have good jobs on farms and in factories. They have pure water and electricity throughout the island. While many people once lived on a diet of corn, beans, and dried meat, today the people eat a greater variety of foods. They enjoy radio and television. Low-cost houses have been built in the cities and in the country. All children go to school and receive free lunches daily. The standard of living of Puerto Ricans has risen until it is one of the highest in all of Latin America. Despite these successes the average income per person in Puerto Rico is still lower than that in any of the U.S. states.

11. What will the future bring to the island? Most people want to keep their present relationship with the United States. There are those who want the island to become a state of the United States, although this would mean paying federal taxes. There are other Puerto Ricans who demand complete independence from the United States, despite the loss of free trade and other forms of aid.

12. Puerto Rico is important to the United States for various reasons. U.S. military bases there are important because the United States does not have friendly relations with Cuba. Puerto Rican industries produce over $5 billion worth of goods a year. Many of these fac-

Testing electronic equipment. Why have businesses such as this been set up in Puerto Rico?

tories are owned by people on the U.S. mainland. Puerto Ricans are also important as Latin Americans who are successfully raising their standard of living. In this manner, the Puerto Ricans are pioneers in an experiment that may affect all the Americas.

UNDERSTANDING WHAT YOU HAVE READ

1. **Which questions are answered in this chapter?**
a. Who is Luis Muñoz Marin?
b. How was Puerto Rico acquired by the United States?
c. Why have some Puerto Ricans left the island?

2. **The main idea of *paragraphs 9 and 10* describes**
a. how Puerto Rico has used its resources
b. the tax problem of Puerto Ricans
c. trade between Puerto Rico and the United States

3. **One of the "cash crops" of Puerto Rican farms is**
a. coconut   b. sugarcane   c. citrus fruit

4. **Puerto Rico is now**
a. a commonwealth
b. a state of the United States
c. an independent country

5. **Puerto Rico is important to the United States because it**
a. supplies U.S. factories with raw materials
b. is rich in mineral resources
c. has U.S. military bases that guard the United States in the Caribbean

6. **Many Puerto Ricans have come to the mainland of the United States to**
a. look for jobs
b. find religious freedom
c. work on the farms of the southwestern states

Building Map Skills——Puerto Rico and Connecticut

Study the maps. Then answer the questions below.

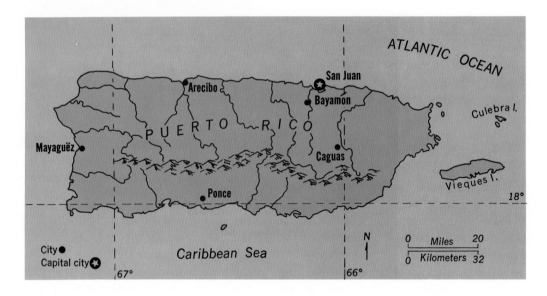

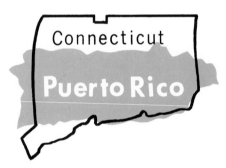

CONNECTICUT	PUERTO RICO
POPULATION: 3.3 MILLION	POPULATION: 3.3 MILLION
LAND AREA: 5,018 SQUARE MILES	LAND AREA: 3,435 SQUARE MILES
12,618 SQUARE KILOMETERS	8,860 SQUARE KILOMETERS
679 PEOPLE PER SQUARE MILE	944 PEOPLE PER SQUARE MILE

Puerto Rico and Connecticut

1. Does Puerto Rico lie in the high, middle, or low latitudes?
2. How wide is Puerto Rico at its widest point?
3. Where are the most important cities on the island located? Why do you think this is so?
4. What is the approximate latitude and longitude of the city of Ponce?
5. Why do you think San Juan is the largest city on the island?
6. In what direction do the streams of Puerto Rico flow? Can you give reasons for this?
7. Which has the greater population, Puerto Rico or the state of Connecticut?
8. Which is more crowded, Puerto Rico or Connecticut?

In Latin America

Zoologists **Roberto Roca** and **Patricia Gutierrez** began to study the oilbirds of Guacharo Cave in Venezuela because they were curious about the birds. Roca, a Venezuelan, and Gutierrez, who was born in Chile, had studied many different animals in their careers. But meeting the oilbirds changed their lives. Oilbirds are the only nocturnal (nighttime) fruit-eating birds. As they feed on the fruit trees, oilbirds spread seeds throughout the forests of northern Venezuela. Because of this, they are vital to the life of the forests. Roca and Gutierrez discovered that the national park in which the oilbirds lived was not large enough for the colony of birds to survive. In 1989, the two zoologists persuaded the Venezuelan government to add 166,000 acres (66,400 hectares) to the park. Since then, Roca and Gutierrez have dedicated themselves to preserving the environment.

Forty-five kinds of coral and hundreds of species of fish live in the barrier reef off the coast of Belize in Central America. The reef, which stretches 150 miles (240 kilometers) along the coast, is a diver's paradise. For this reason, it is in danger. By the middle of the 1980s, too many tourists had fished in the waters of the reef, and too many shell collectors had disturbed its delicate balance of life. Construction and pollution had added to the problem. **Jane Patricia Gibson,** a Belizan botanist and zoologist, refused to let the reef die. She drew up plans for a marine reserve. Then she raised the money she needed for the project. The result is the Kolchan Marine Reserve, the first of its kind in Central America. Its five square miles (12.95 square kilometers) of protected reef are once again a place where fish and coral can grow undisturbed. "We've seen an incredible rise in the diversity of fish life," says Gibson. "If you dive in a similar area that is not protected, you can see the difference."

Governments do not often appoint strong—or vocal—critics to important jobs. That is why the world's environmentalists were shocked when they heard the news from Brazil. **Jose Lutzenberger** had been named as the new Secretary of the Environment in the government of President Fernando Collor de Mello. Lutzenberger had made the previous administration very angry. He had said publicly that the other countries in the world had a right to be worried about what happened to the Amazon rain forest. "If you set your home on fire, it will threaten the homes of your neighbors," he said. Lutzenberger has a tough job now. He must find a way to stop farmers from burning the forests of the Amazon in order to clear more land for their crops.

Many farmers rely on modern science to help them increase food production. But **Bonifacia Quispe** looked to the past. Working with archaeologist **Oswaldo Rivera,** Quispe and her fellow Aymaran Native Americans of Bolivia have rediscovered a thousand-year-old secret. Using the outlines of ancient ridges, the Aymaras rebuilt the platforms of earth used by their ancestors for growing crops. This platform system makes it easier to irrigate and fertilize crops. The people in Quispe's Andean village of Lakaya began planting potatoes in these raised fields in 1986. They now grow 28 times the amount of potatoes they grew six years ago.

Chapter 13

Brazil: The Tropical Giant

How has geography helped and limited the growth of Brazil?

READING FOR A PURPOSE:
1. How has climate helped to influence what crops are grown in Brazil?
2. What mineral resources have helped Brazil build its industries?
3. How are the people of Brazil trying to solve the country's problems?

1. Brazil is the giant country of South America. Brazil has more farmland than all of the European region. It is rich in minerals, and forests cover more than half the land. It has a large, hard-working population. Yet much of the land is empty and many of the people are poor. The following sections describe some of the reasons for this condition.

2. With an area of more than 3 million

Brasília, capital city of Brazil. The building of this new city began in 1957. It was built far from the Atlantic coast to encourage people to develop the country's resources.

square miles (8.5 million square kilometers), Brazil occupies half the continent of South America. It is the fifth largest country in the world. Only Russia, Canada, China, and the United States are larger. Every nation in South America except Chile and Ecuador borders this giant country. To the east, Brazil faces the Atlantic Ocean. The equator crosses the northern part of the country. Most of the nation lies in the low latitudes. The country is so large, however, that the southern part extends into the middle latitudes.

3. Along the Atlantic Coast, there is a narrow lowland that stretches from the Amazon River south to Uruguay. West of the coastal strip are the Brazilian Highlands, reaching far inland to the Amazon Basin. These highlands are made up of hills, low mountains, and large areas of plateau. The other major land form is the lowland of the Amazon. The huge plain of the Amazon reaches from the Atlantic Ocean into Peru and Colombia. It is fed by a thousand rivers and drains almost two-thirds of the nation. The Amazon can be used by ships as far as Peru. Except for this mighty river, most of the rivers of Brazil have rapids and are not useful for transporting goods.

4. Along much of the low coastal area and in the valley of the Amazon, the climate is hot and rainy throughout the year. This area is the rain forest. Inland, where the land is higher, the climate is cooler, but it is still warm. This is the savanna climate with its wet and dry seasons. In the southern part of the country, the humid subtropical climate is found—mild winters and long, warm, and rainy summers.

5. In 1500, Brazil was claimed by Portugal. The colony was set up to grow sugarcane on large plantations worked by African slaves. In the 18th century, sugar was replaced by gold as the main source of riches. Brazil led the world in gold production for 100 years, before the supply ran out. When the world first needed natural rubber, Brazil's forests filled the need.

6. In 1822, Brazil gained its freedom from Portugal. In 1888, slavery was ended in Brazil.

Until 1889, however, the country continued to be ruled by an emperor. In 1889, the country became a republic with an elected president and congress. Despite the rule of a few "strong men" and several revolutions, Brazil still has a government under a constitution. Because Brazil was settled by Portugal, the people today speak Portuguese and are largely Roman Catholic. Brazil is the largest Roman Catholic country in the world.

7. With over 153 million people, Brazil is the sixth largest country in the world in population. There are a large number of descendants of immigrants from Portugal and other countries of Europe. Africans also make up much of the population. The black population is the largest of any country outside Africa. Since there has been much intermarriage among these groups, the color of one's skin is not important in Brazil. When the Europeans first arrived in 1500, it is believed there were about 5 million Indians. Today, there are only about 200,000 Indians in Brazil.

8. Most Brazilians live in the narrow lowlands along the Atlantic coast, in the growing cities and towns. São Paulo, Rio de Janeiro, and Belo Horizonte are the largest of seven cities with more than a million people. The capital city is Brasília, about 400 miles (640 kilometers) from the coast. Brasília was built far inland so that people would move to those areas and help develop them.

9. Brazil has many riches. There is fertile land on which to grow crops and feed animals. Around São Paulo are the large cattle ranches and plantations, or *fazendas,* where coffee is grown. Brazil grows and sells more coffee than any other nation in the world. Sugarcane and corn are common crops here as well. Corn is grown as cattle feed. Citrus fruits are also grown. However, by the end of the 1970s, soybeans became Brazil's leading cash crop. Protein-rich soy is used to make vegetable oil and soy flour. It is also an important animal feed for cattle, hogs, and chicken. Sugarcane is grown to be used as alcohol fuel for cars to be sold abroad. In the northeast, where

sugarcane is king, there has been much drought in recent years. As a result, millions of workers moved to the cities. By 1985, Brazil was importing beans and rice as food for its people.

10. Forests cover about half the country of Brazil. Hardwoods are a product of the Amazon rain forests. So is rubber from rubber trees. There are great pine forests in the milder south. Canauba wax is obtained from the oil palm. This product is used in the finest waxes and polishes. Brazil nuts are also gathered in the tropical forests. Many forests are being cleared around Brasília to make way for cattle raising, tea plantations, and lumber companies.

11. The highland mines produce many minerals, chiefly iron ore and manganese. Brazil has some of the largest deposits of iron ore in the world. As in most Latin American countries, not much coal is mined. Brazil is the world's leader in mining quartz crystals. These are used in electronic equipment. Uranium and gemstones are also mined. There are good supplies of chromium, nickel, tungsten, and bauxite—important metals for the modern world. Large iron and steel plants are located near Rio de Janeiro. São Paulo is the leading industrial city. Since the mid-1960s, many new factories have been built. By 1984, three-fifths of Brazil's exports were manufac-

New kinds of seeds and the long growing season allow farmers to plant two crops a year in some parts of Brazil. What else about the environment of Brazil makes it favorable to farming?

tured goods, cars and trucks, military goods, TVs, and machinery.

12. Brazil is now the world's eighth largest producer of goods and services. But in reaching this point, it has paid a heavy price. Despite modern farms and factories, many people are still poor. The health services do not reach them. One out of four adults still cannot read or write. Millions of people, especially in northeastern Brazil's countryside and in the slums of the large cities, barely get enough to eat. There is more homelessness than ever. Along the Paraná River, Brazil has joined Paraguay in building the Itaipú Dam. When it was completed in 1982, it became the world's largest electric power project. In addition, Brazil bought nuclear power plants from West Germany to supply energy. Yet the high cost of importing oil has created huge debts. Brazil owes foreign countries and banks billions of dollars. Only a few people have benefited from the growth—the large landowners,

the large factory owners, and the military leaders. In the 1970s, Brazil borrowed heavily to pay its bills. Like Mexico, it is deeply in debt. But after many years of military rule, Brazil now has a democratic government.

13. Relations between the United States and Brazil have been friendly. During World War II, Brazil fought on the side of the Allies. Its airfields were used by the United States to send planes to the battle areas of Africa and the Middle East. In the first years of the Alliance for Progress, the United States sent more than a half billion dollars in aid to Brazil. The United States is Brazil's largest trading partner, both in imports and exports. The United States imports coffee, cacao, waxes, hides, and manganese. Brazil imports machinery, autos, trucks, wheat, oil, and coal. The giant of South America has a long way to go to reach its goals. But there is little reason why Brazil cannot become a great source of riches for its own people and for the rest of the world.

UNDERSTANDING WHAT YOU HAVE READ

1. Which questions are answered in this chapter?
a. What produced wealth for Brazil early in its history?
b. What are some problems that face Brazil?
c. Where are cacao and sugarcane grown?

2. The main idea of this chapter is that
a. Brazil has great resources that it is rapidly developing
b. Brazil has a democratic form of government
c. forest products are Brazil's greatest wealth

3. The chief industrial city of Brazil is
a. Brasília   b. Recife   c. São Paulo

4. The chief export crop of Brazil is
a. soybeans   b. wheat   c. sugar

5. Brazil's major industries include
a. steel mills and military goods
b. car and TV factories
c. both a and b

6. Forests are valuable in Brazil because they
a. provide wood for the shipbuilding industry
b. are a source of hardwoods, waxes, rubber, and nuts
c. are the world's only source of rubber

DEVELOPING IDEAS AND SKILLS

Building Map Skills —— Brazil and the United States

Study the maps on this page. Then answer these questions.

1. Does Brazil lie in the high, middle, or low latitudes?
2. How wide is Brazil at its widest point?
3. What is the approximate longitude and latitude of the city of Manaus?
4. In what direction would you be traveling if you flew from your community to the city of Belém? (Use the map on page 173 to help you answer this.)
5. In which parts of Brazil are large cities located? Can you give reasons for this?
6. Which direction is *upstream* on the Amazon River?
7. Which city would have the greater difference in temperature from one part of the year to another—Brasília or Manaus?
8. What countries border Brazil?
9. How can you explain the large number of rivers in central Brazil?
10. Would it be possible to fit all of Brazil inside the boundaries of the United States?
11. Which country is more crowded, Brazil or the United States?

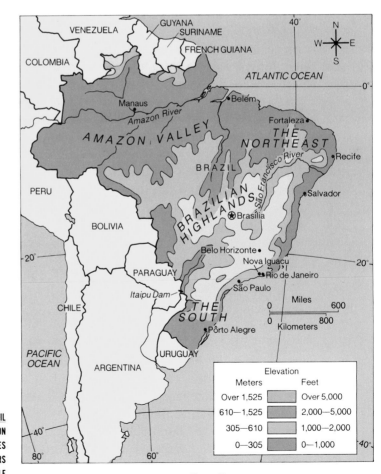

Brazil

UNITED STATES
POPULATION: 253 MILLION
LAND AREA: 3.6 MILLION SQUARE MILES
9.36 MILLION SQUARE KILOMETERS
70 PEOPLE PER SQUARE MILE

BRAZIL
POPULATION: 153 MILLION
LAND AREA: 3.3 MILLION SQUARE MILES
8.5 MILLION SQUARE KILOMETERS
46 PEOPLE PER SQUARE MILE

Brazil and the United States

Save the Rain Forest

 Scientists know that a cancer drug can be extracted from the bark of yew trees found in North America. Yet this breakthrough drug may be lost if the forests where it is found disappear. Forests around the world are disappearing at a rate of 75,000 square miles each year. Tropical forests are at special risk. They occur mainly in the world's developing countries where populations are growing at a rapid rate. Many developing countries see forest clearing as a quick way to provide more jobs, farms, and a better life for their people.

Environmentalists are seeking ways to use the rain forests without destroying them and their rare plant and animal life.

Brazilian Forests on Fire. Much of the battle over tropical deforestation centers on the rain forests of Brazil. Ninety percent of the 2.7 million square miles of rain forest covering the Amazon region is owned by Brazil.

In the 1970s Brazil's leaders began a program to bring settlers and new wealth to the "empty" Amazon region. Many of the first settlers drawn to the Amazon were farmers. The farmers began burning the rain forest to clear land for crops and livestock. The farmers quickly found out, too late for the forest, that fragile tropical soils soon lose their fertility once the trees are gone.

Other government programs in Brazil also encouraged destruction of the rain forest. New roads were pushed through the Amazon and large numbers of trees were destroyed as a result. Ranchers took over many abandoned farm lands and burned more forest to enlarge their landholdings. Mining was encouraged..Forests around some of the new mines were cut and burned to help smelt iron, manganese, copper, and other mineral ores. Loggers, too, found it profitable to chop down ancient trees and transport them over the new highways to add to Brazil's exports.

Threatened Lives. Rain forests contain more than 80,000 different types of plants and 30 million different types of birds, insects, and other animals! All depend on the forest for their survival. Some of the plants and animals found in the rain forest have value for humans. Curare, a muscle relaxant, comes from trees in the rain forest. Rubber is one useful product now collected from trees in the Amazon rain forest. Others are Brazil nuts, palm nuts, and an ivory-like nut used to make buttons.

Indian Rights. Lives of Indians native to the rain forest are also threatened when the rain forest is destroyed. Indians of the Amazon live simply as hunters and gatherers. They cannot survive when their environment is disturbed.What to do? Efforts to save the rain forest must balance the interests of the people who live in the region with the interests of the world as a whole. Environmentalists claim that collecting valuable forest products can yield twice as much income as using the land for grazing or farming. "Debt for nature" swaps may help. Brazil and other Amazon countries borrowed heavily in the 1970s. Now they are having trouble repaying the loans. In "debt for nature" swaps, private organizations raise money from people in industrialized countries. They use the money to pay off loans of debtor countries agreeing to protect areas of the rain forest. **Why might Amazon countries object to international efforts to save the rain forest? What can individual people do to save the rain forest?**

Latin America

Country	Area (Square Miles)	Capital	Population (1991 estimates)	Number of Years to Double Population	Life Expectancy	Per Capita GNP, 1990
Anguilla	35	The Valley	7,000	—	74	—
Antigua/Barbuda	171	St. Johns	100,000	83	—	—
Argentina	1,065,189	Buenos Aires	31,200,000	56	71	$ 2,160
Bahamas	5,380	Nassau	300,000	54	72	$11,370
Barbados	166	Bridgetown	300,000	102	75	$ 6,370
Belize	8,867	Belmopan	200,000	21	70	$ 1,600
Bermuda (UK)	21	Hamilton	—	—	75	—
Bolivia	424,165	La Paz	7,500,000	27	54	$ 600
Brazil	3,286,470	Brasilia	153,300,000	36	65	$ 2,550
Chile	292,257	Santiago	13,400,000	40	74	$ 1,770
Colombia	439,735	Bogotá	33,600,000	35	71	$ 1,190
Costa Rica	19,575	San Jose	3,100,000	21	77	$ 1,790
Cuba	44,218	Havana	10,700,000	62	76	$ 1,940
Dominica	290	Roseau	100,000	34	76	$ 1,670**
Dominican Republic	18,816	Santo Domingo	7,300,000	30	67	$ 790
Ecuador	109,483	Quito	9,600,000	29	66	$ 1,040
El Salvador	8,124	San Salvador	5,400,000	25	62	$ 1,040
Falkland Islands (UK)	4,700	Stanley	2,000*	—	—	—
French Guiana (Fr)	43,740	Cayenne	94,000**	—	—	$ 1,935*
Grenada	133	St. George's	100,000	24	71	$ 1,900
Guadeloupe	660	Basse-Terre	400,000	51	—	—
Guatemala	42,042	Guatemala City	8,600,000	23	63	$ 920
Guyana	83,000	Georgetown	800,000	39	68	$ 310
Haiti	10,579	Port-au-Prince	5,900,000	24	54	$ 400
Honduras	43,277	Tegucigalpa	5,300,000	23	66	$ 900
Jamaica	4,232	Kingston	2,500,000	37	77	$ 1,260
Martinique (Fr)	425	Fort-de-France	300,000	54	76	—
Mexico	761,604	Mexico City	81,700,000	30	72	$ 1,990
Netherlands Antilles (Neth)	385	Willemstad	200,000	59	77	—
Nicaragua	50,193	Managua	3,900,000	21	63	$ 830***
Panama	29,208	Panama City	2,500,000	34	72	$ 1,780
Paraguay	157,047	Asunción	4,400,000	25	70	$ 1,030
Peru	496,222	Lima	22,000,000	30	64	$ 1,090
Puerto Rico (US)	3,435	San Juan	3,330,000	62	72	$ 6,010
St. Christopher-Nevis	101	Brasseterre	40,000	64	67	$ 3,330
Saint Lucia	238	Castries	200,000	44	72	$ 1,810
Saint Vincent/ The Grenadines	150	Kingstown	100,000	43	70	$ 1,610
Suriname	63,037	Paramaribo	400,000	35	69	$ 3,020
Trinidad and Tobago	1,980	Port-of-Spain	1,300,000	44	70	$ 3,160
Uruguay	68,037	Montevideo	3,100,000	83	73	$ 2,620
Venezuela	352,143	Caracas	20,100,000	30	70	$ 2,450
Virgin Islands (US)	133	Charlotte Amalie	101,809	—	—	$ 7,465**

*1985   **1987   ***1988

Sources: 1991 World Population Data Sheet of the Population Reference Bureau, Inc.; The World Almanac and Book of Facts, 1992; and the CIA World Factbook, 1991.

UNIT FIVE

THE EUROPEAN REGION

KEY IDEAS

- The relative location of European countries with easy access to important oceans and seas helped create highly developed economies and made the Europeans leaders in world trade.

- Europe is the smallest world region, and its dense and highly urbanized population has greatly altered the physical environment.

- The human characteristics of the European region include highly skilled farmers and factory workers, great centers of industry and trade, and parliamentary democratic governments.

- Great change is taking place in relationships within the European region and in its relationships with other nations and regions.

- Within the European region, twelve nations have formed a new economic region with a market of 380 million people called the European Community. The European Community will allow free movement of people, ideas, and goods across national borders.

- Within the European region, the countries of Eastern Europe are building new economic and cultural relationships with other European nations.

- In the past, many wars were fought in the European region. Today, the new economic power of the European region is based on cooperation.

- New relationships are being built between the European region and the United States, Japan, and the recently formed Commonwealth of Independent States.

Hundreds of feet underwater, workers put the finishing touches on a project that has long excited Europeans: a tunnel linking Britain with the European mainland.

Chapter 1

The Little Giant

How are the countries of Western Europe and the United States important to each other?

READING FOR A PURPOSE:
1. How are the countries of Europe divided into groups for our study?
2. What have been some contributions of European people to the way of life in North America?
3. How is Western Europe important to the defense of the United States?

1. The map of the world does not show a separate land area called Europe. The continent of Europe is really part of a great land mass called Eurasia. If you look closely at a map, you can see that the continent of Europe is a large peninsula on the west of this vast stretch of land. As such, it is bordered by the Mediterranean Sea on the south, the Arctic Ocean on the north, the Atlantic Ocean on the west, and the Ural Mountains on the east. In this unit we will be studying the *European region*. The European region is part of the continent of Europe. The European region includes all of the continent of Europe except for the European parts of the Commonwealth of Independent States and Turkey.

2. There are 36 independent countries in what we call the European region. All of these nations together make up an area that is less than half the size of the United States or Canada. France, the largest nation of the European region, is almost the size of Texas. The United Kingdom is about the same size as Oregon. Belgium is only a little larger than Maryland.

The Main Areas of the European Region
- British Isles
- Western part of the European Region
- Northern Europe
- Southern Europe or Mediterranean Europe
- Eastern Europe
- Non-essential area

3. The nations of the European region fall into five main groups. One group is made up of the countries of *the British Isles.* The British Isles are separated from the mainland of Europe by the English Channel and the North Sea. The two island nations that make up the British Isles are the United Kingdom and Ireland. The second group of nations is on the mainland in the *western part of the European region.* This western group includes France, Germany, the Netherlands, Belgium, Luxembourg, northern Italy, Austria, Liechtenstein, and Switzerland.

4. The third group is sometimes called *Northern Europe and Scandinavia.* It includes the countries of Norway, Sweden, Denmark, and Finland. The island nation of Iceland is usually considered part of this group also. The fourth part of the European region is the southern part. It is sometimes called *Southern* or *Mediterranean Europe.* It includes Portugal, Andorra, Spain, southern France, southern Italy, San Marino and Greece. It also includes a very tiny nation within Italy—Vatican City—and the small island nation of Malta in the Mediterranean Sea. Hereafter, when we speak of *Western Europe* (with a capital letter W in the word *Western*), we refer to *all four* parts: the British Isles, western Europe, Northern Europe, and Southern Europe.

5. The fifth part of Europe is called *Eastern Europe.* This group of nations includes Poland, Czechoslovakia, Hungary, Romania, Bulgaria, Yugoslavia, Croatia, Slovenia, Bosnia and Herzegovina, Macedonia, Latvia, Lithuania, Estonia, and Albania.

6. For hundreds of years, the countries of Western Europe were the leaders of the world. While this leadership is now shared with other regions, Western Europe is still a very important area.

7. The Northern American way of life owes much to Western Europe. The United States was settled largely by people who came from the United Kingdom and other parts of Western Europe. So was Canada. The settlers brought their ways of living and learning. As a

Canterbury Cathedral, England. Why are many of the buildings in the United Kingdom made of stone?

result, most North Americans speak English, live under a democratic form of government, and are usually Christians.

8. Western Europe is a center of music, art, and literature. The books written by its authors are read all over the world. Millions of tourists from the United States and Canada visit Western Europe each year to see its art galleries, museums, and cathedrals.

9. The Industrial Revolution that became so important in the United States and Canada first began in the United Kingdom and spread throughout Europe. Over the years, the people of this region developed a high standard of living. Because of this high standard of living, the people of Western Europe can afford to buy many things. Today they are the best customers for U.S. goods—more than 85 billion dollars worth a year. The United States also buys more from this group of countries than from any single nation in the world.

10. The United States thought that the Atlantic Ocean would keep it out of European wars. But two world wars have ended this

241

belief. The United States now realizes that what happens in Western Europe also affects Americans. It needs a friendly Western Europe as a place for military bases and other defenses. (In 1990, about 249,565 American troops were stationed there.) The United States also needs Western Europe because it is one of the great industrial areas in the world. It has many natural resources. It is a leader in making steel. It has large, modern factories and many goods, and its people are among the most skilled in the world.

UNDERSTANDING WHAT YOU HAVE READ

1. Which questions are answered in this chapter?
a. Why is a free Western Europe important to the United States?
b. Why is the United States interested in the people of Western Europe?
c. What are the important cities of Europe?

2. The main idea of *paragraph 10* is that Western Europe is
a. isolated from North America
b. important to the defense of the United States
c. threatened by enemies

3. The largest country of Western Europe is
a. France   b. Belgium   c. Spain

4. The northern part of Europe is called
a. the Alpine region
b. Scandinavia
c. Benelux

5. To Western Europe, Americans and Canadians owe
a. their highway systems
b. their public schools
c. their form of government

6. The United States has a large amount of trade with Western Europe because
a. there are no tariffs in Europe
b. these countries use the same money system
c. Europeans have money to buy goods and modern factories to make products to sell

7. Greece is a part of the European region called
a. Mediterranean Europe
b. Northern Europe
c. Eastern Europe

8. A European country that has no coastline is
a. France   b. East Germany   c. Switzerland

DEVELOPING IDEAS AND SKILLS

Building Map Skills — The European Region

Study the map on page 243. Then answer these questions.
1. Is the region north or south of the equator?
2. Is the whole region located east of the prime meridian?
3. How many miles north and south does the region extend?
4. What region or regions are near it?
5. Which chief bodies of water border the region?
6. Which countries in the European region have no outlets to the sea?
7. What is the country that is farthest north?
8. Which countries are island nations?
9. Which countries are located on a peninsula?
10. On which bodies of water would your ship sail if you sailed from Copenhagen, Denmark, to Naples, Italy?

—— Interpreting Color on a Map ——

Maps can be used to show many kinds of information in many ways. Maps can show political boundaries, population, urban population, life expectancies, and so on. These things can be shown in many ways: with rules, dots, shading, color. The map below highlights or illustrates the main areas of the European region.

Look at the map key. See how the mapmaker used different colors to show the different parts of the European Region. The mapmaker used another color to show the lands that border the European region. Since the lands bordering the European region are not being studied here, those lands are referred to in the key as nonessential. The mapmaker uses color on a map to translate what you have read on the printed page.

Copy the following statements into your notebook. Tell whether these statements are *correct* or *incorrect*. If a statement is *incorrect*, rewrite it to make it *correct*.

1. The British Isles are part of Northern Europe.
2. The countries of Eastern Europe lay between the Soviet Union and Western Europe.
3. Germany is in Eastern Europe; Hungary is in Western Europe.
4. Norway, Sweden, and Denmark are located on major peninsulas in Northern Europe.
5. Portugal, Spain, and Italy are located on major peninsulas in Southern Europe.

The Main Areas of the European Region

- British Isles
- Western part of the European Region
- Northern Europe
- Southern Europe or Mediterranean Europe
- Eastern Europe
- Non-essential area

0   250   500 Miles
0   250   500 Kilometers

Chapter 2

Water, Water Everywhere

How does the European region's topography help to explain the activities of the people?

READING FOR A PURPOSE:
1. Why have nations in Western Europe been great sea powers?
2. Where have mountains served to separate people in Europe?
3. How have rivers influenced the way of life in Europe?

1. As you remember, the continent of Europe is a huge peninsula on the great land mass known as Eurasia. Reaching out from Europe's mainland are a number of smaller peninsulas. These smaller peninsulas are the most striking feature of Europe's shape. Spain and Portugal, Italy, Denmark, Scandinavia, and Greece and Albania are all on peninsulas.

If you look closely you will see that these peninsulas have even smaller peninsulas. As a result, the coastline of the European region is very long and is broken into bays and smaller seas. These bays are fine natural harbors for ships.

2. Almost all the people of Western Europe live near water. No part of the entire region is more than one or two days' automobile drive from the sea. Therefore, it should not surprise you to learn that the nations of Western Europe have been great sea powers. They have explored distant lands. Some of the nations—the United Kingdom, France, Spain, Germany, Denmark, Italy, Portugal, Belgium, and the Netherlands—have owned colonies in almost every corner of the world. As you might also expect, many people of Western Europe have made their living through sea trading, fishing, and shipbuilding. Some of them still do.

3. There are important bodies of water around the European region. The Mediterranean Sea, in the south, was an important waterway long before America was reached by Europeans. The Italian cities of Venice and Genoa were great trading centers for products

Some Italian workers make their living from fishing. What are some other advantages that living near a large body of water might provide?

from Asia and North Africa. This sea is still the center of water travel from Western Europe to the countries of eastern Asia. The Strait of Gibraltar, at the western end of the sea, controls the entrance to the Mediterranean from the Atlantic Ocean.

4. The North Sea is a busy trade route from the island of Great Britain to the Scandinavian countries and the Baltic Sea. The Baltic Sea is the main water trading route for Sweden, Finland, Poland, and Germany. Most of the Baltic Sea freezes, however, during the winter months and is not as useful for trade as the more southerly Mediterranean. The English Channel, scarcely 21 miles (34 kilometers) wide at its narrowest point, separates the island of Great Britain from the mainland of the continent. Three world regions touch the shores of the Black Sea: Bulgaria and Romania in Eastern Europe, Turkey in the Middle Eastern region, and Russia, Ukraine, and Georgia in northern Eurasia.

5. Although all parts of Western Europe are near the sea, not every country has an entrance to the large bodies of water. The nations of Switzerland, Austria, and Luxembourg are *landlocked.* That is, they have no coastline. For Switzerland this has been a blessing. There is no entrance to Switzerland except through the mountains. This tiny nation has therefore been able to avoid war for hundreds of years. In Eastern Europe, Czechoslovakia and Hungary are landlocked.

6. Much of the European region is a great lowland, or plain, that stretches from southern Great Britain across Germany, Poland, Russia, and Ukraine. It grows wider toward the east. It is known as the Great European Plain. North of the plain are highlands that stretch from northern Great Britain through the Scandinavian countries.

7. South of the plains, the land is also hilly or mountainous. The mountains of Southern Europe are high and rugged. The Pyrenees Mountains separate Spain from France. They extend from the Atlantic Ocean to the Mediterranean Sea. The Alps stretch from southern

The Swiss Alps. How have these mountains benefited Switzerland?

France, through Switzerland and Austria, to Yugoslavia. The Balkans stretch from western Bulgaria almost to the Black Sea. These mountains separate Southern Europe from the rest of the region.

8. There are many rivers in the European region. Some of the most important ones rise in the Alps—the Rhine, the Rhone, the Po, and the Danube. Compared with the other rivers we have studied, the Mississippi and the Amazon, these rivers are small. However, they are generally navigable. They are joined by many canals to help carry goods, such as iron ore, from mine to mill. Except for the Rhine, these rivers flow south or east. The Rhone flows into the Mediterranean; the Po leads into the Adriatic Sea; the Danube flows east into the Black Sea. Each runs through fertile valleys where many people live. Many of Western Europe's great cities and seaports are located on these rivers. Other important rivers in the European region flow north across the European plain. These include the Vistula and Oder rivers in Poland, which flow into the Baltic Sea. The Elbe River flows through Czechoslovakia, Germany, and then into the North Sea.

Rotterdam is Europe's leading seaport. It is on a river about 15 miles (24 kilometers) from the North Sea. Rotterdam is the center of a system of canals that connect it with the Rhine River. Name two other European rivers.

UNDERSTANDING WHAT YOU HAVE READ

1. Which questions are answered in this chapter?
a. Why did Western Europeans turn to the sea?
b. What is the topography of the European region?
c. How long is the Danube River?

2. The main idea of this chapter describes
a. how people of Europe use the sea
b. the European region's land forms and bodies of water
c. the southern chain of mountains

3. Much of Western Europe is a
a. plateau
b. desert
c. plain

4. Many of the important rivers of Western Europe rise in the
a. Pyrenees
b. Alps
c. northern highlands

5. "There are many bays and many seas. . . ." This tells you that
a. there are many harbors
b. people travel a great deal
c. there are many sandy beaches

6. The rivers of Western Europe are useful because
a. goods are shipped on them between ports and inland cities
b. most of them flow toward the east
c. they are a source of minerals

7. Land that is surrounded by water on three sides is called
a. a peninsula
b. an isthmus
c. an island

8. Venice was a great *trading center.* This means that the city was well known for
a. training soldiers
b. printing books
c. buying and selling goods

Building Map Skills—Land Forms of the European Region

Study the map. Then tell whether these statements are *true* or *false*. Be able to explain your answers.

1. Almost every country of Western Europe may be described as a plateau.
2. The islands of the European region are chiefly plains.
3. Plains make up a small part of the far northern part of the European region.
4. Mountains are found in both the northern and southern parts of this region.
5. Some mountains appear to separate parts of the European region from countries along the Mediterranean Sea.
6. In Southern Europe, Italy and Spain are chiefly one vast plain.
7. Most of Western Europe is part of a large low-land area.
8. In the far north, mountains line the Atlantic coast.
9. The interior of Western Europe is mainly plains.

Land Forms of the European Region

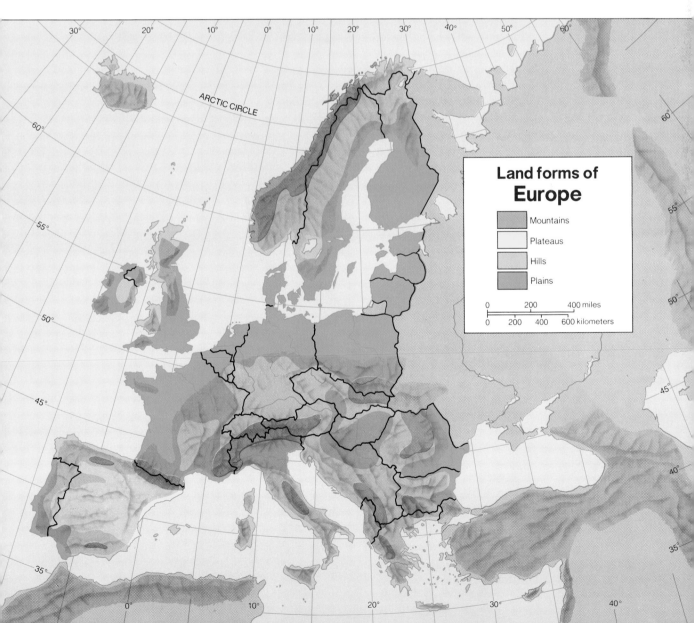

Land forms of **Europe**

- Mountains
- Plateaus
- Hills
- Plains

0   200   400 miles
0   200   400   600 kilometers

REVIEWING AND WRITING

Using the Library

Complete the following chart in your notebook. You may find it helpful to use an atlas or an almanac from your library to find some of the information.

	Comparing Rivers			
	Mississippi	Amazon	Danube	Rhine
1. Length:				
2. Body of water it flows into:				
3. Area drained:				
4. How it is used by the people around it:				

Chapter 3

Green Lands Near the Sea

How does the European region's climate help to explain its standard of living?

READING FOR A PURPOSE:
1. How does the North Atlantic Drift affect the climate of Western Europe?
2. Why does southern Europe have a Mediterranean climate?
3. Why are northern nations called lands of the "midnight sun"?

Ireland has a marine climate. The climate is good for raising beef and dairy cattle and for growing potatoes, barley, sugar beets, and wheat. Why are Ireland's winters usually cool and rainy instead of bitter cold and snowy?

1. Nearly all of the European region is nearer the North Pole than the United States is. Rome is farther north than New York. London is almost as far north as Hudson Bay in Canada. These cities ought to be very cold, but they are not. The countries in the western part of Europe have a mild and rainy climate. They have a marine climate.

2. The climate of Ireland, Great Britain, and the European mainland is much warmer than we would expect because of a current of warm water known as the North Atlantic Drift. The Drift begins far away in the warm waters of the Gulf of Mexico. (See the map of ocean currents on page 36.) There, it is called the Gulf Stream. The Gulf Stream travels northward and eastward. As it nears Europe, it becomes wider and weaker. Eventually, the Gulf Stream current becomes the North Atlantic Drift. The Drift moves eastward until it reaches the shores of Ireland, Great Britain, and much of the western part of Europe.

3. The winds that blow over the countries of the western part of Europe come from the west. Because these winds blow over the Drift, they bring its warmth to the European mainland. Since no part of the region is more than 400 miles (644 kilometers) from the sea, the warm winds are felt through much of Western Europe. Farther inland, the winds begin to lose their warmth. The winters become colder and longer, and snow falls. The summers are shorter. But the presence of water on three sides of the European mainland still tends to keep the winters milder and the summers cooler than they would otherwise be. Because of the rainy winds, the plains of Europe are green with crops.

4. Southern Europe has a Mediterranean climate. The southern coast of France is about the same latitude as Montreal, Canada. Yet this coastal area, far from being cold, has long, hot summers. The winters are mild. Rain falls mainly during the winter. Why is this climate so different? The Alps keep out the blasts of cold air from the north. The winds that blow over Southern Europe come from the deserts of Africa. They are hot and dry. As a result, the climate is the same as that of southern California. The long growing season makes it possible to grow all kinds of citrus fruits. Vegetables grown in Southern Europe are sent to the colder areas farther north.

5. Much farther north is the *taiga*, or northern forest lands. The taiga extends through Norway, Sweden, and Finland—lands of the "midnight sun." Here summers are short and winters are long and very cold. During the cold winter days, there are only a

The Riviera in southern France. Why does this Mediterranean coastline have a warm, dry climate?

few hours of sunlight. Rivers and lakes are icy, and the ground is frozen. But during the summers, the sun shines very late into the evenings. While much of the soil is poor and stony, there are many evergreen forests. In the northernmost parts of Europe there is a tundra climate. It is too cold for trees to grow.

6. In much of Eastern Europe there is a humid-continental climate. As you travel eastward the climate slowly changes. The winters are colder than in the western part of the region. The summers are often hotter. Warsaw, Poland, has a climate similar to that of the north central states of the United States.

7. The high mountainous region of Switzerland, Austria, and parts of France and northern Italy has a vertical climate. Near the bottoms of the mountains there is a warm climate. Peaks are covered by snow and ice.

UNDERSTANDING WHAT YOU HAVE READ

1. Which questions are answered in this chapter?
a. Why is Western Europe mild and rainy?
b. How are fogs caused?
c. Why do many tourists visit Southern Europe?

2. The main idea of *paragraph 4* describes
a. the climate of Southern Europe
b. the effects of the westerly winds
c. the vertical climate of the Alps

3. Most of Eastern Europe is
a. farther from the equator than New York City is
b. in the region of the taiga and the tundra
c. about the same distance from the equator as the United States

4. The Gulf Stream begins
a. at the Arctic Circle
b. in the Gulf of Mexico
c. in the Pacific Ocean

5. Much of Western Europe has a mild, rainy climate because
a. it is near the equator
b. the winds are warm and wet
c. high mountains shut off the eastern winds

6. Southern Europe has a mild climate because
a. it is located far from large bodies of water
b. it is located near the Atlantic Ocean
c. cold northern winds are blocked by the Alps

7. A feature of the Mediterranean climate is
a. frequent rain and fog
b. a long growing season
c. short but very cold winters

8. Winters are longer and colder inland in the European region because
a. the land receives breezes from Africa
b. the mountains bring cold winds to the plains
c. these lands are far from the effects of the ocean currents

DEVELOPING IDEAS AND SKILLS

Building Map Skills — Climates of the European Region

Agree or Disagree. Study the map. Then decide whether or not each statement at the top of this page agrees with the information on the map. If the answer is *disagree,* explain why.

1. The taiga occupies all the European region north of 50° latitude.
2. Spain and Italy are the only countries in Western Europe with an area of Mediterranean climate.
3. The climate of Europe's Atlantic coast is like the climate of the northeastern United States.
4. Nearness to large bodies of water has an effect on the climate of much of Western Europe.
5. The northern part of this region probably has the fewest people for each square mile of land.
6. The greatest part of the European region lies in an area of marine climate.
7. There is no region in Northern Europe where cocoa, cane sugar, or rubber can be grown.
8. Mountains have an effect on the climate of all the countries of the European region.

Climates of the European Region

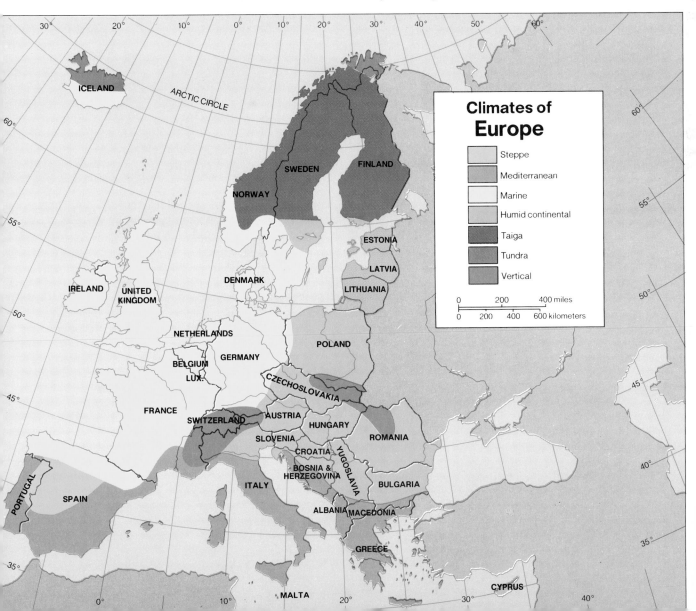

WRITING

Supporting an Opinion

In Chapter 3, you read about the different climates in the European region. In a paragraph, explain in which climate you would prefer to live. Give reasons to support your opinion.

FOLLOW UP

True or False

Tell whether these statements are true or false. The underlined words make the statements true or false. If a statement is false, what words would you place in it to make it true?

1. The rain-bearing winds blow from the east.
2. The North Atlantic Drift is a cold water current.
3. A Mediterranean climate is found on the southern coast of France.
4. Plenty of rain and mild winter temperatures are found in a marine climate.
5. Lands of the "midnight sun" have a winter in which there is almost continuous sunlight.
6. The northern countries have a short growing season.

Growth of Modern Europe

How have the people of Europe changed the world?

READING FOR A PURPOSE:
1. How did lands ruled by different lords become a nation under one ruler?
2. How did European nations benefit from the period of exploration?
3. How did the revolutions in industry and science increase the power of European nations?

1. The lands around the Mediterranean Sea were once part of the great Roman Empire. Even before this huge and powerful empire broke up, people settled wherever there was a good piece of farmland. Later, when Roman rule was replaced by *feudalism*, these settlements were called *manors*. Under feudalism, a lord controlled the life of the manor from his castle. *Serfs* worked for the lord. They lived on the crops they raised on the land. They gave part of their crops to the lord in return for the protection he gave them. These farmers were not free to come and go as they pleased, but had to stay on the land where they were born.

2. In time, this way of life changed. As people began to travel and meet other people, trade began and cities grew. The growth of the cities helped to weaken the power of the lords. Sometimes, the people in the cities paid the feudal lord for their freedom. Some lords became stronger than others. Wars were fought for control of a large territory. The stronger lords began to call themselves princes or kings. This was the beginning of what became European nations.

3. Countries like France and England were brought together by strong lords. The people who lived in the territory of a strong lord, or king or queen, came to think of themselves as part of the ruler's "kingdom"—the ruler's nation. At the beginning, this feeling of belonging to a nation was weak. By the end of the 19th century, it had become very strong. The feeling of belonging to a nation, and of having pride in that nation, is known as *nationalism.*

4. One of the reasons for the development of strong nations was the great period of exploration and discovery. After Columbus made his famous voyage, France, Holland, England, Spain, and Portugal all sent explorers to every corner of the world. The coasts of Africa, the Asian region, and the islands of the Pacific region were explored. Because of these voyages, Europe became rich from the gold, silver, furs, and foods found in these lands.

Bruges (in what is now Belgium) was an important trading and financial center by the 1300s. The city was a center of the cloth industry. Merchants bought their wool from England. Today, Bruges is still a trading center with canals that connect it with the North Sea.

5. As a result of these and later travels, the lives of millions of people in the New World, Africa, Asia, and Australia were changed. People from Europe made settlements in the Americas and Australia. In the past 400 years, millions of Europeans have moved to these areas. The European nations set up trading posts along the coasts of Africa to supply the New World with slaves. The traffic in slaves uprooted the African world for 300 years. In the islands of the Pacific region, Europeans set up plantations to get more of the products they wanted.

6. At the same time there was a great religious change in Europe. Some rulers and

Galileo built a telescope in 1609. He discovered that the moon shines with reflected light and has mountains. He also discovered some of the moons of Jupiter and was the first to see sunspots.

princes who were Roman Catholic changed their religion. In the 16th and 17th centuries, new churches were started. Because these new Christian churches were started in protest against some of the teachings of the Roman Catholic Church, they were called *Protestant.* Martin Luther of Germany was one of the leaders of this Protestant movement.

7. While some people learned more about the land and waters of our earth, others studied the heavens. In 1543, Copernicus of Poland stated that the earth revolved around the sun. For thousands of years people had believed the opposite. They had believed that they were the center of the whole universe. Now Copernicus said that they were wrong. Others looked at the stars and developed new instruments for the study of *astronomy.* People like Galileo and Sir Isaac Newton tested or experimented with such new ideas as gravity. Many facts concerning the world were discovered. This was the beginning of modern science.

8. The advances in science led also to the Industrial Revolution. This great change from handmade to machine-made goods began in the United Kingdom (Great Britain) during the early 1700s. It began with the making of cloth. New machines for spinning and weaving cloth were invented. Goods could be made faster by machine, so they became cheaper. Factories grew and people moved near them to get jobs. Cities grew where there were sources of power to run the machines. At first, machines were run by waterpower. Then the coal-fed steam engine was invented. In it, coal was burned to heat the water to make the steam for power. The steam engine caused a change in methods of manufacturing and transportation. The United Kingdom (Great Britain), where the steam engine and other machines were invented, soon became the first great industrial nation. Its ships carried goods from its factories to people all over the world.

9. At the same time, a different kind of revolution was taking place in France. In 1789, the people of France rose against the

An English textile mill, 1834. Most of the workers in the early factories were women and children. How did the Industrial Revolution change people's lives?

undemocratic government of their king. The new government divided the large estates of the nobility among the peasants. A few years before, in 1776, there had been a revolution in North America out of which the United States was formed. Both the American and French revolutions were part of what is called the Democratic Revolution. Before these revolutions, most people had few rights. The desire of people to be treated equally was one of the

The French Revolution began in 1789 with the storming of the Bastille, a prison. The new government executed the king and queen in 1793.

causes of the revolution. The Democratic Revolution is still going on today. It is based on the desire of all people for the right to "life, liberty, and the pursuit of happiness."

10. The Industrial Revolution spread to other countries of Europe and also to the United States. The machines proved to be "hungry." No one country seemed to have all the resources it needed to feed the machines. Then, too, the goods had to be sold. So industrial nations began to look for materials and markets in other parts of the world. Africa and Asia proved to be areas where the nations of Europe could find the materials they needed. In the 18th and 19th centuries, European countries took control of some of these lands. This development was called *imperialism* or *colonialism.*

11. It was bound to happen that in the race for colonies, one nation would desire the territory another country wanted. Wars over colonies became frequent. Large armies and navies were built. Finally, in the 20th century, two great world wars were fought. Much of the fighting was on the European continent. The great worldwide power of the Western European nations was broken. One by one, both winners and losers gave up their colonies. The United States and the Soviet Union became the most powerful nations in the world.

12. In 1945, after World War II, the United States tried to help the nations of Europe recover from the damages of war. Secretary of State George Marshall announced his plan to lend money to the nations of Europe. The Marshall Plan restored farmlands and rebuilt railroads and factories in Europe. In a few years, the factories and mills of Western Europe were busy again. In 1949, the United States, Canada, and some of the countries of Western Europe formed NATO, the North Atlantic Treaty Organization. These nations agreed to help each other in case of attack. The nations of Western Europe also learned another lesson. They found out that only by working together could they achieve the best life for their people. They set up the European Community (EC). Through the EC (sometimes called the Common Market), they began to cooperate with each other. They began supplying needed raw materials and products to each other without charging any *customs duties.* (Custom duties are a tax charged on goods crossing borders from one country to another.) By this and other means, EC member nations have built up their industries, their trade, and their standard of living.

UNDERSTANDING WHAT YOU HAVE READ

1. Which questions are answered in this chapter?

a. Why did Western Europe want colonies?
b. Who was Adolf Hitler?
c. How did the nations of Europe become rich after 1492?

2. The main idea of this chapter describes how

a. the Marshall Plan helped to restore Europe
b. Europe has influenced the history of the world
c. changes in science began

3. One of the leaders of the early Protestants was

a. Martin Luther
b. Muhammad
c. Copernicus

4. The Industrial Revolution began in

a. the Soviet Union
b. France
c. the United Kingdom

5. In 1789, one of the causes of the French Revolution was that
a. the king of France wanted to explore in America
b. people did not have religious freedom
c. the people of France wanted some rights

6. In the 19th century, one of the most important reasons why European nations wanted colonies was the need for
a. raw materials for factories
b. large armies and navies
c. spreading the idea of equality throughout the world

7. Under *feudalism*, wealth was measured in
a. factory-made goods   b. land   c. waterpower

8. When a country obtains colonies as a source of raw materials, this is known as
a. imperialism   b. feudalism   c. liberalism

9. Member nations of the European Community are sometimes called
a. NATO members
b. the Common Market countries
c. the Roman Empire

DEVELOPING CRITICAL THINKING SKILLS

Making Inferences

Which of the following are inferences you can make based on the information in this chapter?

1. Serfs under feudalism had few rights.
2. Many people in Germany today are members of Protestant churches.
3. Advances in scientific knowledge led to inventions that changed the way goods were produced.
4. All revolutions result in violence and bloodshed.
5. Before the invention of the steam engine, wind and water were among the chief sources of power.
6. Most of the raw materials—especially cotton and silk—that nations wanted for their textile mills were found in Europe.
7. European nations were fortunate because their lands suffered little damage during two world wars.

DEVELOPING IDEAS AND SKILLS

Reading a Time Line

Look at the time line. Write the letter of the period in which you would place each of the following events.

A	B	C	D	E
1500	1600	1700	1800	1900	2000

1. NATO is formed.
2. The French Revolution takes place.
3. Galileo builds a telescope.
4. The World Wars are fought.

5. The American Revolution takes place.
6. Copernicus states that the earth revolves around the sun.
7. The Industrial Revolution begins.

Reviewing Chapter 4 —— Which Does Not Belong?

In each group, select the item that does not belong with the others.

1. Feudalism
   a. Wealth is gained through buying and selling.
   b. Serfs work the land.
   c. Lords protect the serfs.

2. Colonialism
   a. Weaker lands are occupied by stronger nations.
   b. African people have self-government again.
   c. Powerful nations control raw materials.

3. Industrial Revolution
   a. Growth of cities takes place.
   b. New sources of power are found.
   c. Greater use of hand labor is made.

4. Democratic Revolution
   a. More people can vote.
   b. New constitutions are written.
   c. Fewer newspapers are printed.

5. Revolution in Science
   a. New ideas are tested.
   b. The sun revolves around the earth.
   c. New inventions are made.

6. Protestant Reformation
   a. Roman Catholic religion spreads throughout Europe.
   b. New Christian churches are formed.
   c. Martin Luther announces his beliefs.

7. 20th-Century Wars
   a. There is great loss of life and property.
   b. European nations grow in strength.
   c. United States and Soviet Union become leading powers in the world.

8. Plans for Recovery of Europe after World Wars
   a. NATO is organized.
   b. Marshall Plan is put into effect.
   c. Industrial Revolution begins.

Chapter 5

The People of Europe

Who are the people of the European region?

READING FOR A PURPOSE:
1. How is the life of Western Europeans like that of people in Northern America?
2. What are the various languages and religions of the people of Europe?
3. What systems of government do European countries have?

1. The European region is the smallest of all the regions in our study, but it is one of the most heavily populated. About 502 million people live there. This is more than in Northern America or in Latin America. Only in the Asian region are people almost as crowded together. In the Netherlands, there are 1,000 people for each square mile of land. In Belgium, there are 842. In Germany, there are 577; and in the United Kingdom, there are 601. By comparison, the United States has only 70 people per square mile. Only in Scandinavia, where the winters are cold, are there large areas of few people.

2. Because of the large population, there is very little empty land in the crowded European region. Europeans try to make use of all the parts of their land. Throughout Europe, swamps have been drained and soil has been improved by careful fertilizing. In the Netherlands, the people have built dikes, pumped out sea water, and added thousands of new acres of rich soil to their country.

3. Most of the people (seven out of ten) live in or near large cities. By the mid-1980s, about 90 percent of the people of the United Kingdom lived in cities. In Germany, about 85 percent of the people live in cities. Millions of people work in factories making goods that are sold all over the world. The workers of Western Europe are highly skilled. Even before the beginning of factories and the use of machines, the people of Western Europe were making goods to sell. Others work in offices, warehouses, and docks, preparing goods for shipment to distant parts of the world. In most of Eastern Europe, there are similar kinds of jobs for those who live in the cities. Today, many factories and industries

Paris, France. About three-fourths of the French people live in towns and cities. The same is true for the United States and Canada. In what ways is this scene like those in Northern America? What are some differences?

Rowing, sailing, and swimming are popular sports in Germany. So are skiing, hiking, and bicycling. The most popular sport is soccer. How does the climate of a region affect the sports its people play?

that used to be owned by the government are now owned privately.

4. In many ways, the life of the people of Western Europe is like that of the people of the United States and Canada. The standard of living is high. Western Europeans eat and dress much as Northern Americans do. Potatoes, cheese, milk, butter, and bread are important to their diet. They eat more fish and less meat, though, than Northern Americans do. Automobiles, telephones, radios, and television sets are a part of their daily lives. The standard of living in most of Eastern Europe is not as high as that in Western Europe. Still, people there have a higher standard of living than do most of the world's people.

5. Education is important to Europeans, and so all children attend school. In most countries of Western Europe, 99 percent or more of the adults are *literate*—that is, able to read and write. This percentage is as high as that in the United States. In Eastern Europe, the literacy rate in most countries is also high. The people of Europe are great readers. More books and magazines are printed in Western Europe than in any other region in the world, including Northern America.

6. The health care of most Europeans is very good. There are modern hospitals served by well-trained doctors and nurses. Government support of medical services is common in Western Europe. This means that both the poor and rich may enjoy good health care. In Eastern Europe, medical services are run by the government.

7. Many different languages are spoken in this region. Most of the languages come from three main sources. The *Romance* languages come from Latin. These are the languages of France, Spain, Portugal, Italy, and parts of Belgium and Switzerland. (Different languages may be spoken within the same country. In Switzerland, French, Italian, German, and Romansh are each spoken in different areas.) After the fall of Rome, many German tribes occupied different parts of Europe. They left their *Germanic* languages in such countries as Germany, Austria, Luxembourg, parts of Switzerland and Belgium, the Netherlands, the United Kingdom, Iceland, and Scandinavia. The *Slavic* languages are spoken in Poland, Czechoslovakia, Yugoslavia, and Bulgaria. The Romanian language is a Romance language with many Slavic words. Albanian, Finnish, and Hungarian do not belong to the three main European language groups.

8. There are many different religions in Europe, but most of the people are Christians. The Christians are divided into three main groups: *Roman Catholics, Protestants,* and members of the *Eastern Orthodox* churches. Italy, France, Ireland, Spain, Portugal, southern Germany, Poland, Austria, Hungary, much of Czechoslovakia, and parts of Switzerland, Belgium, and Yugoslavia are largely Roman Catholic. Northern Germany, Denmark, Iceland, Sweden, Norway, Finland, the Netherlands, the United Kingdom, and parts of Switzerland and Belgium are largely Protestant. Greece, Bulgaria, Romania, and much of Yugoslavia are largely Eastern Orthodox. In 1967, the government of Albania outlawed all religions. At that time, most of the people were Muslims. For about 2,000 years, many Jewish people lived in Europe. But during the rule of Adolf Hitler in Germany, millions of Jews were killed. Thousands have since moved to Israel and the United States.

9. The countries in Western Europe have democratic governments. The laws are made by representatives of the people. In these nations the people enjoy the same freedoms as Americans and Canadians—freedom of speech, religion, and the press. Although kings and queens still "rule" such nations as the United Kingdom, Norway, Sweden, Denmark, Spain, and Belgium, they have little or no real power.

10. The *parliamentary* form of government is most common among the nations of Western Europe. In such a government there are two lawmaking bodies, but one "house" has most of the power. (In the United States, both house of Congress have great power.) European countries may have presidents, but, except for France, these presidents have little power. The chief officer is the prime minister. The prime minister and the cabinet are the real leaders of the government. In most of these governments the prime minister and the cabinet are members of the parliament. They take part in passing and carrying out laws. (Canada has this type of government. In the United States, there is a separation of the powers held by the president and Congress.)

11. The Communist governments in Eastern Europe did not meet the needs of the people. Therefore, in 1989, the governments of Eastern Europe collapsed. However, the road from communism to capitalism and democracy in Eastern Europe was not without troubles. Since the Eastern European governments do not have a tradition of democracy, the new governments of these countries do not always know how to govern democratically.

The Swedish government provides free dental care for children and low-cost care for adults. High taxes help pay for many programs including free college education. The Swedish people have one of the highest standards of living in the world.

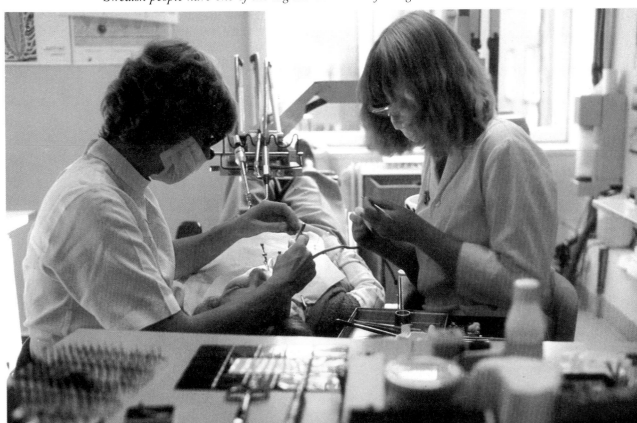

UNDERSTANDING WHAT YOU HAVE READ

1. Which questions are answered in this chapter?

a. What do the people of Western Europe eat?

b. What are the most crowded countries of the European region?

c. Who is the ruler of Spain?

2. The main idea of *paragraph 3* describes

a. the kinds of work in European cities

b. how Western Europeans use machines

c. the importance of trade in the life of the people

3. The religion to which most of the people of the European region belong is

a. Christianity   b. Judaism   c. Islam

4. Dikes have been built to reclaim land in

a. France   b. the Netherlands   c. Norway

5. In which country would you be most likely to hear a *Romance* language spoken?

a. Germany   b. Portugal   c. Austria

6. The people of Europe must use their farmland wisely because

a. there is little fertile land

b. there is a need to feed a large population

c. the soil can easily be washed down the steep mountainsides

7. The nations of Western Europe

a. have parliamentary governments

b. are ruled by kings or queens

c. are governed by dictators

8. This chapter discusses which of the following?

a. Europeans are chiefly farmers

b. Western Europe has a high standard of living

c. the people work hard and are highly skilled

9. In the last sentence of paragraph 10, the term *separation of powers* means that

a. the president and Congress have different powers

b. the U.S. president has more power than Congress

c. the president and Congress have the same powers

10. The countries of Eastern Europe had

a. freedom of speech

b. only one political party to control the nation's government

c. democratic governments

DEVELOPING IDEAS AND SKILLS

Understanding Pictographs——Population, Area, and Standard of Living of the European Region

Study the pictograph on page 263. Then answer these questions.

1. Is the standard of living of this region high or low when compared with that of the United States?
2. Is the region more or less crowded than the United States?
3. Are the people of this region literate compared with the people of the United States?
4. How long may the average person in this region expect to live?
5. What facts tell you the standard of living of the people of the region?
6. How does this region compare with the United States in size?

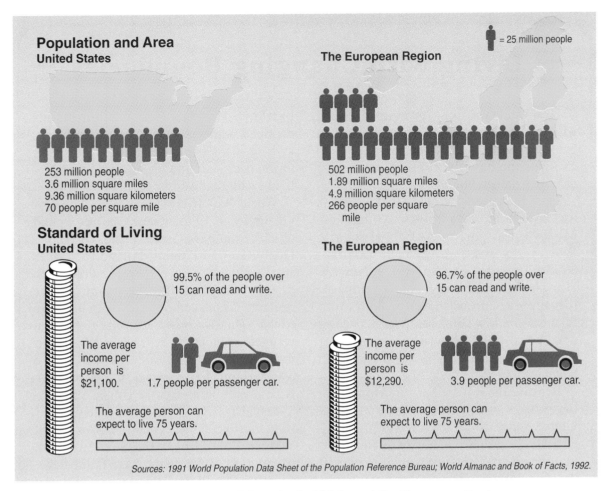

Population and Area
United States

253 million people
3.6 million square miles
9.36 million square kilometers
70 people per square mile

The European Region

= 25 million people

502 million people
1.89 million square miles
4.9 million square kilometers
266 people per square mile

Standard of Living
United States

99.5% of the people over 15 can read and write.

The average income per person is $21,100.

1.7 people per passenger car.

The average person can expect to live 75 years.

The European Region

96.7% of the people over 15 can read and write.

The average income per person is $12,290.

3.9 people per passenger car.

The average person can expect to live 75 years.

Sources: 1991 World Population Data Sheet of the Population Reference Bureau; World Almanac and Book of Facts, 1992.

Population, Area, and Standard of Living of the European Region

DEVELOPING CRITICAL THINKING SKILLS

Do You Agree or Disagree?—— Give reasons for your answers.

1. The European region is small in size and population.
2. The farmlands of Western Europe cover a vast area, much like the midwestern states of the United States.
3. The health standards of Western Europeans are probably very high.
4. Most people in the European region live and work in cities.
5. The religions of the people of Europe are much like the religions of the people of the United States.
6. The prime minister of the United Kingdom and the president of the United States have the same powers.
7. The languages spoken in most of Eastern Europe are Romance languages.

FOLLOW UP

Some of the largest cities in the world are located in Western Europe. Many are at the center of large *metropolitan areas*. (A metropolitan area is a city plus the smaller towns surrounding it.) As you read, think about the kinds of problems and benefits that are presented by the growth of big cities.

— Living with Changing Boundaries —

How would you like to grow up in a place where your country's name and boundaries change every few years? The people of Eastern Europe have learned to cope with changing names, boundaries, and rulers.

Take the case of Victor Horky. Victor was born in Moravia in 1900. At that time Moravia was part of Austria-Hungary. When Victor was 15 years old, he was drafted into the army and fought for Austria-Hungary in World War I. Austria-Hungary lost the war and was later broken up to form several new countries. Victor's village and the rest of Moravia became part of Czechoslovakia. Czechoslovakia came into being in 1918.

Because times were hard in Moravia in the 1920s, Victor decided to emigrate to the United States. From the safety of the United States he watched in horror as Nazi Germany overran Czechoslovakia in 1939 at the start of World War II. Many of Victor's relatives in Moravia died in the war.

In 1949, Victor tried to visit his village in Moravia. However, Communists loyal to the Soviet Union had taken over the countries of Eastern Europe at the end of World War II. The Communist rulers would not allow Victor to cross the "Iron Curtain" to visit Czechoslovakia. Communists ruled Czechoslovakia until the people rebelled and regained their freedom in 1990. By 1990, however, Victor was 90 years old and too feeble to travel. He died in 1992 without ever seeing his homeland again.

Look, too, at events in the life of Karl Kretschmer. Karl was born in Germany on the east bank of the Oder River in 1932. He was seven years old in 1939 when his father was drafted into the German army to fight in World War II. Karl's father was killed in battle in 1941. In 1944, Allied planes dropped bombs on the Kretschmer home, killing Karl's mother and two sisters. Orphaned, Karl and his brother Fritz went to live with relatives.

World War II ended with the defeat of Germany in 1945. Peace treaties signed after the war gave German lands east of the Oder River to Poland. Poland took over Karl's village. Karl and Fritz, along with nearly 2 million other Germans, were declared "displaced persons" with nowhere to live. The two boys received offers from refugee agencies to resettle in West Germany. Instead, they decided to flee to Switzerland. Fritz stayed in Switzerland. Karl later emigrated to the United States.

David and Rose Yashpeh are Jews. They were married in 1929 and lived in an area of eastern Poland near the Soviet border, where most of the people were Polish Jews. Life for David and Rose was shattered when Nazi Germany conquered Poland in 1939 at the start of World War II. The young couple joined the resistance movement and worked to save East European Jews from being sent to concentration camps.

After World War II, lands in eastern Poland, where David and Rose lived, were taken by the Soviet Union. Poles were ordered to move west and settle lands that Poland had taken from defeated Germany. David and Rose moved to Israel.

1. Moravia is now a part of what country?
2. What are two historical events that changed the political geography of Eastern Europe during the mid to late 1900s?
3. Why do you think this area has had so many boundary changes?

Chapter 6

Western Europe— A Workshop of the World

Why is Western Europe a great industrial area?

READING FOR A PURPOSE:
1. How does Western Europe supply power for its industries?
2. What transportation facilities have helped develop industries in Western Europe?
3. Where are Western Europe's steel manufacturing centers?

1. Western Europe is one of the world's workshops. Many raw materials for manufacturing are found in the countries of this region. What they do not have, they import from all over the world. Their factories turn these raw materials into steel, machinery, textiles, and chemicals. Great ships carry these goods to markets everywhere. With the profit from the sale of manufactured goods, Western Europe can pay for the the fuel, raw materials, and food needed by its large population.

2. There are many reasons why industry became so important in Western Europe. This group of nations had an early start. The Industrial Revolution began in Great Britain. The first modern machines and factories were built by the British. By the early 1800s, the use of machines and the factory system had spread across Western Europe. Only in the 20th century did the change from human-made to machine-made goods become important in the Soviet Union, India, China, and Africa.

3. The people of Western Europe are highly skilled. For a long time, Europeans made things to sell at home or in small shops. When the first factories were started, these skilled people were then able to work at the new machines.

4. Western Europe is rich in the sources of power for factories. Western Europe mines about 10 percent of the world's coal. Waterpower is plentiful. France and Italy are two of the countries that make important use of it: Oil is the chief source of energy. Much of it must be imported. Leading industrial nations, such as Germany and France, depend upon Middle Eastern countries for half their supply of oil. However, the United Kingdom and Norway are becoming major world oil producers. Giant oil rigs drill for oil in the

In the 1600s and 1700s, the city of Delft in The Netherlands became famous for its pottery. Delftware began when local craftspeople copied Chinese porcelain. How is delftware an example of cultural mingling?

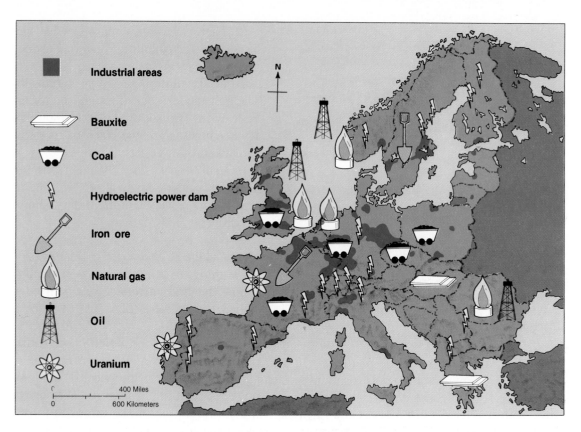

Mining and Industry in the European Region

North Sea. The Netherlands produces huge amounts of natural gas. But much of Western Europe's natural gas is imported, some from Russia. Nuclear power is important in Italy, France, Belgium, the United Kingdom, and Germany.

5. There are great amounts of coal and iron in the region for making steel. Although most countries in Western Europe have some coal or iron ore, the main iron-ore mining areas are in France and Sweden. The main coal mining areas are in the United Kingdom and Germany. One of the richest coal and iron areas is a small triangle of land that includes Belgium, the northern part of France and the southwestern part of Germany.

6. Western Europe has an excellent transportation system. This region is like a spider's web of rivers, canals, highways, and railroads. The chief rivers for trade—the Rhine, the Rhone, and the Elbe—are connected by canals. It is therefore possible to carry goods

Many Western Europeans are skilled factory workers. Others have trained for jobs in the region's businesses, banks, offices, and schools.

easily to any inland city or seaport in this region. Moreover, Western Europe's long, irregular coastline provides many ports. Oceangoing ships can pick up Western Europe's products close to where they are made or grown.

7. There is another reason for Western Europe's early industrial development. Whatever these nations did not have, they could get from their colonies. For example, Western Europe has little cotton, no rubber, and—until recently—little oil. But the United Kingdom, France, Germany, the Netherlands, and Belgium used to have great colonies in far-off lands. They depended on their colonies to supply the raw materials they needed for their factories. Moreover, profit from this trade gave the Western Europeans money to build more factories. It also helped to supply them with machinery and equipment.

8. Workers from the northeastern United States feel at home when they visit the great cities of Western Europe. This is because the making of steel and mining are among the chief industries. There are several main centers of steel manufacture in this region. These include Italy, the United Kingdom, Spain, and the area of the continent known as the Vital Triangle. Italy has more than doubled its steel production since the mid-1960s. Italy imports the coal and iron ore needed to make steel. The United Kingdom's iron and steel district is located in the Midlands in Central England. Birmingham and Sheffield are two of the great steel cities. But many of the United Kingdom's steel plants are old. By the mid-1980s, that country was making only about half the steel it made in 1970. In the 1960s and 1970s, Spain's new steel industry grew rapidly.

9. The Vital Triangle, continental Europe's most famous steel area, includes the Lorraine Valley of northern France, parts of Belgium and Luxembourg, and the Ruhr and Saar basins of Germany. Here the iron ore deposits and the coal mines are close to each other. There are many rivers, canals, and railroads within the Triangle. They connect the iron ore, coal, and steel centers with the nearby seaports. These steel mills with their huge furnaces and smokestacks supply steel not only to Europe, but also to the rest of the world.

10. Europe's factories make use of this steel to produce many goods. Machine tools, electrical equipment, farm machinery, ships, barges, airplanes, and automobiles are only a few of the products. In addition, there are electronics, textile, aerospace, and chemical industries. All of these goods are carried to world markets by Western European ships. These many products tell the story of Europe's leadership in manufacturing.

In most Western European countries, more than half the workers have jobs in services, not in farming or manufacturing. Service jobs include work in repair shops, banks, schools, hospitals, offices, and stores. Why do such a large number of Western Europeans work in services?

UNDERSTANDING WHAT YOU HAVE READ

1. Which questions are answered in the chapter?

a. What is the Vital Triangle?

b. Why is the region of Western Europe a leader in manufacturing?

c. How is steel made?

2. The main idea of this chapter describes

a. how Western Europe makes use of its resources

b. the chief industries of Western Europe

c. why Western Europe's workers are skillful

3. One of Western Europe's chief industries is the making of

a. steel

b. paper and paper products

c. food products

4. Western Europe is called a "workshop of the world" because this region

a. turns raw materials into finished goods

b. makes nearly everything by hand

c. ships goods to all parts of the world

5. The chief source of power in Western Europe is

a. oil   b. natural gas   c. coal

6. The Ruhr Valley became a center of industry because

a. rich coal mines are located there

b. it has good transportation

c. farmland is too poor and thus, people have moved to the cities to live

7. In paragraph 6, the term "a spider's web of rivers" means that

a. ships rush back and forth over many great waterways in the region

b. rivers bring goods far inland

c. the rivers seem to flow out in all directions

8. In paragraph 10, "chemical industries" might include the manufacture of

a. cotton goods

b. light bulbs

c. fertilizer

DEVELOPING IDEAS AND SKILLS

Building Map Skills — The Vital Triangle

Study the map of the Vital Triangle on page 269. Then answer the following questions.

1. Which countries are located in the area called the Vital Triangle?
2. (a) Which countries have great deposits of iron ore?
   (b) Which have great deposits of coal?
3. (a) Which cities are located on the Rhine River?
   (b) Which city is located near the Saar Coal field?
   (c) Which cities are located in the Lorraine Iron District?
4. Based on your reading, name two industries that are affected by steel production in the Vital Triangle.
5. Explain the importance of rivers to the economy of the Vital Triangle.

REVIEWING AND WRITING

Making Outlines — Manufacturing in Western Europe

Use these three headings to make an *outline* of the industries of this region. From what you have read, enter three statements under each heading.

A. Reasons for the Growth of Industry
B. Resources of Western Europe
C. How Europe's Resources Are Used

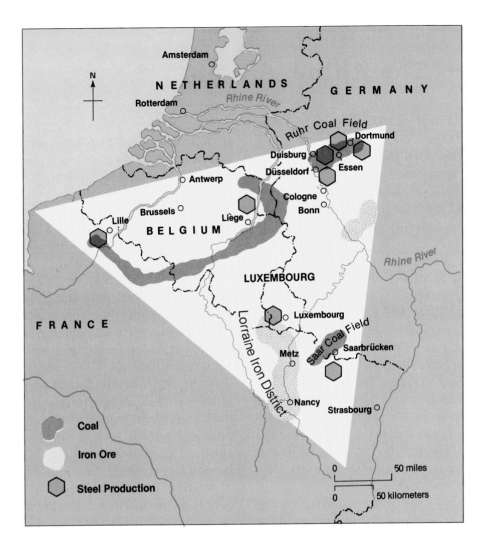

The Vital Triangle

SUMMING UP

True or False

Tell whether these statements are true or false. The underlined words make the statements true or false. If a statement is false, which word or words would you replace the underlined word with to make it true?

1. The Vital Triangle is an important area of <u>steel</u> manufacturing.
2. Western Europe grows little <u>cotton</u>.
3. Norway and the United Kingdom have important oil wells in the <u>Baltic Sea</u>.
4. One of the mining areas of the Vital Triangle is located in <u>Sweden</u>.
5. Most manufactured goods in Western Europe are made from <u>copper</u>.
6. The Industrial Revolution had its start in <u>Great Britain</u>.
7. The United Kingdom's great manufacturing district is located <u>along the northeastern coast</u>.
8. Since the 1960s, Spain and Italy have become important <u>steel</u> producers.

269

The Rhine: A Polluted River

More than 100 years ago, the poet Henry Wadsworth Longfellow described the Rhine in the following words:

O, the pride of the German heart is this noble river! And right it is; for of all the rivers of this beautiful earth there is none so beautiful as this.

Today, however, the once-beautiful Rhine has become polluted with dirt and deadly chemicals.

A Great River The Rhine and its tributaries form a water highway that stretches from the heart of Western Europe all the way to the North Sea. More ships travel on the Rhine every year than on any other waterway in the world. Even so, the river is used for more than shipping and transportation. It provides drinking water for the millions of people who live along its banks. It gives pleasure to thousands more who swim, fish, and boat in its waters.

Pollutants Unfortunately, however, the Rhine also serves as a dumping ground for nearby factories, farms, and cities. In addition to polluting the water, harmful substances dumped into the river cause other serious problems.

Bacteria and other disease-carrying organisms enter the water along with sewage, soil, and fertilizer that has been washed away from nearby farms. The bacteria use up the oxygen that is dissolved in the water. As you probably know, fish and plants need oxygen to survive. Without it, they will die. As a result, great numbers of plants and sea creatures have perished in the polluted waters of the Rhine. Cities that use the river for drinking water have to treat it with strong chemicals such as chlorine before it is safe to drink.

Metals that tend to build up on the river's floor are another serious pollutant. Mercury is especially destructive. It damages the nervous systems of many kinds of fish, which in turn harm the people and wildlife that eat the contaminated fish.

Poisonous chemicals also pollute parts of the Rhine. Although the dumping of waste materials is now forbidden, accidental spills sometimes happen. For example, in 1986 a fire in a chemical factory in Basel, Switzerland, sent out clouds of foul-smelling smoke over the city. The fire also caused millions of gallons of deadly chemicals to pour into the Rhine. Great numbers of fish died in the poisoned waters. As you can imagine, the chemical spill caused problems in areas far beyond Switzerland.

International Cooperation How are the people of the world meeting the challenge of cleaning up the Rhine? In 1963, Switzerland, France, Germany, the Netherlands, and Luxembourg formed the International Commission of the Rhine (ICR) to fight the problems of pollution. Since that time, the commission agreed to limit dumping of pollutants into the river. Fortunately, these agreements have significantly reduced the amounts of untreated sewage, chemicals, and metals from their 1970 levels.

What pollutants are present in rivers near you? What is being done to reduce them? Why should you be concerned about pollutants in U.S. rivers?

Chapter 7

Their Farms Are Their Gardens

How do the Western European farmers use their land?

READING FOR A PURPOSE:
1. Why do farmers of Western Europe produce such a high *yield* from their farms?
2. Why is dairying an important occupation in Western Europe?
3. How is farming in Scandinavia different from farming in the Mediterranean region?

1. The skill of the European farmer matches the skill of the worker in Europe's factories. But in most of the Western European nations, only a small part of the population works on farms. By the mid-1980s, about two in five workers in Ireland worked in agriculture. In the rest of the British Isles and the northern and western parts of Europe, an even smaller percentage of workers worked on farms. In the United Kingdom, Germany, Belgium, France, and the Netherlands, not even two workers in ten were farmers.

2. Most farmers in Western Europe own their own land. The average size of a farm is about 42 acres. (That is only one-tenth the size of the average American farm.) Most of the farmers do not work for others. They live in villages near the fields. Farmers work their small plots with great care. That is why we often say that their farms are their gardens. They care for their land as much as Americans and Canadians might care for their garden crops. Because most farms are small, most of the work used to be done by hand or by animal labor. However, in the northern and western parts of Europe, farmers now use modern farm machinery.

3. Because great care is given to the land, an acre will provide a greater *yield,* or amount of crop, than in other regions. Western European farmers raise more wheat on an acre of land than American farmers do. Because there is a shortage of good farmland, every acre that can possibly be farmed is farmed. In the Netherlands, much land has been reclaimed from the flooding sea. The great dikes that hold back the Atlantic Ocean have given the Netherlands farmers a large area of fertile soil that they could not otherwise have had.

4. Science, hard work, and experience have

The farmers near Bordeaux, France, grow grapes for the area's famous red and white wines.

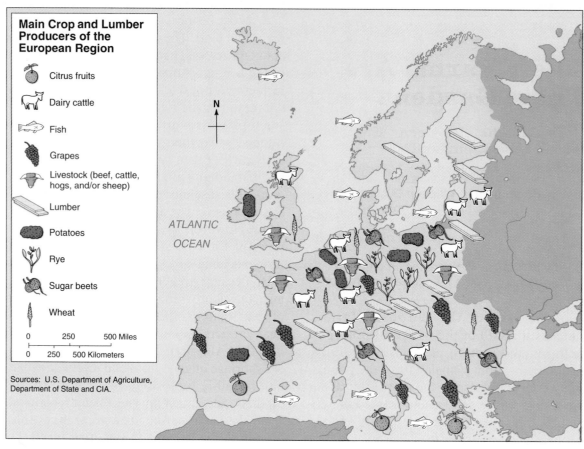

Main Crop and Lumber Producers of the European Region

- Citrus fruits
- Dairy cattle
- Fish
- Grapes
- Livestock (beef, cattle, hogs, and/or sheep)
- Lumber
- Potatoes
- Rye
- Sugar beets
- Wheat

0   250   500 Miles
0   250   500 Kilometers

Sources: U.S. Department of Agriculture, Department of State and CIA.

ATLANTIC OCEAN

N

A variety of crops and livestock are raised in the European region. The lumber industry is also an important part of the economy throughout the region. In which European region are citrus fruits grown?

also helped the farmers of Western Europe to grow large amounts of food. They *rotate,* or change, their crops from year to year. They use fertilizer to enrich the soil. They cultivate the land carefully. They plant crops that grow best in a marine climate. Vegetables are grown in most of the countries. Root crops like potatoes, sugar beets, and turnips are among the chief crops. They are rotated with wheat, rye, and barley. France is one of the world's leading wheat growers. It is also the leading Western European producer of sugar beets, rye, and barley. Wine grapes are a major crop in France, Italy, and Germany.

5. Marine Europe is also one of the great dairying regions of the world. The cool, wet summers provide grass for pasture. The mild winters mean that there is grass for the ani-

mals throughout the year. Oats, hay, and sugar beets are also used as food crops for the animals. As a result, many countries have important dairy industries in which cows are raised for milk, butter, and cheese. France, Germany, the United Kingdom, Denmark, and the Netherlands are leaders in this area. Switzerland is an example of the good use of mountain land. Despite its mountains, much of the land is used for crops or pasture for cattle, sheep, and goats. (Where grass is plentiful and land is flat, cattle are raised. Sheep are found in areas of shorter grass and hillier land. Where grass is thinnest and land is very rugged or mountainous, the hardier and more surefooted goats are raised. Goat's milk and goat cheese are very popular in many parts of Europe.)

6. Many European farmers raise beef cattle, hogs, chickens, and sheep. France and Germany are leading raisers of beef cattle. The United Kingdom and Spain raise sheep in especially large numbers. The United Kingdom alone has almost as many sheep as the United States. The sheep supply both wool and meat for the people.

7. As a whole, Western Europe is one of the world's largest food producers. It supplies most of the food its people consume. However, it still imports coffee, tea, cocoa, cane sugar, bananas, and many other foods from other regions of the world.

8. Many European farmers have joined together to form *cooperatives*. These are organizations of farmers who agree to sell their farm crops together. A cooperative sells all the crops at a certain price. Each farmer who is a member of the cooperative shares in the costs and the profits. The cooperatives also buy goods in large quantities to supply cheaply the farmers' needs for fertilizers, feed, tools, and clothing. By buying in large amounts, the farmers can save money. In the Scandinavian countries, for example, almost all farmers belong to cooperatives.

9. In two of the countries of Southern Europe—Portugal and Greece—slightly less than one-third of the workers are farmers. Farming here, and in Spain and Italy, is different from that of marine Europe. There is little rainfall during the summer. Much of the land is rough and hilly. Because of this, the Mediterranean farmer has a harder time raising enough to feed the people in the region.

10. The income of the average farm family along the Mediterranean is now improving. Large farms were divided and land was provided for many farmers. Aid has been given to farmers in member countries of the European Community. The farmers of the Mediterranean are also "gardeners." They cultivate their small plots of ground very carefully. Many of the farmers do not use the modern farm machinery common in the northern and western parts of Europe. The farms are usually small and there is not enough good farmland. Yet some crops are grown for the market.

11. The farmers of Southern Europe have learned how to farm the steep hillsides. At sea level they grow citrus fruits, if there is water from irrigation. In parts of Italy and Portugal, rice is grown. Tomatoes and vegetables are also important. Higher up, they build *terraces,* or steps, on the sides of hills. Terracing creates more usable farmland. The olive trees and grape vines that are planted here do not need much water or very rich soil. Their roots reach far down into the ground for water. (More than any other crop, the olive tree is a sign of the lack of water.) The grapes are grown to produce wine for drinking and cooking and for raisins. Olive oil is used instead of animal fat for cooking. Wheat and vegetables are also planted among the vines and trees. On the

A cheese market in Edam in the Netherlands. What other European nations are noted for their dairy products?

A fisher woman in Portugal. Are most of the leading fishing nations in Southern Europe or Northern Europe?

higher rocky slopes, sheep and goats graze in pastures. In Italy and Spain, beef cattle are raised.

12. The seas of Western Europe are another source of food. Fish are an important part of the diet in lands of the marine climate. Fish and fish oils contain vitamins and other things necessary for good health. The North Sea in particular has many shallow waters and narrow areas. These fishing banks are rich in tiny plant and animal life. The larger fish come here to feed on the plants and smaller animal life in the water. Herring, cod, and mackerel are found here. The leading European fishing nations are Norway, Denmark, Iceland, and Spain. The fishers of Western Europe catch thousands of tons of fish every year. Some is eaten by Europeans, and the rest is sold to other regions of the world.

UNDERSTANDING WHAT YOU HAVE READ

1. Which questions are answered in this chapter?
a. Why does the Northern European farmer use little machinery?
b. How are the hillsides farmed in the region of Southern Europe?
c. What foods are important in the diet of the Western Europeans?

2. The main idea of this chapter describes
a. the importance of fishing
b. how Western Europeans get their food
c. the importance of dairying

3. Important crops of the farms of Western Europe are
a. wheat, sugar beets, and potatoes
b. rice and beans
c. cotton and tea

4. In the Mediterranean countries, farmers face the problem of
a. little rainfall   b. unbearable heat
  c. heavy summer rains

5. Western European farmers are able to raise large crops per acre because
a. dikes are used for irrigation
b. machinery is not widely used
c. fertilizing and crop rotation are practiced

6. Olives, grapes, and wheat are farm products of which of these regions?
a. Italy
b. Ireland
c. Belgium

7. Good farmers *rotate* their crops—that is, they
a. water them daily
b. change them from year to year
c. use minerals to enrich the soil

8. In an agricultural *cooperative,*
a. people work with others on the farm
b. farmers buy and sell goods together
c. people rent machinery to their neighbors

DEVELOPING IDEAS AND SKILLS

Understanding Bar Graphs — Agricultural Production in Western Europe

Study the graphs below. Then answer the following questions.

1. Which Western European nation leads in raising beef cattle?
2. What are the top two fish-catching countries of the region?
3. In which country would you most likely see wheat fields?
4. Is the Netherlands the main milk-producing country of Western Europe? Support your answer with evidence.
5. Which country of the region is the greatest farming country? On what information do you base your answer?
6. Are Norway and Denmark located near the sea? Support your answer with evidence.
7. What does this chart tell you about the land and climate of France and Germany?

Agricultural Production in Western Europe

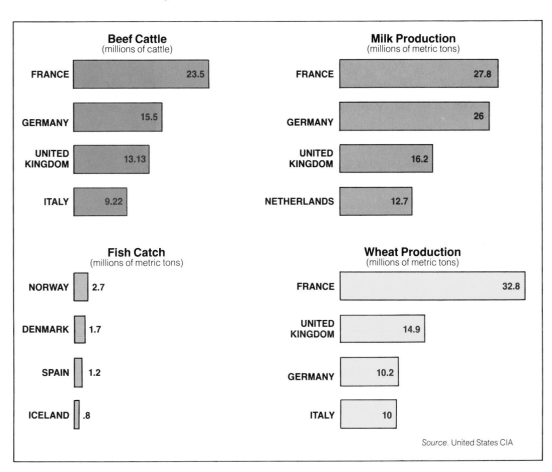

SUMMING UP

Making Charts

Complete the following chart in your notebook.

Farming in Western Europe

	Marine Europe	Southern Europe
1. Climate		
2. Surface of land		
3. Chief crops		
4. Farm animals		
5. Methods of farming		

DEVELOPING CRITICAL THINKING SKILLS

Do You Agree or Disagree?

Decide whether or not each of the following statements agrees with what you have read. If the answer is *disagree,* explain why.

1. Most Western European farmers do not live on their own farms.
2. The skill of the Western European farmer matches the skill of the worker in Western Europe's factories.
3. The countries with a marine climate have a large dairy industry.
4. There are few animals on Western European farms.
5. France is probably better able to provide all the food needs of its people than any other country of Western Europe.
6. The farmers of Western Europe have been slow to join farm cooperatives.
7. The farmers of Southern Europe have learned to farm the hilly lands along the coast.
8. The seas around Western Europe provide much food for the large population.

Chapter 8

Great Centers of Trade

Why does Western Europe need trade with other regions?

READING FOR A PURPOSE:
1. What are Western Europe's major imports and exports?
2. How does Western Europe "balance" its trade?
3. What problems interfered with trade among Western European nations for many years?

A French seaport. Do you live in or near a river port or seaport or have you ever visited one? What kinds of jobs are people likely to have in port cities?

1. Western Europe trades with many regions of the world. It imports raw materials and minerals to feed the "hungry" machines of its industries. It manufactures and exports finished products. Western Europe also exports large amounts of wheat, barley, and wine. It imports corn, rice, and tropical fruits and vegetables. However, most of Western Europe's trade with the rest of the world is with other industrial nations. It buys from them the modern equipment and machinery its own factories do not produce. It sells to them the machinery that they need. By the mid-1980s, trade (both exports and imports) between the United States and the countries of Western Europe amounted to over 135 billion dollars a year.

2. Among Western Europe's important imports are oil from the Middle East, South America, and the United States; cars from Japan; wood, paper pulp, and machinery from the United States and Canada; cotton from the United States and Egypt; tin and rubber from Malaysia; and copper from Chile. In return, ships carry away steel products, machinery, automobiles, chemicals, clothing, shoes, and farming tools. The rest of the world benefits from the factories of Western Europe, for they get the *finished products* in return for their raw materials. Western Europe shows how people can help each other through trade.

3. Nearly everywhere you look in Western Europe, there are busy harbors. The port of Rotterdam, in the Netherlands, handles the most tons of cargo. Huge amounts of oil are shipped into Western Europe through the port of Rotterdam. Among the other large and important ports are London, Glasgow, Belfast, and Liverpool (the United Kingdom); Dublin (Ireland); Helsinki (Finland); Copenhagen (Denmark); Cherbourg and Marseille (France); and Genoa (Italy). Paris (France), the largest city in Europe, is a busy trade and fashion center on the Seine River. Amsterdam (Netherlands), Antwerp (Belgium), Hamburg (Germany), Barcelona (Spain), Lisbon (Portugal), and Athens (Greece) are also important. Day after day, shiploads of raw materials and manufactured goods are unloaded at these ports. The empty ships are reloaded with goods to be shipped all over the world. Among Western Europe's important exports are automobiles (from the United Kingdom, France, Germany, Italy), foods (from France, Germany, Italy, Greece), clothing and textiles (France, Italy, Greece). The many bays and harbors of Western Europe have helped the people to use the nearby waters as highways for trade.

Lucerne, Switzerland, is a major tourist center. What Swiss products have you used in recent months?

4. Germany is the leading nation in trade in Western Europe. The countries of Western Europe together account for almost half of the world's trade. (While the United States leads the world in foreign trade, it is only one nation.) There is usually a balance between the import of foods and raw materials into Western Europe and the export of manufactured goods. Europeans sometimes import more than they export (buy more than they sell). The difference is sometimes made up through the millions of dollars spent by tourists.

5. Much of Western Europe's trade is trade among the nations of Western Europe. The countries of Western Europe are small. (In some cases, a trip of less than 100 miles [161 kilometers] will take you all the way across one country and into another.) There are dif-

ferences in language and also in money systems. In the past, passports were needed as people moved from one country to another. There were tariffs or taxes on goods going from one nation to another. Tariffs are taxes on goods imported into a country. At one time, the prices of goods were raised because of the tariffs paid when goods were shipped from one country to another.

6. In the United States these differences do not exist. Manufacturers in New York can sell their goods in California with little trouble. There is no tax, no passport, no difference in money from one state to another. An American who drives from coast to coast, almost 3,000 miles (4,828 kilometers), has few problems. But if you drove from Italy to Belgium (just a few hundred miles) you might pass through three different countries. In Western Europe, goods often cross several borders before they reach customers. Since the late 1960s, however, the tariffs among many Western European nations have been eliminated. Goods can now be shipped freely from one country to another.

7. Western Europe's resources are divided among many nations and are needed by people in different countries. Therefore, they must be saved and used wisely. In the next chapter, you will learn what has been done to overcome resource problems.

UNDERSTANDING WHAT YOU HAVE READ

1. **Which questions are answered in this chapter?**

a. Why is the Suez Canal important to Western Europe?

b. Why have many cities in Western Europe become important?

c. What does Western Europe export?

2. **The main idea of this chapter describes**

a. how Western Europe depends on trade

b. imports and exports of Western Europe

c. how many people of Western Europe make a living

3. **Western Europe imports large quantities of**

a. wheat   b. coal   c. oil

4. **Most of the food imports to Western Europe are paid for by**

a. the sale of manufactured goods

b. the sale of food products

c. income from tourists

5. Parts of Western Europe import food because

a. the quality of farm products is higher in the United States
b. the food is bought in order to carry on trade
c. farms in parts of the region cannot raise all the kinds of foods the people want

6. There were difficulties in trading among nations in Western Europe because

a. the mountains are too high to cross easily
b. there were many tariffs to pay
c. there was a lack of good transportation

7. A tariff is a tax on

a. imports
b. exports
c. goods made and sold within the country

8. In *paragraph 2,* the term *finished products* refers to

a. highly polished goods
b. only high-priced goods such as linens and watches
c. manufactured goods of all kinds

9. Much oil is imported into Western Europe through the port city of

a. Edinburgh   b. Rotterdam   c. Zurich

DEVELOPING IDEAS AND SKILLS

Understanding Circle Graphs—Industry in Western Europe

Read each of the statements below the graph. Write *true* if the statement is correct. Write *false* if the statement is wrong. Write *not given* if the graphs do not give you the information you need to decide on the statement.

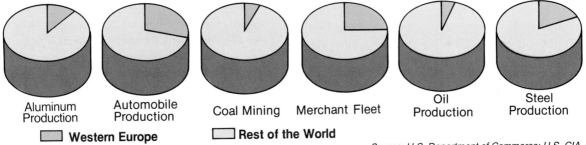

Aluminum Production   Automobile Production   Coal Mining   Merchant Fleet   Oil Production   Steel Production

☐ **Western Europe**   ☐ **Rest of the World**

Source: U.S. Department of Commerce; U.S. CIA.

Industry in Western Europe

1. Western Europe depends heavily on trade.
2. Western Europe probably imports much of the oil it needs.
3. Many people in Western Europe work in auto factories and steel mills.
4. The United States produces more steel and aluminum than Western Europe does.
5. Ships from Western Europe can be seen in harbors all over the world.

SUMMING UP

Indicate whether the following items are mainly *imports* or *exports* of Western Europe. One of the items is both a major import and an export.

1. oil
2. fish
3. dairy products
4. wheat
5. corn
6. textiles
7. machinery
8. rubber
9. bananas and pineapples
10. chemicals

279

Chapter 9

The European Community

How have some European nations overcome some of their problems in trade with each other?

READING FOR A PURPOSE:
1. Why did European nations feel a need for cooperation with one another after World War II?
2. What is the European Community?
3. Why were more nations admitted to the European Community?

1. As you learned in the last chapter, Western Europe is made up of many small nations. Each nation has different resources. For example, France has iron and Germany has coal. By the time the iron ore and coal were brought together in a steel mill, the price of steel was higher because of tariffs. Since World War II, however, the nations of Western Europe have learned that their resources can be used more wisely if they cooperate with each other.

2. Because of World War II (1939–1945), the power of Western European countries in world affairs had declined. The people were exhausted from the wars that had divided and ruined them. They realized that the United States and the Soviet Union were the new powers in the world. They knew they could not be important in world affairs unless they regained their strength. They believed that the United States was successful because of free trade. The powers of Western Europe felt they could create an even larger market for European companies if only they removed the tariff walls between them. The idea of sharing resources through free trade took root in Western Europe.

3. The first steps in this movement started in 1948. At that time, Belgium, the Nether-

Electronics manufacturing in Denmark. How has the European Community's Common Market benefited industry in Western Europe?

lands, and Luxembourg formed a trading union. These nations are called the Benelux nations because their beginning letters are BE-NE-LUX. Through the plan, each country was able to send its goods to the others without paying a tax or tariff. Trade grew so quickly that the idea began to spread. Other countries decided to try it also.

4. In the early 1950s, Jean Monnet and Robert Schuman, of France, drew up a plan for pooling Western Europe's coal and iron resources. In 1951, six countries accepted this plan: the Benelux countries, France, Italy, and West Germany. All of these nations had been hurt in World War II. All of them were willing to give up a little of their national power to join in the plan. This plan led to the idea of the European Community. The leaders of the plan looked to the day when the countries of Western Europe would be united as a single nation.

5. In 1957, the six countries signed several more treaties. These countries agreed to lower and then end tariffs on goods going back and forth among their nations. The result was the Common Market. Trade flows as though there were no borders between member countries. This means that a manufacturer in France makes things not only for the people of France, but also for the people in all countries of the Common Market. For purposes of trade, these countries are almost like one nation. The six nations also agreed to work together to develop nuclear energy for peaceful purposes.

6. The results of the Common Market pleased all members. Trade among the member nations doubled. Tariffs dropped lower and lower. Business people thought in terms of sales to all six nations rather than to only their own country. The standard of living in all member nations rose. People had more money and were able to buy more goods. Trade between Common Market countries and foreign lands also grew.

7. Because the coal and steel agreement, the Common Market plan, and the nuclear energy treaty were so successful, other nations wanted to become part of the European Community. The United Kingdom asked to join, but France blocked its request for membership. (Each country has the right to *veto,* or prevent, the admission of a new member.) Finally, in 1972, France agreed to British membership. Soon after, the British people voted to join. They hoped to share in the benefits that the first six member countries had received. Along with the United Kingdom, Ireland and Denmark were also admitted to the European Community. In 1981, Greece, the tenth member, was admitted to membership. In 1986 Portugal and Spain became members of the European Community. In 1986, this group of 12 nations added up to a market for goods of about 325 million people.

8. Member nations of the European Community are also trying to work closely together to solve farming problems. Members are trying to increase the output of some

The Parthenon, an ancient temple in Athens, Greece. Greece joined the European Community in 1981. What nations have recently asked to become members of the European Community?

crops. They want to be sure that the people will have a good supply of food at reasonable prices. They also want the farmers to have a high standard of living. One of the main goals is to have a common market for food products as well as manufactured goods. The problem is that farmers in one country want to keep out their neighbor country's crop if it sells for less. Another problem is that modern methods of farming result in a surplus. A surplus is extra food that people do not want to buy because of the high prices farmers want. Often the farmers lower the prices of the food so that people will buy the surplus. In some years, wheat, dairy products, sugar beets, wine, olive oil, and citrus fruits have been surplus crops. The European Community is now the world's largest food producer.

9. The 12 members of the European Community have several common political groups. Citizens in each member country vote for representatives to the European Parliament. There is also a council of Ministers, a Commission, and a Court of Justice. The Court handles disputes concerning the European Community's laws and treaties.

10. The success of the European Community has some advantages for the United States. It brings the nations of Europe closer together. It should make them stronger and better able to defend themselves. With more money to spend, Western Europeans buy more from the United States. How much more will depend on whether U.S. business people, factory workers, and farmers can produce the goods Europeans want at prices they will pay.

UNDERSTANDING WHAT YOU HAVE READ

1. Which questions are answered in this chapter?
a. Who is Jean Monnet?
b. What are the benefits of belonging to the European Community?
c. Why did France block the United Kingdom's entry into the European Community?

2. The main idea of this chapter describes
a. how the European Community is changing Western Europe
b. how the European Community affects the United States
c. the work of Monnet and Schuman

3. In 1981, how many countries belonged to the European Community?
a. 6   b. 10   c. 12

4. The Common Market began
a. soon after World War I
b. soon after World War II
c. at the urging of the United Nations

5. The Common Market was formed to
a. share waterpower resources among the member nations
b. increase trade with the Soviet Union
c. share resources and skills of Western Europe

6. The Common Market has been successful in that
a. more farms are needed
b. more and less costly goods are available
c. tariffs on exports have been raised

7. The "Benelux nations" are
a. Poland, Czechoslovakia, and Yugoslavia
b. Belgium, the Netherlands, and Luxembourg
c. England, France, and Germany

8. Member nations of the European Community have signed
a. a coal and steel agreement, the Common Market plan, and a nuclear power agreement
b. an agreement to sell wheat to the United States
c. a military agreement between the United States, Canada, and China

9. The European Community's Common Market

a. deals only with manufactured goods
b. deals with both manufactured goods and farm products
c. is located in the business center of Paris

10. *Surplus* food is food that

a. sells for a low price
b. is in short supply
c. is extra and that people do not want to buy at the prices being offered

DEVELOPING IDEAS AND SKILLS

Building Map Skills — The European Community

Study the map below and review the information in Chapter 9. Then answer the questions below.

1. (a) What is the population of the European Community? (b) What is its area?
2. Who produces more steel, the United States or the European community?
3. Why was the European Community formed?
4. How did free trade among the nations of the European Community raise the standard of living in member nations?
5. How do the agreements among the nations of the European Community affect world peace?

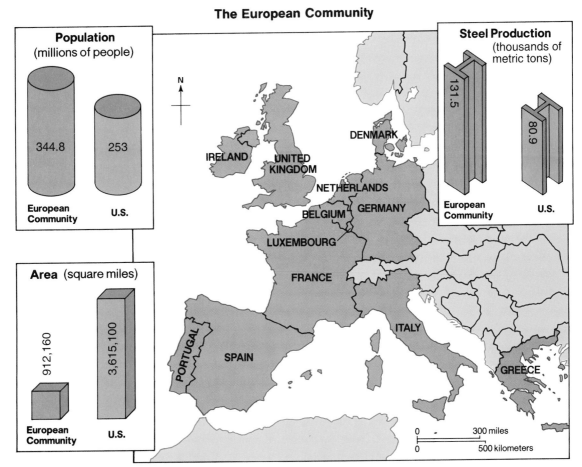

The European Community

Population (millions of people): European Community 344.8, U.S. 253

Area (square miles): European Community 912,160, U.S. 3,615,100

Steel Production (thousands of metric tons): European Community 131.5, U.S. 80.9

Source: 1987 United Nations Statistical Yearbook, ©1990

REVIEWING AND WRITING

Making Outlines

Complete the following *outline* in your notebook.

The European Community

A. How It Started
   1.
   2.
   3.
B. How It Works
   1.
   2.
   3.
C. Results
   1.
   2.
   3.

DEVELOPING CRITICAL THINKING SKILLS

Making Inferences

In our reading, many facts are given to us. From these facts we can draw conclusions. The following are some conclusions, or inferences, that you might make after reading Chapters 6, 7, 8, and 9. Tell whether these conclusions are correct or incorrect. Give reasons for your answers.

1. (Chapter 6) Many of the stoves in the kitchens of the Netherlands are probably gas stoves.
2. (Chapter 6) In some parts of Western Europe, water takes the place of oil or coal in making electricity.
3. (Chapter 6) Coal mines, factories, and large cities of Western Europe are often found near each other.
4. (Chapter 6) Western Europeans have made good use of their rivers and have developed a large system of canals.
5. (Chapter 7) Wheat bread or white bread is commonly found on French dinner tables.
6. (Chapter 7) Europeans eat many kinds of soups made from vegetables, barley, and potatoes.
7. (Chapter 8) Europe has a great many large cities on a small area of land.
8. (Chapter 9) At the present time, there is a movement of the small nations of Europe to join together to solve common problems.
9. (Chapter 9) Manufacturers in Europe can succeed in business only by selling their goods within their own country.
10. (Chapter 9) As a result of World War II, the ability of Western Europe to produce a great amount of goods was weakened for a few years.

A Changing Europe

What will the Europe of the future be like?

1. How has the fall of communism and the breakup of the Soviet Union affected Europe?
2. How will Europe solve its problems?
3. Will Europe be united or divided?

1. It was July 14, 1991—Bastille Day in France. Thousands of French were celebrating the anniversary of the French Revolution, cheering loudly as the parade passed. France's president was about to speak. When he appeared on television, two flags were flying at his side. One was the red, white, and blue banner of France. The other was the flag of the European Community (EC), a circle of 12 gold stars on a field of blue. These two flags symbolize Europe's choices for the future. Will the region be united or will it be divided into individual, competing states?

2. In the early 1990s, Europe was going through a time of great change. It was greater, perhaps, than at any other time in its history. After years of tension and terror, the cold war was over. The Soviet Union existed only in the pages of history books. A new economic and political relationship was formed between the United States and Europe and between Western and Eastern Europe.

3. In Western Europe, important steps had been taken to build a Europe that was united economically. The Western European countries began to cooperate and pooled their strengths. When the nations of Eastern Europe broke free of Soviet control, the EC immediately negotiated new trade agreements with them.

4. Although European nations had formed the European Community that you read about in Chapter 9, Europe was still not unified economically. There were still barriers to free trade between countries. Also, Europe was not yet able to compete economically with the United States or Japan. In the late 1980s and early 1990s, a number of disagreements about trade took place between the United States and the European Community. So, the

A giant piece of the new "chunnel", the direct link between the European mainland and Britain is readied by workers for installation.

On a wintry night in February 1990, crowds watched as workers began taking down the old Berlin Wall.

European Community put together a new plan called "Europe 1992." This plan called for the creation of a single, huge European market with all barriers removed. The goal was an economically united Europe with the free flow of people, goods, and money across national boundaries.

5. The European Community also began talking about a Europe that was not only united economically, but also politically. This might mean a United States of Europe similar to the United States of America. In December 1991, EC leaders met to talk about uniting Europe. After lengthy debate, EC leaders drew up a treaty. They planned for a common currency to be used in all European nations by the year 2000. EC leaders also agreed to let the newly freed nations of Eastern Europe join the community.

6. A centuries-old dream that has become a reality was another sign of a uniting Europe.

That was the construction of a tunnel under the English Channel connecting Great Britain with the mainland of Europe. The project actually consists of three tunnels. Each is approximately 31 miles long. Two carry the trains—one eastward and the other westward. The third tunnel is for maintenance. When the tunnel, nicknamed the Chunnel, is in full operation, passengers will travel between London and Paris in about three hours.

7. While Western Europe was moving toward uniting, parts of Eastern Europe were being split apart. (You will read more about Eastern Europe in Chapter 14.) The Eastern Europe that was created after World War II had already disappeared. Beginning in 1989 with the fall of the Berlin Wall, the Iron Curtain came crashing down. East Germany and West Germany, divided for almost 50 years, were united again. Newly independent nations of Eastern Europe and the Baltic states were finally free from the Soviet Union. Many struggled to set up democracies and free-market economies. Western nations have been sending aid to Eastern Europe to try and relieve the people's misery so that the new governments can survive.

8. Meanwhile, some new nations were also dealing with serious ethnic conflicts. Communism had helped unify the many peoples of Eastern Europe. National and ethnic conflicts were forbidden. However, the revolutions of 1989 saw a return of historic national and ethnic identities. In 1991, the three Baltic states of Lithuania, Estonia, and Latvia broke away from the Soviet Union. In Yugoslavia, fighting between ethnic groups tore the country apart.

9. The new Eastern European governments also had to deal with environmental problems. The communists' drive to build industry had polluted the land, the air, and the water. Many of the forests were dying or severely damaged. Raw sewage and industrial waste filled the Baltic and Black seas and most of the rivers. Thousands of acres of farmland were damaged. Pollution had brought about many birth defects and illnesses, including cancer. Pollution from Eastern Europe had a harmful effect on the environment of the Scandinavian countries to the north. Cleaning up the environment will take years.

10. With all the events taking place in what was the Soviet Union and Eastern Europe, it is easy to overlook what has happened in Southern Europe. Southern Europe also has grown stronger and less dependent on foreign powers. This area is made up of Italy, Spain, Portugal, and Greece. These countries have joined the European Community and enjoyed some prosperity after the hard times of the 1970s. After decades of dictatorships, Spain, Portugal, and Greece have set up democracies. Although once lower than the other areas of Europe, the standard of living in these countries has been improving for some time. There is a new, strong middle class. Society has become less rural as people left the countryside and moved to the cities. The role of women has improved dramatically. Now more women in Southern Europe than ever attend college and work outside the home.

11. One force that has helped unify all the regions of Europe is NATO. As you read in Chapter 4, NATO was formed after World War II to protect its members against the spread of communism. The dramatic political changes in Europe in the late 1980s removed NATO's original reason for being; it needed a new role. Different countries had different ideas about what NATO's new role would be.

12. In July 1990, NATO leaders met to decide the fate of the alliance. At the meeting, they changed the focus of NATO from war to politics. In fact, some of the newly freed nations of Eastern Europe had already asked to join NATO. NATO's leaders also decided to cut down the number of soldiers in its army. By the mid-1990s, the number of U.S. soldiers in Western Europe will be cut in half. This will reduce American influence in the region while Europe becomes stronger and more united.

13. In the years to come, Europe will most likely focus on four major issues. Europeans will be concerned with trade, reform in Eastern Europe, cleaning up the environment, and handling ethnic conflicts.

UNDERSTANDING WHAT YOU HAVE READ

1. Which questions are answered in this chapter?

a. How has the fall of Communist governments changed Europe?

b. What is NATO's new role?

c. How are the Scandinavian countries governed?

2. The main idea of *paragraph 2* is that

a. European nations have colonies all over the world

b. Europe went through a great period of change in the early 1990s

c. Southern Europe has also made progress

3. What did the European nations put together to help them build a united European economy?
   a. NATO
   b. "Europe 1992"
   c. The Chunnel

4. The Chunnel connects which two European nations?
   a. Spain and France
   b. France and Great Britain
   c. Great Britain and Belgium

5. The European Community was formed to
   a. help unite Europe politically and economically
   b. protect Europe from communism
   c. counteract the influence of the United States

6. What is one problem that resulted from the fall of Communist governments in Europe?
   a. Immigrants no longer came to Western European countries.
   b. Raw materials from Eastern Europe were no longer available.
   c. Serious ethnic conflicts tore some Eastern European nations apart.

7. Because of the drive by the communist governments of Eastern Europe to build industry,
   a. a serious pollution problem must be solved by the new Eastern European nations
   b. Eastern Europe has run out of raw materials for manufacturing
   c. Eastern European nations compete successfully against Japan and the United States in the world economy

8. Which nation is *not* included in Southern Europe?
   a. Sweden
   b. Greece
   c. Italy

9. By the mid-1990s, the number of U.S. soldiers in Western Europe will
   a. increase by 25 percent
   b. be zero
   c. decrease by 50 percent

10. Which issue is *not* important to the European nations in the 1990s?
    a. cleaning up the environment
    b. developing a single European language
    c. increasing trade

FOLLOW UP

Reviewing Western Europe

Complete the following statements by using the words or phrases listed below.

Vital Triangle
offices and factories
peninsula
oil
natural harbors
northerly
cities

Common Market of the
   European Community
coal and iron
rivers and canals
finished goods
food and raw materials
North Atlantic Drift
wheat

1. Europe is a _____ on the land mass of Eurasia.
2. Europe has many fine _____.

3. The western coast of Western Europe is warmed by an ocean current, the _____.

4. The United Kingdom and Norway have great mineral wealth in _____.

5. The great steel-making area of Western Europe is known as the _____.

6. Western Europe has a web of _____.

7. Western Europe imports _____; in turn, it exports machinery and other _____.

8. Most people in Western Europe work in _____ and live in _____.

9. Ten nations of Western Europe have increased their trade through the _____.

WRITING

Now that you have completed your overall study of the European region, you should be prepared to make a special report. Select one of the countries of Europe for your special study. In your essay, answer the following questions:

1. Where is the nation located? What is its absolute location? Give evidence about its relative location.
2. What are the physical and human characteristics of the nation? What are some observed characteristics, or characteristics that can be seen?
3. What are the relationships between the people and the environment? What are the cultural and physical relationships? How have people modified and adapted to their natural settings? What have been some consequences for humans, and what have been some consequences for the environment?
4. How has movement contributed to the development of the nation? What are some relationships between and among places?
5. How does the country fit the definition of the European region? In what ways is it an exception?

Chapter 11

The United Kingdom: The Island Nation

How has the United Kingdom become a world power despite its small size?

READING FOR A PURPOSE:
1. How has its island location helped the United Kingdom to become a world power?
2. How has the United Kingdom used its resources to develop a high standard of living?
3. What are the reasons for the troubles in Northern Ireland?

1. The United Kingdom of Great Britain and Northern Ireland is made up of the narrow island of Great Britain to the west of the mainland of Europe and the northeastern part of the island of Ireland. The island of Great Britain is made up of three parts: England, Scotland, and Wales. People often refer to the United Kingdom of Great Britain and Northern Ireland by shorter names. It is sometimes called *the United Kingdom, UK, Great Britain,* or *Britain.* The United Kingdom is about 94,000 square miles (243,460 square kilometers) in area, a little smaller than the state of

Oregon. The population is about 57 million. This makes the United Kingdom one of the world's most densely populated countries. Generally, nine times as many people live on each square mile in Britain as on each square mile in the United States.

2. The northern and western parts of the island of Great Britain are hilly or mountainous. The eastern part is a lowland plain. This is part of the Great European Plain. The coastline is long and irregular. There are many fine harbors.

3. The island of Great Britain has a marine climate. This mild, rainy climate is caused by the warm current (North Atlantic Drift) and winds that come from the west. The weather of London is much like the weather of Seattle, Washington, and Vancouver, British Columbia. The ocean winds bring rain. The heaviest rains fall on the western side of the island. The fogs of London are world-famous. We sometimes talk about fogs so thick that we can hardly see in front of us. In London this is often true.

4. The British have always used the seas around them. In the 17th and 18th centuries, they began to build a great empire. They started colonies in the New World, India, Africa, and Australia. At the same time, the Industrial Revolution was taking place. The British were the first to use machines run by steam engines. Their colonies furnished raw materials. The machines turned these raw ma-

Llangollen, Wales, is a town in the western part of the island of Great Britain. Why does the United Kingdom have a mild and rainy climate?

Trafalgar Square, London, England. London is the capital of the United Kingdom. Which country, the United States or Canada, has a government more like that of the United Kingdom?

terials into finished goods. The goods were then shipped to all parts of the world. The sea has meant life to the British people.

5. After World War I, four of the United Kingdom's former colonies—Canada, Australia, New Zealand, and South Africa—joined with the United Kingdom in a new relationship called the British Commonwealth of Nations. They agreed to help one another by lowering tariffs on goods sent to each other. During World War II, the United Kingdom fought as one of the Allies against Nazi Germany. Germany was defeated, but the United Kingdom had used up much of its resources in the process. Later, the United Kingdom had to give up colonies in Asia, Africa, and Latin America. Many former colonies joined the Commonwealth as free and equal partners.

6. Most of the British live in cities and towns. The largest city is London, the capital, home of 7 million people. Many of the British ways of living are like those of the people in the United States and Canada. The English language came from Great Britain. Much of the clothing is in the same fashion. We use many British products. The British go to movies, listen to the radio, and watch television. Almost all adults can read and write. Medical care is given to the people as a government service. The British standard of living is high.

7. Most American ideas of law and government came from Great Britain, although in the United Kingdom there is no written constitution. The king or queen is the head of state, but holds little power. The lawmaking body of the British government is Parliament. Parliament is divided into two houses, the House of Lords and the House of Commons. The chief official is the prime minister. He or she is the leader of the political party that has the most members in the House of Commons. Prime ministers choose cabinets that will help them pass and carry out laws. (You will recall that Canada's government is a parliamentary one, too.)

8. The British depend on their farmlands and surrounding seas for about half of their food. The best farmland is on the eastern part of the island. Here farmers plant wheat, barley, fruits, and vegetables. Machinery is used wherever possible, and the yield per acre is high. In the northern highlands they also raise dairy cattle and sheep. The wool is used in the textile factories. Besides their farm and grazing land, the British obtain a large supply of herring, cod, and other fish from the nearby waters.

9. The farms and seas do not provide enough food for the United Kingdom's millions of people, though. The British must, therefore, buy more food from abroad. To pay for this food, the United Kingdom turns to its factories. Raw materials are imported. The raw materials are turned into finished goods and sold in world markets. The money earned from these goods pays for the materials and foods that must be imported.

10. The United Kingdom became a leading manufacturing nation for many reasons. Because the United Kingdom is surrounded by water, it has been able to avoid invasion from Europe for centuries. Thus, it has been left alone to develop its industries without interference. Its people are hardworking, skilled, and inventive. It has had great resources of coal and iron ore. (The chief coal and iron fields are in Wales and eastern England.) Using these resources, the United Kingdom's skilled workers turn out a great variety of products: woolen and cotton goods, steel products of all kinds, automobiles, airplanes, farm machinery, chemicals, electronic equipment, and films. Several important industries—steel making, coal mining, railroads—are owned by the government. In 1985, a damaging year-long coal strike finally ended.

11. These manufactured goods are the United Kingdom's exports. Because of its great need for trade, the United Kingdom has long been a leading shipbuilding nation. Its ships sail the seas, trading with nations all over the world. Its greatest trade is with the other members of the European Community. The United States and Canada are also among the United Kingdom's major trading partners.

12. The United Kingdom has a number of problems, though. Its well-being depends

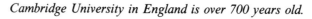

Cambridge University in England is over 700 years old.

upon its selling goods abroad. This is becoming harder because of the growing number of industrial nations that also want to sell goods abroad. Many countries built modern mills and factories to compete with British factories. In the early 1980s, the Soviet Union, the United States, Japan, West Germany, China, Italy, France, and Poland each produced more steel than the United Kingdom did. The loss of colonies after World War II meant that the United Kingdom no longer controlled the raw materials or markets of its former colonies.

13. Large oil and gas fields have been found off the coast of Great Britain in the North Sea. By the mid-1980s, the nation was able to provide for all its oil and gas needs. However, the United Kingdom lacks other important resources such as cotton, copper, and sulphur. And despite its resources, it still must import wool and iron ore. Food is imported at a high cost. In their search for new sources of power, the British were the first to develop a power station using atomic energy.

14. The United Kingdom still plays a leading role in world affairs. It is a member of the NATO alliance with the United States, Canada, and the nations of Western Europe. In 1973, it joined the European Community.

15. The United Kingdom has faced some problems away from home. In April 1982, Argentina invaded the Falkland Islands, a small group of islands in the South Atlantic. The islands are about 750 miles (1,200 kilometers) east of the South American mainland. This little territory was home to about 2,000 Britons. The British sent a naval force from home to reclaim the islands. In June 1982, the Argentine troops surrendered and the Falkland Islands returned to British control.

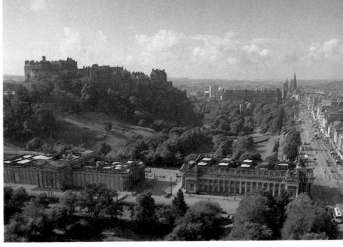

Edinburgh Castle in Edinburgh, Scotland. What valuable resource was discovered off the coast of Scotland? How is this resource a benefit to the people of the United Kingdom?

16. The United Kingdom has faced problems in Northern Ireland. In 1921, the island of Ireland was divided into two parts. Southern Ireland, the larger part, became an independent country, Eire (Irish for Ireland). The smaller part, Northern Ireland, remained part of the United Kingdom. Two-thirds of the people in Northern Ireland are Protestants; the rest are largely Catholics. Because they are in the minority, Catholics feel that they are discriminated against in voting, housing, and jobs. Catholic groups want Northern Ireland to be joined with the nation of Ireland. To speed things up, some Catholic groups, however, have tried to force union by violent means. Some Protestant groups have used violence to oppose them. Since 1970, several thousand people have been killed and injured in rioting and bombings. British troops are stationed in Northern Ireland to try to stop the bloodshed. So far, they have been unsuccessful.

UNDERSTANDING WHAT YOU HAVE READ

1. Which questions are answered in this chapter?

a. How are the British people governed?
b. Where are the coal-mining areas?
c. What are some of the United Kingdom's economic and political problems?

2. The main idea of *paragraph 10* describes

a. the variety of British products
b. how the United Kingdom became a great industrial nation
c. the skill of British workers

3. Most of the British people work

a. on farms
b. in mines
c. in industry and trade

4. The leader of the British government is the

a. prime minister
b. premier
c. chancellor

5. The United Kingdom became a leader in manufacturing for all of these reasons EXCEPT

a. it had an early start
b. it grew a large supply of cotton
c. there have been large coal and iron resources

6. Some of the United Kingdom's problems are now caused by

a. the loss of population since World War II
b. the loss of former colonies
c. problems of wheat farmers on the island

7. England is located on the

a. island of Ireland
b. island of Great Britain
c. peninsula of Europe

DEVELOPING IDEAS AND SKILLS

A. Building Map Skills — The United Kingdom

The United Kingdom

The United Kingdom and Oregon

OREGON
POPULATION: 2.8 MILLION
LAND AREA: 97,073 SQUARE MILES
251,180 SQUARE KILOMETERS
30 PEOPLE PER SQUARE MILE

UNITED KINGDOM
POPULATION: 57.5 MILLION
LAND AREA: 94,226 SQUARE MILES
244,030 SQUARE KILOMETERS
601 PEOPLE PER SQUARE MILE

Study the maps on page 294. Then answer these questions.

1. Does the United Kingdom lie in the high, middle, or low latitudes?
2. What is the distance from the coast of Great Britain to the coast of France?
3. How do you explain the presence of the large cities of Liverpool, London, Glasgow, Dublin, and Belfast?
4. If you flew from your community to London, in which direction would you fly? How do you know this without looking at a world map?
5. Locate the prime meridian. Which city is it near?
6. Name two cities that are not seaports.
7. How many different bodies of water can you find on the map?
8. How does the map tell you that the climate of Great Britain will be milder than the mainland near it?
9. Which is larger, Oregon or the United Kingdom?
10. Which is more crowded, Oregon or the United Kingdom?

B. Understanding Circle Graphs — Where Do Western Europeans Work?

The following graphs show what kind of jobs workers have in the United Kingdom, Ireland, France, and Germany. They show what percentage of the workers have jobs in *agriculture* (growing crops, raising livestock), in *industry* (working in factories, mines, mills), and in *services* (working in offices, stores, banks, schools, hospitals). Study the graphs. Then answer the questions.

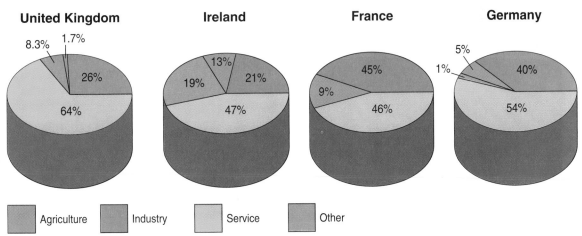

Source: World Almanac and Book of Facts, 1992.

1. In which country does the greatest percentage of workers have jobs in services?
2. In which country does the greatest percentage of workers have jobs in agriculture?
3. In which country does the greatest percentage of workers have jobs in industry?
4. Both the United Kingdom and the United States have only about 2 percent of their workers working on farms. Yet the United States exports huge amounts of food, while the United Kingdom needs to import about half its food. From what you have learned in this chapter, why do you think there is this difference between the two countries?

REVIEWING AND WRITING

Making Outlines

Use these four headings to make an outline of the important facts and ideas concerning the United Kingdom. From what you have learned, write three statements under each heading.

A. How the United Kingdom Compares With the United States in Size and Population
B. How the United Kingdom Compares With the United States in Government and Life of Its People
C. Sources of the United Kingdom's Strength
D. The United Kingdom's Weaknesses and Problems

DEVELOPING CRITICAL THINKING SKILLS

Cause and Effect

In Column A there are six items about the United Kingdom. In Column B there are six results of the items stated in Column A. See if you can match the causes in Column A with the effects or results in Column B.

COLUMN A
1. Warm ocean winds
2. Coal and iron resources
3. Need for raw materials
4. Lack of farmland
5. North Sea oil fields
6. Need for trade

COLUMN B
a. gave an early start in the manufacture of steel
b. led to growth of shipbuilding
c. bring rain and fog to the island
d. help fill the United Kingdom's energy needs
e. led to a great empire of colonies
f. led to the sale of manufactured goods in trade for food

Chapter 12

Spain: Changing Country of Southern Europe

Will Spain be able to regain its place as a leader of the European Community?

READING FOR A PURPOSE:
1. How does the topography of Spain affect the output of its farms?
2. How did Spain lose its position as one of the world's great powers?
3. How has Spain developed its industries?

1. Spain occupies most of the Iberian Peninsula. It shares this peninsula with the smaller country of Portugal. The Pyrenees Mountains in the north separate Spain from the rest of Western Europe. Portugal and the Atlantic Ocean form its western boundary. Aside from the mountains in the north, all of the remaining boundaries are water—the Bay of Biscay on the north and the Mediterranean Sea on the east. Its long coastline of 1,500 miles (2,414 kilometers) is regular and provides few natural harbors. The narrow Strait of Gibraltar separates Spain from North Africa.

2. Spain's nearly 39 million people live in a land somewhat larger than California. Almost all Spaniards are Roman Catholic. For hundreds of years, Spain was a farming nation. Poor soils and lack of rain made farming difficult in much of Spain. But since the 1960s, factories and mills have developed rapidly. Today, more Spaniards work in manufacturing than on the farms. Spain is an industrial nation. Its people have better food, clothing, homes, education, and health care than ever before. Many old customs such as taking a siesta (nap) after lunch, are disappearing.

3. Most of Spain is a wide, treeless plateau called the *meseta* (or little table). The plateau is crisscrossed by low hills and mountains

Spanish beach resort. Spain has more tourists yearly than it has population. Look at the map on page 301. Where do you think the most popular tourist spots are located?

called *sierras.* Madrid, the capital, is in the middle of the meseta. A number of small rivers, such as the Ebro and Guadalquivir, drain the plateau. In the north, the high Pyrenees have few passes through them to France.

4. Spain's climate is varied. In the north it is cool and rainy—the marine climate. The central plateau is hot and dry in the summer and very cold in the winter. Along Spain's Mediterranean coast the summers are hot and dry, but the winters bring some rain.

5. About 2,000 years ago, Spain was part of the Roman Empire. The Romans controlled this land for about 600 years. They gave Christianity and the Roman language, Latin, to the Spanish people. The Moors, a Muslim people from North Africa, then crossed the Strait of Gibraltar and ruled most of Spain for almost 800 years. They were finally driven out in 1492.

6. In that same year Christopher Columbus, sailing from Spain, reached the New

Harvesting olives in southern Spain. Spain exports large amounts of table olives and olive oil. What geographic conditions allow farmers to grow olives in this region of Europe?

World. Spanish conquerors—de Soto, Cortez, Pizarro, Coronado—soon explored and claimed large areas of this New World. Magellan made his famous voyage around the globe and claimed Guam and the Philippines. Spanish ships brought in gold and silver from Mexico and Peru and silks and spices from Asia. Spain became the richest nation in Europe.

7. In 1588, Spain's great navy, or Armada, lost a great sea battle to England. At that time, Spain began to lose its power. By 1825, most of its colonies in the New World had won their freedom. Then it suffered a defeat by the United States in the Spanish-American War of 1898 and lost more territory. Cuba became independent. Puerto Rico and the Philippines were given to the United States.

8. A terrible civil war from 1936 to 1939 ruined Spain. More than a million people were killed as the Spanish fought each other. The winners were the Nationalists led by Francisco Franco. Franco then became the ruler of the nation. For 36 years Spain was ruled by the dictator Francisco Franco.

9. Upon Franco's death in 1975, Juan Car-

los became king. Today Spain is a monarchy with a constitution. The people of Spain are now as free as any other people in Western Europe. There is a parliament elected by the people. It makes the country's laws and chooses a prime minister to be the head of the government. The people enjoy freedom of speech and the press and the right of assembly. For the most part, Spanish life today has adjusted quickly from a dictatorship to the present democratic rule. (The Basques are a group of two and a half million people who live near the French border. Despite self-rule, many Basques want their own nation.) In 1986, Spain was admitted to the Common Market. Spain has a special agreement with the United States. Under this agreement, the United States can use certain airfields and naval bases in Spain.

10. Fewer than one out of five Spanish workers makes a living from farming and herding animals. Most farmers live in irrigated valleys or along the coasts where there is more rainfall. For some, farm work is done by hand or with simple tools. Less farm machinery has been used on Spanish farms than in the farming regions of France. But in recent years, more and more farm machinery and fertilizer have been used. Spain's agricultural growth rate has been the highest in Western Europe during the last 20 years.

11. The chief farm crop is wheat. Not enough is raised for export, however. In some wheat-growing areas, there is so little rainfall that farmers plant their crops only once in two years. Barley, potatoes, and sugar beets rank next to wheat in importance of farm products. Spanish farmers also grow rice and cotton. Much of the meseta is also used for raising sheep. Spain once supplied wool for much of Europe. Large herds of goats graze in the foothills of the Pyrenees as well. In some areas where the land is poor, people tend to raise goats.

12. Citrus fruits, grapes, olives, and vegetables are the chief export crops of Spain. Grapes are processed into wine. Olives are used to make olive oil. Grapes and olives can grow on land that is rocky. They need less water than other crops. They are raised on the hillsides along the Mediterranean coast in the south and east. Spanish farmers also grow oranges near the city of Valencia. Spain has one of Western Europe's leading fishing fleets.

13. There are only a few large cities in Spain. Madrid, Barcelona, Valencia, and Seville are the most important. Madrid has over 3 million people; Barcelona has about 2 million. Almost all city people live in high-rise apartment buildings, dress in Western clothing, drive automobiles, and watch television. Schooling has improved dramatically. Today, over 97 percent of the people can read and write. The Prado, in Madrid, is Spain's best known museum. It has a major art collection.

14. Spain has some mineral wealth. Coal and iron ore are mined along the Atlantic coast. Spain's iron and steel industry is located there. Spain is one of the chief sources of mercury, a silver-colored metal used in thermometers and in electrical equipment. There is also some copper and lead. Water-

power is being developed. The amount of coal is limited. Oil must be imported. There is a good supply of uranium, the chief mineral used in producing atomic energy. As a result, some nuclear power has been developed and more is planned.

15. Spain has become an industrial nation. Barcelona, Bilbao, and Madrid are the country's chief industrial centers. Its leading industries are automobile, steel, shoes, leather goods, and clothing. With the help of two U.S. automobile companies, Spain turns out a million cars a year. *Tourism*, too, is a major industry, employing thousands of people and bringing needed income to Spain. Tourists are attracted by the country's history, museums, warm climate, sandy beaches, and friendly people.

Why do you think Spain's standard of living has increased over the last 20 years?

UNDERSTANDING WHAT YOU HAVE READ

1. Which questions are answered in this chapter?
a. What are the chief farm crops of Spain?
b. Why has Spain developed nuclear power?
c. Where are Spain's leading museums?

2. The main idea of *paragraph 9* is that
a. dictators have ruled Spain
b. Spain has many political problems today
c. Spain now has a democratic government

3. Spain was once ruled by the
a. Mongols   b. Moors   c. Mayans

4. Most of the land in Spain is made up of
a. fertile river valleys
b. a dry, treeless plateau
c. high, rugged mountains

5. Olives and grapes are among Spain's chief farm products because they
a. do not need much water
b. grow best in cool highlands
c. are easy to care for

6. Spain receives a large income from
a. money spent by visitors
b. the production of copper and lead
c. the sale of wheat to developing countries

7. Which statement is most accurate?
a. Spain has a large supply of minerals important in developing industry.
b. Spain has developed its waterpower and coal but needs to import oil to provide energy.
c. Spain has become the leading farming nation of Southern Europe.

8. Which statement about the Spanish people is most accurate?
a. There is a mixture of many religions.
b. The great majority of adults are literate.
c. Half the people live on farms.

DEVELOPING IDEAS AND SKILLS

Building Map Skills — Spain and California

Study the maps on page 301. Then answer these questions.

1. What countries border Spain?
2. How would you describe the land formation of Spain and Portugal?
3. How is Spain separated from France?
4. Is your community farther north or south than the city of Madrid?
5. Why do you think there are few large seaports in Spain?
6. Which direction is *upstream* on the Ebro River?
7. What is the distance from the Pyrenees Mountains to the Strait of Gibraltar?
8. How does Spain compare in size with the United States? with California?
9. Which is more crowded, Spain or California?

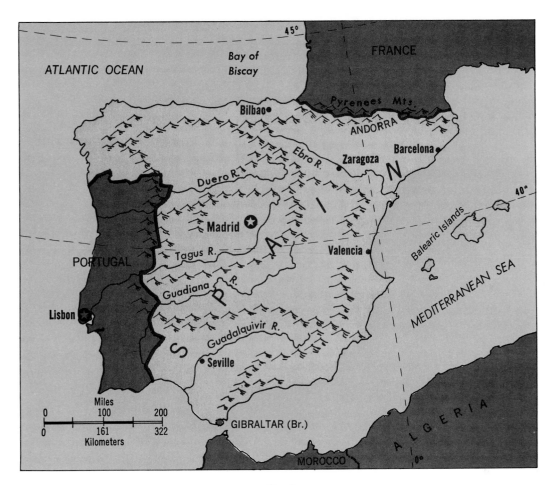

Spain

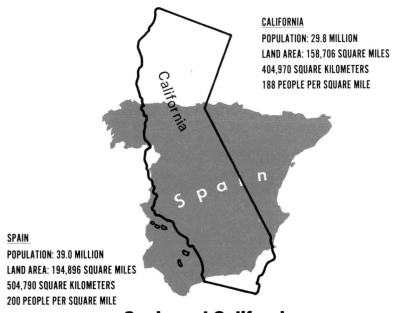

CALIFORNIA
POPULATION: 29.8 MILLION
LAND AREA: 158,706 SQUARE MILES
404,970 SQUARE KILOMETERS
188 PEOPLE PER SQUARE MILE

SPAIN
POPULATION: 39.0 MILLION
LAND AREA: 194,896 SQUARE MILES
504,790 SQUARE KILOMETERS
200 PEOPLE PER SQUARE MILE

Spain and California

In Europe

Britain's **Anita Roddick** is a sharp businesswoman who puts the environment first. She has said publicly that respect for the environment comes before profit for her shareholders. Her company makes its cosmetics mainly from plants. None of its 300 creams and lotions is ever tested on animals. The cosmetics are sold in plastic bottles that customers can return for a refund on their next purchase. The 464 store branches are decorated in wood, but endangered tropical hardwoods are never used. Customers leave the shops with leaflets urging them to help save the ozone layer. Needless to say, the leaflets are printed on recycled paper. Caring about the environment can be very profitable. Sales of Roddick's products average around $90 million per year.

The man who hiked through the Tyrolean Alps that fateful day was warmly dressed. His suit was neatly sewn and made of leather. His boots were filled with straw and birchwood clippings, and he wore birchbark gloves. A quartz jewel hung around his neck on a leather cord, and he carried a knapsack. He might have been hunting. Possibly he was prospecting for minerals. The cutting edge of his hatchet was made of copper, and so were the tips of the arrows he carried, although some of the arrowheads were made completely of stone. No one will ever know why **Tyrolean Man** died on that glacier near the border between Italy and Austria. Two German climbers found his body in 1991. At first, scientists estimated that Tyrolean Man might be 4,000 years old. Further tests showed that he is probably about 5,000 years old.

The discovery of Tyrolean Man, the oldest complete body ever found in Europe, shows us how earlier humans used their environment.

Janos Vargha was fired from his job for being a "green anarchist." Vargha got himself into trouble for criticizing a dam that was going to be built on the Danube River. He recognized that the dam would have a bad effect on the environment. At that time in Hungary, criticizing public policy invited trouble from the Hungarian Secret Police. However, Vargha was determined to be heard. He published a newsletter about the dam and circulated a petition against it. Over 10,000 people signed. The government did not like it, but history was on Vargha's side. When the Communist government give up its control of Hungary, Vargha increased his efforts. Public protest finally forced Hungary to cancel the dam.

The first political party devoted to the environment began in Germany in 1979. Its founders, **Herbert Gruhl** and **Petral Kelly,** created Die Grunen, or The Greens, by merging 250 separate environmental groups. At first, no one took them seriously. They were proposing "Green" taxes on products that pollute, and they demanded controls on air and water pollution. The Green message got through, however. Die Grunen became a national political party in 1980, and in 1984 the first representatives of the Green party were elected to the legislature. Green parties now exist in France, the Netherlands, and Canada.

Chapter 13

Germany: United Once More

How have Germany's central location, history, and resources made it one of the world's leading powers?

READING FOR A PURPOSE:
1. How has the past influenced Germany?
2. How have Germany's physical features and climate shaped its economy?
3. What issues are facing Germany today?

1. People all over the world sat glued to their television sets in November 1989, watching as the German people tore down the Berlin Wall piece by piece. That wall, stretching 99 miles, had been built by the government of East Germany to keep its citizens from escaping to the West. Thousands of men, women, and children lined both sides of the Wall as it came tumbling down. Using hammers and chisels, they began to break off chunks of concrete. Soon they destroyed the hated symbol of a divided Germany. Less than a year later, East Germany and West Germany were officially reunited.

2. Although it is united now, during most of its history, Germany was an area of many small territories. It did not become a united nation until the 1800s. Under the leadership of Chancellor Otto von Bismarck, Germany became a major European and colonial power, with a powerful military force. When World War I began in 1914, it was the most powerful nation in the world.

3. When Germany was defeated in that war, it lost lands in Europe and was stripped of its colonies overseas. The country sank into severe economic depression in the early 1930s. In 1933, Adolf Hitler and his Nazi party came to power by promising to make Germany great again. Hitler spread hatred to increase his power. He blamed all of the country's troubles on the Jews.

Flowing through Germany to the North Sea, the Rhine River passes many historic towns built for trade in the Middle Ages.

4. In 1939, Hitler began World War II by invading Poland. During World War II, Hitler had 6 million Jews and many other innocent people murdered in what became known as the *Holocaust.* However, by 1945, Germany again lay defeated and in ruins. The combined force of the Allies—France, the United Kingdom, the United States, and the Soviet Union—now occupied it.

5. To make sure that Nazi Germany would never rise again, the Allies divided the country and its capital, Berlin, into four zones. The Soviet Union controlled eastern Germany, and the other three nations controlled the west. In 1949, two Germanies were created. One was the Federal Republic of Germany, which was composed of the three western zones. It had a democratic government. The other was the communist German Democratic Republic, created from the Soviet zone.

6. The two Germanies became enemies immediately. Divided Berlin presented a special problem for them. It lay about 100 miles (160 kilometers) inside East Germany. Like the rest of Germany, it was divided into a democratic zone and a communist zone. Between 1949 and 1961, thousands of East Germans fled to West Berlin. To stop people from fleeing to the West, the East German government built a wall splitting the city. This wall became a symbol of a divided Germany.

7. Over the years, communist power slipped. Thousands of people, unhappy with the communist government, marched for free elections. Because so many people either protested the government or fled the country, East Germany finally was forced to open all its borders, including the Berlin Wall, in November 1989. In March 1990, East Germans held their first free elections and voted the communists out of power. On October 3, 1990, East and West Germany became a united country—the Federal Republic of Germany.

8. Today, the Federal Republic of Germany is a powerful nation of more than 79 million people. It is divided into 16 states: eleven from the former West Germany and five from the former East Germany. The country is headed by a chancellor who has real power to govern and a president who carries out the ceremonial duties. The new Germany also has a *bicameral,* or two-house, legislature, called Parliament.

9. Though Germany is one of the world's leading countries, it is actually a little smaller than the state of Montana. Because of its nearness to the sea, much of Germany has a marine climate. Warm, wet winds from the ocean bring warm winters, cool summers, and a lot of rain. Winter temperatures generally do not fall below freezing, while summer temperatures rarely rise above 70° F (21° C). The mild marine climate is ideal for farming. Although small areas of Germany in the south and east have a more extreme humid continental climate, they still produce a variety of crops.

10. Most of Germany is made up of mountains, hills, and plains. The high, rugged mountains of the south level off to become the hills and plateaus of central Germany. Then the land flattens into level plains that reach the North Sea.

11. Along Germany's southern border lie the Alps, with many high, snow-covered peaks, which attract many skiers in the winter. The hills and plateaus of central Germany have many forests. The most famous is called the Black Forest because of its huge, dark pine trees. In the summer, hikers enjoy the spectacular beauty of the hills, forests, and rivers. Tourists explore Munich [MYOO-nikh], the largest city in the south and one of Germany's important cultural centers.

12. The central region also contains rich coal and iron ore deposits. These resources have helped make the country into a highly

With gaping holes in the Berlin Wall at their backs, Germans in what was East Berlin stand in line in March 1990, waiting to vote in their first free elections.

industrialized nation. The Ruhr [ROOR] Valley, which has the richest of the coal and iron deposits, has long been Europe's leading industrial center. The area specializes in steel and iron production as well as chemicals and automobiles. These high-quality automobiles have made Germany one of the leading car manufacturers in the world.

13. Most of Germany's cities lie near its central zone. Two major rivers, the Rhine and the Elbe [EL-buh], flow through this rugged section. Cities such as Essen and Duesseldorf [DOOS-uhl-dawrf] are located near the rivers and the country's natural resources. In fact, the cities of the Ruhr have grown so much that they now form one huge metropolis called Ruhrstadt [ROOR-shtaht] or Ruhr City.

14. North of this area is a broad, flat plain where much of the land is barely above sea level. This is called the North German Plain and is part of the Great European Plain. Although much of the plain is used for farming, trade and manufacturing are also important to the economy. Hamburg, Germany's second largest city, is its leading port. Northern Germany contains the capital and largest city of Germany, Berlin, which has over four million people.

15. Important rivers such as the Rhine, the Elbe, and the Danube [DAN-yoob], flow through Germany. In areas where there are no *navigable* rivers (rivers deep enough for large ships), canals have been built to help the flow of goods and people. German rivers and canals link most of the major cities and ports, providing an excellent transportation system.

16. Today, Germany is one of the most urbanized nations in the world. As the Germans rebuilt their economy and industrial centers after World War II, many people again began moving from farms to cities looking for jobs. Today, 85 to 90 percent of all Germans live in cities. There, its people enjoy a high standard of living. Most live in apartments and own their own cars, televisions, and radios. Large numbers of men and women work outside the home in offices, stores, and factories. In their leisure time, people enjoy sports, especially soccer.

17. With a population of over 79 million, Germany needs a great deal of land to feed its people. However, only one-third of its land is fit for agriculture, and only 10 to 15 percent of its people are employed in farming. German farms, which produce grains, potatoes, sugar beets, and livestock, manage to supply about 75 percent of the food necessary for the people. The rest must be imported.

18. United Germany is a leading economic and political power in Europe. However, there are great challenges ahead. It is costing vast amounts of money to unite East Germany and West Germany. The new nation has had to take over East Germany's large debt, clean up pollution, and modernize transportation and telephone systems in the former communist nation. The final price tag to unite Germany is expected to be between $70 and $300 billion! Germans are committing much of their wealth and energy to make the new nation work.

As the two Germanys were united, East Berliners stood in line outside a West Berlin bank to receive "welcome money."

UNDERSTANDING WHAT YOU HAVE READ

1. **Which questions are answered in this chapter?**
    a. What is the climate of Germany?
    b. What three important rivers flow through Germany?
    c. What is the German national anthem?

2. **The main idea of this chapter describes**
    a. how Germany's history has affected its people today
    b. the Black Forest
    c. Germany's lead in car manufacturing

3. **A good description of Germany would include mention of**
    a. hills and plateaus covered with many forests
    b. rivers flowing through central zones
    c. warm climate with little rainfall

4. **Along Germany's southern border lie(s)**
    a. the Alps
    b. the Black Forest
    c. major Seaports

5. **Many sections of Germany are ideal for farming because of**
    a. the mild marine climate
    b. the large population
    c. the high, rugged mountains

6. **What industry has made Germany one of the leading exporters of the world?**
    a. automobiles
    b. wheat
    c. gold

7. **Germany's governing body includes**
    a. a chancellor, a president, and a parliament
    b. a king or a queen
    c. the people and the military

8. **The Ruhr Valley is rich in**
    a. coal and iron deposits
    b. bauxite and lead
    c. silver and chromite

DEVELOPING CRITICAL THINKING SKILLS

Do You Agree or Disagree?

1. Germany has a mild marine climate.
2. Germany lies next to the Commonwealth of Independent States.
3. The climate of Germany is affected by its nearness to the sea.
4. Germany has huge supplies of oil and natural gas.
5. In 1949, East and West Germany became a united country—the Federal Republic of Germany.
6. Germany is closer to the United States than it is to the Commonwealth of Independent States.
7. Much of the land is covered with forests and rapid mountain streams.
8. Rich soils make Germany the greatest wheat-growing country of Europe.
9. Germany has rich iron-ore deposits.
10. Electricity is a great source of power in Germany.

DEVELOPING IDEAS AND SKILLS

Building Map Skills — Germany

1. Does Germany lie in the high, middle, or low latitudes?
2. Berlin, the largest city and capital, is located in what part of Germany?
3. If you flew from your community to Germany, in what direction would you be traveling?
4. What city is located near 53 degrees north latitude and ten degrees east longitude?
5. What is the distance from Munich to Nuremberg?
6. Where are the large cities of Germany located? Why is this so?
7. Into what seas do the broad rivers of Germany flow? In which direction do they flow?
8. What is Germany's second largest city and leading port?
9. What countries border Germany on the east?
10. What countries border Germany to the west?

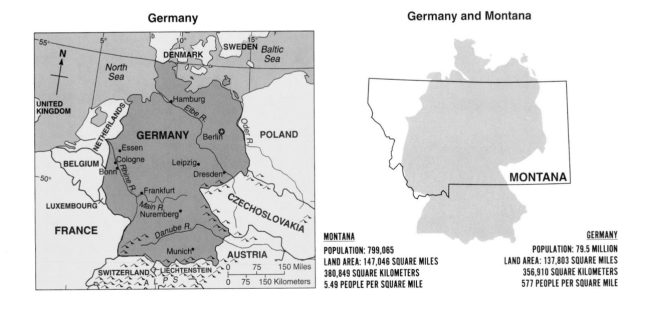

Germany

Germany and Montana

MONTANA
POPULATION: 799,065
LAND AREA: 147,046 SQUARE MILES
380,849 SQUARE KILOMETERS
5.49 PEOPLE PER SQUARE MILE

GERMANY
POPULATION: 79.5 MILLION
LAND AREA: 137,803 SQUARE MILES
356,910 SQUARE KILOMETERS
577 PEOPLE PER SQUARE MILE

WRITING

Now that you have completed your study of Germany, you have an opportunity to describe the nation. Use the following questions to help you organize facts to show what Germany is like. Use the five themes of geography to help you uncover the answers. Then combine your answers in a paragraph that describes Germany.

1. What is the location of the city of Munich?
2. What are some physical and human characteristics of the land and people of Germany?
3. In what positive way have human/environmental interactions occurred in Germany?
4. How has movement affected Germany's rise to industrial leadership?
5. How has Germany's place in Europe affected its accessibility to the rest of the world?

Chapter 14

A New Age in Eastern Europe

What changes have taken place in Eastern Europe since the 1980s?

READING FOR A PURPOSE:
1. How do land forms and climate changes affect the economies of Eastern Europe?
2. What conditions led to the fall of communism in Eastern Europe?
3. How does geography affect the problems the new governments of Eastern Europe are facing?

1. It was the late 1980s. The winds of change were blowing fiercely across Eastern Europe. Eastern European citizens took to the streets demanding democratic reforms. Ultimately, their demands were met and communist governments came toppling down. Eastern Europe entered a new age.

2. Throughout the history of eastern Europe, the area has experienced frequent changes. Such physical features as mountain passes, valleys, and lowland plains made Eastern Europe easy to invade. Many groups of people have moved into and out of the region, making it a crossroads of many cultures. Eastern Europe has been the site of a number of wars because of its location, fertile soils, and natural resources. National boundaries and governments have shifted many times.

3. Eastern Europe stretches from the Baltic Sea in the north to the Adriatic Sea in the south. It is sandwiched between the Commonwealth of Independent States and the countries of Western Europe. The region includes Poland, Czechoslovakia [chek-uh-sloh-VAHK-ee-uh], Hungary, Romania, Bulgaria, Yugoslavia, and Albania. Three states that border the Baltic Sea, Estonia, Latvia, and Lithuania, declared independence from the Soviet Union in September 1991. Other states in Eastern Europe have an uncertain status.

Croatia, Bosnia and Herzegovina, and Slovenia, which had been a part of Yugoslavia, have declared their independence.

4. Since Eastern Europe is made up of so many countries, you might think that it is very large. Actually, the combined area of all the countries in Eastern Europe is smaller than the state of Alaska. Although Eastern Europe is small in size, it has a remarkable variety of land forms. In the south, the Balkan Peninsula is filled with rugged mountain ranges and steep valleys. The Balkan Mountains and the Dinaric Alps have acted as barriers that prevent invasion, but they have also contributed to the ethnic divisions. Today, dozens of languages are spoken on the peninsula.

5. North of the Balkans, the Danube River dominates the land. The Danube is the longest river of Eastern Europe and the second largest river in Europe. It flows from Germany's Black Forest, through Eastern Europe, across a huge plain that covers most of Hungary, and

The Danube River flows through the middle of Budapest, the capital of Hungary. More than 2 million people live in this city. It is noted for its museums, historic houses, colleges, and libraries.

Not all of Eastern Europe has a humid-continental climate. Check the map on page 251 to find out what the climate is along the coast of Croatia.

empties into the Black Sea. This plain, called the Hungarian Basin, is mostly farmland.

6. North of the basin is a twisting set of mountain ranges called the Carpathians [kahr-PAY-the-uhnz], which divide Poland from the rest of Eastern Europe. The range curves through mountainous Czechoslovakia into southern Poland. In Romania, the southern branch of the Carpathians is called the Transylvanian Alps. This is an historic area that is said to be the home of the fictional character Dracula!

7. The northernmost section of Eastern Europe is dominated by the North European Plain. Flowing through the plain is the Vistula River. Most of Poland occupies the plains surrounding the Vistula and its tributaries. Lithuania, Estonia, and Latvia also lie on the North European Plain. Here, especially, many different people have fought to control the plains for hundreds of years.

8. Most of Eastern Europe has a humid continental climate. The winters are cold, and the summers are hot. There is also plenty of rain for the crops. Up to 20 inches (50 centimeters) per year falls in many places. Parts of Yugoslavia, Bulgaria, and Albania have a Mediterranean climate, or long, hot summers and short, mild winters. Therefore, the growing season in these Mediterranean areas lasts all year.

9. Eastern Europe has a variety of natural resources. There is iron ore in Czechoslovakia, Poland, Romania, and Hungary. There is oil and natural gas in Romania and Bulgaria. Poland's forests provide lumber. Eastern Europe's mines are rich in coal and copper.

10. Some of the richest most fertile soil on earth lies on Eastern Europe's plains. Eastern Europe's main crops are grains, such as wheat, rye, barley, and oats. Farmers also grow potatoes and sugar beets. Romania is Eastern Europe's leading wheat and wool producer. Poland produces the most potatoes, barley, oats, rye, sugar beets, hogs, beef, and dairy cattle.

11. Eastern Europe is a region of great cultural diversity. There are about 131 million people living in Eastern Europe. Albania, the least populous country, has a little more than 3 million people while Poland, the most populous, has more than 38 million people. Most Eastern European nations are *multiethnic,* or composed of many different ethnic groups.

The largest ethnic group is Slavic. The Slavs themselves consist of a number of groups, including Poles, Czechs, Slovaks, and Bulgarians, Croatians [kroh-A-shuns], Slovenes [SLOH-veens], and Serbs. So, most Eastern Europeans speak a Slavic language, such as Polish, Czech, Bulgarian, or Serbo-Croatian. The people of Hungary make up another group. They speak Magyar [MAG-ee-ahr], a language they brought with them from Central Asia about 1,000 years ago. The Romanians speak a Romance language that is based on Latin.

12. Serious challenges lay ahead because of the many ethnic differences in the region. In Yugoslavia, ethnic conflict in the early 1990s tore the country apart as Serbs, Croatians, and Slovenians fought for their independence. Such countries as Czechoslovakia and Hungary faced similar prospects. Gypsies and Jews, who are other groups living in Eastern Europe, face discrimination that has existed for hundreds of years.

13. Religious differences also divide Eastern Europe. Today, most people are either Eastern Orthodox or Roman Catholic. The

This palace in Prague, Czechoslovakia, used to be the home of the royal family. Now it is the home of the president of the republic. What major changes have taken place in the past few years in the way leaders are chosen in Eastern Europe?

people of Poland, Hungary, and Czechoslovakia are mainly Roman Catholic. Most of the people in Bulgaria, Romania, and about half of Yugoslavia are Eastern Orthodox. Albanians are largely Muslim. The Jewish religion is also practiced in Eastern Europe.

14. Eastern Europe has been a land conquered again and again by foreign powers, such as the Romans, the Turks, and the Germans. After World War II, the Communists took control of much of this area. Estonia, Latvia, and Lithuania were forced into the Soviet Union. Hungary, Poland, Czechoslovakia, Romania and Bulgaria became *satellite* states, nations dependent on the Soviet Union. Only Yugoslavia and Albania, though communist, remained somewhat independent. The Eastern European governments were modeled after the Soviet Union's government. This meant the communist party controlled the government. In most countries, the government ran the economy and also controlled the newspapers, the radio, and television stations.

15. Soviet leaders used strong measures to control its satellites. Revolts in Hungary in 1956 and Czechoslovakia in 1968 were quickly crushed by Soviet tanks and troops.

16. However, a revolution in Poland set an example for the people of Eastern Europe. In 1980, Polish workers formed a free labor union, called Solidarity. It was led by Lech Walesa [LEK vah-LEN-sah]. Hoping to lower prices and receive higher wages, union workers began striking. At first, the unions forced the government to recognize them. When workers increased their demands, the government outlawed the union and jailed its leaders. By about 1983, the government had released the union leaders. The government's treatment of Solidarity was an important reason the communists lost power in 1989. In December 1990, Lech Walesa was elected president of Poland in the country's first free elections.

17. Democracy gained strength in Eastern Europe as communism weakened throughout the 1980s. In 1989, communist governments in East Germany, Czeckoslovakia, Hungary, Romania, and Bulgaria also fell. Soon, Hungary opened its border with Austria. Hungarians helped tear down the barbed-wire fence, sometimes with their bare hands. Thousands of Eastern Europeans fled to the West through this opening in the Iron Curtain. Even Albania, the last communist holdout, opened its borders and set up free elections for 1991.

18. An important reason for the decline of communism was the collapse of the economies of Eastern Europe. As communist countries, the Eastern Europe nations had planned economies. The government decided what and how much to produce. State-controlled farms were not well organized, and they used outdated farming methods and machinery. Therefore, the farms did not produce enough food for the people.

19. The governments also controlled industry. The communists ran the factories and decided what and how much to make. They were more interested in producing heavy machinery and equipment than consumer goods. Items such as shoes and meat were often in short supply.

20. Today, the level of economic development differs from country to country. In general, the northern part of Eastern Europe is urban and industrial, and the southern part is rural. The countries with the most industry, Poland, Czechoslovakia, and Hungary, are the wealthiest. Others, like Albania which depend mostly on farming, are poorer. However, even the wealthier nations do not have a standard of living that is equal to Western Europe's.

21. At the start of the 1990s, the new governments of Eastern Europe faced many challenges. Having rid themselves of their communist governments, they now had to change their planned economies into free-market economies. Industrial production was down, unemployment was up, prices soared, and there were severe housing and food shortages. People often stood in line for hours just to buy basic necessities. Some governments even began *rationing,* giving out limited amounts, of sugar, flour, dairy products, soap, toilet paper, gasoline, and electricity.

22. The new governments of Eastern Europe are trying to do something about the pollution that has plagued the region. The Danube was once one of the world's most beautiful rivers. Today, the Danube is heavily polluted. Cities along the river dump raw sewage and industrial wastes. Industrial air pollution has destroyed thousands of acres of trees and endangered human lives. Cleaning up the river and the air will be a huge task.

23. Ending communism in Eastern Europe was an historic change, but the people of the region face enormous economic problems, ethnic hostilities, and environmental dangers. Solutions to these difficulties will bring true freedom.

UNDERSTANDING WHAT YOU HAVE READ

1. Which questions are answered in this chapter?
a. Why is the Danube River important to the people of Eastern Europe?
b. What physical features have made Eastern Europe easy to invade?
c. Which countries are landlocked?

2. The main idea of this chapter describes
a. trade in Eastern Europe
b. the lands and people of Eastern Europe
c. how the satellite countries are ruled

3. The following states border the Baltic Sea
a. Estonia, Latvia, and Lithuania
b. Romania, Bulgaria, and Lithuania
c. Greece, Albania, and Italy

4. Poland, Czechoslovakia, and Hungary are the countries in Eastern Europe with the
a. least wealth
b. lowest standards of living
c. most industry

5. The Slavic ethnic group consists of
a. Poles, Czechs, and Serbs
b. Germans, French, and Belgians
c. Scottish, Irish, and Welch

6. Why is there unrest in Eastern Europe?
a. The people may want to be free from foreign control.
b. There are many ethnic and religious differences in the region.
c. These countries are not members of the United Nations.

7. The dominant religious groups in Eastern Europe are
a. Eastern Orthodox or Roman Catholic
b. Buddhist or Muslim
c. Orthodox Jews and Shinto

8. A major steel-producing country of Eastern Europe is
a. Albania
b. Poland
c. Bulgaria

9. Poland's farms produce
a. cotton, rice, and citrus fruits
b. olives and wine grapes
c. potatoes, sugar beets, and beef and dairy cattle

313

DEVELOPING IDEAS AND SKILLS

Building Map Skills — Eastern Europe and The United States

1. How many countries do we include in Eastern Europe?
2. Which of these countries border the Commonwealth of Independent States?
3. Which of these countries are landlocked?
4. Locate the capital city of each country. Which ones are sea or ocean ports?
5. Locate the Danube River. Through which countries does it flow?
6. The Danube forms the boundary or part of the boundary between which countries?
7. In which direction does the Vistula River in Poland flow?
8. The United States is how many times as large as the entire region of Eastern Europe?
9. How does Eastern Europe compare with the United States in the density of population?
10. Locate the four states bordering the Baltic Sea.

Eastern Europe

Eastern Europe and the United States

UNITED STATES
POPULATION: 253 MILLION
LAND AREA: 3.6 MILLION SQUARE MILES
9.36 MILLION SQUARE KILOMETERS
70 PEOPLE PER SQUARE MILE

EASTERN EUROPE
POPULATION: 131.9 MILLION
LAND AREA: 517,600 SQUARE MILES
1.35 MILLION SQUARE KILOMETERS
255 PEOPLE PER SQUARE MILE

The European Region

Country	Area (Square Miles)	Capital	Population (1991 estimates)	Number of Years to Double Population	Life Expectancy	Per Capita GNP, 1989
Albania	11,100	Tiranë	3,300,000	36	72	—
Andorra	185	Andorra la Vella	51,000	—	—	—
Austria	32,375	Vienna	7,700,000	770	75	$17,360
Belgium	42,822	Brussels	9,900,000	495	74	$16,390
Bosnia and Herzegovina	19,741	Sarajevo	4,200,000	90	72	—
Bulgaria	44,365	Sofia	9,000,000	630	67	$ 2,320
Croatia	21,829	Zagreb	4,600,000	1,386	72	—
Czechoslovakia	49,371	Prague	15,700,000	408	72	—
Denmark	16,629	Copenhagen	5,100,000	1,732	75	$20,510
Estonia	17,413	Tallinn	1,600,000	365	70	—
Finland	130,127	Helsinki	5,000,000	239	75	$22,060
France	211,208	Paris	56,700,000	169	77	$17,830
Germany	137,803	Bonn	79,500,000	—	75	$16,200
Greece	50,942	Athens	10,100,000	770	77	$ 5,340
Hungary	35,919	Budapest	10,400,000	—	70	$ 2,560
Iceland	39,768	Reykjavik	300,000	62	78	$21,240
Ireland	27,135	Dublin	3,500,000	117	74	$ 8,500
Italy	116,305	Rome	57,700,000	1,155	76	$15,150
Latvia	24,695	Riga	2,700,000	630	70	—
Liechtenstein	61	Vaduz	30,000	98	70	—
Lithuania	25,170	Vilnius	3,700,000	158	72	—
Luxembourg	992	Luxembourg	400,000	385	74	$24,860
Malta	124	Valletta	400,000	83	75	$ 5,280
Monaco	.6	Monaco-Ville	29,000*	—	—	—
Netherlands	15,770	Amsterdam and the Hague	15,000,000	165	77	$16,010
Norway	125,181	Oslo	4,300,000	204	76	$21,850
Poland	120,727	Warsaw	38,200,000	144	72	$ 1,760
Portugal	36,390	Lisbon	10,400,000	315	74	$ 4,260
Romania	91,699	Bucharest	23,400,000	131	70	—
San Marino	24	San Marino	23,000**	144	76	—
Slovenia	7,819	Ljubljana	1,900,000	267	73	—
Spain	194,896	Madrid	39,000,000	308	76	$ 9,150
Switzerland	15,942	Bern	6,800,000	231	78	$30,270
United Kingdom	94,226	London	57,500,000	330	75	$14,750
Vatican City	.17	Vatican City	750**	—	—	—
Yugoslavia	39,449	Belgrade	10,890,000	133	71	$ 2,490

* 1989 ** 1990

Sources: 1991 World Population Data Sheet of the Population Reference Bureau, Inc.; The World Almanac and Book of Facts, 1992.

KEY IDEAS

- Rapid political and economic change is taking place in the region located in the heart of Eurasia. Democratic ideas have replaced communist governments and leadership.

- A number of newly independent nations have emerged from the collapse of the Soviet Union. These nations are experiencing new freedoms.

- The chief physical characteristic is a huge lowland plain which allows open movement of people, ideas, and goods.

- North-flowing rivers and a lack of warm-water seaports make this a vast landlocked region with few easy outlets for world trade.

- Many national or ethnic groups live in the heart of Eurasia, but the largest groups are Slavic-speaking Russians, Ukranians, and Belarussians.

- Change is underway in the way farms and factories are organized. People are free to attempt free enterprise by growing their own food for profit.

- The people of the heart of Eurasia face many critical problems in changing to democracy and free enterprise.

The Russian people fill Red Square in Moscow to celebrate the end of communism. The citizens of newly free republics in the heart of Eurasia face many challenges.

Chapter 1

The Commonwealth: A Eurasian Giant

Why is the new Commonwealth of Independent States one of the most important areas of the world?

READING FOR A PURPOSE:
1. What is the Commonwealth of Independent States (CIS) and how is it different from the Soviet Union?
2. What are some of the problems the Commonwealth is facing?
3. How does the size of the Commonwealth and its different ethnic groups affect life in this region?

1. In 1991, the Soviet Union fell apart at the seams. As each of the republics that formed the Soviet Union declared its independence, the world looked on anxiously. This enormous region stretches across two continents: Europe and Asia. Its 8,600,000 square miles (22,000,000 square kilometers) occupy one-sixth of the earth's land area. Disorder in this vast territory affects everyone in the world. That is why the world was relieved when 11 of the 15 republics agreed to become the Commonwealth of Independent States. A commonwealth is a loose organization of independent states that gives limited power to the central government.

2. The largest and most powerful republic in the Commonwealth is Russia. It covers about three-fourths of the land area of the former Soviet Union. Large parts of Russia are located in Asia, but most of the people live in the European portions of Russia. The three major republics in Europe—Russia, Ukraine (yoo-KRANE), and Belarus (bel-ah-ROOS)—have about three-fourths of the Commonwealth's population. Tiny Moldova (mahl-DOH-vuh) is the fourth European republic in the Commonwealth. Three republics located along the shores of the Baltic Sea—Estonia (e-STOH-nee-uh), Latvia (LAT-vee-uh), and Lithuania (lith-uh-WAY-nee-uh)—had earlier gained their independence from the Soviet Union and did not wish to join the Commonwealth.

The Kremlin in Moscow. The fortress contains many ancient buildings. Parts of the walls are almost 500 years old.

3. The Central Asian republics in the Commonwealth have smaller populations. These republics are Kazakhstan (kuh-ZAHK-stahn), Uzbekistan (uz-BEK-i-stahn), Kyrgyzstan (kir-GEEZ-stahn), Tajikistan (tah-JIK-i-stahn), and Turkmenistan (tuhrk-MEN-i-stahn). Farther west, in the Caucasus mountain area, are Armenia (ahr-MEE-nee-uh) and Azerbaijan (az-uhr-bye-JAHN), both of which joined the Commonwealth. Georgia, also in this region, did not join the Commonwealth.

4. Even without all of the former Soviet republics, the Commonwealth extends almost halfway around the world. Its population of almost 280,000,000 people is made up of more than 100 different ethnic groups. Compared with the nations of the world, the Commonwealth ranks third in population.

5. The nations of the Commonwealth have many natural resources. Russia has large reserves of oil, much of which is exported by pipeline to Western Europe. One-fifth of the world's forests grow in the European republics. The vast prairies of the European republics contain rich farmland. There are major mineral resources in addition to oil. Like much of the oil, many of these resources are in Siberia, which is in the Asian part of the Russian republic. Siberia's climate is harsh, and distances are great. Because the mineral deposits are often hard to reach and difficult to move, mining them is costly.

6. In spite of their natural wealth, the republics have serious problems to solve. Many of the different national and ethnic groups in the republics do not get along with each other. Under the iron rule of the Soviet government, these rivalries were kept under strict control. For example, Armenia and Azerbaijan in Central Asia have been enemies for most of their history. However, Soviet armies maintained order for many years. Now there is no central army to prevent outbreaks of violence between these two republics. The rivalries are often bitter because ethnic minorities within each republic are sometimes persecuted. Now that travel to the West is permit-

Time out for workers on a state farm near Rostov. Which area of the Unites States is similar to this flat farming area of Russia?

ted, many educated members of minorities are leaving the republics.

7. Questions about boundaries are another problem. Under the previous government, boundaries were not an issue. The individual republics had no reason to press their claims for more territory. Now that the republics are independent, such things matter. Russia, for example, wants to change the border that separates it from Ukraine. Many other republics have similar claims. These disputes must be settled peacefully if the fragile Commonwealth is to survive.

8. If the new Commonwealth enjoyed a prosperous economy, it would be easier for the republics to resolve their differences. But poverty and the breakdown of the economy have increased rivalries. The Soviet Union did not have a free-market economy. In a free-market economy, prices are determined by demand rather than being set by a central committee. The Soviet Union had a Communist economy. Soviet currency was based on the ruble, just as currency in the United States is based on the dollar. The Soviet government controlled the value of the ruble. As the government needed more money to pay workers, it printed more rubles. As more rubles were circulated, the value of the

Reading a Map with a Pie Graph

The Eurasian region and Northern America are alike in one way. They both have many national or ethnic groups. The groups in Eurasia have different backgrounds, customs, and languages. The members of each ethnic group generally tend to live with other members of their group in the republics that make up the Eurasian region. (A republic is like a province or state.)

The largest national groups are the three that are Slavic-speaking—the Russians, the Ukrainians, and the Belorussians. The Russians are the largest group among them, making up about half the population of the

Eurasian region. Members of the Russian ethnic group live throughout the region and are large minorities in many republics. The Ukrainians, the second largest Slavic group, live in the southern part of the Commonwealth. The Belorussians, the third largest Slavic group, live in the western part of Eurasia.

As you look at all the pie graphs, you will see that, except in Kazakhstan, the majority of the people living in each republic are from that region. In Kazakhstan, the Kazakhs make up only 40 percent of the people living there. Most of the area around the Caspian Sea is a mountainous region called

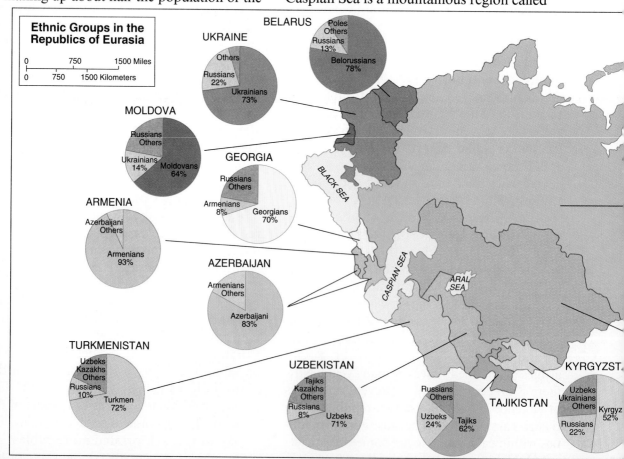

the Caucasus. The major national groups in this area are the Georgians, the Azerbaijanis, and the Armenians.

In central Asia, are the Muslim and Turkic-speaking peoples. The Uzbeks are the largest among these groups. Other Turkic groups include the Kazakhs, Kyrgyz, and the Turkmen. Their ancestors were once nomads in this region. (Another Turkic group is the Tatars who live mainly in the Volga River valley in European Russia.) The Tajiks also live in central Asia.

Many national groups do not have their own republic. They include large numbers of German-speaking and Polish-speaking people and Jews.

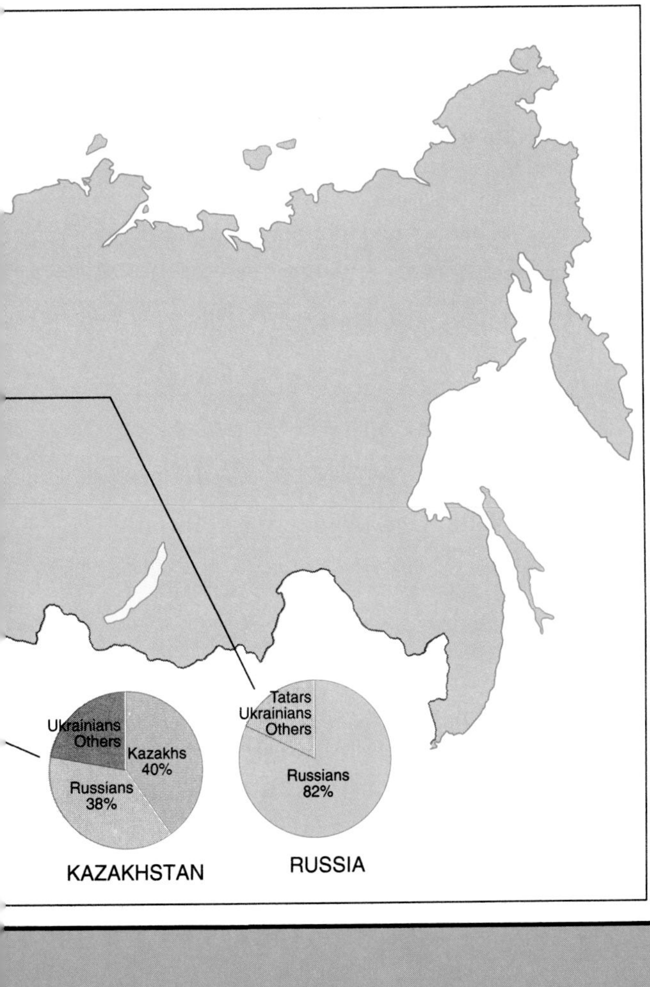

Look at the map shown here. It names the 12 republics of Eurasia. The percentages of national groups living in each republic is shown through *pie graphs*. A pie graph is a circle that is divided into parts. The pie or circle must add up to 100 percent. Look at the pie graph for the Republic of Uzbekistan. It shows that 71 percent of the republic is made up of Uzbeks; therefore, 71 percent of the circle is shaded. The rest of the pie graph shows the remaining ethnic groups in the region. What is the percentage of Russians in the Uzbek regions? What ethnic groups make up the remaining part of the pie graph?

1. Name the republics of the Eurasian region.
2. Which is the largest republic?
3. What is the percentage of Armenians in the Republic of Armenia?
4. What national groups live in the Ukraine? What is the percentage for each?
5. Where is the Republic of Georgia located?
6. Which republics were annexed during World War II?
7. Which ethnic groups do not have their own republic?
8. Which major ethnic groups are in the Caucasus region?
9. What is the percentage of Russians in the Republic of Kyrgyzstan?
10. Which is the major ethnic group in Kazakhstan?

Ukrainians
Others
Kazakhs 40%
Russians 38%

KAZAKHSTAN

Tatars
Ukrainians
Others
Russians 82%

RUSSIA

ruble fell. It is now worth very little. As a result, the people of the Commonwealth now suffer from inflation, or rapidly rising prices.

9. The Soviet Union was considered a superpower. Under communism, the nation poured its resources into building its military strength. Soviet foreign policy was designed to extend Soviet influence around the globe. The Soviet Union's nearest neighbors lived nervously in the shadow of this giant. Now that the Soviet Union no longer exists, the republics of the Commonwealth must build new relationships among themselves and with the nations to the east and west.

UNDERSTANDING WHAT YOU HAVE READ

1. Which of the following questions are answered in this chapter?
a. Are there forests in the Commonwealth of Independent States?
b. Why is the Commonwealth important in the world today?
c. Who are the leaders of the Commonwealth today?

2. The main idea of *paragraphs 6 through 8* is that
a. the Commonwealth of Independent States is an important member of the United Nations
b. the Commonwealth has used its troops in many parts of the world
c. the republics of the Commonwealth must build new relationships among themselves

3. The Soviet Union fell apart in
a. 1956   b. 1991   c. 1919

4. The Commonwealth of Independent States stretches across all the following continents EXCEPT
a. Asia   b. Europe   c. Africa

5. Which statement is TRUE of the population of the Commonwealth of Independent States?
a. It has more people than any country in the world.
b. It includes more than 100 different ethnic groups.
c. It has few people despite its large size.

6. All of the following statements are true of the Commonwealth of Independent States EXCEPT
a. it is equal in size to the United States
b. eleven of the fifteen republics of the former Soviet Union belong to the Commonwealth
c. the Commonwealth has many natural resources

7. From what you have read, which of the following statements are TRUE?
a. Rivalries among the republics are no longer a problem.
b. The people of the Commonwealth of Independent States speak the same language, dress the same, and worship in the same church.
c. Many of the republics want more territory.

8. In a *commonwealth,*
a. independent states give limited power to a central government
b. independent states give all power to a central government
c. the largest and most powerful state runs the central government

9. All of the following republics of the former Soviet Union joined the Commonwealth of Independent States EXCEPT
a. Ukraine
b. Lithuania
c. Azerbaijan

Chapter 2

The Land of the Commonwealth

How does the nature of the land affect Eurasia's people?

READING FOR A PURPOSE:
1. How large is the Commonwealth of Independent States?
2. What is the surface of the land like?
3. How do the rivers affect the movement of goods in this area?

1. From western Ukraine to Russia's eastern border on the Sea of Japan is a distance of almost 6,000 miles (9,600 kilometers). This distance is about twice the distance between the Atlantic and Pacific coasts of the continental United States. The Commonwealth of Independent States is so big it spans 11 different time zones! So when the sun is making its appearance in Ukraine, it is disappearing below the horizon in eastern Siberia. The Commonwealth also has the longest coastline in the world. However, the northern part of this great coast is on the Arctic Ocean. That means that most northern harbors are frozen much of the year, making the coast useless for shipping.

2. This huge region is located far north of the equator. In fact, some of the area lies above the Arctic Circle. St. Petersburg, one of the largest cities in Russia, is on almost the same line of latitude as Anchorage, Alaska. The southernmost point of the Commonwealth, in Tajikistan, is only 35° north latitude. This means that the *entire region* is farther north than Memphis, Tennessee.

3. The largest geographic feature in Eurasia is a lowland plain that was once the bottom of an ancient sea. This plain, part of the Great European Plain, stretches across Europe and into Asia as far as the Yenisei (ye-nuh-SA) River in central Siberia. The low hills of the Ural (YUHR-uhl) Mountains rise in the middle to separate the European and Asian sides of the plain. The lowlands on the Asian side of the Urals are some of the flattest in the world, and much of it is swampy.

4. The plain is bordered on the north, south, and east by mountain ranges. The mountains in the east block any rain clouds coming from the Pacific. This means that the moisture from the oceans cannot blow west. For this reason, there are enormous deserts in the eastern part of the Commonwealth.

The Nurgush Range in the Southern Urals.

A wheat harvest in the steppes, or plains of the Central Asian republic of Kazakhstan.

5. Eurasia has many long rivers. These rivers help connect the interior with the countries of Western Europe and the Mediterranean Sea. West of the Ural Mountains, the largest rivers are the Dnieper (NEE-puhr), the Don, and the Volga. The Volga is the longest river in Europe. It empties into the Caspian (KAS-pee-uhn) Sea, which is really a salt lake. The Dnieper and Don rivers empty into ports of the Black Sea. At its southeast corner, the Black Sea is connected to the busy Mediterranean Sea by waterways that include narrow straits called the Dardanelles (dar-duh-NELZ). These straits, controlled by Turkey, are used to move goods to world markets. Another outlet for shipping is the Baltic Sea. However, the Baltic is partly frozen during much of the year.

6. Eurasia's longest rivers can be found east of the Urals in Asia. These include the Ob (AHB)—the region's longest river—the Yenisei, the Lena (LEE-nuh), and the Amur (AH-muhr). These rivers rise, or begin, in the higher lands to the south. Except for the Amur, they flow toward the Arctic Ocean in the north. These rivers are frozen for many months of the year. This means that ships cannot travel down the rivers to the ocean and to ports around the world. The Amur is the only river that reaches the warmer waters of the Pacific Ocean.

7. As you can see, the republics find it hard to reach the rest of the world with their goods. East of the Urals, in Asia, high mountains separate the southern part of the Commonwealth from warmer lands. In the north, the icy waters of the Arctic Ocean make the rivers and harbors hard to use for much of the year. The ports on the Pacific Ocean are far from the major trade routes of the world, and mountain ranges separate them from the region's industries. The most convenient ports are on the Black Sea. Their one drawback is that Commonwealth ships must pass through the narrow Dardanelles to get to the Mediterranean.

The Yenisei River flows into the Kara Sea, an arm of the cold Arctic Ocean.

On December 21, 1991, 11 republics of the Soviet Union signed a declaration forming the Commonwealth of Independent States. Only Georgia refused to join the Commonwealth. Which state in the new Commonwealth is the largest? Which city lies in Belarus? Which states border China? Where are most of the large cities located? Why do you think this is so?

UNDERSTANDING WHAT YOU HAVE READ

1. **Which of the following questions are answered in this chapter?**
   a. Why are the rivers of the Commonwealth of Independent States not very useful for trade?
   b. Which countries border the Commonwealth?
   c. Which is the longest river in Europe?

2. **The main idea of *paragraphs 5 and 6* is to describe the**
   a. use of the water resources of Eurasia
   b. rivers of Eurasia
   c. problems of the inland seas

3. **The vast Eurasian lowland plain is divided by the**
   a. Caucasus Mountains
   b. Ural Mountains
   c. Alps

4. **Why are Eurasia's rivers east of the Urals in Asia not highly useful for trade?**
   a. They are very short in length.
   b. Rapids prevent boats from using them for long distances.
   c. They are frozen for many months of the year.

5. **The Ural Mountains**
   a. make travel from Europe to Asia almost impossible
   b. guard the Commonwealth of Independent States against invasion from the south
   c. are low and easily crossed

6. **All of the following statements about the Commonwealth of Independent States are true EXCEPT**
   a. it spreads across 11 time zones
   b. people in one part of the country may be on their way to bed while those in another part are going to work
   c. the Commonwealth has more people than any country in the world.

7. **It is likely that the Great European Plain**
   a. contains few people
   b. is mostly flat to gently rolling
   c. contains rich soil for the growing of crops

8. **All of the following statements are true of trade in the Commonwealth of Independent States EXCEPT**
   a. the Commonwealth has the longest coastline in the world
   b. many seaports have to be cleared of ice in the winter
   c. the most convenient ports are on the Baltic Sea

9. **Some parts of the Commonwealth of Independent States lie**
   a. south of Memphis, Tennessee
   b. south of the equator
   c. north of the Arctic Circle

10. **The longest river in Europe is**
    a. the Dardanelles
    b. the Volga
    c. the Dnieper

11. **All of Eurasia's longest rivers flow north toward the Arctic Ocean EXCEPT**
    a. the Amur
    b. the Yenisei
    c. the Lena

12. **The most convenient ports of the Commonwealth of Independent States are located on**
    a. the Black Sea
    b. the Mediterranean Sea
    c. the Arctic Ocean

Building Map Skills—Land Forms of the Independent Republics

Tell whether these statements are *true* or *false*. Be able to explain your answers.

1. Comparing the climate map of the Republics with the map of land forms below, you will see that nearly all the tundra is mountainous.
2. The eastern part of the Republics has several different land forms.
3. The western part of this region is largely lowland.
4. The plains of the Republics cover thousands of miles from east to west.
5. The plateau is the most important land form along the southern border.
6. Most of the mountains of this region are near its outer edges.

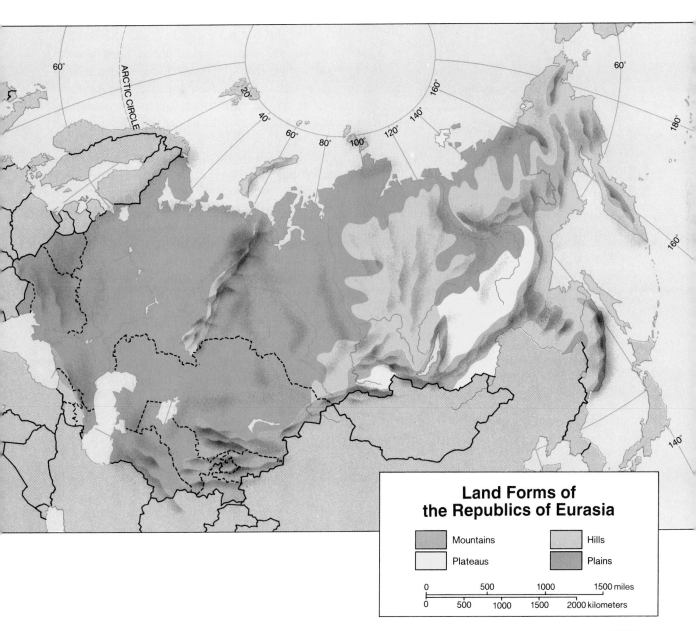

Land Forms of the Republics of Eurasia

Mountains	Hills
Plateaus	Plains

0   500   1000   1500 miles

0   500   1000   1500   2000 kilometers

Chapter 3

Land of Many Climates

How is life in the Commonwealth of Independent States affected by its climates?

READING FOR A PURPOSE:
1. Why do few people live on the tundra or taiga?
2. Where is the best farmland in the Commonwealth?
3. Where are the warmer lands of the Commonwealth?

1. In northern Russia, it is so cold that in some places the ground is frozen 3,000 miles (4,800 kilometers) deep. Car engines must run all the time, for if they stop, they freeze. Milk is sold in frozen slabs, and people can work outside for only a half hour before they must go inside to warm up. In winter, the temperatures hover around -60°F (-52°C).

2. In general, the Russian climate is much like that of Canada, although winters in the northern areas are even colder than those in Canada. Russians call their winter weather "General Winter," because it has helped them defeat invaders. In 1812, the French armies of the Emperor Napoleon had to retreat after a bitter winter in Moscow. Thousands of soldiers died of cold or starvation. In World War II, the Russian winter helped to defeat the armies of Adolf Hitler. However, not all of the countries of the Commonwealth have a cold climate. Because of its vast size, the Commonwealth has many climates.

3. The coldest part of the region is the tundra, found in the far north, where temperatures are cold year round. The flat and treeless land of the tundra extends along the Arctic coast as much as several hundred miles inland. Cold winds from the Arctic Ocean blow across it to reach the lands farther south. The temperatures of the tundra are below freezing as much as eight months of the year. Even in the summer, the ground is frozen beneath a thin layer of thawed earth. This frozen ground is called permafrost. The permafrost allows just a short growing season for crops. Only plants with short roots can thrive there.

4. Few people live on the tundra. Those who do brave the cold make their living by

Hotel at Sochi, on the Black Sea. Even though Sochi is as far north of the equator as is New York City, its climate is more like that of Los Angeles. Why?

The taiga is a land of dense forest, flowing rivers, and wide temperature changes.

hunting, fishing, and herding reindeer. These nomads, or wanderers, move from place to place as their reindeer herds graze the tundra. The reindeer furnish the people with nearly everything they need. The herders eat reindeer meat and drink reindeer milk. They make tents and clothing from reindeer skins. They use the reindeer to carry their belongings. Some who live on the tundra also hunt wild animals, such as the ermine and fox, for their valuable furs.

5. South of the tundra are the forest lands, or taiga. Taiga is a Russian word for "dense forest." The Commonwealth has more acres of forest than any nation in the world. The taiga area alone is nearly as large as the entire United States! It has many rivers, lakes, and ponds. A greater range of temperature is found in the taiga because the land is farther from the waters of the Arctic Ocean. In winter, a temperature of -60°F (-52°C) is common. During the summer, the temperatures may reach 80° to 90°F (27° to 32°C). At that time, the frozen waters melt and the land becomes soft and marshy. Fuel and metals are mined in the taiga. However, few people live in the taiga because of the cold winter climate.

6. South of the taiga is a belt of land with a humid-continental climate. Temperatures are lower in the winter and cooler in summer than the climate of most of the continental United States. Many large, important cities—Moscow, St. Petersburg, and Kiev (KEE-ef)—have this climate. The soil is fertile here, and much of the land is used for farming. The growing season lasts five months or longer.

7. Southward, the climate is drier and the summers are longer and warmer. Here, the dry grasslands are found. The Russians call this area the steppes. The steppes reach from

Reindeer herder of the Russian tundra. Parts of the tundra have valuable minerals beneath the frozen soil.

the Black Sea eastward into central Asia. Only 10 to 20 inches (25 to 50 centimeters) of rain fall in the steppes each year. Despite this lack of rain, the steppes have fertile soil that is well suited to farming. Part of the western steppes lies in Ukraine, which supplies over one-fifth of the Commonwealth's grain, including crops like wheat and barley. Thus, the steppes are similar to the dry prairies of the United States.

8. In the south, from the Caspian Sea eastward to Lake Balkhash (bahl-KASH), the land is largely desert. There is little rain and it is very hot. As you can imagine, few people live in this area because it is hard to make a living. In some parts, the mountains provide water for irrigation so that cotton and tobacco can be grown. These irrigated areas support more people than the rest of the desert.

9. In the northern part of the Black Sea lies an area with a different kind of climate, the Crimean (cry-MEE-uhn) Peninsula. This peninsula, with its hot, dry summers and mild, wet winters, has a Mediterranean climate like that of southern California. Many fruits are grown here, including oranges, figs, and grapes. This warmer pocket of land has become a favorite vacation spot for many people of the Commonwealth. Thousands of visitors fill its large hotels every year.

10. Most of the Commonwealth landmass is made up of frozen wastelands, forests, and mountains. Temperatures in some areas often drop below -50°F (-46°C), and snow covers more than half the region most of the year. The region has too short a growing season for many crops. There are also many areas in which there is not enough rain for farming. For these reasons, much of the land has not been settled. The richest land is west of the Ural Mountains, where most people live.

UNDERSTANDING WHAT YOU HAVE READ

1. Which of the following questions are answered in this chapter?
a. Why is most of this region cold?
b. In what climate region are many of the Commonwealth's large cities?
c. What crops are grown on the steppes?

2. The main idea of this chapter is to describe
a. how people live in northern lands
b. the different climates of this region
c. where the steppes are located

3. The best farmlands of this area are found in the
a. taiga
b. steppes
c. irrigated desert

4. Some people of the tundra herd
a. reindeer
b. llamas
c. caribou

5. This region has no climate in which a farmer can grow
a. wheat
b. cotton
c. bananas

6. The summer climate near the city of Moscow is
a. warmer than that of New York City
b. colder than that of Chicago
c. much like the climate of New Orleans

7. A taiga is a
a. treeless plain
b. dense forest
c. tropical rain forest

8. On the steppes, people usually make a living by
a. farming
b. fishing
c. lumbering

Climates of the Republics of Eurasia

Desert
Steppe
Mediterranean
Humid continental
Marine
Taiga
Tundra
Vertical

0   1000   2000 Miles
0   1000   2000 Kilometers

DEVELOPING IDEAS AND SKILLS

Building Map Skills — Climates of the Commonwealth of Independent States

Study the map above. Then answer the following questions.

1. a. Which states have a desert climate?
   b. Which have a humid-continental climate?
2. a. Which climates are found in Ukraine?
   b. Which are found in Kazakhstan?
3. a. In which part of the region is the tundra located?
   b. Describe the climate of the tundra.
   c. How do people in the tundra survive?
4. Check the land form map on page 327. Which land forms are found in the humid-continental climate in the west?
5. a. What role did climate play during the invasions of Napoleon in 1812 and Adolf Hitler in 1941?
   b. Do you think climate would be as important to an invading army today?

SUMMING UP

Matching

Match the descriptions in column B with the terms in column A. There is one extra item in column B.

COLUMN A
1. tundra
2. humid-continental
3. taiga
4. permafrost
5. steppes

COLUMN B
a. layer of permanently frozen ground beneath the earth's surface
b. fertile, dry land like the prairies of the United States
c. flat, treeless land with cold temperatures year round
d. Russian word for "dense forest"
e. arid, barren desert
f. warmer climate of Moscow, St. Petersburg, and Kiev

REVIEWING AND WRITING

Using Research Skills

Plan an imaginary trip to a republic in Eurasia. Visit your school or local library and find travel books about this area. Then answer the following questions. Write your answers in one or two paragraphs.
1. Which part of this region would you like to visit? Why?
2. What clothing would you take with you? Why?
3. What historic sites or places of cultural interest would you like to visit? Why?

DEVELOPING CRITICAL THINKING SKILLS

Generalizations to Watch Out For

Even the most careful thinkers sometimes make sweeping generalizations. ("Everyone was watching the ball game on TV." "Absolutely the best movie in town is _____!") Such statements seem very definite and clear, but they are seldom true. Some kinds of sweeping generalizations are called stereotypes, because people use them over and over again. ("The British eat the dullest food." "Italians love spaghetti.") They are used so often that people believe they must be true. Below are some stereotypes about the former Soviet Union. With which do you agree? With which do you disagree? Keep them all in mind. We will come back to them in a later chapter.

1. There are no rich people in the Commonwealth.
2. In the CIS, no one believes in any religion.
3. This region has a cold, unbearable climate.
4. The people of this region are suspicious and warlike.

Chapter 4

A Long and Varied History

Why is the Commonwealth being rocked by such massive changes today?

READING FOR A PURPOSE:
1. How did Communists come to power in the Soviet Union?
2. How did the relationship between the Soviet Union and the United States change from World War II to the 1990s?
3. How do the republics of the Commonwealth plan to change their economies?

1. Over the centuries, many peoples—from the Slavs to the Vikings to the Mongols—invaded and settled on the great Eurasian plain. In the mid-1300s, Moscow became the center of a new state called Russia. Ivan IV, who ruled in the 1500s, was the first Russian ruler to be crowned czar. This term comes from the word Caesar and means "emperor." Under Russian czars such as Peter the Great and Catherine the Great, Russia steadily moved its borders eastward. It expanded into Siberia and across the Bering Strait into Alaska for a time. Peter the Great made

tremendous efforts to modernize his empire. However, after his death, Russia failed to keep up with Western Europe, which began to change with the Industrial Revolution in 1750. Industrialization did not begin in Russia for another hundred years.

2. The czars were the absolute rulers of Russia from the 1600s to the beginning of the 1900s. But Russia's terrible losses in World War I set the stage for its downfall. The nation had not been prepared for war when it started in 1914. In three years, almost 2 million Russians lost their lives. The Russian people were starving, and they blamed Czar Nicholas for their troubles. In March 1917, the people rebelled, and Czar Nicholas abdicated (gave up the throne).

3. After the czar's fall, a republic was formed. The new government had little power, and it never gained much support. In November 1917, a revolutionary group known as the Bolsheviks overthrew the government. The Bolsheviks, who were later called Communists, wanted to end the private ownership of land, factories, and railroads. The government, or state, would own all property and means of production. Once in power, the Bolshevik leader, Vladimir Ilyich Ulyanov—

Two rulers who increased Russian power: above, left, Peter the Great (1682-1725). Below, Catherine the Great (1729-76).

who called himself Lenin (LEN-uhn)—tried to extend his power. For the next four years, civil war raged across Russia as the Communists fought other groups to stay in power. In 1918, the Communists executed the czar and his family. By 1921, the Communists had taken control of a vast portion of the czar's old empire. The next year, they formed the Union of Soviet Socialist Republics (USSR), or the Soviet Union. The Soviet Union brought together under a Communist government the great variety of land and people once ruled by the czar.

4. Lenin died in 1924. Soon after, Joseph Stalin took his place. Under Stalin, who ruled until his death in 1953, the Soviet Union became a brutal police state in which millions were sent to prison or executed. Stalin stopped at nothing in his attempt to turn the Soviet Union into a major industrial and military power.

5. By the late 1930s, the shadow of war loomed over Europe. In 1939, Stalin signed a treaty with his greatest enemy, Adolf Hitler, the dictator of Nazi Germany. In this treaty, Stalin and Hitler agreed not to attack each other. They also agreed that each of their countries could occupy a piece of Poland, dividing up between them an entire independent country. In 1941, without warning, Hitler broke the treaty, and the German army invaded the Soviet Union. The army was soon stopped by the harsh Russian winter and the people's fierce resistance. The Soviet Union then joined the Allies (the United States, Britain, and France). While the Allies attacked from the west, Soviet forces pushed the Nazis back toward Germany from the east. Soviet armies overran Estonia, Latvia, and Lithuania, and the Soviet Union made these three countries an official part of the Soviet Union. By 1945, the war was won, but over 20 million Soviet citizens had died.

6. After World War II, a cold war (nations opposing each other without actually fighting) grew between the Soviet Union and its former allies. The Soviet Union refused to give up

Lenin takes control of the Russian government. Note the red flag of the Bolsheviks behind him. What has the artist of this painting tried to convey about Lenin? What has he tried to convey about this moment in history?

control of the Eastern European countries it had occupied during the war. Soon there were Communist governments in Poland, Romania, Hungary, East Germany, Bulgaria, Yugoslavia, Czechoslovakia, and Albania. Many of these governments were kept in power by the armed might of the Soviet Union. Others were supported by local Communist governments. The British leader, Winston Churchill, noted that an "Iron Curtain" had been placed between Eastern and Western Europe. Under the Marshall Plan, the United States sent Western Europe billions of dollars worth of aid. The aid helped Western European countries recover and prevented them from falling to communism.

7. In order to further protect Europe from Soviet expansion, 12 Western nations formed the North Atlantic Treaty Organization (NATO) in 1949. The member nations agreed to help one another in case of attack. They also created a military organization to guard Western Europe. To counter NATO, the Soviet Union formed the Warsaw Pact with most of its Eastern European satellites a few years later. A satellite is a country that is economically dependent on and therefore controlled by a more powerful country.

8. Meanwhile, Germany continued to be a trouble spot in the cold war. The Soviets set up the Berlin Blockade in 1948 to try to get the Western Allies to leave Berlin. This city, like the rest of Germany, had been divided into occupation zones. When the Soviets closed off all land and water routes into Berlin, the United States flew supplies in by airplane. Finally, the Soviet Union lifted the blockade. Then, in 1961, the East German Communist government built a wall between East and West Berlin to stop people from escaping into West Germany through West Berlin. This concrete and barbed-wire wall was a stark symbol of the cold war.

9. The cold war was carried on in Asia, too. In China, Chinese Communists took power after a long and bloody civil war. Korea, which had been ruled by Japan, was divided into two parts after Japan's surrender in World War II. The Soviet Union occupied North Korea and set up a Communist government there. The United States occupied South Korea and allowed the people to set up their own government. In 1950, the North Koreans invaded South Korea. United Nations and U.S. troops drove back the Communist attack. China sent soldiers to help North Korea. A truce was finally signed, but no agreement was reached until years later.

10. In the 1960s, Communists controlled North Vietnam, and anti-Communists ruled South Vietnam. When fighting broke out between the two, the Soviet Union and China backed North Vietnam. The United States eventually sent troops to fight beside the South Vietnamese. In 1973, after about ten years of involvement, the United States agreed to a cease-fire and began to leave the country. Not long after, the Communists gained control over Vietnam and all of Indochina. At least 2 million people, including 58,000 Americans, lost their lives in this long and painful war.

11. In Cuba, the United States faced a threat only 90 miles (144 kilometers) from home. In 1959, Fidel Castro (KAHS-troh) became the dictator of Cuba. The Soviet Union supplied Cuba with money, food, and arms. In 1961, the United States tried to over-

throw Castro but failed. Then, the Soviets placed missile bases in Cuba. After President John F. Kennedy ordered a blockade of Cuban ports, Soviet Premier Nikita Khrushchev ordered the missiles removed.

12. In the early 1970s, relations between the United States and the USSR, the two superpowers, improved for a while. The two countries agreed to limit nuclear weapons and increase trade. However, the Soviet invasion of neighboring Afghanistan (af-GAN-uh-stan) in 1979 revived the cold war. In the early 1980s, the United States and the USSR backed opposite sides as a struggle broke out in Nicaragua over control of the government. These situations increased tension between the Soviet Union and the United States. But soon, events in the Soviet Union put an end to the cold war.

13. In 1985, the cold war began to wind down when Mikhail Gorbachev (gor-buh-CHOF) became the leader of the Union of Soviet Socialist Republics. Although he was a Communist, it was clear to him that Soviet communism was not working. Years of inefficient government control of industry and heavy military spending had left the Soviet economy in very bad shape. Gorbachev recog-

As leader of the Soviet Union, Mikhail Gorbachev tried to boost his popularity by speaking with workers on a collective farm.

nized that the Soviet Union could no longer afford to give financial support to its Eastern European satellites. As he eased control over these nations, Communist governments throughout Eastern Europe fell. In 1989, the Berlin Wall was torn down. Germany was reunited. The Warsaw Pact ended.

14. Meanwhile, in the Soviet Union, conditions went from bad to worse. Gorbachev was not moving fast enough with his economic reforms to suit leaders like Boris Yeltsin (YELT-sin), president of the Russian republic. However, Gorbachev was going entirely too fast for some of the old-time Communists. In August 1991, these Communists, called hard-liners, formed a conspiracy to take over the government. They arrested Gorbachev and announced that they were in charge. Tanks rumbled through the streets of Moscow and up to the Russian Parliament building. Boris Yeltsin emerged. But instead of giving in to the hard-liners, he accused them. The people of Moscow rallied behind Yeltsin. Moscow's defiance inspired other cities to resist the takeover. The nations of the world did not support the hard-liners.

15. Yeltsin was successful. Through his efforts, Gorbachev was returned to office. But Gorbachev's position had been damaged beyond repair. Although he quit the Communist party and banned it from taking part in the Soviet government, he could not regain his power and support.

16. The Soviet Union started breaking apart. Republic after republic declared its independence. In December 1991, the Commonwealth of Independent States was formed. A few days after the birth of the Commonwealth, Gorbachev resigned as Soviet president. He had helped end the cold war. But he was not able to deal with economic conditions in the Commonwealth. Events had swept him away—as well as Soviet communism and the nations it had ruled.

UNDERSTANDING WHAT YOU HAVE READ

1. Which of the following questions are answered in this chapter?
a. How did Russia reach North America?
b. Why was there a revolution in 1917?
c. How was Russia ruled by the Mongols?

2. The main idea of *paragraphs 5 through 7* is to describe
a. how the czars ruled from the 1600s to the 1900s
b. the Soviet Union during and after World War II
c. Russia's defeat in World War I

3. A *czar* is the same as
a. a representative
b. an explorer
c. an emperor

4. In a *cold war,*
a. major military powers attack each other
b. several nations invade and occupy a weaker nation
c. nations oppose each other but do not actually fight

5. In 1949, to protect Europe from Soviet expansion, 12 Western nations formed
a. the Warsaw Pact
b. NATO
c. the Marshall Plan

6. The purpose of the Berlin Blockade was
a. to divide Germany into occupied zones
b. to get the Western Allies to leave Berlin
c. to send billions of dollars' worth of aid to Berlin

7. Paragraphs 9 through 11 discuss
a. communism in Asia, the Vietnam War and Cuba
b. the economic dependence of the Eastern European satellites on the Soviet Union
c. how the Cold War wound down after the end of the Vietnam War

8. In December 1991, after the Soviet Union broke apart, all of the following took place EXCEPT
a. Gorbachev resigned as Soviet president
b. Gorbachev regained his power and support
c. the Commonwealth of Independent States was formed

FOLLOW UP

Who Am I?

Below are statements about some famous people. Can you tell who is described in each statement? Choose your answers from the list of names below.

Mikhail Gorbachev   Stalin   Lenin
Ivan IV   Catherine the Great   Peter the Great
Boris Yeltsin   Nikita Khrushchev   Czar Nicholas

1. I was the first Russian to be crowned czar. I ruled in the 1500s. I am _____.
2. In 1917, I led a revolutionary group called the Bolsheviks. I wanted the state to own all means of production. I am _____.
3. I moved Russian borders eastward. I tried to modernize my empire. I am _____.
4. Under my rule, the Soviet Union was a brutal police state. My goal was to make the Soviet Union a major industrial and military power. I am _____.
5. I was the last czar of Russia. I abdicated in 1917. I am _____.
6. I became the Communist leader of the USSR in 1985. When I realized that Soviet communism was not working, I tried to make reforms. I am _____.
7. I was president of the Russian republic. I was against the hard-liners in 1991. I am _____.
8. I was Premiere of The Soviet Union when the Cuban Missle Crisis took place. After the U.S. blockade, I ordered Soviet missiles removed. I am _____.
9. Like Peter the Great, I steadily moved Russian borders eastward. I am _____.

Chapter 5

A New Government Is Formed

Who now has the power that once belonged to the Soviet Communist party?

READING FOR A PURPOSE
1. What was the government like in the Soviet Union?
2. How has the government changed now that the Soviet Union has fallen?
3. What problems must the Commonwealth of Independent States solve in order to become a world power?

1. On paper, the Soviet constitution seemed as democratic as the U.S. Constitution. The Soviet constitution provided for an elected lawmaking body, a high court, and a president. What the constitution did not mention, however, was that there was only one legal political party in the Soviet Union, the Soviet Communist party. The Party was headed by the general secretary, who was the most powerful person in the country.

2. The Soviet Union was a *totalitarian state,* a nation with a dictatorship that completely controls the lives of its people. The Communist party ran everything—from nuclear weapons factories to nurseries. Not only were opposition parties illegal, but criticism of the Communist party was also against the law. The Soviet secret police, known as the KGB, had informers everywhere. Complaining about the government was dangerous. Then Mikhail Gorbachev announced a new policy. It was called *glasnost* (GLAZ-nohst), which means "openness." People began to criticize the government and its policies openly. Suddenly, millions of people were demanding change. Within a few years, the Soviet Communist party was destroyed.

3. The Communist way of life was all that the Soviet republics had in common. Under communism, everyone worked for the state and did whatever the Communist party dictat-

Delegates to a Communist party convention in 1986. Despite its small size, the Communist party was able to rule the Soviet Union until its collapse in 1991.

Statue of Lenin is removed in Leningrad, which took back old name, St. Petersburg.

5. One of the Commonwealth's most serious problems concerns its nuclear weapons. There are about 27,000 nuclear missiles left in the former Soviet republics. Other countries want to reduce the number of weapons and keep them under tight control to make sure there is no nuclear war. In early January 1992, the Commonwealth leaders met in the city of Minsk (mentsk), the new headquarters, to talk about the problem. They set up a united command to handle nuclear weapons. Over the next few years, the states with nuclear weapons—Belarus, Ukraine, and Kazakhstan—would move the weapons to Russia. The leaders made less headway deciding what to do with *conventional,* or regular, non-nuclear, weapons and forces. They finally decided that each republic could set up its own armed forces. Three decided to do so, while the others planned to give control to a joint command.

6. All the republics want to change to free-market economies. In Russia, President Boris Yeltsin took government controls off prices so that demand could regulate prices. This

Despite its troubles, Russia remains a strong military power in the world.

ed. Without the Party in control, each of the republics began to declare its independence. Unfortunately, not all of the republics got along with each other, and several of them had arsenals of nuclear weapons. When the leaders of Russia, Ukraine, and Belarus announced that they had formed the Commonwealth of Independent States, they invited the other republics to join them.

4. The new government is really a loose alliance of *sovereign,* or independent, states that are trying to make important decisions together. The CIS has a Council of Presidents made up of the presidents and premiers of each of the member republics. Below this council is a general coordinating body that sets joint military, economic, and foreign policy. The states, however, have all the power and must agree on all decisions.

caused great hardship, but it was the only way to solve the nation's economic problems, he believed. Yeltsin began to *privatize* (to make privately owned) government-owned industries and break up government-owned farms. But the task of overturning one economic system and getting another one to work could be beyond the ability of any person.

UNDERSTANDING WHAT YOU HAVE READ

1. Which of the following questions are answered in this chapter?

a. How do farmers in the Commonwealth of Independent States live?

b. What do the Communists think of religion?

c. What is the governing body of the Commonwealth?

2. In a *totalitarian* state,

a. people openly criticize the governments and its policies

b. the government owns the industries and farms

c. a dictator completely controls people's lives

3. How many legal political parties were there in the Soviet Union?

a. 3

b. 1

c. 4

4. The first republics to form the Commonwealth of Independent States were Russia, Ukraine, and

a. Belarus

b. Kazakhstan

c. Mensk

5. In the Commonwealth of Independent States, which bodies have all the power and must agree on all decisions?

a. the members of the Council of Presidents

b. the member states

c. the general coordinating body

6. The most powerful person in the Soviet Union was

a. the general secretary

b. the president of the high court

c. the dictator of the secret police

SUMMING UP

Matching

Match the description in column B with the terms in column A. There is an extra item in column B.

COLUMN A	COLUMN B
1. totalitarian state	a. an elected lawmaking body
2. sovereign state	b. a nation with a dictatorship that control the lives of its people
3. glasnost	c. a policy of openness
4. privatization	d. the Soviet secret police
5. KGB	e. an independent state
	f. private ownership

Chapter 6

The People of the Commonwealth

Who are the people of the CIS?

READING FOR A PURPOSE:
1. What ethnic groups make up the population of the Commonwealth?
2. Why did "Russification" fail?
3. What is life like in the Commonwealth of Independent States?

1. The Commonwealth has a tremendous variety of ethnic groups among its almost 283 million people. The republics that form the Commonwealth are divided to a great extent along ethnic lines. Approximately 75 percent of the people are Slavic, speaking one of a number of Slavic languages. Most of them live in Russia, Ukraine, or Belarus. Another 18 percent of the people of the Commonwealth live in the Central Asian republics of Kazakhstan, Turkmenistan, Uzbekistan, Tajikistan, and Kyrgyzstan. The people in these republics speak languages similar to Turkish. In the Caucasus region, the people of Armenia and the Azerbaijani speak entirely different languages. The European republic of Moldova once belonged to Romania, and the people there speak a language similar to Romanian.

2. The reason that there are so many different languages spoken in the CIS can be found in history. Under the czars, Russia conquered the nations that became republics in the Soviet Union. The Soviet government did not want these nations to keep their national identities. The government wanted to create a nation with a single language and culture, and it wanted that language and culture to be Russian. This policy was called Russification. Russification succeeded outwardly in stamping out the smaller ethnic cultures and languages. Under the surface, however, the people kept their cultures alive.

3. The Communist party disapproved of religion. No one who practiced a religion could have a career in the Party. Even though the government closed Christian churches and persecuted Jews, religion survived in the Soviet Union. The Soviets were also unsuccessful in stopping the practice of Islam in the Central Asian republics.

4. The Soviet Union was very successful in educating the population. Under the czars, most people could not read or write. But the Soviet government made certain that everyone went to school for at least eight years. In the large cities, students were required to stay in school for at least 10 years. They began the study of a foreign language—usually English—

Russian women proudly display the red, white, and blue banner of Russian Republic.

341

in the fifth grade. By the time they were in eighth grade, many Soviet students knew more math and science than most U.S. high school graduates.

5. Under the Soviet government, the average citizen made about 400 rubles a month, about $4 in the world economy. Because a free-market economy has been introduced in the CIS, prices now rise to meet demand. Prices are rising faster than incomes because food and other goods are scarce. The people of the Commonwealth must go through hard times before their economy begins to work properly.

6. Russia has the greatest resources of all the republics in the Commonwealth. Yet its people lead difficult lives. For example, there is not enough housing in the large cities. Often two or three families must share an apartment. Families wait for years to get an apartment to themselves. There are waiting lists for cars, too. Since there are no service stations, Russians who want a driver's license must pass a mechanic's test as well as a driving test.

7. Even when Russians have enough rubles, they must wait in long lines to buy such items as shoes, small appliances, and soap. Most of these products are poorly made. Russians often use the barter system—trading—to get the things they need. Many educated Russians take simple, unchallenging jobs rather than the careers for which they are trained. Careers mean long hours at work, which does not leave enough time for standing in line or bartering.

8. Career choices are particularly hard for Russian women. According to law, they can enter any profession they choose. But when many women enter a profession, the profession loses status and salaries go down. Because most Russian doctors are women, the status of the medical profession in Russian is much lower than it is in the United States. Over 85 percent of Russian women work outside the home. Most of them work at manual labor. Yet they cannot afford such labor-saving appliances as washing machines and clothes dryers

A group of Russians stare at a piece of beef they cannot afford to buy.

in their homes. Since many Russian men do not help with the housework or the children, many Russian women work much longer hours than their husbands do.

9. According to Communist theory, a Communist society is a classless society. Everyone is supposed to be equal. In reality, in the Soviet Union there were two classes—ordinary citizens and Communists, particularly Communist leaders. Important Party members and their families did not have to deal with the problems that ordinary citizens faced. They shopped in special stores that had well-made Western products. They received the best medical care and lived in the nicest apartments. They vacationed in houses that were kept just for them and paid for by the government. Their children had no trouble getting into the finest universities. About 3 million Russians belonged to this privileged class. Now that the Communist party has been banned in Russia, former Communists stand in line just like their fellow citizens.

UNDERSTANDING WHAT YOU HAVE READ

1. **Which of the following questions are answered in this chapter?**
   a. What ethnic groups live in the Commonwealth?
   b. What is life like for the people of Russia?
   c. What land forms are present in the CIS?

2. **The main idea of this chapter is to describe**
   a. the religious beliefs of the Russian people
   b. the people of Russia and the republics
   c. the growing cities of the CIS

3. **The Communist policy that was designed to create a single culture and language was**
   a. Marxism
   b. education for everyone
   c. Russification

4. **In general, the republics are divided along**
   a. ethnic lines
   b. meridians and parallels
   c. rivers

5. **One problem in Russia and the republics is**
   a. prices are rising faster than incomes
   b. the people are poorly educated
   c. an increase in automobile production

6. **What do Russians do to get things they need when they cannot buy them?**
   a. Make the things themselves.
   b. Barter for them.
   c. Use a neighbor's.

TAKING A SURVEY

Now that you have read the chapter on the people of the Commonwealth, you know that the ethnic groups that make up the Commonwealth speak many different languages.

Make a list of the languages mentioned in the chapter. Put a check next to those that are spoken in your community. What other languages are spoken in your community? Add these languages to your list. What other ways can you think of in which different cultures leave their mark on a community?

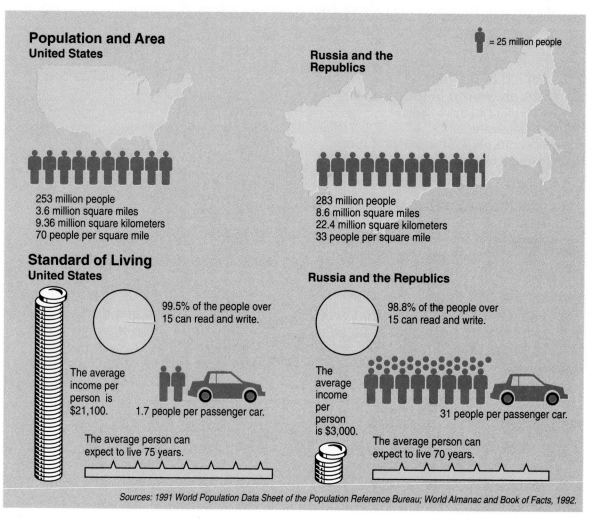

Population and Area
United States

🧍 = 25 million people

Russia and the Republics

253 million people
3.6 million square miles
9.36 million square kilometers
70 people per square mile

283 million people
8.6 million square miles
22.4 million square kilometers
33 people per square mile

Standard of Living
United States

99.5% of the people over 15 can read and write.

The average income per person is $21,100.

1.7 people per passenger car.

The average person can expect to live 75 years.

Russia and the Republics

98.8% of the people over 15 can read and write.

The average income per person is $3,000.

31 people per passenger car.

The average person can expect to live 70 years.

Sources: 1991 World Population Data Sheet of the Population Reference Bureau; World Almanac and Book of Facts, 1992.

Population, Area, and Standard of Living of Russia and the Republics

DEVELOPING IDEAS AND SKILLS

Understanding Graphs — Population, Area, and Standard of Living of Russia and the Repub

Use these graphs to answer the following questions:

1. Is the standard of living of this area high or low compared with that of the United States? Is is a low-income or underdeveloped area?
2. Is the area as crowded as the United States?
3. Are the people of this area literate compared with the people of the United States?
4. How long may the average person in this area expect to live?
5. What facts tell you the standard of living of the people of the area?
6. How does this area compare with the United States in size?

Living in Uzbekistan

The Eurasian region is divided into many national groups. In central Asia, there are large numbers of Muslim peoples, descendants of nomads that once roamed these lands. At one time, their way of life was similar to Muslims living in Iran, Afghanistan, and Pakistan. Even when they were Soviet citizens, Muslims retained some of their Muslim culture: their clothing was not westernized, but native to their region; within the family they said prayers and observed other Islamic customs; children grew up modest, obedient, and attentive to their elders. For the most part, however, they were greatly changed by Communist rule. Today, the young people study Russian as well as their Uzbek language. They go to public schools. They look for jobs that will allow them to advance in the new economic system. Here is a brief story about one Uzbek city that has a Muslim flavor.

Bukhara is a city in the central Asian republic of Uzbekistan, south of the Aral Sea. It is as far from Moscow as Moscow is from London. It is a sun-baked land, different from the cold Siberian Taiga in the far north.

The local nomads have given up their tents for apartment houses, topped by television antennas. The large mosaic domed mosques (places of worship) in the city are open today. When Bukhara was a Soviet city, the few mosques that remained open were in the back streets, rotting from lack of care.

Usman Aliyev is a member of the local government. He keeps an eye on the mosques in Bukhara. The Communist party, he explains, was officially against religion. They closed most churches, mosques and synagogues throughout the land. However, they did not dare to close every place of worship. They knew that many older people would never give up their religion. Today, Usman believes that the young people are returning to the Islamic faith. He proudly admits he was married by a mullah, a Muslim religious leader, even when he was a Communist. He is happy that he will have his funeral in a mosque.

On Sunday, Usman and other Bukhara families go to the bazaar, or local market. Uzbek music pours from the loudspeakers. The people crowd around stalls loaded with vegetables, live chickens, and fruits. It is always a time to talk with your friends and neighbors. Usman proudly shows his medals, won for bravery in World War II. He is, like many other Uzbeks, happy to return to the traditional way of life.

Copy the following into your notebook. If you agree with the statement, mark it with an *A*. If you disagree, mark it with a *D*. Rewrite the statements you disagree with to make them correct.

1. The Eurasian region has many groups of people who have many different ways of life.
2. The people who live in Bukhara have a way of life similar to people in Moscow.
3. Bukhara is a city with Muslim culture.
4. The Soviet government discouraged the practice of religion in the Soviet Union.
5. Education is an important goal of the Uzbek republic.

Chapter 7

Eurasia's Farmland

How is farming in the CIS different from farming in the United States?

READING FOR A PURPOSE:
1. Where is the chief farming area of the Commonwealth of Independent States?
2. What is the difference between a collective farm and a state farm?
3. Why do farmers in the CIS have shortages in grain production?

1. Soviet dictator Joseph Stalin destroyed private farming in the Soviet Union in the 1920s. Successful farmers were forced to turn over their land to the state. Those who resisted were killed. Millions died as the farms in the Soviet Union were collectivized, or joined together to make larger farms. Under Soviet rule, the government—not the individual—owned all the land. Government planners decided what to grow on Soviet farms, how much would be grown, and where it would be sold. Farmers were hired help, and most of the profit from the farms went to the government.

2. The breakdown of this farming economy was one of the chief reasons for the break-down of the entire Soviet economy. However, the Commonwealth of Independent States has inherited the Soviet system of agriculture. There are two kinds of farms in the CIS—the state farm and the collective farm. A state farm is very large—usually about 42,000 acres (17,000 hectares). The land in these huge farms makes up about two-thirds of all the Commonwealth's farmland. State farms are owned and run by the government. They are very much like factories. Each of the thousands of workers does a certain job on the farm and receives a set wage for his or her work.

3. The collective farm is also large but smaller than a state farm. A collective farm averages about 16,000 acres (6,475 hectares). Usually, about 400 families live on a collective farm. The farmers work together, plowing the soil and harvesting the crops. The harvest is then sold to the government. The money received goes to pay for expenses, such as machinery and seed. After that, each farmer shares in the remaining profits from the harvest. The size of a farmer's share depends upon the success of the crops. If the harvest is large, the reward is good. Farmers on collective farms also receive a wage.

4. Farmers in the CIS live in villages near their fields. Farmers own their houses and tools. However, the large pieces of farm machinery are owned by the farm. Farmers plant fruits

Homes in a kolkhoz village. Private plots of land surround each house.

A shepherd tends his flock in the Republic of Georgia. More and more herds are now privately owned. Why is this so?

and vegetables for themselves on small garden plots. They sell whatever they do not need from their gardens and keep the profits. Often, they also keep a cow, goats, and chickens. The diet of farmers in Russia and Ukraine usually consists of black rye bread, borscht (a beet soup), cabbage, potatoes, salt pork, buckwheat, and tea.

5. The greatest farming area in this region is known as the Fertile Triangle (see map page 325). This belt of farmland begins near the Black Sea. It stretches across Ukraine eastward to the southern Ural Mountains and beyond. In this triangle, the soil is rich and dark. The area is flat and suitable for the use of machinery. The major crop of this belt of rich soil is wheat. The CIS is a world leader in wheat production.

6. Besides wheat, the chief farm products of the area are rye, potatoes, sugar beets, cotton, and wool. Rye is an important grain product of the region because it can grow in the north, where the climate is cooler. It is used in the black bread that is eaten by many of the people of the area. Potatoes, another important food in the local diet, also grow in the cooler areas. Only China grows more potatoes than this part of the world.

7. Very fine cotton is grown in the dry lands east of the Caspian Sea. Nearly all the cotton is produced on irrigated land in the dry regions of Central Asia. The CIS is a world leader in the production of cotton. This region is second only to Australia in wool production. The main grazing lands of the area are found along the border of the steppes and the southern Caucasus Mountains. These are the old grazing grounds of the Mongols.

8. Despite these successful crops, collective and state farms have never been able to produce enough food or a great variety of foods. The choice of foods is limited, and shortages of grain often occur. There are several reasons for these problems. First, much of the region is too cold or too dry to produce good crops every year. Only if the weather is mild and wet will the land yield good harvests. Second, although one-fourth of the area's land is farmed, the land is less fertile than farmland in the United States. Third, farmers have had little desire to grow larger amounts of crops or to try new farming methods because they have not owned the land on the state and collective farms. Most important, the system was and still is inefficient. The state has had too much control over decisions. Soviet farmers have not had the authority to decide when to plant, what fertilizer to use, or even when to harvest. Until recently, government ministers in Moscow made these decisions.

9. The shortages of grain have meant that there often has not been enough food for cattle and pigs. This, in turn, has led to meat

Scientists at the Plant Biology Institute at Tashkent. They are studying cotton plants.

shortages. Beginning in 1972, the Soviets bought large amounts of grain from the United States. In 1990, the Soviet Union was the world's largest buyer of U.S. wheat.

10. To increase farm production, the Soviet government began to allow farmers more freedom to sell for a profit the foods they grew in their own small gardens. These thousands of tiny plots, making up only 3 percent of all farmland, provided 60 percent of the nation's potatoes and fruits. They also produced 30 percent of the nation's eggs, vegetables, meat, and milk. Yields from these private farms were almost 10 times as high as the yields from state and collective farms.

11. As change sweeps through the Commonwealth, farmers have been quick to take advantage of the situation. In Russia, farmers held back produce from the market as the Soviet government began to collapse. The government urged the farmers to bring their stored food to market. However, even though the prices of many foods rose, the food supply did not increase immediately. The shelves of the government-owned food stores remained empty. Farmers did not want to sell their produce for rubles.

12. Russia is planning to break up unprofitable state farms and give the land to independent farmers. In 1992, Russia's agriculture minister announced plans to create 150,000 new private farms by the end of the year. It remains to be seen whether the system can be changed to become more efficient.

UNDERSTANDING WHAT YOU HAVE READ

1. Which of the following questions are answered in this chapter?
a. Why did the government "collectivize" the farms?
b. Why is most of the former Soviet Union's land not good for farming?
c. Where is cotton grown?

2. The main idea of this chapter is to describe
a. what is grown on the former Soviet Union's farms
b. how Soviet farms were organized
c. the use of machinery on Soviet farms

3. What is the most important crop of the Fertile Triangle?
a. potatoes
b. rice
c. wheat

4. On a state farm, the farmers worked for
a. a share of the crops
b. wages
c. the profits from their own gardens

5. Part of the food problem in what was the Soviet Union is caused by a lack of
a. machinery
b. seed
c. fertile land

6. In the former Soviet Union, cotton is grown in dry areas where
a. mountain soil is rich
b. water is supplied through irrigation
c. it needs only a small amount of labor at picking time

7. On a Soviet collective farm, people
a. owned the business that ran the farm
b. sold the crops to the government and shared the profits
c. gathered the crops from nearby farms for sale

8. One difference between a state farm and a collective farm is
a. on a state farm, workers own machinery
b. on a collective farm, workers get a share of the profit
c. a state farm is smaller

SUMMING UP

Making Charts

Complete the following chart in your notebook.

	UNITED STATES	THE REPUBLICS
Ownership of land:		
Kinds of farms:		
Farming methods:		
Crops:		
Animals:		
Standard of living:		

WRITING

In paragraph 4, reread the typical menu of Russian and Ukranian farmers. How is their diet similar to or different from what farmers usually eat in the United States? Write out a typical menu for farmers in the plains area of the United States.

Chapter 8

Industry in the Commonwealth

Why is the CIS a major industrial nation?

READING FOR A PURPOSE:
1. How did the Soviet government help the growth of industry?
2. Where are the main industrial regions of the Commonwealth of Independent States?
3. What changes are occurring in manufacturing in the CIS?

1. Before the Revolution of 1917, Russia was largely a farming nation. While the countries of Western Europe were building large factories, Russia was still a long way from industrialization. In 1928, the Soviet Union began planning the use of its natural resources. Within a few years, the Soviet Union had changed from a nation that relied on farming as its major economic activity to a land of mills and factories.

2. There were several reasons for this change. First, Eurasia has a greater variety of mineral resources than any other region in the world. There are large deposits of coal, iron ore, copper, manganese, platinum, and bauxite. Many of the area's mineral resources are important sources of power.

3. Second, there are many sources of power: oil, coal, natural gas, and peat—a soft, inexpensive, coal-like material found just underneath the surface of the ground. (Oil is now the chief source of power in the CIS.) Waterpower resources were also developed. The region has four of the world's five largest hydroelectric plants, which produce electricity from the power of falling water. There is also uranium, from which nuclear power is developed. The Soviet Union continued to build nuclear power plants even after the major 1986 nuclear accident at Chernobyl (cher-NOH-buhl) in Ukraine.

4. Third, the Communist government owned all the natural resources and factories in the Soviet Union. As a result, it planned the use of these resources. Planners decided how many houses, dams, or factories would be built. Wherever possible, factories and cities were located near the source of raw materials. These areas are called industrial regions.

A power station in Tajikistan

A chemical plant in the Republic of Kyrgyzstan

Factories were built and run by the government. Soviet planners decided how and where goods were to be sold.

5. The Soviet Union developed four major industrial regions. The most important one is the Donets (duh-NETS) Basin, or Donbas (duhn-BAS), in Ukraine. The Donets coal field supplies fuel for steel mills. Iron ore and manganese are also mined there. Dams on the Dnieper (NEE-puhr) River provide electrical power. All these things together make this region very much like the Vital Triangle in Western Europe. It also resembles the steel centers of the northeastern United States.

6. The Moscow/St. Petersburg area is one of the oldest industrial regions. It has become a key region for industry because it is a transportation center. Railroads, rivers, and canals connect it to the resources and provide highways for shipping finished goods to market. Factories in Moscow make automobiles, chemicals, steel, and textiles. Factories in St. Petersburg produce ships, light machinery, textiles, and medical equipment.

7. The Volga River/Ural Mountain area is another important industrial region. There are large deposits of oil and natural gas, which are carried by pipeline to markets at home and abroad. Coal is found there, and the mountains are rich in iron, copper, manganese, bauxite, and platinum. Magnitogorsk (mag-NEET-eh-gorsk) is one of the leading iron and steel cities in this region.

8. Siberia's Kuznetsk (kuz-NETSK) Basin, or Kuzbas (KUZ-bas), is about 1,200 miles (1,920 kilometers) east of the Ural Mountains. This area of Russia is rich in coal. At first, coal from Kuzbas was taken by rail to the Urals, and iron ore was brought back from the Urals to Kuzbas. This two-way shipment of coal and iron between the two regions made both of them leading iron and steel centers. But the long shipping distances made the steel very expensive. This problem was solved when iron ore was discovered near Kuzbas and coal was found at Karaganda (kar-uh-gun-DAH), a city much closer to the Urals. Novosibirsk (no-VO-suh-bersk) became a great steel making city.

Trans-Siberian Railroad, shown in 1927, is still Russia's link with desolate Siberia.

9. The Soviets left many problems for the Commonwealth of Independent States. Moving goods to markets is difficult. There are not enough railroads, and the extreme cold in many areas makes it hard to build and repair the lines. Unlike the United States, the CIS has no interstate highway system. This means that there is no long-haul trucking industry. Manufactured goods often sit for months waiting to be shipped to cities that desperately need them.

10. Factory equipment is another problem for the CIS. While the equipment in most factories was new in the 1930s, today it is badly outdated. Using new technology would help many industries. The Soviet Union lags far behind the West in computer technology. As a result, CIS factories are not computerized. Most people in the CIS have never seen a computer. Even when computers are brought from abroad, there is no one to fix them when they break down.

11. CIS workers have had a problem turning out quality products. One reason has to do with work quotas. Quotas are given to each factory by the central planners. The monthly work schedule is divided into three ten-day periods. In the first ten days of each cycle, the workers usually wait for raw materials, which are increasingly hard to get. In the next ten days, workers manufacture what they can, even though some raw materials still are not at the factory. In the last ten days of the cycle, workers labor long, hard hours to fill the quota. Since the central planners do not accept excuses for missed quotas, the workers do not have time for quality checks. Because products are always stamped with the date of manufacture, wise consumers do not buy anything that was made during the last ten days of the month. How the system will change and evolve remains to be seen.

12. The end of the cold war is forcing major changes in industry. Stalin developed Soviet industry because he wanted his armies to be as well equipped as those in the West. In the years that followed, Soviet industry continued to turn out more military equipment than consumer goods. Now, the demand for tanks

An iron mine in the Ukraine's Donets Basin, the most important industrial region in the Commonwealth. What are the major industrial regions in the United States?

and weapons has fallen. The CIS will need to start producing quality consumer goods, such as washing machines and television sets, if it wants to compete in the world market.

13. Even before the fall of Soviet communism, some Russian industries began to look for foreign help. The idea was to have other nations supply money, knowledge, technology, and marketing. In return, the Soviet factories offered the energy, metals, and cheap work force needed to produce goods. Today, a few U.S. firms are helping one industry make the transition from manufacturing military aircraft to building planes and helicopters for export. A Japanese company has promised to sell scrap metals from another factory that now dismantles Soviet submarines. It remains to be seen, however, whether this kind of investment in the republics will allow a free-market economy to grow and thrive.

UNDERSTANDING WHAT YOU HAVE READ

1. Which of the following questions are answered in this chapter?
a. Why were steel goods expensive in the Soviet Union?
b. What were the Five-Year Plans?
c. How rich was the Soviet Union in natural resources?

2. The main idea of this chapter is to describe
a. working conditions in the Soviet Union
b. how planning was used
c. the resources and industries of the Soviet Union and the CIS

3. Some steel goods were expensive because
a. high wages were paid to workers
b. there was a lack of machinery in the factories
c. iron ore and coal often had to be transported great distances

4. One reason the Soviet Union was a successful industrial nation is that
a. it had many useful resources
b. factories were owned by individuals who made a profit
c. the railroads made transportation of goods easy

5. The Soviet Union had large deposits of
a. bauxite, gold, tin
b. coal, iron ore, copper
c. platinum, uranium, tin

6. The Donets Basin and Kuznetsk Basin were important
a. farming regions
b. industrial regions
c. tourist regions

7. The Moscow/St. Petersburg area was known for its
a. agricultural goods
b. fishing industries
c. industrial products

8. The former Soviet Union is trying to boost its economy by entering into partnerships with
a. other factories
b. individual citizens
c. companies from other nations

DEVELOPING IDEAS AND SKILLS

Building Map Skills — Industrial Resources of the Republics of Eurasia

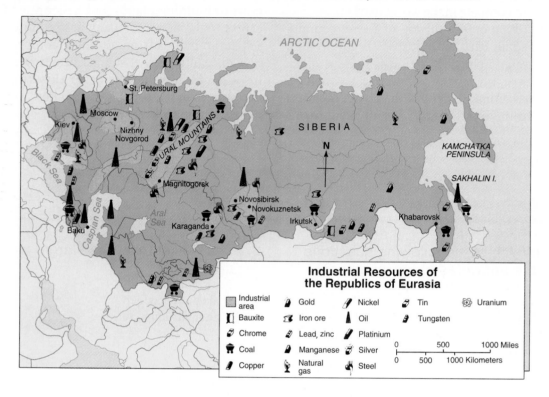

Study the map above. Then answer the following questions.

1. Which resources are found in the eastern part of the Eurasian region?
2. Which cities lie in industrial areas?
3. Which resources are found in Kiev?
4. Which industrial city has the most resources? The least?
5. How do you think the distribution of resources will affect the republics of the Eurasian region?

Chapter 9

Staying Together

How strong is the Commonwealth of Independent States?

READING FOR A PURPOSE:
1. Do Communists still have any power in the lands of the Commonwealth?
2. What must the republics do to repair their economies?
3. Why do the republics need one another?

1. The Soviet Union was founded on December 30, 1922. At the time, Joseph Stalin listed the problems facing the new nation. Among them, he said, were "devastated fields, factories at standstill, destroyed productive powers and exhausted economic resources." Seventy years later, the leaders of the new Commonwealth of Independent States are facing the same problems.

2. The world was shocked when the Soviet Union collapsed in December 1991. The end was so sudden that it took a while for people to realize what changes were in store. One major change was the end of the cold war, which was welcomed by the United States and its NATO allies. China was left as the only major Communist power in the world. Fidel Castro of Cuba became the only Communist dictator outside Asia. Those countries that had depended on the Soviet Union for money and weapons began to look for new allies.

3. The new leaders of the different republics told the world what many had suspected for a while. The Soviet Union was almost bankrupt. The 1991 Gulf War had revealed something else. Soviet military equipment and weapons, long feared in the West, were inferior to those of the United States.

4. Many of the republics in the former Soviet Union chose new leaders. Some of them had very recently been Communists. Most of the people in the republics wanted democracy and a free-market economy. In a free-market economy, prices are controlled by demand rather than being set by a central planning committee. Individuals make decisions about what to make and where to sell it. But the people were not certain about how to achieve these goals. Besides, many of their leaders, especially on the local level, continued to be the same Communists who had always run things.

5. The people who had government positions under the Communists naturally wanted

At a rally in Vilnius, Lithuania, Lithuanians call for complete independence from the then Soviet Union.

School in this Siberian boomtown is crowded because the building cannot keep pace with the fast growing population.

to keep their jobs. When President Boris Yeltsin of Russia promised to break up many of the state and collective farms, the well-paid managers of those farms resisted his plan. Other changes were also necessary. Factories that produced the huge farm machinery used on the state farms needed to buy equipment to make smaller tractors for the private farms. But these factories did not have the money to make changes. So the old planners, who were often still in charge, continued to run things as they always had. It will take time to make many of these changes.

6. Feeding the population of the Commonwealth is a top priority. Famines happened regularly during the 70 years of Communist rule. Many of the children of the Commonwealth are still undernourished.

7. In order to feed its citizens adequately, the Commonwealth must solve its transportation problems. The CIS desperately needs more railroads to move food and manufactured goods among the republics. A good highway system to connect the republics is also necessary.

8. One of the most dangerous situations left behind by the Communist central planners is the state of the environment in the former republics. In Kazakhstan, for example, government planners decided to create an industrial center out of farmland that was rich in

mineral resources. In the 1960s, the government began to build huge factories in the area. Giant industrial centers were filled with iron and steelworks and factories that processed copper, lead, and zinc. Kazakhstan became the leading producer of lead in the Soviet Union. But the republic paid a price. Many of its cities are among the most polluted in the Commonwealth. In summer, the air in these cities stings the eyes and smells like rotten eggs.

9. The republics were not really ready for the sudden change from government control of the economy. The Soviet Union had never had a strong banking system. In a capitalist economy, banks attract depositors by offering to pay them interest on their money. Meanwhile, the banks lend the money. The people who borrow the money use it to start new businesses or to expand old ones. The banks make money because they charge higher interest to the borrowers than they pay to their depositors. The Commonwealth has not had the time to develop such a system. In 1987, there were seven commercial banks in the Soviet Union. In 1992, there were 1,500. There still are not nearly enough banks to serve the needs of all of the privately owned farms and businesses that the republics will have.

10. In the past, the Soviet Union shared a common currency, the ruble. Now, some republics, like Ukraine, are creating their own

At a market in Alma Atta food is plentiful. But manufactured goods are in short supply.

currencies. As a result, the Commonwealth may face many new problems. Who will determine the values of the different currencies? As the new money is created, will the Commonwealth have to deal with the rising prices of inflation or the reduced business activity of a depression? Will the republics pass laws that restrict or protect their own trade? The republics must find a way to make their economies work together. Otherwise, the challenge to the Commonwealth may be too great.

11. Working together is the key to the Commonwealth's survival. The republics have been interdependent for 70 years. This means they have depended on one another. Today, they still need one another. Russia produces 90 percent of the oil in the CIS. Ukraine produces 25 percent of the grain. Kazakhstan's industrial output, however, is needed in Ukraine. If the republics do not work together to preserve the Commonwealth, they may not survive separately.

UNDERSTANDING WHAT YOU HAVE READ

1. Which of the following questions are answered in this chapter?
a. What does Russia export?
b. What problems with their economies do the republics face?
c. Why must the republics work together?

2. The main idea of the chapter is to describe
a. the strengths and weaknesses of the newly free republics
b. the relations between China and Russia
c. the relationship of Cuba to the CIS

3. One of the chief weaknesses of the CIS is
a. their leaders' lack of experience with a free-market economy
b. the growing armed forces
c. the lack of natural resources

4. A top priority of the republics is
a. feeding the population

b. forming alliances with African nations
c. helping China

5. A dangerous situation left by Communist leaders is
a. lack of petroleum
b. environmental pollution
c. overproduction by farmers

6. Which of the following is NOT an economic problem for the new republics?
a. the banking system
b. a common currency
c. too much oil

7. In order to survive, the republics of the CIS must
a. work together
b. build a strong military
c. produce less food

WRITING

In this chapter, you have read about some of the problems that Russia and the republics must solve in order to survive. Imagine that you are one of the leaders in a newly-free republic. What problem would you solve first? Write a "position paper" that defines the problem and then expains how to solve it.

In the Heart of Eurasia

Valentin Rasputin is considered the spiritual leader of the ecological Green Movement in the Commonwealth. This writer lives near Lake Baikal in Siberia. Thus, it was especially fitting that the first target of his Green Movement was a paper mill on the lake. Lake Baikal contains at least one-sixth of all the fresh water on earth. Unlike most lakes, Baikal was not formed by the retreating glaciers of the last Ice Age. Instead, it is a water-filled giant crack in the earth's crust. The paper mill that the Greens opposed is at the southern end of the lake. The mill was pouring slimy black discharge into the lake, and its chimneys belched black, greasy smoke. The Soviet government was not pleased with the public protest about the mill. Furthermore, Lake Baikal is known as the Pearl of Siberia. Within a very short time, the protest paid off. The Soviet government came up with ways to clean up the paper mill.

In the late 1980s, radio and television stations suddenly began saying what most Soviet citizens already knew: Soviet industry was making the country very dirty and very unhealthy. **Moscow Radio** drew attention to many of the worst polluters. One of its programs exposed conditions at a gas-processing plant in the Ural Mountains. The factory was discharging 100,000 tons of poisonous substances into the air every year. Sometimes clouds of gas covered entire villages, causing sore throats and nosebleeds. Although the government promised to do something about the factory, Radio Moscow was not satisfied. The station reported that it would "keep an eye on these promises." Because of this publicity, the plant was shut down.

Nikolay Vavilov was a giant among the world's botanists. Working during the 1920s and 1930s, he understood how important it was for a nation to have many different kinds of seeds for food plants. Having such a variety of seeds determines whether a nation can feed itself. His fellow botanists were loyal to his ideas. During the 900-day siege of Leningrad in World War II, no food could be brought into the city. Even so, Vavilov's staff refused to eat the precious seeds and root vegetables they had gathered from all over the world. Many of the scientists died of starvation in the laboratories. The sacks of seed and potatoes that they had been saving to plant had not been touched. Unfortunately, Vavilov did not live to learn of the sacrifice of his associates. He had a dispute with Stalin's favorite agricultural scientist. Vavilov died in prison, accused of spying and agricultural sabotage.

History's worst nuclear accident happened at Chernobyl, near Kiev, on April 25, 1986. The Soviet government asked the world for help in treating hundreds of victims who had been exposed to deadly doses of radiation. The only hope for these people was a bone marrow transplant. A United States expert on bone marrow transplants, **Dr. Robert Gale,** was invited to the Soviet Union to advise local doctors. Working around the clock, Dr. Gale finished his work by the middle of May. Before returning to the United States, Dr. Gale agreed to continue working with the 100,000 people who lived near Chernobyl at the time of the accident. The effects of high doses of radiation can continue to harm the human body indefinitely.

Chapter 10

Armenia

What are Armenia's major economic resources?

READING FOR A PURPOSE:
1. How does the elevation of the land affect the crops grown by Armenia's farmers?
2. How did Armenia's religion affect its history?
3. What problems does the future hold for an independent Armenia?

1. Armenia (ar-MEE-nee-uh) is a tiny nation in the Caucasus Mountains. Only a little larger than the state of New Hampshire, Armenia occupies about 11,500 square miles (29,800 square kilometers) of rocky land. This makes it the smallest republic in the Commonwealth of Independent States. Landlocked Armenia is bordered by Georgia in the north, Azerbaijan (az-uhr-bi-JAHN) in the east, Turkey and Azerbaijan in the west, and Iran in the south.

2. The Caucasus Mountains run through Armenia from the northwest to the southeast. Some of these mountains reach heights of more than 10,000 feet (3,000 meters). The highest peak soars 13,418 feet (4,090 meters). The average elevation of the whole region is about 5,900 feet (1,800 meters) above sea level. South of the mountains lies the Armenian Plateau, a flat land broken by lakes and rivers. Lake Sevan (suh-VAHN) lies on the plateau and from it flows the Razdan (rahz-DAHN) River. The Aras (uh-RAHS) River and its valley split the plateau along the Armenia-Turkey border. Although most of the region is settled, some of this land is still wild. Jackals, wild pigs, and snakes roam in the drier areas. About 10 percent of the region is forest, where wildcats and bears still live.

3. Earthquakes are a fact of life to the people of Armenia. Legend says that the land is caught between the horns of an enormous bull, and that the earth quakes when the bull shakes its head. The Armenians were devastated by a quake that hit on December 7, 1988. More than 25,000 people died—500 students in one school alone—and a half million lost their homes. Part of the reason the quake did so much damage was that many of the houses were very poorly built. Official reports blamed most of the deaths on the "shoddy construction" of many high-rise apartment buildings "that fell apart like matchboxes" in the quake. The apartments were built during the Soviet Union era. They had been put up quickly and cheaply to meet the severe housing shortage.

4. Armenia's location high in the mountains affects its climate. In general, the republic has cool, dry summers and cold, dry winters. The summer temperature averages about 54°F (12°C), while January temperatures average about 10°F (-21°C).

5. Armenian farmers fit their crops to the land. The rich volcanic soil of the warmer river valleys, aided by irrigation, yields good crops of grapes, cotton, peaches, tobacco, apricots, and vegetables. As the elevation changes, so do the crops. The Caucasus foothills are warm enough during the growing season for the farming of figs and grains. Grains also grow higher up the mountains. Even higher on the mountainsides, meadows provide pastures for herds of goats, sheep, and cattle.

6. Although in the past Armenia has been a farming country, over half of its people now live in its cities. Most came to the cities seeking jobs in the growing number of factories. These factories manufacture chemicals, electrical products, and textiles. Yerevan (yeer-uh-VAHN), the capital and largest city, has about 1 million people.

7. Mining was important to Armenia even in ancient times. Archaeologists have found what may be the world's oldest steel furnace—built 3,000 years ago—in Armenia. Today, Armenia is one of the world's leading producers of copper. Many other metals, including molybdenum, lead, and zinc, are mined there as well.

8. Hydroelectric power plants have been built to provide power for Armenia's growing industries. Five of these plants operate along the 65-mile downhill course of the Razdan River. Still, only 50 percent of the waterpower of the region has been developed. Armenia must import power to provide electricity for its citizens.

9. Armenia is located in the Caucasus region, along with Georgia and Azerbaijan. The Caucasus is home to more than 50 ethnic

Over half of all Armenians live in its cities. Yerevan, capital of Armenia, is a modern city with and educated population.

Parts of this Armenian Apostolic Church were built as far back as the fifth century.

groups. Yet, in Armenia, almost 90 percent of all the people are Armenian. A very few groups—mostly Azerbaijani, Russians, Ukrainians, and Kurds—make up the other 10 percent.

10. Only about half the world's 6 million Armenians live in Armenia itself. Over the years, others have been forced to leave their homeland by different conquerors. They have set up Armenian settlements in many other countries. About 1 million Armenians live in Azerbaijan and Georgia. Over 600,000 Armenians live in the United States. Nearly 100,000 Armenians have settled in France.

11. The Armenian Plateau was first settled during the 800s B.C. The name Armenia was found carved in three different languages on a 2,500-year-old stone. But people occupied this land even earlier than that. Tools used by humans more than 10,000 years ago have been found in the Armenian mountains. A wooden, wheeled cart—one of the oldest wheeled objects ever discovered—was found in an ancient Armenian grave.

12. Armenia has always been attractive to invaders. Its location on the trade routes between Europe and Africa made it a prize worth having. First ruled by Persia, then

Greece, Armenia finally fell under Roman rule in 55 B.C. While part of the Roman Empire, Armenia became a Christian nation. Much of Armenian culture is based on its religion. This has caused conflict with Armenia's neighbors. In an effort to wipe out Armenia's Christianity, the Persians and later the Mongols and the Turks invaded Armenia again and again. By the 1500s, the Turks held all of Armenia.

13. In 1828, Russia took most of eastern Armenia from the Turks. Between 1894 and 1916, the Turks killed hundreds of thousands of Armenians in western Armenia. Many of the survivors fled to Russian Armenia, the Middle East, and the United States. Russian Armenia was independent for a very short time in 1920, but then it fell under Communist control. In 1921, Armenia became a republic in the Soviet Union.

14. Although Armenia welcomed Soviet protection from the Turks, Armenians were not happy under Soviet rule. Despite Soviet disapproval, Armenians continued to practice their religion openly. As early as 1965, Armenians protested Soviet control of the Armenian economy. When Moscow declared that Russian would be Armenia's official language, demonstrations in Yerevan caused the government to back down. In 1991, when the Soviet government began to lose control of the republics, there was little surprise when 95 percent of Armenian voters chose independence. Few were surprised, either, when the Armenians elected a non-Communist president.

15. Independence will bring new challenges for the Armenian people. One problem that must be solved involves a region called Nagorno-Karabakh (nuh-GOHR-noh-KAHR-uh-bahk). This region lies not in Armenia but in Azerbaijan, Armenia's neighbor to the west. Most of the people in Nagorno-Karabakh are Armenians. Many have been persecuted by the Muslim Azerbaijani. This has caused much bloodshed. For years, Soviet troops kept peace in the area. However, when both Armenia and Azerbaijan declared their independence, the troops could not stop the bloody clashes.

16. Other members of the Commonwealth have encouraged the feuding republics to negotiate. In 1991, Armenia and Azerbaijan agreed to a cease-fire. Unfortunately, the agreement lasted no more than two months. When a helicopter carrying some Azerbaijani officials crashed—or was shot down—in November 1991, the two republics stopped negotiations. The lingering hostility between Armenia and Azerbaijan is one more example of how ethnic rivalries endanger the existence of the Commonwealth of Independent States.

UNDERSTANDING WHAT YOU HAVE READ

1. Which of the following questions are answered in this chapter?

a. What are the physical characteristics of Armenia?

b. What is Armenia's relationship with Cuba?

c. Why has Armenia been invaded throughout history?

2. The main idea of this chapter is to describe

a. Armenia's historical relationship with the Russian Empire

b. Armenia's resources

c. Armenia's official language and religious practices

3. Armenia is

a. a large republic

b. a small nation

c. a country the size of Texas

4. Physical characteristics of Armenia's location that have caused devastation for the population are

a. earthquakes

b. floods

c. tornadoes

5. Armenia's farmers

a. grow very little food

b. grow citrus fruits and bananas

c. fit their crops to the elevation of the land

6. The capital of Armenia is

a. Yerevan

b. Kiev

c. Azov

7. A major source of energy for Armenia is

a. hydroelectric power plants

b. solar power panels

c. nuclear power plants

8. Armenia has attracted invaders because

a. it has gold and silver mines

b. it is located on trade routes between Europe and Africa

c. it has many natural harbors on the Mediterranean Sea

9. One problem that Armenia must solve

a. involves a dispute with Azerbaijan over Nagorno-Karabakh

b. is uniting the many different ethnic groups

c. is establishing diplomatic relations with the United States

10. Most Armenians are

a. Muslims

b. Buddhists

c. Christians

WRITING

In this chapter, you have learned about Armenia. You recall that about half of the Armenian people live outside the republic. If you were a citizen living in Armenia, what would you want Armenians who live outside the country to know? Write a letter to a relative who lives in the United States and inform your relative about the new Armenia.

Chapter 11

Ukraine: Breadbasket of the Commonwealth

Why is Ukraine an important member of the Commonwealth?

READING FOR A PURPOSE
1. How have its climate and physical features shaped Ukraine's economy?
2. What economic problems does Ukraine face?
3. Why must Ukraine and Russia get along with each other?

1. Ukraine is located in the western part of the Commonwealth of Independent States. On its southern border are the Black Sea and the Sea of Azov (AZ-ahf). Belarus lies to the north. Moldova, Romania, Hungary, Czechoslovakia, and Poland form its western border. Russia is to the east. With a land area of 603,700 square miles (1,569,620 square kilometers), Ukraine is about as large as France. It is the third largest republic in the CIS.

2. Much of Ukraine is a large plain, though in the north, there are wooded, swampy lowlands. In the south and west, there are hills, plateaus, and mountains. Farther south, the steppe, or treeless plain, begins. The land here

has dark, fertile soil. Several major rivers flow through Ukraine. The Dnieper (NEE-puhr), which is the third longest river in Europe, flows for 1,320 miles (2,112 kilometers). Other important rivers are the Dniester (NEES-tuhr) and the Desna (duh-SNAH). Ukraine's location is critical to most of the republics of the Commonwealth. This is because the Black Sea and the Sea of Azov that border Ukraine are the Commonwealth's only warm-water outlets to the West. Odessa (oh-DES-uh), on the Black Sea, is Ukraine's major port.

3. Much of Ukraine has a humid-continental climate with warm summers and cold winters. The area around the Black Sea has a Mediterranean climate with mild, short winters and hot, dry summers. This climate makes the area a popular vacation spot.

4. Ukraine is the "breadbasket" of the Commonwealth. In addition to producing more than a quarter of the grain in the CIS, Ukraine grows sugar beets, sunflowers, potatoes, tobacco, and tea. Ukrainian farmers also raise livestock. As in the other republics, much of the farming is done on state and collective farms.

5. Ukraine is also a strong industrial nation. The land is rich in natural resources, such as coal, iron ore, mercury, manganese, uranium, oil, and natural gas. Ukraine's factories produce metal products and heavy machinery. The leading industrial cities are Kiev (KEE-ef), Kharkov (KAHR-kof), and Rostov (ruh-STOF).

6. Approximately 51.8 million people live in Ukraine. This makes it the fifth largest nation in Europe and the second largest republic in the CIS. The people of Ukraine practice the Roman Catholic religion, and their language is Ukrainian. About three-fourths of the people are Ukrainians. The rest are mostly Russians. Ukrainians, like Russians and Belorussians, are Slavs.

7. Today, over half of all Ukranianians live in cities. Kiev, Ukraine's capital, is set among lush, green hills on the banks of the Dnieper River. Kiev has a long history. It was in Kiev

Historic Kiev is a city of fountains and squares, with an active cultural life.

that Christianity was first introduced to Russia, by Prince Vladimir I of Kiev in A.D. 988. It was from Kiev that medieval traders set out every spring in their longboats. They traveled down the Dnieper River and across the Black Sea to Constantinople. There they traded furs for the luxury goods of the East. When they returned to Kiev, they brought with them the culture of the Byzantine civilization. Moscow eventually became the powerful center of the Russian Empire, but Kiev was a major source of Russian culture. The region was not called Ukraine until the 1200s. It meant "border region," and it described the vast area of land between Poland and the many small kingdoms around Moscow. Ukraine came under Russian control in the late 1700s. It became independent in 1918 after World War I, but it was overrun by the Communists and made part of the Soviet Union in 1922.

8. The new leaders of Ukraine have many challenges ahead of them. The first, as in all the republics of the Commonwealth, is the economy. Ukraine took price controls off all products but found that prices rose so fast that most people could not afford simple items. Although Ukraine and Russia agreed to maintain trade relations with each other, Russia is now limiting shipments of gasoline and timber to Ukraine. Ukraine is shipping less food to Russia. These cutbacks hurt both republics.

9. Russia and Ukraine also have a disagreement over the Crimean Peninsula. The government of the Soviet Union gave the Crimea to Ukraine in 1954. The Russian parliament is now questioning whether that was legal, since the Crimea had belonged to Russia. Meanwhile, 350 ships of the former Soviet navy are stationed at a Crimean port in the Black Sea. Ukraine says that the ships now belong to Ukraine. Russia also claims the ships on behalf of the Commonwealth.

10. Added to the naval question is the problem of the former Soviet army. There were 450,000 soldiers stationed in Ukraine when the Soviet Union collapsed. Since then, about 300,000 soldiers have taken the oath of allegiance to Ukraine. Ukraine probably cannot afford such a large army, but the soldiers want to remain in Ukraine because they know that conditions in Russia are worse than in Ukraine.

11. Ukraine and Russia must settle their differences if either of them—and the Commonwealth—is to survive. The economies of all the republics have been tied together for so long that the republics are truly dependent on one another. There are also the emotional ties of the 12 million Russians who live in the Ukraine. Because it has both industry and fertile farm land, Ukraine may be the only republic that is strong enough to survive economically on its own. But if the Commonwealth falls apart, the Ukrainians, already hard pressed, will suffer further hardships.

The giant market at Kiev reflects Ukraine's role as the "breadbasket" of Eurasia.

UNDERSTANDING WHAT YOU HAVE READ

1. Which of the following questions are answered in this chapter?
a. What are the physical characteristics of Ukraine?
b. What are some economic problems that Ukraine is facing?
c. Why does Ukraine produce little food on its farms?

2. The main idea of this chapter is
a. Ukraine is a very small country
b. Ukraine is ruled by a prince
c. Ukraine is an important member of the Commonwealth

3. The major port of Ukraine is
a. Odessa
b. Kiev
c. Desna

4. Most of Ukraine has what kind of climate?
a. humid-continental
b. marine west coast
c. taiga

5. Which of the following natural resources does Ukraine NOT have a good supply of?
a. gold and diamonds
b. coal and mercury
c. uranium and natural gas

6. The capital and largest city is
a. Moscow
b. Vladimir
c. Kiev

7. Ukraine became a part of the Soviet Union in
a. 1922
b. 1200s
c. 1700s

8. What is the major challenge for Ukraine in the 1990s?
a. its relationship with China
b. growing enough food for the population
c. the economy

9. Russia and Ukraine have a disagreement over what area?
a. the Balkans
b. the Crimean Peninsula
c. the Sea of Azov

10. Ukraine is called the "breadbasket" of the Commonwealth because
a. it has the largest baking factories in the CIS
b. it produces more than a quarter of the grain in the CIS
c. it has many natural resources

WRITING

In Chapter 11, you have learned about Ukraine's wealth of natural resources and productive agriculture. You have also discovered that Ukraine, like other republics in the CIS, has a troubled economy. How do you think Ukrainians can use their resources and agriculture to improve their economy? In a small group, decide what Ukrainians might produce. Then write a description of the product and explain how it will help make the Ukrainian economy better.

The Disappearing Aral Sea

Thousands of years ago, irrigation changed the way people lived. By diverting lakes and rivers, human beings were able to transform desert areas into grassy plains. These new plains of dark, rich soil bore crops for the farmers. Yet if irrigation has helped the farmer, it has sometimes harmed rivers and lakes. This is what happened in the Aral-Caspian Lowland in Central Asia.

Once, the Aral Sea was part of an ancient seabed connected to the Mediterranean. Today, however, it is an inland sea with no outlet to the ocean. The Aral is fed by two large rivers, the Amu Darya (ah-moo DAHR-yah) and the Syr Darya (seer DAHR-yah). The water filling these rivers comes mainly from melting snows in the mountains in and near Afghanistan and from an occasional desert rain.

Diverting the Waters In 1918, Soviet leaders decided to irrigate more of the dry lands of Central Asia. As a result, farming and trade in the former Soviet Union increased dramatically. Farmers were able to grow several kinds of subtropical crops, including cotton, rice, and tobacco, in the warm climate of Central Asia. Because farmers grew a variety of different products, there was less need to import them from other countries.

Irrigation in Central Asia also helped protect the southern border of the former USSR. New jobs in construction and other areas helped win the loyalty of the people of the region.

Irrigation brought industry to the region as well. Dams needed for irrigation also provided electricity. Now local textile factories could process the cotton grown locally.

Environmental Damage Although they expected that the Aral would lose some water, Soviet leaders never expected that the whole region might someday turn into a desert. Since 1960, the level of the sea has dropped almost 9 feet (3 meters) Today, farmers have drained off so much water from the Amu Darya and the Syr Darya for irrigation that the Aral Sea is in danger of disappearing.

With so much less water, the Aral has become too salty for fish to survive. The fishing industry in the area has completely collapsed. In addition, as the coastline moved inland, many ports and harbors have become useless.

Concern for the Future The Aral Sea is likely to keep shrinking and to get saltier. One way to reverse the damage is to end irrigation in some areas. However, such a move would probably be very unpopular. Another way is to use more efficient types of irrigation. A third way is to bring water to the Aral Sea from other rivers. Some people have suggested transporting water from the Ob and Irtysh (eer-TIHSH) rivers in Siberia. Under this plan, water would be pumped from Siberia to the Aral Sea along a new 1,600-mile (2,574-kilometer) irrigation canal.

What advantages and disadvantages do you think there are in pumping water from Siberia to save the Aral Sea?

What other solutions do you see?

The Republics of Eurasia

Country	Area (Square Miles)	Capital	Population (1990)	Per Capita GNP, 1989
MEMBERS OF THE COMMONWEALTH OF INDEPENDENT STATES				
Armenia	11,306	Yerevan	3,300,000	$4,710
Azerbaijan	33,400	Baku	7,100,000	$3,750
Belarus	80,200	Minsk	10,300,000	$5,960
Kazakhstan	1,049,200	Alma-Ata	16,700,000	$3,720
Kyrgyzstan	76,642	Bishkek	4,400,000	$3,030
Moldova	13,012	Kishinev	4,400,000	$3,830
Russia	6,592,800	Moscow	148,000,000	$5,810
Tajikistan	54,019	Dushanbe	5,300,000	$2,340
Turkmenistan	188,417	Ashkhabad	3,600,000	$3,370
Ukraine	233,100	Kiev	51,800,000	$4,700
Uzbekistan	172,700	Tashkent	20,300,000	$2,750
NONMEMBER OF THE CIS				
Georgia	26,911	Tbilisi	5,500,000	$4,410

Sources: The World Almanac and Book of Facts, 1992, and Time Magazine, September 9, 1991

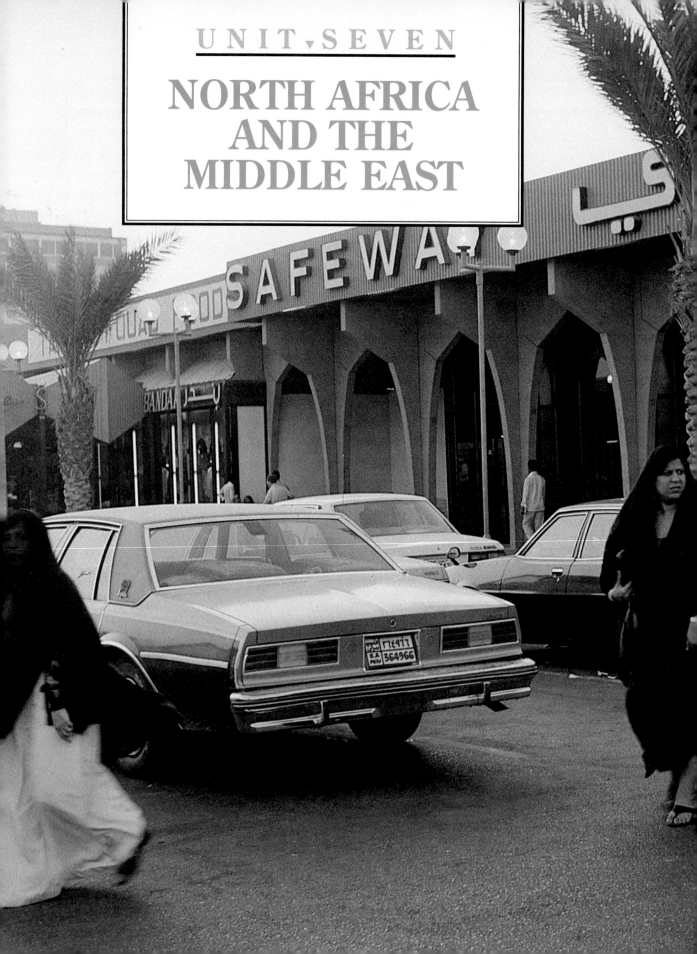

UNIT·SEVEN

NORTH AFRICA AND THE MIDDLE EAST

KEY IDEAS

▪ North Africa and the Middle East make up one of the world's most vital oil producing regions.

▪ Located at the crossroads of three continents, North Africa and the Middle East contain some of the busiest trading routes in the world. These ports move both ideas and goods.

▪ The physical characteristics of North Africa and the Middle East also make this a desert region where water is even more important than oil.

▪ The world's earliest civilizations arose in North Africa and the Middle East. Three world religions began in the Middle East: Judaism, Christianity, and Islam.

▪ Though the highest living standards in the world are found in the small oil-rich countries of the Persian Gulf, masses of people in the other countries of this region are poor.

▪ Unrest in North Africa and the Middle East stems from the lack of democracy, health care, and education and from problems in modernizing a traditional way of life.

▪ The conflict between Israel and the Arab states is a longstanding problem for the region.

Saudi Arabian women wearing traditional abayah *shop at a Western-style supermarket. The culture of the region combines modern influences with traditional ones.*

Chapter 1

The Crossroads of the World

Why are the Middle East and North Africa important to us?

READING FOR A PURPOSE:
1. How are the lands of North Africa and the Middle East alike?
2. What is the main resource of this region?
3. What religions had their beginning in the Middle East?

1. Many books have been written and movies have been made about the Middle East and North Africa. They usually showed the region to be a land of mystery, adventure, and romance. Americans have a different picture of that region today. Some see a once poor land made rich by huge reserves of oil. Others see a region torn apart by continuous wars and violence. Which picture is the true one?

2. The region known as North Africa and the Middle East begins on the west coast of northern Africa. It stretches across North Africa and southwestern Asia to the mountains of central Asia. It may be divided into two parts, the Middle East and North Africa. The Middle East includes the Asian countries as far north as Turkey (which is partly in Europe too), as far east as Afghanistan, and as far south as the Indian Ocean. It includes Egypt, which is located mostly in Africa. North Africa includes the countries west of Egypt—Libya, Tunisia, Algeria, and Morocco. When referring to the Middle East, many people include North Africa.

3. These lands are studied as one region because they are alike in several ways. The climate of the region is generally hot and dry. In fact, much of the land is barren desert. Getting enough water for everyday needs is a problem. Most of the people are farmers, town dwellers, or nomads. Most speak Arabic and follow the Muslim religion.

4. The United States has a great interest in North Africa and the Middle East. First, parts of the Middle East are rich in oil. Most of the oil is needed by U.S. allies in Europe and by Japan. The United States wants to be sure that it will always be able to get this oil. Second, the United States uses much more oil than it produces. It, therefore, also depends on oil from this region. The Arab nations of the Middle East are among the most important suppliers of oil to the United States. (Large U.S. oil imports also come from Mexico, Canada, and Venezuela.)

5. Third, this region is sometimes called the "crossroads of the world." Many of these countries border the Mediterranean Sea. This is one of the busiest trading routes in the world. The Suez Canal connects the Mediterranean Sea with the Red Sea. It shortens the distance from Europe to India by almost 5,000 miles (8,000 kilometers). The countries of Western Europe and the United States send their products to Asia and parts of Africa through the Suez Canal. In turn, oil, tin, and other materials from those lands are shipped through the canal to European and U.S. factories. The control of the land and sea routes around the Mediterranean Sea by friendly nations is important to the United States.

6. Fourth, three of the world's great reli-

An oil refinery in Saudi Arabia. How do the large reserves of oil in Saudi Arabia make it important to people in the U.S.?

gions—Judaism, Christianity, and Islam—began in this part of the world. Judaism is the oldest of these three religions. The religious beliefs and customs of millions of Americans began in this area on the eastern side of the Mediterranean Sea. Christianity began in the hills around Jerusalem where Jesus lived, taught, and died. In Jerusalem there are places Jews, Christians, and Muslims regard as holy.

7. Fifth, under communist rule, the Soviet Union was very interested in the Middle East for two reasons. It too wanted to benefit from the rich oil fields of the Middle East. Also, the Soviet Union needed to maintain a tie to the Middle East in order to reach the busy trade routes of the Mediterranean Sea. Since the 1991 collapse of the Soviet Union, the CIS has not taken a great interest in the Middle East because it has chosen to concentrate on its own economic and political problems.

History will determine the CIS's future interest in this region.

8. Finally, the Jewish state of Israel stands in the middle of the Arab countries of this region. Israel was formed in 1948, largely through the help of the United Nations. Its people's religious and political beliefs are different from other nations in the region. Since the little country was formed, most Arab nations have been opposed to Israel. A war was fought between them in 1948. During this war, many Arabs, called Palestinians, fled their land. The Palestinians would like their own state. Since the 1948 war, border fights have broken out. Again in 1956, 1967, and 1973, and 1982, Israel and some of its Arab neighbors went to war. A peace agreement between Israel and Egypt was signed in 1979. Israel is still involved in conflicts with its neighbors, especially Lebanon.

UNDERSTANDING WHAT YOU HAVE READ

1. Which of the following questions are answered in this chapter?

a. Why is this region important to the United States?

b. Why is the Suez Canal important?

c. Who owns the city of Jerusalem?

2. The main idea of this chapter is to describe the

a. resources of the Middle East

b. reasons why we should study this region

c. importance of religion in the lives of the people

3. Most of the people in North Africa and the Middle East are
a. Christians
b. Jews
c. Muslims

4. The greatest need of people living in this region is
a. water
b. wood
c. a home

5. A reason why North Africa and the Middle East are important to the United States is that
a. their coal and iron are needed for U.S. factories
b. the United States has agreed to protect the Arab nations
c. this region is the birthplace of three great religions and is a source of oil

6. The Suez Canal is an important waterway because it
a. gives the Commonwealth an outlet to the Mediterranean Sea
b. connects the Mediterranean and Black seas
c. carries a great amount of trade between Europe and Asia

7. The *Middle East* is a region in
a. southwestern Asia
b. central Africa
c. southwestern Africa

8. The *Dardanelles* is a narrow strait that makes up part of the water

route connecting the Mediterranean Sea and the
a. Atlantic Ocean
b. Red Sea
c. Black Sea

9. Many Middle East nations have become wealthy because of
a. wise investments
b. oil
c. a good growing season

10. The three religions that began in this region are Judaism, Christianity, and
a. Islam
b. Hinduism
c. Hebrew

11. Religions and political beliefs are different from the other nations in this region in
a. Egypt
b. Libya
c. Israel

12. Arabs who fled their land during the 1948 war in Israel are known as
a. Israelis
b. Palestinians
c. Jews

13. North Africa includes the nations of Egypt, Libya, Algeria, Morocco, and
a. Tunisia
b. Israel
c. Saudi Arabia

DEVELOPING IDEAS AND SKILLS

Building Map Skills——North Africa and the Middle East

Study the map. Then answer these questions.

1. Is the region north or south of the equator?
2. Is the region east or west of the prime meridian?
3. How far north and south does the region extend?
4. Does the region extend farther from east to west or from north to south?
5. What region or regions are near it?
6. What is the largest country? The smallest?
7. What bodies of water border the region?
8. Which country has no outlets to the sea?
9. What are some of the important rivers in the region?
10. Which countries are located on peninsulas?
11. What are the capital cities of the countries in this region?
12. Are there large rivers that form the boundary lines between these countries?

North Africa and the Middle East

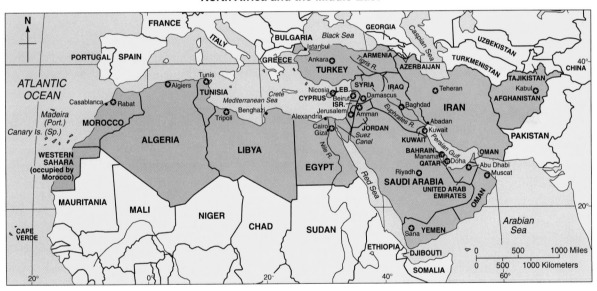

Chapter 2

Warm, Dry Lands

How does the geography of the region affect the life of the people?

READING FOR A PURPOSE:
1. How does the desert really look and feel?
2. Why are the mountains important?
3. How does the Nile benefit Egypt?

1. North Africa and the Middle East are lands that include much desert. There are mountains and plateaus as well, but the desert most affects the life of the people. The largest desert area is the Sahara in North Africa. The Sahara is almost as large in area as the United States. It reaches from the Atlantic Ocean eastward to the Nile River. East of the Red Sea is more desert. The Arabian peninsula, large parts of Iran, Jordan, and southern Israel are all desert. Thus, a dry region extends for 5,000 miles (about 8,000 kilometers) from the Atlantic to the Indian Ocean. Except for the coast and the area around a few rivers, fertile land is scarce.

2. Some people have mistaken ideas about deserts. For example, some believe that the desert is all sand. This is not true. While there are large hills of sand (called sand dunes), most of the desert either is bare rock or is covered with small pebbles and sandstones. Some also believe that the desert is flat. In some places the desert *is* a large, flat plain. However, in other areas there are mountains and high peaks. Some people believe that the desert is always hot. This is partly true. During the day, the sun bakes the sand and bare rock until they are very hot. At night, however, the earth cools quickly and may become very cold. Thus, temperatures may range from 100°F or hotter during the day to 40°F at night—a change of 60 degrees in a single day.

3. Life on the desert is very difficult. The hot sun bakes the earth and the winds blow continually. There is almost no rain. Except for small animals like lizards and snakes, there is very little life. There is not enough grass to support life, not even the herding of animals. Humans living on the desert move from one oasis to another. (An oasis is a fertile spot in the desert where water can be found. Some oases are quite large and support many crops.)

4. Parts of the Middle East and North Africa are hilly or mountainous. The highest mountains are the Hindu Kush in Afghanistan. Other high mountains are in Turkey and Iran. These are the Taurus, Elburz, and Zagros mountains. In northwestern Africa are the Atlas Mountains of Morocco and Algeria. They lie between the desert and the Mediterranean Sea.

5. The mountains are very important to the people of this region. What little rain there is falls in the mountains. Water trapped by the mountain peaks travels for hundreds of miles underground. In some places it comes to the top of the earth in springs. In others it is reached by digging wells at the base of the mountains.

6. Because of the water from the mountains, there are two great river systems: the Tigris and Euphrates rivers in Iraq and the Nile River in Egypt. The Tigris and Euphrates rivers rise in the mountains of Turkey. The Euphrates is west of the Tigris River. The two rivers flow almost parallel or next to each

Part of the Sahara is in Algeria. The name Sahara *comes from the Arab word for "desert."*

other as they wind through Iraq. Where the rivers almost meet on their flow southeastward, the ancient city of Baghdad is located. About 200 miles (320 kilometers) southeast of Baghdad, the rivers join together and flow into the Persian Gulf. For thousands of years the people living along these rivers have used the waters to irrigate their lands.

7. The Nile is the longest river in the world. It begins south of Egypt in the highlands of central Africa. The Nile River is joined by other streams that rise in Ethiopia and East Africa. This giant river flows northward through Sudan and Egypt until it reaches the Mediterranean Sea, over 4,000 miles (6,400 kilometers) from its source. The river brings water to the people of the Nile Valley. The Nile also brought rich soils until the Aswan Dam was built stopping the overflow of the river. Without the Nile, few people could live in Egypt. Beyond the waters of the Nile there is desert. Thus you can see that Egypt is truly the "Gift of the Nile."

8. While most of the Middle East and North Africa is hot and dry, the lands along the Mediterranean Sea have a more pleasant climate. This is the Mediterranean climate. The summers are long, hot, and dry; the winters are mild and moist. Because there is more rainfall, more crops can be grown. Olives, fruits, and grapes are grown on the hillsides of the coastal lands. This area has a mild climate because of the surrounding mountains and the warm Mediterranean waters.

UNDERSTANDING WHAT YOU HAVE READ

1. **Which of the following questions are answered in this chapter?**
a. Why are the rivers of this region important?
b. Why is this region largely a desert?
c. How do people live in the desert?

2. A good title for paragraph 2 would be
   a. Hot and Cold Regions
   b. Clearing Up Some Ideas About Deserts
   c. Traveling in the Sand

3. The largest desert in the world is the
   a. Atacama
   b. Gobi
   c. Sahara

4. The Nile River flows in which direction?
   a. South
   b. North
   c. East

5. Mountains are important in the Middle East because they are
   a. the source of rivers and springs
   b. rich in minerals
   c. the population centers

6. More crops can be grown along the coast of the Mediterranean Sea because
   a. there is greater rainfall
   b. the dry winds from the desert pick up moisture over the Mediterranean Sea
   c. some of the world's richest soils are found there

7. An *oasis* is a
   a. mountain spot where water is collected
   b. place where rivers flow into the sea
   c. place in the desert where water can be found

8. "Rivers *parallel* each other." This statement means that the rivers
   a. touch each other
   b. flow next to each other
   c. rise in the same mountains

9. The highest mountains in the region are the
   a. Hindu Kush
   b. Atlas Mountains
   c. Taurus Mountains

10. The great river systems in this region are the Nile and the
    a. Tigris and Euphrates
    b. Jordan
    c. Amazon

11. The Elburz Mountains are located in
    a. Turkey
    b. Iran
    c. Algeria

12. The Nile River flows into
    a. the Mediterranean Sea
    b. the Persian Gulf
    c. Sudan

SUMMING UP

True or False

Tell whether these statements are true or false. The underlined words make the statements true or false. If a statement is false, what word or words would you place in it to make it true?

1. The Sahara is located in underlined northern Africa.
2. The Tigris and Euphrates rivers flow through Iraq.
3. Potatoes are a major crop near the Mediterranean Sea.
4. Egypt has fertile soil because of the Nile River.
5. There are two great river systems in this region, the Tigris and Euphrates rivers in Iraq and the Nile River in Egypt.
6. On the desert, groups of people have gathered to live near the tin mines.
7. The Nile River flows into the Persian Gulf.
8. Some of the highest mountains in this region are found in Egypt.

DEVELOPING IDEAS AND SKILLS

Building Map Skills — Land Forms of the Middle East and North Africa

Study the map of land forms on this page. Then choose the item that best completes each of the following sentences.

1. Saudi Arabia is mostly made up of
a. mountains
b. plateaus
c. plains
2. The highest mountains are in
a. Afghanistan
b. Egypt
c. Oman

3. The Tigris and Euphrates rivers flow through Iraq's great
a. desert
b. plains
c. hills
4. The Tropic of Cancer falls through
a. Egypt
b. Turkey
c. Lebanon
5. Libya is covered with
a. hills and plains
b. plateaus and mountains
c. plains and plateaus

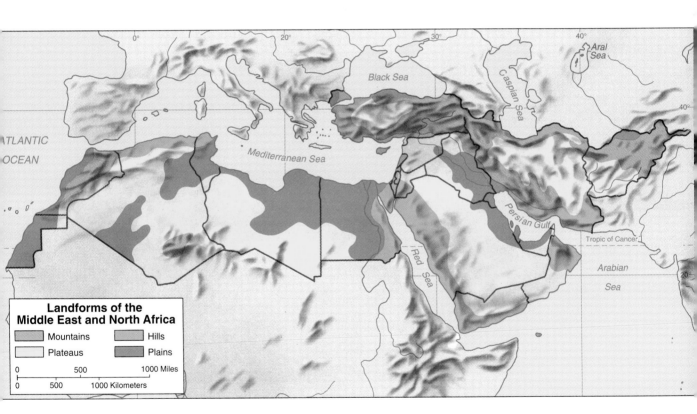

Landforms of the Middle East and North Africa

Mountains   Hills
Plateaus   Plains

0   500   1000 Miles
0   500   1000 Kilometers

377

Building Map Skills — Climates of The Middle East and North Africa

Study the climate map on this page. Then answer the questions below.

1. (a) Which countries have a Mediterranean climate?
   (b) Where can a vertical climate be found?
2. Which climate region is the largest?

3. (a) Which climates can be found in Iran?
   (b) Which climates can be found in Morocco?
4. How does latitude affect climate in the Middle East and North Africa?
5. List two ways the climate has affected the way of life in the Middle East and North Africa.

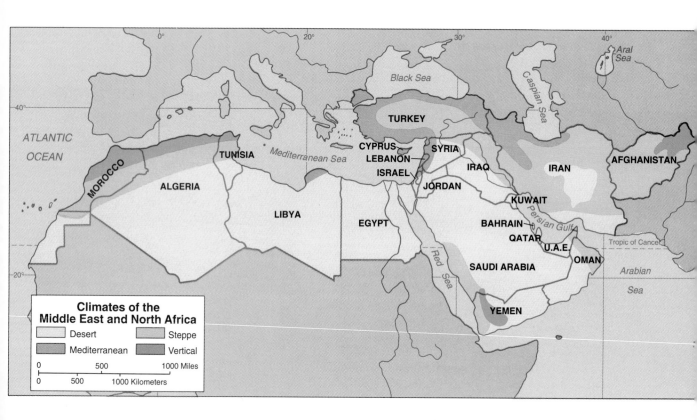

Climates of the Middle East and North Africa

- Desert
- Mediterranean
- Steppe
- Vertical

0   500   1000 Miles
0   500   1000 Kilometers

Chapter 3

Where Civilization Began

How has this region contributed to a changing world?

READING FOR A PURPOSE:
1. Where were the first civilizations in this region?
2. What have Egypt and Babylonia given to the world?
3. Where did the religion of Islam start? Where did it spread?

1. This is a region with a very long history. Many kinds of farm animals we now have—oxen, sheep, goats, pigs, and dogs—were tamed by the early hunters and farmers of the Middle East. They also tamed wild donkeys and camels and used these animals to cross the desert. They knew where to find water in the desert and how to grow crops on the oases. Some of the crops that first came from this part of the world are wheat, barley, and melons. This is the region where figs and dates were first grown.

2. Farmers settled early in the great river valleys of North Africa and the Middle East. They noticed that the rivers flooded the land every year at a certain time. They learned how to dam the water when it flooded and how to let it out when they needed it. They made up rules for the use of the water. Before long, they had the first government in which laws were being enforced. The first civilizations we know of began in the river valleys of the Nile and the Tigris and Euphrates.

3. Babylonia was one of the great civilizations along the Tigris-Euphrates valley. The people of Babylonia and Egypt learned to do many things. They learned how to grow crops and irrigate their farmlands. They lived in cities. Both had a form of picture writing. The Egyptians wrote on the treated leaves of the *papyrus* plant. (We get our word *paper* from *papyrus*.) The Egyptian writing was called *hieroglyphics*. The Babylonians used a chisel to "write" on clay tablets. The Egyptians built great tombs, burial places for their rulers. These were called *pyramids*. The Babylonians built great temples. The Egyptians used a calendar of 365 days. The people around the Tigris and Euphrates rivers were the first to count in units of 60. From them comes our method of counting 60 seconds in one minute and 60 minutes in one hour.

The Rosetta Stone. This slab has enabled people to figure out early Egyptian writing (hieroglyphics). The message on the stone is written in three different languages. The writing at the top is hieroglyphics.

The ancient Romans conquered Tunisia in the second century B.C. There, they build this colosseum for games and athletic contests.

4. The Jews also contributed to the civilizations of the Middle East. The ancient Jews were called Hebrews. They lived in different parts of the region—first Iraq, then Egypt, and later Palestine, much of which is now called Israel. Their religion taught for the first time the belief in one God. This is called *monotheism.* The history of the Jewish people and their religious beliefs are written in one of the world's most famous books, the Bible.

5. The Middle East was ruled at different times by the Persians, the Greeks, and the Romans. While the land of Palestine was under Roman rule, Christianity, a religion based on the teachings of Jesus, began. He also taught the belief in one God. He taught that people should love one another. His followers spread Christianity to all parts of the world.

6. Late in the 6th century, a man named Muhammad was born at Mecca in Arabia. As a young man, he was a trader or merchant. Muslims believe that he was a prophet or messenger of God. He taught a new religion called Islam. Muhammad gradually *converted* the people of Arabia and united them. After Muhammad's death, the Muslims (followers of Islam) began to spread eastward and westward, bringing their religion to many lands.

7. Within 200 years, the Muslims controlled a vast area extending from Spain across North Africa to India. The Arab lands became centers of a great civilization. In time, most of the people of these lands became fol-

lowers of Islam and used the language of the Arabs. Arab traders carried ideas and goods of Asia throughout their lands and into Europe. In this way they transferred beliefs and products between the civilizations of Asia and Europe. Arabic words such as soda, alcohol, coffee, algebra, and magazine became part of the English language. In the 11th century, Turkish peoples from central Asia invaded Arab lands. The Mongols were the next people to conquer the region. Most of North Africa and Southwest Asia then came under the control of the Ottoman Turks. They controlled much of the area into the early 20th century. But by 1500, European explorers had found an all-water route to the riches of Asia. European traders could bypass the overland routes. Therefore, the Middle Eastern traders were no longer as important as they once were.

8. Europe became very much interested in North Africa and the Middle East in the middle of the 19th century. In 1869, a French company finished building the Suez Canal, greatly shortening the sea route between Europe and Asia. The British soon took control of the canal. Other European nations began to take parts of the Turkish empire that had conquered the Arabs. France took Algeria in 1830, Tunisia in 1881, and Morocco in 1909. Italy took Libya after a war with Turkey in 1912.

9. During World War I, the Arabs helped

the United Kingdom and the Allies. When the Allies won, the Arabs had been promised that their lands would be made free. However, after the war the League of Nations was formed. The League gave some of the Arab lands to the Allies, who were to govern them until the Arabs were ready for self-government. These territories were called *mandates.* Among the governing nations, France was given Syria and Lebanon. The United Kingdom controlled Iraq, Palestine, and Jordan. Egypt did become free in 1922.

10. The fact that some of their lands were held by nations of Europe made the Arabs want their freedom even more. This dislike of control by foreign nations has carried over to the present day. It is true that France and the United Kingdom built some dams, railroads, schools, and hospitals in the lands they held. It is also true that they probably knew more about democratic government than did the Arabs. But this did not stop the desire of Arab people to govern themselves. During World War II, Syria and Lebanon gained their independence. Since that war, independence has been gained by Jordan, Israel, Libya, Morocco, Tunisia, and Algeria. The new nations have worked to establish stable governments.

UNDERSTANDING WHAT YOU HAVE READ

1. Which of the following questions are answered in this chapter?
a. How did Islam begin?
b. How did world wars change this region?
c. How was the Suez Canal built?

2. The main idea of paragraph 3 is that
a. Egyptians and Babylonians built great temples
b. ancient Egyptians lived in cities
c. ancient people of the Middle East were highly civilized

3. The Suez Canal was built by
a. a French company
b. the British government
c. the United States

4. Both of the old civilizations along the Nile and Tigris-Euphrates rivers had
a. a system of writing
b. the Christian religion
c. great trade with the countries of western Europe

5. One of the reasons Arab civilization has been important in world history is because
a. Arabs started the belief in one God

b. Arab traders brought goods and ideas from East to West
c. Arabs first developed a system of reading and writing

6. The contributions of the old civilizations of the Middle East include all of these EXCEPT the
a. use of gunpowder and printing thousands of years ago
b. beginning of cities and governments
c. discovery of methods to irrigate land

7. A *monotheist* believes in
a. one God
b. no gods
c. many gods

8. "Many Arabs were *converted* to Islam." The best meaning for *converted* is
a. "changed their beliefs"
b. "opposed something new"
c. "spoke roughly about"

9. The best meaning for *mandates* in paragraph 9 is
a. "orders given by a ruler"
b. "backward territories"
c. "lands taken care of by other nations"

DEVELOPING IDEAS AND SKILLS

Reading a Time Line

Look at the time line. In your notebook, write the letter of the period of time in which each of the following events took place.

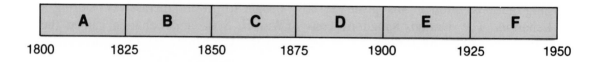

1. France takes control of Tunisia.
2. End of World War II.
3. France takes control of Algeria.
4. The Suez Canal is completed.

5. Egypt becomes independent.
6. France takes control of Morocco.
7. Italy takes control of Libya.

REVIEWING AND WRITING

Writing a Report

The history of North Africa and the Middle East is filled with so many interesting events and people that you will want to know more about it. Special reports may be made on many of the following:

1. How have ancient ruins given us a knowledge of life in Egypt, Babylonia, Israel?
2. Contributions of these civilizations include buildings and statues. Find out about the pyramids, sphinx, Hanging Gardens of Babylon.
3. How Islam spread from Arabia to western Europe can be found in most world history books.

Find out what you can about it and report to the class.
4. The religious leaders of this region have been very important in its history. Report to the class on one of them. You may also be interested in such political leaders as Lawrence of Arabia, David Ben-Gurion, Kemal Ataturk, Anwar el-Sadat, Ayatollah Khomeini.
5. The resurgence of Islam in the late 1970s and 1980s and its impact on Middle Eastern society and politics.

Chapter 4

How the People Live

Who are the people of the dry lands?

READING FOR A PURPOSE:
1. Where do most people of North Africa and the Middle East live?
2. How do people live in the cities?
3. Who are the nomads?

1. About 280 million people live in the Middle East and North Africa. Except for those in Israel, most are Muslims. However, they do not all speak the same language. In Arabia, Syria, Lebanon, Jordan, Iraq, parts of Egypt, and most of North Africa the people speak Arabic. In Turkey, Iran, and Afghanistan other languages are spoken. In parts of North Africa, there are some people who have come from Europe. As a result, European languages and customs may be found in this area. This is because the nations of North Africa were once European colonies.

2. Population is scattered unevenly throughout the Middle East and North Africa because of the uneven distribution of water. Where there is water, there are people. Many live along the shores of the great rivers, the Nile and the Tigris-Euphrates. (For example, nearly all of Egypt's 50.5 million people are crowded around the Nile River.) Others live near the borders of the seas or at the foot of mountains where there is more rainfall. In some mountain areas, farmers dig tunnels to catch the streams. These tunnels carry water into the desert. Along the tunnels are farm villages that depend on this method of getting water.

3. Finally, other farmers live near a well or spring that will give them the water they need for growing crops. Such a green place in the middle of the desert is called an oasis. Beside oases there are farm villages. The fields are planted for grains. Date palms also grow. There is even grass for sheep and goats.

4. About 51 percent of the people in the Middle East and North Africa are laborers who till the soil. About 47 percent are town and city dwellers. The rest are nomads, who travel from place to place to get water and food for their herds of animals. Farmers, townspeople, and nomads live very different lives. Few farmers own their own land. The landowner supplies them with water, farm tools, and work animals. In return for working the land, farmers keep a part of the crop.

5. The second largest group of people live in towns and cities. These cities are very different from the small villages of the farmer. These cities are a fascinating mixture of the old and the new. There are new buildings and old quarters with narrow streets and crowded houses. Automobiles clog the streets. Modern Western dress is seen along with the long, flowing cotton robes that Middle Easterners and North Africans have worn for years. There are modern schools and hospitals, but many of the women still wear veils to cover their faces. There are television antennas, radio stations, and newspapers. The largest and most important cities are Cairo and Alexandria in Egypt, Teheran in Iran, Baghdad in Iraq, Istanbul and Ankara in Turkey, Algiers in Algeria, Tunis in Tunisia, Tripoli in Libya,

Visitors to the great pyramids at Giza, near Cairo in Egypt, often photograph and ride the camels. But camels are no longer widely used for transportation in the Middle East.

A store in Saudi Arabia. In the past 20 years, oil wealth has rapidly changed the ways of living in Saudi Arabian cities.

Casablanca in Morocco, Damascus in Syria, and Tel Aviv and Jerusalem in Israel.

6. The towns and cities are the homes of factory workers, government officials, doctors, merchants, and craftspeople. The factory workers are often farmers who have moved to the cities in search of a better life. Crafts-people are those with special skills who make all kinds of beautiful and useful things. They turn cotton into cloth, wool into rugs, skins into leather, and silver into jewelry. Their articles are sold by merchants in the marketplace, called the *bazaar* or *souk*. The bazaar is the meeting place where goods are sold or ex-

Tel Aviv, the largest city in Israel. Tel Aviv means "Hill of Spring." The city was built on sand dunes along the sea in the early part of this century.

An Arab pottery maker. Why may skilled craft workers sometimes take greater pride in their work than do factory workers? What other crafts are important in this region of the world?

changed with the oasis farmer and other workers. At one time, the bazaar was a place where ideas and news from the outside world would reach the Muslim world. Today, the radio or television set brings news of what is happening.

7. The nomads are the smallest group of people in the region. They are disappearing rapidly. At one time, nomadic peoples were always traveling over deserts and dry grasslands in search of food for their sheep, goats, and camels. They lived in tents of tanned skins or cloth. They carried all their belongings with them. The camel was their chief means of transportation. Today, they load their belongings and their animals on trucks in order to move from place to place. It is not unusual to see a young camel in the back of a truck. Many are giving up the nomadic way of life, preferring to find work in the oil fields or the growing cities. The largest number remain in the countries of the Arabian peninsula.

UNDERSTANDING WHAT YOU HAVE READ

1. Which of the following questions are answered in this chapter?
a. How do the people of the region make a living?
b. How do the nomads use their animals?
c. Who are the rulers of the Arab countries?

2. A good title for paragraphs 5 and 6 would be
a. The Bazaar—Meeting Place of the World
b. Booming Factories of the Middle East
c. The Cities—Where the Old Meets the New

3. Most of the people of this region are
a. farmers
b. city dwellers
c. nomads

4. The people get most of their water from
a. rainfall
b. the ocean
c. springs and wells

5. Some people have moved to the cities to
a. learn about the modern world
b. find work in factories and mills
c. be near the oil fields

6. Nomads are always moving because they are
a. looking for minerals
b. warlike people
c. looking for water and pasture

7. *Craftspeople* earn a living through
a. making goods by hand
b. working in the oil fields
c. building irrigation ditches

8. "The person purchased some pots at the *bazaar*." A *bazaar* is a place where
a. clothes are washed
b. goods are bought and sold
c. movies are shown

DEVELOPING IDEAS AND SKILLS

Understanding Graphs — Population, Area, and Standard of Living of the Middle East and North Africa

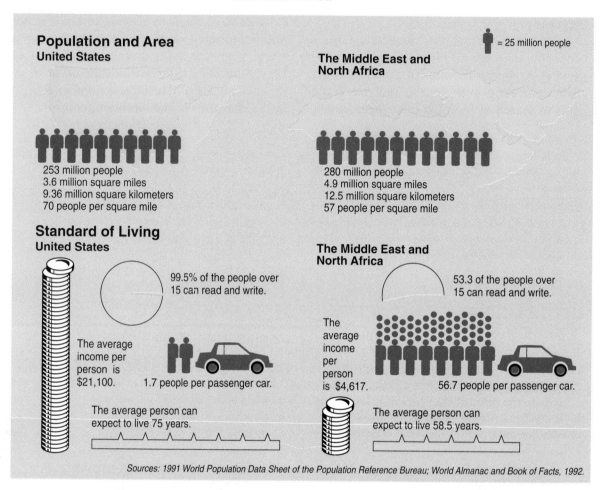

Population, Area, and Standard of Living of the Middle East and North Africa

Study the graphs. Then answer these questions.

1. Is the standard of living of this region high or low compared with that of the United States? Is it a developing area?
2. Is the region as crowded as the United States?
3. Are the people of this region literate compared with the people of the United States?
4. How long may the average person in this region expect to live?
5. What facts tell you the standard of living of the people of the region?
6. How does this region compare with the United States in size?

386

Chapter 5

Islam—Religion of the People

How does the Muslim religion unite the people of the Middle East?

READING FOR A PURPOSE:
1. How did Islam begin?
2. What are the chief duties of Muslims?
3. What is the Koran?

1. More than 700 million of the world's people are believers in Islam. Far less than half of these live in the "crossroads of the world," the Middle East and North Africa. Yet in every country in this region, except Israel, most of the people are Muslims. (In Algeria, Kuwait, Libya, Morocco, Tunisia, Afghanistan, Saudi Arabia, and Turkey, more than 95 percent are Muslim.) In Lebanon, almost half the people are Arabic-speaking Christians. The Arabic language is common to most of these countries except for Turkey, Iran, Afghanistan, and Israel. The belief in Islam affects almost everything the people do.

2. The Muslim religion was founded by Muhammad early in the 7th century. Muhammad lived in Mecca, in present-day Saudi Arabia. Mecca is holy for Muslims all over the world. Muhammad called the religion Islam. Islam means "surrender to the will of God." Those who follow Muhammad's religion are called Muslims, or "surrendered ones." It is not correct to call them Muhammadans, for Muhammad did not put himself before his people as God. He said that he was a prophet or messenger from God.

3. Muhammad taught that there was only one God. The Arabic word for God is "Allah." There could be no images or idols of Allah. Muhammad set up some rules that all Muslims had to follow, and that they still follow today. First, all Muslims believe in one God. Second, each Muslim must pray five times a day. (When Muslims pray, they turn toward Mecca, the holiest Muslim city.) Third, Muslims are expected to fast (go without food) from dawn to sunset during the holy month of Ramadan. Fourth, they are required to give help to the needy and poor of the community.

4. Finally, each member of the Muslim faith should make a trip to the sacred mosque,

The interior of the Dome of the Rock in Jerusalem. The Dome of the Rock is one of the holiest sites in Islam. Muslims believe Muhammad ascended to heaven from this spot.

or place of worship, at Mecca. This religious trip is called a pilgrimage. This pilgrimage should be made at least once during the life of each Muslim. Every year, hundreds of thousands of Muslims from different parts of the world travel to Mecca to fulfill this duty.

5. After his death, Muhammad's followers put his words and beliefs into a book called the Koran. This holy book is considered by Muslims to be the word of God. It is the book used by most Muslim children in learning to read.

6. Each Muslim city has at least one mosque or place of worship. Every morning the Muslim is awakened by a call to prayer from the mosque. Every Friday, the faithful Muslim goes to the mosque and listens to a reading from the Koran. There are no idols or images in the mosque. (In some places nonbelievers may not enter the mosques.) The religious beliefs that Muslims share have brought

Artists and craft workers in Iran combined brilliant colors and designs in this mosque.

them close together. This entire region is the heart of a larger Muslim world that stretches eastward to the Philippines.

UNDERSTANDING WHAT YOU HAVE READ

1. **Which of the following questions are answered in this chapter?**
a. How does Islam differ from other religions?
b. What is a mosque?
c. What is the meaning of "Islam"?

2. **The main idea of this chapter is to describe the**
a. Muslim religion
b. duties of Muslims
c. life of Muhammad

3. **The holiest city of the Muslim religion is**
a. Rome
b. Cairo
c. Mecca

4. **Muhammad lived in**
a. Egypt
b. Arabia
c. Turkey

5. **The Muslim religion is important in the Middle East because it**
a. affects the actions of the people in all walks of life
b. forces members to travel great distances
c. is the religion of all Arabs

6. **Islam, Judaism, and Christianity are alike in that they**
a. have many statues and holy pictures
b. teach belief in one God
c. require their members to make a pilgrimage to a holy city

7. **"The people visited a *mosque* to pray." A *mosque* is**
a. a place of worship
b. a school
c. an office

8. **"The old man went on a *pilgrimage* to see the Holy Land." A *pilgrimage* is a trip taken for**
a. health
b. study
c. religious reasons

The Muslims' Pilgrimage to Mecca

The principal elements that make up the worship of Muslims are called the Five Pillars of Islam. These are duties that Muslims are expected to perform. You have already read about these duties in this chapter. The last of the five pillars is the *hajj,* or pilgrimage to the Great Mosque in Mecca. The mosque encloses a shrine that is said to have been founded by Abraham. Every able Muslim is expected to make the pilgrimage at least once in his or her lifetime. Many Muslims try to go each year. Here is a brief story of a Muslim family that makes the pilgrimage.

Saadia owns a small cake shop in a bazaar in Jerusalem. One day his son, Ahmed, came into his shop. "Father," Ahmed said, "it's almost the eighth day of the 12th month" (the time of the pilgrimage to Mecca). "Are we going to make the hajj this year?" Saadia smiled and said, "Yes, my Koran scholar, we are going this year." Ahmed turned to his mother, Salwa, and asked, "How will we get there, Mother?" "First, we will take a flight from Jerusalem to Cairo. From there we will fly to Jidda. Then we shall go by bus to Mecca," she said.

The family's pilgrimage was soon underway. Before taking the bus to Mecca, Saadia and his family bathed, took off their jewelry, and changed their clothing. They put on the *ihram,* a white seamless garment. In this simple dress, all Muslims, rich or poor, are equal in the eyes of God. The bus to Mecca was crowded with people. As they approached the city, Saadia and his family saw rows and rows of tents. "What is that?" asked Saadia. "That is where you will live while you are on hajj," said the bus driver.

Saadia and his family were soon settled in one tent.

As part of their pilgrimage Saadia and his family went to Arafat, a large open plain nearby. From noon until sunset, they stood and prayed. In the evening, they went to Muzdalifah, to gather stones "for the throwing of pebbles." Exhausted, they said a final prayer and went to sleep. The next day, they threw their pebbles at the stone pillars at Mina and made sacrifices. (The pillars represent evil. The sacrifices symbolize a Muslim's willingness to sacrifice what is dearest to him.) Once these ceremonies were over, Saadia and his son shaved their heads. His wife cut off a lock of her hair. They then entered Mecca and circled the Kaaba seven times as is the custom. They were also able to kiss the sacred black stone of the Kaaba. The hajj over, they put on their regular clothing and returned home, feeling that this had been a very rewarding time.

Write the statements below in your notebook. If a statement is true, mark it with a *T*. If it is false, mark it with an *F* and cross out the incorrect word or words, putting in the word(s) that make the statement true.

1. The hajj is a practice of the *Christian* religion.
2. The purpose of the hajj is to *raise money for starving people.*
3. The holy city of the Muslims is *Riyadh.*
4. Saadia and his family had to wear a special dress, called the *ihram,* before they could take part in the hajj.
5. As part of the hajj, the Kaaba is circled four times.

Chapter 6

The Farmer

How do farmers use their land to meet their needs?

READING FOR A PURPOSE:
1. How do subsistence farmers live on their small plots of land?
2. What are the problems of Middle East and North African farmers?
3. How is farming in Israel different from that of other countries in the region?

1. A large number of the people in the Middle East and North Africa work on small farms. The farmers in this region are often called *fellahin,* an Arabic word that means "farm laborers." Most of the farmers live in villages. Where there is plenty of water (as in the Nile Valley), the villages are close together. Where there is little water, the villages are farther apart. Most villages are small. A large village may have electricity. The fields are outside the village.

2. Some *fellahin* continue to be subsistence farmers. They raise crops to feed themselves and to have enough left over to buy what they need from town. Everyone in the usual farm family works in the fields. The average farmer turns the soil with a wooden plow drawn by an ox or a buffalo. Some farmers have tractors. Farmers harvest grain with hand sickles. They also thresh grain by hand or use animals to trample it. The boys help in the never-ending job of drawing water. Because of poor soil, simple tools, and lack of fertilizer, most farmers can raise very little food despite hard work.

3. The average farmer's small house may shelter not only the family but also their animals—water buffalo, goats, or chickens. They own little clothing and know few comforts. Because wood is scarce, their house has wood only in the door or window frames, if at all. The family usually eats from low tables and sleeps on mats and rugs on the floor.

4. The farm family eats little meat. Its chief foods are bread, goat's cheese, fruits, and vegetables. The girls of the family help their mother prepare the food. They milk the family goats and make the cheese. They grind the wheat or millet into flour for bread.

5. Many of the peasants are always in debt.

Fresh water from drilled wells pours into an irrigation project in Saudi Arabia. Why is irrigation necessary for farming in desert areas?

Irrigated farms and fish ponds in Israel's Jezreel Valley, once desert and swamp land. Today Israel's chief crops include oranges, grains, olives, fruits, and grapes.

Sometimes the land in an Arab village may belong to a rich landowner, who most likely lives in the city. The landowner also owns the water that the village uses. In return for the use of the land, water, seed, and sometimes fertilizer, village farmers must turn over most of their crops to the landlord. Some countries have started land reform. For example, in Egypt, no family is allowed to own more than 100 acres.

6. The main crops of the region are cereals such as wheat, barley, and millet. Fruit, corn, and rice are also grown. Rice must be grown on irrigated land, for there is not enough rain to produce it otherwise. The most important cash crop is cotton, which is raised in the irrigated fields of the Nile valley. The waters of the Nile River and the warm climate have made Egypt a leader in the growing of cotton.

7. Poverty causes many problems in vil-

lages of some countries which also lack teachers and schools. While the cities might have good drinking water, some villages cannot afford pure water. The few sources of water are used by the people of the village not only for cooking and drinking, but for bathing their children and washing their clothes as well. Also, the farmers throw their garbage into the irrigation ditches. There are few doctors. As a result, some villagers suffer from diseases of many kinds.

8. Farming in Israel is very modern. Many farming families use modern machines and good farming methods. As in the rest of the region, many Israeli farmers live in villages. The land is mostly evenly distributed. In some cases, these people work together and share in the goods and services of the community. This community is called a *kibbutz,* or cooperative farm.

UNDERSTANDING WHAT YOU HAVE READ

1. Which of the following questions are answered in this chapter?

a. Why is the Arab farmer poor?
b. Why is fertilizer important?
c. Why are Arab families often sick?

2. The main idea of this chapter is to describe

a. the simple tools of the village farms
b. land ownership in the Middle East and North Africa
c. the life of the village farmer

3. Most of the farmers in North Africa and the Middle East

a. own their own farms
b. rent their farms
c. work on land belonging to the government

4. The chief crop of the small farm is

a. wheat
b. corn
c. rice

5. Cotton is grown in the Nile River valley because

a. the climate of Egypt is different from the rest of the Middle East
b. a warm climate and irrigated land are best for growing cotton
c. farmers in Egypt are richer than farmers in the rest of the region

6. On a *kibbutz,* people

a. keep all the crops they raise
b. are paid wages for farming
c. are provided with all the goods and services they need

7. When farmers *thresh* grain, as described in paragraph 2, they

a. remove the weeds
b. gather it into a shed
c. separate the grain from the straw

8. The average farmer in the Middle East and North Africa lives in a

a. hut
b. small house
c. two-story home

9. The chief foods of most farm families are bread, goat's cheese, fruits, and

a. vegetables
b. meat
c. fish

10. Most rich Arab landowners live

a. on their land
b. in the city
c. in the village

11. The main crops of the region are cereals such as wheat, barley, and

a. soybeans
b. rye
c. millet

12. Egypt is a leader in growing

a. cotton
b. corn
c. cattle

SUMMING UP

Making Charts

Complete the following chart in your notebook.

	CIS FARMER	MIDDLE EAST FARMER
1. Who owns most of the farmland?		
2. What kinds of tools are used?		
3. What are the chief crops?		
4. What do farmers do with the crops they grow?		
5. What animals are on the farm?		
6. What is the size of the farm?		
7. What is the climate of this farm region?		
8. What comforts does the farm family have?		

DEVELOPING CRITICAL THINKING SKILLS

Do You Agree or Disagree?

Give the reasons for your opinions.

1. Farmers in Morocco face the same problems as farmers in Russia and Ukraine.
2. A dishwasher would often be found in a farm home in Algeria.
3. Wheat can be grown only in a region of heavy rainfall or where irrigation is used.
4. Millet is a cereal that can grow in a dry climate.
5. Few people in North Africa and the Middle East would find work in lumber mills.
6. A farmer in a kibbutz would have little use for a tractor.
7. A large number of Arab farmers grow a cash crop.
8. The best chance for a boy or girl in the Middle East to get an education is to live in one of the large cities.
9. People in North Africa and the Middle East would have little use for a snowmobile.
10. Most countries of North Africa and the Middle East need land reform very badly.

Chapter 7

Nomads

How do the nomads make use of their few resources?

READING FOR A PURPOSE:
1. How does the nomad make a living?
2. What are the different kinds of nomads?
3. Why are the nomads disappearing?

1. Beyond the village fields and the oasis farms of North Africa and the Middle East are the dry, lonely lands of the desert. The people who live in these desert lands are different from the farmers. They are the nomads, the wanderers. They live in large groups that are made up of smaller family groups. Their leaders are called sheiks. These nomadic groups roam over the dry lands in search of water and pasture for their herds of sheep, goats, and camels. Nomads make up less than 2 percent of the people of the region.

2. There are two kinds of nomadic peoples. The first group are those who live in and around the mountains. In the winter, they graze their herds in the valleys. In the summer, they move the herds into the mountains to find grass. The second group of nomads are those who live in the desert. They move every few days or weeks in search of grass and water. These desert nomads are called *Bedouin.* The Bedouin often split into smaller groups because the pastures they find are too small to feed all their animals. When water is found, the group settles down to enjoy its newfound riches.

3. Because they are always on the move, nomads have few goods besides their cooking pots, loose clothes, rugs, radios, and blankets. They live in tents. They sleep and eat on rugs. The men and boys of the family live in one half of the tent, and the women and girls in the other half. When they are ready to move, the tents are folded up and packed on the camels along with their other belongings. Many now use trucks instead of camels.

4. The animals—sheep, goats, and camels—provide the nomads with most of what they need. Goat's milk and cheese are their main foods. Like the region's farmers, they rarely eat meat. Their blankets, tents, and most of their clothes are woven from the hair of goats or camels. Leather from the hides of the animals is used to make baskets and sandals. Whatever their animals do not supply,

Why must Bedouins move throughout the desert to find grass and water?

Bedouin rider on his camel. Some well-to-do Bedouin use small trucks to travel from place to place.

the nomads buy when they reach an oasis. The nomads' wealth used to be judged by the number of camels and horses they owned.

5. During the hot summer months when desert wells are dry, Bedouin go to an oasis. Here they exchange camels, wool, and woven rugs for dates or flour raised by the farmer. They buy other goods that are needed—knives, tea, clothing, sugar, and coffee.

6. In the past, the herders of the desert were the rulers of the region. They crossed and recrossed borders as they pleased. They were able to conquer the oasis farmers because they could attack swiftly on their horses and camels. The farmers were forced to give their crops to the desert nomads. Today, only a few Bedouin groups remain on the desert. They want many of the goods available to town dwellers such as watches and television sets. To get these goods, many are giving up their nomadic life and settling near oil fields and cities.

UNDERSTANDING WHAT YOU HAVE READ

1. Which of the following questions are answered in this chapter?
a. Why does the nomad live in a tent?
b. Why is the camel important to the nomad?
c. Why is the nomad's way of life disappearing?

2. The best title for paragraph 6 would be
a. Herders of the Oases
b. Dashing Riders of the Desert
c. Border Leaders

3. ALL of the following make up an important part of the Bedouin diet EXCEPT
a. cheese
b. meat
c. dates

4. Bedouin wealth is judged by the
a. camels and horses owned
b. clothes worn
c. amount of crops grown

5. "Bedouin wear loose, white clothing." This tells you that the Bedouin
a. dislike suits
b. live where the temperature never changes
c. have clothing that protects them from the sun and sand

6. Nomads go to the oases because
a. it is too hot in the desert at certain times
b. they wish to trade with the farmers
c. they want to buy land

7. A *herder* makes a living through
a. grazing animals
b. farming
c. fishing

8. A *sheik* is a
a. skilled weaver of rugs
b. a city merchant
c. leader of a group that is or was nomadic

DEVELOPING IDEAS AND SKILLS

Building Map Skills — A Desert Oasis

Study the map on this page. Then answer the questions below.

1. Identify three methods of transportation that could be used in this oasis.
2. How might goods be transported to the marketplace?
3. What natural resources are available in the oasis?
4. (a) What kind of crop is grown in this oasis?
   (b) How are the crops watered?
5. How is oil transported from this oasis?
6. (a) What religious buildings are present?
   (b) What other public buildings can be seen?
7. Describe how life in an oasis is a blend of traditional and modern influences.

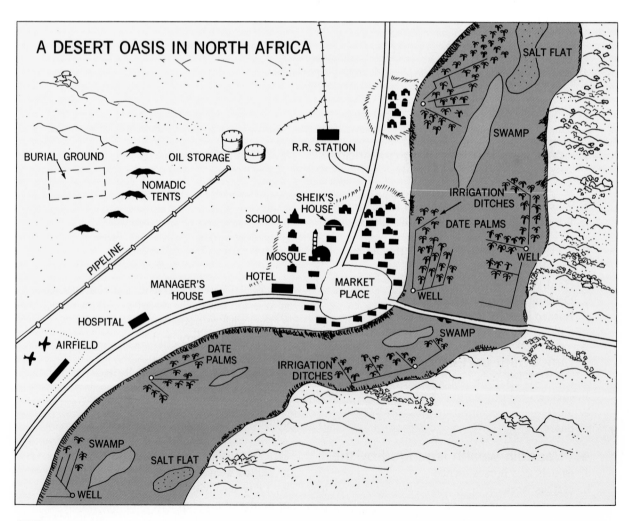

Oil Pollution in the Persian Gulf

 Have you ever seen pictures of fish or seabirds covered with thick, black, greasy oil? It's a very upsetting sight. Yet oil spills happen all too often—especially in the Persian Gulf.

An Oil Highway Today, the Persian Gulf has become an "oil highway." Over one-fifth of the world's oil moves across its waters every year. First, the oil is loaded from pipelines onto huge oil tankers. Then, the tankers carry the oil down the gulf and out through the Strait of Hormuz.

Accidental and Deliberate Oil Spills Every year, about 250,000 barrels of oil spill into the waters of the Persian Gulf. Some spills happen as oil is loaded onto the tankers. Others occur when tankers collide or when pipelines delivering the oil accidentally break.

One of the worst spills took place in 1983 when planes from Iraq bombed Iranian oil wells during the Iran—Iraq War. About 4,500 barrels of oil spilled from the damaged wells every day for two months. The oil created a gigantic slick that covered nearly 7,500 square miles (19,425 square kilometers) of gulf waters.

Another disastrous oil spill occurred in 1991 during the Persian Gulf War. As Iraqi soldiers retreated, they slashed pipelines filled with oil in the port of Kuwait City. As a result, more than 6 million barrels of crude oil poured into the Persian Gulf. The world was shocked as it watched the spilled oil spread slowly across 600 square miles (1,554 square kilometers) of gulf water.

The Shape of the Gulf Because of its long, narrow shape, the Persian Gulf keeps spilled oil from spreading out quickly. The Strait of Hormuz, the gulf's outlet to the Indian Ocean, is too narrow to allow much polluted water to flow out to sea. As a result, oil spills can stay locked up in the Persian Gulf for as long as five years.

Climatic and Tidal Effects About half of the oil spilled in the Persian Gulf evaporates in the hot, dry climate. The rest turns into a thick oil sludge, or slimy mass, that sits on top of the water. Some of the oily sludge sinks and coats the ocean floor. The remainder is blown across the gulf by the wind. Twice a day, tides carry the oily sludge onto the coast. Once it reaches the shore, the sludge blackens everything in sight, from fish and seabirds to stones and sand. This oily slime quickly hardens in the dry climate to form a thick "tar mat."

Water Depth The shallow depth of the Persian Gulf makes oil spills especially harmful. Wide coastal shelves reach out for miles from the mainland into the gulf. At low tide, large portions of these shelves are exposed or are under less than four feet (1,219 millimeters) of water. Covered with thick growths of sea plants, or algae, sea grasses, and coral, the shallow coastal shelves provide an ideal home for shrimp, fish, oysters, and turtles. As oil flows in with the tide, it smothers and kills many of these valuable sea creatures.

Cleanup and Prevention Small oil spills can be vacuumed up by special machines or broken up with strong detergents. Larger spills, however, are impossible to clean up completely. One way to reduce the number of spills is to ship oil in double-walled tankers. Another way is to bring peace to the region. **How can oil spills in this region affect the United States? Why should we be concerned if sea life is killed by an oil spill? What measures do you think are necessary to prevent oil spills and limit damage?**

Chapter 8

Oil Brings Change

Why is oil so important in North Africa and the Middle East?

READING FOR A PURPOSE:
1. Where are the large oil fields located?
2. How is oil carried to the seaports?
3. The wealth from oil has brought about what kinds of problems for the region?

1. At one time it was thought that the deserts of the Middle East and North Africa were almost worthless. But with the discovery of oil under the desert sands, this region has become one of the most important in the world. In this region are almost two-thirds of the world's entire oil reserves. (Oil reserves are the amounts of oil that can profitably be removed from the ground.) Not all of the countries of the region have oil. Most of the oil comes from countries around the Persian Gulf. There are also large oil reserves in North Africa in Algeria and Libya. Smaller reserves are in Egypt and Turkey.

2. Most of the oil fields in the Middle East used to be owned by oil companies from Europe or the United States. In return for working the oil fields, these companies shared part of their profits with the governments of the region. By the early 1980s, most Middle Eastern and North African governments had taken over the oil industry. Most of the oil companies continue to work closely with these governments. The European and U.S. oil companies have oil experts and modern equipment. These are needed to explore for, refine, transport, and sell the oil. Today, many specialists are native born. Five countries—Saudi Arabia, Iran, Iraq, Libya, and Kuwait—produce about 95 percent of the oil from North Africa and the Middle East.

3. Oil must be refined before it can be used. Oil refineries are huge chemical plants that turn the oil into gasoline and other oil products. Many are located in Europe and the United States. With their new oil wealth, some of the Middle Eastern and North African countries have built their own modern oil refineries. Both oil and oil products are carried by pipelines to seaports along the Mediterranean Sea and the Persian Gulf. Every few miles along the lines there are pumps to keep

Exploring for oil in Saudi Arabia. Why are the United States and other industrialized countries dependent on oil from the Middle East?

Some oil-rich nations in the Middle East have used their wealth to set up schools and hospitals. These girls attend school in Saudi Arabia. The older girls wear long skirts and head coverings. What aspects of both Western and Middle Eastern culture does this scene show?

the oil moving to the sea. Oceangoing ships called tankers carry the oil from the region to ports all over the world.

4. Most of the oil produced in this region is sold to the countries of Europe and to Japan. The United States is also a big importer of oil. These industrial nations need oil to keep their factories running. Oil is also used in many products, from gasoline to human-made fibers and plastics. In 1960, the Arab oil nations had joined with other oil-producing nations of the world to form the Organization of Petroleum Exporting Countries. OPEC, as the group is known, tries to set the price of oil for its 13 members. During the 1973 Arab-Israeli War, the Arab nations cut off oil supplies to certain industrial nations. The price of oil rose sharply.

5. The new oil wealth led to many problems. Of course, the main problem was how and on whom to spend the money. Should the money be spent on weapons and armies? Should it be spent on improving farming or on building up industry? Should it be spent on helping the poor living in the countryside or on the city people? Should money be spent on buying goods from other countries? Or should the money be invested in making products (and jobs) within the oil-rich countries?

6. The greatest changes brought about by

oil took place in the nations along the Persian Gulf. The Kingdom of Saudi Arabia changed from a country of nomads into one of automobiles, roads, high-rise buildings, air-conditioned supermarkets, power lines, and international airlines. Kuwait supplied its almost two million citizens with fine schools and good health care. It suddenly had one of the highest living standards in the world. The region was flooded with all kinds of military weapons. More than two million workers from the nearby poorer countries moved in to help build the many new projects. Most of these countries depended largely on oil to bring money into their land.

7. By the early 1980s, it was clear that oil prices were going down. First, as prices rose too high, the demand for oil dropped. Second, the industrialized nations took steps to use oil more carefully and efficiently. Third, new sources of oil were found in Great Britain, Norway, Mexico, and the United States. On the other hand, the countries of OPEC did not reduce their production of oil. There was soon an oversupply of oil in the world. So oil prices fell. Many oil-producing countries of the Middle East have realized they need to reduce their dependence on oil by developing other industries that will provide much-needed jobs for their people.

Understanding An Oil Flow Chart and Map

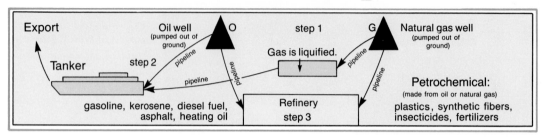

The diagram above shows how crude oil and natural gas are "processed" into useable products. Diagrams of this type are called flow charts.

The flow chart for oil begins with the crude oil being pumped from the ground (step 1). Pipelines carry the oil directly to tankers for export or to nearby refineries (step 2). Refining the crude oil produces useful products (step 3). The flow chart for natural gas follows the same steps as crude oil except that natural gas must be liquefied (made into a liquid) before it can be loaded onto a tanker for export.

These steps can also be shown on a map. The map below uses symbols for the steps oil goes through to become useful. One symbol represents oil fields in the Middle East. Another symbol represents pipelines.

A shaded box represents oil refineries. A blank box represents important tanker terminals.

Use the map and the flow chart to answer the following questions.

1. Is the oil that comes from the ground ready to be used in a car?
2. Name four fuels produced in an oil refinery.
3. What must be done to natural gas before it can be loaded onto a tanker?
4. Name three oil-producing countries in the Middle East.
5. How many oil well symbols are shown in the Persian Gulf region?
6. Name a country with oil refineries on the Persian Gulf.

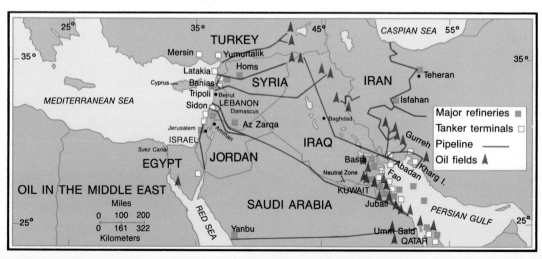

UNDERSTANDING WHAT YOU HAVE READ

1. **Which of the following questions are answered in this chapter?**
   a. Why is oil important in the Middle East and North Africa?
   b. How are oil wells drilled?
   c. What changes have taken place in the oil-rich nations of the region?

2. **The main idea of paragraph 5 is to describe**
   a. the high standard of living in Iraq
   b. some of the problems in the oil-rich nations of the region
   c. how the United States imports oil

3. **Most of the oil fields in the region were first developed by**
   a. European and U.S. companies
   b. Arab governments
   c. the shah of Iran

4. **Because of oil wealth, the people of which country suddenly had one of the highest standards of living in the world?**
   a. Israel   b. Kuwait   c. Afghanistan

5. **Member nations of OPEC are**
   a. only Arab countries
   b. countries in the Middle East or North Africa
   c. from both the Middle East and North Africa and the rest of the world

6. **At present, oil refineries are found**
   a. only in Europe and the United States
   b. in the Middle East, North Africa, Europe, the United States, and other parts of the world
   c. only in the Middle East and North Africa

7. **Tankers used to carry oil from the Middle East and North Africa travel by**
   a. land   b. air   c. sea

8. **How the oil money is spent by the governments in the region is decided by**
   a. the people in free elections
   b. European countries and the United States
   c. the rulers of the oil-rich countries

9. **Oil reserves are the amount of oil**
   a. a country has
   b. that can profitably be removed from the ground
   c. produced in one year

10. **The major oil-producing countries in the region are Saudi Arabia, Iran, Iraq, Kuwait, and**
    a. Libya
    b. Egypt
    c. Turkey

11. **Oil is also used to make**
    a. steel
    b. rubber
    c. plastics

12. **Those nations most affected by oil are**
    a. Egypt and Turkey
    b. the Persian Gulf states
    c. the Mediterranean states

Chapter 9

Challenges for the Future

How are the people of this region facing their problems?

READING FOR A PURPOSE:
1. Why are many village farmers poor?
2. How are some countries increasing their water supply?
3. How can health care be improved?

1. Except for Israel and Turkey, the great majority of farmers in the Middle East and North Africa are poor. There are many reasons why this is so. Most farmers do not own their own land. Egypt, Iran, Syria, and Iraq have made some land reforms. Many large landowners live in the city and have no real interest in farming. But in this region, many farmers must still give much of their crops to large landowners for the use of land and for seed. Although farmers work hard, their crop yields (the amount of crops per acre) are small (except for Israel and Egypt). This is because the same crops are raised year after year. The soil wears out unless fertilizer is used. But there is little money to buy fertilizer. Plot sizes are often small and scattered, so that modern equipment cannot easily be used. Thus, lack of land, small plots, high rents, and poor soil keep many farmers in extreme poverty.

2. Besides these problems, the farmer of this region must always worry about the water supply. Important as oil is, water is still more important. Water is the most needed natural resource of the region. The future of the Middle East and North Africa depends upon the full use of its scarce water resources.

3. The Aswan Dam on Egypt's Nile River was an early effort to make use of water in a desert land. This dam "saves" or holds back a part of the Nile's yearly flood. The water is then used for irrigation. The first Aswan Dam was built in 1902. Egypt, with Russian aid in

the 1950s, built a higher dam at Aswan. This Aswan High Dam holds back an even larger supply of water and creates new farmlands through irrigation. The water spilling over the huge dam also provides electric power for areas that never had it before. Using a different method to solve its problems, Kuwait has one of the world's largest plants for removing salt from seawater and making it into fresh water.

4. Israel would also like to increase its water supply. Most of southern Israel is a desert. The Israeli government has taken control of all water resources within the country. They have brought the waters of the Jordan River in the north to the drier south and the Negev (the desert area). As a result of careful planning of wells and pipelines and strict control of all water resources, they have been able to increase Israel's farm land and provide running water for all people.

5. Many of the people of North Africa and the Middle East are in poor health. Because the rivers and irrigation ditches are used for bathing and washing, pure drinking water is scarce. In the waters of irrigation canals are snails that carry tiny worms. These worms enter the skin of barefoot farmers and weaken their bodies. Such diseases as snail fever, tra-

An Egyptian farmer hauling water from the Nile River to irrigate his fields.

A grape harvest in Algeria. About 2,000 farms are owned by the government. These farms were left by the French settlers in 1962, the year Algeria became independent of French rule.

choma, malaria, typhoid fever, and hookworm are common in the farming villages. Most of the region's countries are trying to solve this problem of poor health among their people.

6. To escape some of these problems, many people in the region are moving to the cities. Cairo, with a population of over 13 million, is the largest city in the region. Teheran, the capital of Iran, now has over 6 million. Baghdad, Iraq, has over 4 million. Algiers, Tunis, Istanbul, and Casablanca are also growing cities. Although their housing may be poor, many of the newcomers are able to get better health care and schooling for their families in the cities. Living side by side with the poor of

the cities are a few wealthy families and a growing middle class. While all people of the region would like to enjoy the goods of the West, they also want to keep the best of their traditions and to modernize in their own ways.

7. In addition, most people in the countries of the region cannot choose their own leaders or make their own laws. Most of the countries are ruled by military leaders, kings, or dictators. Only in Israel, Turkey, and Egypt are people able to vote for their leaders in free elections. This lack of freedom is another reason why there is often unrest in the Middle East and North Africa.

Shops in a bazaar in Tunis, Algeria. What things might draw villagers to the cities of the Middle East?

UNDERSTANDING WHAT YOU HAVE READ

1. Which of the following questions are answered in this chapter?

a. Who are the rulers of the Middle Eastern countries?

b. Why are dams important in North Africa?

c. Why is there often unrest in the Middle East?

2. The main idea of this chapter is to describe

a. the problems of people in North Africa and the Middle East

b. the need for more electricity

c. how land can be divided among the farm laborers

3. Many people in the region are moving to the cities because there they can get

a. more land

b. better health care

c. more Western ideas

4. The Aswan High Dam is bringing water and power to the people of

a. Saudi Arabia

b. Lebanon

c. Egypt

5. A big problem in government in this region is that

a. only men are allowed to vote

b. few leaders are elected by the people

c. Arab nations believe in communism

6. Water is called the most important resource of this region because

a. so much water is needed for refining oil

b. it is needed by people merely to stay alive and in good health

c. without waterpower, the people could not improve their standard of living

7. In paragraph 1, "crop yields" means

a. profit gained

b. amount produced

c. time saved

DEVELOPING CRITICAL THINKING SKILLS

Do You Agree or Disagree?

Give reasons for your answers.

1. Fertilizer is widely used by North African farmers.
2. Farmers in some of the nations of North Africa and the Middle East now own their own land.
3. Although three religions began here, Christianity is the center of life for most people.
4. Arab countries of the Middle East are friendly with Israel.
5. There is little democracy in North Africa and the Middle East.
6. A lack of many natural resources helps to cause the poverty in this region.
7. Many different ways of saving water are being tried in the countries of the Middle East and North Africa.

— In North Africa and the Middle East —

When the Persian Gulf War ended in 1991, 580 oil wells were still burning from fires deliberately set by the retreating Iraqis. Smoke from the well fires darkened the Kuwaiti sky and made breathing dangerous. Kuwait did not have the equipment or the professional firefighters needed to stop the fires. But Texas had both. Firefighters like **Red Adair** arrived in Kuwait as soon as the war ended. Tons of equipment were airfreighted from Houston, and the work began. First, the fires had to be put out. Then the wells had to be capped. The firefighters had a dirty job. Oil gushed into the sky from many of the wells. Installing caps on the wells meant working in a downpour of oil. The firefighters spent their days drenched to the skin in oil, but their work paid off. Originally, experts had said that it would take four to five years to control the fires. In fact, it took less than a year.

The Bible mentions many different animals that once roamed freely in Israel. For centuries, these animals were not disturbed. Then the Ottoman Turks cut down the forests to build railroads. Goats and camels were allowed to overgraze in the area. By the early 1960s, no more ostriches, lions, fallow deer, oryx, or wild bears lived in Israel. People believed that the desert leopard was extinct, too. Fifty other species, such as the long-fingered bat, the Persian squirrel, and the sand cat, were on the endangered list. In 1963, the **Israeli Nature Reserve Authority** was created to restore the biblical animals to the area. The authority has replanted forests and vegetation and has set aside areas where the animals can be protected. Because of these nature reserves, the gazelle population has increased by 10,000 and the ibex population by 2,000. The desert leopard has returned, and wild boars once again roam the area.

The Kurds want a place to call their own. The problem is that for many years the nations in which the Kurds live have been hostile to them. For the Kurds in some countries, life is bearable. But the Kurds of northern Iraq are persecuted by the government. During the Gulf War, the Kurds rose up against the Iraqis. In return, the Iraqis bombed their villages and drove thousands of Kurds into the mountains. Many Kurds died during the harsh winter, but many others were saved by the efforts of the **United Nations High Commissioner for Refugees.** The commissioner arranged for winter shelter and brought the Kurds and Iraqis together for talks. If it were not for the UN's help, the Kurds might not have survived at all.

The ancient Cendere bridge in Turkey, which was built 2,000 years ago by Roman armies, will soon be lost. It will be underwater, along with many other historic treasures on the Harran Plain. The Turkish **Southeast Anatolia Project** is building a series of dams that will change the land and culture of most of southeastern Turkey. The Turkish government believes that the benefits will outweigh the losses. The dams will provide one-third of Turkey's electricity needs each year. Farmers will be able to plant cash crops in newly irrigated areas. Increases in revenue will allow the government to improve such services as housing and education. The people of the Harran Plain hope that completing the Southeast Anatolia Project is the right thing to do.

Chapter 10

A Disputed Region

Why are the problems of North Africa and the Middle East so important to the peace of the world?

READING FOR A PURPOSE:
1. What is meant by Arab nationalism?
2. What events in the Middle East have threatened world peace?

1. The presence of the Suez Canal alone would make the Middle East and North Africa one of the most important regions of the world. The canal is one of the busiest of all water routes. For years, the United Kingdom controlled the canal. In 1956, Egypt took it back. Now the Suez Canal brings money to Egypt. Most countries want to make sure that the canal is always open for their ships.

2. Nationalism—the pride people have in their country—is strong in the Middle East and North Africa. For years, this region was under the control of foreign nations. In the early 20th century, the United Kingdom and France held much of the area. Since the 1940s, all the countries in North Africa and the Middle East have become independent. Some of the people are bitter about the many years their nations spent under foreign rule. Western nations are often blamed for all the troubles of the region.

3. Probably no other single problem in North Africa and the Middle East causes as much trouble as the dispute over the State of Israel. Israel was formed in 1948 as a homeland for the Jews. The Arabs of the area did not agree to this. A war was fought and Israel won. The two sides agreed to a truce—a stopping of the fighting. This truce was arranged by Ralph Bunche of the United Nations.

4. But there has been no lasting peace since then. Some Arab leaders still do not accept the state of Israel. They view Israel as a Western creation at the expense of Arabs. Fighting broke out again in 1956. In 1967, Israeli forces

Lebanon is a war-torn nation in the Middle East. Here, a bomb exploded in Beirut, the capital.

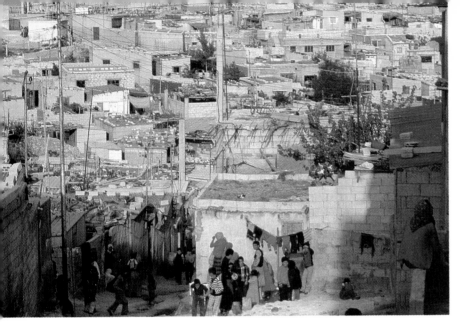

What problems in the Middle East led to the formation of refugee camps? What problems do the camps still cause?

won a victory in six days of fighting. They occupied Arab territories including Egypt's Sinai Peninsula and the Gaza Strip, Jordan's West Bank region, and Syria's Golan Heights. In 1973, Egypt and Syria began a surprise attack against Israel on the holiest day of the Jewish religion. Although the actual fighting ended in three weeks, meetings to reach a settlement lasted for almost two years. Through the leadership of President Carter, Israel and Egypt signed a peace agreement in 1979. Israel completed its withdrawal from the Sinai desert in 1982. Egypt and Israel continue to discuss the differences that have caused wars between them but the problems of the West Bank are harder to settle.

5. Another problem resulted from the Arab-Israeli conflict. During the 1948 war, thousands of Arabs left Israel. Israelis say that these Arabs fled the war zone and thought they would return with the conquering Arab armies. Arabs say they were forced to leave Israel. Today there are more than 2 million of these people. They call themselves Palestinians since they or their parents once lived in Palestine. (Palestine is the ancient name of the region that is now Jordan and Israel.) Most of these refugees want to return to their homeland. At present, many live in the cities of nearby Arab countries. Others live in refugee camps. The United Nations continues to support these camps with food and other supplies. Some Palestinians formed armed bands and attacked Israelis in Israel and around the world. Their group is known as the PLO, the Palestinian Liberation Organization. However, some Palestinians believe the problems must be solved by talking instead of through terrorist acts.

6. Arab nations have not given most Palestinians a permanent home within their borders. They say the refugees lived in Israel and should return there. Israel says these people cannot return because they are unfriendly to Israel. Most of the Arab states (except Egypt) do not recognize Israel. They say that Israel must recognize a Palestinian state first. Israel says that it took in hundreds of thousands of Jewish refugees from Arab countries after 1948 and so Arab countries should take in Arab refugees. The issue is a major reason for fighting between Israel and Arab nations.

7. In 1970, the PLO was thrown out of Jordan. They moved to Lebanon, where thousands of fellow Palestinians already lived in refugee camps. As years went by, the PLO created military bases in Lebanon to attack Jewish settlements in northern Israel. Many Lebanese resented this use of their county by the PLO. To protect their bases, the PLO was drawn into a civil war going on in Lebanon. In August 1982, Israel invaded Lebanon. They hoped to get rid of the PLO. After a bitter fight, the PLO left Lebanon. In September 1982, President Reagan sent marines to Lebanon, as did the French and Italians, to help keep the peace. In April 1983, the U.S. embassy in Beirut was bombed. In October 1983, the U.S. Marines' barracks in Beirut was bombed. After much loss of American troops, the marines were withdrawn in 1984. By 1990, much of the fighting between armed groups had ceased because of peace accords and new legislation. But there was still fighting within some groups.

8. The revolt that overthrew the shah (ruler) of Iran in 1979 brought about another series of events that threatened world peace. The shah fled Iran. When he came to the United States for treatment of an illness in 1979, a group of Iranian students stormed the U.S. embassy in Teheran, Iran's capital city. They held Americans prisoner in the embassy because, they said, the United States had interfered in Iran many times to support the shah. The students and the new Iranian government leaders demanded the return of the shah to Iran before the *hostages* (those being held) would be freed. The United States refused to do this. The General Assembly of the United Nations and the International Court of Justice condemned the taking of hostages and ordered their release. The United States stopped buying oil from Iran. In 1981, the Iranians finally freed the 52 hostages.

9. Late in 1979, Soviet troops invaded Afghanistan, which borders Iran on the east. The United States feared that the Soviet attack was the beginning of a further move on the oil fields along the Persian Gulf. It slowed its sale of wheat to the Soviets. U.S. naval forces and marines were sent to the area of the Persian Gulf. Under a United Nations agreement, Soviet troops finally withdrew from Afghanistan in 1989. The communist leader was later overthrown. But the fighting continues today. Now different Afghan groups are competing for power.

10. On September 22, 1980, Iraq attacked Iran. In response, the Ayatollah Khomeini, the leader of Iran, called for a holy war against the Iraqi invaders. Thousands of Iranians, some as young as 12 years old, often threw themselves against Iraqi tanks. They were ready to sacrifice their lives for Iran and their leader. In 1988, Iran and Iraq finally agreed to a cease fire. However, the cost of the war was devastating in both countries. Iran was affected particularly badly because of a major earthquake in 1990. The country did not have the huge amount of money necessary to repair the damage caused by the war and the earthquake.

11. The Persian Gulf crisis was the most serious situation to date in the Middle East. In August 1990, Iraq invaded and captured the small country of Kuwait. Saddam Hussein, the leader of Iraq, said that Iraq had the right to take over Kuwait because Kuwait had been stolen from Iraq by colonial powers. He also said that Kuwait was plotting with the West to keep oil prices low and that Kuwait had stolen oil from Iraq. The United States government was worried that Hussein would gain control of most of the world supply of oil. Diplomats from many nations tried to persuade Hussein to remove his forces from Kuwait. When he refused, a multinational force, led by the United States, went to war against Iraq. In February of 1991, Iraqi forces were defeated and finally left Kuwait. The Persian Gulf crisis dramatically demonstrated that the Middle East is a crucial but unstable region.

UNDERSTANDING WHAT YOU HAVE READ

1. Which of the following questions are answered in this chapter?
a. How is the Suez Canal operated?
b. Why have Arab nations worked together in world affairs?
c. Why is the United States interested in this part of the world?

2. The main idea of this chapter is that
a. there is no unity among Arab leaders
b. Palestinians want their own homeland
c. affairs of the Middle East and North Africa affect the rest of the world

3. A person's pride in his or her country may be called
a. nationalism
b. militarism
c. imperialism

4. Palestine is the ancient name for the region that is now
a. Libya and Egypt
b. Israel and Jordan
c. Saudi Arabia and Israel

5. Arabs fought Israel in 1948 because
a. they did not agree to the formation of Israel as a homeland for the Jews
b. they wanted new farm land near the Red Sea
c. freedom came to the people of Arabia

6. The PLO is pledged to attack and destroy
a. Egyptians
b. Israelis
c. Jordanians

7. The United States has taken all of these actions EXCEPT
a. placing a boycott on oil imports from Iran
b. sending military forces to stop the Soviet invasion of Afghanistan
c. slowing its wheat sales to the Soviet Union

8. Persons who leave their homes to escape danger are called
a. pioneers
b. traitors
c. refugees

DEVELOPING CRITICAL THINKING SKILLS

Fact or Opinion

Which of these statements are fact and which are someone's opinion?

1. The Commonwealth of Independent States has the same right as the United States to be interested in the Middle East.
2. The United States should not send arms either to Israel or to the Arab nations.
3. The Suez Canal is one of the most important waterways in the world.
4. Many Arab refugees live on the borders of Israel and Jordan.
5. The independence of the nations of North Africa and the Middle East will bring the needed improvements to the region.
6. The United States helped Greece and Turkey in 1947 because of the threat of the spread of communism.
7. Some Arab states do not recognize the State of Israel's right to exist.
8. A single Arab nation may solve most of the problems of the region.

Chapter 11

Egypt:
From Pharaohs to
Presidents

What aspects of life in Egypt are affected by the Nile River?

READING FOR A PURPOSE:
1. Why is the Nile River so important to the people of Egypt?
2. How are Egypt's cities a mixture of the old and the new?
3. Why is Egypt one of the most important countries in the Middle East and North Africa?

1. It has been said that Egypt is the Nile and the Nile is Egypt. Without the Nile, this North African country would be a vast desert. Except for a few scattered nomads, nearly all of Egypt's 55.7 million people live and work in the Nile River valley. It has always been so in Egypt. The Nile has been the center of Egyptian life for thousands of years. One of the earliest civilizations in the history of the world grew up around this great river.

2. More than 5,000 years ago, the Egyptians had learned to irrigate the land in the Nile Valley and raise crops. They built large stone temples to their gods. The great pyramids, one of the wonders of the ancient world, were huge stone burial places for their rulers, the *pharaohs.* The pyramids have lasted to this day. In the 7th century, the Egyptians were conquered by the Arabs. They gradually became Muslims and were ruled by Muslim kings or sultans for more than a thousand years. There is also an important Christian Arab minority.

3. In 1869, the Suez Canal was built on Egyptian land. In time, the United Kingdom gained control of the canal. The government of Egypt grew weaker, and in 1952 it was overthrown. A new government was formed by Gamal Nasser. When the United Kingdom withdrew its soldiers from guarding the canal in 1956, Nasser seized it. France, Britain, and Israel attacked Egypt after this act. The United States and United Nations forced these nations to remove their troops, and Nasser kept control of the canal. Because of the attack, Egypt was angry with the West for many years.

4. Egyptians today, like Egyptians long ago, depend upon the Nile. It is the longest river in the world, flowing from central Africa through the Sudan and Egypt into the Mediterranean Sea. Each year there are heavy summer rains in the mountains to the south. As a result, the Nile floods its banks each fall, bringing rich soil to the lands near it.

5. Egyptian farmers no longer depend upon the yearly flood alone to water their land. In 1902, the first Aswan Dam was built. The second, the Aswan High Dam, was completed about 70 years later. It holds back the water of the Nile until it is needed. When the water is released, it is carried to fields by a system of canals. In this way, water is available for irrigation throughout the year and can cover more distant farms. Egypt's chief products are cotton, wheat, and rice. The dams were given credit for saving these crops during very dry years. The dams have made it possible to grow several crops a year. This al-

Irrigation in the Nile Delta. The lives of the fellahin are linked completely with the Nile and its life-giving waters.

most doubled the crop yield. Power from the Aswan High Dam runs Egypt's huge fertilizer plant. Fertilizer is a major need of Egyptian farmers.

6. Egyptian *fellahin* or farmers live in the many small villages that lie in the Nile Valley. If they are lucky, they own their own farm. Land reform laws have lessened the power of large landowners. Laws forbid families from owning more than 100 acres. Even so, many farmers have to rent land or work for others. They use simple tools on their small plots. Despite hard work, they do not make a lot of money. They earn about $100 a year from the sale of cotton or wheat. The Egyptian farmer's chief foods are corn and vegetables. Animals provide a little milk and cheese. Farmers rarely eat meat. Poor sanitary conditions and lack of enough food cause much sickness among farm families. Most of them can neither read nor write.

7. Though Egypt is mainly a farming country, it has some large and well-known cities. Cairo, its capital, is the largest city in all of Africa. The city of Cairo marks the beginning of the delta of the Nile. Northwest of Cairo is Alexandria, its second largest city. It is also Egypt's chief seaport. Both cities have huge textile mills.

8. The cities of Egypt contain both the old and the new. There are new shops, offices, and apartment buildings, as well as large hotels

A Cairo street scene. What mixture of traditional life and modern life can you see in this photo?

411

and department stores. There are both factories and smaller workshops. There are schools and several universities. The older sections have dark, narrow streets, dried brick houses, and small shops. These sections are crowded with fellahin who can neither find jobs in the city nor obtain land in the country.

9. Like several other nations in North Africa and the Middle East, Egypt is a poor country. There is not enough fertile land for its rapidly growing population. Second, many of the people suffer from sicknesses and have little education. However, this is changing. The Aswan High Dam has made it possible for more land to be irrigated. More electricity is being provided for the villages. Pure water is becoming available. Although there is a shortage of mineral resources, new industries are being started. More children are going to school than could in the past.

10. Egypt's chief imports are wheat to feed its people and machinery that its own factories cannot make. Egypt pays for some of the goods by the sale of cotton. This dependence upon one export crop can cause trouble. A drop in the price of cotton can seriously hurt the Egyptian farmer and the income of the nation. In the 1970s, oil was discovered in Egypt. It is gradually becoming Egypt's leading export. Tourism is also bringing money into the country. Thousands of tourists visit the ancient pyramids and temples every year.

11. With all its problems, Egypt is still important to the world. First, Egypt is the largest Arab nation. Anwar el-Sadat, president of Egypt until his assassination in 1981, made peace with Israel though it led to the diplomatic isolation of his country from the rest of the Arab world. His policies may have a great impact on the peaceful future of the Middle East. Second, Egypt owns the Suez Canal. This is one of the world's important trade routes. Egypt gets income from the canal, and also controls the passageway between the Mediterranean Sea and the Indian Ocean.

UNDERSTANDING WHAT YOU HAVE READ

1. Which of the following questions are answered in this chapter?
a. How long is the Nile River?
b. Where is the source of the Nile?
c. Why does the Nile River flood?

2. The main idea of paragraphs 4 through 6 is to describe
a. how the Suez Canal has changed the government of Egypt
b. improvements in irrigation along the Nile
c. how people live along the Nile

3. The Nile River begins in the
a. Mediterranean Sea
b. highlands of east and central Africa
c. Sahara

4. Most people of Egypt live
a. along the route of the Suez Canal
b. in the valley of the Nile River
c. in the cool southern mountains

5. Dams are of great importance to the people of Egypt because
a. atomic power is provided in this way
b. farmers will be able to use more of the water
c. a larger amount of land can be used for grazing cattle

6. Egypt's income from selling goods is never certain because
a. its machinery often breaks down
b. the Suez Canal can easily be closed to ships
c. it depends largely upon the sale of cotton

7. The largest city in Africa is
a. Cairo
b. Alexandria
c. Jerusalem

8. *Fellahin* are the same as
a. doctors
b. teachers
c. farmers

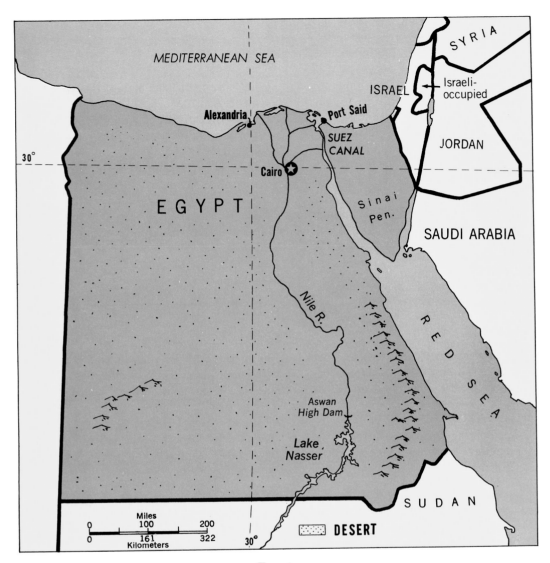

Egypt

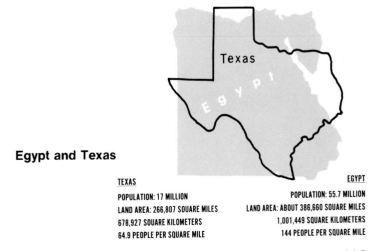

Egypt and Texas

TEXAS

POPULATION: 17 MILLION
LAND AREA: 266,807 SQUARE MILES
678,927 SQUARE KILOMETERS
64.9 PEOPLE PER SQUARE MILE

EGYPT

POPULATION: 55.7 MILLION
LAND AREA: ABOUT 386,660 SQUARE MILES
1,001,449 SQUARE KILOMETERS
144 PEOPLE PER SQUARE MILE

413

DEVELOPING IDEAS AND SKILLS

Building Map Skills — Egypt and the United States

Study the maps. Then answer these questions.

1. What is the distance from the Mediterranean Sea to the southern border of Egypt?
2. What bodies of water are connected by the Suez Canal?
3. What direction is *downstream* on the Nile River?
4. To what continent is the Sinai Peninsula connected?
5. What continent lies north of the Mediterranean Sea?
6. Describe the topography of Egypt.
7. Where do you think most of Egypt's 55.7 million people live?
8. How would you compare Egypt with Texas in size and population?
9. What city is located at latitude 31°N and longitude 30°E?
10. What countries border Egypt?

SUMMING UP

True or False

Tell whether these statements are true or false. The underlined words make the statements true or false. If a statement is false, what word or words would you place in it to make it true?

1. Egypt is located on the continent of Africa.
2. Until 1956, the Suez Canal had been controlled by the United Kingdom.
3. The president of Egypt who worked for peace with Israel was Gamal Nasser.
4. The Nile River flows north through Egypt.
5. An Egyptian farm family usually has a meal of meat and vegetables.
6. Egypt's chief seaport is Alexandria.
7. Egypt's chief export crop is wheat.
8. Most of Egypt's land is desert.

DEVELOPING CRITICAL THINKING SKILLS

Fact or Opinion

Which of these statements are fact and which are someone's opinion?

1. The Aswan High Dam has made Egypt one of the most powerful nations in the world.
2. Egypt's people should irrigate and develop enough farm land to feed all the people.
3. Dams along the Nile will provide more water for irrigation.
4. Most of Egypt's land is too dry to grow crops.
5. Egypt should lead a union of Arab states.
6. The Nile River will always be important in the life of the people of Egypt.
7. The peace treaty between Egypt and Israel means there will be peace all over the Middle East.
8. The United Kingdom ought to regain control of the Suez Canal.

Chapter 12

Israel: The Jewish State

Can Israel and its Arab neighbors live in peace?

READING FOR A PURPOSE:
1. How is Israel different from most countries in the Middle East and North Africa?
2. How did Israel become an independent nation?
3. What problems does Israel face with the Muslim nations of the region?

1. Israel is a tiny land (about 8,000 square miles—or 20,700 square kilometers—in area) at the eastern end of the Mediterranean Sea. Most of Israel has a desert climate, as do the other nations in the Middle East. Nevertheless, Israel is different from them in several ways. First, most of its people are Jews rather than Muslims. Second, most Israelis live in towns and cities rather than in farm villages. Many work in factories. Third, Israel has one of the few democratic governments in this re-gion. Fourth, a rather high percentage of its people can read and write. It is a land of newspapers, books, schools, and modern hospitals.

2. Israel is bordered by four countries: Lebanon on the north, Syria on the northeast, Jordan on the east, and Egypt on the south. To the west lies the Mediterranean Sea. At its southernmost end, Israel has a seaport on the Red Sea. Despite its small size, this country is important to the United States. It lies close to the Suez Canal. And it is a bridge for three continents: Europe, Asia, and Africa.

3. Israel has a fertile inland plain near the Mediterranean Sea. East of the plain, the land rises and then drops sharply to the valley of the Jordan River. Much of this valley is below sea level. Part of the river valley lies in the West Bank, territory Israel took from Jordan during the 1967 war. The Jordan River flows south and empties into the Dead Sea, the low-est spot on earth. The waters of the Dead Sea are very salty because they do not flow out to the sea. South of the sea is the Negev Desert. It takes up a large part of Israel.

4. Along the coast, the climate is Mediter-ranean. In the summer it is hot and dry; in the winter it is mild. The winter season is the sea-son of rain. However, much of southern Israel is desert—the Negev.

A view of Jerusalem, capital of Israel. Why is Jerusalem an important city for Muslims, Jews, and Christians alike?

5. Israel was once called Palestine. It was the home of the Jewish people for centuries. The Romans conquered it in A.D. 70. Over the centuries, the number of Jews in other parts of the world increased. As one nation or another conquered Palestine, the number of Jewish people there decreased. Beginning in the 16th century, Jews in many countries were forced to live apart in sections of cities called *ghettos.* They dreamed of returning to their homeland. In the 19th century, Theodor Herzl, a Hungarian Jew, urged the Jews to return to Palestine. His followers were called Zionists.

6. Palestine became a mandate of the United Kingdom after World War I. (This meant Britain had the power to administer the government and affairs of the territory then known as Palestine.) With the permission of the British government, Jews began to settle in Palestine alongside the Arabs. (The Arabs also had been living there for many centuries with their own religions and customs.) The number of Jews in Palestine grew yearly. From 1933 to 1945, the Nazi government of Germany carried out Hitler's terrible program to destroy the Jewish people. During this time, 6 million Jews were killed by the Nazis in Europe. After the war, many Jews who survived this Holocaust came to Palestine. Arab leaders wanted the movement of Jews to the Middle East to stop.

7. When the United Kingdom gave up its control of Palestine after World War II, the United Nations wanted to settle the problem growing in Palestine. It was suggested that Palestine be divided into two states, one Jewish and one Arab. In 1948, the nation of Israel was formed. This started a war. Arabs and Israelis fought and the Israelis won. Parts of what was to have been the new Arab state in Palestine were taken over by Israel, Egypt, and Trans-Jordan (now called Jordan). This left no homeland for the Palestinian Arabs. This has not ended the warfare between Israel and the Arab nations. There have been periods of fighting since then. The Arab states have sided with the Palestinians against Israel.

Ethiopian Jews being married by a rabbi.

Since the late 1950s, the United States has supported Israel; the Soviet Union first supported Israel, then the Arabs. In 1979, Israel and Egypt signed a peace treaty.

8. The people of Israel have come from all over the world—Europe, Asia, North Africa, even America. They speak mainly Hebrew and have different customs. Some are highly skilled; others cannot even read or write. Some are from poor lands; some come from rich, industrial nations. Some are farmers; others are factory workers. The one thing most of them have in common is that they are Jews. (Israel is a Jewish state, but nearly 600,000 Muslims and some Christians live there.) The newest immigrants have come from the Commonwealth (CIS) and Ethiopia.

9. Like other places in the Middle East, Israel is short of water and fertile land. Despite these difficulties, more and more land is being reclaimed through irrigation.

10. Most Israeli farms are found along the fertile coast and on the reclaimed land—land made useful again—of the desert. The chief crops are olives, grapes, citrus fruits (lemons and oranges), and flowers. Some of these are exported. The farms do not produce enough meat for the people, however, so much must be imported. In some parts of Israel, the peo-

416

All Israeli citizens who are 18 or older are required to serve in the army. Why does the location of Israel make this necessary?

ple live in *moshavim* (cooperative settlements) or *kibbutzim*. (In a kibbutz the land belongs to the people who live there.)

11. There are many small factories in Israel, despite the fact that it lacks coal and iron. These factories depend upon the skills of the people, such as watchmaking, metal work, or diamond cutting. By bringing water to the Negev, Israel is now able to mine there. Near the southern tip are the copper mines first worked by King Solomon more than 3,000 years ago. The Dead Sea is also rich in minerals used for fertilizer. There is a rapidly growing electronics and arms industry. Israel gets more of its income from industry than any other country in the Middle East.

12. Israel's cities have grown in size with the increase in factories. The cities are different from the border settlements. One of the largest cities, Tel Aviv, is less than 75 years old, yet it has about 350,000 people. Northward along the Mediterranean Sea is Haifa, the main seaport. The capital of Israel is Jerusalem. This very old city contains the holy places of three religions—Judaism, Christianity, and Islam. It is also the home of the famous Hebrew University. From 1948 to 1967,

the city of Jerusalem was divided between Israel and Jordan. In the 1967 war, Israel captured Jordan's half of the city and still controls it.

13. Of all the problems faced by this tiny desert nation, the most serious is the hatred shown by its Arab neighbors. Since 1948, when the State of Israel was created, there have been several wars between Israel and its neighbors. In the 1967 war, Israel occupied the Gaza Strip and Jordan's West Bank. Today, about 1.5 million Arabs live in this Israeli-controlled land. There are ongoing clashes between Israel and Palestinians in the occupied territories. There are also attacks by commandos who slip into Israel from neighboring Arab countries. Israel has often felt it necessary to attack Palestinian camps in search of suspected terrorists. Because of these dangers, Israel believes it must keep a large, modern and expensive armed force. All over Israel you see young people in uniform. Almost all Jewish citizens—male and female—and some of the Arabs—must serve in the army upon reaching the age of 18.

14. Another problem derives from the fact that the Jews come from different lands. About one-third of the Jews are skilled and educated Europeans. They have good jobs, live in the cities, and control the government. Some of the other Jews, chiefly from North Africa and the Middle East, are unskilled and illiterate. Many of them are poor and live in small towns and villages. Attempts are being made to educate these people and improve their living conditions.

15. The citizens of Israel are showing the world that a skilled and hardworking people, with help from abroad, can develop even the poorest land. This has brought respect for Israel from other new nations in Asia and Africa. And Israel has a democratic way of life, unlike many other nations of North Africa and the Middle East.

UNDERSTANDING WHAT YOU HAVE READ

1. Which of the following questions are answered in this chapter?
a. Why is there trouble between Arabs and Jews?
b. What are Israel's problems?
c. How large is Israel?

2. The main idea of this chapter is to describe
a. how Israel began
b. Israel's growth
c. Israel's farms

3. The founder of Zionism was
a. Ben-Gurion b. Einstein c. Herzl

4. One reason Israel is important in this region is because it
a. has the highest standard of living in the region
b. is located near the oil fields
c. has the only river near the Mediterranean

5. The Arab states of the Middle East dislike Israel because
a. Israel has the only iron and coal resources in the region
b. Israel has a large and modern army
c. they feel Israel is a state on land that belongs to the Arabs

6. If farmers *reclaim* a swamp, they have
a. made it into useful land
b. watered it
c. sold it

7. A section of a city in which people of a particular race or religion live apart from others is often called a
a. ghetto
b. slum
c. province

DEVELOPING CRITICAL THINKING SKILLS

I. Do You Agree or Disagree?

Give reasons for your answers.

1. People of many different religions are visitors to Jerusalem.
2. To support a growing population, Israel must irrigate more land.
3. The land along the Mediterranean coast provides much of Israel's food.
4. The people of Israel have little use for the Suez Canal.
5. Israel became an independent state in the 1960s.
6. The Dead Sea is a source of water for future irrigation.
7. The people of Israel have in common religion, customs, and skills.

II. Making Comparisons

Tell whether the following items refer to Israel, Egypt, or to both countries. If the item applies to Israel only, write the letter **I**. If the item applies to Egypt only, write the letter **E**. If the item applies to both Israel and Egypt, write the letter **B**.

1. Oil pipelines
2. Suez Canal
3. Export of cotton
4. Most people live in cities.
5. Coastline on the Mediterranean Sea
6. Many skilled workers
7. Much of the land is desert.
8. People have come from many countries.
9. Larger than the state of Texas
10. Fertile river valley
11. Most people of the Muslim religion
12. Dependence on one export crop

418

DEVELOPING IDEAS AND SKILLS

Building Map Skills — Israel and New Jersey

Israel and New Jersey

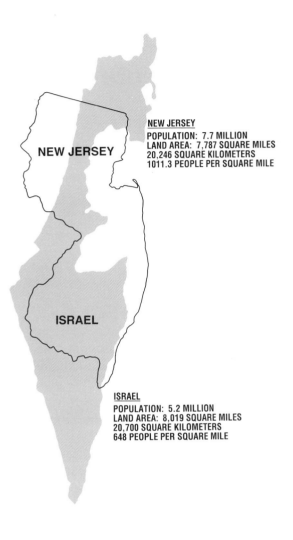

NEW JERSEY
POPULATION: 7.7 MILLION
LAND AREA: 7,787 SQUARE MILES
20,246 SQUARE KILOMETERS
1011.3 PEOPLE PER SQUARE MILE

ISRAEL
POPULATION: 5.2 MILLION
LAND AREA: 8,019 SQUARE MILES
20,700 SQUARE KILOMETERS
648 PEOPLE PER SQUARE MILE

Study the map above. Then answer the questions that follow.

1. How long is Israel in a north-south direction?
2. What kind of land is found in the Negev?
3. What river is important to the people of Israel?
4. Is Israel in the high, middle, or low latitudes?

5. What Israeli city is a port on the Gulf of Aqaba?
6. What countries border Israel?
7. Where are the large cities of Israel located? Why?
8. Which has more people per square mile or kilometer, Israel or New Jersey?

419

Chapter 13

Saudi Arabia: Modern Development and an Islamic Tradition

How has the development of Saudi Arabia brought both improvements and problems to its people?

READING FOR A PURPOSE:
1. What makes Saudi Arabia such a rich country?
2. What does Saudi Arabia do with its wealth?
3. What do the United States and Saudi Arabia disagree about?

1. Visitors to Saudi Arabia might find it hard to believe they are in a country of great wealth. Fifteen and one-half million people live in Saudi Arabia in a land one-fourth the size of the United States. There are more people in the metropolitan area of New York City than there are in Saudi Arabia. About 5 percent of its people are nomads. They travel across the desert with their goats and camels depending on the season of the year. Nearly 14 percent of the population are farmers. They work hard trying to scratch a living from land that is a vast desert. About three-quarters of the people live in cities. Only a small part of the population has had an education. But Saudi Arabia has the largest known oil reserves in the world. In today's world of machinery and technology, oil is precious.

2. Saudi Arabia is the largest country on the Arabian Peninsula. In the north and northeast, it is connected to the continent of Asia. On the west is the Red Sea. On the east is the Persian Gulf around which are the important oil fields of the Middle East. On its southern and eastern borders are the countries of Yemen, Oman, Qatar, Bahrain, and the United Arab Emirates. Highlands line the western coast. Some run as high as 9,000 feet (2,700 meters). The land then slopes eastward toward the Persian Gulf. Throughout the land there are some 2 million people, traveling from place to place, setting up their tents wherever grass can be found.

3. Other Saudis live in oasis areas, or in a small region in the southwest where farming is possible. Dates are the chief crop of the oases. They are part of the daily diet and are exported as well. Coffee is a product of the highlands. Some barley, millet, cotton, and fruits are also grown. The remainder of the people live in the growing cities, which are scattered throughout the country. Cities have started in places where there is enough underground water for large numbers of people to survive.

4. Saudi Arabia is the center of the Muslim world. It was in Saudi Arabia that Muhammad was born and first taught his beliefs. Mecca, the city of Muhammad's birth, is the most sacred Islamic city. Medina, where Muhammad died, is also sacred. More than a million Muslims make the pilgrimage to Mecca each year. Caring for the needs of the pilgrims is an important business in Mecca.

Irrigation canals in Saudi Arabia. How has irrigation helped the Saudi Arabian economy?

5. The king is the head of the Saudi government. The country's constitution is the Koran, the Muslim holy book, and its law is the law of Islam as interpreted by religious scholars. The king is advised by a council of ministers. One member of the council is the prime minister. King Fahd became king in 1982. He is also the prime minister. The Saud family has ruled Saudi Arabia since defeating a rival family in the early 1900s. The country is named for them. The capital of Saudi Arabia is Riyadh (REE-yahd).

6. The law of the land is based on the Koran. Religious law tells the Islamic people how to live their lives. The king makes sure that these rules are carried out. Drinking of alcohol is forbidden. So is public dancing. Although public education is free, boys and girls study separately. Only recently have young women been allowed to enter colleges. Women almost always wear veils in public. They are not allowed to drive cars and only certain jobs are open to them. Islamic law touches all parts of private life. For example, construction of a new apartment building in Jidda was stopped because it did not have separate elevators for men and women.

7. Oil is the source of Saudi riches. Americans discovered oil in Saudi Arabia in the 1930s. American engineers and technicians were the leaders in developing the oil fields. Then, other foreign companies also gained control of Saudi oil reserves. The Saudi government has since regained control of the country's oil. The oil fields are centered in an area about 100 miles (161 kilometers) long and 40 miles (64 kilometers) wide along the Persian Gulf. The fields produce between 6 and 10 million barrels of oil a day. Income from oil pays for the Saudi development of their country and for military equipment. Jubail (joo-BYL) and Damman (dah-MAM) are the chief gulf ports. Pipelines carry oil from refineries at the Persian Gulf ports to the port of Yanbu' (YAN-boo) on the Red Sea.

8. The transporting of oil has made the Persian Gulf one of the world's most important waterways. Tankers from all parts of the

A busy street scene in a Saudi Arabian city.

globe enter and leave the gulf daily. Keeping the Persian Gulf open for the oil trade is important to the United States. Saudi Arabia is one of the United States' largest suppliers of oil. Other countries like Japan, Germany, and France depend heavily on oil from Arabian ports. Income from oil sales has made Saudi Arabia one of the richest countries in the world.

9. What does Saudi Arabia do with its wealth? It is building a modern country in a short period of time. More construction is going on in Saudi Arabia than in any other country in the world. The skylines of Saudi cities are full of cranes. New high-rise buildings for offices, schools, and hospitals are going up all over the country. At Jubail, on the Persian Gulf, and Yanbu', on the Red Sea, two new cities have been built. Refineries, factories, steel mills, roads, airports, and deep-water ports for oil tankers are being built. The Saudi government gives billions of dollars to poorer nations in the Middle East and Africa. It also spends billions buying the latest weapons and airplanes for its armed forces.

10. The signs of change appear all over Saudi Arabia. But change often creates new problems. One of the most serious seems to be the conflict between the old ideas and customs and the new ways of life. Saudi Arabia has a shortage of skilled workers. Almost half of its workers come from foreign countries. With their families, they make up more than one-third of the total population. They often do

What aspects of both western and traditional Middle Eastern life are shown in this photo?

not have the same customs as the native Saudis. Some Saudis have gone to school in Europe. There they learned Western ideas and may have followed Western customs. Modern buildings, cars, highways, television, movies, and supermarkets are all changes in Saudi life. *Traditionalists* (those whose practices and customs were handed down for generations) fear changes in their ways of life. They want to save the values and beliefs of Islam even as their country develops.

11. The United States and Saudi Arabia do not agree about Israel, though. Israel and the United States are close friends. The Saudis' chief aim in Middle-East affairs is to return Israel to its pre-1967 borders. It wants the lands Israel occupied in 1967 returned to Arab rule. In 1948, the Saudis supported the fight against the creation of Israel. In 1973, they supplied funds to Egypt and Syria during the war against Israel. In 1973, Saudi Arabia participated in a brief cutoff, or embargo, against oil shipments to the United States.

12. The United States and Saudi Arabia have had a long history of friendship. Many wealthy Saudi families have sent their children to school in the United States. In turn, the United States has been a chief exporter of goods to Saudi Arabia. To the Saudis, the United States is the nation that can stop the spread of communism in the world. The United States looks upon Saudi Arabia as a leader in resisting communism in the Middle East.

UNDERSTANDING WHAT YOU HAVE READ

1. Which of the following questions are answered in this chapter?
a. How did Saudi Arabia become a nation?
b. What were Saudi Arabia's actions during the revolution against the shah of Iran?
c. How has Saudi Arabia used its wealth?

2. Which statement best describes the ideas in *paragraphs 11 and 12?*
a. The United States has been a good customer for Saudi oil.
b. Saudi Arabia will always support the United States, despite the Saudis' feelings about Israel.
c. Saudi Arabia has to measure its feelings for Israel against its friendship with the United States.

3. We can infer from Chapter 13 that
a. some believers in Islam do not like what is taking place in present-day Saudi Arabia
b. most Saudis live on a diet much like that of the people of the United States
c. money from the sale of oil barely covers the cost of running the Saudi government

4. If a pipeline carried oil from the Persian Gulf directly westward, it would end at the
a. Indian Ocean
b. Mediterranean Sea
c. Red Sea

5. Saudi Arabia's problems include all of these EXCEPT:

a. a lack of seaports from which oil can be shipped
b. a shortage of skilled Saudi workers
c. less than half its people have had an education

6. The head of the Saudi government

a. is elected by men only
b. is the king
c. is chosen by a council of ministers

DEVELOPING IDEAS AND SKILLS

Building Map Skills – Saudi Arabia and the Southern United States

1. Is Saudi Arabia north or south of the equator? How do you know?
2. Is Saudi Arabia located in the high, middle, or low latitudes?
3. If you flew from your hometown to Riyadh, in which direction would you be traveling?
4. Are there any major rivers in Saudi Arabia? How do you know?
5. What is Saudi Arabia's capital city? Which cities are seaports?
6. Which is more thickly populated, Saudi Arabia or the United States?
7. What is the distance from Dhahran to Jidda?
8. Why are most cities in Saudi Arabia near large bodies of water?
9. Through which important bodies of water would a ship pass on leaving the port of Dammam and traveling to a port in Lebanon?

Saudi Arabia and the Southern United States

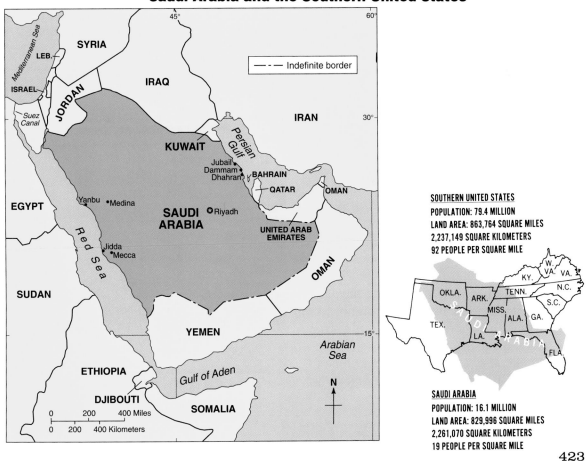

SOUTHERN UNITED STATES
POPULATION: 79.4 MILLION
LAND AREA: 863,764 SQUARE MILES
2,237,149 SQUARE KILOMETERS
92 PEOPLE PER SQUARE MILE

SAUDI ARABIA
POPULATION: 16.1 MILLION
LAND AREA: 829,996 SQUARE MILES
2,261,070 SQUARE KILOMETERS
19 PEOPLE PER SQUARE MILE

Women in Saudi Arabia

In Saudi Arabia, the women must follow a set of rules laid down by the government. These rules, the government feels, are part of the Islamic faith. Saudi women are not allowed to drive cars or work with men. When they leave their homes, they must wear the *abayah* (aba for short), a black robe that covers their arms, legs, and body. They must cover their faces with veils of black gauze or chiffon.

Hend al-Khuthaila is a young woman from Riyadh. She attends King Saud University Women's Center. The school is surrounded by iron gates and guarded by elderly men. Inside, the young women can remove their abas and veils. They wear T-shirts, long skirts, lots of gold and silver jewelry, and make-up. They are taught only by women. Sometimes they watch male teachers lecture on television. Most of the 500 women students at the university are studying to be teachers, social workers and nurses. But not Hend. She wants to go into the banking business, but for women only.

The Islamic faith allows women to own property and money separate from their husbands. There are already ten banks in Saudi Arabia that do business only with and for women. Hend's best friend, Soad, works in such a bank. Once inside the bank, Soad removes her aba and wears Western-style dress. She handles deposits and withdrawals for 900 women customers. Hend and Soad often talk about life in Riyadh. They do not like the separation of men and women in the work force. They do not like to depend on male relatives or shuttle buses to drive them from place to place. They would like, they say, to see change come to their land. But not, they add, as quickly as it has for women in the West.

Copy the statements below into your notebook.

If you agree with a statement, mark it with an *A*. If you disagree, mark it with a *D*. Rewite any sentence you disagree with to make it accurate.

1. Women and men are treated equally in Saudi Arabia.
2. Saudi women must cover their faces when they go out in public.
3. Women do not receive higher education in Saudi Arabia.
4. Men and women cannot work together in Riyadh.
5. Hend would like to marry, raise a family, and stay at home after she graduates.
6. There are businesses for women only in Riyadh.
7. The Saudi interpretation of Islam places some restrictions on women.
8. More Saudi women are getting an education and going to work.

A Saudi woman in abayah and veil. Many Saudi women use heavy eye makeup because their eyes are often the only part of their face visible.

– North Africa and the Middle East –

Country	Area (Square Miles)	Capital	Population (1991 estimates)	Number of Years to Double Population	Life Expectancy	Per Capita GNP, 1990
Afghanistan	250,000	Kabul	16,900,000	27	41	$ 220
Algeria	919,591	Algiers	26,000,000	28	66	$ 2,060
Bahrain	239	Manama	500,000	29	72	$ 6,360
Cyprus	3,571	Nicosia	700,000	71	76	$ 8,040
Egypt	386,660	Cairo	55,700,000	28	60	$ 600
Iran	636,293	Teheran	59,700,000	21	65	$ 2,450
Iraq	167,923	Baghdad	17,100,000	26	64	$ 1,950
Israel	8,019	Jerusalem	5,200,000	45	76	$10,970
Jordan	37,737	Amman	3,600,000	20	71	$ 1,240
Kuwait	6,880	Kuwait	1,400,000	23	74	$16,380
Lebanon	4,015	Beirut	3,400,000	33	68	$ 690
Libya	679,359	Tripoli	4,500,000	23	67	$ 5,410
Morocco	172,413	Rabat	26,200,000	29	64	$ 950
Oman	82,031	Muscat	1,600,000	20	66	$ 5,220
Qatar	4,247	Doha	500,000	28	72	$15,860
Saudi Arabia	829,996	Riyadh	16,100,000	20	65	$ 6,230
Syria	71,498	Damascus	13,700,000	18	65	$ 990
Tunisia	63,170	Tunis	8,400,000	33	66	$ 1,420
Turkey	301,382	Ankara	59,200,000	32	67	$ 1,630
United Arab Emirates	32,278	Abu Dhabi	2,500,000	25	71	$19,860
Yemen	205,356	Sana'a	10,400,000	20	50	$ 640

UNIT·EIGHT

AFRICA

KEY IDEAS

- Both young and ancient countries in Africa are striving to use their rich natural resources for economic development.

- Africans are meeting the challenges created by the climate, their land, and an inhospitable coastline.

- The hundreds of different ethnic and language groups have created diverse ways of life in Africa.

- Although urbanization is increasing, most Africans live in rural areas.

- In the past, Europe colonized most of Africa. The present-day borders they established often ignored geographic boundaries and disrupted ethnic groups.

A busy bus station in the city of Khartoum, Sudan, reveals a growing population. Increasing numbers of Africans are moving to the cities.

Chapter 1

Africa: The Giant Continent

Why are we interested in Africa?

READING FOR A PURPOSE:
1. How does the Sahara divide Africa?
2. Why is Africa important to the world?

1. Algeria, Nigeria, Tanzania, Zimbabwe, Sudan, Namibia! These are only a few of the nations on the giant continent of Africa. Forty years ago, these countries did not exist. Now they appear almost daily in our newspapers. Since World War II, Africa has undergone many changes. In our changing world, few regions have changed as much as this one.

2. Africa's geography really makes it two regions. Stretching eastward from the Atlantic Ocean to the Red Sea is the Sahara, a vast desert. The Sahara divides Africa in two. North of the Sahara, the people are mainly Arabs and Berbers. They have a way of life much like that of Middle Eastern peoples. South of the Sahara, there is a great variety of peoples and cultures, whose ways of living are different from those to the north.

3. While geography tends to divide Africa, history unites it. People north and south of the Sahara have been in contact from very early times. Early peoples on opposite sides of the desert traded goods—and also ideas. Sometimes they cooperated, and sometimes they fought against each other. Because of the many links between northern Africa and sub-Saharan Africa, many experts believe the continent should be treated as a single region. Other experts disagree. They say it makes more sense to group northern Africa with the Middle East. An argument can be made for each approach. While you have already read about northern Africa in Unit 7, you will find many references to that area in this unit, too.

4. There are several reasons why the world is interested in the continent of Africa. First, since World War II, many African nations have won their freedom. Most had been colonies of European countries. In African nations like Algeria and Mozambique, the struggle for independence was as hard as the American fight for independence from Britain. Now, new African nations want to take their place among the older nations of the world. They are trying to do in a few years many of the things that took the United States 200 years to do. They need to maintain stable governments and develop their natural resources. They need to give their people a better way of life. They want new roads, factories, and schools. In these tasks, they sometimes receive help. The United States, the former Soviet Union, China, Japan, and the countries of Europe have given money and low-cost loans to African nations. They have helped to build factories and schools. But most Africans would prefer to build up their nations by their own efforts.

5. Second, Africa is rich in mineral resources. No one knows just how great those resources are, for it has been difficult to explore and develop the region. We do know that oil, gold, diamonds, uranium, copper, bauxite, cobalt, iron ore, and manganese can be found in parts of the continent. All of those minerals are important to the modern world.

An auto factory in Côte d'Ivoire. This factory is run by a major French automobile manufacturer.

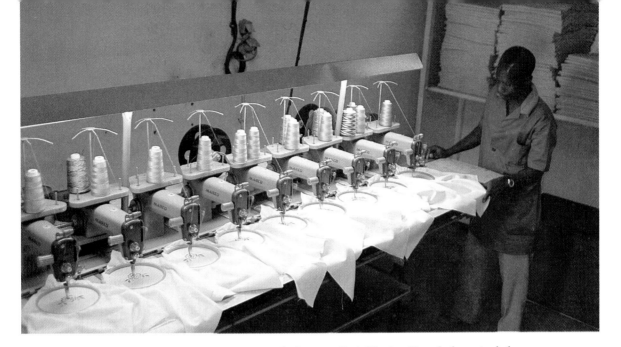

An embroidery machine in a textile factory, Côté d'Ivoire. How do factories help develop the economies of African nations?

Many of them are part of our daily lives.

6. Third, many private and government-owned businesses from other parts of the world have invested money to develop Africa's resources. For example, private American companies and banks have huge investments in Liberia, Nigeria, Angola, and Morocco. The French government owns an oil company with large oil projects in Gabon. A Chinese company built a railroad across Tanzania and Zambia.

7. Fourth, the forming of so many new nations in Africa has made that region important in world affairs. African nations now have the largest voting bloc in the United Nations General Assembly. This large vote is one reason why the United States and other important nations want to hold their friendship.

8. Fifth, unrest has troubled much of Africa. Many nations have had difficulty maintaining stable governments. Civil wars have raged in nations such as Ethiopia and Liberia, with several groups fighting one another for power. Moreover, some governments in Africa allowed only one political party. In the 1990s, Africans gained more political freedoms. Algeria and Zambia, among other nations, let new parties form.

9. Sixth, the problem of hunger in Africa has become a worldwide concern. People see pictures of starving babies on television and in newspapers and magazines. They see lands, once fertile, that have turned dry and dusty from lack of rain. They see animals either dead or too weak to move. People have learned that large amounts of food and medicine are needed in order to save people's lives. Africans are working to overcome hunger by improving food production.

10. Finally, events in the nation of South Africa continue to draw world attention. South Africa contains about seven million whites and 33 million nonwhites. Although a minority, the whites have long run the country. The all-white government dictated a form of strict racial separation called apartheid [uh-PAR-tayt]. This policy meant that schooling, health care, jobs, and wages were much better for whites than for nonwhites. Black South Africans, as well as Asians and people of mixed race, suffered greatly. In March 1992, the people of South Africa voted to end apartheid. Soon people of all races will have a say in the government of South Africa.

UNDERSTANDING WHAT YOU HAVE READ

1. **Which of the following questions are answered in this chapter?**
   a. How many people live in Africa?
   b. What is the great change taking place in Africa?
   c. Why should we know more about Africa?

2. **The main idea of this chapter is to describe**
   a. Africa's needs
   b. Africa's resources
   c. why Africa is important to the rest of the world

3. **The continent of Africa is divided into two parts by the**
   a. Sahara
   b. Atlas Mountains
   c. Congo River

4. **One problem many nations in Africa face is**
   a. hunger
   b. lack of mineral resources
   c. continued colonization by European powers

5. **One of the reasons Africa is so important to the rest of the world is that it**
   a. is rich in natural resources
   b. supplies most of the world's food
   c. is made up of many colonies

6. **African nations want to**
   a. be admitted to the United Nations
   b. have guidance from colonial rulers
   c. develop their resources themselves

7. **In paragraph 8, the term *stable governments* means governments that are**
   a. new
   b. lasting
   c. changing

DEVELOPING CRITICAL THINKING SKILLS

Do You Agree or Disagree?

Give reasons for your answers based on what you have read in Chapter 1.
1. In North Africa and sub-Saharan Africa we find different ways of living.
2. Few businesses from the rest of the world have invested money to develop Africa's resources.
3. Africa has many mineral resources to help its nations develop.
4. Much of Africa was once ruled by European countries.
5. Apartheid is a policy followed by all African governments.
6. Since World War II, many African nations have won independence.
7. Governments in modern Africa have always allowed their citizens a great deal of political freedom.

DEVELOPING IDEAS AND SKILLS

Building Map Skills — Africa

Study the map below. Then answer these questions.

1. Is the region north or south of the equator?
2. Is the region east or west of the prime meridian?
3. What region or regions are near it?
4. What are the chief bodies of water that border the region?
5. Which countries have no outlets to the sea?
6. Which large rivers form boundary lines between countries?
7. Which countries are island nations?

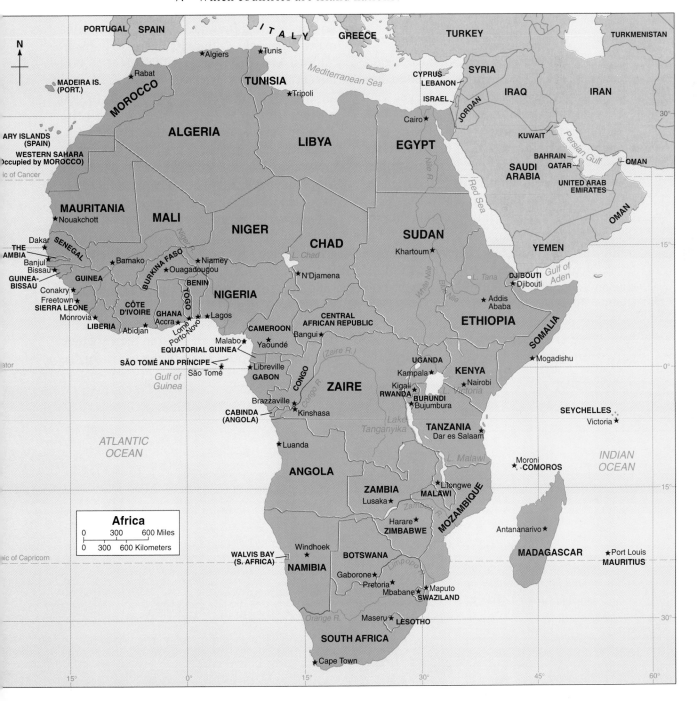

Chapter 2

The Land

What is the geography of Africa?

READING FOR A PURPOSE:
1. In what way is Africa shaped like a tilting table?
2. Where are Africa's tallest mountains?
3. How do large African lakes differ from the Great Lakes in North America?

1. The continent of Africa is a huge region. It is almost 12 million square miles (30 million square kilometers) in area. It is larger than either North or South America.

2. The land of Africa resembles a giant, tilting table. The lower edge of the table lies to the west. To the east, the land gradually becomes higher and higher. Most of Africa lies on this "table," which is actually a series of plateaus. There is very little coastal plain for lowlands. The plateaus vary from 1,000 to 5,000 feet (300 to 1,600 meters) above sea level. Near the coasts, the plateaus fall off sharply to a narrow band of land that is only slightly above sea level.

3. The plateaus of Africa are drained by four large rivers; the Nile, the Zaire (also called the Congo), the Zambezi, and the Niger. On these plateaus, these rivers are broad and deep in many places. Boats use them—especially the Zaire and the Niger—as highways for travel. But before they reach the sea, the rivers often flow downhill in roaring rapids and falls. Boats must stop at the rapids. Passengers then go by land to the next place where they can board a boat. Where the rivers flow into the sea, some of them form muddy deltas or sandbars.

4. On the eastern coast, a range of mountains extends from South Africa northward to Ethiopia. This range contains many high peaks. Mount Kilimanjaro [kihl-uh-muhn-JAH-roh] is over 19,000 feet (6,000 meters) above sea level. Mount Kenya reaches an altitude of more than 17,000 feet (5,000 meters). Both are located almost on the equator, yet they are so high that ice and snow blanket their tops. There are other mountains in western North Africa. These are the Atlas Mountains, which are actually part of a range that includes the Alps of Europe.

5. Powerful natural forces have pushed and pulled at the African continent. These forces created a long *rift* or trench. Called the Great Rift Valley, this spectacular series of deep valleys stretches north to south through most of eastern Africa.

6. Some huge lakes have been formed in the deep Rift Valley. The snow from the very high mountains provides some of the water for the

Sugar cane fields, South Africa. What is the flat land form that makes up much of Africa's surface?

432

Mount Kilimanjaro is the highest peak in Africa. How does the climate in the mountains differ from the climate in lower areas?

What are the benefits and problems caused by falls, such as this one at Lake Tana in Ethiopia?

lakes. Lake Victoria is the largest lake. It is almost the size of Lake Superior, the largest of the North American Great Lakes. Lake Tanganyika and Lake Malawi are other important lakes in the eastern highlands. These lakes also can be compared in size to the Great Lakes of North America.

7. Lakes and rivers allow travel within the African interior. But travel from the coast to the interior is more difficult. First, crossing the Sahara from the north is not easy. A trip requires careful planning, because water is scarce in the desert. Second, much of the African coastline is smooth and straight so that there are few harbors where boats can stop. (Africa has fewer miles of coastline than Europe, though it is almost three times larger than Europe.) Third, many of the mouths of Africa's rivers are difficult to navigate because of the deltas and sandbars. These barriers have created some difficulties in travel and communication in Africa.

UNDERSTANDING WHAT YOU HAVE READ

1. Which of the following questions are answered in this chapter?
a. What is the Great Rift Valley?
b. Why is it often hard to travel by water throughout the African interior?
c. Where do most Africans live?

2. The main idea of this chapter is to describe
a. the rivers of sub-Saharan Africa
b. African land forms
c. the mountains of sub-Saharan Africa

3. Most of Africa is a
a. lowland
b. plateau
c. rain forest

4. Africa's highest mountains are located in the
a. east
b. north
c. west

5. Africa's rivers are sometimes of little help in transporting goods because
a. there is a lack of boats
b. most of the rivers flow inland
c. many of the rivers have falls and rapids

6. African lakes are
a. too small for boat travel
b. found mainly in the west
c. about as big as the Great Lakes of North America

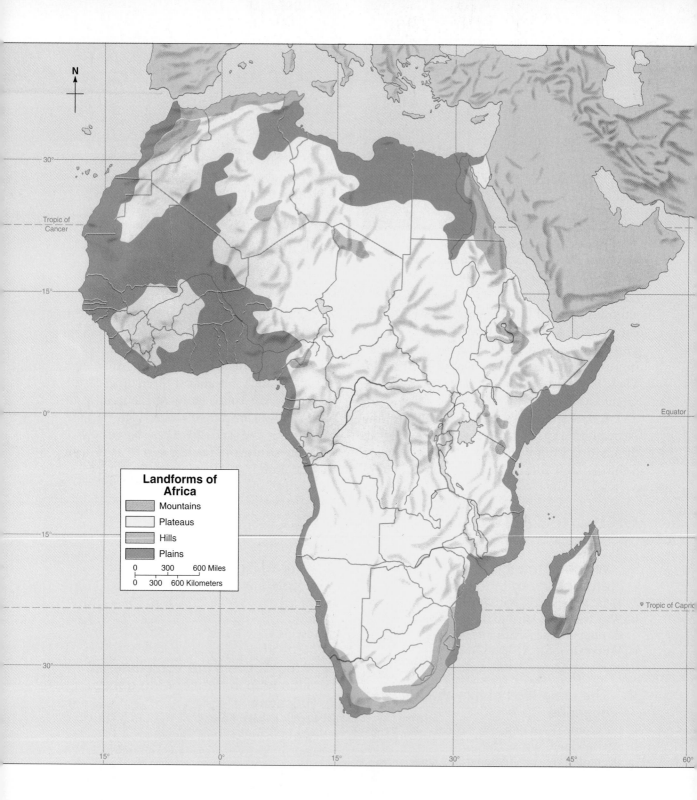

DEVELOPING IDEAS AND SKILLS

Building Map Skills — Land Forms of Africa

Study the map on the opposite page. Then answer the questions below.

1. What land form fills most of the interior of Africa?
2. Approximately how wide, in miles, is the area of plains along Africa's western coast at the equator?
3. In what parts of Africa are the most extensive plains located?
4. Locate three areas of Africa that contain mountains.
5. At what latitude does Africa's northernmost point lie?
6. Approximately how wide, in miles, is Africa at the equator?
7. In what parts of Africa are hills found?
8. Where are Africa's biggest lakes located?

DEVELOPING CRITICAL THINKING SKILLS

Drawing Conclusions

Write the following list in your notebook. Then place an X next to the reasons that explain how Africa's land forms made it hard for people from outside Africa to reach the interior of the continent.

____ 1. a vast desert in the north
____ 2. many rivers difficult to travel on
____ 3. southern tip near the cold southern ocean
____ 4. few openings into the land for harbors
____ 5. lack of natural resources
____ 6. unfriendly people
____ 7. not near other continents
____ 8. large inland lakes
____ 9. disease-carrying insects
____ 10. cliffs and mountains near the coasts

REVIEWING AND WRITING

Making Outlines — Land forms of Africa

Use these three headings to make an outline of the land forms of Africa. From what you have read, enter three statements under each heading.

A. Africa's Plateaus
B. Mountains of Africa
C. Lakes of Africa

Chapter 3

The Climate Areas

What are the climates of Africa?

READING FOR A PURPOSE:
1. How is the way of life on the savannas different from that in the rain forest?
2. How is the climate of southeastern Africa similar to the climate of southeastern United States?
3. What environmental problems do Africans fight to overcome?

1. The equator runs through the middle of Africa. This means that most of the continent is in the tropics. As you have read, temperatures near the equator tend to be warm. However, it is always cooler in highlands than at sea level. Therefore, parts of tropical Africa are cooler than you might expect because they lie at high elevations. Still, most of Africa is warm. This simple statement can help you remember Africa's climate: "Africa is warm, but some places are warmer than others."

2. Africa's climate and vegetation zones form an interesting pattern. If you were to travel north of the equator for a certain distance, and then you traveled south of the equator for about the same distance, you would find yourself in similar climate areas. Generally, the climate gets drier in regular bands as you move away from the equator.

3. Near the equator in Africa is a large rain forest. It extends from the Gulf of Guinea on the west to the highlands of East Africa. The rain forest of the Congo River is very much like the rain forest of the Amazon River in South America. It is always hot and rainy. The air is still, and there is rarely a wind of more than ten miles an hour. The treetops are so thick that leaves keep sunlight from reaching the forest floor. Thus, there are few bushes. Along rivers the sun gets through to the ground. The tangle of heavy undergrowth makes travel along the riverbanks difficult. Many animals—birds, snakes, monkeys, and apes—live in the rain forest. So do mosquitoes that carry malaria and yellow fever.

4. Most of Africa is made up of dry grasslands called *savanna*. Savannas lie north, south, and east of the rain forests. Here summer is the rainy season, and the winters are dry and dusty. It is always hot. During the dry

The Lobe River, Cameroon. This equatorial nation contains thousands of acres of unspoiled rain forest.

Clifton Beach, near Capetown, South Africa.

season, the grasses turn brown. Cattle and people grow thin as food becomes scarce. During the rainy season the earth is green again and grain grows. Cattle and people find more food and begin to fill out. Most African farms and pasture lands are in the savanna areas. This is the area where Africa's large animals—antelopes, lions, elephants, giraffes, and zebras—live.

5. In the area of western Africa called the Sahel, the savanna is turning into desert. Overgrazing and cutting firewood stripped the land of plants and trees. When drought hits, as it has in the 1980s and 1990s, the remaining vegetation is lost. Desert spreads over pastures and farms. This destructive process is called *desertification.* Losing good farm land has made producing enough food for the population almost impossible.

6. North and south of the savannas are the deserts. The great Sahara occupies nearly all the northern part of the continent. Days in the desert are very hot. However, nights can be extremely chilly. That is because there are no clouds to keep the day's heat from escaping into space. The smaller Kalahari Desert lies in southern Africa. The edges of the desert may receive as much as ten inches (25 centimeters) of rain a year, but most of this area rarely has rainfall. Very little can grow in the dry, barren desert regions.

7. You will remember from your study of North Africa that the lands of the northern coasts border the Mediterranean Sea. They have the sunny climate of the Mediterranean. The same climate is found at the southwestern tip of Africa near Cape Town. The summers are almost rainless. Whatever rain there is comes during the winter months.

8. The southeastern coast has a humid-subtropical climate. Southeastern Africa is about 35 degrees of latitude from the equator and is on the east coast of a large continent. It has the same climate we find in other regions that are similarly located. Such regions include Argentina and Uruguay in South America, and the southeastern region of the United States. Summers are hot and winters mild to cool. There is enough rainfall for farming.

9. Rainfall is a problem in most of Africa. Some parts get too much, while others get too little. The savanna and the Mediterranean

437

regions both have very dry seasons. One year the rains may come early and soak the earth. In other years they may be too late and too skimpy. There are few ways of storing water for the dry season. What is worse, the heavy rains wash important minerals out of the soil. These rains make the land difficult to farm.

10. Africa's environment affects Africa's population and economy. A deadly disease called malaria is caused by a mosquito that thrives in the warm, moist climate of the African coast. Africans who survive childhood cases of malaria will be weakened as adults and have shorter lives. Another disease called sleeping sickness affects humans and animals. The disease is spread by the tsetse fly, which lives in the savanna. Infected cattle cannot be used for food, and infected horses and oxen cannot be used for transportation or plowing. These and other diseases, such as AIDS, have prevented economic development and slowed progress in parts of Africa. Massive efforts by Africans and worldwide health organizations are being directed at controlling and preventing these destructive diseases in sub-Saharan Africa.

UNDERSTANDING WHAT YOU HAVE READ

1. Which of the following questions are answered in this chapter?
a. Why isn't it always hot in the tropics?
b. Where is the Kalahari Desert?
c. Why is life difficult in sub-Sahara Africa?

2. The main idea of this chapter is to describe
a. the climate of Africa
b. the animals of Africa
c. how people live in the Sahara

3. Most of Africa has the climate of the
a. rain forest
b. savanna
c. desert

4. The tsetse fly causes
a. malaria
b. sleeping sickness
c. smallpox

5. One reason why life is hard in parts of Africa is that
a. it is too cold in the mountains
b. there are many sandstorms
c. diseases are common

DEVELOPING CRITICAL THINKING SKILLS

Making Inferences

The following statements are conclusions, or inferences, that you might make after reading this chapter. On a separate piece of paper, tell whether these conclusions are correct or incorrect. Give reasons for your answers.
1. The mountains of eastern Africa are usually cooler than the plains of western Africa.
2. A person is more likely to get malaria in a rain forest than in a savanna.
3. If you walk north from an African rain forest, you will probably reach a savanna.
4. A good time to plant around Cape Town would be in May.
5. Both the east and west coasts of a large continent at about 35 degrees of latitude probably have similar climates.

DEVELOPING IDEAS AND SKILLS

Building Map Skills — Climates of Africa

Study the map below. Then answer the following questions.

1. Where are Africa's tropical rain forests found?
2. (a) Which climates are in Mali? (b) Which are in Tanzania? (c) Which are in Botswana?
3. (a) Which nations have a humid subtropical climate? (b) Which have a vertical climate?

4. (a) Describe the savanna climate. (b) What is the summer like in the savanna? (c) What is the winter like? (d) What health problems do people and animals in the savanna face?
5. (a) List two similarities between the climates in Africa and the climates in South America. (b) List two differences.

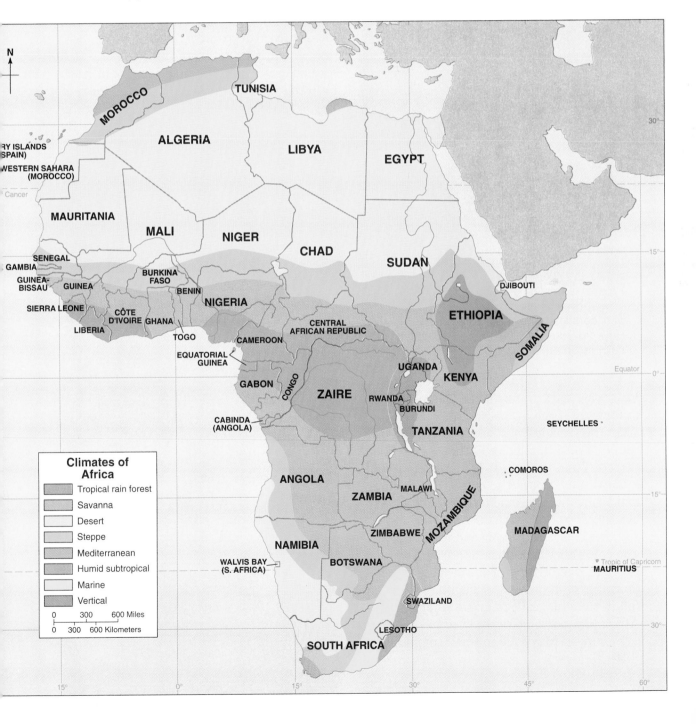

Climates of Africa

- Tropical rain forest
- Savanna
- Desert
- Steppe
- Mediterranean
- Humid subtropical
- Marine
- Vertical

0   300   600 Miles
0   300   600 Kilometers

Chapter 4

Empires Rise and Fall

What great empires arose in early Africa?

READING FOR A PURPOSE:
1. What was the first great civilization in Africa?
2. What riches did Africa have that made outsiders interested in the continent?
3. How did European nations come to have colonies in Africa?

1. In 1959, scientists Mary and Louis Leakey were excavating in the Olduvai [OHL-duh-way] Gorge, in present-day Tanzania. There they made a surprising discovery—the remains of a human skull that was almost three million years old! That evidence and other discoveries led scientists to conclude that East Africa was the birthplace of human life.

2. Africa has had a long and varied history. The Nile Valley in northeastern Africa was the home of one of the world's earliest civilizations: Egypt. Empires and kingdoms rose and fell in the Nile Valley and in other parts of Africa. But not all Africans lived in kingdoms or empires. Many lived in small communities

440

without a strong central government.

3. The great Egyptian civilization arose about 3500 B.C. Egyptians developed some of the earliest systems of mathematics, astronomy, writing, and religion. They also pioneered in engineering, architecture, and medical knowledge. Egyptians and other Africans braved the dangerous *cataracts,* or powerful rapids, of the Nile River to trade and travel, so ideas spread. People from many parts of Africa contributed to Egyptian culture. Meanwhile, Egyptian customs, skills, and ideas reached deep into Africa.

4. As early as 750 B.C., other empires had formed in eastern Africa. The empire of Kush (also called Nubia) lay along the Nile south of Egypt. At one point Kush became so powerful it conquered and ruled southern Egypt. By 200 B.C., Meroë [MER-uh-way], the capital of Kush, was an important iron-producing area. Meroë traded with the Middle East and other parts of Africa.

5. The empire of Axum [AHK-soom] (in what is now Ethiopia) was also a trading nation. Traders from Axum and other parts of Africa bought ivory and other products from

The ancient Zimbabwe ruins located in present-day Zimbabwe were built about 1,000 years ago.

the African interior. These products were then sold to India and countries around the Mediterranean. In about A.D. 350, Axum's army destroyed Meroë. About the same time, Axum's king became a Christian. To this day, many of Ethiopia's people are Christians.

6. The religion of Islam swept through northern Africa in the A.D. 600s. Over hundreds of years, Islam gained many followers. Islam became the leading religion of eastern and northern Africa. Along the east coast, Muslim cities such as Kilwa carried on trade in gold, ivory, cotton, and slaves with the Middle East, India, and China.

7. South of the Sahara, in the grasslands and forests of western Africa, a succession of empires arose. The most important of these empires were Ghana, Mali, and Songhai. Ghana formed about A.D. 700. From about 1300 Mali dominated the region. By 1500 Songhai had replaced Mali as the leading power. These empires had cities and powerful governments. They carried on a busy trade across the Sahara with North Africans. The traders from the north introduced the religion of Islam to West Africa. Today, many West Africans are Muslims.

8. In southeast Africa, a city called Zimbabwe [zihm-BAHB-way] became the center of a trading empire. This empire reached its height in the 1400s. Huge stone buildings and walls were constructed without mortar or cement. From these large structures, Zimbabwe's rulers carried on a successful trade in gold and copper.

9. Until the late 1400s, the people of Africa had few contacts with Europe. Then the rulers of Portugal began a search for an all-water route from Europe to India. They were interested in trade. The Portuguese sea captains sailed along the coast of Africa. They traded with the Africans and returned with shiploads of gold and ivory.

10. Soon, Portugal had established trading posts or stations along the eastern and western coasts of Africa. To those stations, Africans brought goods for sale. Other nations besides Portugal set up their own trading posts. Several European countries divided up the land along Africa's coasts. In 1652, Dutch farmers settled at the southern tip of the continent in what is today called Cape Town. Other whites came to settle in Africa. They planted crops from the Americas such as corn, peanuts, tobacco, potatoes, and tomatoes. African farmers soon started farming those crops.

11. Meanwhile, the Atlantic slave trade had begun in West Africa. In the 1500s, Europeans began to capture or buy Africans to enslave them. Ships carried African captives to European colonies in the Americas. The Europeans did not go into Africa's interior for their captives. They bought most of them from powerful African groups that raided their neighbors, carrying off men, women, and children. The slave trade lasted into the 1800s. It caused great suffering among those who were enslaved and destroyed many once wealthy African societies.

12. Slowly, Europeans extended their control. First, they learned more about Africa's interior. During the 1800s, explorers like Mungo Park, John Speke, and David

Did Stanley and Livingstone improve life for Africans, or did they change Africans' lives for the worse? Why?

441

Livingstone traveled through many areas. They drew maps so that other Europeans could find their way. The explorers' reports called attention to Africa's riches: gold, ivory, animal skins, fine tropical woods. This was a time when European nations were looking for raw materials for their factories. They also wanted places to sell their manufactured goods.

13. Next, Christian missionaries came. They wanted to convert Africans to the Christian religion. They also established schools and hospitals.

14. Then, European soldiers arrived to take control. Sometimes they had to fight African armies, or the armies of other European nations. Africans won some important battles. In the end, however, the European armies with their modern weapons were too strong. By the late 1880s, Great Britain, France, Belgium, Germany, and Italy had divided most of Africa into colonies.

15. The Europeans drew borders without regard to boundaries already established by existing African kingdoms and ethnic groups. Some boundaries divided African peoples who spoke the same language or shared the same culture. Some lumped many different peoples together in one colony. Some of those unfair and senseless boundary lines are still causing problems today, as you will read in the next chapter.

16. For a time, Ethiopia and Liberia were the only independent countries on the entire continent. Liberia, on the west coast, had been started in 1822 by American Africans who had formerly been enslaved. After winning their freedom, they chose to return to Africa. Until the mid-1950s, only two other nations—South Africa (ruled by whites) and Egypt—had gained independence. However, within the past four decades, African peoples have shaken off European rule and established their own governments.

UNDERSTANDING WHAT YOU READ

1. Which of the following questions are answered in this chapter?
a. What famous empires arose in Africa?
b. What are the Great Lakes of Africa?
c. Why were Europeans interested in Africa in the 1600s?

2. The main idea of this chapter is to describe
a. the exchange of goods between Europe and Africa
b. how missionaries opened Africa
c. the history of Africa

3. The first great African civilization was in
a. Egypt
b. Axum
c. Zimbabwe

4. An African empire that ruled over Egypt for a time was
a. Kush

b. Ghana
c. Ethiopia

5. An ancient empire of West Africa was
a. Songhai
b. Axum
c. Egypt

6. Europeans became interested in Africa in the 1600s chiefly because they
a. needed raw materials for factories
b. wanted slaves and ivory
c. wished to make the land safe for missionaries

7. Two African countries that never fell under European rule were
a. Egypt and Zimbabwe
b. Liberia and Ethiopia
c. Ghana and Portugal

Save the Animals

Can you imagine an Africa without elephants, gorillas, or zebras? These and many other animals in Africa are threatened with *extinction* in the next century unless given special help by humans. Extinction means the animals will be lost forever.

Endangered Animals. Wildlife experts classify animals at greatest risk as "endangered." Endangered animals are the most likely to become extinct in the near future.

Africa's rhinos are endangered. Hunters have killed so many that no white rhinos now live in Africa except in zoos, national parks, and special reserves. Black rhinos also face extinction. There are now only about 3,500 black rhinos in Africa, down from 65,000 in 1970. Many rhinos are killed each year for their horns. Some people believe that powdered rhino horns restore health and are willing to pay high prices for them.

Africa's gorilla population is also at risk. Wildlife experts estimate that only between 5,000 and 15,000 gorillas are now left in Africa. Farmers clearing new land for crops have destroyed much of the environment; gorillas need to survive.

Threatened Animals. Wildlife experts list animals at lesser risk as "threatened." Threatened animals are not in immediate peril, but are having trouble surviving in the wild. Zebras, leopards, and chimpanzees are among Africa's threatened wildlife.

Save the Elephant. Africa's elephants are considered at a special risk. The number of elephants in Africa is now only 625,000, down from 1.3 million in 1979. Elephants are illegally hunted in Africa for their valuable ivory tusks.

Reaching a Balance. Protecting the balance of nature is a major reason to save animals at risk. Extinction upsets natural food chains established over millions of years.

Saving a valuable global resource is another reason to save animals at risk. Many animals may now appear to be of little value to humans, but they may become important new sources of food and medicines in the future.

Conservation Efforts. One way to conserve, or save, Africa's animals is to protect their environment. Many African countries now have preserves and national parks where farming and ranching are forbidden.

Another way to save the animals is to make them more valuable alive than dead. The East African nation of Kenya encourages tourists to come and see animals living in protected areas. "Ranching" or "harvesting" animals is also used. In ranching, animals are raised for hunting and food, but their numbers are always kept high enough to guarantee survival.

A third way to save the animals is to stop or limit trade in threatened and endangered animals. An international agreement now bans all trade in raw ivory, leopard skins, and rhino products. **Why might some countries oppose wildlife conservation? How can people in the United States save Africa's wildlife?**

Chapter 5

The African World

How are Africa's people building a modern society with traditional roots?

READING FOR A PURPOSE:
1. How do the lives of people in Africa show great diversity?
2. How are traditional ways changing in modern-day Africa?
3. What challenges do Africans face today?

How might classes for these Muslim students in Kenya differ from a classroom in the United States?

1. About 680 million people live in Africa, with about 570 million of those people living in the region south of the Sahara. Africa is the third most populated and the fastest-growing region in the world. This is a region of great *diversity,* or variety of ethnic groups. There are over 2,000 ethnic groups. These groups are united by their own customs and their own language. Language experts have identified over 800 African languages. Many are part of a language group called Bantu. Besides African groups, small numbers of Asians, whites, and people of mixed heritage (or parentage) live in Africa.

2. Each ethnic group or community has its own cultural characteristics, customs, and traditions. The way groups live can be very different. This is especially true for those who live in traditional rural communities, such as the two we will study in this chapter: Bangway of Cameroon and the San of southern Africa. (At the end of this chapter, you will read how traditional ways are fast changing in the cities of Africa.)

3. The Bangway of Cameroon in West Africa base their economy on coffee, palm oil, pig rearing, and trade. Many young men have migrated to cities in search of jobs. Therefore, women play an even more important role in

Bangway society than usual. Women are both farmers and traders, controlling their own farms and crops. They are the primary source of labor. The Bangway encourage women's education. Female teachers and midwives make important contributions to their families' income.

A chief of Ghana with members of his group. Today in Africa there are many hundreds of ethnic groups, each with its own language and culture.

4. The Bangway's traditional religion centers on ancestor worship. People pray to their ancestors for help in solving the problems of everyday life. The traditional political system centers on a chief. While only men can be chiefs, women can serve as *princesses royale.* A princess royale is highly respected by the chief and often influences him. Ordinary people form groups where they can discuss events, dance, and socialize.

5. The San culture in southern Africa is different from that of the Bangway. Traditionally, the San *subsist,* or survive, by hunting and gathering. They practice *collective ownership* of resources—all members of a group share equally. Usually, women gather food, carry water, collect firewood, cook, and raise children. Men hunt, gather food on the way home from hunting, prepare skins, and make the clothes. Young people are close to their elders, who serve as role models.

6. In the San culture, decisions are made by members of the various groups involved. For example, hunters make decisions about hunting, while gatherers may decide about food collection.

7. Although a majority of Africans today live in rural areas, urban growth is increasing rapidly. Between 1950 and 1979, the population in the cities grew from 21 million to 93 million, an increase of 450 percent. For the 30 years from 1980 to 2010, the United Nations predicts the urban population will increase another 475 percent, to 441 million!

8. Many Africans have left the countryside to earn a living in cities. Men and women work in a variety of occupations. Some work in factories that produce cloth, furniture, canned goods, or shoes. Others work for businesses in such fields as photography, electronics, construction, and machine repair. Because opportunities in education are greater in the city, Africans study to become lawyers, doctors, engineers, and teachers. Members of the growing middle class often own their own businesses or work for the government.

445

A day care center in Harare, the capital of Zimbabwe. As more Africans move to cities, the need for services such as day care centers for the children of working mothers increases.

9. City life can be lively and exciting. Modern conveniences such as telephones and electricity are more common in the city. However, there are problems. Sometimes there are too few jobs. Often, there are not enough houses, and people end up living in crowded slums.

10. In both rural areas and cities, Africans are working to improve their lives. In the cities, Africans are building economies that can compete with other nations of the world.

Improvements in housing, transportation, education, and health care have made cities better places to live. In rural areas, Africans are fighting to improve health care while they are learning how to increase agricultural production in the face of drought. All over the continent, Africans are successfully adapting their traditional patterns to modern ways of life. They are building societies for the future that are deeply rooted in Africa's past and present.

UNDERSTANDING WHAT YOU HAVE READ

1. Which of the following questions are answered in this chapter?

a. Why have many Africans left the countryside and moved to cities?

b. How are African governments organized?

c. What are the important land forms in Africa?

2. The main idea of this chapter is to describe

a. the varieties of occupations in Africa

b. the traditional ways and modern changes in Africa

c. the role of women in African societies

3. The Bangway of Cameroon in West Africa base their economy on
   a. fish, salt, and trade
   b. yams, peanut oil, and leather
   c. coffee, palm oil, and pig rearing

4. Today women play an even more important role in Bangway society because
   a. they have more free time than men
   b. many men have migrated to the cities
   c. only women can be chiefs

5. Traditionally, the San in southern Africa subsist by
   a. slash-and-burn agriculture
   b. wage labor
   c. hunting and gathering

6. One of the problems in African cities is
   a. lack of educational opportunities
   b. not enough jobs
   c. too many factories

7. Most Africans live in
   a. mining regions
   b. rural areas
   c. cities

8. Africans are working to improve their lives in rural areas by
   a. building factories
   b. focusing on health care
   c. rejecting their traditional way of life

DEVELOPING CRITICAL THINKING SKILLS

Do You Agree or Disagree?

Tell whether you agree or disagree with the following statements. Give reasons for your answers.

1. The population of Africa south of the Sahara is growing rapidly.
2. There are many different ethnic groups in Africa.
3. Communication among groups is easy because Africans speak the same language.
4. There are large groups of Asians and whites living in Africa.
5. All Africans are either Christian or Muslim.
6. The traditional religion of the Bangway of Cameroon centers on animal spirits.
7. Traditionally, San hunters own individual plots of land.
8. The urban population in Africa is expected to decrease.
9. One problem that Africans have worked to improve is health care.
10. Africans think that their traditional ways of life are important.

WRITING

Now that you have read about two African ethnic groups, the Bangway and the San, write an essay that answers the following questions.

(a)Where are these groups located? (b)How do the different environments in these two areas affect the way that they make a living? (c)How might the migration of young men to the cities affect the way they make a living in the future?

DEVELOPING IDEAS AND SKILLS

Building Map Skills — Population, Area, and Standard of Living

Can you answer these questions?

1. Is the standard of living of this region high or low compared with that of the United States? Is it a developed or developing area?
2. Is the region as crowded as the United States?
3. Are the people of this region literate compared with people of the United States?
4. How long may the average person in this region expect to live?
5. What facts tell you the standard of living of the people of the region?
6. How does this region compare with the United States in size?

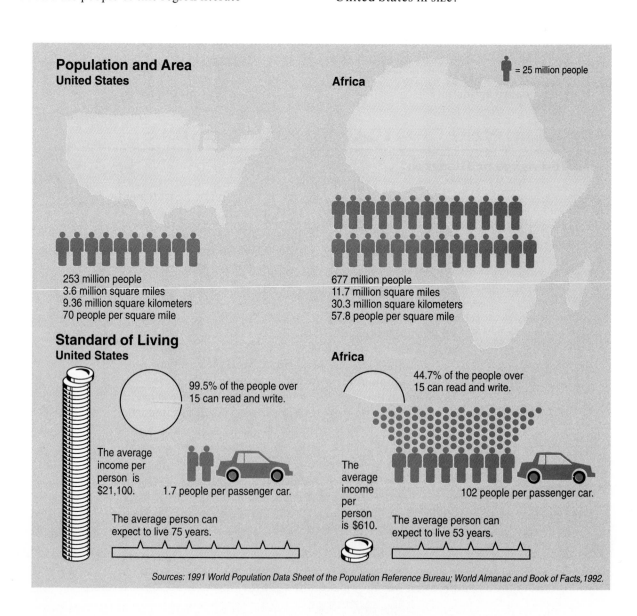

Population and Area

United States

Africa

= 25 million people

253 million people
3.6 million square miles
9.36 million square kilometers
70 people per square mile

677 million people
11.7 million square miles
30.3 million square kilometers
57.8 people per square mile

Standard of Living

United States

99.5% of the people over 15 can read and write.

The average income per person is $21,100.

1.7 people per passenger car.

The average person can expect to live 75 years.

Africa

44.7% of the people over 15 can read and write.

The average income per person is $610.

102 people per passenger car.

The average person can expect to live 53 years.

Sources: 1991 World Population Data Sheet of the Population Reference Bureau; World Almanac and Book of Facts, 1992.

Chapter 6

The Rain-Forest Farmer

How do African farmers meet their needs?

READING FOR A PURPOSE:
1. How do the rain-forest people live?
2. What is migratory farming?
3. What is plantation farming?

1. As you have learned, much of the climate in sub-Sahara Africa is either rain forest or savanna. These climates are not good for farming. Despite this fact, most people in Africa south of the Sahara are either farmers or herders of cattle. Starting with the rain forest, let us see what kind of farming is carried on by the people who live there.

2. The rain-forest people live in small villages near a stream or river. The village houses are small and dark. They have cone-shaped roofs made of grass and leaves. The shape of the roof allows the rain to run off quickly. Around the village are the clearings for the main food crops, such as bananas, yams, rice, and manioc. Manioc is a plant with a root like a potato. It is the source of the bread of rain-forest peoples. Besides these crops, the people grow fruits and vegetables in small gardens.

3. Usually the women do the farming. The women farm the clearing with simple tools like the hoe and digging stick. The yields from their fields are very low. The men fish and hunt, but meat is hard to get. There are few cows in the rain forest because they die of the tropical diseases. When the crop or the hunt is good, there is plenty to eat. However, the food cannot be kept long because it spoils in the heat. When the crops are poor, the problem of having enough food is serious. Some men earn money by gathering palm-oil nuts or rubber.

4. Rain-forest people farm in a region where the soil is poor. Usually they cannot afford to buy fertilizer or farm machinery. So many Africans use a kind of farming called *migratory* or *shifting* farming. This involves moving from place to place over a number of years. When the soil is no longer productive in one area, the farmers move. They clear new fields. The trees are cut down, but the stumps remain. The thick undergrowth is cut and burned. The ashes enrich the soil. Crops are planted among the tree stumps. These crops grow well for about two or three years. Then the farming group moves out and looks for a new place to clear. The thick brush returns to the old fields and puts back in the soil some of the minerals crops need. After a number of years, the area is ready to be farmed again.

5. Most rain-forest people are subsistence farmers. When families grow more food than they need, the extra, or surplus, is sold at the village market. In this way, they can obtain products not available in their area. Plantation farming is also found in the rain forest. Coffee, tea, peanuts, timber, and rubber are important cash crops. At one time, many of the plantations were owned by foreigners but were worked by Africans. Today a growing number of farms and plantations are owned by Africans or African governments.

6. The palm nut, from which oil is made, is

one of Africa's leading cash crops. The soap or cosmetics you use today may be made from Africa's palm oil. The oil palm grows wild in the Congo rain forest. Plantations are also located along the river valleys. Africa produces 90 percent of the world's supply of palm nuts. Most of the nuts are shipped to Europe for processing—that is, changing into oil products such as margarine and cooking oil. Other uses for palm oil include palm wine, lubricants, and medicine. The leading producers of palm nuts are Nigeria and Sierra Leone.

7. Most likely the chocolate you eat comes from the cacao trees of Africa. Côte d'Ivoire, Ghana, Nigeria, and Cameroon, produce about *half* the world's total supply of cacao beans. The cacao trees grow best in the tropical climate. People gather the pods from the trees and remove the beans. Then the beans are carried to the trading stations located along the rivers. The bulk of the crop is shipped to the United States and Europe where cacao beans are made into chocolate. The money earned in Africa from selling cash crops is often used to import food from other parts of the world.

"Wheels" of chocolate at a factory in western Africa.

UNDERSTANDING WHAT YOU HAVE READ

1. Which of the following questions are answered in this chapter?
a. Why is the oil palm important?
b. How do the Africans work with iron?
c. What crops are raised on plantations?

2. The main idea of this chapter is to describe
a. how the African makes use of wood products
b. the major products of the rain forest
c. how rain-forest people travel

3. Among the most important plantation crops of the African rain forest are
a. palm nuts and cacao beans
b. olives and oranges
c. corn and millet

4. The chief foods of the rain-forest people are
a. proteins, like meat and beans
b. starches, like manioc and yams
c. sugars, like chocolate and oranges

5. Farming is difficult in the rain forest because
a. the land is hilly
b. weeds grow rapidly
c. soils are poor

6. The oil of the palm nut is important because
a. Africans use it for heating their homes
b. it is used to help make machinery run more smoothly
c. it is an important export crop

7. Throughout the African continent, much of the farming is done by
   a. men
   b. women
   c. machines

8. Which statement is TRUE of African farming?
   a. There are many forms of farming in Africa south of the Sahara.
   b. In general, African farmers grow more food than they can use.
   c. African farmers never leave the land idle.

9. Which crop is not matched properly with the country where it is grown?
   a. Sierra Leone—palm oil
   b. South Africa—rubber
   c. Côte d'Ivoire—cacao beans

10. Which statement is TRUE of Africa's farming today?
    a. Europeans are becoming more active on Africa's farms.
    b. African farmers may often sell some crops in the local market.
    c. Most cash crops are raised by women.

DEVELOPING CRITICAL THINKING SKILLS

I. Making Generalizations

Below are several generalizations based on Chapters 4, 5, and 6. After you read each generalization, see if you can offer *proof* from these chapters to support the statement.

1. Where people live decides in part how they live.
2. The culture in which people live has an influence on their thoughts and actions.
3. Family organization is not the same in all societies, nor in all periods of history.
4. People develop their own rules and laws to live together depending upon the place where they live and how they live.
5. Change in one part of the world affects people in other parts of the world.

II. Making Inferences

In our reading, many facts are given to us. From these facts we can draw conclusions. The following are some conclusions or inferences that you might make after reading this chapter. Tell whether these conclusions are correct or incorrect. Give reasons for your answers.

1. Farmers of the rain forest use little fertilizer on their land.
2. Wheat bread is little known to rain-forest families.
3. At night, after a hard day's work, rain-forest families probably spend some time reading.
4. When Africans go to the city, they will probably look for other people from their own ethnic group.
5. Apple orchards are probably found in the rain forest.
6. Some customs of American men and women might change if the United States stopped trade with Ghana and Nigeria.
7. The African rain forest grows back almost as fast as people can clear it away.
8. Drier areas of Africa usually have the greatest number of insects.
9. Most people in the rain forest have plenty to eat.
10. Most rain-forest people live near rivers.

451

The Savanna Farmer and Herder

How do many Africans adapt to the wet and dry lands?

READING FOR A PURPOSE:
1. What farming methods are used by the Hausa?
2. What is the difference between herding in western Africa and on the plateaus of East Africa?
3. Why are cattle important to the herders of East Africa?

1. Africans of the savannas are usually farmers or herders. In the northern grasslands of western Africa live the Hausa people. They are farmers who live in houses of dried mud thatched with grass. Like most African farmers, the Hausa use only a hoe or digging stick. They build ridges on their farmland to catch the water during the rainy season and hold it for the dry season. Their chief crop is corn. They use the grain for food and the stalks for roofs and fences. They also grow wheat, millet, and yams. The Hausa grow crops to feed

themselves and their families. Some of them may grow a cash crop such as peanuts to get money for other goods.

2. Some of the farming peoples of western Africa are also herders. However, raising cattle is difficult in this area. Good cattle cannot be grazed on the western savannas because of the disease-carrying tsetse fly. The cattle are thin, particularly in the dry season. The little milk they give is used to make butter and cheese. When the animals die, their hides are sold and tanned to make clothing.

3. In the highlands of eastern Africa, safe from the tsetse fly, herding is the chief occupation. Two typical herding groups are the Masai of Tanzania and Kenya and the Karamojong of northeast Uganda. The Masai wander with their herds. They are nomads like the Bedouins of the Middle East. The Masai measure their wealth in cattle. They rarely kill their animals for food or use them to provide fertilizer. Their chief use for cattle is their milk.

4. During the rainy season, Masai herders keep their cattle in the valleys. During the dry season, they move to the highlands where there is more rain and more grass. The cattle have a hump of fat on their backs. When there isn't enough food to eat during the dry season, the cattle "use" the fat they have stored. In this, they are like the camels of North Africa. The Masai have so many cows on the grazing lands that the grass is soon killed and the soil is washed away when the rains come. While

A Hausa village and cattle in Niger. In this dry country, there are few good places for growing crops. Raising good cattle is also difficult.

A Masai family in Tanzania.

A Masai girl in Kenya.

the men are away, the women care for any crops that are planted.

5. When several Masai families decide to live in a group, they set up a small village, called a *kraal*, for themselves and their animals. To keep out enemies and wild animals they build a circular fence of thorny bush around the kraal. Inside the fence, the women build round houses of branches and grass. In the center of the kraal is a large open space for the cattle. Each morning the men of the group drive the cattle out into the grazing land. The cattle are watched carefully during the day and returned to the village at night. Whenever there is a need for new pasture, the herders move on and set up a new village.

6. The Karamojong live on a plateau. They also live in thatched villages near wells or a river bank where they can raise crops as well as tend herds of cattle, goats, and sheep. The men and boys take care of the herds. The women and girls tend the fields, grind the grain, fetch the water, and collect the firewood. The chief food is a grain called *sorghum*. It is planted in the dry season and ripens in the rainy season. It is eaten with sour milk or vegetables. During the dry season the men move the cattle far from the village in search of grass and water. As with the Masai, guarding cattle is the Karamojong way of life. The animals make it possible for the men to marry and support their families.

7. Unfortunately, the Masai way of life is passing. The industrialized world is closing in upon them. The lion hunts and cattle raids in which the Masai warrior proved his courage are no longer permitted. As time goes on, more land is taken from them to use for farming or as national parks. As they continue to lose grazing lands there will be fewer and fewer cattle. The Masai and other herding groups will be forced off the land into the big cities. They will then have to get jobs and learn to live in the modern world. Will these people be able to survive in a modern Kenya and Tanzania?

8. As you have learned, many of sub-Sahara Africa's people are herders or subsistence farmers. As such, their incomes are low and they cannot buy many goods. In recent years there has been an increase in the number of cash crops such as cacao, coffee, sisal, palm oil, peanuts, and cotton. These crops are grown on both small farms and plantations.

453

UNDERSTANDING WHAT YOU HAVE READ

1. Which of the following questions are answered in this chapter?
   a. What is sorghum?
   b. How do peanuts grow?
   c. Why do herding groups move?

2. The main idea of this chapter is to describe
   a. how Africans use the dry grasslands
   b. the customs of the Masai
   c. life in African villages

3. The chief form of wealth of the Masai is their
   a. corn
   b. camels
   c. cattle

4. An important food crop of the grasslands is
   a. palm oil
   b. cacao
   c. corn

5. The Masai are always on the move because they
   a. fear attacks by other tribes
   b. need to find new pastures
   c. are looking for fertile farmland

6. Few cattle are grazed in certain parts of the grasslands because
   a. rubber trees have been planted
   b. Africans have little use for cattle
   c. the tsetse fly kills many of the cattle

7. The houses of the savanna farmers are made of
   a. stones
   b. cement blocks
   c. dried mud

8. All of these are food *grains* grown in the grasslands EXCEPT
   a. yams
   b. sorghum
   c. millet

DEVELOPING IDEAS AND SKILLS

Making Comparisons

Complete the following chart in your notebook.

MASAI HERDERS		BEDOUINS
	Wealth	
	Use of Land	
	Foods	
	Clothing	
	Shelter	
	Goods for Trade	

Mixing Old and New Ways

Many young Africans are caught between worlds, the traditional or the new, the group or the individual. In the villages, people take care of each other. Village members have rules about making a living, building a house, or getting married. The group system is still working well for many Africans. But what happens when the young people leave their homes in the villages and move to the cities? Here is the story of Eremina Mvura, who is trying to mix both worlds, old and new.

Eremina Mvura was born in a small village in Zimbabwe. She was one of seven daughters. Her parents did not want to spend money on educating daughters. Desperate for an education, she pleaded for admission to a convent school. Luckily the convent school took her in. As she got older, she became a "community development officer," a person who helps to bring certain basic services, such as health clinics and schools, to poor villages. Eremina was a community development officer first with the nuns and later with the Zimbabwe government. In 1978, she went to Skiaobou, a small town near the Zambian border.

In Africa, many women do much of the hard work in the village. To win the confidence of the women in Skiaobou, Eremina began to share their life. Like other women, she would awaken at 3:00 in the morning to pound grain into flour on a mortar. At sunrise, she would go to the river to get water. Then she would go into the fields to remove weeds. Sometimes Eremina would also climb the watchtower to chase away wild animals like elephants and lions. At sunset, she would prepare supper, gather more water and wood, and if she had energy, bathe herself. In the evening, Eremina would sleep lightly in her thatched hut, listening for wild animals.

Eremina is working hard with the women. The burdens of the village women are even harder now than before. Many of the young men have left for the large towns, leaving women behind to take over more of the village jobs. When Eremina saw the need for a school and clinic, she worked alongside the women to mold bricks. The government sent doors, building supplies, medicines, and books. Now they are digging wells to save trips to the river. Eremina Mvura feels she is successfully mixing both worlds. With her early morning and evening chores, she is working like millions of African farm women. With her community work, she feels she is making the best use of her education.

Copy the following statements into your notebook. If you agree with the statement, mark it with an *A*. If you disagree, mark it with a *D*. Correct the statements you disagree with.

1. This story is taking place in South America.
2. Many Africans are now members of two worlds.
3. In many parts of Africa, a person's entire way of life depends upon the group he or she belongs to.
4. The group way of life is no longer part of Eremina Mvura's life.
5. Eremina is using her education to help the poorer members of the village.
6. As the men depart for the towns, women have become more involved in running the village.
7. The government has been helpful in meeting the demand for better health care and education.
8. As more people become educated, new ways of doing things open up for them.

Chapter 8

Africa's Resources

What problems have held back the development of Africa's resources?

READING FOR A PURPOSE:
1. What are the important forest and mineral resources of Africa?
2. Why have Africa's resources not been fully used in the past?

1. Africa south of the Sahara has many resources: animals, forests, minerals, and falling water. There are more different kinds of wild animals in Africa than in any other region. The animals have both helped and harmed Africans. Some peoples of the forest still depend upon hunting for their meat supply. Wild animals are becoming fewer in number, as place after place is cleared for settlement. Most remaining large wild animals now live in special areas set aside for them. Thousands of tourists visit these parks each year.

2. Of more importance to the people of Af-

rica are the trees and plants. Great forests still cover about one-third of Africa. From certain trees come the raw materials for many waxes and medicines. In the rain forests are valuable hardwood trees: mahogany, ebony, and many others. Many trees are being cut down. International companies use the trees to make wood products. Many Africans use the trees to supply their fuel needs. Some governments, such as Nigeria's and the Côte d'Ivoire's, are planting thousands of new trees.

3. The land contains great mineral riches. The most important industry in Africa is mining. Many of the mineral deposits are found in the highland areas. One of the world's richest mining areas is in the southeastern part of Zaire and in Zambia. Zaire leads all regions of the world in the mining of industrial diamonds. (Because diamonds are so hard, they are used in high-speed drills in factories.) Zaire and Zambia are also leading copper producers. Cobalt, used in the manufacture of jet engines and special steel, is also mined in Zaire and Zambia.

4. Important mining areas also extend south into Zimbabwe and the Republic of South Africa as well. South Africa has long been famous for its gold and diamonds. These diamonds are large and very beautiful. They are made into jewelry. Gold mines are located near the city of Johannesburg. For this reason it is sometimes called the "City Built on Gold." Uranium, now one of the world's most important minerals, is also mined in South Africa. Uranium is used in producing atomic power.

5. West Africa is one of the world's major oil-producing areas. Nigeria and Gabon are members of OPEC. Angola, Congo, Cameroon, Zaire, and the Côte d'Ivoire are also developing their oil resources. In West Africa, Ghana has large deposits of manganese, gold, diamonds, and bauxite. The small nation of Guinea has about one-third of the world's supply of bauxite, from which aluminum is made. Nigeria has rich supplies of tin. Iron

Akosombo Dam in Ghana.

ore deposits are found in South Africa, Guinea, Liberia, and Sierra Leone.

6. Mining is big business in Africa. Thousands of workers are needed in the mines. Mining companies bring Africans from a wide area to live in the villages built by the mining companies. The Africans come because more money can be earned in the mines than on the farms. The movement of people from the farms to the mines has done much to change the life of Africans. More and more, they work for wages and have new needs.

7. Most of Africa's riches have not been fully used. There are several reasons. First, until recently, most mines were directed by foreigners, and most of the profits went back to owners in Europe and America. While Africa's new leaders still allow foreigners to develop their resources, Africans keep a bigger share of the profits. In this way they are raising money for the needs of their people.

8. Second, fuel to supply power is scarce. Parts of West Africa are now producing oil. Yet most sub-Sahara countries are importing millions of dollars worth of oil. Except in South Africa, there is little coal. Waterpower could be used, for Africa has the greatest waterpower resources in the world. But waterpower projects are expensive. Some nations are developing their water resources. For example, there are big power projects in Zaire, Zambia, and Zimbabwe. Ghana has its huge Akosombo Dam and plans other dams on the Volta River.

9. Third, factories need skilled workers. However, a great number of Africans have not had the opportunity to go to school. African leaders today recognize the need for education and are building schools and universities for their citizens.

10. Fourth, there are few good highways and railroads in sub-Sahara Africa. What railroads there are do not connect with other roads to form a large transportation system. Then, too, Africa's rivers have many falls and rapids that make them difficult to navigate. The coastline has few good harbors. The highways, railroads, and now airplanes are often in need of repairs because of the beating they take in Africa's difficult climates. Transportation improvement is an important goal for modern Africa.

11. Fifth, the local market for African products has been small. Most of the people do not have the income to buy the products of the farms and mines. Foods and minerals have been shipped to Europe or America,

457

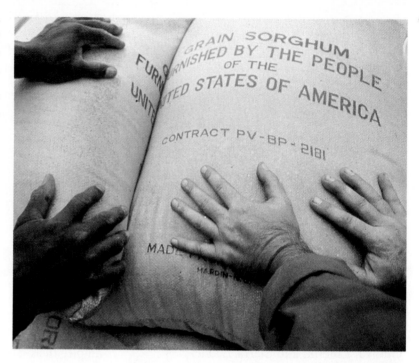

A bag of sorghum is delivered from the United States to African farmers and villagers. Many African nations are working with foreign specialists to find ways to grow more food and thus free themselves from dependency on outside aid.

where they were sold. Now, however, there is a growing number of factories to make use of the products of the continent. Processing plants will use the oils of palm nuts and coconuts. Refineries will use the raw tin, copper, bauxite, and manganese. Textile mills will produce cotton goods.

12. Almost all African countries depend on foreign aid to help them develop their resources. Much of this aid comes from France, the United States, Great Britain, China, Japan, and Israel. Besides aid from individual countries, Africa gets help from the United Nations and low-cost loans from the World Bank. In most cases, the money is used to start new plants, build roads and dams, set up hospitals, and feed the hungry. In some cases, the money is used to buy weapons and build up the armies of military chiefs. In exchange, Africa is a rich and steady source of crops and raw materials needed by the industrial nations.

UNDERSTANDING WHAT YOU HAVE READ

1. Which of the following questions are answered in this chapter?
a. How has mining changed the life of the African?
b. Why are Africa's riches not fully used?
c. How are the minerals brought to the coast?

2. The main idea of this chapter is to describe
a. how Africa trades with the world
b. how Africans work in the mines
c. the variety of riches in Africa

3. Zaire leads in the production of
a. nickel
b. gold
c. industrial diamonds

4. One of the world's major oil-producing areas is located in
a. West Africa
b. East Africa
c. South Africa

5. Zaire has been an important section of Africa because
a. it lies along the trade routes from north to south
b. its mines have copper, cobalt, and diamonds
c. it has the only oil-processing plants in Africa

6. Africa's forests are useful because
a. soils are fertile
b. they contain good grazing lands
c. they provide raw materials for furniture, waxes, medicine, and fuel

DEVELOPING CRITICAL THINKING SKILLS

Do You Agree or Disagree?

Tell whether you agree or disagree with the following statements. Give reasons for your answers.

1. Africa south of the Sahara has few mineral resources.
2. Most of Africa's large wild animals can be found mainly in parks.
3. There are few forests left in sub-Sahara Africa.
4. Fishing is the most important industry in Africa.
5. Zaire and Zambia are rich mining areas.
6. Many Africans work in mines because they can earn more money than if they farmed.
7. African governments are now receiving a larger share of the mining profits.
8. Africa has an adequate transportation system.
9. Many of Africa's raw materials are shipped out of Africa.
10. African countries receive aid from many Western countries.

REVIEWING AND WRITING

Making an Outline

Complete the following outline in your notebook.

Resources of Sub-Sahara Africa

A. Types of resources
   1.
   2.
   3.
   4.

B. Important Minerals
   1.
   2.
   3.
   4.
   5.
   6.
   7.
   8.

C. Reasons why Africa's riches have not been fully used
   1.
   2.
   3.
   4.
   5.

Interpreting a Map and a Bar Graph

This map shows three things: the important exports of Africa south of the Sahara, the leading trading nations in sub-Sahara Africa, and the amount of trade these countries have with the United States. The focus of the map is on the leading exports of the region. The symbols in each country stand for the important exports of that country. (See the map key.)

The map also includes a chart that shows the leading trading nations of the region. Two bar graphs are used for each major trading country. They show the value of both imports and exports. The shaded part of the bars show the amount of trade the country has with the United States. The graph shows at a glance which nations sell more (export) than they buy (import). Nations that sell more than they buy have a "favorable balance of trade." Nations that sell less than they buy have an "unfavorable balance of trade."

Study the map and graphs. Then tell if these statements are true or false.

1. Nigeria sends more goods to the United States than any other sub-Sahara nation.
2. Gabon is a petroleum exporter.
3. Kenya grows coffee for export.
4. South Africa exports more goods to the United States than it imports.
5. Most nations in sub-Sahara Africa export more goods than they import.

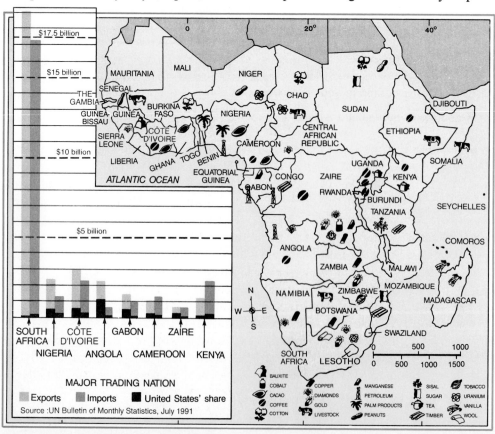

Source :UN Bulletin of Monthly Statistics, July 1991

Chapter 9

From Colonies to Free Countries

How are Africans building new nations after years of being ruled by foreign powers?

READING FOR A PURPOSE:
1. What changes did European rulers make in Africa?
2. How was the "freedom explosion" accomplished?
3. What problems face the new African nations?

1. In 1950, only three nations in Africa were free—Ethiopia, Liberia, and South Africa. Egypt was only partially free, because British troops were on its soil. Today, 53 African nations are independent. A true "freedom explosion" has taken place, ending colonial rule in Africa. Now the nations of Africa can deal with the rest of the world's nations as equals.

2. As you remember, European nations seized control of Africa during the 1800s. Explorers had found great riches there. The leading countries in Western Europe needed raw materials for their factories. Because of this, almost all of Africa was divided into colonies. Three countries—Great Britain, France, and Germany—had the most colonies. Belgium, Italy, Portugal, and Spain also had possessions in Africa.

3. When the Europeans first came to Africa, they made Africans help them develop the riches of mines and forests. Europeans took the best lands for themselves. They laid out roads and railroads to carry the ore and other products to the sea. They trained Africans to run the railroads and to work in the offices. They brought schools and health care to many Africans. They educated Africans for a limited amount of leadership. Although Europeans made life better in some ways, they decided what Africans could learn and what Africans could do. This system is called *imperialism* or *colonialism.* The Africans objected vigorously to their loss of freedom.

4. The European nations planned to keep ruling Africa as long as possible. But World War II seriously weakened the ruling nations. Also, the war disrupted the system of colonialism in many ways. It loosened the ties between European nations and their colonies. During the war, many Africans served in the armies of the Allies. After the war, they saw that people in India, Indonesia, and other European possessions were gaining their freedom. Africans too wanted freedom to make a better life for themselves.

5. The year 1956 was the beginning of the great freedom movement in Africa. Sudan and Morocco were the first African possessions to gain independence. After that, freedom came rapidly to other nations. Compare the map in this chapter with the map in Chapter 1 to find all the changes since 1914. One of the most recent countries to gain its independence is Zimbabwe. Until its independence in 1980, it was known as Southern Rhodesia. An even newer nation is Namibia, once called South-West Africa. After World

An independence day celebration in Somalia.

War I, this territory came under South Africa's rule. It was the last colony in Africa. The United Nations helped to oversee elections that led to Namibia's independence in 1990.

6. The newly formed nations of Africa faced many problems. First, the European nations—especially Belgium and Portugal—had done little to prepare the way for self-rule. In the Belgian Congo (now Zaire) the Belgians allowed only a few Africans to attend universi-

ties. Few people had training in government affairs. The people of the country were surprised when Belgium suddenly announced that it was granting Zaire independence in 1960. Fighting broke out. It flared up many times in the years after independence. Much of the fighting was over the rich mineral deposits the country contains. Today, in some African countries, people recall with resentment their treatment under foreign rule. They believe that European nations took African resources for their own use. They believe that Europeans had little interest in educating Africans for self-government.

7. Second, the new national governments of Africa were troubled by the fact that many people were still loyal to their ethnic groups. Within any one country, there may be many groups, each with its different language and customs. These groups may be very large—as in Nigeria. During the 1960s, a bitter civil war broke out in Nigeria. Some of the leaders of the Ibo people did not want to give up their power to the leaders of the national government. The national leaders belonged to the Hausa people. Civil wars have also broken out in Ethiopia, Liberia, and other nations.

In Africa today, modern comforts are part of the daily life of many. How may problems result when people try to combine their traditional ways with new ways?

462

Loyalty to rival ethnic groups and to rival religions still causes problems today in many African nations.

8. Another problem is that national boundaries separate people of the same background, culture, and language. When the European nations divided Africa in the 19th century, they placed boundary lines in places that were convenient to them. The lines sometimes ran through the middle of ethnic groups. As a result, hundreds of ethnic groups have members in two or more nations. The Somali people of East Africa are divided in this way. Some groups have tried to change the national boundaries that now exist, in order to form new countries based on ethnic groups. Bloody wars have resulted.

9. In addition, many of the governments of the continent do not allow free elections or rival political parties. Some rulers do not protect their citizens' civil liberties. They do not allow freedom of the press. They punish people who hold meetings to discuss political questions. They jail people without a fair trial. In some places, rulers use terror to silence those who criticize them. Terror also occurs when a group within a country uses violence against another group. In recent years, Africans in many countries have been able to change governments that took away their freedoms. They have tried to establish rules that would guarantee those freedoms in the future.

10. Nations outside Africa sometimes try to influence African events. Nations that once had African colonies have kept close ties to the new countries. France, for example, keeps soldiers in many African countries. It does this with the permission of African governments. Other countries have sent weapons or soldiers to Africa at various times. For instance, the United States and the former Soviet Union armed opposite sides in a civil war in Angola in the 1980s.

11. African nations are trying to build a better future for their people. They want to make people forget old hatreds and work together for the good of all. When Zimbabwe became independent in 1980, its president, Robert Mugabe [muh-GAH-bee], urged people to forget the wrongs of the past. He said black peo-

Winnie Mandela, an activist in South Africa.

ple should not hate white people for what had happened during the colonial era. They should not oppress the white citizens of Zimbabwe now that blacks were in charge. "An evil remains an evil whether practiced by white against black or by black against white," said Mugabe. In Zimbabwe and other African nations, people of different racial and ethnic groups are trying to learn to live together as partners.

UNDERSTANDING WHAT YOU HAVE READ

1. Which questions are answered in this chapter?

a. What did European countries do for their African colonies?

b. What happened when Zaire became free?

c. What are the leading ethnic groups of Africa?

2. The main idea of this chapter describes

a. the religions of new African nations

b. how Africa changed from colonies to independent countries

c. why European countries were interested in Africa

3. Much of Africa in 1914 was controlled by

a. the United Kingdom and France

b. Spain and Portugal

c. the United States and the Soviet Union

4. Today, almost all African territory is

a. colonized by European nations

b. controlled by European nations

c. free and independent

5. The first African countries to gain their independence after 1950 were

a. Ghana and Mali

b. Sudan and Morocco

c. Ethiopia and South Africa

6. A big problem that faced many new nations of Africa was that

a. the new governments were ruled by Europeans

b. ethnic groups gave up their old customs

c. few people had the opportunity for an education

DEVELOPING IDEAS AND SKILLS

Building Map Skills — Africa in 1914 and Today

Study this map and the one on page 431. Then answer the questions below.

1. (a) Which nation ruled Egypt?
   (b) Which ruled Libya?
2. Which modern nations emerged from French West Africa?
3. Which nations were free in 1914?
4. (a) Which nation controlled most of West Africa?
   (b) Which controlled most of East Africa?
5. (a) Name one reason why Europeans colonized Africa.
   (b) Name two effects of colonialism on Africans.

SPANISH MOROCCO

ALGERIA

LIBYA

EGYPT

RIO DE ORO

FRENCH WEST AFRICA

ANGLO-EGYPTIAN SUDAN

ERITREA

FRENCH SOMALILAND

BRITISH SOMALILAND

GAMBIA

PORTUGUESE GUINEA

SIERRA LEONE

LIBERIA

GOLD COAST

TOGO

NIGERIA

CAMEROON

EQUATORIAL AFRICA

ETHIOPIA

ITALIAN SOMALILAND

UGANDA

BRITISH EAST AFRICA

FRENCH

BELGIAN CONGO

GERMAN EAST AFRICA

NYASALAND

ANGOLA

NORTHERN RHODESIA

MOZAMBIQUE

MADAGASCAR

GERMAN S.W. AFRICA

BECHUANALAND

SOUTHERN RHODESIA

SOUTH AFRICA (Dominion)

SWAZILAND

BASUTOLAND **Africa in 1914**

Legend:
- ■ FREE COUNTRIES
- ITALIAN COLONIES
- FRENCH COLONIES
- ENGLISH COLONIES
- GERMAN COLONIES
- PORTUGUESE COLONIES
- SPANISH COLONIES
- BELGIAN COLONIES

465

Chapter 10

Developing Africa

What are the problems to be solved in a developing Africa?

READING FOR A PURPOSE:
1. For a region so large in size, why doesn't Africa support a larger population?
2. Why has there been a food problem in Africa?
3. How is present-day Africa meeting its problems?

1. Africa south of the Sahara has many resources. Its gold, diamonds, uranium, oil, and copper already play an important part in world affairs. Yet, people ask, why is Africa south of the Sahara so poor? (The average income in most of these countries is about $581 a year.) Why do so few people live there? By this time, we should be able to supply some of the answers to these questions.

2. First, life is hard in much of Africa. Much of the land is dry. The Sahara is as large as the United States, and the dry lands in the south are as large as most of western Europe. Much of the continent is hot. In the heart of Africa is the steaming rain forest. North and south of the tropical forest is the savanna area, with its wet and dry seasons. The tsetse fly and other harmful insects are present in much of these areas. As a result, large sections of land cannot be used.

3. Second, the heat and rainfall affect everything. The possessions of the African family often rust or rot. The climate makes it hard to get a good "set" in chocolate, so that Ghana must export most of its cacao beans in their raw form. Many kinds of cattle cannot be raised in this heat. Those that are raised give little milk and less meat. The climate makes it difficult to raise crops like peas and beans, which the people of the middle and high latitudes depend on for body growth. Rain-forest people must depend on starchy foods such as bananas, yams, and manioc.

4. In the last 10 years, the countries that lie between the Sahara Desert and the rain forest have suffered new disasters. Slowly, the Sahara Desert has pushed southward. There has been little or no rain in these years—a drought. As a result of the lack of rain, the desert has begun to cover the oases—islands of green—that have provided farmland for the people of the region. In addition, people are no longer able to graze their herds. A nomadic way of life thousands of years old is coming to an end. The drought affected many other parts of Africa as well. But as the rains finally arrived, a new problem developed—locusts. Swarms of locusts threatened to destroy the crops of much of sub-Sahara Africa. Experts hope that the millions of dollars spent on pesticides will help avoid massive damage to the crops.

5. Third, from the voyage of Vasco da Gama to recent times, the world's main interest in Africa was in taking things out of the continent. European nations seized and divided among themselves the vast lands of the continent. They profited from the slaves, gold, ivory, and raw materials that Africa provided. As a result, Africa remained underdeveloped for hundreds of years.

6. *Underdeveloped* means that most Africans must make a poor living by simple farming methods. The main tool is the hand hoe. There are few work animals because of the tsetse fly and the thick rain forest. Farmers use little or no fertilizer. There is also a lack of water at certain times. The result, of course, is low crop yield. In some places, Africans do not even produce enough food to feed themselves. Wars in Ethiopia, Chad, Sudan, and Mauritania have also added to the problem of hunger. Only the sorghum, wheat, powdered milk and medicines brought in by international relief organizations have kept the people from starving.

Students in Zimbabwe using a scale they made themselves.

7. Underdeveloped also means the poor use of human resources. Until now, most Africans were not taught how to read and write. Part of this failure can be traced to the colonial governments that did not provide enough schools. However, there is a strong drive to change this situation at once. Aware of the need to read and write, many African governments are setting aside more and more money to build elementary schools for their children. A large part of their budget is spent on education. Africans feel that schooling will help them to be better farmers, to operate machines in factories, to run railroads, or to pilot airplanes. Education also will train people to run businesses and government agencies. Every African country now has at least one university.

8. Underdeveloped means poor health for most Africans. Good health for all the people is another important goal of African governments. Diet is being improved. Through the use of sprays and other methods, mosquitoes that carry diseases are being killed. The brush and forests where the tsetse fly breeds are being burned. More children are being vaccinated. Hospitals are being built and more doctors are being trained. People are moving to the cities where modern healthful practices are in effect. The "old Africa" is slowly being limited to the villages far inland. Even there, rural health centers are being set up.

9. Underdeveloped also means few factories. Most African countries have exported their raw materials. But this situation is changing. Africans now want to process their own goods and materials at home and then ship them abroad or use them at home. More Africans are now managing their own factories. For example, in Nigeria recent laws list those kinds of businesses that must be run entirely or partly by Nigerians rather than by foreigners. Nigeria, the Côte d'Ivoire, and other countries have made great economic progress. Air transportation is a big factor in African communication and trade. Now there are "crash programs" to improve roads and railroads. Africa is becoming developed. In fact, it is more proper today to call these countries developing countries rather than underdeveloped ones.

10. Finally, many African countries are going through a bad time because they depend too much on one product. At one time, Nigeria was one of the wealthiest countries in sub-Sahara Africa. It was rich in oil. But as oil prices dropped, Nigeria's troubles began. Jobs were lost. Government services were cut back. Other countries in sub-Sahara Africa rely equally on one product. For example, Ghana relies on cocoa, Zaire on copper, Mali on cotton, Gambia on peanuts, Mauritania on iron ore, Guinea on bauxite, to name a few. As the prices for these goods fall, the people will suffer loss of jobs and cutbacks in services. These countries must learn to vary their products and not rely on only one product or crop to make money.

UNDERSTANDING WHAT YOU HAVE READ

1. **Which of the following questions are answered in this chapter?**
   a. How can we help African nations solve their problems?
   b. How is the health of Africans being improved?
   c. What are Africa's major problems?

2. **The main idea of this chapter is to describe**
   a. the greatest needs of the African people
   b. the effect of climate on the African people
   c. Africa's relations with the rest of the world

3. **One of the chief needs of African nations today is to**
   a. export food
   b. encourage the growth of their armies
   c. begin a factory system to use their resources

4. **The main tool of most African farmers is the**
   a. tractor
   b. bulldozer
   c. hand hoe

5. **One of the reasons Africa supports such a small population is because**
   a. few minerals are found anywhere
   b. most of Africa is desert, rain forest, and dry grasslands
   c. mountains line the coast of the oceans

6. **Africa has remained underdeveloped for so long because**
   a. it lacks mineral resources
   b. there is little use for electric power
   c. raw materials are not used at home

7. **In nations that are now called *developing,* most of the people are**
   a. poor, in poor health, unable to read, and workers on rural farms
   b. rich, in good health, able to read, workers in factories of crowded cities
   c. poor, in good health, able to read, workers in office buildings in towns

8. **What are the regions's major strengths?**
   a. food crops and raw materials
   b. a well-developed transportation system
   c. a large number of factories.

9. **What are the region's major weaknesses?**
   a. reliance on one crop or product
   b. many people are in poor health and lack education
   c. both of these

10. **What is a major problem facing sub-Sahara Africa today?**
   a. hunger affects a large number of people
   b. there are too many nuclear-powered plants
   c. air pollution

In Africa

"Women are concerned about children, about the future," says **Wangari Maathai.** That is why this Kenyan biologist turned to the women of her country to help stop the advancing desert. Years of tree cutting and population growth had stripped the Kenyan forests. The result was soil erosion, lack of firewood, malnutrition, and poverty. Maathai helped create the Green Belt Movement to do something about the problem. So far, about 50,000 women have been trained to raise tree seedlings in small village nurseries. When the seedlings reach the right height for transplanting, these "foresters without diplomas" persuade local farmers to accept and raise the young trees. For each tree they grow, the women receive 2 cents. By 1990, the Green Belt Movement had planted over 10 million trees. That is not enough for Wangari Maathai, however. Her goal is 24 million trees, one for every person in Kenya.

One day a game warden brought a pair of 110-pound elephant tusks into the Kenyan Game Department office where **Michael Werikhe** worked. Poachers had killed an elephant for the ivory. Werikhe decided that he had to do something to save African wildlife. "Being an African, I see wildlife as part of my heritage," says Werikhe. "If wildlife goes, then part of me is dead. I wanted to campaign for wildlife in my own private way." In the past 10 years, Werikhe has walked thousands of miles across Africa, Europe, and North America to raise money for his cause. He is trying to save the black rhino. In 1975, there were 1,000 black rhinos left in Africa, and the number kept dropping until there were only 400. In 1991, there were 500 rhinos, and the

population is growing, thanks in part to the millions of dollars raised by Werikhe's one-man crusade.

Sometimes the most obvious solutions are overlooked. That is what a team of researchers in the United States discovered. **Glen Green** and **Robert Sussman** were studying the rain forests of Madagascar. The variety of animal and plant life in Madagascar is one of the richest in the world. However, because the island's rain forests are shrinking, its thousands of species of plants and animals are greatly endangered. But no one had an accurate idea of how bad the situation was. Green and Sussman turned to a powerful tool that everyone had overlooked: satellite pictures. By comparing satellite images over the past 20 years, the team of researchers made a sad discovery. The amount of vegetation on the island in 1985 was only half of what it had been in 1950. The vegetation in 1950 was only 34 percent of what would have existed if humans had not come to the island 1,500 years earlier.

Back in the early 1970s, the Mossi people of Burkina Faso (then called Upper Volta) were in trouble. They were in the midst of a long drought. Not only that, but they seemed to have lost faith in themselves. **Bernard Ledea Ouedragoo** believed that his people had to learn how to help themselves. He founded **Naam,** an organization that is based on self-help and village-level cooperation. Today, the Mossi culture is alive again. New dams have been built and new trees planted. As conditions have improved, the Mossi have regained their ability to take care of themselves.

Chapter 11

Republic of South Africa: A Land Divided

Why is this richest of southern African lands troubled?

READING FOR A PURPOSE:
1. What are the resources of the Republic of South Africa?
2. How did the South African region come under British rule?
3. How has apartheid set the Republic of South Africa apart from the other nations of the world?

1. For a long time it seemed that the Republic of South Africa was not aware of the "freedom explosion" in Africa. White people in the republic make up only 18 percent of the population of 40 million. A large majority of the people—73 percent—are black. Yet South Africa's blacks have had almost no share in the government of their country. Only in the past few years has South Africa's government begun to admit the need to give *all* South Africans a voice in their country's affairs.

2. The Republic of South Africa is located at the southern end of the African continent. It is made up of four provinces. South Africa is the only country on the continent that is almost entirely in the middle latitudes. Except for a narrow belt of lowland along the coast, the country occupies a great plateau. The northwestern part of the plateau is desert. The rest is a grassy prairie land known as the *veld* [felt]. Winds from the Indian Ocean provide this area with enough rain for farming and grazing.

3. The San people were among the first settlers of South Africa. Then Bantu-speaking peoples moved in from the north. At about the same time, Europeans began to establish settlements in the far south. Before long, the three groups were fighting each other for control of the land.

4. The Dutch were the first European settlers in South Africa. They set up a trading post at Cape Town in 1652. In the early 1800s, the British took over Cape Town, and the Dutch moved north, away from British rule. The Bantu-speaking peoples did not want to give up their land to the Dutch and fought against them. In spite of strong Bantu resistance, the Dutch settled on the veld. They called their new lands the Orange Free State and Transvaal.

5. The Dutch farmers and herders on the veld called themselves *"Boers,"* or farmers. In 1886, gold and diamonds were discovered in the land of the Boers. As a result, the British tried to gain control of the area. Before long, a

A fine home on Berea in a whites-only part of Durban, South Africa. How does this scene represent South Africa's troubles?

Workers pour gold at a South African mine.

war broke out between the Dutch and the British. After several years of fighting, the Boers were defeated in 1902. All the provinces were united into a new, self-governing part of the British Commonwealth. Today, about three fifths of the white people in South Africa are descended from the Boers. Most of the other whites have British ancestors. In 1961, South Africa cut all its ties to the British Commonwealth and became a republic.

6. Largely because of its natural resources, South Africa has become the richest country in Africa. South Africa mines large quantities of gold, uranium, and diamonds. Gold fields near Johannesburg are the richest in Africa. South Africa also has iron and coal. Factories produce textiles, chemicals, and automobiles. Wealth from these industries makes South Africa a powerful country.

7. South Africa has the highest standard of living on the continent—for its white people. It has a modern transportation system. Its largest city, Johannesburg, has two million people counting its suburbs. Other large cities are Cape Town, Durban, and Pretoria.

8. Despite the fact that it is the richest nation on the continent, the Republic of South Africa has been seriously troubled. The government long followed a policy of *apartheid,* or separate development of racial groups. Whites held most of the power; blacks had no

power at all. In between were Asians and people of mixed race. For many years, the government did not consider black people to be South Africans at all. Instead, the government set up homelands, areas where blacks would live and govern themselves. Black leaders opposed the idea of being forced to live in certain areas. Furthermore, the homelands were never accepted by other nations of the world.

9. This system ignored the fact that many blacks worked in cities or at mines, away from their homelands. They lived in all-black townships or in dormitories. In addition, the whites kept the best lands for themselves. The soil and pasture land in the homelands were poor, and it was hard to make a living there.

10. What did apartheid mean to the black workers of South Africa? It meant living in two different worlds. During the day, they worked in the white world of skyscraper offices, department stores, factories, warehouses, and mines. When night came, they returned to the all-black townships or dormitories. They received lower wages than other workers. Most received poor health care. Blacks could not vote or take part in South Africa's government.

11. Most of South Africa's whites supported apartheid. They felt that South Africa was theirs because they had worked and lived in it for many years. They feared what might happen if blacks could vote as equals. After all, there were many more blacks than whites. Whites feared that South Africa's blacks would take control of the government and take away whites' rights.

12. Black Africans felt that apartheid was close to slavery. They struggled to put an end to it. Groups like the African National Congress (ANC) formed to fight apartheid. When the government broke up their meetings and arrested their leaders, such groups went underground. They got weapons and planned for war. Sometimes they set off explosions that killed innocent people. Blacks and other South Africans held meetings to protest apartheid. Sometimes police broke up the meetings with brutal force. Hundreds of people died in bloody riots.

13. People outside South Africa wanted to help end apartheid because they thought it was wrong. During the 1980s, several nations decided to impose *sanctions,* meaning they stopped selling goods to South Africa. They did this to pressure South Africa's government to end apartheid. The United States was among the nations that restricted trade with South Africa during this period.

14. The combination of protest within South Africa and pressure from outside had an effect. The country's leaders decided they would have to make big changes. They began by giving Asians and people of mixed race a say in government. Then they gave more freedoms to blacks. In 1990, the government released an important ANC leader, Nelson Mandela, from prison. The government also said it was ending apartheid. White officials began holding meetings with Mandela and leaders of rival black groups. The goal was to try to agree on a new and democratic constitution that blacks, whites, and other groups could accept. In March 1992, white South Africans voted to let people of all races participate in government. Leaders of all groups said they would work for a new spirit of partnership among the races.

UNDERSTANDING WHAT YOU HAVE READ

1. Which of the following questions are answered in this chapter?
a. Why do we say that South Africa is rich?
b. Where do many black people live?
c. When did apartheid begin?

2. The main idea of this chapter is to describe
a. the meaning of apartheid
b. the large cities of South Africa
c. how South Africa became what it is today

3. The largest group in South Africa is made up of
a. blacks
b. whites
c. people of mixed race

4. The largest city in South Africa is
a. Nairobi
b. Cape Town
c. Johannesburg

5. The first settlers of South Africa were the
a. Boers
b. British
c. San

6. A policy of apartheid means
a. equal rights
b. separation of races
c. black rule

7. Under apartheid, black South Africans were considered to be citizens of
a. the cities in which they lived
b. homelands set aside for ethnic groups
c. no nation

8. One reason that South Africa's government agreed to end apartheid was
a. pressure from South African whites
b. pressure from South African blacks
c. a need for more black workers

472

DEVELOPING IDEAS AND SKILLS

Building Map Skills —— Republic of South Africa and the United States

Use the map to answer these questions.

1. In which direction is the equator from the Republic of South Africa?
2. Is the Republic of South Africa in the high, middle, or low latitudes?
3. The Orange River flows into which body of water?
4. Are there any independent countries bordering the Republic of South Africa? If so, name them.
5. What is the latitude and longitude of the city of Durban?
6. Why do you think there are only a few large seaports in the Republic of South Africa?
7. What country is completely surrounded by the Republic of South Africa?
8. The United States is how many times as large as the Republic of South Africa?
9. If you flew from your community to Capetown, in which direction would you be traveling?
10. Why has a large city grown inland at Johannesburg?

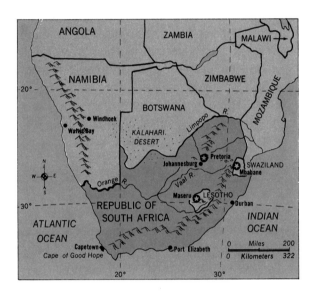

UNITED STATES
POPULATION: 252.8 MILLION
LAND AREA: 3.6 MILLION SQUARE MILES
9.36 MILLION SQUARE KILOMETERS
70 PEOPLE PER SQUARE MILE

REP. OF SOUTH AFRICA
POPULATION: 40.6 MILLION
LAND AREA: 472,400 SQUARE MILES
1,221,037 SQUARE KILOMETERS
86 PEOPLE PER SQUARE MILE

Republic of South Africa and the United States

SUMMING UP

Making Charts

Complete the following chart in your notebook.

	REPUBLIC OF SOUTH AFRICA
1. Location	
2. Size	
3. People	
4. Resources	
5. Problems	

Chapter 12

Nigeria: Africa's Most Populous Nation

How has Nigeria come to be a powerful nation in West Africa?

READING FOR A PURPOSE:
1. How have ethnic groups influenced Nigeria's history?
2. How has Nigeria used its wealth from the sale of oil?
3. Why must Nigeria import food?

1. A leader of an African nation has said, "Whenever an important issue arises in Africa, everyone wants to see what Nigeria will do. You may not agree with it. But you always listen to it." Such is the standing of Nigeria in present-day Africa. Nigeria has more people than any other nation in Africa. Its great oil reserves are important to the industrialized nations of the world. One of these nations is the United States. Nigeria is a major supplier of oil to the United States.

2. Nigeria's area is as large as the combined size of Texas and Arizona. In 1991, it had a population of over 122 million. This is a greater number than the combined population of all the states of the United States west of the Mississippi River. Among its millions of people are a number of different ethnic groups. The largest group is the Hausa-Fulani in the north. Most are Muslims, believers in the religion of Islam. Other major ethnic groups are the Yoruba in the southwest and the Ibo in the southeast. Many of the people of these groups are Christians. Others follow traditional African religions. There are many other ethnic groups with smaller numbers of people. Each group has customs and languages that are different from other groups. It is estimated that over 250 different languages are spoken in Nigeria. English, however, is the official language of the Nigerian government.

3. The Niger River and the Benue (BANE-way) River are the two most important rivers in Nigeria. They form Nigeria's main river system. These rivers divide Nigeria into three sections: the north, the southeast, and the southwest. The north is largely a dry plateau. It is the home of the Hausa-Fulani. The southeast is a region of heavy rainfall. In this area, near the coast, there are large mangrove trees growing in swampy land. This is the home of the Ibo. Large oil reserves are also located in this region. In the southwest, the rainfall is not so heavy. The Yoruba live in this area. The Niger and Benue rivers carry a huge amount of mud along with them, piling up a delta at the river mouth on the Gulf of Guinea. Because of the shifting sand in the rivers and the differences in rainfall, large boats cannot use the rivers the year round.

4. Early cultures in Nigeria reach back into history thousands of years. Remains of 2,500-year-old clay sculptures from central Nigeria have been identified as part of the Nok culture. North African traders crossed the Sahara in camel caravans as early as A.D. 400. By about A.D. 1100, most of northern Africa had

A 16th-century ivory carving from the kingdom of Benin.

been conquered by Arabs. Soon the Arabs came in contact with western Africa. The Arabs brought with them into western Africa their language, customs, and the Muslim religion. They traded in the markets of Kano in northern Nigeria. Many Africans became followers of Islam. By the 13th century, civilization in northern Nigeria showed the influence of Muslim customs and beliefs. During the 1400s, the kingdom of Benin was powerful in what is now southern Nigeria. Benin produced some of the world's outstanding bronze and brass sculptures.

5. Some Arab traders were interested in trading their goods for people—slaves. In the 15th century, slave traders from Portugal and Great Britain appeared in West Africa. In the 19th and early 20th centuries, parts of Nigeria became colonies of the United Kingdom. Not until 1960 did Nigeria become an independent nation.

6. The government of the new republic of Nigeria was headed by members of the Hausa-Fulani and Ibo cultures. In 1966, the government was overthrown by a group of Ibo army officers. Soon thereafter, some leaders of

ethnic groups in the north and west were killed. Some blamed these deaths on the Ibos. Rioting and killing of innocent people followed. Thousands of Ibos died in the violence. In 1967, the eastern region of the Ibos withdrew from the Nigerian nation and tried to form an independent country called Biafra.

7. Biafra was not able to keep its independence. A terrible war broke out between Nigeria and Biafra. Thousands of homes and farms were destroyed. The Nigerian army was able to keep the Biafrans from getting food and supplies by land or sea. It is estimated that 2 million Biafrans (Ibos, chiefly) died of starvation in over two years of war. Torn by hunger and the loss of the land they had claimed, the Biafrans surrendered. Biafra again became a part of the national government of Nigeria.

8. Sixty percent of Nigerians are farmers or herders. Most family farms are small. Some farmers say they could not farm larger plots of land. In recent years, many young people have left to look for jobs in the city. Yams and corn are the chief food crops of the rainy southeast. Palm nuts from the oil palm tree are a major cash crop. In the west, cacao, tobacco, and peanuts are grown for export. In the north,

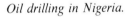

Oil drilling in Nigeria.

Nigerian woman dressed for a festival dance. In southern Nigeria, women control the markets and run many of the trade organizations.

where there is less rainfall, peanuts, wheat, and cotton are grown. The north, too, is the region of the Hausa herders, tending their goats and cattle.

9. In spite of the many small farms, Nigeria must import food. There are several reasons why this is so. The growing population in the cities has created a demand for more food. There are more people to feed, and less land is being used for farming. Then, too, there are fewer workers on family farms, and less food is produced. Another reason is that the family farms are still producing food with methods used for hundreds of years. Finally, when Nigeria was a colony of the United Kingdom, the greatest effort was placed into growing cash crops for export—cacao, coffee, sugar, palm nuts, peanuts, and rubber. Less attention was given to raising food for their own needs. One of the goals of the Nigerian leaders today is to make their country able to produce enough food to feed all its citizens.

10. Nigeria has great wealth in mineral resources. There are tin mines in the northern plateau. There are also stores of natural gas, coal, iron ore, and limestone. But the most valuable resource is *oil.* In the 1970s, the sale of oil brought in a lot of money for improvements. For awhile, it seemed as though all kinds of improvements were going on at once. There were new roads, schools, and hospitals. There was telephone service, apartment and office buildings, factories, and new facilities for handling the great number of ships that came to its harbors. The effects of the oil boom spread throughout the cities and country. But in the 1980s, the price of oil began to drop. Oil production had to be cut. Many people lost their jobs. Government services were cut. For the time being, the great wealth had ended.

11. In the past 25 years large numbers of people have left the farmlands to live and work in the cities. The largest cities are Lagos, the capital, Ibadan, Kano, and Enugu. (Nigerian leaders plan to move the capital to the city of Abuja in the near future. Abuja is a new city being built in the center of the country.) Housing, water, and sewage facilities have not kept up with the expanding city population. Houses are crowded together. The water supply is poor. The streets cannot keep up with the large increase in cars and trucks. In the cities, the few rich live side by side with the increasing numbers of poor.

12. For much of its brief history, independent Nigeria was ruled by military leaders. In 1979, a new constitution reestablished a democratic form of government. The leader of the government was Shehu Shagari. It lasted less than five years. The government was overthrown by the armed forces led by General Mohammed Buhari. They gained control of the major cities without bloodshed. Buhari ran the country through a Supreme Military Council. In 1985, Buhari's government was overthrown by another general. The people can only hope that the new leaders will better solve the nation's problems.

UNDERSTANDING WHAT YOU HAVE READ

1. Which of the following questions are answered in this chapter?
a. What are the most important ethnic groups in Nigeria?
b. What kinds of goods are exchanged in trade between Nigeria and the United States?
c. How do Nigeria's resources compare with those of Ghana?

2. The main idea of paragraph 9 is that
a. fertilizer is expensive for most farmers
b. food production has not grown as fast as industry
c. there has been a steady movement of people to Nigerian cities

3. The main idea of paragraph 12 is that
a. a variety of ethnic groups are represented in the government
b. a general heads the Nigerian government
c. the Hausa-Fulani control the government

4. The land of northern Nigeria is chiefly

a. tropical rain forest
b. a fertile river valley
c. partly dry plateau

5. The history of Nigeria contains all of these events EXCEPT
a. trade with Arab caravans
b. rule by France for hundreds of years
c. violent civil war

6. A large number of believers in Islam would be found among the
a. Hausa-Fulani   b. Ibo   c. Yoruba

7. You might expect to find crops of the tropical rain forest grown in the
a. southeast
b. southwest
c. northwest

8. Wealth from Nigeria's oil has been used chiefly to
a. improve farming methods
b. provide for the growth of industry
c. develop meat-packing plants

FOLLOW UP

True or False

Tell whether the following statements are true or false. The underlined words make the statements true or false. If a statement is false, what word or words would you place in it to make it true?

1. The Ibos are the largest tribal group in Nigeria.
2. Lagos is a Nigerian city reached by early Arab traders.
3. A major export crop of Nigeria is cacao.
4. In 1967, the eastern region of Nigeria declared itself the independent country of Guinea.
5. Before 1960, Nigeria was a colony of the United Kingdom.
6. Yams are an important food crop in Nigeria.
7. Nigeria's government is headed by a prime minister.
8. English is the official language of Nigeria's government.

DEVELOPING IDEAS AND SKILLS

Building Map Skills—Nigeria

1. What large body of water forms Nigeria's southern border?
2. Does Nigeria have any mountains?
3. What countries border Nigeria?
4. In what direction do the Niger and Benue rivers flow?
5. Where are Nigeria's oil resources located?
6. Which is more thickly populated, Nigeria or Texas–New Mexico?
7. Which is farther from the equator, Nigeria or the United States?
8. What is the distance from the northern border of Nigeria to the city of Lagos?

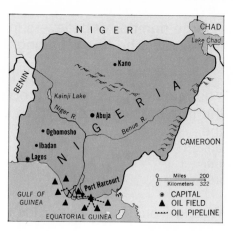

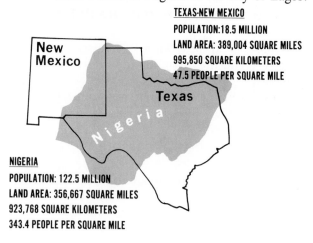

TEXAS-NEW MEXICO
POPULATION: 18.5 MILLION
LAND AREA: 389,004 SQUARE MILES
995,850 SQUARE KILOMETERS
47.5 PEOPLE PER SQUARE MILE

NIGERIA
POPULATION: 122.5 MILLION
LAND AREA: 356,667 SQUARE MILES
923,768 SQUARE KILOMETERS
343.4 PEOPLE PER SQUARE MILE

SUMMING UP

Making Charts

Complete the following chart in your notebook. Head it, "Some Important African Nations." Use an almanac, encyclopedia, or atlas to get additional facts.

NATION	AREA	ETHNIC GROUPS	MAJOR CROPS	MINERAL RESOURCES	GOVERNMENT
Ghana					
Côte d'Ivoire					
Nigeria					
Tanzania					
Zambia					
Zimbabwe					

Africa

Country	Area (Square Miles)	Capital	Population (1991 estimates)	Number of Years to Double Population	Life Expectancy	Per Capita GNP, 1990
Angola	481,353	Luanda	8,900,000	25	44	$ 620
Benin	43,483	Porto-Novo	5,000,000	23	47	$ 360
Botswana	231,804	Gaborone	1,400,000	23	59	$ 2,040
Burkina Faso	105,869	Ougadougou	9,600,000	21	52	$ 330
Burundi	10,759	Bujumbura	5,800,000	21	52	$ 210
Cameroon, United Republic of	179,714	Yaounde	12,700,000	22	57	$ 940
Cape Verde	1,557	Cidade de Praia	400,000	21	61	$ 890
Central African Republic	240,534	Bangui	3,200,000	27	47	$ 390
Chad	495,755	Ndjamena	5,200,000	28	46	$ 190
Comoros	838	Moroni	500,000	20	56	$ 480
Congo, People's Republic of the	132,046	Brazzaville	2,400,000	24	46	$ 1,010
Côte d'Ivoire	124,503	Abidjan	12,500,000	20	52	$ 790
Djibouti, Republic of	8,950	Djibouti	400,000	24	48	—
Equatorial Guinea	10,832	Malabo	400,000	26	50	$ 430
Ethiopia	471,776	Addis Ababa	53,200,000	24	46	$ 120
Gabon	103,346	Libreville	1,200,000	31	52	$ 2,770
Gambia	4,127	Banjul	900,000	27	43	$ 230
Ghana	92,098	Accra	15,500,000	22	55	$ 380
Guinea	94,964	Conakry	7,800,000	28	42	$ 480
Guinea-Bissau	13,948	Bissau	1,000,000	35	42	$ 180
Kenya	224,960	Nairobi	26,200,000	19	61	$ 370
Lesotho	11,716	Maseru	1,900,000	24	58	$ 470
Liberia	38,250	Monrovia	2,800,000	22	54	$ 450**
Madagascar	226,657	Antananarivo	11,900,000	22	54	$ 230
Malawi	45,747	Lilongwe	8,700,000	20	49	$ 200
Mali	478,764	Bamako	8,500,000	23	45	$ 270
Mauritania	397,954	Nouakchott	2,100,00	25	48	$ 500
Mauritius	790	Port Louis	1,100,000	48	69	$ 2,250
Mozambique	303,769	Maputo	16,600,000	26	48	$ 80
Namibia	317,818	Windhoek	1,500,000	22	60	—
Niger	489,189	Niamey	8,300,000	22	45	$ 310
Nigeria	356,667	Lagos	122,500,000	25	48	$ 250
Rwanda	10,169	Kigali	7,700,000	20	50	$ 310
São Tomé and Príncipe	372	São Tomé	100,000	28	66	$ 380
Senegal	75,750	Dakar	7,900,000	25	48	$ 710
Seychelles	171	Victoria	100,000	44	70	$ 4,670
Sierra Leone	27,925	Freetown	4,400,000	27	43	$ 240
Somalia	246,300	Mogadishu	8,300,000	24	46	$ 150
South Africa, Republic of	472,400	Capetown, Pretoria & Bloemfontein	41,600,000	26	64	$ 2,520
*Bophuthanswana	16,988	Mmabatho	1,959,000***	—	—	—
*Ciskei	2,996	Bisho	844,000***	—	—	—
*Transkei	16,855	Umtata	3,301,000***	—	—	—
*Venda	2,771	Thohoyandou	518,000***	—	—	—
Sudan	966,757	Khartoum	26,500,000	22	53	$ 420
Swaziland	6,704	Mbabane	800,000	22	55	$ 820
Tanzania, United Republic of	364,886	Dar-es-Salaam	27,400,000	20	52	$ 120
Togo	21,622	Lome	3,800,000	19	55	$ 410
Uganda	93,354	Kampala	17,500,000	19	51	$ 220
Zambia	290,586	Lusaka	8,400,000	18	53	$ 420
Zimbabwe	150,803	Harare	10,300,000	22	60	$ 640

*These former "black homelands" are now considered by South Africa to be independent nations. Other nations have not recognized these areas as being free from South Africa. **1988 ***1984

Sources: 1992 World Population Data Sheet of the Population Reference Bureau, Inc.; The World Almanac and Book of Facts, 1992.

UNIT·NINE

THE ASIAN REGION

KEY IDEAS

■ The Asian region is the largest and most populous on the earth.

■ Movement within the Asian Region is difficult because of the highest mountains in the world. However, its many peninsulas and islands help promote trade with the other world regions.

■ Asian cultures are shaped by the ancient religions and philosophies of Hinduism, Islam, Buddhism, and Confucianism.

■ Some Asian countries lead the world in industrializing, but the largest Asian countries and others are slow in developing factories and mines.

■ Although most Asians live as farmers in small villages, urbanization is increasing rapidly.

■ The rate of population growth is great in the Asian Region.

A swift bullet train races across the landscape of Japan. Beautiful Mount Fuji stands in the background.

Chapter 1

Asia: A Region of Many Parts

Why are we interested in Asia?

READING FOR A PURPOSE:
1. What are the countries of Asia?
2. Why was this region called the Far East?
3. Why is the United States interested in Asia?

1. Asia is the home of more than half the people of the world. Over 3 billion people live in a vast region extending over 4,000 miles (6,400 kilometers) from east to west. In this unit, *Asia* will refer to the Asian region from Pakistan on the west to the Philippines, and southeast to Indonesia. (The actual continent of Asia also includes countries of the Middle East and a large part of the Commonwealth of Independent States, which you have studied.) This region used to be called the Far East because it lies far to the east of Europe. These lands were visited by Marco Polo in the 13th century. When he returned to Europe, he described the riches of these faraway lands.

The term *Far East* was used by early merchants who traveled to these lands in search of the goods described by Marco Polo. Part of this region was called the *Orient,* because the word means "the East."

2. The Asian region is often divided into several parts. First, there is the Indian peninsula, which is so big that it is sometimes called a subcontinent—that is, almost a continent. This area includes the countries of India, Pakistan, Bangladesh, Nepal, Bhutan, the island nations of the Maldives and Sri Lanka. Eastward are the nations of Southeast Asia, the second part. This includes the island republics of Indonesia and the Philippines and a peninsula divided among the countries of Myanmar, Thailand, and Malaysia. It also includes the countries of what was Indochina (Cambodia, Laos, and Vietnam). Northward are the countries of eastern Asia: China, Mongolia, North and South Korea, and the island nations of Japan and Taiwan (Republic of China).

3. Asian countries vary in size. The largest country in the region, and the third largest in the world, is China. (In terms of population, China is the largest country in the world.) The second largest country in Asia is India. The nations on the Indian subcontinent are about half the size of the United States. Indonesia is

Hong Kong is a densely populated area. How do high-rise apartment buildings help people adapt to high population density?

not much larger than the U.S. state of Alaska, but its many islands extend over 3,000 miles (5,000 kilometers) from east to west. The Philippines is not much larger than the state of Colorado. Yet its islands extend about 1,100 miles (1,800 kilometers) north and south. Japan, the richest country of Asia (with the third largest GNP in the world), is about as large as the state of Montana. Part of the Commonwealth is in the continent of Asia. But the CIS is considered a region separate from the rest of Asia. The smallest nation in Asia is the Maldives, which is twice the size of Washington, D.C.

4. The rest of the world is interested in Asia for many reasons. First, the rest of the world gets many valuable raw materials from the peoples of Asia—tin, rubber, silk, jute, timber, sugar, minerals, and metals. It also gets electronic equipment, machinery, cars, textiles, and other manufactured products from Asian industries. In exchange, the rest of the world sells Asian countries a variety of things. Oil-rich countries send their much needed oil. Industrial nations sell machinery and transportation equipment to them. Many Asian countries need to import food from grain-rich nations such as Canada and the United States.

5. A second reason why the rest of the world is interested in Asia is that the region has been the scene of continued conflict. Civil war between Nationalists and Communists in China ended with a Communist victory in 1949. The Nationalist party of Chiang Kai-shek moved to the island of Taiwan. In the early 1950s, Communist North Korea invaded South Korea. The United Nations sent soldiers to help the South Koreans. The Communists were prevented from taking over South Korea.

6. There was much other fighting in Asia. In the early 1950s, Indochina was still a French colony. Fighting between the French and the Vietnamese continued until the French left Indochina in 1954. Soon, however, fighting developed between Communist

Unloading jute at a mill in Calcutta, India. Jute fibers are removed from the stalk and are taken to the mill for processing into burlap and twine.

northern Vietnam and American-supported southern Vietnam. In the 1960s and early 1970s, hundreds of thousands of U.S. troops fought in Vietnam. In 1973, the United States withdrew its troops. In 1975, Communist northern Vietnam defeated the south and united the country. In nearby Cambodia about two million people died as a result of fighting between rival forces in the country. In 1978, Vietnam invaded Cambodia and placed in power a government friendly to Vietnam. Besides the war in Indochina, there has also been border fighting or wars between India and Pakistan, India and China, and China and Vietnam.

7. Many Asian countries have gained independence from European nations only since World War II. Having experienced colonial domination from the 1500s through World War II, the Philippines gained its independence from the United States in 1946. In 1986, President Marcos of the Philippines was forced to leave the country when the people claimed that the election results of 1984 had been tampered with. Corazon Aquino took control of the government, and was recognized as the rightful president of the Philippines. In 1989, some members of the military staged an unsuccessful attempt to overthrow President Aquino.

UNDERSTANDING WHAT YOU HAVE READ

1. Which of the following questions are answered in this chapter?
a. Why are we interested in Asia?
b. What were the results of the Korean War?
c. What government has headquarters on Taiwan?

2. The main idea of this chapter is to describe
a. how the new nations of Asia have won their freedom
b. why Asia is important to the rest of the world
c. the growing power of Japan

3. The richest country in Asia is
a. Taiwan
b. Myanmar
c. Japan

4. Thailand and Malaysia are located at least partly on a large
a. island
b. peninsula
c. delta

5. The Asian region used to be called the Far East because
a. it was far to the east of Europe
b. the sun rises in the east
c. the Pacific Ocean is east of the mainland

6. Which of these nations is made up of many islands?
a. India
b. Indonesia
c. Bangladesh

7. The term *the Orient* was used to describe Asia because it means
a. "the West"
b. "the East"
c. "the North"

8. A subcontinent is
a. like an archipelago
b. land "below," that is, south of the equator
c. a body of land almost as large as a continent

SUMMING UP

True or False

The following statements are true or false. The underlined words make the statements true or false. If a statement is false, what word or words would you place in it to make it true?

1. Over half the people of the world live in Asia.
2. Since World War II, the power of communism has spread in Asia.
3. Asian countries are customers for American grain and manufactured goods.
4. There are no democratic countries in Asia.
5. Most Asian countries gained their independence from European powers before World War II.
6. United States troops have fought in Asia since 1945.
7. American troops have fought in wars in Korea and Vietnam.
8. Japan is the largest nation in size in Asia.
9. One country occupies the Indian subcontinent.
10. In 1949, the Nationalist party of Chiang Kai-shek moved to the island of Taiwan.

Building Map Skills—The Asian Region

The Asian Region

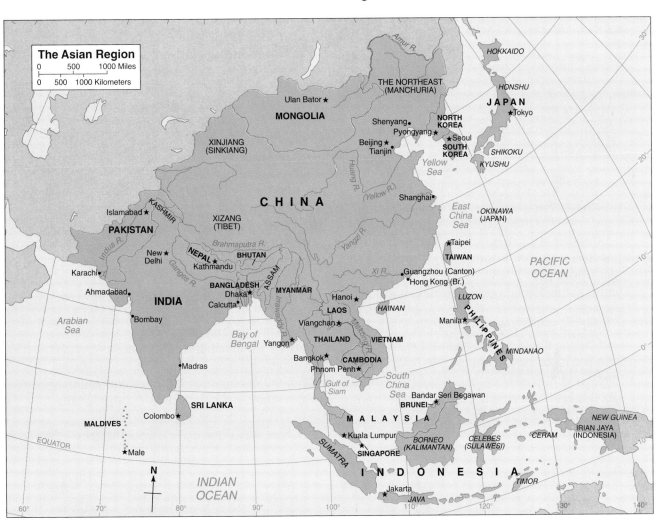

Study the map above. Then answer these questions.

1. Is the region north or south of the equator?
2. Is the region east or west of the prime meridian?
3. How far north and south does the region extend?
4. Does the region extend farther from east to west or from north to south?
5. What region or regions are near it?
6. What is the largest country? The smallest?
7. What are the chief bodies of water that border the region?
8. Which countries have no outlets to the sea?
9. What are some of the important rivers in the region?
10. Are there large rivers that form boundary lines between countries?
11. What is the capital city of each country? How do you know they are the capitals? How many are sea or river ports?
12. Which are island nations?
13. Which countries are located on peninsulas?
14. What countries are found in Borneo?

485

Chapter 2

Crowded Islands and Valleys

What is the topography of Asia?

READING FOR A PURPOSE:
1. What are the great rivers of Asia?
2. What effect do rivers have on life in this region?
3. What are the important island groups?

1. Much of Asia is mountainous. The inner highlands of Asia are the highest in the world. In the south are the Himalaya Mountains. These mountains extend east and west for 1,500 miles (2,400 kilometers), separating India from the countries to the north. Mount Everest, in the Himalayas, is the highest mountain peak in the world. To the north of these great mountains is the lonely Plateau of Tibet. This plateau, about 16,000 feet (4,800 meters) above sea level, is sometimes called the "roof of the world."

2. Ranges of high mountains continue from Tibet southward across the Malay Peninsula. There they drop below the surface of the seas and appear again above water to form the main islands of Southeast Asia. Another mountain range runs eastward through the center of China, dividing it into two regions. In general, however, the land slopes downward from the inner highlands until it reaches the great Chinese plains in the north, and the Pacific Ocean in the south.

3. Many rivers rise in the mountains of Asia and form plains as they flow toward the oceans. The lowlands formed by these rivers are bordered by hills and low mountains. The millions of people in Asia tend to be crowded into these river valleys because the land is fertile. The rivers bring the rich soil of the mountains into the valleys and supply water to irrigate the crops.

4. Three major rivers rise in the Himalayas—the Ganges, the Brahmaputra, and the Indus. The Ganges flows across northern India, forming a great lowland plain. It flows southeastward and empties into the Bay of Bengal, which is a northern part of the Indian Ocean. The Brahmaputra flows southwestward from the northern mountains and joins the Ganges in Bangladesh. The Indus flows through the dry lands of Pakistan and empties into the Arabian Sea, which is the part of the Indian Ocean between Oman and India.

5. China has three great rivers that rise in

A fertile terraced area in Bali, Indonesia.

The Himalayas of northern India.

the mountains to the west. The Huang, or Yellow, River begins in the Plateau of Tibet and flows through northern China to the sea. (The region through which it flows is covered with a yellow, dusty soil called *loess*. As the river flows through the loess hills, it picks up the yellow soil. Thus, it has been given the name Yellow River.) The Huang is not a deep river. When there are heavy rains, the river overflows its banks and floods the land, sometimes spoiling crops and drowning people. For this reason it is sometimes called "China's Sorrow."

6. The Yangzi, the third longest river in the world, is China's longest and most useful river. It rises in Tibet and flows eastward to the sea near the city of Shanghai. The Yangzi is comparable to the Mississippi. Along this waterway, one-tenth of the world's people live. The Yangzi is connected to the Huang by a canal. Farther south is the Xi River, flowing into the sea near the city of Canton.

7. Several large rivers also flow southward across the vast peninsula of Southeast Asia. The Irrawaddy, Mekong, and Red rivers rise in the high mountains east of the Himalayas. They form broad valleys and deltas as they flow toward the sea. These valleys are separated by rugged mountain ranges.

8. Off the mainland of southern and eastern Asia are thousands of islands. These groups of islands are called *archipelagoes*. The main archipelagoes are Japan, the Philippines, and Indonesia. Many islands have volcanoes.

The Li River in Hunan province, China.

The lava from the volcanoes has kept the soil of some of these islands very fertile. The island nation of Sri Lanka is located off the southeastern tip of India. It is not part of an archipelago.

9. Finally, one of the most striking features of this region is that, like western Europe, it has so many peninsulas. Southern India is almost completely surrounded by water as it reaches out into the ocean. The Malay and Indochina peninsulas are very heavily populated. They are near the important trade routes that lead to the great city-state of Singapore. The Korean peninsula has long been a center of disputes between nations in Asia and Europe. Many of these peninsulas are near much-traveled bodies of water and are therefore important in world trade.

UNDERSTANDING WHAT YOU HAVE READ

1. Which of the following questions are answered in this chapter?
a. Why are the rivers of Asia important?
b. When was Mount Everest first climbed?
c. How has the Yellow River caused sorrow?

2. The main idea of this chapter is to describe
a. the topography of Asia
b. the chief rivers of Asia
c. the mountains of Asia

3. The highest mountain chain in the world is the
a. Rockies
b. Andes
c. Himalayas

4. The Ganges, the Brahmaputra, and the Indus rivers all start as small streams in the
a. Himalayas
b. Indian Ocean
c. high mountains of Japan

5. The rivers are important to the people of Asia for all these reasons EXCEPT
a. They furnish rich soil for farming.
b. They serve as boundaries between countries.
c. They provide water for farming.

6. Rivers are said to have the opposite effect of mountains because
a. rivers are a source of great mineral wealth
b. mountains have kept people apart; rivers have brought people together
c. the mountains of Asia have the best soils

7. The word *loess* would have most meaning to
a. farmers
b. factory workers
c. fishers

8. A group of islands surrounded by a large body of water is
a. a continent
b. an archipelago
c. a peninsula

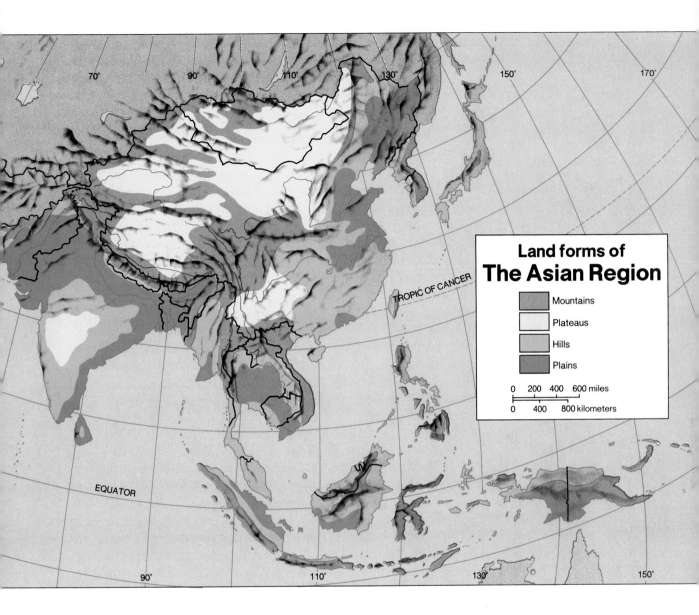

Land forms of
The Asian Region

Mountains
Plateaus
Hills
Plains

0   200   400   600 miles
0   400   800 kilometers

TROPIC OF CANCER

EQUATOR

DEVELOPING IDEAS AND SKILLS

Building Map Skills — Land Forms of the Asian Region

Study the map. Then answer the following questions.

1. Which land forms are found on the islands of the Asian region?
2. Which land forms make up India?
3. Which countries contain large plateaus?
4. China is almost completely surrounded by mountains and sea. How do you think these borders might have affected the development of China?
5. How has the presence of many peninsulas in the Asian region helped trade and travel?

489

To Feed the World

Imagine these newspaper headlines for the year 2020. "Experts' Predictions Come True. World Population Hits 8.2 Billion." How do you think we will feed so many people?

The Green Revolution Over the past 30 years, a system of farming called the Green Revolution has helped the world's farmers produce more food for our growing population. The Green Revolution is a "high-tech" scientific approach to farming.

Scientists have created new, high-yielding seeds that farmers plant to grow more food faster. Farmers also rely on better irrigation to farm lands that were once too dry for crops. Often, farmers can grow a second crop on lands that once were left idle during the dry season. Sprays protect crops against pests and diseases.

As a result of the Green Revolution, many nations have increased food production tremendously. India, for example, produces three times more rice and eight times more wheat than in 1950. Despite its increased population, India has less hunger today than it had in the 1950s.

The Problems of the Green Revolution The high-yield seeds require vast amounts of pesticides, irrigation water, fertilizer, and other additives. Once cheap and widely available, fertilizer from fossil fuels is now expensive and much in demand.

Success has brought other problems with it. First, soil loss is a serious problem. The United States, for example, has lost more than 30 percent of its best topsoil. Second, chemicals in fertilizers and pesticides create serious water pollution. Third, irrigation is using up water supplies.

In addition, the gap is widening between rich farmers and poor farmers. Poorer farmers cannot buy the special seeds and fertilizers. Their crops do not sell for enough money to support their families. Many poorer farmers lose their land.

A New Gene Revolution The so-called Gene Revolution may bring important changes in farming. More research in farming methods and types of plants will bring new kinds of fertilizers and pest control and new ways of irrigating. Scientists are breeding food plants to grow in almost any environment, even in the desert. New strains of wheat, barley, and tomatoes now can thrive when irrigated with seawater. However, we cannot expect scientific discoveries alone to solve the problem of feeding the planet.

China, today, is a country that has a lot to show the developing world about producing food. Chinese farming methods waste little. The Chinese recycle farm wastes for inexpensive fertilizer. They rely on human labor rather than expensive machines. They try to choose crops that fit the environment. They have also developed "fish farming" as an efficient way to produce animal protein.

We will have to pay more attention to protecting the land, the water supply, and our sources of energy. Our attitudes toward what we eat probably need to change. We will need to provide more grain for people and less as feed for cattle.

The Green Revolution has only given us a few years to solve the larger problems that cause hunger. Additional strategies are needed.

Why is it important to continue to improve crop production?

How can governments ensure that their people have enough food?

What can individuals do to help provide food for the hungry?

Chapter 3

Monsoon Asia

How do the climates of Asia affect the ways people live?

READING FOR A PURPOSE:

1. Where is the Asian rain forest?
2. What are monsoons?
3. In which areas of Asia are climatic regions like those in the United States?

1. As you might guess, a region as large as Asia has many kinds of climate. The part of Asia we are studying here extends from just below the equator a great distance north. (CIS Asia is discussed in another unit.) From Indonesia in the south to the Chinese-CIS border is a distance of about 60 degrees. This is the same distance as from the tropics of Brazil to Newfoundland, Canada. In addition, much of the region is mountainous. Also, many of the land areas border or are surrounded by large bodies of water.

2. The equator passes through the southern part of this region. Indonesia, Malaysia, Sri Lanka, and much of the Philippines, Southeast Asia, and southern India are all within 15 degrees of the equator. Indonesia, Malaysia, and the Philippines are hot and rainy the year round. (Mountains provide some relief from the heat.) There is thick forest and a year-round growing season. The heavy rains wash minerals from the soil. This is the same kind of climate as is found in the Amazon River basin in South America and the Zaire (Congo) River basin in Africa. It is the rain forest.

3. In many ways, however, the rain forest of Southeast Asia is different from the others we have studied. One of the chief differences is caused by their location. The Amazon and Zaire rain forests are in the hearts of their continents. In Southeast Asia, this climate is found largely on islands off the mainland. Again, in the Amazon and Zaire river basins, the land is largely lowland plains. The Asian rain-forest lands are mountainous. Around the mountain "centers" of the islands is a narrow belt of hilly lands, next to which are the coastal plains.

4. The rain forests of Asia support a huge population. Some of the fertile areas of rain forest in Southeast Asia have more people for each square mile of land than any other farming area in the world. These people have cleared more land in the Asian forests than have the people of either the Amazon or the Zaire.

5. North of the rain forest, the tropical savanna climate is found. As in other savanna regions, there is a wet and a dry season. This climate is found in most of India, Sri Lanka, Myanmar, Thailand, and the countries of Southeast Asia. These lands are affected by winds called *monsoons*. The monsoons are winds that blow steadily either from the water or from the land for several weeks at a time. During the summer, the winds blow from the ocean to the land; they are hot and rainy. During the winter, they blow from the land to the sea; they are dry and cold.

6. The reasons for the monsoon winds are easy to understand. Land heats more quickly than water. During the summer months, the hot rays of the sun beat down on the lands of

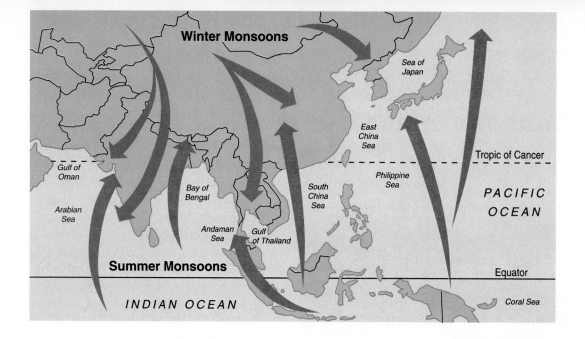

southern Asia. The air is also heated. The warm air then rises because it is lighter. Because the ocean waters are cooler than the land, the ocean air remains cool and heavy. When the warm land air rises, the cool air over the oceans rushes toward the land to take the place of the rising warm air. It brings rain to the land. This rainfall takes place from May to October. During the winter months, the monsoon winds change because the land becomes cooler than the water. The air over the ocean is then warmer than the air over the land. The warm ocean air rises, and the cooler land air moves in to take its place, making dry winds. These blow from November to March.

7. The people of southern Asia cannot get along without the monsoons. In May, they begin to watch the skies for the coming of the summer monsoons. The summer winds bring rain, and the land becomes green again. Without this rain, the crops would fail. The farmers try to save some of the water in small tanks or reservoirs. If there is too little or too much rain, or if it is too late, crops can be ruined.

8. In southeastern China and in parts of Japan, the climate is humid subtropical. This area is like the southeastern United States. The summers are long, hot, and rainy. The winters are mild and there is less rain. This makes for a long, moist growing season. Southern China is a rice-growing region. (Rice can also be grown in the U.S. southeastern states from South Carolina to Louisiana.)

9. Farther north in China and Japan, the climate is humid continental like that of the northeastern United States. Beijing (Peking), China, is the same distance from the equator as New York City is. There are long, cold winters, hot summers, and enough rainfall to support crops. Near the sea, the temperatures are milder throughout the year. In the mountains, the cold of winter is very severe. The lower rainfall in the north has made this an area of wheat growing.

10. Most of western China lies in the dry regions of Asia. A large part of this land is desert; the other part is a region of grassy steppes. (Grass will grow where the rainfall is at least 10 inches—25 centimeters—a year.) The desert areas are almost completely surrounded by mountains, which keep out the rain-bearing winds. The Gobi Desert of northern China and Mongolia is one of the loneliest places on earth. Few people live there. In Pakistan, there is another vast dry region. The Indus River is important, for it provides water for irrigation in this dry region.

UNDERSTANDING WHAT YOU HAVE READ

1. Which of the following questions are answered in this chapter?

a. When was the Asian rain forest cleared?

b. What causes the monsoon winds?

c. Why is the Gobi Desert such a dry place?

2. The main idea of this chapter is to describe

a. the effects of the monsoons

b. the various climates of Asia

c. how mountains affect climate

3. The climate of many lands of southern Asia is affected by the

a. monsoons

b. Atlantic Ocean

c. winds from Siberia

4. Southeastern China has a climate like that of

a. Oregon and Washington

b. Massachusetts and New York

c. South Carolina and Louisiana

5. Monsoons are important to the people of Asia because they

a. bring rain for crops

b. bring cool weather

c. bring fine soil from the interior

6. The rain-forest area that supports the greatest population is the

a. Asian rain forest

b. Zaire (Congo) rain forest

c. Amazon rain forest

7. People in *monsoon* lands have

a. rain throughout the year

b. a wet and dry season

c. only 10 inches (25 centimeters) of rain a year

DEVELOPING CRITICAL THINKING SKILLS

I. Making Comparisons

Complete the following lists in your notebook.

I. How the Zaire (Congo) and Asian Rain Forests Are Alike.

1.   3.

2.   4.

II. How the Zaire (Congo) and Asian Rain Forests Differ.

1.   3.

2.   4.

II. Making Inferences

In our reading, many facts are given to us. From these facts we draw conclusions. The following are some conclusions or inferences that people might make after reading Chapter 3. Tell whether these conclusions are correct or incorrect. Give reasons for your answers.

1. Farmers in Indonesia and in the Amazon River valley could grow the same crops.

2. In the Gobi Desert, life would be very different from life in the Sahara of Africa.

3. A large part of the population of Pakistan probably lives near the Indus River.

4. In Indonesia and the Philippines, temperatures throughout the year might vary from 20°F (−7°C) to 100°F (38°C).

5. Throughout China, farmers will grow rice.

6. If the wet monsoon should arrive later than usual, millions of Asian people might starve.

7. The growing season in Indonesia is shorter than the growing season in northeastern China.

493

DEVELOPING IDEAS AND SKILLS

Building Map Skills — Climates of the Asian Region

Study the map. Then answer the following questions.

1. (a) Where is a humid subtropical climate found?
   (b) How does this climate affect farming?
2. Which climates are found on the islands of the Asian region?
3. (a) Where is a desert climate located?
   (b) Which countries have a humid continental climate?
4. How does wind affect climate in the Asian region?
5. Do you think that people in the United States are more or less affected by climate than the people in the Asian region? Explain your answer.

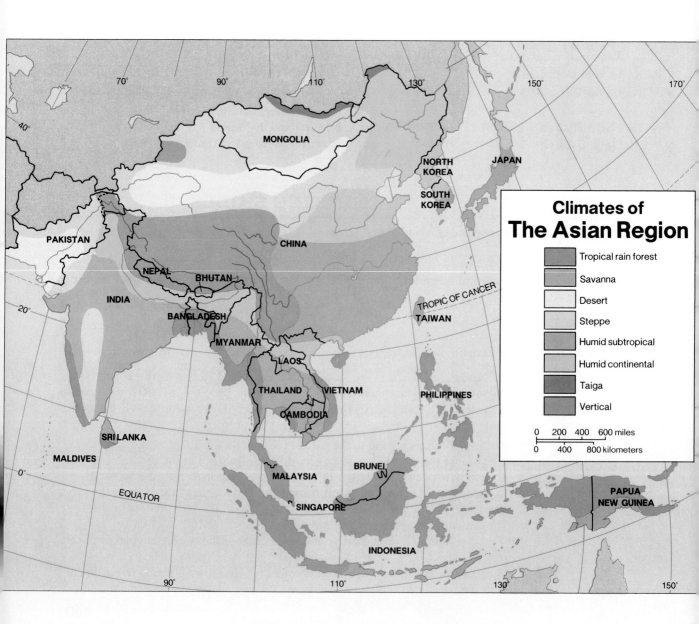

Climates of
The Asian Region

- Tropical rain forest
- Savanna
- Desert
- Steppe
- Humid subtropical
- Humid continental
- Taiga
- Vertical

0   200   400   600 miles
0   400   800 kilometers

Monsoon India

Hindus rely on the sea, for it is from the sea that the monsoon winds come—the rain-laden winds without which the crops would fail. Here is the story of Nathan and his wife Rukmani. They own a few acres of land in southern India. (However, they have a mortgage on the land, part of which must be paid yearly to a local landowner.) They live, like most villagers, in a two-room house made of sun-dried mud bricks. The roof is of thatched grass and branches. Nearby is a small fruit and vegetable patch and their rice fields.

Like most Hindu farmers, Nathan depends on the monsoon winds for rain. Although the rains have always fallen, there are always the moments of mounting anxiety if they do not come on time. Here is a brief description of the tragedy that can befall a small farmer if the rains fail to come on time.

. . . That year the rains failed. A week went by, two. We stared at the cruel sky, calm, blue, indifferent to our need. We threw ourselves on the earth and prayed. But no rains came.

Each day the level of the water dropped . . . the river had shrunk to a trickle, the well was as dry as a bone. Before long the rice shoots were tipped with brown. Harvesting time had come and there was nothing to harvest. The paddy had taken all our labor and lay before us in heaps of dry, yellow shoots.

Sivaji, the overseer, came to collect the money lender's interest.

"There is nothing this year," said Nathan.

"What do you mean," Sivaji answered. "You have had the land this year; you have contracted to pay for its use. I must have the due interest."

Nathan went into the mud hut and Rukmani followed. "The bullocks must be sold," said Nathan. "That is better than having the land taken from us." And so the oxen were taken.

The drought continued. Day after day, the pitiless sun blazed down. The earth cracked, plants died and the grasses rotted. The cattle and sheep crept to the dry river and died there for lack of water . . . .

Then, too late to do any good, Nathan and Rukmani saw the storm clouds gathering. Before long the rain came down in a fury, making up for the long drought and giving the land as much as it could drink. But, for Nathan and Rukmani, there was nothing left. There was no joy for the monsoon had come too late.

1. How did Nathan and Rukmani make a living?
2. Why was the monsoon important to them?
3. Where did the monsoon come from?
4. What happened to Nathan and Rukmani when the monsoon failed to come?
5. What can the government do to bring water to these farmlands?
6. Why was there no joy for Nathan and Rukmani when the monsoon came?

Chapter 4

Early History

How did people live in the ancient lands of China and India?

READING FOR A PURPOSE:
1. Who were the early peoples of China and India?
2. What were some of the achievements of the early civilizations of China and India?
3. Why were Europeans interested in the Asian region?

1. The Chinese developed one of the oldest continuous civilizations in world history. Because of their geography, they were somewhat shut off from the outside world. To the east lay the great Pacific Ocean. To the south was a dense tropical forest where elephants, tigers, and other wild animals lived. The high Himalayas and the highlands of Tibet shut off invaders from the west. The only way into China was through the Gobi Desert to the north. From time to time, China was invaded by tribes from the desert. These groups brought other ways of living. However, China's culture and traditions were strong. Usually the foreign invaders ended up adopting a Chinese way of life.

2. Some of the earliest of all civilizations started in the Asian region. It is believed that government began in the valley of the Yellow River and spread southward to the Yangzi River Valley. The early Chinese people worked together to fight floods and build canals. It was near the Yangzi that rice was grown and became the main food for the southern Chinese people. The rice growers changed the land. They built terraces on the hillsides. They divided the land into hundreds of small fields bordered by dikes.

3. For much of its history China was ruled by powerful families. These ruling families were called *dynasties.* The head of the dynasty was called the emperor. The emperor obtained power over the people by means of a strong army. Over the years, however, the emperor's descendants would lose their power and a new family would become the rulers of China. Another emperor would build up a powerful army and a strong government. Then that dynasty or family would rule for a while. This change of ruling family took place many times in the history of China.

4. The history of China is also a history of invasions. On the northern steppes were tribes of nomads who raised goats and sheep. These nomads often moved southward in search of better pastures for their herds. About 215 years before the birth of Christ, the Chinese built a Great Wall along their northern border to keep out the nomads. The wall did not succeed. Again and again, Chinese armies had to battle these invaders from the north. Finally, a very strong tribe called the Mongols overran large parts of Asia and Russia. Their leader was Genghis Khan. In 1279, the Mongols

In the third century B.C., the Great Wall of China was built to keep out invaders from the north. This 1,500-mile (2,414-kilometer) wall is a symbol of the isolation that for years China tried to maintain. Why is isolation from other countries almost impossible in today's world?

Chinese civilization dates back thousands of years. This wine vessel was made by a highly skilled craftworker around 1,400 years ago.

completed their conquest of China. They were led by Kublai Khan, the grandson of Genghis Khan.

5. The stories of Marco Polo tell us much about the size and riches of China during this time. Marco Polo went from Italy to East Asia with his father and uncle and lived in Cathay, as China was then called by Europeans. He stayed in China for twenty years, from 1275 to 1295. He was amazed by the beauty and wealth of the Chinese court. When he returned to Europe, he described all he had seen. Marco Polo told the people of Europe about such Chinese inventions as printed money, gunpowder, the compass, and the *abacus,* a counting machine. He told how the Chinese made silk and paper and printed with wood blocks and movable type. He told of the Grand Canal, which connected northern and central China.

6. The Chinese civilization, however, did not remain within the borders of China. It spread to Korea and later to Japan. The Japanese, over a period of years, imitated the Chinese in many ways. They used their system of writing. They adopted their religion and copied their form of government. In time, the Japanese people were taught to obey their emperor because he was supposed to have descended from the gods.

7. There were other early civilizations in the Asian region, as we know from certain ruins that still exist. Within the past 60 years, experts discovered that India had a civilization as old as China's. In India's long history, many different groups have ruled the country. More than 4,000 years ago, the people who spoke Dravidian lived in India. The Aryans, who were wandering herders, invaded from the northwest and conquered the land. They became farmers and divided the land into small kingdoms. Most Indians today follow the Hindu religion and philosophy. The Hindu religion began with the ideas of the early peoples of India. More than a thousand years later another religion, Buddhism, began in India.

8. In 327 B.C., India was conquered by Alexander the Great from Greece. Shortly after that, an Indian family called the Mauryas ruled northern India. Under the Guptas, still another family, India reached a time of greatness. During that time, there were many great scientists, thinkers, and craftworkers. Indian mathematicians invented the zero and the decimal point. Indian craftworkers wove cotton, invented the waterclock, and found a way to forge rustproof iron. Later rulers included Muslims and an Asian people called the Mongols, whom Indians called the Moguls.

9. Meanwhile, the ships of Europe were beginning to sail to the Far East. Since the time of Marco Polo, the people of Europe wanted the jewels, cloth, and spices of the Asian region. (Europeans sometimes called the region the Orient.) Most of the Asian goods were

497

The Taj Mahal was built in the 1600s by an emperor of India. It is built entirely of white marble. For many, it symbolizes the beauty of India.

reaching Europe over land routes. The rulers of Europe wanted an all-water route that would be quicker, safer, and less expensive. This all-water route was found, in 1498, by the Portuguese explorer Vasco da Gama, who sailed around Africa to India. After the Portuguese established a colony in India, the British, the Dutch, and the French followed the same route and set up their own trading posts in the Asian region.

UNDERSTANDING WHAT YOU HAVE READ

1. **Which questions are answered in this chapter?**
   a. Why did the Chinese build a great wall?
   b. Why did Europeans want an all-water route to the Far East?
   c. Who built the Taj Mahal?

2. **The main idea of *paragraphs 2 through 5* describes the**
   a. early history of China
   b. importance of Mongol invasions
   c. journeys of Marco Polo

3. **The Koreans and Japanese adopted many beliefs and ways from the**
   a. Aryans
   b. Chinese
   c. Greeks

4. **An early invader of India was**
   a. Kublai Khan
   b. Vasco da Gama
   c. Alexander the Great

5. **The Chinese built a great wall to**
   a. keep out nomad tribes
   b. keep their people from moving west
   c. stop trade with European nations

6. **Europeans wanted an all-water route to the Asian region because they**
   a. wanted more knowledge of the oceans
   b. wanted the spices and jewels of the Asian region
   c. were looking for adventure

7. **A *dynasty* is in many ways like**
   a. a democracy
   b. the dictatorship of a few
   c. a royal family or monarchy

8. **In *paragraph 6,* the phrase "descended from the gods" means**
   a. "following a tribal religion"
   b. "the gods were his ancestors"
   c. "ruled according to the teachings of the Bible"

498

— An Amazing Discovery in China —

As we leaf through our textbooks we read about the history of ancient peoples: Egyptians, Jews, Greeks, and Romans. We find out how these people lived in peace and war. We learn the names of rulers. But from where does this knowledge of the past come? Much of it comes from the work of archaeologists, people who search through the ruins of cities, tombs, and temples to bring us a better understanding of human life in the past. A recent discovery in China shows us how the work of archaeologists adds to our understanding of history.

China probably gets its name from the dynasty, or ruling family called the Qin (Ch'in [Chin]). They came to power about 250 B.C. At that time, China was divided into many small kingdoms, each one trying to gain control of the others. By 221 B.C., the ruler of the Qin dynasty succeeded in conquering the small kingdoms. He then formed them into one empire. The ruler of this new empire gave himself the name Qin Shihuangdi, or First Sovereign Emperor of Qin. Not satisfied with his conquests, the First Emperor decided to take on larger and larger projects. Before he came to power, many separate walls had been built by earlier peoples to keep out invaders from the north. The First Emperor decided to join all these walls together to form one great wall. When it was finished, it wound its way 1,500 miles (2,400 kilometers) across the tops of the rugged northern mountains like a huge stone dragon!

Before he died, the First Emperor planned one more huge project: he planned to have himself buried with an entire life-size army of 7,500 warriors, servants, and horses to serve and guard him. This project was discovered accidentally in 1974, near Qin's ancient capital of Xi'an (Sian). Farmers, digging wells, uncovered a vast underground burial place filled with hundreds of clay warriors and horses. The figures were made of terra cotta, a kind of clay that is hardened and painted like pottery. Most of the figures were standing at attention, as if waiting for the First Emperor to inspect them. From this tomb, historians were able to learn a great deal about China's past.

The Chinese leaders have always placed a high value on their nation's past history. Upon hearing of the accidental discovery, they quickly sent a trained labor force to dig further and to restore whatever they could. The work was carried out in well-planned stages. As they dug further, the workers carefully removed more and more layers of soil. Gradually, they were able to clear the figures themselves. Some had been toppled or broken. These were repaired and reassembled. Heads, fingers, and other parts of the body were joined together. Finally, each figure was lowered back into its original position.

Other huge earth mounds were dug up near the First Emperor's tomb. One revealed bronze horses, chariots, and chariot drivers. Together, these finds have been transformed into a large on-site museum that attracts thousands of visitors within China and from abroad.

1. Who are archaeologists?
2. Why is the Qin dynasty important?
3. What was uncovered near Qin Shihuangdi's burial place?
4. How was it gradually restored?
5. How has it added to our knowledge of early China?

Chapter 5

Years of Struggle

How did the lands of the Asian region win their independence?

READING FOR A PURPOSE:
1. Why did European nations try to control parts of the Asian region?
2. How did World War II affect the Asian region?
3. How did China come to be divided between the People's Republic of China and Taiwan?

Modern Japanese dressed in the kind of clothes worn by fighters in feudal Japan. Such warriors were called samurai.

1. After Vasco da Gama's voyage, the European nations rushed to obtain the riches of the Asian region. Gradually, they gained control of many lands. By 1858, the United Kingdom had won control of the Indian subcontinent. The Dutch ruled the Netherlands East Indies. The French were powerful in Indochina, the lands of the southeast peninsula. Portugal never became as strong as the others and held only small territories.

2. At first, Europeans and Americans knew very little about China and Japan. China was ruled by an all-powerful emperor and a strong army. Japan was divided among powerful landowners called feudal lords. Each lord ruled the peasants who worked his fields. The most powerful lord, or *shogun,* was stronger than the emperor who ruled the land. The Chinese emperor and the Japanese shogun kept their lands shut off from the rest of the world.

3. The Western nations, however, could not be kept out of Asia forever. In the 19th century, they began to produce large amounts of goods by machine. They looked to Asia as a place where these goods could be sold. Their ships began to appear in the waters off the Asian coast. At the same time, American sailors who had been shipwrecked on Japanese shores reported that they had been poorly

treated. To protect American sailors, Commodore Matthew Perry was sent to Japan to make a treaty. Impressed by the modern arms and machines he brought them as gifts, the rulers of Japan agreed to give American sailors better treatment. They also agreed to allow American ships to trade in some Japanese harbors.

4. Perry's visit had an important effect on the history of Japan. The Japanese rulers saw that they could no longer keep their country shut off from other nations. In 1868, the turning point came. The emperor took power away from the shogun, who had become weak. In a short time, Japan learned how to use the machines of the Western nations. Factories were started. A powerful army and navy were built up. Within a short time, Japan became the strongest nation in Asia.

5. At the same time, China was growing weaker. The British, French, Russians, Germans, and Japanese soon gained control over parts of China. To protect American trade with China, the United States announced the Open Door policy in 1899. This meant that China should be equally open to all nations for trade and also for business. For a time the nations stopped dividing China among themselves.

6. In 1911, revolution broke out in China.

Commodore Matthew C. Perry met with Japanese officials in 1853 and 1854. In 1854, the Japanese agreed to open up trade between the United States and their nation. How did Perry's visit affect the economy of Japan?

The emperors' rule was ended. The Chinese people set up a republican form of government, that is, one with no monarch. One of the revolutionary leaders was a young doctor, Sun Yat-sen. He led the Nationalist party that set up the government. But Sun Yat-sen died in 1925, before he could unite China. He was followed by General Chiang Kai-shek. To strengthen his rule, Chiang fought to rid his government of Communists. He was able to drive them into hiding in northern China.

7. To the east of China, the island nation of Japan continued to grow in strength. It set out to build a large overseas empire. In 1895, it took Taiwan (Formosa) from China. In 1904–5, it defeated Russia and conquered Korea. It officially took over Korea in 1910. In 1931, it invaded China and added the Northeast (Manchuria) to its empire. The Japanese said they needed places to sell their goods and more land for their rapidly growing population. They especially wanted Southeast Asia because of its rich natural resources. In the late 1930s, Japan attacked China again. The United States protested these attacks. On December 7, 1941, Japan made a surprise attack on an American naval base at Pearl Harbor in Hawaii. Because of this attack, the United States officially entered World War II.

8. Fighting against the United States during World War II, the Japanese held much of Southeast Asia. However, in 1945, the United States dropped atomic bombs on the Japanese cities of Hiroshima and Nagasaki. Japan was then defeated by the Allies and lost all its colonies. After the war was over, a new government was started with the help of the United States. In time, Japan recovered from the war. Today it is a great industrial power.

9. Following the war, the colonies of European nations demanded their independence. In 1947 India gained its freedom from Britain. Pakistan was carved out of British India to give India's Muslims a land of their own. Sri Lanka, Malaysia, and Myanmar also broke away from the United Kingdom and became self-governing. France's possessions were broken up to form the nations of Cambodia, Laos, and North and South Vietnam. The Philippines, a possession of the United States, was given its freedom in 1946. Korea, which was taken from Japan, was divided into North and South Korea. Indonesia became free after a long struggle with the Netherlands.

10. After World War II ended in 1945, civil war broke out again in China. The Nationalists were led by General Chiang Kai-shek, and the Communists were led by Mao Zedong. In 1949, the Communists won and set up the People's Republic of China. The Nationalists retreated to the island of Taiwan, which they called the Republic of China. Both governments claim the right to rule all China.

11. In 1950, the Communist government of North Korea directed an invasion of South Korea. The United States and other members of the United Nations sent armed forces to help South Korea. The Communist government of China helped the North Koreans. The end of fighting did not bring victory for either side, however. Korea remained divided. But the action of the United States and United Nations saved the independence of South Korea.

12. There was still no peace in some parts of the Asian region. In the 1960s and early

501

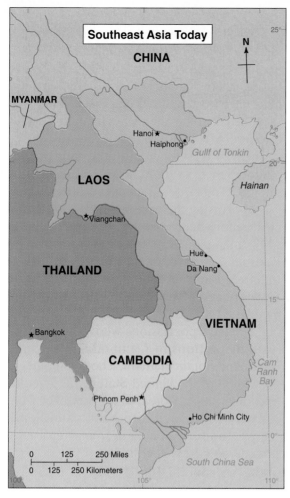

Southeast Asia Today

The nations of Southeast Asia are valued for their rich supply of natural resources. Which countries share a border with China?

1970s, the United States took part in a war in Vietnam. It tried to stop the Communist North Vietnamese and the Communists in South Vietnam from taking over South Vietnam. More than 46,000 Americans and a million and a half Vietnamese were killed. In 1973, American forces were brought home. In 1975 North Vietnam defeated South Vietnam, and Vietnam became one country. Communist governments soon controlled Kampuchea (Cambodia) and Laos. When Soviet-supported Vietnam invaded Communist Kampuchea (Cambodia) and took over its government, China invaded Vietnam as a "punishment." China's troops later withdrew.

13. More bloodshed came to this region in 1971, when the eastern and western parts of the Muslim nation of Pakistan went to war. The main government was in West Pakistan, though more than half of the people lived in East Pakistan. The two parts of Pakistan were divided by about 1,000 miles (1,600 kilometers) of India's land. The people of East Pakistan wanted a stronger voice in the government. The western rulers refused and sent an army to the eastern half to crush the movement toward self-government. A bloody war followed. However, with the help of India's army, the people of East Pakistan fought back and won their freedom. Their new nation is now called Bangladesh.

UNDERSTANDING WHAT YOU HAVE READ

1. **Which questions are answered in this chapter?**

a. Why did Europe become interested in the Asian region?

b. How did India become British?

c. How did Japan become a modern nation?

2. **The main idea of *paragraphs 5 through 13* is that**

a. new nations were formed in Asia and Africa at the same time

b. wars among people of the Asian region fill its modern history

c. there are two Chinas and two Koreas today

3. **European nations established colonies in Asia in the 19th century because they**

a. needed lands for their growing populations

b. wanted to try out their new ideas of government

c. wanted markets for their goods

4. All of the following have
   Communist governments EXCEPT:

a. China
b. Cambodia
c. India

5. U.S. troops fought in wars against
   all of the following EXCEPT:

a. India
b. Japan
c. North Vietnam

DEVELOPING IDEAS AND SKILLS

Reading a Time Line

Look at the time line. Write the letter of the period of time in which each of the following events takes place.

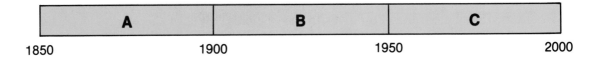

| A | B | C |

1850   1900   1950   2000

1. Japan takes Taiwan from China.
2. Bangladesh is created.
3. The United States drops atomic bombs on Japan.
4. The United States announces Open Door policy.
5. Korean War begins.
6. Sun Yat-sen dies; General Chiang Kai-shek leads the Chinese Nationalists.
7. The United Kingdom takes control of the Indian subcontinent.
8. India becomes independent; Pakistan is created.
9. Shoguns lose power in Japan.
10. American troops withdraw from Vietnam.
11. The Philippines become independent.
12. The United States enters World War II.

Chapter 6

The People of the Asian Region

Who are the people of Eastern Asia?

READING FOR A PURPOSE:
1. What are the chief groups of Asia?
2. What are some problems of village people?
3. How important is the family unit in Asia?

1. Asia has over one-half the people of the world. China, with more than 1.1 billion people, and India, with about 859 million people, are the two most populous countries in the world. Since a great part of Asia is covered with either mountains or desert, most of its people are crowded into the fertile river valleys and coastal plains. The island of Java in Indonesia, one of the most densely populated areas in the world, has nearly 1,500 people for each square mile of land. In Japan, there are about 848 people for each square mile. Compare these figures with the United States, which has about 70 people for each square mile!

2. Not only are there many different racial and national groups in Asia, there are many languages spoken as well. Different groups of people within a country often speak different languages. For example, most of China's 67 million people who are not ethnic Chinese speak other languages. Even the Chinese spoken throughout the country is very different from one area to another. However, more than 90 percent of the people speak or understand Mandarin, the nation's standard language. India and Indonesia are also countries with many different languages.

3. Most of the people of Asia are farmers. They live in thousands of small villages, not in widely separated houses as in the United States. The farmers have a deep love for their fields. Most of the work is done by hand on small, scattered plots. The main crop in the warm areas is rice. Many of the families raise barely enough food for themselves. Often they cannot afford to pay enough taxes to build the hospitals and schools that are needed.

4. Yet even where schools have been built, children are often kept at home. Many parents need the help of their children in the fields to raise enough food for the family. In many villages there is no pure water. People use the water of village "ponds" and tanks, where animals are brought to drink. Poor diet, over-

How does farming in China differ from farming in more industrialized nations?

How does the city-nation of Singapore differ from much of the rest of Southeast Asia?

crowded houses, dirt, and disease-carrying insects are a few of the reasons there is often poor health. In much of Asia, people can only expect to live about 63 years. In China, it is 70 years; in Japan, 79.

5. The nations of Japan, South Korea, and Singapore have become highly urbanized. Three-quarters of the Japanese live in cities and towns. Japan's capital, Tokyo, has about 8.3 million people. There are 11 other cities in Japan with over a million people. South Korea's capital, Seoul, has about 9.6 million people. Singapore is a city-nation of 2.7 million people. Hong Kong, a British colony and port, has about 5.8 million people.

6. All other Asian nations have more people living in the countryside than in their cities. However, even these nations have very large cities. China has 39 cities with over a million people. China's port city of Shanghai,

There are many means of transportation in Asia. Asians do not all own cars. Many walk, ride bikes, or use scooters.

including its suburbs, has 12 million people. Beijing (Peking), the capital of China, has 9.7 million people. Just a few of the other large Asian cities are the following: Bombay, Delhi, and Calcutta in India; Bangkok in Thailand; Jakarta in Indonesia; Karachi in Pakistan; Yangon in Myanmar; Ho Chi Minh City (Saigon) in Vietnam; and Taipei in Taiwan. Each year, more and more people come to live and work in the cities. Not all of them find the better way of life they are looking for.

7. Family life is important in Asia. In some parts of Asia, boys and girls in thousands of villages are taught to think of their families before themselves. Families are usually large. When a daughter marries, she joins the family of her husband. The father is the head of the family and is respected by all. All members of the family share what the family owns. Each family is expected to look after its own affairs and help each of its members. It is not unusual to find whole villages made up of just a few families, with all the relatives living together. These large families with many relatives are called extended families.

8. The family in China is still important. But it is smaller—usually parents, children, and sometimes grandparents. In China, the Communist government is trying to lessen the importance of the extended family because of the huge populations. The government is trying to get couples to limit the size of their families. Couples are encouraged by the government to have only one child. Those who agree to have only one child are given money every month until the child is 14. If the couple has a second child, their salary is reduced until that child is 14.

UNDERSTANDING WHAT YOU HAVE READ

1. Which of the following questions are answered in this chapter?
a. How many people live in Japan?
b. What food do many people in the Asian region eat?
c. What is family life like in the Asian region?

2. A good title for *paragraphs 5 and 6* would be
a. Asia: A Region of Many Villages
b. Cities of the Asian Region
c. The Races and Ethnic Groups of the Asian Region

3. The country in the world with the most people is
a. India
b. United States
c. China

4. Most people in the Asian region are
a. fishers
b. farmers
c. factory workers

5. Many Asian farmers keep their children home from school because
a. school is too expensive
b. the children are needed to help in the fields
c. the schools are too far away

6. In China, the Communist government has
a. increased the importance of the extended family
b. urged couples to have large families
c. lessened the importance of the extended family

7. The nations of Japan, South Korea, and Singapore have become
a. Communist
b. urbanized
c. Muslim

8. In China, India, and Indonesia,
a. many different languages are spoken
b. only one language is allowed
c. English is the official language used for all government business

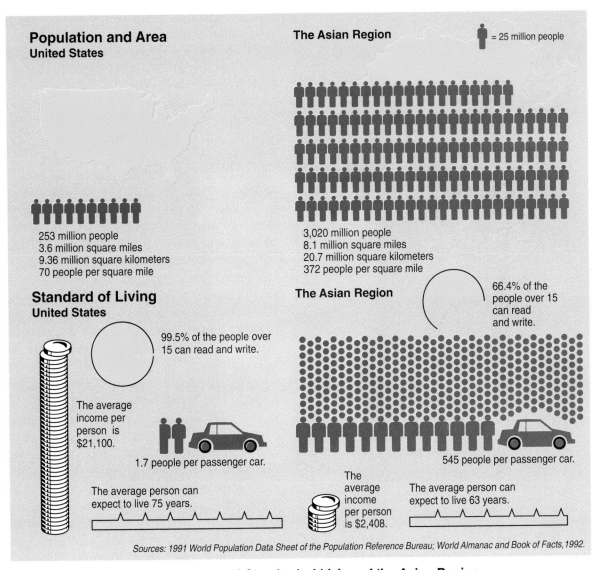

Population and Area
United States

253 million people
3.6 million square miles
9.36 million square kilometers
70 people per square mile

The Asian Region

= 25 million people

3,020 million people
8.1 million square miles
20.7 million square kilometers
372 people per square mile

Standard of Living
United States

99.5% of the people over 15 can read and write.

The average income per person is $21,100.

1.7 people per passenger car.

The average person can expect to live 75 years.

The Asian Region

66.4% of the people over 15 can read and write.

545 people per passenger car.

The average income per person is $2,408.

The average person can expect to live 63 years.

Sources: 1991 World Population Data Sheet of the Population Reference Bureau; World Almanac and Book of Facts, 1992.

Population, Area, and Standard of Living of the Asian Region

DEVELOPING IDEAS AND SKILLS

Understanding Charts and Diagrams — Population, Area, and Standard of Living of the Asian Region

Answer these questions by using the charts and diagrams above.

1. Is the standard of living of this region high or low compared with that of the United States? Is it a low-income or developing area?
2. Is the region as crowded as the United States?
3. Are the people of this region literate compared with the people of the United States?

4. How long may the average person in this region expect to live?
5. What facts are clues to the standard of living of the people of the region?
6. How does this region compare with the United States in size?

Chapter 7

Religions of Asia

What religions are most important in Asia?

READING FOR A PURPOSE:
1. What do Hindus believe?
2. Who was the Buddha?
3. What is the Confucian way of life?

1. In North and South America and Europe, most people are members of Christian religions. This is not true of the Asian region. (The southwestern corner of the continent of Asia was the starting place of Judaism, Christianity, and Islam. We studied that area as part of the Middle East region.) Most of the people in the Asian region—the part of Asia east of Iran and Afghanistan—are not Christians or Jews. They are followers of other religions and philosophies. Most practice Hinduism, Islam, Buddhism, or Confucianism. These religions and philosophies have played a great part in the history of Asia and in the lives of the people. To understand the people of Asia and how they live, we must know something of their beliefs.

2. The religion of the great majority of people in India is Hinduism. The Hindu religion had its beginnings in the ideas of early peoples who came to India more than 4,000 years ago. Hinduism is not only a religion. It is a philosophy and a way of life. Most Hindus believe in many gods or spirits. They believe that these gods may be different forms of one spirit called Brahma. Hindus believe that certain pools and rivers, like the Ganges, are sacred. Among their important beliefs are *karma, dharma,* and *reincarnation.* The *caste* system is still widely followed by Hindus. It is based on the belief that a person, from birth, has the same caste or place in society that his or her father had. A person cannot change caste and is expected to do the same work as his or her father. Certain work can be done only by certain castes.

3. From earliest times there were four main castes. The highest caste was that of the priests or Brahmins. The second was made up of the warriors. The third caste was that of the craftworkers, traders, and farmers. The lowest caste was the unskilled workers. These four main groups were divided into many smaller castes. These were formed as new jobs were needed in the village or town. Each caste had its own rules by which its members lived. (These rules are called *dharma.* Dharma is knowing what is the right thing to do and what should not be done.) Members of one caste did not eat with or marry members of another caste. They did not mix at social affairs. Lower than even the fourth caste were people called "untouchables." They belonged to no caste and did the jobs that no one else would do. (The "untouchables" make up about 10 percent of India's population. It is illegal to discriminate against them.)

4. Another major belief of Hinduism is *reincarnation.* According to this belief, a person's soul never dies. After death, people can be born again. The kind of life people can expect after they are reborn depends on how they have lived before. A Hindu believes that

508

people can be reborn many times until their soul reaches its final resting place. The number of times that people are reborn depends on *karma,* the way they lived before. (According to the idea of karma, every action brings about certain results. In short, if people act badly, the results will be bad. If they act well, the results will be good.) For example, if people have worked and followed the rules of their caste *(dharma),* they will be rewarded. If they have been evil and broken the rules of the caste, they may be reborn into a lower caste. In the next life they might become an untouchable or even an animal. (According to Hindu belief, people have no one to blame but themselves for their place in life. Instead of complaining, they should lead a good life so that they can be reborn into a higher caste.)

5. Islam is another religion of the Indian subcontinent. Islam was brought to India by the followers of Muhammad. When India was ruled by the United Kingdom, the Hindus and the Muslims lived side by side. Now it is

(top) A Hindu worshipping in a temple.
(bottom) Hindus bathing in the Ganges River,
which they regard as sacred.

divided into three countries: India, Pakistan, and Bangladesh. Today, India and Nepal are largely Hindu, while Pakistan and Bangladesh are chiefly Muslim. However, a large minority of Hindus live in Bangladesh and millions of Muslims live in India.

6. When the followers of Hinduism and Islam lived together in British India, there were many disputes because of their different beliefs. Most Hindus worship many gods; Muslims believe in one. Muslims have one sacred book, the Koran; Hindus read many sacred texts. Muslims have no images or statues of gods in their mosques; the temples and shrines of Hindus are for individual worship and are filled with images. Muslims eat beef but not pork; Hindus believe the cow is sacred and often will not eat other animals either. There are many holy places in the Hindu religion. In Islam, the main holy place is Mecca. The Sikh religion, started about 1500, began as an effort to combine Hinduism and Islam. Today, about 2 percent of India's population are Sikhs.

7. Buddhism began in India more than 2,500 years ago. It was started by a young prince called Gautama. He decided to spend his life helping others. People called Gautama "Buddha," or the "Enlightened One." The Buddhists have no God such as is found in Christianity, Islam, or Judaism. Buddhism teaches that humans have many desires that lead to suffering. They must fight themselves to drive away these desires and do what is right. The best way to do this is to forget oneself and help others. Buddhism spread throughout Asia. Millions of people in China, Tibet, Japan, Bhutan, Sri Lanka, and Southeast Asia are Buddhists. A Buddhist temple is sometimes called a *pagoda.*

8. While Buddhism and other religions became part of Chinese life, it was really the teachings of a wise man called Confucius that guided the everyday life of the Chinese people. Confucius lived in the 6th century B.C. and began his teachings about the same time as Gautama in India. He did not teach about

A mosque in Delhi. What are some major differences between the followers of Islam and Hinduism? Why have religious differences so often been the cause of hatred and war?

a life after death but about how to live on earth. He believed that people should be more concerned about their responsibilities to others. These responsibilities included respect for learning; love and obedience to parents and family; loyalty to a good emperor; and understanding one's "place" in society. As a result of Confucius's teachings, the Chinese form of government developed. Power was in the hands of a small, educated group, while the majority of the people worked hard, lived simply, and loyally supported them. This way of life lasted far into the 20th century.

9. There are other groups of people who follow different religious beliefs or philosophies in the Asian regions. Lao-tse was another famous teacher in China. The book of Dao (Tao) contains many of his teachings. In time, Daoism (Taoism) became a religion with many gods, priests, and ceremonies. There are many Christians in Asia, too. Yet they are few in number when compared with the number of people who practice other religions. The Philippine people are mostly Christian. Their early Spanish rulers brought Christianity to the islands. Christian missionaries teach in many Asian countries. About 22 million people in India are Christian. Many Japanese are followers of both the Buddhist and Shinto religions. Shinto, Japan's oldest religion, is centered on the worship of nature and the spirits within nature.

UNDERSTANDING WHAT YOU HAVE READ

1. Which of the following questions are answered in this chapter?
a. When did Buddhism begin?
b. What is Shintoism?
c. How do Hinduism and Islam differ?

2. The main idea of this chapter is to describe the
a. beliefs of people in the Asian region
b. importance of Buddha
c. teachings of Confucius

3. Most of the people of India are
a. Hindus   b. Buddhists   c. Muslims

4. The Christian religion was brought to the Asian region by
a. nomads   b. explorers   c. missionaries

5. The Confucian teachings include all of the following EXCEPT
a. respect for learning
b. belief in a god and an afterlife
c. love and obedience to parents

6. There have been disputes between Hindus and Muslims because they
a. are both warlike people
b. try to spread their beliefs throughout the world
c. have different religious beliefs

7. Under a *caste system*, people are
a. united in one group   b. divided   c. Communists

8. *Reincarnation* is the belief in
a. many lives after death
b. one God
c. giving help to needy people

DEVELOPING CRITICAL THINKING SKILLS

Do You Agree or Disagree?

Tell whether you agree or disagree with the following statements. Give reasons for your answers.

1. Most of the people of Asia belong to one of three great religions.
2. All religions of Asian people have a belief in one God.
3. India is the only Asian country in which cattle are raised for their meat.
4. There are more Christians than non-Christians in the world.
5. The caste system has divided the Indian people into various groups.
6. Hindus believe in sacred rivers and pools.
7. In Buddhism the main belief is that humans may be born again several times.
8. Confucius is known as a great teacher rather than as a religious leader.
9. Since the caste system was ended in India, all people are considered equal by their fellow Indians.
10. Because Buddhism was founded by an Indian prince, its followers are found only in India.

FOLLOW UP

Making Comparisons

In your notebook, complete the following chart.

	HINDUISM	BUDDHISM	CONFUCIANISM
1. How it began			
2. Major beliefs			
3. How it affects the lives of the people			

Buddha

Buddhism, like Christianity and Islam, is a world religion. Its followers live in a huge part of Asia: India, Sri Lanka, Thailand, Mongolia, Tibet, China, Korea, and Japan. It also has many followers in Europe and North America. Here is a brief story of its founder and his beliefs.

Siddhartha Gautama was born about 565 B.C. in what is today southern Nepal. He came from a noble family and spent his early years inside the grounds of lovely palaces. He knew nothing about sorrow and suffering in the world. He married and had a son. Despite his isolation from the real world, Siddhartha began to think of the unhappiness and suffering that many people faced. At 29, he left his palace and family. For six years he wandered seeking the reasons for sorrow. Then, one night, sitting under a pipal, or bo, tree, he gained insight or wisdom. He became the Buddha, or "Enlightened One." He discovered why people suffered and how they could avoid suffering and unhappiness. For the next 45 years, the Buddha traveled up and down India, teaching. His closest followers were organized into an order (sangha) of monks and nuns. Dressed in saffron or orange robes, they set out to spread the Buddha's ideas throughout the world.

According to the Buddha, all sorrow or suffering came from desires. In turn, desires came from the quest for and possession of worldly goods. Desire meant sorrow and suffering in life after life. He believed in the cycle of death and rebirth, where a person's behavior in life would determine his or her position in the next life. The way to escape from these successive lives was to overcome desire. Once this was done, the person would be released and be absorbed or drawn into the All, a state of happiness and peace called Nirvana. This is the aim of all Buddhists.

Write the statements below in your notebook. If the statement is true, mark it with **T.** If the statement is false, mark it with an **F** and change the underlined word or words to make it correct.

1. The Buddhist religion was begun by Confucius.
2. The Buddhist religion began in India.
3. Buddha means "wise or enlightened" one.
4. As a young man, Siddhartha lived in palaces and studied hard.
5. Siddhartha left his palace in order to learn more about sorrow and suffering.
6. The Buddha believed that people must go through successive lives because of their desires.
7. Buddhist monks and nuns have spread the ideas of their religion throughout the Far East.

Buddhist monks at prayer.

Farmers of Asia

How do most Asians meet their daily needs?

READING FOR A PURPOSE:
1. What are some practices of intensive farming?
2. What is subsistence farming?
3. How is farming carried on in a commune?

1. Good land in Asia is like a precious gem. This is because so much of the land is not suited for farming. Most of the people in Asia live in thousands of small villages. Each of these villages is a little world of its own. These subsistence farmers use nearly everything they raise and rarely have any products left over for sale. As a result, little is brought into the village from other areas. Many villages probably have no electricity, schools, or hospitals. There are few roads to the big cities.

2. The farmer's fields are outside the village. These may be a dozen or more scattered plots. The farmer tends these small plots of land very carefully. Almost everything is done by hand: planting the seeds, removing the weeds, and harvesting the crops. Since much of the region is hilly, it is not unusual for farming families to work on terraces carved out of the hillsides. Many plots are too small to use large farm machinery. Small machines such as hand tractors are in use. But even these machines and their fuel are expensive. However, because of the methods of farming, the yields per acre are sometimes higher than those of American farmers. This kind of farming is called *intensive* farming.

3. Except for a few pigs and chickens, most Asian farmers do not raise animals for food. They must use all their land to raise food for themselves; they cannot afford to graze animals on it. As a result, the people of Asia eat much less meat than those of the Americas and Europe. While India has more cattle than any other nation, most Indians are Hindus who do not eat beef. According to their religion, cows are sacred. However, the cattle are useful. They provide milk and their dung is used as fuel and fertilizer.

4. Despite their hard work, farmers have low incomes. Many farmers do not own their own land. They rent it from large landowners. Tenant farmers pay their rent with part of the crop they grow. If it is a good year, they have enough to pay debts to the village moneylender or to the government. If the farmers are very lucky, they may have enough left over to buy a water buffalo, some fertilizer, or a hand tractor. Many farmers stretch their small in-

Farming in Asia is done chiefly by hand or with the aid of animals, as in this rice paddy.

comes by bartering (trading) food and services with other villagers.

5. In the monsoon region, water is as precious as land. Every effort is made to save it during the dry season. In some places the fields are irrigated by water brought from the rivers through canals. In other places there are wells. In India there are many ponds or "tanks." For some villages, these tanks are the only source of water. The people wash their clothes in the tanks and bring their cattle to them to drink.

6. Besides the subsistence farmer, there are both migratory and commercial (plantation) farmers in the rain forest. Migratory farmers go about their work much the same as the rain-forest farmer in central Africa or South America does. To clear a field, they first burn the thick underbrush. Then they dig holes in the ground with a stick and drop in seeds. When the crop ripens, they pick it. After two or three years, the soil is no longer fertile. The farmer leaves the field and clears another. After about 15 years, the brush and grasses in the old field have made it fertile again.

7. There are also many plantations scattered throughout the rain forest. Each plantation raises a cash crop such as rubber, tobacco, coffee, tea, or sugarcane. These crops are not grown for use by the people in the home countries. They are exported to other lands throughout the world. Plantations are big businesses with directors and hundreds of workers. Many have stores and shops, a school, a hospital, and a water and electric plant on the plantation property. Many of the plantations are owned by people in Europe and North America.

8. In China, as in other countries, most people are farmers. For a time, the Communist Chinese introduced a new way of farming to Asia. In 1958, they formed *communes*. Each commune was made up of many farming villages, ranging in size from 500 to 70,000 members. Managers directed the farmers to carry out government plans. What was left after the government got its share of the crops was divided among the farmers. In the 1980s, the government began to rent parcels of land to individual farmers. This is known as tenant farming, and it is replacing the commune.

India is the world's leading tea exporter. The woman shown here is picking tea leaves in the Himalayan region. What are some other countries in which tea is grown?

UNDERSTANDING WHAT YOU HAVE READ

1. **Which of the following questions are answered in this chapter?**
   a. Why can Japan provide enough food for its people and Bangladesh can't?
   b. Why don't many Asian people eat much meat?
   c. Why are most farmers in Asia poor?

2. **The main idea of this chapter is to describe**
   a. a new kind of farming in China
   b. how farmers of the rain forest meet their needs
   c. different kinds of farming in Asia

3. **The chief farm animal of Asia is the**
   a. camel
   b. water buffalo
   c. horse

4. **Most of the work on Asian farms is done by**
   a. hand
   b. machinery
   c. animals

5. **There are few farm animals in Asia because**
   a. there is a lack of water for them
   b. religious beliefs forbid owning animals
   c. farmers use all the land to raise crop foods for their families

6. **In Asia, farm machinery has not been widely used because**
   a. the religions are against it
   b. the farms are too small
   c. climates are not favorable for the use of machines

7. **In *intensive* farming, the farmer**
   a. uses machinery and plants crops a distance apart
   b. uses hand labor and plants seeds close together
   c. gets a smaller amount of grain from each acre planted

8. **Communists combined farming villages into communes in**
   a. Taiwan
   b. China
   c. India

9. **Plantations in Asia raise crops for**
   a. nearby towns
   b. export
   c. the entire country

10. **Cash crops grown in Asia include**
    a. tobacco and sugarcane
    b. corn and sugarcane
    c. tobacco and corn

11. **Many of the plantations in Asia are owned by**
    a. Indians and Chinese
    b. Americans and British
    c. Europeans and North Americans

12. **Communes are being replaced by tenant farms in**
    a. China
    b. Taiwan
    c. India

— Developing Areas of Indonesia —

More than 90 percent of Indonesia's 170 million people live on three islands, Java, Madura, and Bali. There are about 1,500 people per square mile on Java. This is too much for the land to support. There are however, vast areas on Indonesia's other islands, such as Borneo, the Moluccas, and Irian Jaya, which are available for development. The government of Indonesia is encouraging people to go to these undeveloped areas. Here is the story of one such pioneer.

Sukardji was a 42-year-old landless farm laborer on Java. He lived with his wife, Sukartini, and their three children in a house he did not own. In 1984, he accepted the Indonesian government's offer and moved his family to Irian Jaya, the western half of the island of New Guinea. He would go with 600 other families to West Irian. Together, they would clear the jungles and create new farmlands. Sukardji knew what he wanted: his own home, his own piece of land, a kerosene lamp, a radio, and a new life. He hoped to find these in West Irian.

After laboring for a year Sukardji was beginning to realize part of his dream. Friends came to visit him to see his progress. Luckily, Sukardji's farm was near the town of Koya Timus so they could reach him by truck. When his friends arrived, Sukardji was preparing his rice fields for the year's second crop. Sukardji took his friends into his new home, a three-room house with a dirt floor. He had filled it with furniture he and his wife made from wood cleared from the fields. His first crop of rice had brought him enough money to buy a lamp and a radio.

The Indonesian government hopes its new program to populate the area will succeed. Each family gets a plot of land, a

house, a year's supply of food, and fertilizer. In return, each family must promise to open new territory. Not all of the pioneers were as pleased as Sukardji. Some families quit when their lands did not prove fertile. In the meantime, Sukardji is busy building a coop for chickens. He hopes to buy them with money he will earn from selling his second rice crop.

1. Where is West Irian located?
2. Why does the Indonesian government want to move people to this area?
3. Why did the Sukardji family volunteer to be pioneers?
4. How well did Sukardji do in West Irian?
5. In what ways is Sukardji a pioneer? Would you follow him to this new clearing? Why or why not?
6. What crop gives him money to buy other goods?

Chapter 9

Making Use of the Land

How do Asian farmers make use of their lands?

READING FOR A PURPOSE:
1. How is rice grown?
2. What are the important forest products?
3. Why are the seas important?

1. Wherever the climate of Asia is warm and wet, rice is the chief crop. Rice crops mean life for millions of people in this region. There are many reasons why this is so. First, in a region where there are many people and little fertile land, rice provides more food for each acre planted than any other grain. Second, in a hot climate, rice can be stored without spoiling. Third, rice has many uses. It is the staple or main ingredient in the Asian diet, just as wheat and potatoes are in the United States. When boiled, rice is eaten with meat or fish. It can be used to make wine. Animals can also be fed rice straw.

2. The rice plant is grown in small fields called *paddies*. The paddy is surrounded by dikes, or walls, made of earth. While the rice seedlings are growing, the paddies are flooded with water. The dikes control the supply of water. On the hillsides, terraces are built for the paddies.

3. Farmers first plant the rice seeds in a small plot of ground. As the plants start to grow, they clear the rest of the land. They use a wooden plow pulled by a water buffalo (carabao). The fields are flooded by means of dikes. When the young rice plants are about six inches (15 centimeters) high, they are transplanted, or moved, to the flooded fields. In a monsoon area, there may not be enough rainfall. Therefore, the farmer gets water by digging ditches from nearby streams or pumping water from a well. In four months, the rice plants are fully grown. The water is then drained from the paddy, and the rice is threshed. In Myanmar, Pakistan, and Thailand, some farmers produce enough rice to export to neighboring countries.

4. The warm, rainy climate of Asia is good for other crops as well. Scattered throughout the rain forest are many plantations on which are grown special crops such as rubber, tea, bananas, coconuts, tobacco, coffee, and sugarcane. Southeast Asia is the largest rubber-producing area in the world. Malaysia is the world leader. The rubber is gathered by hundreds of workers. The worker first makes a cut

Cotton field in southern India. Which area of the United States is also an important cotton-growing region?

517

Farmers bringing their crops to market in Thailand. Can you identify any of the crops?

in the tree. The sap of the rubber tree, *latex,* drips out of this cut into small pails. The latex is collected and then processed, or turned into rubber. It is then shipped to factories all over the world.

5. The rain forest has other valuable products. *Quinine,* a medicine used to treat the disease of malaria, is obtained from the bark of the cinchona tree. *Kapok* is a light waterproof fiber used to fill mattresses and life preservers.

Wood from the *teak* tree is used in making furniture. *Rattan* is a palm that is made into baskets, chairs, and furniture. *Bamboo* is a tall grass with hard stems. It is used to make poles, furniture, and even houses. And then there are spices. Indonesia produces more than half the pepper used by Americans. *Cinnamon* comes from the inner bark of a tree grown in Sri Lanka, Myanmar, and India.

6. *Jute* is a wet-season crop grown in India, Bangladesh, and China. It is a fiber that is made into burlap bags and rope. In the Philippines, *abacá,* another rope fiber, is grown. This product is often called Manila hemp and is used in making the strongest natural rope.

7. China, India, and Pakistan are leading growers of cotton. Indian cotton was among the first products to be introduced to the countries of the Western world. The silk products of China and Japan have long been famous. Silk is obtained from a worm that eats the leaves of the mulberry tree. A great amount of labor is needed to care for the silkworms and the mulberry trees. Silk is not as important in world trade as it once was. The development of nylon and other such products has reduced the demand for silk throughout the world.

8. Where it is too cool or dry for rice to grow, such foods as wheat, barley, millet, potatoes, and corn are raised. China is among the world leaders in the production of wheat.

These women are checking silkworm cocoons. The cocoons are made into silk fibers. How is silk that you find in stores in your area an example of cultural borrowing?

518

Spring wheat is planted in northern China and in the northeast (Manchuria), where the climate is cooler. Winter wheat is grown in much of the central part of eastern China. China's northeast is a leading producer of *soybeans*. This vegetable has many uses. It provides flour and breakfast food, and its oil is used for cooking. Soups and sauces are also made from it. Soybeans are high in protein. The plant is valuable, too, for it can be used to feed animals. The soybean plant enriches the soil where it is grown, restoring minerals to the earth.

9. As you have learned, most people in Asia eat little meat because farmers lack the land to raise large animals. Therefore, the people along the coast have turned to the sea for other sources of food. Fish is more important in the diet of many Asians than meat. Thousands of fishing boats sail along the coasts of China and Japan every day to catch fish. Japan has some of the finest fishing grounds in the world. Japan also has very

Japanese fishing people unloading the day's catch. Why does the diet of many Asians include more fish than meat?

modern fishing boats that can sail far from land. The fish are not only carried aboard these boats, they are also prepared for sale on board.

UNDERSTANDING WHAT YOU HAVE READ

1. Which of the following questions are answered in this chapter?
a. What is a *paddy*?
b. What is jute used for?
c. Why does India import rice?

2. The main idea of this chapter is to describe
a. how the people of Asia use the seas
b. the products of the rain forest
c. how Asian people make use of their land

3. The warm, rainy climate is suited to the growing of rice and
a. millet   b. tea   c. olive trees

4. The Asian rain forest has plantations that grow
a. rubber   b. bananas   c. corn

5. How do Asian farmers provide water in the dry season?
a. They plant only near rivers that are filled with water all year.
b. They draw water through canals.
c. They plant only in the highlands.

6. Wheat is grown instead of rice in places where
a. the growing season is longer
b. the growing season is shorter
c. rainfall is steady throughout the year

7. A *paddy* is important to
a. rice farmers
b. fishers
c. rubber planters

8. Southeast Asia is the largest producer of
a. rubber
b. cotton
c. wheat

9. Quinine is a
a. valuable mineral
b. medicine made from the bark of the cinchona tree
c. light waterproof fiber used to fill mattresses

10. Teak, rattan, and bamboo are all used to make
a. furniture
b. rope
c. boats

11. China is a leading producer of
a. cinnamon
b. kapok
c. wheat

SUMMING UP

Match the statements in Column B with the Asian products listed in Column A.

COLUMN A	COLUMN B
1. wheat	a. Indonesia produces more than half of this spice used by Americans.
2. tea	b. Plantation crop of Sri Lanka.
3. cotton	c. From the sap of trees grown on plantations of Southeast Asia.
4. jute	d. High-protein Chinese crop of many uses.
5. rubber	e. Grain grown in northern China.
6. soybeans	f. Chief food crop of the Malay Peninsula.
7. pepper	g. Special fiber obtained from worms raised in Japan.
8. rice	h. China, Pakistan, and India have been leaders in exporting this crop used to make cloth.
9. silk	i. Produced in Bangladesh and used in making rope.

Chapter 10

Industrial Resources of Asia

How can the nations of Asia best use their resources?

READING FOR A PURPOSE:
1. How did Japan become a leading industrial nation?
2. What are the chief mineral resources of Asia?
3. Why have some Asian nations been slow to develop industry?

1. The population of many nations in Asia is continuing to grow rapidly. Since much of the land is not suitable for farming, the problem of feeding this growing population becomes more and more serious. In most cases, food must be imported. In order to buy food from abroad, a country must have goods to sell. These are products of the nation's mines, fields, or factories. Japan was the first nation in Asia to realize it could not depend on its land alone to feed its large population. As a result, it changed its ways of living.

2. The change in Japan came rapidly. The Japanese bought machines from the West and built factories. They imported raw materials from other nations. They used their small amount of coal and their swift-flowing mountain streams as sources of power for their factories. The country's large population provided plenty of workers for the factories. They were sent to schools and trained for their new jobs.

3. Japan is a world leader in the production of goods and services. It has built a steel industry nearly as large as that of the United States. It has become the world's biggest producer of motorcycles, cars, bicycles, cameras, watches, transistor radios—to name a few. Its giant tankers carry much of the world's oil. By the 1980s Japanese television sets could be seen in the homes of Saudi Arabia; its cars on the streets of Buenos Aires, Argentina; its cameras in the hands of tourists throughout the world.

4. The rapid growth of mills and factories is not limited to Japan. In the past 15 years, many of the countries in eastern Asia have moved ahead faster than some industrialized countries in the West. Hong Kong, Singapore, Taiwan, and South Korea have become major exporters of textiles, clothing, toys, watches,

A car factory in Japan. How has the growth of car manufacturing in Japan affected the U.S. automobile industry?

This woman is making a batik print. Batik is a kind of fabric designing in which wax is placed on areas that are not to be dyed. The wax is removed after the cloth has dried.

and small electronic goods. Indonesia, Thailand, Malaysia, and the Philippines are following close behind. There are still many agricultural villages in these countries, but they are rapidly changing.

5. Southeast Asia has other riches. Malaysia, Thailand, and Indonesia mine about half the world's supply of tin. Indonesia earns about two-thirds of its export money from oil. Both Indonesia and Malaysia export oil, but it is not enough to supply the needs of all Asia. In Southeast Asia, some of the mines and oil fields are still managed with the help of foreign companies. Many governments have trained their own people to take over. In this way, they feel they are using their resources for their own benefit rather than for the benefit of companies in other countries.

6. Unlike its neighbors, the two other giants in the region, China and India, are not moving ahead quickly. Both nations have great reserves of raw materials. China has huge coal deposits. India has large amounts of iron ore. Some believe their failure to move ahead is caused by too much government interference. Under Mao Zedong, Chinese officials drew up a master plan each year telling the state-owned industries what and how

much to produce. In India, many businesses, public and private, are tightly controlled by the government. Today, government officials in both countries are trying to improve the output of their factories and mines.

7. Although progress has been great in some countries, more needs to be done. Millions of people must be trained in schools before they can work the machines in factories. Many do not want to work in factories. They prefer to work at home, making things by hand for people they know. Many people cannot afford to buy the goods made in factories. Since there is little demand for machine-made goods, factories are not built. Money is also needed to start factories and businesses.

8. Transportation throughout much of Asia is poor. The mountains, jungle, and desert make roads and railways very difficult and expensive to build and maintain. Some areas do have good transportation, but most do not. Japan and Taiwan have built fine networks of highways and railroads. India has a large railway system too. In China, the rivers are an important means of shipping goods and materials. China is improving its roads and railroads. Good transportation is needed if raw materials and manufactured goods are to flow

522

back and forth between buyers and sellers in Asia. Asian leaders and business people realize that without good transportation, the cost of moving goods is high.

9. Many Asian nations trade with each other. For example, Indonesia sells oil to Japan, and India supplies cotton to Japanese mills. China, Malaysia, Pakistan, Bangladesh, Thailand, and Indonesia have Japan as their main trading partner. China also trades heavily with Hong Kong and the United States. Japan, Taiwan, South Korea, India, and the Philippines have the United States as their main trading partner. Nepal and Bhutan do most of their trading with India. On the other hand, Vietnam carries on a large portion of its foreign trade with the Commonwealth. North Korea also has the Commonwealth as a main trading partner.

10. Two of the greatest seaports in the world are centers of trade in Asia. Both are islands. The island of Singapore is located off the southern coast of the Malay Peninsula. Trade from the Indian Ocean to the Pacific Ocean passes through the straits near Singapore. Hong Kong is a British colony on the southeast coast of China. Part of the colony is an island off the coast. Most of Hong Kong's food and water supplies come from China. Besides being a center of world trade and shipping, Hong Kong has important banks and textile and electronics industries. Hong Kong is expected to be returned to China in 1997 when the United Kingdom's treaty ends.

UNDERSTANDING WHAT YOU HAVE READ

1. **Which of the following questions are answered in this chapter?**
a. What is Japan's chief source of power?
b. What are the resources of Asia?
c. Why did Japan go to war in 1941?

2. **Many Asian nations have not developed industries as quickly as Japan has because**
a. many people have not been trained to work in modern factories
b. many people are too poor to buy the factory-made goods
c. both a and b

3. **The Asian nation that is a world leader in the production of goods and services is**
a. China   b. India   c. Japan

4. **A reason land transportation has been poor in Asia is that**
a. no nation has had good railroads
b. there are few materials to be shipped
c. roads are difficult and expensive to build and keep in good condition

5. **In spite of the large population of this region, there is no great market for factory goods because**
a. too many people work in the mines
b. people have little money to buy goods
c. schools train people for office work rather than for factory work

6. **China and India are not moving ahead quickly in industry because they**
a. lack raw materials
b. have had too much government interference
c. lack the necessary skilled workers

7. **Many Asian nations trade with**
a. other Asian nations
b. the Commonwealth of Independent States
c. Germany

8. **Though Hong Kong is a British colony, it will come under China's control in 1997 because**
a. The United Kingdom sold it to China
b. the people of Hong Kong voted to become part of China
c. The United Kingdom's treaty ends in 1997

9. **The two great centers of trade in Asia are**
a. Hong Kong and Taipei
b. Singapore and Hong Kong
c. Bangkok and Bombay

WRITING

Imagine that you are a business person from the United States. Your company has decided to expand its business into Asia. You must decide in which nation you wish to build your factory. As you decide, think about what your company wants to produce. Consider such important things as transportation possibilities, available raw materials, and the type of labor force you need. Write a letter to your stockholders and explain in which country you have chosen to build your plant. Include the reasons that support your decision.

SUMMING UP

Developing Industry in Asia

Place a check before each item that is *true* about Asia.

_____ 1. Good water-power resources
_____ 2. Coal reserves in every country
_____ 3. Enough oil for the entire region
_____ 4. Few trained workers for factories
_____ 5. Many raw materials to sell
_____ 6. Money to invest in new industries
_____ 7. Good seaports
_____ 8. Large population
_____ 9. Iron ore deposits in India
_____ 10. Large, modern highway system
_____ 11. Minerals that other nations need
_____ 12. More trade with Europe than with any other region

Chapter 11

Toward a Better Way of Life

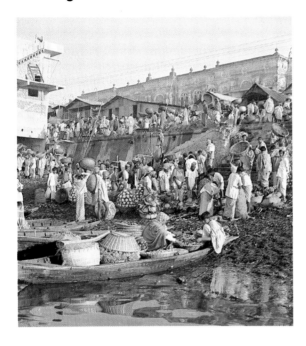

What are some of the needs of the people of Asia?

READING FOR A PURPOSE:
1. Why are there food shortages?
2. Why is a growing population a problem?
3. What problems do cities face?

1. Despite the fact that they are hardworking, many of the people of Asia are poor and hungry. The farms are too small, and many farmers do not own their own land. They cannot grow enough food. Farmers are often in debt to village moneylenders or large landowners. Throughout Asia, people are working for a better way of life. Can they achieve this in a democratic way while keeping many of their traditions and old ways of life?

2. Asian leaders realize that improving people's education can lead to a better way of life. In most Asian countries, most adults can now read and write. However, the countries of Laos, Cambodia, Bangladesh, India, Pakistan, Indonesia, Nepal, and Bhutan are lagging behind. Yet even in these countries, the improvements have been rapid over the past few years. For example, in India in 1950, only one adult in six could read and write. Thirty-five years later, one in three could. As part of the drive to improve literacy, Asian countries have built thousands of new schools and many universities. However, education is not the whole solution to the problems Asian nations face.

3. Many of the people are in poor health, and death at an early age is common. Many of the countries are improving the health of their people through better water supplies, immunization, and the use of insect killers. World Health Organization (WHO) teams have visited many of the small villages, giving medical help and advice. As health improves, however, the population grows at an even faster rate. This raises a new problem—namely, will the growing of food keep pace with the growing population?

4. There is a need to improve the water supply in the monsoon lands. In many of the countries affected by the monsoon, there is either too little or too much water. More reservoirs and tanks are being built so that rain water can be stored during the wet season for

As in the United States, cities in Asia are growing rapidly. What are some problems that are found in both U.S. and Asian cities?

use during the dry season. More dams are also being built to hold back water and provide irrigation for the dry lands. If more water is available, more food can be raised for the fast-growing populations of Asian countries.

5. Because fertile land is scarce and the population is growing, many people are leaving their villages to go to the cities in search of work. Cities are growing at a faster rate than farmlands. The movement of the people to the cities increases the need for more homes, better schools, and better health care. For the most part, cities like Seoul, Hong Kong, Taipei, and Singapore have been successful in providing for the needs of their people. Yet while some people find work in the cities, million of others are jobless. It is not unusual to find people sleeping in the streets of some cities in India. The governments of India and China have pointed out their problems in providing work for millions of their people.

6. Many of the nations—India, Myanmar, Malaysia, Vietnam, and others—gained their independence after World War II. Many of these people had lived under foreign rule for centuries. Some of these countries are still trying to set up stable governments. They are trying to feed, educate, and provide health care for millions of people.

7. To reach these goals and to have a democratic government seem even more difficult. Japan and India have governments that protect their people's political rights. This means they allow free elections. The people can freely choose candidates from more than one political party. There is a free press and free speech. Not all democratic countries provide their people with these rights. The people in the Philippines, for example, had their civil liberties severely restricted by President Ferdinand Marcos. Accusations of election tampering, restricted civil liberties, and the military-backed assassination of opposition leader Benigno Aquino led to protests and a revolt. In 1986, the people of the Philippines forced Marcos to flee the country. Marcos's successor, Corazon Aquino (the widow of Benigno Aquino) has been able to set up a more democratic government, although there have been several attempts to overthrow her administration. Other nations of Asia, however, do not give their people a voice in the government. The governments are run by a small group of people who usually belong to one political party. Among these nations are China, Vietnam, and Myanmar.

Former President Corazon Aquino of the Philippines.

UNDERSTANDING WHAT YOU HAVE READ

1. **Which of the following questions are answered in this chapter?**
   a. Why are millions of Asians moving from the countryside to the cities?
   b. Why have all the nations in Asia increased their trade with Europe?
   c. What are the problems that Asian nations face?

2. **The main idea of this chapter is to describe**
   a. the greatest needs of the peoples of Asia
   b. conditions in the crowded cities
   c. the plans of India and China to improve the life of the people

3. **An important problem for many of the nations of Asia is the**
   a. lack of food for a growing population
   b. need for foreign aid
   c. use of the sea for transportation

4. **A nation in Asia that fully protects its people's political rights and civil liberties is**
   a. China
   b. North Korea
   c. Japan

5. **The group that has sent medical teams to give help and advice to the people of small Asian villages is the**

   a. North Atlantic Treaty Organization (NATO)
   b. Warsaw Pact
   c. World Health Organization (WHO)

6. **In which group of countries can most adults read and write?**
   a. Bangladesh and India
   b. Pakistan and Laos
   c. Japan and Taiwan

7. **A problem in countries affected by the monsoon is**
   a. too many reservoirs
   b. too little or too much water
   c. too many dams

8. **Many people are leaving the villages and going to the cities because**
   a. there is little fertile land in the villages
   b. the village populations are not growing fast enough
   c. there are plenty of jobs in the cities

9. **To increase the amount of food grown, the countries of Asia need more**
   a. land
   b. water
   c. people

In Asia

Sundarlal Bahuguna is a tree hugger. This 60-year-old environmentalist is trying to save the forests of the Himalaya region in northern India. He is the driving force behind *Chipko,* which means "hug" or "embrace" in the Hindi language. Chipko is helping villagers to protect their forests. As Bahuguna walks from village to village, he urges the villagers to plant trees. Bahuguna is on an important mission. Half of the Himalayan forests have been cut down in the past 30 years. The loss of the forest threatens to strip away the topsoil in one area of the Ganges Plain—where one-third of India's 785 million people live. "The forest must be restored as soon as possible," says Bahuguna, "[or] all of India will be a desert."

In 1977, several thousand Penan people lived in the forests of Malaysian Borneo. Then the loggers came. Now only 500 Penans are still living on the fish, animals, and vegetation of the rain forests that remain. In the late 1970s when he was still in his teens, **Harrison Ngau** noticed what was happening to the Penan people. He set up a branch of Friends of the Earth, an environmental organization. Since then, he has been annoyed by the government, arrested, and put in prison for trying to stop the loggers from destroying the Penans' way of life. Only in recent years has the government begun to negotiate with the Penan people. Because of Harrison Ngau's efforts, the Malaysian people are learning to respect these people who live in the forest.

In the 1100s, religious pilgrims must have stood in awe when they first saw the temples at Angkor (ahn-KOHR). Larger than the pyramids, these huge temples are one of the masterpieces of world architecture. Since the time of the pilgrimages, however, the temples have been neglected. **Uong Von,** a native Cambodian, began working with a group of French researchers to restore the temples in 1960. Then the Khmer Rouge government came into power, and Uong Von was forced to work as a laborer in the countryside. When he returned to Angkor after the fall of the Khmer government, he was saddened by the state of temples. He quickly organized groups of volunteers to clean up the temples. Since then, Uong Von and his team have restored over 2,400 statues and sculptures.

During the Vietnam War, chemicals rained down on the country's rain forests. Canals were dug to drain water from the Plain of Reeds, a watery plain that is vital to the ecology of the Mekong River Delta. **Dr. Vo Quy** of the University of Hanoi has dedicated his life to repairing the terrible damage that the war did to Vietnam's natural environment. One of his greatest accomplishments is the Tram Chim Reserve in the Plain of Reeds. Once the home of hundreds of thousands of birds, the reserve had little life at first. Then the birds slowly began to return. One hopeful sign is the reappearance of the sarus crane. To Buddhists, the crane is a sacred symbol of happiness and long life. Although they were once almost extinct, over 1,000 sarus cranes now live in the reserve.

Chapter 12

Japan: An Industrial Leader

How has this small land become one of the leading nations in the world?

READING FOR A PURPOSE:
1. How does Japan's location affect its climate?
2. What are the chief occupations and industries of the Japanese?
3. How does Japan support its people?

1. Off the eastern coast of Asia is the archipelago of Japan. Japan has four main islands, all of which are very mountainous. While only a small part of the land is good for farming, the Japanese have achieved the highest standard of living in the Asian region. They have become the world's third largest industrial power. They have done this without the huge size, population, or wealth of raw materials enjoyed by the United States and the Commonwealth of Independent States.

2. While Japan is narrow, it stretches for a long distance north and south—as far as the distance from Maine to Georgia. In the northern islands, the climate is humid continental, like that of the northeastern states of the United States. In the winter, cold air from Asia blows over these islands and brings heavy snows. In the southern islands, the climate is milder, or humid subtropical. Rainy winds from the Pacific Ocean blow across Japan. Like the United Kingdom, Japan is surrounded by water and is affected by a warm ocean stream, the Japan Current. This current comes from east of the Philippines and warms the southern coast of Japan. Therefore, Japan's year-round temperatures are milder than those of the lands in the same latitude on the Asian mainland. Occasionally, strong winds and rains rise in the Pacific Ocean and sweep over southeastern Japan. These storms with strong winds are called *typhoons*. They do heavy damage.

3. Japan's chief lawmaking body is called the Diet. It is made up of two houses. Members of both houses are elected by citizens 20 years of age and over. The chief officer is the prime minister, who is chosen by the Diet. The Japanese still have an emperor. However, like the British king or queen, he is now a symbol of the country but has no real power. Tokyo is the capital city.

4. In 1947, Japan, under United States guidance, drew up a new constitution. Article 9 of the constitution ordered Japan to renounce, or give up, war. As a result, Japan has "walked softly" since World War II. It has limited its armed force to the size needed to defend itself. Over the years, the United States has come to regard Japan not as a defeated enemy but as a valuable friend in the Asian region. The United States government would like Japan to increase its armed forces. They want more help from Japan in counterbalancing instability in the northwest Pacific.

5. Japan, with a population of 124.4 million people, is one of the world's most densely populated countries. It has about 848 people

for each square mile of land. That is slightly less than the Netherlands. The Japanese are largely descendants of people who came from the mainland of Asia. Most Japanese have straight, black hair, almond-shaped eyes, and medium complexions. About one out of 10 working people farm or fish. Most Japanese people live in the cities and towns. They work in factories or in the rapidly growing service industries, such as banking, transportation, trade, and insurance. The major large cities are Tokyo (the capital), Yokohama, Osaka, Nagoya, Kyoto, and Kobe. All except Kyoto are seaports on the main island of Honshu. In large cities, the streets are filled with crowds of busy people (in Western-style dress), neon lights, and cars and buses. There are subways and tall buildings. Almost all homes have electricity and TV. Many people live in small homes and apartments made of wood, brick, and cement. Wherever possible, there is a small garden in the back of the house.

6. The Japanese place a very high value on

Tokyo's Shinkansen, or "Bullet Train," carries people to and from the suburbs at about 130 miles per hour.

education. This means that they believe a young person should spend time studying, not watching television or playing video games. From an early age, Japanese parents prepare their children to pass the exams they are required to take in the ninth and twelfth grades. For the ninth graders, the exams determine which high school they will attend; and for twelfth graders, which university. Japanese companies offer their best jobs to graduates of the best universities. The school system has made the Japanese people among the most literate people in the world. They are big readers of books, newspapers, and magazines. Their focus on education has helped Japan become the great industrial power it is.

7. The Japanese enjoy many of the same sports as Americans, such as baseball, tennis, and swimming. Most Japanese are both Buddhists and Shintoists. Shinto teaches respect for nature and for one's ancestors. Many Japanese practice Shinto customs at birth and marriage, and Buddhist customs at funerals. The Christian religion was brought to Japan about 400 years ago. There are more than one million Christian followers today. The temples, shrines, and churches of these religions are seen throughout the islands.

8. Because most of Japan's land is hilly, only about one-sixteenth is good for farming. Each acre is used in the best possible way to produce the greatest amount of food. Japanese farmers use every bit of land and cut terraces into the hillsides to make the land level. They use much fertilizer. Such heavy use of small amounts of land is called *intensive farming.* A large part of Japan's crop output is rice. Another major part of farm production is hogs, cattle, and poultry. Other important crops include vegetables, wheat, and tea. Because of their farming methods, Japanese farmers lead the world in the amount of food grown on an acre of land. Yet, because of its large population and shortage of farmland, Japan imports about half of its food supply.

This family is having a traditional meal. What can you learn about the Japanese way of life from this photograph?

9. Until recently, the Japanese have not been a meat-eating people. They still consume much less meat than most Americans do. Next to rice, fish is the most important food. There are many fish to be found in the fresh-water lakes and streams of Japan. The warm, shallow waters around Japan also make good fishing grounds. The many inlets along the coast make it easy for village fishing people to put out to sea and return. Big ships go far out to sea and roam all over the Pacific. On these ships, fish are cleaned, packed, and even canned. Since fish are as nourishing as meat, the people of Japan have a well-balanced diet. In fact, the Japanese are the best-fed people of Asia. Much fish is also exported to the United States in exchange for cotton, oil, and wheat.

10. Compared with India and China, Japan is not rich in natural resources. Its chief minerals are gold, magnesium, and silver. To keep its factories going, Japan imports oil, cotton, wood, rubber, coking coal, iron ore, copper, and bauxite. Imported oil is Japan's chief fuel. But coal is still an important source of power. So is falling water, from the many streams that flow down the mountainsides. (These are fed by Japan's heavy snows and rains.)

11. Its need for food and raw materials has not stopped Japan from becoming the third greatest industrial power in the world. How has Japan done this? Japanese factories have the latest equipment and tools. Billions of dollars are spent on research for new products. Its workers are highly skilled and take great pride in their work. Japanese companies take good care of their workers. Workers and factory managers work as a team. The Japanese people are among the world's biggest savers. Much of this money is invested in Japanese industries.

12. Today Japanese products are known all over the world. Japan is a world leader in making passenger cars, ships, motorcycles, and bicycles. It is a world leader in steel manufacturing and textiles. Japan is best known for its electronics industry. Its televisions, stereo and video equipment, cameras, radios, watches, and computers are known and respected for their high quality.

13. Foreign trade is very important to Japan. Japanese factories produce more goods than the Japanese people can buy. So Japan sells its automobiles, motorcycles, steel, and electronic equipment all over the world. In turn, Japan must import important raw materials like oil and wood, and also food. Still, Japan exports more than it imports. One-third of all automobiles made in Japan are exported

531

to the United States. Japan has been selling more to the United States than it has been buying. It ranks second only to Canada as the chief trading partner of the United States.

14. Although it is the most modern nation in the Asian region, Japan is not without problems. The United States and countries in Western Europe would like Japan to open its markets to their goods. They want Japan to import more goods. In 1992, President Bush traveled to Japan and tried to secure a trade agreement. However, he did not get the agreement he wanted. The United States would like its ally to take a more active role in defense. Although Japan now gives more than four billion dollars in foreign aid to some Asian neighbors, the United States would like Japan to increase this aid. Many Japanese women working outside the home want better jobs, better pay, and better labor laws. Men and women both want a change in their way of life. Many of them now have more money, but they want to work less. They want more time to relax and spend their money. However, it is foreign trade that is more important to the Japanese. Many of the materials and fuels it needs to run its factories must be imported. Although its farmers grow rice and its fishers have huge catches of fish, the Japanese depend on billions of dollars of imported foods: wheat, meat, sugar, and soybeans. If foreign trade was disrupted, the well-being of the Japanese people would be threatened, and the nation would suffer hardship.

UNDERSTANDING WHAT YOU HAVE READ

1. Which questions are answered in this chapter?
a. How is Japan governed?
b. How did the United States help Japan after World War II?
c. How do the Japanese make use of the waters around their islands?

2. The main idea of *paragraphs 5 through 7* describes
a. how the topography affects Japan's climate
b. the farm life in a Japanese village
c. the work and ways of life of the Japanese

3. The population of Japan is about
a. 78 million
b. 50 million
c. 124 million

4. There is intensive farming on the islands of Japan because
a. the Japanese know little of scientific farming
b. farmers do not have machinery
c. there is very little farmland and the Japanese use the most modern methods to get the most crops from it

5. Japan is a major exporter of
a. finished goods
b. wheat
c. oil

6. A *densely populated* area means
a. the population is spread out
b. many people are crowded close together
c. people live mostly near the seacoast

7. Japan's chief fuel is
a. imported oil
b. coal
c. waterpower

8. The climate of most of Japan is
a. tropical and steppe
b. humid continental and humid subtropical
c. savanna and marine

Building Map Skills — Japan

Japan

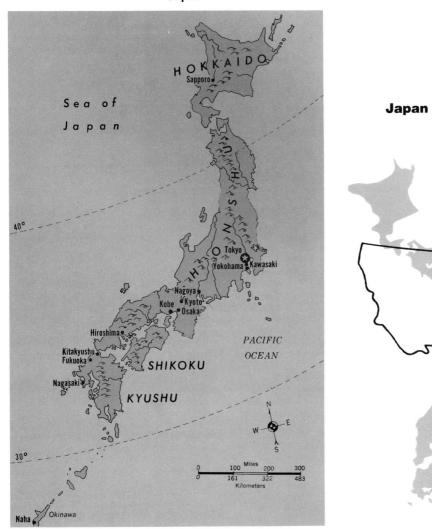

Japan and Montana

MONTANA
POPULATION: 799,065
LAND AREA: 147,046
377,000 SQUARE KILOMETERS
5.4 PEOPLE PER SQUARE MILE

JAPAN
POPULATION: 124.4 MILLION
LAND AREA: 143,749 SQUARE MILES
372,313 SQUARE KILOMETERS
823 PEOPLE PER SQUARE MILE

Study the maps on this page. Then answer the following questions.

1. Is Japan located in the high, middle, or low latitudes?
2. What is the distance from the northernmost tip to the southernmost tip of the Japanese islands?
3. On which of the islands are the largest cities located?
4. Osaka, Kobe, Yokohama, and Nagoya are all large cities. What else do they have in common?
5. How would you describe the topography of Japan?
6. Which area is more crowded, Montana or Japan?
7. Why do you think there are few rivers of great size on the Japanese islands?
8. If you traveled from Osaka to Tokyo, in which direction would you be traveling?
9. In which direction is the equator from Japan?

533

DEVELOPING CRITICAL THINKING SKILLS

A. Do You Agree or Disagree?

Decide whether or not each of the following statements agrees with what you have read. If you *disagree* with the statement, explain why.

1. The Japanese eat the same kinds of foods Americans and Canadians eat.
2. Japan's islands are very mountainous; there is little lowland for farming.
3. Most of Japan's large population is crowded into the narrow lowlands.
4. Most Japanese are fishers or farmers.
5. The Japanese depend upon manufacturing and trade to pay for the food and various goods they import.
6. Japan has built a modern nation despite its shortage of natural resources.
7. Japan sells over half its goods to China, the Commonwealth, and African nations.
8. Most Japanese are Hindus.
9. Japan's factories produce more than those of any other nation in the Asian region.
10. About one out of every four Japanese adults cannot read and write.

B. Which Does Not Belong?

Select the item in each group that does not belong with the others.

1. The main islands of Japan: a. Hokkaido b. Honshu c. Taiwan d. Kyushu
2. The weather in Japan: a. humid continental b. monsoons c. heavy snows d. humid subtropical
3. The lawmaking body of Japan: a. queen b. Diet c. two houses d. prime minister
4. The population of Japan: a. wear Western-style dress b. most work in factories or service industries c. most farm or fish d. one of the most densely populated countries
5. Major religions of Japan: a. Shinto b. Buddhist c. Christian d. Muslim
6. Diet of Japanese: a. fish b. rice c. vegetables d. meat
7. Seaports: a. Kyoto b. Kobe c. Osaka d. Yokohama
8. Chief minerals: a. gold b. silver c. platinum d. magnesium

Chapter 13

India: A Land Rich in Resources and Traditions

How are Indians working to end the poverty in their country, a land rich in resources and traditions?

READING FOR A PURPOSE:
1. How does India's geography affect its climate?
2. How does India make use of its available farmland?
3. What are India's largest industries?

1. South of the Himalaya Mountains of Asia is a large triangle-shaped peninsula. This large area, about half the size of the United States, is the Indian subcontinent. While it is occupied by five countries—India, Pakistan, Bangladesh, Nepal, and Bhutan—the nation of India covers most of the subcontinent. India is the seventh largest nation in the world, taking up about 1,300,000 square miles (3,300,000 square kilometers). With about 883 million people, it is the world's second largest nation in population.

2. The Himalaya Mountains form the northern border of India. South of the mountains, a great plain stretches east and west across the subcontinent. The western part of the plain is drained by the Indus River. The eastern part of the plain is the valley of the Ganges and Brahmaputra rivers. Many people live in this valley because the land is so fertile and well watered. The southern edge of the plain is bordered by the Vindhya Mountains. Although these mountains are low, they have divided India. The customs, languages, and dress of the people living north of these mountains are often different from those living south of them. South of the mountains is the Deccan Plateau. On the eastern and western edges of the Deccan there are ranges of low mountains. Along the east and west coasts are long, narrow coastal lowlands, or plains.

3. India lies mainly in the low latitudes. (Its latitude is about the same as that of Mexico and Central America.) The climate is generally hot and humid except in the highlands and mountains. (Because of the Himalayas in the north, the cold winds of Central Asia do not reach India.) The rainfall varies throughout the country from the heaviest in the world to the least. The rainfall is controlled by the seasonal winds called *monsoons*. During the summer (from July to September), the southwest winds blow from the Indian Ocean. They bring rain to the land. During this rainy season, there may be heavy rains every day. In the winter (from October to February), the northeast monsoon takes over and blows from the land to the sea. Since it blows from the land, it brings little rain. The dry season is from March to June. In many parts of India the temperature often reaches 100°F (38°C).

4. In 1601, the British came to India. They built trading posts and in time ruled almost all of India. There were many changes under British rule. Roads, canals, railroads, schools, and some factories were built. Much of the land was given to large landholders. Many raw materials were shipped out of the country. As British rule continued, many Indians began to turn against the British and to desire freedom. One of the great leaders for Indian independence was Mohandas K. Gandhi,

Mohandas Gandhi, shown here with two followers, became world famous for his successful campaign of non-violent resistance to British rule in India.

called the Mahatma, or "great-souled one." He urged the people to resist British rule, but not to use violence. He asked the people to boycott (refuse to buy) British goods and to disobey British laws. He was put in jail many times, but this only made him a greater hero to his people. It was largely because of Gandhi that the United Kingdom gave India its freedom in 1947.

5. The government of India is partly like that of the United Kingdom and partly like that of the United States. There is a written constitution. The chief lawmaking body is the Parliament, which has two houses. The chief officer is the prime minister. He or she has the power to suggest laws and to carry them out when they are approved by Parliament. Like the United States, India has a federal government. The powers of the government are divided between the national government and the 22 states. The capital city is New Delhi. Jawaharlal Nehru was the first prime minister and leader of India through the first 17 years of its independence. His daughter, Indira Gandhi, led the country as prime minister in most of the 1970s and early 1980s. Assassinated in 1984, she was succeeded by her son, Rajiv Gandhi.

6. India is one of the most crowded nations in the world. It has over 677 people for each square mile of land. Most of the people live in the Ganges River valley and along the coasts. India's people speak many different languages, wear different clothing, eat different foods, and have different ways of living from one part of the country to another. About 83 percent of the Indians are Hindus. Muslims make up the next largest group. There are smaller religious groups such as Christians, Sikhs, Parsis (Zoroastrians), Jains, and Buddhists. There is no single language for all of India. There are 16 recognized languages and also hundreds of small dialects. The government of India has made Hindi the official language for all of India. Many educated people also speak English. (English is the associate official language.)

7. Most Indians are farmers who live in small villages. Indian farmers work in fields that surround their villages. The average Indian farm is small and is often separated into tiny fields scattered about the countryside. Most farm work is done by hand. Farmers may use a light wooden yoke or frame, a wooden plow tipped with iron, a spade, and a sickle. The light wooden yoke is usually placed on a water buffalo or a humped white ox called the *zebu*. These are the chief work animals. Members of farm families work together in the fields whenever possible. Chemical fertilizer and new seeds are now in use. With new seeds and chemicals farmers have been able to boost the yield of the land.

8. The chief food crops of the Indian people are the grains rice, millet, sorghum, barley, corn, and wheat. Rice is grown in the lower Ganges valley and in the coastal lowlands. Millet is grown on the Deccan Plateau where it is too dry for rice. Wheat is grown in the drier western part of the Ganges Plains. Here many irrigation canals bring water to the fields. Where wheat is grown, it is used to make *chapatti,* a flat bread of baked flour and water, shaped like a pancake. India's cattle produce one of the world's largest supplies of milk. Cheese is also important. Although India's Muslims may eat beef, most Hindus do not.

9. The chief exported farm products of India are cotton, jute, and tea. Cotton is grown mostly on small farms in the Deccan. Jute is grown in the Ganges-Brahmaputra delta. It is a canelike plant that is used to make burlap sacks. India leads the world in growing and exporting tea. It is grown in the Assam province and in southern India on plantations started by the British. Other important crops include sugarcane, peanuts, cashews, tobacco, and coffee.

10. For years, Indian farmers could not raise enough grain to feed the huge population. That picture changed in the late 1970s. By that time, India had made much progress in its farm production. India now stores some

Bombay is an island city and a chief seaport.

of its rice and wheat crop as grain reserves. If a season's crops are poor, the grain reserves can be used as food. However, this does not mean that all Indians have enough to eat. Part of the reason why there is extra grain to add to reserves is that it is too expensive for the very poor people to buy.

11. Although India is largely a nation of farmers, the number of Indians who live and work in the cities is growing. Calcutta, at the delta of the Ganges River, is the gateway to the fertile farming lands of the north. It has some of the worst housing of any city in the world. With a population of over 9 million, it is also the largest city in India. Bombay is a seaport on the western coast. Madras is the chief seaport on the eastern coast. In the cities, old India and new India live side by side. The new India can be seen in the many cars and trucks, the Western style of dress, and the modern office buildings and shops. Old India is seen in the buffalo carts, the old bazaars, and the poor that crowd the streets.

12. For hundreds of years, the Indian people turned out wonderful handmade goods in their villages. About 2 million village craftworkers still produce fine silver objects, jewelry, wood carvings, carpets, and pottery. However, today India is an industrial power. A major industry is textiles, made mostly from India's own cotton. The largest textile mills are near the city of Bombay. Building on its many mineral resources (large deposits of iron and coal in the Deccan Plateau and around Calcutta). India's engineering and steel-making industries are growing fast. These include businesses that make machinery for steel mills, coal mines, and chemical and cement factories. The growing electronics industry now produces modern equipment, TVs, and calculators. Though these industries bring jobs, there are some occasional drawbacks. The worst industrial accident in history occurred in India. In December 1984, a deadly chemical gas escaped from a chemical plant at Bhopal, killing over 2,500 people and sickening thousands.

537

How has transportation improved in India since it became an independent nation?

13. India has made great strides since it became an independent nation. Its farms are now able to feed its people. It is building modern industries. Irrigation and electric power projects are going up throughout the country. The villages, in which 3 out of 4 Indians live, are now worlds apart from those of 1950. Almost all villages now have running water and most have electricity. Nearly every large village has a health center. Most of the young children attend school. Despite these gains, many Indians are still poor. They are often forced to borrow money to make ends meet.

14. India has other problems that divide the country. So many different languages are spoken that Indians have a difficult time communicating with one another. Hindi is the most widely used of the recognized languages. Religious differences are equally troublesome. Since the division of India in 1947, Hindu and Muslim tensions have continued. Lately, however, Hindus have had to focus their attention on the Sikhs from the state of Punjab. Many Sikhs, a religious group that began as a movement to combine Hinduism and Islam, want their own nation. In 1984, a group of militant Sikhs took over the Golden Temple, the most sacred shrine of the Sikh religion. Indira Ganhi ordered her army to capture the sacred temple. In revenge for the many Sikhs killed during the attack, Sikhs claimed to have been behind Gandhi's assassination. India is still trying to solve its internal religious problems.

UNDERSTANDING WHAT YOU HAVE READ

1. **Which questions are answered in this chapter?**
a. Where are Kashmir and Goa?
b. What are the chief food crops of India?
c. What are India's farm problems?

2. **A good title for *paragraphs 7–10* is**
a. "Mining Giant of the East"
b. "Too Much From Too Little"
c. "Farming in India"

3. **India gained its freedom largely through the efforts of**
a. Clive   b. Churchill   c. Gandhi

4. **The winds that bring rain to India's farmers are the**
a. monsoons   b. easterlies   c. hurricanes

5. **Millet is grown on the Deccan Plateau because**
a. water is more plentiful
b. in a drier climate it can grow better than rice
c. machinery can be used

6. **India was ruled for a long time by the**
a. French   b. British   c. Japanese

7. **India's major natural resources include**
a. tin and rubber
b. iron and coal
c. tungsten and asbestos

8. **India's largest industries produce**
a. textiles and steel   c. cars and trucks
     b. canned fish and frozen vegetables

DEVELOPING IDEAS AND SKILLS

Building Map Skills—India and the United States

India

India and the United States

UNITED STATES
POPULATION: 253 MILLION
LAND AREA: 3.6 MILLION SQUARE MILES
9.36 MILLION SQUARE KILOMETERS
70 PEOPLE PER SQUARE MILE

INDIA
POPULATION: 882.6 MILLION
LAND AREA: 1.3 MILLION SQUARE MILES
3.3 MILLION SQUARE KILOMETERS
679 PEOPLE PER SQUARE MILE

Study the maps. Then answer these questions.

1. Is India located in the high, middle, or low latitudes?
2. How does India compare in size with the United States?
3. In which direction is the equator from India?
4. What are two important port cities of India?
5. How is India separated from China?
6. The rivers of India flow in many directions. Why is this so?
7. What is the great river of northern India?
8. What nations border India?
9. How does the topography of northern India differ from that of the southern half of the country?
10. What is the approximate latitude and longitude of Bombay?
11. Which country is more crowded, India or the United States?
12. What word would you use to describe the land formation of India?

SUMMING UP

In your notebook, place before each statement the word that makes the statement correct:

Most, Some, Few

1. _____ Indians live in river valleys.
2. _____ of India's people live in small villages.
3. _____ people are able to read and write.
4. _____ Indians are of British descent.
5. _____ people in India are poor.
6. _____ people in India work in steel mills.
7. _____ people speak the same language.
8. _____ large cities are seaports.

— Understanding a Land Use Map —

This is a land use map of India. It shows how the people of India use their land. The map key tells us that five different land uses are shown on the map.

Manufacturing is one of the land uses shown on the map. These are areas where goods are made.

Forestry is another land use shown on the map. It occurs mainly in India's high mountains.

Grazing is the third land use shown on the map. Most of the grazing lands are in India's dry regions.

Farming is shown as two separate land uses on the map. Farmers in rainy lowlands along the coasts and the Ganges River get enough rain to grow two or more crops a year.

Farmers in inland areas of India get less rain than farmers along the coasts. They can only grow one crop a year unless the land is irrigated.

1. Is rice one of the chief food crops of the Indian people? Where is it grown?
2. Cotton is grown on small farms in the Deccan Plateau. What manufacturing industry is based on this crop?
3. Is India largely an agricultural or industrial country?
4. Name three manufacturing centers located on the coast. How might the ocean have helped their development?

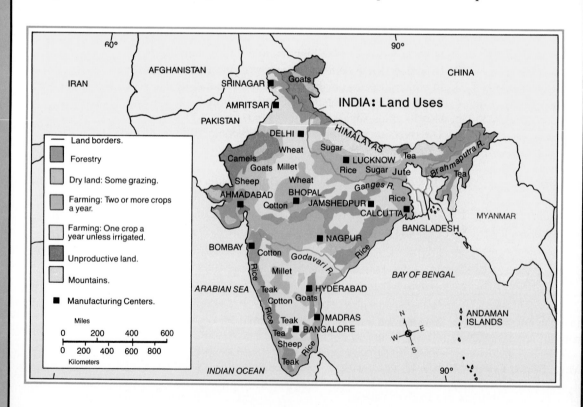

Chapter 14

China: The Most Populous Country

Can China become a leading industrial nation?

READING FOR A PURPOSE:
1. Why do most Chinese live in the eastern section of the country?
2. How is China governed?
3. What are China's chief industries and farm crops?

1. The People's Republic of China is the largest country in Asia and the third largest country in the world. Most of China's one billion two hundred million people live in the eastern section of the country. In the southwest are the giant Himalaya Mountains. The cold, empty plateau of Xizang (Tibet) lies in these mountains. North of Xizang is Xinjiang (Sinkiang), a dry land bordered by mountains. East of Xinjiang is Inner Mongolia, a dry plateau. In the eastern part of this region is the Gobi Desert, one of the loneliest spots on earth. These dry, mountainous lands, in which few people live, make up about one-third of China's land area. On the north, China is bordered by the Commonwealth, and on the east, by the Pacific Ocean.

2. Unlike the high, dry areas of western China, the southeast is lined with fertile river valleys and plains. This is the busy center of rice farming and trade. Thousands of canals connect streams and have been the chief avenues of travel for hundreds of years. The major lowlands are the plains formed by the Xi and Yangzi rivers. The winds bring plenty of rain to the rice fields here. The climate of this part of China is the same as in the southeastern part of the United States. The largest cities in this region are Shanghai and Guangzhou (Canton).

3. The lands farther north are sometimes called North China. They include the valley of the Huang Ho (Yellow River) and the fertile North China Plain. There is less rainfall here than in southeastern China. The climate is cold, and there is a shorter growing season. For these reasons, this is the wheat-growing region of China. Most of the land is covered by a fine yellowish-brown dust, which is called *loess*. The Huang Ho (Yellow River) gets its name from the yellow loess it picks up. The Huang Ho frequently overflows its banks, causing great damage to the nearby farmlands. The largest cities of North China are Beijing (Peking) and Tianjin (Tientsin). Beijing is the capital of China.

4. The northernmost part of China is called the Northeast (Manchuria). The climate is humid continental, like that of the northeastern states of the United States. Shenyang (Mukden), the iron and steel center, is about the same distance from the equator as New York City. Here iron ore and coal are found near each other. This area has long been wanted by both Japan and the former Soviet Union. The Northeast also has fertile farmland where wheat and millet take the place of rice as the chief food. Fewer people live here than in the warmer southeast.

5. China is the last major world power to retain a Communist form of government. The

Students enjoy an open-air cafe in Chengdu. About 5 percent of high school graduates go on to higher education. How might these students help the nation become economically successful?

means that there are two governments, the "acting" government and the "real" government. Under the "acting" government, the chief lawmaking body is the National People's Congress. It meets yearly and has little power. The executive branch is the State Council or Cabinet, headed by a premier.

6. The real rulers are the leaders of the Communist party. That is the only political party allowed. The Party has about 40 million members, just about 4 percent of the nation's people. Party members are chosen carefully. Only people who are willing to work hard and follow the orders of the Party leaders are accepted. Party members hold the most important jobs in the government, in the factories, and also on the farms. The Party controls the army. The leaders of the Party make up a group called the Politburo. The real power is held by the Politburo Standing Committee of six. Party leaders make important decisions. These decisions are put into effect by the Party members at all levels. The "party line" is continually made known to the people through the newspapers, radio, and television.

7. For hundreds of years, the custom was for all members of a Chinese family to live together in the same house. The oldest male was the head of the home and the family worked for him. Most people could not read or write, so the village scholar was a respected

person. Furthermore, the people followed the teachings of Buddhism, Confucianism, and Daoism (Taoism). Buddhism, which came from India, teaches that pain and suffering are caused by attachment to worldly things. Confucianism is concerned with the ways in which people live and deal with each other. Daoism teaches that people can gain peace by being at one with the natural order. Mixed with these beliefs are certain religious practices that are also very old. One such practice is respect for the spirits of the dead. The Chinese, according to custom, visited the graves of their ancestors to sweep the area and pay their respects. They also felt that mountains and rivers had spirits or souls.

8. The Communists are changing the ways of living in China. Today, the government tries to discourage some of these religious practices. Almost three out of every four persons can now read and write. But the schools also teach loyalty to the Communist party. Instead of working for the family, people used to work for the state. Today, people are starting to work for their own benefit as well as for the state. Women work at the same kinds of jobs as men.

9. In China, as in most Asian countries, most of the people are farmers. For centuries, much of the land was owned by rich landlords. The Communists took land away from the landlords and gave it to those who had little or no land. In the mid-1950s, collective groups became the owners of the land. Each collective was like a small farming village. It owned the land, tools, and animals. In 1958, the collectives were gathered into larger units called *communes*. Some communes had as many as 10,000 acres and 20,000 people. Communes were directed by members of the Communist party. After the harvest, part of the crop was sent to the government. The farmers divided what was left.

10. The commune system did not work. In 1978, the party decided to try a new system. They began to experiment in enterprise economy. The government still owns the land, but the fields have been divided into small plots that individuals farm. The farmers, not the government, decide what to plant and when. Farmers must sell a share or quota of their harvest to the government. They are free to sell whatever is left over and to keep the profits. In short, Chinese farmers are now working for themselves as well as for the government. This form of tenant farming is spreading across China.

11. Under the Chinese Communists, all businesses, large and small, belonged to the government. Government officials drew up plans telling businesses what and how much to produce. Roughly three out of four people had jobs at salaries set by the state. All profits belonged to the state. The system did poorly.

Starting in 1979, the Chinese leadership made changes. They gave more responsibility to the managers of small shops and large plants. The managers were able to decide what was best for the business. If they were right, they made profits for the government. They were also able to keep a good part of the profits for themselves and for their workers, and to buy needed raw materials and equipment. There has been a big increase in production in both heavy and light industries. By the year 2000, China hopes to equal the industrial achievements of its neighbors in the Asian region.

12. China has rich deposits of coal, iron, antimony, tungsten, tin, and other minerals. It is one of the largest producers of coal in the world. Rich deposits of oil have recently been

Resources and Industrial Areas of China

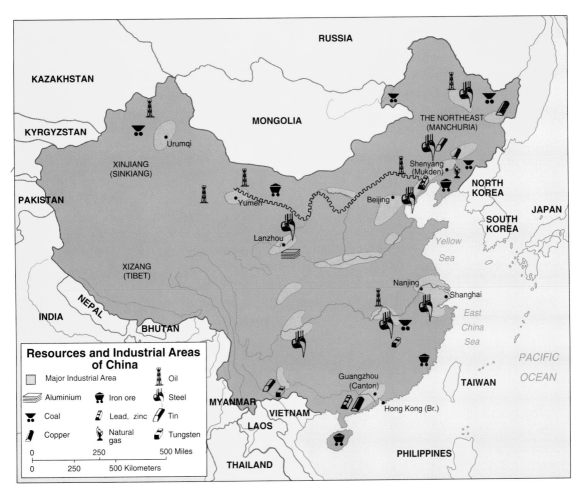

discovered. China's large and growing steel industry supplies the steel for heavy machinery. Chinese factories also produce textiles, radios, and bicycles. China's industry has been growing at a rapid rate. But there are also problems that must be overcome. China has a poor transportation system. Many advanced machines like computers must be imported. There are not enough skilled workers to run advanced machinery and plan new programs. The Chinese government is working to solve these problems.

13. As part of its turnaround, China's leaders are taking a new look at education. In the mid-1960s, China went through a "cultural revolution." It turned its back on education. Scholars were made fun of and pushed out of work. Many universities and colleges were closed. Today, school competition is as fierce as it is in Japan. Students are admitted to the "key" schools only if they pass difficult examinations. The Communist party is starting to reward its scientists and scholars with high salaries and good housing. China's leaders now look to education, science, and technology as the road to success for the nation.

14. Since 1949, China has become a major world power. At first, the Chinese were close friends with the Soviet Union. The USSR loaned China money. Soviet advisors helped build Chinese industry. By the late 1950s, though, jealousy had begun to grow between the two Communist powers. China competed with the USSR in lending money and giving advice to developing nations around the world. Each claimed to be the true leader of communism. Both developed atomic weapons. The Chinese, alarmed over Soviet forces on its borders and by Soviet influence in the world, have built up the world's largest land army (the People's Liberation Army).

15. From 1949 until the early 1970s, the United States and China had only limited contact with each other. In fact, Chinese and American troops fought against each other during the Korean War of the early 1950s. The United States had supported the Nationalist government on Taiwan. President Nixon's trip to Beijing in 1972 was a breakthrough in United States-Chinese relations. In 1979, the United States and the People's Republic of China established full diplomatic relations. Trade between the two nations has grown. The United States began to supply China with military and high-tech equipment. The main problem in United States-Chinese relations remains Taiwan. The Communists claim Taiwan is part of China and should be returned to them.

16. The Nationalist Chinese government is still located on Taiwan. When Communist China joined the United Nations in 1971, Taiwan was removed from membership. In 1979, the United States stopped recognizing Taiwan as the official Chinese government. But the United States and Taiwan are still close trading partners. Taiwan's standard of living is rising very fast. It exports textiles and modern electronic equipment. Several of the big businesses are owned by the government, but most businesses are in private hands. Land reform laws divided up the rich landowners' farms. About 90 percent of the land is now owned by the people who farm it. The United States has agreed to continue to provide Taiwan with weapons to defend itself.

UNDERSTANDING WHAT YOU HAVE READ

1. Which questions are answered in this chapter?

a. How did the Communists come into power?
b. Where do most of the people of China live?
c. Where is Hong Kong?

2. The main idea of *paragraph 9* describes

a. the purpose of a commune
b. how China differs from the CIS
c. the strength of China today

3. On Chinese farms

a. farmers live as they have for centuries
b. families own and run their own farms
c. farmers give a share of the crops to the government and keep the rest

4. The United States and the People's Republic of China

a. have been friends since 1949
b. established diplomatic relations in 1979
c. are sworn enemies

5. Since 1979, changes have come to China's

a. farming methods
b. methods of doing buisness
c. both of these statements

6. China and the United States differ over

a. Hong Kong
b. Singapore
c. Taiwan

DEVELOPING IDEAS AND SKILLS

Building Map Skills — China

China

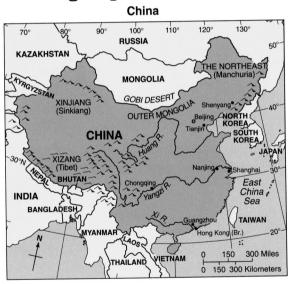

China and the United States

UNITED STATES
POPULATION: 253 MILLION
LAND AREA: 3.6 MILLION SQUARE MILES
9.3 MILLION SQUARE KILOMETERS
70 PEOPLE PER SQUARE MILE

CHINA
POPULATION: 1.2 BILLION
LAND AREA: 3.7 MILLION SQUARE MILES
9.5 MILLION SQUARE KILOMETERS
311 PEOPLE PER SQUARE MILE

Study the maps. Then answer these questions.

1. Is China in the high, middle, or low latitudes?
2. Which is larger in size, the United States or China?
3. What is the capital of China?
4. How would you describe the topography of China?
5. What countries border China?
6. Where do both the Huang Ho and Yangzi rivers begin?
7. How far is Taiwan from the mainland of China?
8. What is the approximate latitude and longitude of Shanghai?
9. If you traveled by air from California to Beijing, would it be quicker to travel east or west?
10. What is the British-held city on the coast of southern China?

545

DEVELOPING CRITICAL THINKING SKILLS

A. Making Comparisons

I. Tell whether the following items refer to China, India, or to both countries. If an item applies to China only, write **C** in your notebook; if it applies to India only, write **I;** if it applies to both countries, write **B.**

1. Not enough food is grown to feed all the people of the country.
2. More than half the people cannot read or write.
3. Rice is the chief food crop.
4. There is a population of more than one billion people.
5. This nation is larger in area than the United States.
6. There are fertile river valleys.
7. Farms are organized into communes.

B. Do You Agree or Disagree?

Tell whether you agree or disagree with the following statements. If you disagree with a statement, rewrite it so you agree.

1. China is the second largest country in size.
2. The northernmost part of China has a humid continental climate.
3. Manchuria makes up about one-third of China's land area.
4. The Xi and Yangzi rivers are located in the southeastern part of China.
5. The government of China is similar to the government of Russia.
6. The leaders of the Party make up a group called the Politburo.
7. Real power in China is held by the president.
8. Most people in China are farmers.
9. Most Chinese follow the teachings of Buddhism, Confucianism, and Daoism.
10. Most land belongs to the people.
11. China has rich deposits of coal, iron ore, and gold.
12. The Nationalist Chinese government is located on Taiwan.

The Nations of Southeast Asia

How do the land, climate, and history of Southeast Asia affect its people?

READING FOR A PURPOSE:
1. What are the lands of Southeast Asia?
2. What kinds of farming are found in Southeast Asia?
3. What are some problems the people of Southeast Asia are trying to solve?

1. The world has long been interested in the lands of Southeast Asia. Early explorers looked for a water route to the "Spice Islands," as part of Southeast Asia was once called. European nations were so eager for the resources of this region that they made many of these lands their colonies. Great as the interest of the world may have been in this area in past centuries, it is even greater today. Independence has come to the small countries of Southeast Asia. But since independence, wars and hunger have made news from this part of the world. Communism has spread to many of the countries of the region.

2. Southeast Asia is made up of lands east of India and Bangladesh and south of China and Japan. Part of this region lies on the continent of Asia, ending in the Malay Peninsula that extends southeast from the continent (map, page 551). On the mainland of Asia are the nations of Myanmar, Thailand, Laos, Vietnam, Cambodia, and part of the nation of Malaysia. The rest of Malaysia is on a large island. To the south of the mainland's Malay Peninsula is the island of the small, prosperous city-nation of Singapore. (Besides the main island, Singapore also includes many small islands.) To the south and east are the archipelagoes of the nations of Indonesia and the Philippines. The tiny, oil-rich land of Brunei shares an island with parts of Malaysia and Indonesia. The total land area of Southeast Asia is about one-half that of the United States, although it stretches across a greater distance from east to west.

3. Southeast Asia is a crowded region. About 400 million people live in an area about half the size of the United States. The country of Indonesia, with about 168 million people, is the largest in population. The island of Java, part of Indonesia, has more than 1,500 people for each square mile of land. Most of the people of Southeast Asia live on the coastal lowlands and the river plains. (In Java and the Philippines, however, some mountainsides are terraced for farming, and people live almost to the very top.)

4. There are many waterways in this region. (Much trade passes through these waters on its way to and from Asia. The amount of trade is almost equal to that going through either the Suez Canal or the Panama Canal.) The most important water passage is the Strait of Malacca, which separates the Malay Peninsula from the island of Sumatra. It connects the Indian Ocean and the South China Sea. The city-nation of Singapore, located on this strait, is one of the world's leading ports. Another important waterway is the Sunda Strait between the islands of Sumatra and Java. It is used by ships coming to eastern Asia from lands south of the equator. Whatever country holds these straits can control trade and the movement of ships in this area.

5. After the early explorers found the Spice Islands, European nations divided almost the entire region among themselves. The Dutch held control over many of the islands, chiefly the ones that make up Indonesia today. The United Kingdom held Myanmar, the Malay Peninsula, and Singapore. (The United Kingdom still has close ties with its former colonies.) The French colonized Indochina. This region is now the countries of Cambodia, Laos, and Vietnam. Because of Magellan's voyage, the Spanish claimed the Philippines and ruled them until the 1898 war with the United States. After that, the United States controlled the Philippines until 1946, when freedom was granted. Thailand has been ruled by its own kings for hundreds of years. Beginning in 1946, all the nations of Southeast Asia that were once colonies have gained their freedom.

6. This is a tropical region. Only the northern part of Myanmar lies outside the low latitudes. Yet, because the lands are mountainous, almost any kind of climate may be found. The hardships are greatest in the lowlands where most of the people live. Here there are heavy rains, thick forests, poor soils in many places, and the ever-present tropical diseases. Myanmar, Thailand, Vietnam, and parts of the Philippines have the monsoon climate as in India. There may be little or no rain during the winter months, but 60 to 80 inches (150 to 200 centimeters) of rain may fall from June to September. The archipelagoes of Indonesia and the Philippines were partly formed by volcanoes. On the Indonesian island of Java, the volcanic soils are fertile. Because of them, much food can be grown, and there is a huge population on the island.

7. Most of the people of Southeast Asia are Malays. However, in most countries there is a mixture of ethnic groups, nationalities, and religions. Chinese influence on these nations has been very strong. The Chinese are the largest minority group in Southeast Asia. In Malaysia, Chinese and Indians make up almost half

Rice harvesters in Myanmar. Which Southeast Asian nation is a major rice-exporting country?

the population. Southeast Asia is an area of many different religions. Most of the people are Buddhists. This religion is found chiefly in the countries that are located quite close to China—Thailand, Myanmar, Cambodia, Laos, and Vietnam. In these countries, Buddhist temples called *pagodas* or *wats* can be seen in almost every village. In Malaysia and Indonesia, the chief religion is Islam. In the Philippines, 83 percent of the people are Roman Catholics as a result of the long Spanish rule. On the island of Bali in Indonesia, the people worship the gods of the Hindu religion. In the remote hills, many people still worship their ancestors. Many of the later religions have been changed by the people to fit some of their older beliefs and customs. As a result, many villagers pray to the good and evil spirits that they believe affect their lives.

8. Most of the people of Southeast Asia are farmers. They live in villages near their fields. The Southeast Asian farmers earn little money and live chiefly on the food they raise themselves. Many farmers are also part-time fishers. The village, in which people of different cultures live side by side, has been a striking feature of this part of the world. One of the

548

problems of this region now is the movement of people from the villages to the cities. The old family and village ties are breaking up.

9. Cities are growing in size. Some of the largest are the following: Jakarta, Indonesia; Bangkok, Thailand; Singapore; Yangon, Myanmar; Ho Chi Minh City and Hanoi, Vietnam; and Manila, the Philippines. Many of these cities are located on large deltas. The outside world comes to Southeast Asia through the cities. Many are modern, with wide, paved streets, tall buildings, electricity, and air conditioning. The wealth of Singapore is seen by the visitor in the grand homes and beautiful avenues of the city. Behind the main streets, however, are the slums that are a large part of many Asian cities.

10. Most of the people make their living growing rice. The best rice-growing areas are the river valleys: The Irrawaddy in Myanmar, the Chao Phraya in Thailand, and the Mekong in Vietnam. The fertile river valley of Thailand makes it one of the leading rice-exporting nations in the world. Most of the rice is exported to neighboring countries where it is badly needed. In areas of less rainfall, corn, millet, beans, and sweet potatoes are grown.

Which nations produce much of the world's natural rubber? What is the climate of these countries?

How does this camera factory show changes that have made Singapore prosperous?

11. Plantation farming is also important in Southeast Asia. Plantation products are sold mainly to foreign countries. This kind of farming was begun by European and American business people. Each of the large farms specializes in one crop. The rubber plantations supply 90 percent of the world's needs of natural rubber. Malaysia and Indonesia are the leading producers. Indonesia is also a large exporter of tea. More than half the world's coconut oil is produced in Malaysia and the Philippines. Palm oil, sugar, coffee, and pepper are other plantation crops. Teakwood and quinine (used as medicine in treating malaria) are products of the forests.

12. Southeast Asia has rich mineral resources, too. Half the world's supply of tin is produced here. Malaysia and the Philippines mine iron ore. From Thailand comes tungsten, the long-burning metal in light bulbs. Oil is found in Indonesia, Malaysia, and Brunei. Indonesia is building oil refineries to process its own oil. It is also building steel mills and aluminum plants. In the 1970s and the early 1980s, about 150 electronics plants were built in Malaysia. Singapore has oil refineries, textile mills, and factories that build electronic equipment and electric machinery. In recent years, the countries of Singapore, Malaysia, and Thailand have done well industrially.

13. The problems of Southeast Asian nations are similar in many ways to the problems of other developing regions around the world. Many people are poor and hungry. They cannot afford the improved seeds, fertilizer, and insect killers that could double their crops. Many do not receive good health care. Many adults still cannot read and write. Singapore, Malaysia, and the Philippines, however, have made great gains in educating their people. Most of the area's raw materials are sent overseas to pay for needed goods. When Southeast Asia was under foreign rule, local factories were not built to process the raw materials. Now there are a growing number of factories in Southeast Asia. Many of the countries are passing laws that permit foreigners to invest in but no longer control the natural resources.

14. Most Southeast Asian leaders have not allowed their people to have full political rights. They have not allowed completely free elections with more than one political party. Civil liberties like free speech, a free press, and fair trials are often not protected. This is especially true in the Communist countries of Vietnam, Cambodia, and Laos, and in non-Communist Myanmar.

15. Because of frequent wars, the people of Southeast Asia are not doing as well as some of their neighbors. First there was the long and bitter struggle to gain freedom from the French and Dutch. During World War II, Southeast Asia was occupied by the Japanese. Then there was the bloody war in Vietnam. That ended with a united, Communist Vietnam. In 1978, Vietnam invaded Cambodia. The terror caused by the Cambodian rulers and the invasion by Vietnam laid waste to most of Cambodia. In the 1980s, there was political upheaval in the Philippines. The people of Southeast Asia need peace if they are to develop their mineral resources, produce enough food to feed themselves, and improve their education and health facilities.

UNDERSTANDING WHAT YOU HAVE READ

1. Which questions are answered in this chapter?
a. Why is the city of Singapore important?
b. How do people farm in Southeast Asia?
c. What countries are located on the mainland of Asia?

2. The main idea of *paragraphs 10 through 12* describes
a. the chief products of Southeast Asia
b. reasons for our interest in this region
c. kinds of rice farming in Southeast Asia

3. Most of the people of Southeast Asia live in
a. large cities   b. fertile lowlands
c. hilly woodlands

4. All of these are countries of Southeast Asia EXCEPT
a. Malaysia   b. Laos   c. Iran

5. All of these are important minerals of Southeast Asia EXCEPT
a. mercury   b. tungsten   c. tin

6. All of these are large exports of Southeast Asia EXCEPT
a. wheat   b. rubber   c. tin

7. One reason Southeast Asia is important in world affairs is that
a. it has large deposits of coal
b. its people have a high standard of living
c. a great amount of trade passes in and around these lands

8. One problem facing Southeast Asia today is
a. rule by European countries
b. few minerals or other natural resources
c. undemocratic governments

Building Map Skills— Southeast Asia and the United States

Southeast Asia

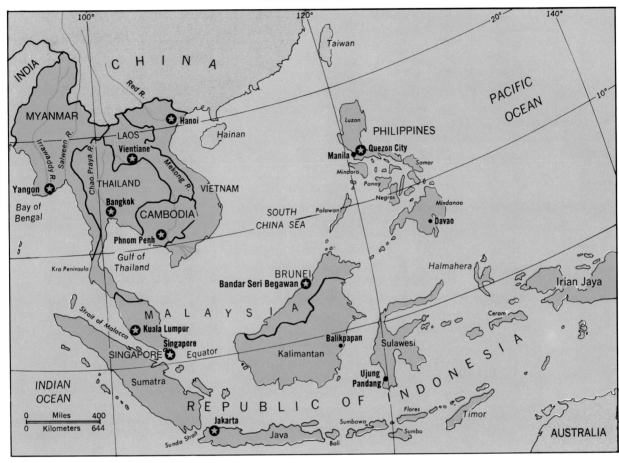

Southeast Asia and the United States

UNITED STATES	SOUTHEAST ASIA
POPULATION: 253 MILLION	POPULATION: 450 MILLION
LAND AREA: 3.6 MILLION SQUARE MILES	LAND AREA: 1.7 MILLION SQUARE MILES
9.36 MILLION SQUARE KILOMETERS	4.4 MILLION SQUARE KILOMETERS
70 PEOPLE PER SQUARE MILE	264 PEOPLE PER SQUARE MILE

Study the maps on this page. Then answer the questions on page 552.

1. Is the area north or south of the equator?
2. Is the area east or west of the prime meridian?
3. Does the area extend farther from east to west or from north to south?
4. What region or regions are near it?
5. What are the chief bodies of water that border the area?
6. Are there countries in it that have no outlets to the sea?
7. What are some of the important rivers in the area?
8. What is the capital city of each country? How do you know they are the capitals? How many are sea or river ports?
9. Are there any island nations? If so, name them.
10. Are there countries that are located on peninsulas? If so, name them.

DEVELOPING CRITICAL THINKING SKILLS

Do you Agree or Disagree?

Decide whether or not each of the following statements agrees with what you have read. If the answer is *disagree,* explain why.

1. The lands of Southeast Asia were ruled by one nation until 1946.
2. It would be unusual to find a Hindu temple or Muslim mosque in Southeast Asia.
3. Some of these lands were once known as the "Spice Islands."
4. Only since 1950 has the world become interested in Southeast Asia.
5. In some countries of this region, there is more than enough rice to feed the nation's people.
6. Mountains and large bodies of water have kept the people of Southeast Asia free from the influence of China.
7. Most of the countries of Southeast Asia allow freedom of speech, free elections, freedom of the press, and fair trials.
8. Some Southeast Asian countries have modern oil-refining plants, textile mills, and factories that make electronic equipment.

REVIEWING AND WRITING

Writing a Report

Make a report on one of the countries of Southeast Asia. You may prepare your report using these headings:

a. Land and Climate
b. The People
c. Progress in Farming and Industry
d. Leading Figures of the Country's History
e. Population Centers and Cities
f. Problems Faced by the Country
g. Plans for the Future

Groups in the class may study individual countries. Assemble pictures or bulletin-board displays of the nation you are studying. Current magazines, travel folders, government information agencies, or magazines that deal with geography will provide you with information. Use the same headings for your display as you did for the written report.

552

The Asian Region

Country	Area (Square Miles)	Capital	Population 1992 estimates)	Number of Years to Double Population	Life Expectancy	Per Capita GNP, 1990
Bangladesh	55,598	Dacca	111,400,000	29	53	$ 200
Bhutan	18,147	Thimphu	700,000	35	47	$ 190
Brunei	2,228	Bandar Seri Begawan	300,000	28	71	$14,120
Cambodia	69,900	Phnom Penh	9,100,000	32	49	—
China, People's Republic of	3,705,390	Beijing	1,165,800,000	53	69	$ 370
China, Republic of (Taiwan)	12,456	Taipei	20,800,000	62	74	—
Hong Kong	402	—	5,700,000	99	77	$11,540
India	1,266,595	New Delhi	859,200,000	34	59	$ 350
Indonesia, Republic of	735,355	Jakarta	184,500,000	40	61	$ 560
Japan	143,749	Tokyo	123,800,000	217	79	$25,430
Korea, Democratic Republic of (North Korea)	46,451	Pyongyang	21,800,000	39	69	—
Korea, Republic of (South Korea)	38,023	Seoul	43,200,000	79	71	$ 4,400
Laos	91,429	Vientiane	4,100,000	32	50	$ 170
Macao (Portug.)	8	—	400,000	51	77	—
Malaysia	127,317	Kuala Lumpur	18,300,000	28	68	$ 2,130
Maldives	116	Malé	200,000	19	61	$ 420
Mongolia, (Mongolian People's Republic)	604,247	Ulan Bator	2,200,000	25	64	—
Myanmar	261,216	Yangon	42,100,000	36	55	$ 2,130
Nepal	54,363	Kathmandu	19,600,000	28	52	$ 170
Pakistan	310,402	Islamabad	117,500,000	23	57	$ 370
Philippines	115,830	Manila; Quezon City	62,300,000	27	64	$ 700
Singapore	224	Singapore	2,800,000	55	75	$10,450
Sri Lanka	25,332	Colombo	17,400,000	47	70	$ 430
Thailand	198,456	Bangkok	58,800,000	53	66	$ 1,170
Vietnam, Socialist Republic of	127,253	Hanoi	67,600,000	31	63	—

KEY IDEAS

- The Pacific World covers more of the earth's surface than any other region, but it is an ocean world of islands.

- The largest country in the Pacific World is Australia. Although the land is mostly desert, Australians have developed mines, factories, and large cities.

- Australia and New Zealand are democracies with a high standard of living, but thousands of Pacific islands depend on fishing, subsistence farming, and cash crops.

- Use of Pacific islands by modern armed forces in World War II exposed the people to many modern ideas and goods.

- Movement of modern people, ideas, and goods throughout the Pacific World has increased rapidly since the mid-1900s.

The Pacific Ocean stretches out as far as the eye can see from Papeete, on Tahiti. Advances in communication have helped modernize the Pacific Islands in the past few years.

Chapter 1

The World of Water

Why are we interested in the Pacific world?

READING FOR A PURPOSE:
1. What do we mean by the Pacific world?
2. How was Australia settled?
3. How did World War II affect this region?

1. The Pacific world is the "world of water." In this region we find Australia, New Zealand, and the thousands of islands of the Pacific Ocean. The Pacific world covers an area of 69 million square miles (176 million square kilometers), more than all the land areas on the earth put together. The Pacific Ocean is the most important influence in the life of the people. Australia, the island continent, is the largest mass of land in the region.

2. The entire region of the Pacific world is made up of islands. These range in size from the large continent of Australia to the tiny coral reefs or *atolls*. Most of these islands are now parts of independent countries. Their people have different ways of making a living, from simple hunting, fishing, and farming to the most modern kinds of manufacturing. Some of the people live very poorly, while others have a high standard of living.

3. It is thought that Australia was once connected to the mainland of Asia. Long ago, part of the land between them sank and the ocean waters covered it. All that remained above water were the islands of Indonesia and New Guinea. Over these island "bridges" from Asia came the ancestors of animals and people who now live in the Pacific world. In addition, over thousands of years, people sailed eastward from island to island. Early people lived by hunting, fishing, gathering fruits, and sometimes farming. In Australia, these people are known as Aborigines. They arrived in Australia about 40,000 years ago.

4. In 1606, long after Europeans had sailed to the New World, the Dutch reached Australia. In 1770, Captain James Cook, an English explorer, sailed along the eastern coast of Australia and claimed the land for the United Kingdom. The first British colony in Australia was founded in 1788—years after the American Declaration of Independence from the United Kingdom. This colony was mainly made up of convicts or prisoners. Free settlers set up other colonies in Australia. They raised sheep and grew corn. In New Zealand, the Maoris, an island people, arrived about A.D. 750. New Zealand was settled by a few Europeans in the late 18th and early 19th centuries. In 1840, the United Kingdom took it over. Settlements did not grow quickly because it was felt that the lands had few resources.

5. In the middle of the 19th century, whaling ships began to sail throughout the Pacific world in search of whales for oil. They stopped at the islands to get fresh water and food. In exchange for these items, they gave the island peoples such goods as cloth, tobacco, and glass beads. At the same time, missionaries began to go to the islands. The ways of life of the island peoples began to change as contact with westerners increased.

6. In 1851, gold was discovered in Australia. This was two years after the gold rush in California. People hurried in great numbers to

People of the Pacific islands were often glad to see traders from Europe and America. Why?

Australia drew many people during the early gold rush days.

the continent. In less than seven years, Australia's population doubled. The Europeans pushed the native people farther inland.

7. Later in the 19th century, European nations took a new interest in the Pacific world. They wanted the raw materials of this area. They also wanted places of supply for ships sailing across the Pacific Ocean. In the 1880s and 1890s, the British, French, and Germans took over many of the Pacific islands. When the west coast of the United States was settled after 1850, the United States also increased its trade with Asia. As early as 1867, the United States took over the Midway Islands. In 1898, the United States gained Hawaii. As a result of the Spanish-American War, it took the Philippine Islands and Guam from Spain in 1898. Wake Island and the islands of American Samoa were obtained in 1899.

8. After World War I, Japan was given many islands in the Pacific as mandates by the League of Nations. Before World War I, the Germans had controlled them. The Japanese fortified these islands with guns. After attacking Pearl Harbor in Hawaii in 1941, Japan overran other Pacific islands and lands in Southeast Asia. Bloody battles were fought throughout the Pacific before the war ended in August 1945. The islands of Tarawa, Guadalcanal, and Iwo Jima are familiar to Americans as battlegrounds in the Pacific during the war with Japan. After World War II, the Northern Mariana Islands, the Caroline Islands, and the Marshall Islands were made a United Nations trust territory under the care of the United States. Other trust territories in the Pacific were assigned to New Zealand, Australia, and some of the European nations.

UNDERSTANDING WHAT YOU HAVE READ

1. **Which of the following questions are answered in this chapter?**

a. Who were Tasman and Bougainville?

b. What event in the 19th century caused an increase in the population of Australia?

c. Why were Europeans slow to settle in Australia?

2. The main idea of this chapter is to describe

a. early settlements in New Zealand
b. Australia's part in World War II
c. important events in the history of the Pacific world

3. Australia was claimed by the United Kingdom because of the voyages of

a. Cook   b. Magellan   c. da Gama

4. The first European settlers in Australia were

a. traders   b. farmers   c. convicts

5. Europeans were slow to explore Australia because

a. the native people were unfriendly
b. Europeans thought it had no riches
c. there were no good harbors

6. The earliest people to live in Australia were the

a. Dutch
b. Aborigines
c. British

7. After Japan was defeated in World War II, many of the Pacific islands

a. became trust territories
b. declared their independence
c. once again became British colonies

8. *Atolls* are

a. early people of New Zealand
b. small coral islands of the Pacific
c. early whaling ships

The Pacific World in the 1990s

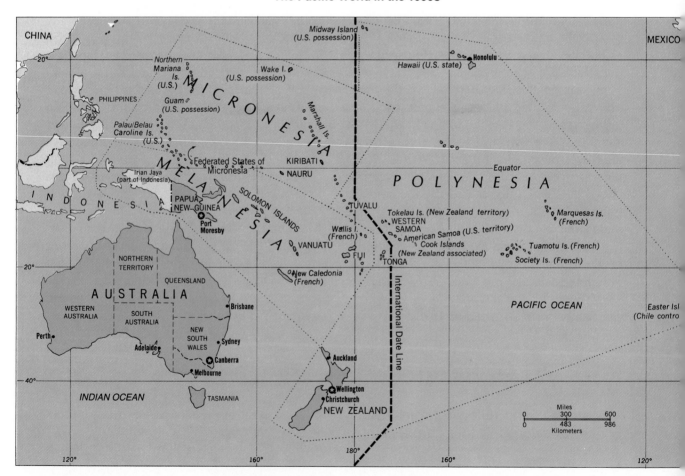

DEVELOPING IDEAS AND SKILLS

Building Map Skills — The Pacific World in the 1990s

Study the map on page 558. Then answer the questions below.

1. What are the three main island groups labeled on this map?
2. Which Asian nations are located near the Pacific region?
3. Where are the most of Australia's large cities located?
4. (a) Which Polynesian island is a part of the United States?
   (b) Which Polynesian island is labeled a U. S. territory?
   (c) Which is labeled a U.S. possession?
   (d) Which other nations control territories in the Pacific region?
5. How does the map show that the Pacific world is the "world of water?"

DEVELOPING CRITICAL THINKING SKILLS

Do You Agree or Disagree?

Tell whether or not you agree with each of these statements. Give reasons for your answers.

1. Australia was settled long after our New World was first reached by Europeans.
2. Nearly all people in the Pacific world do the same kind of work.
3. Most of the people of the Pacific islands govern themselves.
4. As a result of several wars, the United States now has a real interest in the Pacific world.
5. In the years just before World War II, the most powerful nation in the Pacific world was Japan.
6. Between Australia and Asia there are many islands.
7. In the last few years, whaling ships have begun to visit the Pacific lands for the first time.

DEVELOPING IDEAS AND SKILLS

Reading a Time Line

Look at the time line. Write the letter of the period of time in which each of the following events takes place.

| A | B | C |

1750   1800   1850   1900

1. The United States gains possessions in the Pacific.
2. Britain begins the first colony in Australia.
3. The United States gains possession of Guam.
4. The United Kingdom takes over New Zealand.
5. Captain Cook claims Australia for the United Kingdom.
6. Gold is discovered in Australia.

559

Chapter 2

The Lands Down Under

What are the topography and climate of Australia and New Zealand?

READING FOR A PURPOSE:
1. How is Australia's importance in world affairs affected by its location?
2. How does Australia's climate explain, in part, its small population?
3. How does New Zealand's climate differ from that of Australia?

1. Australia is called the island continent. It is the only country to occupy an entire continent by itself. You could call Australia the smallest continent or the largest island on earth. With approximately 3 million square miles (not quite 8 million square kilometers), it is the sixth largest country in the world in area. Australia is also called the "land down under," for it is entirely south of the equator. Therefore, its seasons are the opposite of ours. Australia's summer lasts from December to March; winter is from June to September.

2. Australia is located partly in the low latitudes and partly in the middle latitudes. Its location can be compared with that of Mexico and Central America, except that it is south of the equator instead of north. The city of Melbourne, on the southeast tip of the continent, is 37° south—not as far south of the equator as Cincinnati, Ohio, is north. Australia is farther from the United States than any other major country. The air distance from San Francisco to Sydney, Australia, is 7,500 miles (12,000 kilometers).

3. Along Australia's east coast is a narrow coastal plain. A few miles inland, the land rises to become the eastern highlands or Great Dividing Range. These are the highest mountains in Australia. They are not as high as the Rocky Mountains. West of the mountains is a great central plain. This is called the *outback.* Farther west, the land rises to form a vast, dry plateau. This plateau extends all the way to the western coast. Off the northeastern coast is a long coral reef called the Great Barrier Reef. It has been built up over the ages by millions of tiny sea animals.

4. Lack of water is a serious problem in most of Australia. There are no great rivers like the Congo (Zaire), Mississippi, or Amazon leading into the continent. The largest river is the Murray-Darling, which rises in the eastern highlands and flows southwest into the Indian Ocean.

5. Australia has a varied climate. The north and northeast have a savanna climate. In these areas there is a rainy season and a dry season. During summer, monsoons bring rain. During winter, the wind shifts and the area is dry. It is always hot. Soil is poor because of the heavy rains. As you might guess, few people live in this part of the continent.

6. Most Australians live along the eastern coast. In general, this part of the country has a mild, damp climate. There is plenty of rainfall for farming. The largest cities are also located here. North of Sydney, the climate is humid subtropical. South of Sydney, it is a marine

Kangaroos are found in Australia and the nearby islands.

climate similar to the states of Oregon and Washington.

7. West of the mountains there is less rainfall. The winds that blow over the mountains have lost much of their moisture by the time they reach this area. This is a region of dry grasslands where the rainfall is from 10 to 20 inches (25 to 50 centimeters) a year. It is a steppe climate. The region is almost too dry for farming, but it is good for sheep grazing.

8. Farther west, the land becomes drier. The western half of Australia is a vast desert of sand and rock. (In fact, 40 percent of the country is desert.) Because of the mountains, no rain-bearing winds can reach this part of the continent. No regular winds blow from the Indian Ocean to the east. South of the desert, the coastal areas have a Mediterranean climate—warm, dry summers and mild winters.

9. New Zealand lies about 1,200 miles (1,900 kilometers) southeast of Australia. It is located entirely in the middle latitudes. This country is made up of two main islands, North Island and South Island. Although they are each nearly 1,000 miles (1,600 kilometers) long, the islands are narrow, scarcely more than 200 miles (320 kilometers) wide. This means that the climate of the islands is affected by the ocean around them. These are mountainous islands; there are no deserts as in Australia. The winds blow from the west, so the west coast has more rain than the east coast. New Zealanders enjoy a marine climate, with mild and rainy summers and winters. The land and climate are excellent for raising sheep and cattle. The climate of New Zealand may be compared with that of its "parent country," the United Kingdom.

UNDERSTANDING WHAT YOU HAVE READ

1. Which of the following questions are answered in this chapter?

a. How do the people live in the northeast of Australia?

b. Why is it warm in Australia at Christmas time?

c. How do the mountains of Australia affect its climate?

2. The main idea of this chapter is to describe

a. New Zealand's climate

b. the desert area of Australia

c. the land and climate of Australia and New Zealand

3. New Zealand's climate is chiefly

a. marine b. desert c. rain forest

4. A great part of Australia is very

a. wet b. dry c. cold

5. Seasons in Australia and New Zealand are the opposite of those in North America because these countries are in the

a. Northern Hemisphere
b. Southern Hemisphere

c. Eastern Hemisphere

6. The heart of Australia is dry because

a. rain-bearing winds are blocked by eastern mountains
b. there are few rivers
c. the country is too near the equator

7. The *outback* refers to

a. the coral reefs along the Australian coast
b. the dry central plain
c. reservations where the Aboriginal peoples live

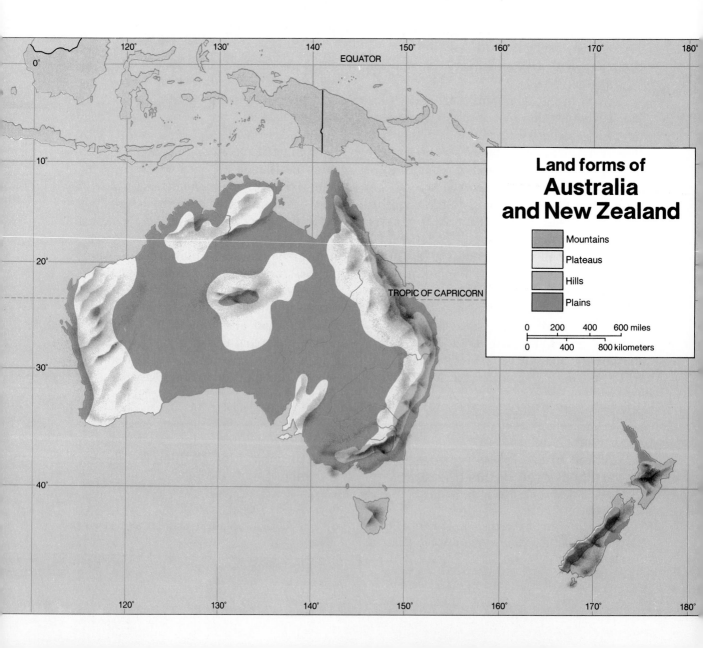

Land forms of
Australia and New Zealand

- Mountains
- Plateaus
- Hills
- Plains

0 200 400 600 miles

0 400 800 kilometers

DEVELOPING IDEAS AND SKILLS

Building Map Skills — Land Forms and Climates of Australia and New Zealand

Study the maps of land forms and climates. Then answer the questions below.

1. Which two land forms make up most of Australia?
2. Which climate is found on New Zealand?
3. Where on Australia is a humid subtropical climate found?
4. (a) Where is the outback located? (b) What is the climate of the outback?
5. Look at the map on page 558. (a) Where are New Zealand's large cities located? (b) Why do you think they are located there?
6. (a) Where do most people in Australia live? (b) Why?
7. How do land forms and climates affect the economic activities that take place in Australia and New Zealand?
8. How is Australia's climate different from the climate in the region where you live?

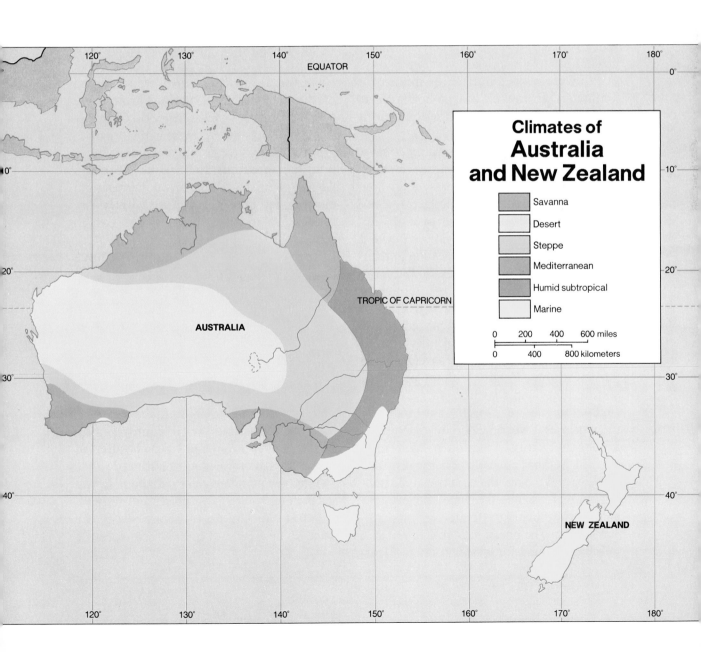

Climates of Australia and New Zealand

- Savanna
- Desert
- Steppe
- Mediterranean
- Humid subtropical
- Marine

0   200   400   600 miles

0   400   800 kilometers

Are the Oceans at Risk?

Did you know that oceans and seas cover 70 percent of the earth's surface? That is why the earth is sometimes called the "blue planet." The oceans interact with the atmosphere, affect climates, provide a source of energy, and contain vast amounts of food and minerals. But like the land and air, the oceans need to be protected.

Who Owns the Oceans? For thousands of years, nations have argued about the control of nearby waters. Since the 1600s, coastal nations have claimed control over ocean waters stretching three miles (4.8 kilometers) from their coasts. Beyond that limit, ships of all other countries have been free to fish and travel.

In 1945, the United States claimed that it owned all mineral resources discovered on its continental shelf. This shelf is the shallow part of the sea floor that slopes gently away from the continents. In order to avoid any future disputes, the United Nations decided to sponsor an international meeting to regulate the use of the world's seas. So far, three conferences have attempted to come up with a Law of the Sea Treaty. But, as of 1992, no agreement had been passed.

Several nations, including the United States, refuse to sign the UN agreement. In particular, they disagree with the provision stating that deep seas beyond a 200-mile (320-kilometer) territorial limit belong to the world as a whole. The United Nations argues that profits from deep-sea mining should be shared between the United Nations and the mining countries. The mining nations, on the other hand, believe that all the profits belong to them.

Pollution The ocean has long served as a dumping ground for waste products. Nearly everything that is crammed down sinks, toilets, and sewers eventually ends up in the world's oceans. Sewage, household wastes, plastics, and industrial chemicals are the worst offenders. They pollute coastal areas, where fish and other seafood breed. In addition, ocean currents often carry pollutants far from where they entered the water. Unfortunately, it is not uncommon to read about trash or waste products that have been discovered in the middle of the ocean.

Oil spills from tankers and ship collisions also pollute the sea. So do radioactive wastes that, for years, have been dumped offshore by industrial nations around the world. Today, it is illegal to get rid of deadly waste products such as these in the ocean.

Overfishing Overfishing is another problem that threatens our oceans. It occurs when more fish are taken from the sea than can be replaced naturally. Overfishing leaves few mature fish in the ocean to rebuild the marine populations.

Today, advances in technology have made fishing very efficient. Huge motor-driven nets haul in everything from the sea within their reach, including dolphins and porpoises. Fortunately, the United Nations banned this type of net fishing after 1991. Most nations, including the United States, have agreed to the ruling. Japan, however, which catches more fish than any other country, continues to object to the ban.

How might tiny Pacific countries like Nauru (nah-OO-roo) and Tuvalu be affected by the new laws forbidding net fishing?

Why are people concerned about saving sea mammals such as porpoises and whales?

What can you do to help protect the oceans?

Chapter 3

The People

What other countries are similar to Australia and New Zealand?

READING FOR A PURPOSE:
1. Who are the original inhabitants of Australia and New Zealand?
2. How are the customs and standard of living of Australians much like that of the people of Canada and the United States?
3. How would you describe the governments of New Zealand and Australia?

1. The populations of Australia and New Zealand are both small. Australia has about 17.5 million people and New Zealand has about 3.5 million. These are mostly white people whose language, customs, and ways of living are like those of the United Kingdom, Canada, and the United States.

2. Australia is one of the most lightly populated countries in the world, with an average of about 7 people for each square mile of land. Because so much of the country is dry, most of the people live around the "rim" of the continent. Until well after World War II, most people who came to Australia were from Great Britain. In the last 25 years, however, over 3 million new settlers have come to Australia. Many have come in search of jobs and a new life; others have come as refugees from Indochina.

3. The first people to come to Australia were the Aborigines. They lived by gathering wild fruits and hunting. The Aborigines were pushed off their land by the white settlers in much the same way the Native Americans were in North America. Today, the Aborigines make up more than 1 percent of the people of Australia. Some are nomads in the outback. Others live on reservations or in the large cities. In the past, many were forced to change their way of life. Today, the Australian government has given them a choice between their old ways and a modern lifestyle.

4. The first people to arrive in New Zealand were the Maoris, a brown-skinned people from the islands of Polynesia. They fought against the white settlers. After a while, they accepted the newcomers and their ways of life. However, they have kept some of their customs. Today, the 290,000 Maoris have the same rights as other New Zealanders. Many are lawyers, doctors, and teachers.

5. While most of the land is used for raising sheep and cattle, most Australians live in cities where they work in factories, offices, and shops. Most of the large cities are located in the southeast. (The port city of Perth on the west coast is the only large city outside the east.) The largest city is Sydney, which has over 3.4 million people. Melbourne, in the mild marine climate of the southeast, is a seaport

A pedestrian mall in Perth, a city on the west coast of Australia. Why are there few cities on the western part of the continent?

Beach and water recreation are popular in modern Sydney, Australia. What areas of the United States might have a similar scene?

with about 3 million people. Other large cities are Brisbane, Adelaide, and Canberra, the capital. About 85 percent of New Zealanders live in that nation's uncrowded towns and cities.

6. The cities of Australia and New Zealand are modern. They are remarkably clean and have very few areas that could be called slums. The people enjoy the comforts of modern living. Washing machines, refrigerators, radios, and television sets are part of most city homes. The streets are wide and automobiles are everywhere. The Australians love to travel. If one considers the small population, Australia has more miles of highway and railroad track for its people than any other nation in the world. (However, the roads and railroads are found mostly in the populated areas.) Most major airlines have routes to Australia.

7. Much of the success of the people of Australia and New Zealand can be traced to their governments. Both countries have a democratic form of government modeled after that of the United Kingdom. The chief law-making body in each is a parliament, elected by the people. The head of each government is the prime minister. They and the members of their cabinets lead their countries with the help of the parliaments. The governments of Australia and New Zealand were the first to pass many laws that have since been adopted by the United States and other countries: the secret ballot, the right of women to vote, and pensions for workers. Both countries are members of the Commonwealth, an organization of countries that were once part of the British Empire.

8. The people of these two nations are

Most Australian cities are modern. This is Sydney, capital of the province of New South Wales.

among the most highly educated in the world. Children must attend school until the age of 15. It would be difficult to find an adult in either country who cannot read and write. (In the outback of Australia, teachers reach their pupils through radio.) The citizens of both nations enjoy a free press and watch American as well as Australian and New Zealand television shows.

9. Both Australians and New Zealanders are great sports-loving people. In Australia, tennis is a favorite sport. Great tennis players have represented Australia in tournaments around the world. In track meets, swimming contests, and boating events among nations, runners, swimmers, and sailors from Australia have also become world-famous. Cricket, rugby, and horse racing draw large crowds everywhere in the country.

10. In many ways, Australia is much like Canada. Both countries are very large but have small populations. Most of the people live along the "rim" of each country. In one case, the interior is largely a cold, watery wilderness; in the other, it is a dry, sandy desert. Both peoples have a high standard of living, with most of them living in cities and working in offices, shops, or factories. Despite their small populations, they are able to export foodstuffs and raw materials. Much of their trade is with the United States, Japan, and Great Britain.

UNDERSTANDING WHAT YOU HAVE READ

1. Which of the following questions are answered in this chapter?
a. What are the large cities of New Zealand?
b. How are the Maoris treated in New Zealand?
c. How are the people of Australia governed?

2. The main idea of this chapter is to describe the
a. cities of the Pacific world
b. ways of living of people "down under"
c. life of the Aborigines

3. Most people in Australia work
a. on farms and plantations
b. on ranches
c. in factories and offices

4. Both Australia and New Zealand have ways of life that can be traced back to the
a. Spanish b. British c. Dutch

5. Australia and New Zealand are similar to the United Kingdom in all of the following ways EXCEPT
a. government
b. Commonwealth members
c. size of population

6. Australia may be called a "hollow continent" because
a. most people live along the coasts
b. it is shaped like a saucer
c. there are no rivers in the interior

7. *Aborigines* refer to the
a. earliest people in Australia
b. original plants and trees of a region
c. earliest European settlers

DEVELOPING IDEAS AND SKILLS

Understanding Graphs and Diagrams — Population, Area, and Standard of Living of Australia and New Zealand

Study the chart on page 568. Then answer these questions.
1. Is the standard of living of this region high or low compared with that of the United States? Is it a low-income area?
2. Is the region as crowded as the United States?
3. Are the people of this region literate compared with the people of the United States?

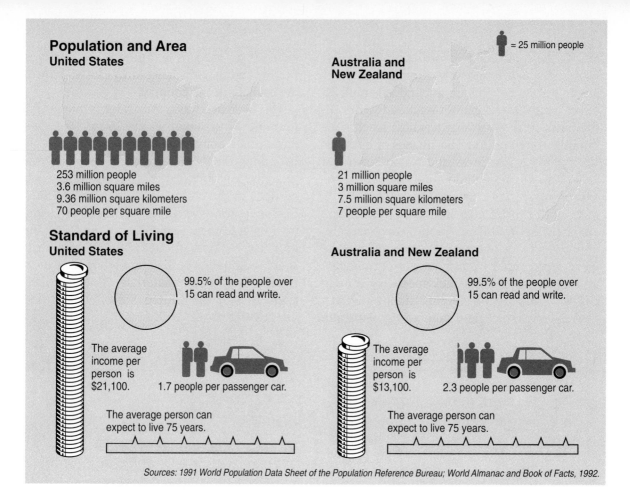

Population and Area
United States

= 25 million people

253 million people
3.6 million square miles
9.36 million square kilometers
70 people per square mile

Australia and
New Zealand

21 million people
3 million square miles
7.5 million square kilometers
7 people per square mile

Standard of Living
United States

99.5% of the people over 15 can read and write.

The average income per person is $21,100.

1.7 people per passenger car.

The average person can expect to live 75 years.

Australia and New Zealand

99.5% of the people over 15 can read and write.

The average income per person is $13,100.

2.3 people per passenger car.

The average person can expect to live 75 years.

Sources: 1991 World Population Data Sheet of the Population Reference Bureau; World Almanac and Book of Facts, 1992.

Population, Area, and Standard of Living of Australia and New Zealand

4. How long may the average person in this region expect to live?
5. What facts tell you the standard of living of the people of the region?
6. How does this region compare with the United States in size?

DEVELOPING CRITICAL THINKING SKILLS

Making Inferences

In our reading, many facts are given to us. From these facts we can draw conclusions. The following are some conclusions or inferences that you might make after reading Chapters 1, 2, and 3. Tell whether these conclusions are correct or incorrect. Give reasons for your answers.

1. The early Maori settlers in New Zealand were good sailors.
2. The early settlers of Australia did not travel far inland.
3. There are few highways in the outback.
4. Visitors from a large city in the United States or Canada would find few things in an Australian city that would be familiar to them.
5. Automobiles would not be as important in New Zealand as in Australia.

A Sheep Station

Sheep are among our most important animals because they provide both food and clothing. Australia and New Zealand are among the leading sheep-raising countries. In each country, there are more sheep than people. Sheep are raised on ranches called sheep stations.

Cecil Peak Station is in the rolling hills near Queenstown, a town on South Island, New Zealand. Scott Barnett, 10 years old, lives on the station. His father is the stockman, or manager. As on other stations, the sheep graze over miles of rangeland, eating grass wherever they find it. From time to time, Scott goes out on patrol with a rangeman (shepherd) and his dogs. He spends most of the day on his horse. He looks for sheep that are ill or in need of help. There are three types of sheep on the station: merino, Corriedale, and Romney. They produce plenty of fine wool and are also good for meat.

Scott is excited. Today the men are going to round up the sheep and bring them in for shearing (cutting their wool). Scott was up early in the morning. The dogs, too, are restless to get going. When all is ready, the men whistle for the dogs and the *muster*, or roundup, begins. In the hills, the men split up, search the fields, and check each corner of the station to find the sheep. The dogs keep the sheep in one pack, moving them gently to the home paddock, or pen. Once home, Scott, who is exhausted, washes, eats, and goes to sleep.

The following days are even busier. It's time to shear the sheep. The shearers, or cutters, are ready to work. The shearing takes place in a large wooden shed that is topped by an iron roof. The sheep jostle one another in the pens beside the shed. As they are led in, each shearer grabs a sheep, upends it (feet in air, head in the lap), and begins cutting swiftly with his electric clipper. In a few minutes, the sheep is stripped of its fleece or wool. Another person carries off the fleece for skirting and grading. Someone is continually sweeping away the scraps of wool, keeping the floor clean. The shorn sheep are marked with paint for identification before they are returned to the pastures. Scott will have to leave the sheep station soon. Since there are no schools nearby, he is going to a boarding school on North Island, to continue his education. Wherever he is, however, he will always think of his horse, his dog, and his life on the station.

A New Zealand sheep ranch.

1. Where does this story take place?
2. Why are sheep important?
3. How are sheep raised?
4. What are the duties of the range-man during most of the year?
5. Why are dogs important on the station?
6. Why is so much land needed to raise sheep?
7. What happens on a muster? What happens during shearing?

569

Chapter 4

Wealth in Lands Dry and Humid

How do the people of Australia and New Zealand make use of their resources?

READING FOR A PURPOSE:
1. Why are Australia and New Zealand good for raising sheep?
2. What is Australia's chief farm crop?
3. How has Australia been able to develop its resources and industries?

1. Much of Australia's land is too dry for farming. What's more, there are not enough people to work the land. Nevertheless, Australia produces more food than its population needs. It is one of the world's great food exporters, sending shiploads of meat and wheat to Europe every year. Let us find out why.

2. Northern Australia is hot and rainy. It has many plantations on which sugar-cane and tropical fruits—pineapples, bananas, and coconuts—are raised. Large amounts of these fruits are exported. The sugarcane lands reach almost to Brisbane, about halfway between northern and southern Australia. Sugar is another food export.

3. South of Brisbane, fruit and dairy farming takes place along the narrow coastal plains. The summers are cool and there is plenty of rain from the winds of the Pacific Ocean. As a result, there is good pasture land. The dairy farmers have good cattle and modern equipment and barns. They supply the people of nearby cities with many dairy products.

4. On the western side of the mountains and also in southwestern Australia are the wheat lands. Here the fields are large and the land is level. Therefore, machinery can be used. In this way, a few farmers can grow a great deal of wheat. Wheat is the chief farm crop of Australia. Next to wool, it is the most important farm export. Many wheat farmers also raise sheep.

5. Farther west from the mountains it is too dry to grow wheat, but there is enough grass for sheep grazing. This is the area of the huge sheep ranches called *stations*. These stations are very large because sheep have to roam far and wide to get enough to eat. The poorer the land, the larger the station. The few ranchers who live here are far apart. The nearest neighbor might be 100 miles away. Travel is difficult and water is scarce. It is not unusual for the sheep rancher to travel by jeep or airplane to look over his vast station. Most sheep are raised for their wool rather than their meat.

6. The sheep rancher has many problems. First, there is not enough water for the people

A cattle muster, or roundup, in northern Australia. Cattle as well as sheep are important to the economy of Australia.

A copper mine at Mount Isa in Queensland forms a deep pit in the ground. What are the benefits and problems associated with such mines?

and animals. This problem has been partly solved by digging deep wells called *artesian* wells. These wells are dug through a layer of rock. The water shoots to the surface. If it were not for the artesian water, many stretches of desert and "bush land" would have no water at all for people or sheep.

7. Second, the sheepherder must fight all kinds of animal pests. There are wild dogs, rabbits, cattle ticks, and kangaroos. The wild dogs, or *dingoes,* were first brought to Australia as pets. They are hated because they kill the sheep—even more than they need for food. Rabbits are the worst enemies of the sheepherders, however. They eat the precious grass and the bark of the bushes. Rabbits limit the number of sheep that the pastures can feed. Another great pest is that unusual creature, the kangaroo. Kangaroos like to eat the grass and brush, too. Australians are doing their best to fight the problems these animals cause.

8. In the northern plains, cattle are raised. The cattle feed on the coarse grass that grows during the rainy summers. From these cattle Australians get large amounts of hides and beef. The cattle ranches are far from railroads and seaports. The animals are driven to market across the country in specially designed cattle trucks.

9. Unlike Australia, New Zealand is a rainy country that is always green. The hills and lowlands of New Zealand are good for raising dairy cattle and sheep. The dairy farms are among the best in the world. New Zealand ranks high in the export of cheese, lamb, butter, and wool. Because of their exports, the people of New Zealand have a very high standard of living.

10. While sheepherding, cattle raising, and wheat growing produce much of its exports, Australia is also a leading mining and industrial nation. There are several reasons for this. First, because many machines are used on the farms and ranches, fewer people are needed there. They can work in the mines and mills.

11. Second, Australia is rich in minerals. It is a world leader in bauxite, used to make aluminum, and iron, used to make steel. It also mines much coal, gold, and uranium. Diamonds, natural gas, and oil have been discovered. The area of Broken Hill, in southeast Australia, produces lead, zinc, and copper. The nation's mills turn out steel for making cars, ships, planes, and trains.

12. Third, Australia has many sources of power: coal, falling water, oil, and natural gas. So much coal and gas is produced that they can be exported. Although there is a water shortage in much of Australia, waterpower is available in the eastern part of the country. The snow and rain from the Great Dividing Range cause many small streams to flow down the mountainsides toward the ocean. Finally,

571

Queenstown, New Zealand. Lake Wakatipu is in the background.

good roads and railroads have been built so that raw materials from the mines and farms can easily be sent to the factories and seaport cities.

13. New Zealand does not have as many mineral resources as Australia. Therefore, it does not have as many large factories. Because much of New Zealand is mountainous, power from falling water is used. Most of the factories make use of the products of New Zealand's farms; there are wool and flour mills, meat-packing plants, and dairies. New Zealand's chief trading partners are the United Kingdom, Australia, the United States, and Japan. Australia does about 40 percent of its foreign trade with Japan and the United States. New Zealand does most of its trading with Australia and Japan.

UNDERSTANDING WHAT YOU HAVE READ

1. Which of the following questions are answered in this chapter?
a. How is water obtained in the outback?
b. Why can Australia grow large amounts of wheat?
c. What animals bother the sheep rancher?

2. The main idea of paragraphs 5 through 7 is to describe
a. how the people of Australia use their resources
b. the sheep country of Australia
c. wheat growing on the plains

3. Water is obtained in the outback through
a. artesian wells
b. irrigation canals
c. dams

4. Australians are able to grow large amounts of wheat because
a. the fields are large, flat, and suited to the use of machinery
b. fields are far from the smoke-filled cities
c. they have a large labor supply and plenty of rainfall

5. The chief exports of New Zealand are
a. bauxite, coal, and uranium
b. beef, sugar, and fruits
c. cheese, butter, lamb, and wool

6. A good reason why Australia has been able to develop industries is that
a. there is a large supply of workers
b. mineral resources are in good supply
c. there are also many farmers

7. An *artesian* well is
a. dug on the side of a mountain
b. a spring in which water is pumped to the surface
c. dug deep in the soil through a layer of rock

8. The word *station,* as used in this chapter, refers to
a. land and buildings used in raising sheep and cattle
b. a position in line
c. a regular stopping place on railroads

REVIEWING AND WRITING

Making an Outline

Complete the following outline in your notebook.

Australia

A. Agricultural Products
  1.
  2.
  3.
B. Problems of sheep ranchers
  1.
  2.
C. Major Exports
  1.
  2.
  3.

D. Minerals
  1.
  2.
  3.
  4.
  5.
  6.
  7.
  8.
  9.
  10.
  11.

E. Sources of Power
  1.
  2.
  3.
  4.

FOLLOW UP

Reviewing Chapters 1 through 4

Which does not belong? Choose the item that *does not belong* with the others in each group.

1. Important animals of Australia: sheep, cattle, hogs, kangaroos
2. Mineral resources of Australia: coal, chrome, copper, iron ore
3. Climates of Australia: desert, savanna, humid subtropical, taiga
4. Cities of Australia: Auckland, Melbourne, Sydney, Perth
5. Events in Australian history: colonies in Africa, discovery of gold, voyage of Capt. Cook, World War II
6. Farm products of Australia: wheat, sugarcane, citrus fruits, peanuts

Chapter 5

Life on the Islands

What is life like on the Pacific islands?

1. How are the Pacific islands divided?
2. What is the difference between "high" and "low" islands?
3. What are the main crops of Pacific islands?

1. The great world of the Pacific Ocean is made up of thousands of islands. You will not be able to find most of them on a map. Most of these islands are located in the tropics, north and south of the equator. The islands are divided into three parts: *Melanesia* or "black islands"; *Micronesia* or "small islands"; and *Polynesia* or "many islands."

2. The islands of Melanesia lie south of the equator and northeast of Australia. They extend southeastward as far as New Caledonia and the Fiji Islands. The largest island in the group is New Guinea, which covers about 300,000 square miles (770,000 square kilometers). The western part of New Guinea is part of Indonesia. The eastern part is the independent country of Papua New Guinea. Most of the people of Melanesia are dark-skinned Melanesians. Almost all Melanesians live in

newly independent countries. These include the nations of Fiji, Vanuatu, Papua New Guinea, and the Solomon Islands.

3. Micronesia lies north of Melanesia. Micronesians have somewhat lighter skin than Melanesians. They live on groups of islands made up chiefly of coral atolls, barely above sea level. Some important battles during World War II took place on the islands of Micronesia. Until the 1980s, the United States cared for the Caroline, Mariana, and Marshall Islands as part of the UN Trust Territory of the Pacific Islands. The United States owns Wake Island and Guam with its fine harbor. Nauru is an independent nation. So is Kiribati, which is made up of the Gilbert Islands in Micronesia and other islands hundreds of miles away in Polynesia.

4. Polynesia is the eastern part of the Pacific world. New Zealand is the largest country in this group. Other independent nations in Polynesia include Tonga, Tuvalu, and Western Samoa. American Samoa is an American territory. The United States owns Midway Islands; Hawaii, of course, is part of the United States. A few other islands in the region are controlled by the French, British, and New Zealanders.

5. All of the Pacific islands are near the equator. This means that the climate is warm throughout the year. The waters tend to keep the temperatures even, so that there is little

Thatched huts are reflected in the waters near Western Samoa.

Cutting sugarcane in Fiji.

How might life be difficult for the persons who live in this house on a coral atoll? How might it be pleasant?

change in temperature from one season to another. The average temperature on most of the islands is near 80°F (27°C). There is plenty of rainfall. The winds blow from the east. If there are mountains on the islands, the eastern or windward side is the part that receives the heaviest rain. This part of the Pacific often has severe storms called *typhoons*.

6. The Pacific islands fall into two groups, the "high" islands and the "low" islands. The "high" islands are usually larger. They are either the tops of underwater mountains or volcanoes that have been built up from the ocean floor. These islands contain more fertile land and support more people. The people who live on them have a higher standard of living than their "low"-island neighbors.

7. There are several reasons for this. First of all, "high" islands get more rainfall because their mountains can catch the winds. The rainy hillsides are covered with forests that are used to build boats and houses. Because of the rain and the fertile soil, a great variety of crops are grown: rice, yams, corn, coconuts, bananas, tobacco, and taro (a starchy root made into a pastelike food called *poi*). The people live in the valleys. Each valley supports a village. (The larger islands have cities.) Many of the people also raise pigs or cattle to

use for food along with fish and fruit. Whatever they grow is needed for themselves; there is little to be sold.

8. The "low" islands are usually reefs or atolls. Many of them are barely above the surface of the water. The atolls are chains of small coral islands. They have been formed by millions of tiny coral animals that live in the ocean. These animals produce a limy shell that hardens to form the atoll. In the center of the atoll is a lagoon, a body of water like a pond. The coral reefs act as protection for the lagoon, and the heavy ocean waves do not enter it. During World War II, these lagoons were places where hundreds of ships lay at anchor. Because the atolls are hard-surfaced, they have been used as landing fields for airplanes.

9. Life on the "low" islands is much harder than on the "high" islands. There is little or no drinking water. The soil is thin, for it is washed away or broken by wind and waves. Many people live on their own small farms. They use simple digging sticks to plant their crops. Their chief food crops are coconuts, taro, and yams. They also catch fish.

10. The coconut palm is the chief resource of both "high" and "low" islands. It is a source of food, clothing, and shelter for many of the islanders. For the outside world, it is a source of *copra*. Copra is dried coconut meat. Oil is pressed out of the copra to make margarine, cooking and salad oils, fine soaps, and cosmetics. Coconut-shell charcoal is also exported for use in cigarettes and gas masks as a filter.

11. Along with subsistence farming and fishing, there are also plantations on many islands that grow crops for export. There are coconut or copra plantations. On New Cale-donia, coffee is raised; on Fiji, sugarcane; on Hawaii, sugarcane and pineapples. A number of "low" islands use the birds that have flown over them for thousands of years as a natural resource. As the birds fly over, their droppings fall on the islands. These droppings mix with the coral limestone and have changed it to a mineral called phosphate rock. This phosphate rock is important for use as a fertilizer. The countries that own these islands are able to export phosphate rock to other lands.

UNDERSTANDING WHAT YOU HAVE READ

1. Which of the following questions are answered in this chapter?
a. Which islands are controlled by the Dutch?
b. What are the many uses of the coconut?
c. How does the Pacific Ocean affect the climate of the islands?

2. The main idea of paragraphs 8 through 10 is to describe
a. life on the "low" islands of the Pacific
b. export crops of the "low" islands
c. the government of the "low" islands

3. The most valuable resource of most island peoples is
a. phosphate rock   b. pineapples   c. coconuts

4. The United States has control of
a. Fiji, the Solomon Islands, Vanuatu
b. Guam, Midway Islands, Wake Island

c. Western Samoa, Tonga, Tuvalu

5. Few people live on the "low" islands because
a. there is little fertile soil
b. the Pacific winds are too strong
c. the islands are too mountainous

6. The coconut palm is important in the life of the island peoples because it is
a. a source of oil for machinery
b. used in building boats
c. a source of food, shelter, and clothing

7. *Copra* is the dried meat of
a. the coconut   b. manioc   c. sorghum

8. An *atoll* is built from
a. volcanoes   b. glaciers   c. tiny sea animals

SUMMING UP

Tell whether the following refer to "high" islands (*H*) or to "low" islands (*L*):

well watered	volcanoes
small in size	little fertile soil
fewer people	mountainous
higher living standards	more minerals
variety of crops	people depend upon the coconut

576

In the Pacific World

When a mining company tried to explore for minerals on her family's sheep ranch on North Island, New Zealand, **Catherine Wallace** objected. That was just the first protest for Wallace, who teaches economics at Victoria University. She is now fighting for the preservation of Antarctica. She wants it to be declared a "world park." As a world park, Antarctica would be protected from industry and mining and, Wallace hopes, from too many tourists.

"Warra, warra [Go away]," a group of **Australian Aborigines** shouted on that fateful day in 1788. But the British ship with its boatload of British convicts did not go away. Instead, the convicts were followed by settlers looking for new opportunities in the vast Australian continent. The Aborigines, who have lived in Australia for 40,000 years, were pushed aside as the British settlers moved in. Now the Aborigines are demanding their rights as the true first settlers of Australia. The Aboriginal Land Rights (Northern Territory) Act of 1976 created controversial land trusts that returned one-third of the 178,000 square miles (461,020 square kilometers) to Aboriginal control. The Northern Territory is now home to 29,000 Aborigines who control the tourist centers and receive rental payments from uranium mines and hotels.

Dr. Bob Brown became a environmental activist quite by accident. He was vacationing in a remote area of western Tasmania. For 12 days, he traveled along the Franklin River, gazing at natural beauty that very few humans had ever seen. Then, as he approached the headwaters of the river, he heard sounds that chilled his blood. A construction crew was ripping into the ground with jackhammers. Drilling barges and bulldozers joined the noisy scene. The Australian physician was horrified. Someone was building a dam that would destroy all of the beauty that he had just seen. He decided that he would practice preventive medicine for the environment. He gave up his medical practice and joined the Tasmanian Wilderness Society. During the seven-year battle to save the Franklin River from the state power commission dam, Dr. Brown was assaulted, robbed, and shot at. In spite of the personal danger, he kept on fighting against the project. He won, and the dam was never built. Today, Dr. Brown is a member of the Tasmanian parliament.

Pao Kele O Puna is the last tropical rain forest in the United States. It covers the sides of the Hawaiian volcano Kilauea. But the forest is in danger. Engineers are planning to sink hundreds of geothermal wells into the volcano. These wells will generate electricity for the islands. Unfortunately, deadly gas from these wells will also poison the rain forest. According to the native Hawaiian religion, the wells will violate the goddess Pele. So Pele's defenders have joined forces with scientists who want to preserve the rain forest. They formed the **Pele Defense Fund** in 1983 to try to stop the developers. Environmentalists hope they win the fight. They believe the United States must stop the destruction of its last rain forest.

Chapter 6

The Pacific World Today

What is the future of Australia and the Pacific islands?

READING FOR A PURPOSE:
1. How can Australia solve problems caused by its vast desert?
2. How has Australia's immigration policy affected relations with its neighbors?
3. How did World War II affect the lives of the island people?

1. Australia is one of the largest countries in the world, yet it is one of the driest. A great desert occupies about 40 percent of the land area. There are few important lakes and rivers. The lack of water means that only a small part of the land can be farmed. In order to solve this problem, Australians are trying to use their few rivers for irrigation and power. One of the most remarkable projects is to make use of the Snowy River in the southeastern highlands. Rather than letting the river flow out to the sea, Australians have built dams, aqueducts, and tunnels so the water can be used. The runoff from the dams is channeled into another river (the Murray) for use in irrigating the dry land.

2. Parts of the Australian continent have hardly been explored. The great desert has separated the people of the eastern coast from other people in the country. Only one railroad crosses the continent to the city of Perth on the west coast. There is a need for more roads, railways, and air routes spanning the continent. (Since air routes are easier than railroads to establish, air travel will probably increase in Australia in the future.)

3. Australia has the problem of defending itself. Before World War II, both Australia and New Zealand felt safe from invasion. They thought they were too far from the rest of the world. However, during the war, Japanese forces came close to the borders of Australia, capturing islands around the continent. Japan bombed the city of Darwin in the north. In the Battle of the Coral Sea the American navy stopped the advance of the Japanese and saved Australia from invasion.

4. After World War II, Australia and New Zealand realized that they needed allies, or friends, to help them keep their freedom. The United States joined these nations in a defense treaty in 1951. It is called ANZUS, after the first letters of the three nations. Its members agreed to help each other in case of war in the Pacific. This friendship has been threatened in recent years. In 1984, however, New Zealand adopted a law saying that it would no longer allow any nuclear-armed or nuclear-powered ships, including U.S. ships, into its ports. The United States, therefore, said that it could no longer guarantee New Zealand's security.

5. The lives of the people of the Pacific islands changed greatly during World War II. Many of the islands of Melanesia and Micronesia were occupied by United States and Australian troops. Many of the Pacific islanders helped to build runways for airplanes and to load and unload ships. The people also sold food to feed the troops. Many of the island

Change is coming to the islands. Here, villagers are going to a health clinic for a checkup.

A football (rugby) game being played on Fiji.

people received more money than they had ever had before. They bought Western clothing, tobacco, chewing gum, canned beef, and other goods.

6. After World War II, some Pacific islanders began giving up their old ways of living. By the 1980s and 1990s, many of the island groups had become independent nations—The Marshall Islands, Fiji, Kiribati, Western Samoa, Vanuatu, Tonga, Tuvalu. Little towns on these islands have become capital cities. Many people left their farms to work at high-paying government jobs. An increasing number of tourists have come to the islands. Small

shops have opened to sell goods to the tourists. With their new incomes, islanders are buying the products of the industrialized world: color television sets, motorbikes, frozen foods.

7. Most Pacific islanders still depend on cash crops. For example, Fiji's main export is sugar. Tonga grows coconuts and exports copra and bananas. The new governments are improving their citizens' education and health. Some countries are trying to improve farming conditions. Others seek to develop the fishing and tourist industries. Several of the island nations have called in foreign companies to help search for oil offshore.

UNDERSTANDING WHAT YOU HAVE READ

1. Which of the following questions are answered in this chapter?

a. Why did Australia and New Zealand join ANZUS?

b. Why does Australia have some fear of the lands to the north?

c. How were the Pacific islands prepared for self-government?

2. The main idea of this chapter is to describe

a. how World War II changed the island peoples

b. the problem of the peoples of the Pacific world

c. the relationship between Asia and Australia

3. The lands to the north of Australia are

a. crowded   b. small   c. far away

4. Both Australia and New Zealand belong to the organization known as

a. OAS   b. NATO   c. ANZUS

5. Australia joined in a treaty with the United States because

a. its population is small

b. it has a fear of attack

c. it needs to trade for food

6. By the 1980s, many of the Pacific island groups had

a. become independent nations
b. been made a part of Australia or New Zealand

c. developed steel mills and new factories

7. If a nation works with its *allies*, it is working with its

a. neighbors   b. suppliers   c. friends

DEVELOPING CRITICAL THINKING SKILLS

Which of these statements are facts and which are someone's opinion?

1. Opening its doors to people of all lands has caused problems in Australia.
2. Someday the atolls of the Pacific will be crowded with people.
3. American soldiers brought new goods and ideas to the people of the Pacific islands.
4. The Pacific islands should join together to develop industries and share their resources.
5. Australia really has little to fear from the countries of Asia.
6. Many of the Pacific islands are too far away to concern the American people.
7. Many of the island people depend upon the sea for a living.
8. Japanese forces came close to invading Australia in World War II.

FOLLOW UP

Tell whether the following items refer to the United States, Australia, or both countries. If the item applies to the United States only, write US; if it applies to Australia only, write *A;* if it applies to both countries, write *B.*

An island country
High standard of living
Modern cities
Near the world's greatest trade routes
Few people living in center of the country
Many large, useful rivers
Cattle raising is important
Democratic government
Large supplies of coal and iron
Desert region
More sheep than people
Women having equal rights with men
Smaller than China
Took part in World War II

The Pacific World

Hikers on a volcano

Country	Area (Square Miles)	Capital	Population (1991 estimates)	Number of Years to Double Population	Life Expectancy	Per Capita GNP, 1991
Australia	2,966,200	Canberra	17,500,000	91	76	$ 14,440
Fiji	7,054	Suva	700,000	35	62	$ 1,640
French Polynesia	1,544	Papeete	200,000	28	69	$ 8,210**
Kiribati	266	Tarawa	65,000****	—	—	—
Marshall Islands	70	Majuro	100,000	18	63	—
Nauru	8	Yaren	8,100****	—	—	$ 21,400*
New Caledonia	7,359	Nouméa	200,000	37	67	—
New Zealand	103,736	Wellington	3,500,000	75	74	$ 11,800
Papua New Guinea	300,000	Port Moresby	3,900,000	31	59	$ 900
Solomon Islands	10,640	Honiara	300,000	20	69	$ 570
Tonga	270	Nuku´alofa	108,000***	70	—	—
Tuvalu	10	Funafuti	9,000	—	62	—
Vanuatu	5,700	Port-Vila	200,000	22	69	$ 860
Western Samoa	1,133	Apia	200,000	25	67	$ 720

*1981   **1986   ***1989   ****1990

Sources: 1991 World Population Data Sheet of the Population Reference Bureau, Inc.; The World Almanac and Book of Facts, 1992.

ATLAS

MAPS

Since ancient times, mapmakers have used their art to show the known world. This 1640 Dutch map is fairly accurate for the Eastern Hemisphere, but inaccurate for the Americas.

Reviewing Basic Skills

Nobody knows when map making began. We do know that when people began to move from place to place, either by land or sea, they needed maps to help them find their way. It is not uncommon for archaeologists to find maps on ancient ruins, tombs, and clay tablets. When Captain Cook reached the islands of the South Pacific, for example, he found that natives were very familiar with maps.

What is a map? It is a special way of recording and communicating information about the earth. Some maps give us information about the physical environment, the kind of land and climate an area has. Some maps locate towns and cities, the boundaries of countries, and coastlines (where land and water meet). Other maps give special information about certain aspects of the world, such as where people live, how long people can expect to live, and the number of people living in cities.

For a map to be useful, you must first know how to read one. The ability to read and understand maps is a matter of knowledge and practice. To understand a map you must know how to interpret the symbols (key), compass rose or directional indicator, scale, lines of longitude and latitude, and colors. You have already learned many of these skills. Let's review some of them.

The first thing you must do when reading a map, is find out what information the map is showing. You can do this by reading the title. Then you must know what each of the symbols on the map represents. Some basic symbols include:

▬▬▬	national boundary,
▬ ▬ ▬	state boundary,
•	city,
⊙	capital city,
∿	river,
∧∧∧	mountain,
✈	airport.

Many maps use color to indicate things such as agricultural areas, urban areas, climate, population, rainfall, and land forms. The map key explains what the symbols and the colors on the map represent.

You have already learned that the full-size of the earth is not shown on a map. The earth is reduced to a smaller scale in order to fit on paper. The scale is usually shown on the map. It tells you how many miles (kilometers) each inch or half inch of space represents. The scale enables you to measure the real distance from one place to another. For example, a half inch on this scale

Miles	500		2,000
Kilometers	800		3,219

is equal to 500 miles (800 kilometers). According to this scale, two inches on a map would equal 2,000 miles (3,219 kilometers). Not every map has the same scale. A scale will vary depending on the size of the map and the amount of earth being shown.

This atlas unit contains six maps, which show world climates, land forms, political borders, urban areas, life expectancy, and population. Two of these maps picture the physical aspects of the earth, the land and water areas, the land forms, and the climate. Another map identifies the names of countries and country borders. The remaining three present different aspects of human culture.

Before using the atlas, use the map on the next page to answer the following questions.

1. What does the map show? What would be another good title for this map?
2. What symbols are shown on the map? Make a map key for the symbols.
3. What bodies of water are shown?
4. What river flows through the state of South Dakota?
5. What river forms the border between Mexico and Texas?
6. What major Californian cities are shown?
7. How far is it from Jacksonville, Florida, to Memphis, Tennessee?
8. In which direction is Dallas, Texas, from New York?
9. What city is located at 90°W, 29°N?
10. What state is farthest north?

584

Northern America

585

World Political Map

The map below is a political map of the world. It shows the boundaries of all the countries of the world. It also shows the major bodies of water. A map like this is useful in finding the relationship of one country to another. For example, is Australia located near Europe? With this map you can see all of the countries that border a particular country. For example, which countries border Libya?

Look at the map key. It is different from the other map keys used in this text. Because there are so many countries, there is not enough room on the map to label each. Therefore, some countries are indentified by letters. For example, Burundi, Africa, is labeled B. Now look at the continent of Africa. Find the letter B. This is where Burundi is located. Some countries are so small that they cannot

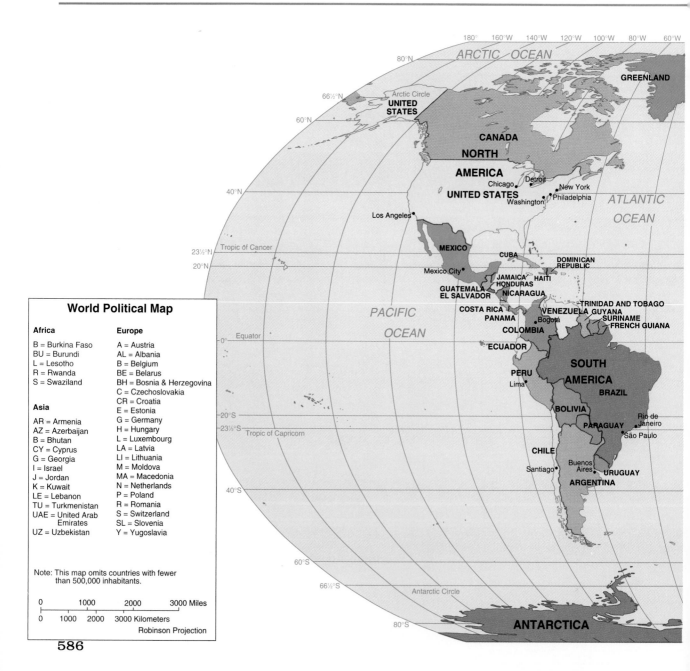

World Political Map

Africa

B = Burkina Faso
BU = Burundi
L = Lesotho
R = Rwanda
S = Swaziland

Asia

AR = Armenia
AZ = Azerbaijan
B = Bhutan
CY = Cyprus
G = Georgia
I = Israel
J = Jordan
K = Kuwait
LE = Lebanon
TU = Turkmenistan
UAE = United Arab
    Emirates
UZ = Uzbekistan

Europe

A = Austria
AL = Albania
B = Belgium
BE = Belarus
BH = Bosnia & Herzegovina
C = Czechoslovakia
CR = Croatia
E = Estonia
G = Germany
H = Hungary
L = Luxembourg
LA = Latvia
LI = Lithuania
M = Moldova
MA = Macedonia
N = Netherlands
P = Poland
R = Romania
S = Switzerland
SL = Slovenia
Y = Yugoslavia

Note: This map omits countries with fewer than 500,000 inhabitants.

| 0 | 1000 | 2000 | 3000 Miles |

| 0 | 1000 | 2000 | 3000 Kilometers |

Robinson Projection

be shown on this map. These have been listed to the left of the map.

Answer the following questions using the World Political Map.

1. What country is bordered by Brazil, Bolivia and Argentina?
2. Which countries are too small to show on the map?
3. What country is north of China?
4. Which country is bordered only by ocean?
5. What country in Europe is labeled with the letter L?
6. Which countries border India?
7. Is Spain closer to France or Germany?
8. Which country is contained entirely in South Africa?
9. What countries border the United States?

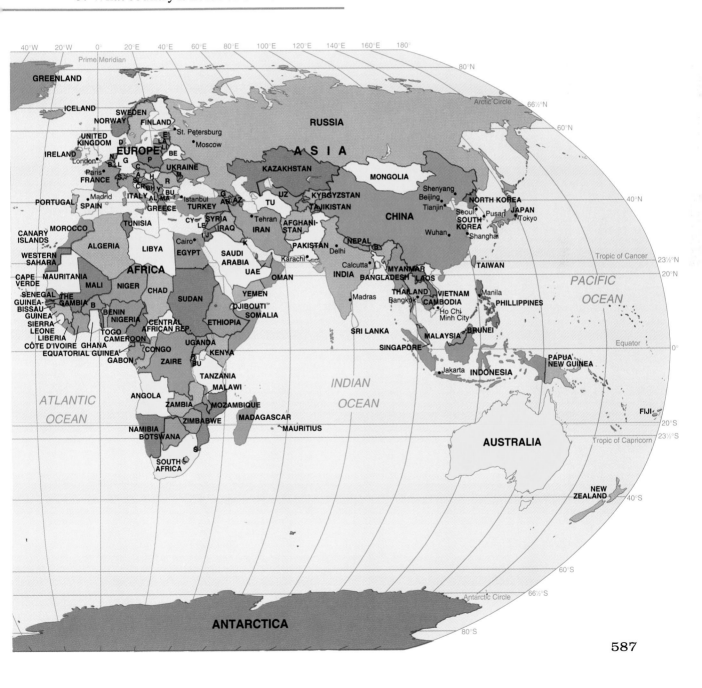

World Climate Map

This is a world climate map. Climate is the kind of weather an area has over a long period of time. This map shows the type of climate in each part of the world. Look at the map key. It shows the color used for each of the 11 world climate regions. (Refer to Unit 1, Chapter 10, for a discussion of each climate region.) To determine the climate of a region you must first locate the region on the map. Find Australia on the map. What colors do you see? Look at the map key. Find the colors that are shown on Australia. What type of climate does each of the colors represent?

Now answer the following questions using the world climate map.

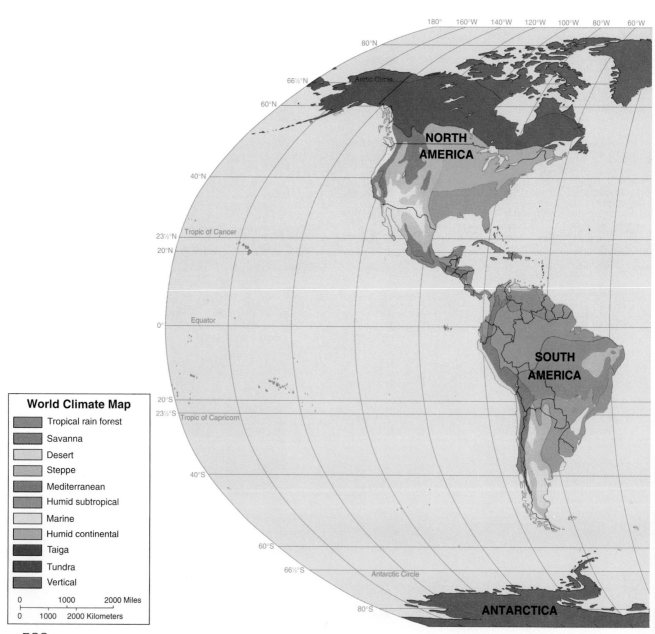

World Climate Map

- Tropical rain forest
- Savanna
- Desert
- Steppe
- Mediterranean
- Humid subtropical
- Marine
- Humid continental
- Taiga
- Tundra
- Vertical

0   1000   2000 Miles

0   1000   2000 Kilometers

1. How many climate types are found in the Commonwealth? What are they?
2. What is the climate of the eastern part of the United States?
3. In what part of the United States would you find a desert climate?
4. What countries of Europe have a Mediterranean climate?
5. What is the main climate region in Europe?
6. What areas of the world have a humid continental climate?
7. What is the main climate region in Asia?
8. What climate region is colored pink?
9. Where would you find a vertical climate?
10. Would you be able to grow wheat along the northern border of Niger? Explain.
11. What color is used to show taiga?

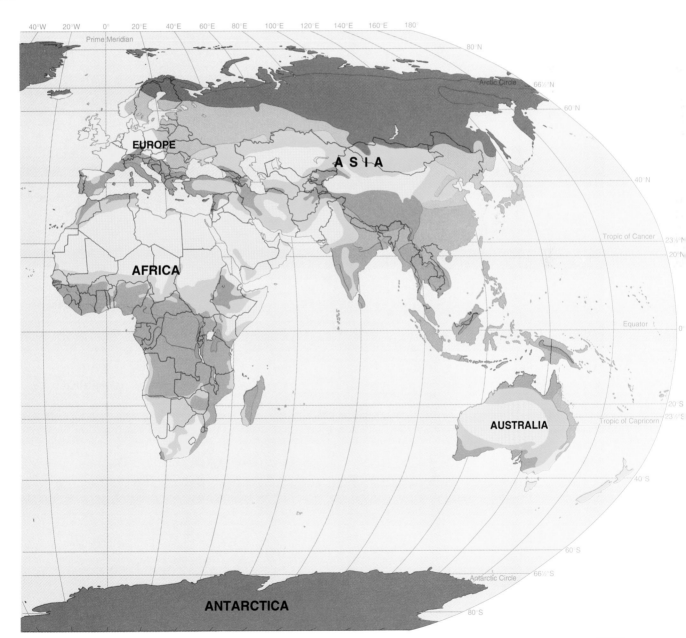

World Land Forms Map

In Unit 1 the four main kinds of land forms were explained. These are mountains, hills, plateaus, and plains. Mountains are usually 1,000 feet (300 meters) or higher. Look at the map key. The orange areas are mountains. Find a mountain area on the map. Hills are the light green areas. Hills are usually lower than mountains. Locate hills on the map. Plateaus are flat land forms that rise above the level of the land around them.

Plateaus are also called tablelands, or mesas. These are the yellow areas on the map. Where are the plateau regions? The last land form are plains. They are the dark green areas. These are areas of level land. Plains are not always flat; they may be slightly rolling. An-

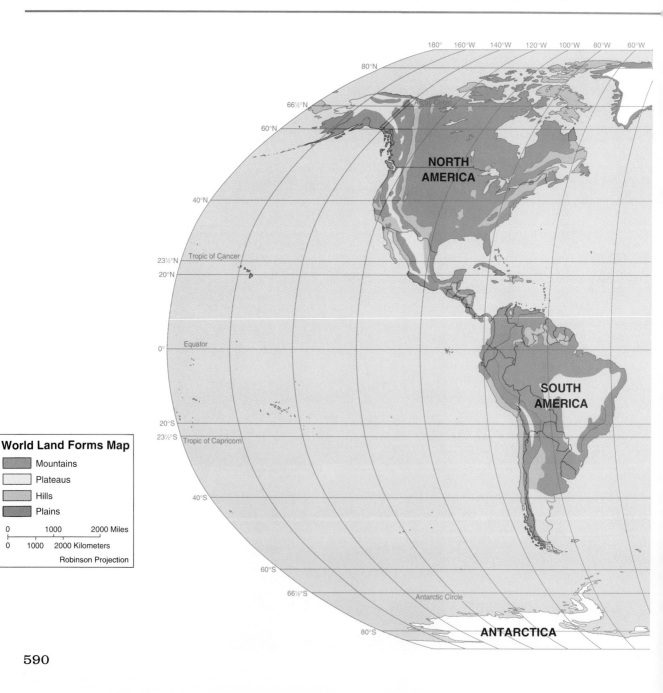

World Land Forms Map

- Mountains
- Plateaus
- Hills
- Plains

0   1000   2000 Miles
0   1000   2000 Kilometers
Robinson Projection

NORTH AMERICA

SOUTH AMERICA

ANTARCTICA

other name for the plains is lowlands. Find the plains on the map. Most of the earth's people live on the plains.

Answer the following questions using the World Land Forms Map.

1. What are the major world land forms?
2. What do the light green areas show?
3. What are the main land forms in the United States?
4. Where are the plains in South America?
5. What is the main land form in Asia?
6. What is the main land form in Europe?
7. Are there more mountainous or plains areas in the Commonwealth?
8. What colors are the mountain areas?
9. Is the west coast of South America generally flat? Explain.
10. Do you think there is much farming in Switzerland? Explain.

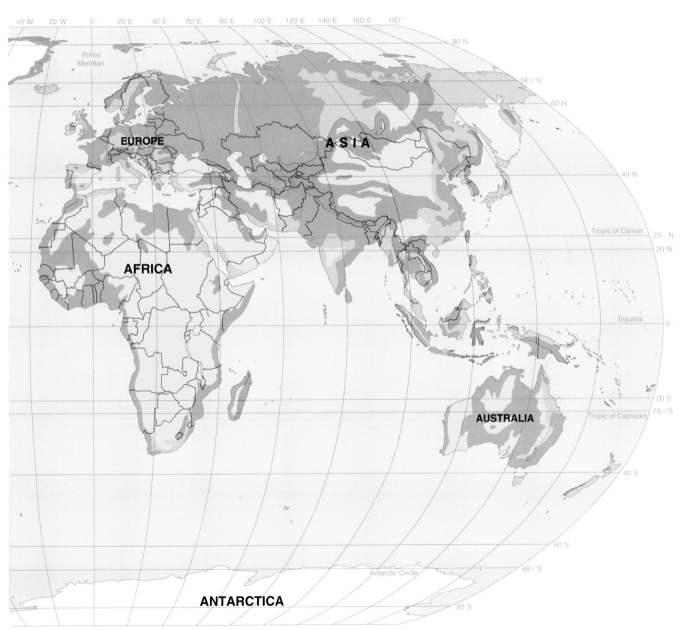

World Population Map

This is a world population map. It shows the number of people living in a certain area. In this case, the number of people living in each country is shown. (However, this map does not show population density, the parts of the country the people live in.)

Look at the key. It is divided into four population ranges—

over one billion ◼
75 million to one billion ◼
15 million to 75 million ◻
under 15 million ◻

It also shows those areas for which this information is not available.

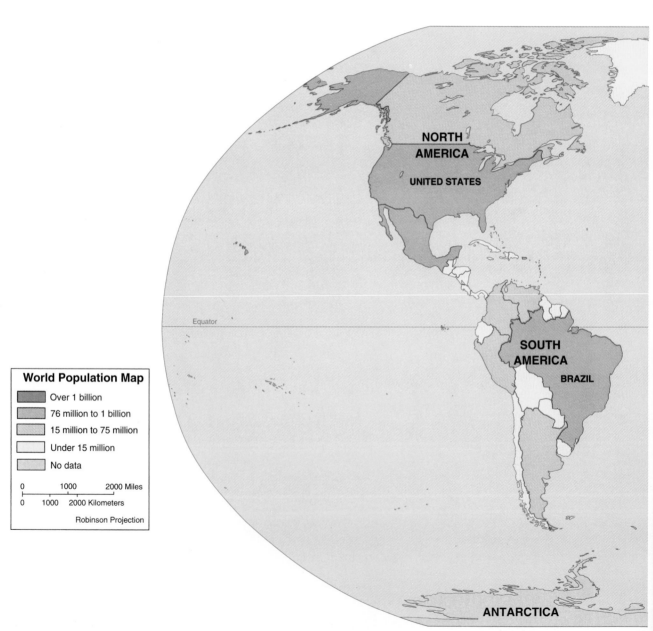

World Population Map

◼ Over 1 billion
◼ 76 million to 1 billion
◻ 15 million to 75 million
◻ Under 15 million
◻ No data

0   1000   2000 Miles
0   1000   2000 Kilometers
Robinson Projection

Answer the following questions using the World Population Map.

1. What does this map show?
2. What does the color  represent?
3. For which countries is there no population information available?
4. What does the color ▢ represent?
5. List some countries with a population of over one billion.
6. What is the population of the United States?
7. List four countries with a population of over 15 million but less than 75 million.
8. What is the population of France?
9. List four countries with a population of under 15 million.
10. What is the population of Argentina?
11. List two countries with a population of 75 million but less than a billion.

593

World Urbanization Map

Color can be used to show many things on a map. On this map, color is used to show the percentage of people in each country who live in urban or city areas. This type of map is a world urbanization map. Look at the map key. The 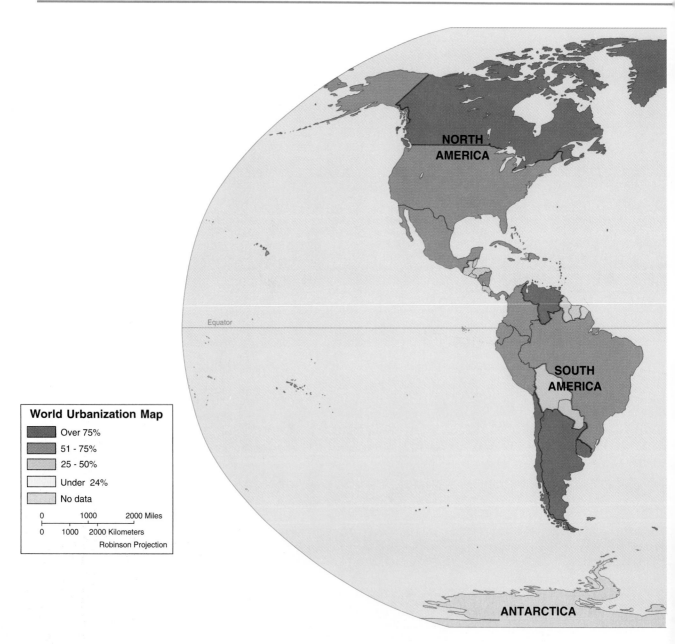 areas are those where more than 75 percent of the people live in cities. Look at the map. Find New Zealand. It is ■ . That means that more than 75 percent of the people living in New Zealand live in cities.

The ■ areas are those where 50 percent to 75 percent of the people live in cities. Find a country that is shaded ■ . Now find ☐ areas. In these areas, 25 percent to 50 percent of the people live in cities. Bolivia is a ☐ area.

NORTH AMERICA

Equator

SOUTH AMERICA

ANTARCTICA

World Urbanization Map

■ Over 75%
■ 51 - 75%
☐ 25 - 50%
☐ Under 24%
☐ No data

0   1000   2000 Miles
0 1000 2000 Kilometers
Robinson Projection

594

The areas where less than 25 percent of the people live in cities are shaded ▭ .

The percentage of people living in cities is not available for some countries. These countries are shaded ▬ .

Answer the following questions using the World Urbanization Map.

1. What does urbanization mean?

2. What color is used to show countries where more than 75 percent of the people live in cities?

3. What does the color ▬ show?

4. Are there more countries with 50 percent to 75 percent of the people living in cities or more with under 25 percent?

5. List four countries where 25 percent to 50 percent of the people live in cities.

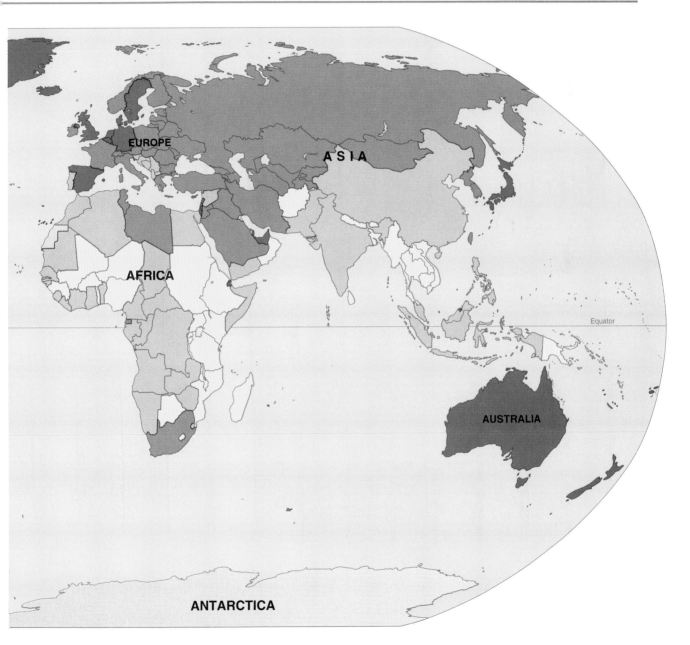

World Life—Expectancy Map

The World Life-Expectancy Map below shows the number of years a person in a particular country can expect to live if he or she was born in 1991. For example, a baby born in the United States in September 1991 will probably live to be more than 65 years old. But a baby born at the same time in India will probably live to be only 45 to 65 years old. As you have read in the text, there are many reasons for this difference.

Look at the map key. It shows three colors for three age groups: those who can expect to live to be more than 65 years old, those who can expect to live between 45 and 65 years

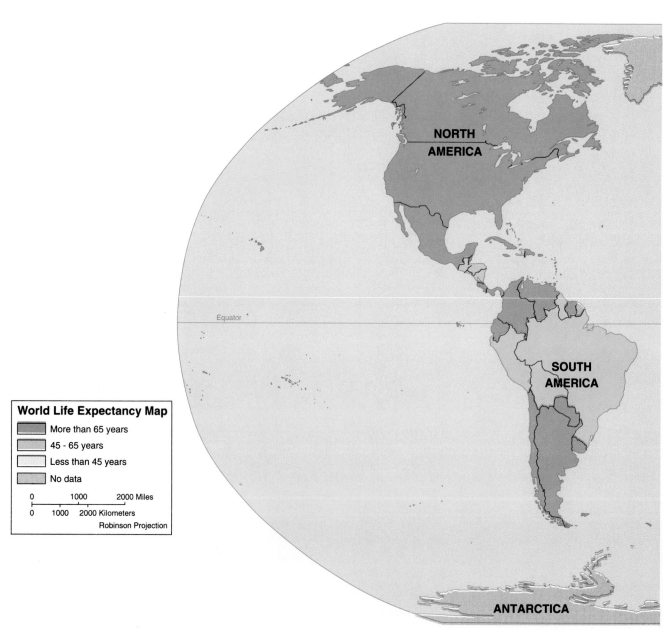

World Life Expectancy Map

- More than 65 years
- 45 - 65 years
- Less than 45 years
- No data

0   1000   2000 Miles
0 1000   2000 Kilometers

Robinson Projection

NORTH AMERICA

Equator

SOUTH AMERICA

ANTARCTICA

old, and those who can expect to live to be less than 45 years old. Another color is used to show those countries for which this information is not available.

Answer the following questions using the World Life-Expectancy Map.

1. What does life expectancy mean?
2. For what year is the information on this map?
3. What does the color ☐ stand for on this map?
4. What color is used to show the countries in which people will live to be 65 years old?
5. What is the life expectancy for the people living in Italy? Spain? China? Ethiopia?
6. For which countries is there no information available?

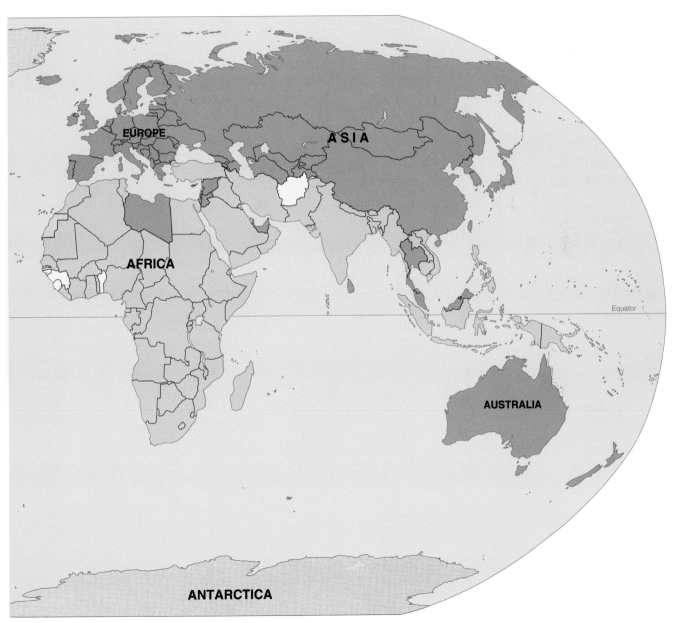

Major World Languages and Currency

Country	Official Language(s)	Currency
Afghanistan	Pashto; Persian	afghani
Albania	Albanian	lek
Algeria	Arabic, French	Algerian dinar
Andorra	Catalan	franc and peseta
Angola	Portuguese	kwanza
Antigua and Barbuda	English	East Caribbean dollar
Argentina	Spanish	new Argentine peso
Australia	English	Australian dollar
Austria	German	schilling
The Bahamas	English	Bahamian dollar
Bahrain	Arabic	Bahrain dinar
Bangladesh	Bengali	Bangladesh taka
Barbados	English	Barbados dollar
Belgium	Dutch, French, German	Belgian franc
Belize	English	Belize dollar
Benin	French	CFA franc
Bhutan	Dzongkha, Bhutanese	ngultrum
Bolivia	Spanish, Aymara, Quechua	Bolivian peso
Botswana	English	pula
Brazil	Portuguese	cruzeiro
Brunei	Malay	Brunei dollar
Bulgaria	Bulgarian	lev
Burkina Faso	French	CFA franc
Burundi	French, Kirundi	Burundi franc
Cambodia	Khmer	riel
Cameroon, United Republic of	French, English	CFA franc
Canada	English, French	Canadian dollar
Cape Verde	Portuguese	escudo
Central African Republic	French	CFA franc
Chad	French	CFA franc
Chile	Spanish	peso
China, People's Republic of	Mandarin Chinese	renminbi (yuan)
China, Republic of (Taiwan)	Mandarin Chinese	New Taiwan dollar
Colombia	Spanish	peso
Comoros	Arabic, French	Comorian franc
Congo, People's Republic of the	French	CFA franc
Costa Rica	Spanish	Costa Rican colón
Côte d'Ivoire	French	CFA franc
Cuba	Spanish	peso
Cyprus	Greek, Turkish	Cyprus pound
Czechoslovakia	Czech, Slovak	koruna
Denmark	Danish	krone
Djibouti, Republic of	Arabic, French	Djibouti franc
Dominica	English, French	East Caribbean dollar
Dominican Republic	Spanish	Dominican peso
Ecuador	Spanish	sucre
Egypt	Arabic	Egyptian pound
El Salvador	Spanish	colón
Equatorial Guinea	Spanish	ekwele
Estonia	Estonian	ruble
Ethiopia	Amharic	Ethiopian birr
Fiji	English	Fiji dollar
Finland	Finnish, Swedish	markka
France	French	franc
French Guiana (Fr)	French	franc
French Polynesia	French	CFP franc
Gabon	French	CFA franc
Gambia	English	dalasi

CFA franc - Communauté financière africaine (African Financial Community)
CFP franc - Comptoir Français du Pacifique (French Bank of the Pacific)

Country	Official Language(s)	Currency
Germany	German	mark
Ghana	English	cedi
Greece	Greek	drachma
Greenland	Greenlandic, Danish	Danish krone
Grenada	English	East Caribbean dollar
Guadeloupe (Fr)	French	franc
Guam	English	United States dollar
Guatemala	Spanish	Guatemalan quetzal
Guinea	French	Guinean syli
Guinea-Bissau	Portuguese	peso
Guyana	English	Guyana dollar
Haiti	French	gourde
Honduras	Spanish	Honduran lempira
Hong Kong (Br)	Chinese, English	Hong Kong dollar
Hungary	Hungarian	forint
Iceland	Icelandic	króna
India	English, Hindi	Indian rupee
Indonesia	Bahasa Indonesia	Indonesian rupiah
Iran	Farsi	rial
Iraq	Arabic	Iraqi dinar
Ireland	Irish, English	Irish pound
Israel	Hebrew, Arabic	Israeli shekel
Italy	Italian	lira
Jamaica	English	dollar
Japan	Japanese	yen
Jordan	Arabic	Jordanian dinar
Kenya	Swahili	Kenyan shilling
Kiribati	none	Australian dollar
Korea, Democratic People's Republic of (North Korea)	Korean	won
Korea, Republic of (South Korea)	Korean	won
Kuwait	Arabic	Kuwaiti dinar
Laos	Lao	kip
Latvia	Latvian	ruble
Lebanon	Arabic	Lebanese pound
Lesotho	Sesotho, English	loti
Liberia	English	Liberian dollar
Libya	Arabic	Libyan dinar
Liechtenstein	German	Swiss franc
Lithuania	Lithuanian	ruble
Luxembourg	French, German	Luxembourg franc
Macao (Port.)	Portuguese	pataca
Macedonia	Macedonian	dinar
Madagascar	Malagasy, French	franc
Malawi	Chichewa, English	Malawi kwacha
Malaysia	Malay	ringgit, or Malaysian dollar
Maldives	Divehi	Maldivian rufiyaa
Mali	French ·	Mali franc
Malta	English, Maltese	Maltese lira
Martinique (Fr)	French	franc
Mauritania	Arabic, French	Mauritanian ouguiya
Mauritius	English	Mauritian rupee
Mexico	Spanish	peso
Monaco	French	French franc or Monégasque franc
Mongolia (Mongolian People's Republic)	Khalkha Mongolian	tugrik
Morocco	Arabic	Moroccan dirham
Mozambique	Portuguese	metical
Myanmar	Burmese	kyat
Namibia (South West Africa)	Afrikaans, English	South African rand
Nauru	Nauruan	Australian dollar
Nepal	Nepali	Nepalese rupee
The Netherlands	Dutch	Netherlands guilder
Netherlands Antilles (Neth.)	Dutch	Netherlands Antilles guilder
New Caledonia	French	CFP franc

Country	Official Language(s)	Currency
New Zealand	English	New Zealand dollar
Nicaragua	Spanish	Nicaraguan córdoba
Niger	French	CFA franc
Nigeria	English	Nigerian naira
Norway	Norwegian	Norwegian krone
Oman	Arabic	rial Omani
Pakistan	Urdu	Pakistani rupee
Panama	Spanish	balboa
Papua New Guinea	English	Papua New Guinea kina
Paraguay	Spanish	Paraguayan guarani
Peru	Spanish, Quechua	Peruvian sol
Philippines	Pilipino, English	Philippine peso
Poland	Polish	zloty
Portugal	Portuguese	escudo
Qatar	Arabic	riyal
Romania	Romanian	Romanian leu
Russia	Russian	ruble
Rwanda	French, Kinyarwanda	Rwanda franc
Saint Christopher and Nevis	English	East Caribbean dollar
Saint Lucia	English	East Caribbean dollar
Saint Vincent and the Grenadines	English	East Caribbean dollar
San Marino	Italian	Italian lira
São Tomé and Principe	Portuguese	dobra
Saudi Arabia	Arabic	Saudi riyal
Senegal	French	CFA franc
Seychelles	English, French, Creole	Seychelles rupee
Sierra Leone	English	leone
Singapore	Chinese, English, Malay, Tamil	Singapore dollar
Solomon Islands	English	Solomon Islands dollars
Somalia	Somali, Arabic	Somali shilling
South Africa, Republic of	Afrikaans, English	rand
Spain	Spanish	peseta
Sri Lanka	Sinhala	Sri Lanka rupee
Sudan	Arabic	Sudanese pound
Suriname	Dutch, English	Suriname guilder
Swaziland	siSwati, English	lilangeni
Sweden	Swedish	Swedish krona
Switzerland	French, German, Italian	Swiss franc
Syria	Arabic	Syrian pound
Tanzania, United Republic of	Swahili, English	Tanzanian shilling
Thailand	Thai	Thai baht
Togo	French	CFA franc
Tonga	Tongan, English	pa'anga
Trinidad and Tobago	English	Trinidad and Tobago dollar
Tunisia	Arabic	dinar
Turkey	Turkish	Turkish lira
Tuvalu	none	Tuvalu dollar
Uganda	English	Uganda shilling
United Arab Emirates	Arabic	U.A.E. dirham
United Kingdom	English	pound sterling
United States of America	English	dollar
Uruguay	Spanish	Uruguayan new peso
Vanuatu	French, English	vatu
Venezuela	Spanish	bolívar
Vietnam, Socialist Republic of	Vietnamese	dong
Western Samoa	Samoan, English	tala
Yemen	Arabic	rial
Yugoslavia	Serbo-Croatian	Yugoslav dinar
Zaire	French	zaire
Zambia	English	Zambian kwacha
Zimbabwe	English	Zimbabwe dollar

Age Distribution for Selected Countries (percent of population)

Country	0-14 years	15-64 years	65 and over	Country	0-14 years	15-64 years	65 and over
Afghanistan	43.3	54.2	2.4	Ethiopia	45.8	51.7	2.6
Albania	35.4	59.7	4.9	Falkland Islands (UK)	NA	NA	NA
Algeria	45.9	50.6	3.5	Fiji	35.5	60.9	3.5
Andorra*·	29.2	61.7	9.1	Finland	19.0	68.7	12.3
Angola	44.6	52.4	3.0	France	20.9	66.7	12.4
Anguilla	NA	NA	NA	French Guiana (FR)*···	34.9	58.1	13.1
Antigua and Barbuda	NA	NA	NA	French Polynesia*·	38.5	56.5	5.0
Argentina	31.0	60.5	8.5	Gabon	35.5	58.5	6.1
Australia	24.2	66.1	9.7	Gambia	42.5	54.5	3.1
Austria	18.3	67.5	14.2	Germany*	14.7	64.7	20.6
The Bahamas*·	43.6	50.9	5.5	Ghana	46.5	50.6	2.8
Bahrain	33.3	64.7	2.0	Greece	21.9	64.8	13.3
Bangladesh	45.7	51.2	3.1	Greenland*···	27.4	67.0	5.6
Barbados	27.6	63.0	9.3	Grenada*··	39.4	50.5	10.1
Belgium	18.7	68.0	13.3	Guadeloupe (FR)*··	27.8	61.7	10.5
Belize	46.1	49.2	4.7	Guam*··	34.9	60.5	4.6
Benin	46.5	50.7	2.8	Guatemala	43.1	53.9	3.0
Bermuda (UK)*	21.3	65.7	13.0	Guinea	43.1	54.0	2.9
Bhutan	40.0	56.6	3.3	Guinea-Bissau	40.7	55.0	4.3
Bolivia	43.8	53.0	3.2	Guyana	37.0	59.1	3.9
Botswana	49.7	48.3	2.0	Haiti	43.6	53.0	3.4
Brazil	36.4	59.3	4.3	Honduras	46.9	50.2	2.9
Brunei*···	38.1	57.5	4.4	Hong Kong (Br)*···	24.8	65.0	10.2
Bulgaria	22.3	66.3	11.4	Hungary	21.8	65.8	12.3
Burkina Faso	44.4	52.8	2.8	Iceland*·	26.7	59.5	13.8
Burundi	44.3	52.4	3.3	India	37.3	59.2	3.5
Cambodia	32.6	64.7	2.6	Indonesia	38.5	58.1	3.4
Cameroon, United Republic of	42.9	53.2	3.9	Iran	43.1	53.5	3.4
				Iraq	46.4	50.9	2.7
Canada	22.5	67.9	9.6	Ireland	30.5	58.6	10.9
Cape Verde	31.4	64.7	3.9	Israel	32.8	59.0	8.2
Central African Republic	42.5	53.7	3.8	Italy	19.9	66.7	13.4
Chad	42.3	54.1	3.6	Jamaica	36.8	57.4	5.9
Chile	31.2	63.1	5.7	Japan	21.5	68.6	9.9
China, People's Republic of*	30.7	64.1	5.2	Jordan	47.8	49.4	2.8
China, Republic of (Taiwan)····	31.2	58.8	7.6	Kenya	52.5	45.7	1.8
Colombia	37.2	59.1	3.8	Kiribati	NA	NA	NA
Comoros	46.2	51.0	2.8	Korea, Democratic Republic of (North Korea)	38.1	58.1	3.8
Congo, People's Republic of the	43.6	53.0	3.4	Korea, Republic of (South Korea)	29.7	65.9	4.4
Costa Rica	36.7	59.5	3.8	Kuwait	41.1	57.4	1.5
Côte d'Ivoire	45.1	52.0	2.9	Laos	42.8	54.1	3.1
Cuba	26.4	65.7	7.9	Lebanon	37.5	57.4	5.1
Cyprus	24.9	65.0	10.1	Lesotho	42.3	54.1	3.6
Czechoslovakia	24.5	64.4	11.1	Liberia	46.8	50.2	3.0
Denmark	18.8	66.4	14.8	Libya	46.5	51.2	2.3
Djibouti, Republic of··	42.3	54.3	3.4	Liechtenstein*·	27.9	60.2	11.9
Dominican Republic*···	44.8	50.9	4.3	Luxembourg	17.5	69.1	13.5
Ecuador	44.2	52.4	3.4	Macao (Port.)	NA	NA	NA
Egypt	39.4	56.2	4.4	Madagascar	44.2	52.4	3.4
El Salvador	44.6	52.0	3.4	Malawi	48.1	49.6	2.4
Equatorial Guinea	41.4	54.4	4.2				

Malaysia	36.7	59.5	3.9
Maldives* ·	44.9	51.3	3.8
Mali	46.1	51.2	2.7
Malta	23.9	67.1	9.0
Martinique (Fr)* ···	28.4	59.7	11.9
Mauritania	46.4	50.8	2.8
Mauritius	31.6	64.9	3.5
Mexico	42.2	54.3	3.5
Monaco	NA	NA	NA
Mongolia (Mongolian People's Republic)	41.0	55.6	3.3
Morocco	45.6	51.4	3.0
Mozambique	44.8	51.8	3.4
Myanmar	41.3	55.0	3.7
Namibia	44.0	50.7	5.3
Nauru	NA	NA	NA
Nepal	43.3	53.8	2.9
The Netherlands	19.0	69.0	11.9
Netherlands Antilles (Neth.)	NA	NA	NA
New Zealand	24.7	65.7	9.6
Nicaragua	46.7	50.7	2.5
Niger	46.7	50.0	3.3
Nigeria	48.3	49.3	2.4
Norway	20.1	64.5	15.5
Oman	44.2	53.4	2.5
Pakistan	44.2	53.0	2.8
Panama	37.5	58.0	4.5
Papua New Guinea	42.6	54.1	3.3
Paraguay	41.7	54.8	3.6
Peru	40.5	55.9	3.6
Philippines	38.6	58.3	3.1
Poland	25.0	65.6	9.4
Portugal	24.8	64.7	10.4
Qatar	33.8	63.6	2.6
Romania	25.1	65.4	9.6
Russia and the Republics	36.7	50.5	12.7
Rwanda	48.8	48.8	2.5
Saint Christopher and Nevis* ··	37.2	49.3	13.5
Saint Lucia**	49.6	42.7	7.7
Saint Vincent and the Grenadines	NA	NA	NA
San Marino* ·	24.4	60.3	15.3
São Tomé and Príncipe* ··	37.3	55.3	7.4
Saudi Arabia	43.1	54.1	2.7
Senegal	45.0	52.1	2.9
Seychelles* ·	39.7	51.1	9.1
Sierra Leone	41.4	55.6	3.0
Singapore	24.8	70.1	5.1
Solomon Islands* ·	49.0	47.5	3.5
Somalia	43.7	52.3	4.0
South Africa, Republic of	41.0	54.9	4.0
Spain	24.6	64.3	11.1
Sri Lanka	34.2	61.4	4.4
Sudan	45.1	52.1	2.8
Suriname	42.6	53.0	4.5
Swaziland	46.0	51.0	3.0
Sweden	17.8	65.2	17.0
Switzerland	15.7	68.6	15.7
Syria	47.5	49.3	3.2
Tanzania, United Republic of	48.8	48.9	2.3
Thailand	36.7	60.0	3.3
Togo	44.5	52.3	3.2
Tonga* ·	44.4	50.5	5.1
Trinidad and Tobago	31.6	62.6	5.8
Tunisia	39.6	56.1	4.3
Turkey	37.1	58.6	4.2
Tuvalu	NA	NA	NA
Uganda	48.5	49.0	2.5
United Arab Emirates	30.7	66.8	2.4
United Kingdom	19.3	66.0	14.7
United States of America	21.9	66.7	11.5
Uruguay	26.9	62.4	10.7
Vanuatu	NA	NA	NA
Venezuela	41.0	56.0	2.9
Vietnam, Socialist Republic of	40.2	55.9	3.9
Western Samoa* ·	50.4	45.4	4.3
Yemen	45.3	51.4	3.3
Yugoslavia	23.4	68.1	8.4
Zaire	45.1	52.0	2.9
Zambia	47.3	50.0	2.7
Zimbabwe	47.6	49.6	2.7

NA   Not available
  * Age distribution breakdown is 0–14, 15–59, and 60 and over
 ** Age distribution breakdown is 0–20, 21–64, and 65 and over; year 1984
*** Age distribution breakdown is 0–19, 20–59, and 60 and over; year 1984
  · 1984 figures
 ·· 1980 figures
··· 1982 figures
···· 1981 figures

Glossary

The meanings given for the following words are the ones used in this book.

A

abacá
(ah-bah-KAH) Manila hemp plant; its fibers are used to make rope.

abacus
(AB-uh-kus) A counting tool made up of a frame set with rods on which beads are moved.

abdicate
(AB-dih-kayt) Give up the throne.

absolute location
(AB-suh-loot loh-KAY-shun) An exact, precise spot on the earth.

altitude
(AL-tih-tood) Height above sea level.

aluminum
(uh-LOO-mih-num) Lightweight metal made from bauxite.

apartheid
(uh-PART-hayt) Policy of separating people of different races that was followed in the Republic of South Africa.

archipelago
(ar-kuh-PEL-uh-goh) Any large group of islands.

artesian well
(ar-TEE-zhun WEL) A well dug deep in the earth through a layer of rock, which causes the water to shoot to the surface.

Asian region
(AY-zhun REE-jun) Countries of eastern and southeastern Asia.

atoll
(AT-tol) Small coral island with a body of water at its center; most often found in the South Pacific.

automation
(aw-tuh-MAY-shun) Use of machines and other technology in the manufacture of goods, often replacing or reducing human labor.

B

barter system
(BAR-tur SIH-stum) The direct trading of one kind of goods for another, with no use of money.

bazaar
(buh-ZAR) Marketplace or shopping area in a Middle Eastern town.

bicameral
(by-KAM-uh-rul) Consisting of two chambers or houses.

Boers
(BOHRZ) Dutch settlers in South Africa.

C

capital
(KAP-ih tul) Seat of government in a country; or money and goods used to make more goods.

capitalism
(KAP-ih-tu-liz-um) System under which people are free to own and develop their own property in order to make a profit.

cash crops
(KASH KROPS) Crops raised for sale by farmers; with profits from these sales, farmers buy the goods which their farms do not supply.

castes
(KASTS) Hindu groups in Indian society that are divided by work/jobs. Each caste has its own customs and jobs that are passed on from parents to children.

cataracts
(KAT-uh-rakts) Powerful rapids in a river.

census
(SEN-sus) Periodic population count.

circumference
(sir-KUM-fruns) The distance around the earth at the equator.

climate	**(KLY-mit)** Average weather in a given region.
cold war	**(KOLD WOHR)** Conflict between nations without actual fighting; military and economic rivalry.
collective farm	**(kuh-LEK-tiv FARM)** Large farm worked by people in common; often under government control.
collective ownership	**(kuh-LEK-tiv OHN-ur-ship)** System in which all members of a group share equally.
collectivize	**(kuh-LEK-tih-vyz)** Join together under group control.
colonialism	**(kuh-LOH-nee-uh-liz-um)** Rule of a group of people by a foreign power.
commercial farming	**(kuh-MUR-shul FARM-ing)** Raising crops for sale.
commonwealth	**(KOM-un-welth)** An association of self-governing autonomous states loosely associated in a common allegiance.
commune	**(KOM-myoon)** Large state-owned farm in Communist China; the people work for wages.
competition	**(kom-peh-TISH-un)** When two or more businesses try to make and sell the same kinds of goods or services.
conformal	**(kun-FOHR-mul)** Term used to describe maps in which areas are represented in their true shape.
consumer	**(kon-SOO-mur)** Anyone who buys and uses a product.
continental climate	**(KON-tuh-nen-tul KLY-mit)** Climates located in the center of continents, including humid-continental and taiga.
continental drift theory	**(kon-tuh-NEN-tul DRIFT THEER-ee)** Theory that a single, original continent broke apart into the continents we know today. All of which continue to move.
convection	**(kun-VEK-shun)** The transfer of heat.
conventional	**(kun-VEN-shu-nul)** Non-nuclear weapons or forces.
converted	**(kun-VER-tid)** Changed from one religion or faith to another.
cooperative	**(koh-OP-uh-ruh-tiv)** Group of farmers who agree to sell their crops together and share all gains and losses.
copra	**(KOP-ruh)** Dried meat or pulp of a coconut.
crop rotation	**(KROP roh-TAY-shun)** Growing different crops on a piece of land from year to year in order to keep the soil from "wearing out."
crop yields	**(KROP YEELDZ)** The amount of a plant or animal that can be raised per area of land.
crust	**(KRUST)** The outer skin of the earth, under continents and oceans.
cultural diffusion	**(KUL-chur-ul di-FYOO-shun)** The spread of culture from one society to others.
cultural features	**(KUL-chur-ul FEE-churs)** Additions people make to the land, such as cities and irrigation systems.
culture	**(KUL-chur)** The characteristic behaviors and beliefs of a particular group.

D

deforestation	**(dee-fawr-uh-STAY-shun)** Destruction of forests.
deposited	**(dee-PAWS-uh-tid)** Let fall in a new location.
desert	**(DEH-zirt)** Dry area where annual rainfall is less than ten inches (25 centimeters).
desertification	**(duh-ZERT-uh-fuh-kay-shun)** Loss of vegetation caused by mismanagement and/or climate change.

dharma	(**DAR-muh**) Hindu belief that a person's destiny is carried out by following customs and laws.
dingo	(**DING-goh**) An Australian wild dog.
distortion	(**dih-STOR-shun**) Alteration of the actual shape of something for the sake of representation, as on a map.
diversity	(**duh-VIR-suh-tee**) Variety.
dry climates	(**DRY-KLY-mits**) A grouping comprising desert and steppe climates.
dynasty	(**DY-nuh-stee**) A succession of rulers who are members of the same family.

E

Eastern Hemisphere	(**EE-sturn HEM-ih-sfeer**) The half of the earth east of the prime meridian.
elevation	(**el-uh-VAY-shun**) Height above sea level or above the surface of the earth.
environment	(**en-VY-run-munt**) The sum of all surroundings and influences that affect human beings.
equal-area map	(**EE-kwul AIR-ee-uh MAP**) Map showing the correct size of land and water areas.
equator	(**ee-KWAY-tur**) Imaginary line around the middle of the earth, halfway between the North and South poles.
erosion	(**ee-ROH-zhun**) Wearing away of the soil through the action of wind, water, or glaciers.
estancia	(**eh-STAN-see-uh**) Large piece of land or cattle ranch in Latin America.
European region	(**yoor-uh-PEE-un REE-jun**) Countries of Europe, excluding the Commonwealth of Independent States and Turkey.
evaporation	(**ee-vap-uh-RAY-shun**) Process by which water is changed into water vapor.
exports	(**EK-sports**) Goods or raw materials sent out of a country.
extinct	(**ek-STINKT**) No longer in existence.

F

fazenda	(**fah-ZEN-dah**) Large Brazilian farm on which coffee is usually grown.
fellahin	(**fel-uh-HEEN**) Peasants or farmers in the Arabic-speaking countries of North Africa and the Middle East.
feudalism	(**FYOOD-uh-liz-um**) System in which land is owned by a powerful lord and worked by people called serfs who exchange their labor for the lord's protection.
floodplain	(**FLUHD PLAYN**) A fertile area of flat land built up by the deposits from streams.
folding	(**FOHLD-ing**) The creation of a bulge in the earth's crust caused by the action of two plates pushing against one another.
fossils	(**FAW-suls**) Hardened remains of plants and animals from a previous geologic age.

G

gaucho	(**GOW-choh**) Cowboy of the South American pampas, or grassy plains.
geography	(**jee-OG-ruh-fee**) Study of the earth and how people have adapted to all of its varying conditions.
geothermal energy	(**JEE-oh-thir-mal EH-nir-jee**) Power derived from heat within the earth.

605

glacier	**(GLAY-shur)** Large mass of ice and snow that moves slowly over the land.
glasnost	**(GLAZ-nohst)** Term used to describe Mikhail Gorbachev's policy of allowing openness, including criticism of the state, in the former Soviet Union.
grid system	**(GRID SIH-stum)** Crisscrossing lines on a map that help to locate any place on the earth.

H

hacienda	**(hah-see-EN-duh)** Large plantation or farm in Latin America.
hajj	**(HAJ)** The pilgrimage to Mecca that Muslims are supposed to make at least once in their life.
heavy industry	**(HEH-vee IN-duhs-tree)** Manufacturing that uses heavy materials such as iron and steel.
hemisphere	**(HEM-ih-sfeer)** Half the earth or globe.
hieroglyphics	**(HY-ruh-GLIF-iks)** A way of writing, used by the Egyptians, in which picture symbols are used to represent words, sounds, and ideas.
hill	**(HIL)** Elevated piece of land, no higher than 1,000 feet (305 meters) above sea level.
Holocaust	**(HOH-luh-kawst)** Mass slaughter of European civilians, including six million Jews, before and during World War II.
hostages	**(HAWS-tuh-jiz)** Persons held by one party in a conflict until promises are kept or terms are met by the other party.
humid	**(HYOO-mid)** Damp or wet.
humid-continental climate	**(HYOO-mid kon-tuh-NEN-tul KLY-mit)** Climate found inland or on the eastern coast of continents, marked by cold winters, hot summers, and some rain throughout the year.
humid-subtropical climate	**(HYOO-mid sub-TROP-ih-kul-KLY-mit)** Climate typical on the eastern coast of continents in the middle latitudes, marked by long, warm summers; short, mild winters; and rain throughout the year.
hydroelectricity	**(hy-droh-ee-lek-TRIS-ih-tee)** Electricity made from the energy of falling water.

I

illiteracy	**(ih-LIT-ur-uh-see)** Inability to read or write.
imperialism	**(im-PEER-ee-uh-liz-um)** Domination by one nation over others.
imports	**(IM-ports)** Goods or raw materials brought into a country.
inflation	**(in-FLAY-shun)** An increase in the volume of available money relative to goods, which causes rapidly rising prices.
intensive farming	**(in-TEN-siv FARM-ing)** Growing crops in a small area with a great deal of hand labor, usually resulting in high yields.
interaction	**(in-tir-AK-shun)** Mutual influence.
interconnected	**(in-tir-kuh-NEK-tid)** Mutually joined or related.
investment	**(in-VEST-ment)** Spending money in the hope of gaining a profit.
irrigation	**(eer-uh-GAY-shun)** Bringing water to dry land through canals, ditches or pipes.

J

jute   (**JOOT**) Plant fiber used in making rope and burlap bags.

K

kapok   (**KAY-pok**) A light, waterproof fiber used to fill mattresses and life preservers.

karma   (**KAHR-muh**) According to Hindu belief, all human conduct has consequences, either good or bad, in this life or a future life; fate.

kibbutz   (**kih-BOOTS**) Farming community in Israel owned by the people who live and work on the land.

kraal   (**KRALL**) A Masai settlement.

L

landlocked   (**LAND-lokt**) Without a coastline or opening to the sea.

latex   (**LAY-teks**) Milky fluid from which rubber is made.

latitude   (**LAT-uh-tood**) Imaginary lines running east and west around the earth and parallel to the equator; they measure in degrees the distance north and south of the equator.

leeward   (**LEE-wurd**) Away from the wind; the side of a mountain that receives less rain.

legislature   (**LEJ-is-lay-chur**) Lawmaking body.

light industry   (**LYT IN-duh-stree**) Manufacturing that uses raw materials of light weight, such as fibers.

llanos   (**LAH-nos**) Lowlands in South America that are good for grazing cattle.

location   (**loh-KAY-shun**) A position or site marked by some distinguishing feature.

loess   (**LES**) Fine, yellow dust or soil found in the Huang River valley in China and in parts of the Mississippi River valley.

longitude   (**LON-jih-tood**) Imaginary lines running north and south from pole to pole; they measure in degrees the distance east or west of the prime meridian, which passes through Greenwich, England.

M

mandate   (**MAN-dayt**) Authorization by the League of Nations to one nation to govern or care for other lands.

manioc   (**MAN-ee-ok**) Starchy food of a tropical plant, made into food by rain forest peoples; also called cassava.

mantle   (**MAN-tul**) The thick layer of very hot rock which lies beneath the earth's crust.

map projections   (**MAP proh-JEK-shuns**) Different versions of a map.

marine climate   (**muh-REEN KLY-mit**) Wet climate on the western side of continents in the middle latitudes, marked by cool summers, mild winters, and rain throughout the year.

mass production   (**MAS proh-DUK-shun**) Method of making large amounts of goods at low cost.

Mediterranean climate   (**med-ih-tuh-RAY-nee-un KLY-mit**) Climate marked by hot, dry summers, mild winters, and rain throughout the year.

meridian	**(muh-RID-ee-un)** Line of longitude.
mestizo	**(meh-STEE-zoh)** Person who is partly European (Spanish) and partly Native American.
migrate	**(MY-grayt)** To move from one place to another to live.
migratory farming	**(MY-gruh-toh-ree FARM-ing)** Shifting farming; type of farming in which the farmer moves from place to place in search of better soil; after a number of years the land is ready to be used again.
migrant workers	**(MY-grunt WUR-kurz)** Field laborers who move from one farm to another to obtain work. They follow the seasons in order to harvest a variety of crops.
mild climate	**(MYLD KLY-mit)** A grouping comprising the Mediterranean, marine, and humid-subtropical climates.
money crop	**(MUH-nee KROP)** (*See* cash crop.)
monoculture	**(MON-oh-kul-chur)** A farming economy mainly dependent on one crop for its income.
monotheism	**(MON-oh-thee-izm)** The belief in and worship of one God, a doctrine that is common to Judaism, Christianity, and Islam.
monsoon	**(mon-SOON)** Wind that changes direction with the seasons, especially those winds blowing to and from the Indian Ocean.
moraine	**(muh-RAYN)** Low hill consisting of piles of rock and soil deposited by melting ice.
mosque	**(MOSK)** Muslim house of worship.
movement	**(MOOV-mint)** A geographical theme used to understand the relationship between places.
muezzin	**(MWEZ-in)** A Muslim crier who calls the people to prayer.
multicultural	**(mul-tee-KUL-chir-ul)** Made up of many cultures.
multiethnic	**(mul-tee-ETH-nik)** Composed of many different ethnic groups.

N

nationalism	**(NASH-uh-nuh-liz-um)** Loyalty and devotion to one's nation above all others and promoting and praising its culture and interests.
natural features	**(NA-chir-ul FEE-churs)** Those things provided by nature, such as lakes and mountains.
navigable	**(NA-vi-guh-bul)** Deep and wide enough to allow the passage of ships.
nomads	**(NOH-mads)** People who have no fixed home but move from place to place in a regular pattern to fill their flocks' need for grazing land.
nonrenewable	**(non-ree-NYOO-uh-bul)** Term used to describe those resources which cannot be replaced once they are used.
Northern Hemisphere	**(NOR-thirn HEM-ih-sfeer)** The half of the earth north of the equator.
nuclear energy	**(NYOO-klee-ur EH-nir-jee)** Energy released through the splitting of atoms.

O

outback	**(OWT-bak)** Dry lands of Australia where there are few settlers.

P

paddy	**(PAD-ee)** Small rice field, enclosed by dikes of mud.

pagoda	**(puh-GOH-duh)** An Asian temple or sacred building, usually shaped like a pyramid or forming a tower with upward-curving roofs over the individual stories.
pampas	**(PAM-puz)** Large grassy plains in the southeastern part of South America, especially inArgentina.
papyrus	**(puh-PY-rus)** An ancient Egyptian writing material made from thin strips of the papyrus plant that have been soaked, pressed, and dried.
parallel	**(PAR-uh-lel)** Line of latitude.
parliament	**(PAR-luh-munt)** Lawmaking body such as those in Canada and the United Kingdom.
peon	**(PEE-awn)** A member of the landless worker class in Latin America.
permafrost	**(PUR-muh-frawst)** Soil just below the earth's surface in Arctic regions that never thaws or melts.
pharaoh	**(FAY-roh)** Title used by ancient Egyptian rulers.
place	**(PLAYS)** A geographical theme used to describe the natural and cultural features of a place.
plain	**(PLAYN)** Broad stretch of level or nearly level land.
plantation	**(plan-TAY-shun)** A large farm on which one chief crop is grown.
plate	**(PLAYT)** Huge, slowly moving piece of the earth's crust.
plateau	**(pla-TOH)** Large area of level highland, not as rough as mountains.
plaza	**(PLAH-zuh)** Public square in a Latin American village, town, or city.
poi	**(POY)** A Pacific region food made from taro, a starchy root.
polar climates	**(POH-lur KLY-mits)** Those climates located in the highest latitudes.
precipitation	**(pruh-sih-pih-TAY-shun)** Water falling to the ground in the form of rain, snow, sleet, or hail.
prevailing winds	**(pree-VAY-ling WINDZ)** Winds that blow most frequently in certain directions.
prime meridian	**(PRYM muh-RID-ee-un)** The first, or beginning, line of longitude, running through Greenwich, England; 0° (zero degrees) longitude.
princess royale	**(PRIN-tses roi-AL)** Position of respect and influence held by some women among the Bangway people of Cameroon in West Africa.
privatize	**(PRY-vih-tyz)** To change from public to private control or ownership.
pyramid	**(PEER-uh-mid)** A huge stone building, usually forming a square at ground level, with triangular-shaped sides, meeting at a point on top; used as a tomb in ancient Egypt.

Q

quinine	**(KWY-nyn)** A medicine obtained from the bark of the cinchona tree; used especially against malaria.

R

race	**(RAYS)** A large group of humans who share many of the same physical features and body chemistry.
rain shadow	**(RAYN SHA-doh)** An area which receives little rain because it is sheltered or leeward.
rain forest	**(RAYN-faw-rist)** A tropical woodland which receives an annual rainfall of at least 100 inches (250 centimeters).

rationing	(**RA-shun-ing**) Distributing limited amounts.
rattan	(**ruh-TAN**) The tough stems of climbing palm plants, whose fiber is used for making baskets or furniture.
refine	(**ree-FYN**) To remove the impurities from raw materials such as oil, sugar cane, or minerals.
region	(**REE-jun**) An area distinguished from others by virtue of certain cultural or natural characteristics.
reincarnation	(**ree-in-kar-NAY-shun**) Hindu belief which holds that the spirit is reborn after death in a new form.
relative location	(**RE-luh-tiv loh-KAY-shun**) The location of a place expressed in terms of its relation to other places.
remote sensing	(**ree-MOHT SEN-sing**) Gathering data, or pictures, by satellite.
renewable	(**ree-NYOO-uh-bul**) Term used to describe those resources that are constantly replaced by nature, such as water.
revolves	(**ree-VAWLVZ**) Moves in a curved path around a central point or body.
rift	(**RIFT**) A trench, fissure, crevasse, or fault.
rotation	(**roh-TAY-shun**) Turning of the earth on its axis; also crops planted in turn in the same fields.
Russification	(**ruh-sih-fih-KAY-shun**) Policy of the former Soviet Union designed to create a single language and culture, Russian, throughout the disparate Soviet republics.

S

sabotage	(**SA-buh-tawj**) The intentional damage or destruction of buildings or other property.
sanctions	(**SANK-shuns**) Refusals to trade or do business with another country until that country changes certain policies.
satellite country	(**SAT-uh-lyt KUN-tree**) A country politically or economically controlled or dominated by another more powerful country.
savanna	(**suh-VAN-uh**) Hot climatic region of two seasons, rainy and dry, found both north and south of the tropical rain forests. Grassland containing scattered trees and drought-resistant undergrowth.
sediment	(**SE-dih-munt**) Fine grains of sand and soil deposited by water, wind, or glaciers.
serfs	(**SURFS**) People who work for a lord or a large landowner, and who are bound to the land and may be sold with it to a new owner.
service occupations	(**SUR-vis ok-yoo-PAY-shuns**) Vocations that do not produce actual goods but that serve human desires and needs; examples include medicine, hair styling, and plumbing.
sharecropper	(**SHAIR-krop-ur**) One who farms the land of another and must pay a share of the crop as rent.
shogun	(**SHOH-gun**) The title given the chief Japanese military commander from the 8th to the 12th centuries; after that, until 1867, the term referred to the actual ruler (not the emperor) of Japan.
solar energy	(**SOH-lir EH-nir-jee**) Energy provided by the sun.
sorghum	(**SAWR-gum**) A kind of grain.
souk	(**SOOK**) An Arab market or bazaar.

Southern Hemisphere	**(SUH-thirn HEM-ih-sfeer)** The half of the earth south of the equator.
sovereign state	**(SAWV-rin STAYT)** An independent state free from external control.
soybean	**(SOY-been)** The oil-rich seeds of the soybean plant, which are used to make a variety of protein-rich foods.
state farm	**(STAYT FARM)** A large government-owned farm in the former Soviet Union on which farmers worked for wages.
station	**(STAY-shun)** A large ranch in Austalia, usually used for sheep and cattle.
steppe	**(STEP)** Large treeless plain with cold winters and hot summers, and with from 10 to 20 inches (25 to 51 centimeters) of annual rainfall. In the United States, a prairie.
subsist	**(sub-SIST)** Survive.
subtropical	**(sub-TROP-ih-kul)** Between the temperate and the tropical zones.
surplus	**(SUR-plus)** Amount left over after needs are met, or after people cannot buy any more, such as a surplus of wheat or clothing.

T

taiga	**(TY-guh)** Large cold forests of subarctic regions.
tariff	**(TAR-if)** A tax placed on goods coming into a country.
teak	**(TEEK)** A kind of hardwood used for shipbuilding and furniture making.
temperature	**(TEM-pur-uh-chur)** Amount of heat or cold in the air, measured by degrees on a thermometer.
terraces	**(TAIR-uh-siz)** Steps of earth cut into hillsides to increase the amount of land that can be farmed.
totalitarian state	**(toh-tal-ih-TAIR-ee-un STAYT)** A nation ruled by a political regime based on subordination of the individual to the state and strict control of all aspects of citizen life.
trade	**(TRAYD)** Exchange of goods between nations or persons.
traditionalists	**(truh-DIH-shun-uh-lists)** Those who adhere to practices and customs handed down for generations.
tropical climate	**(TRAW-pih-kul KLY-mit)** Hot, damp, and sticky climate, typical at sea level.
tundra	**(TUN-druh)** Level, treeless region of the Arctic that has long, severe winters and short summers. The ground is frozen nearly all year.
typhoon	**(ty-FOON)** Violent storm of the western Pacific Ocean.

U

urbanization	**(ur-buh-ny-ZAY-shun)** The development of those characteristics common to a city.

V

vegetation	**(vej-uh-TAY-shun)** The natural plant life that grows in a region.
veld	**(FELT)** High grassy plain or tableland in southern Africa, used for sheep and cattle grazing.
vertical climate	**(VUR-tih-kul KLY-mit)** Climate of mountainous regions in which temperatures are warmer lower down and colder higher up.

veto	**(VEE-toh)** Power to prevent an action by refusing to agree.

W

wat	**(WAT)** A Buddhist temple.
weather	**(WETH-ur)** Variations in temperature, wind, cloudiness, and moisture in an area over a short period of time; the day-to-day changes in the condition of the air.
weathering	**(WE-thuh-ring)** The breaking down of rock into pieces; sometimes caused by wind and rain.
Western Hemisphere	**(WE-sturn HEM-ih-sfeer)** The half of the earth west of the prime meridian.
windward	**(WIND-wurd)** Toward the wind; the rainy or wet side of a mountain.

Y

yurt	**(YOORT)** A circular tent made of goatskin, used by Mongol nomads.

Z

zebu	**(ZEE-byoo)** An ox-like animal with a large hump over the shoulders.

Index

Tropical climate, 42–43, 181
Tropical rain forest climate, 42–43
Tropical regions, 36
Tropical savanna climate, 42–43, 204, 491
Tropic of Cancer, 42
Tropic of Capricorn, 42
Trust territories, 557, 574
Tsetse fly, 438, 452, 466, 467
Tundra, 45, 328–29. *See also* Plains
Tungsten, 233, 543, 549
Tunis (Tunisia), 383, 403
Tunisia, 370, 380–83, 387
Turkey, 240, 245, 361, 370, 371, 374, 380, 383, 387, 398, 405
Turkmen, 321
Turkmenistan, 319, 341
Turquoise, 200
Tuvalu, 574, 579
TVA (Tennessee Valley Authority), 122
Type, moveable, 497
Typhoid fever, 403
Typhoons, 529, 575
Tyrolean Man, 302

U

Uganda, 452–53, 463
Ukraine, 318, 330, 339, 341, 347, 357, 363–64
Ukrainian (language), 363
Ukrainians, 320, 363
Underdevelopment, 466–67
Unemployment, 70, 213, 223
Unions, 126, 312
Union of Soviet Socialist Republics. *See* Soviet Union
United Arab Emirates, 420
United Kingdom. *See* Great Britain
United Nations, 162, 335, 407, 429, 458, 461–62, 483, 501, 544, 557, 564, 574
United Nations Environment Program (UNEP), 50
United Nations High Commissioner for Refugees, 405
United States, 42, 68, 70, 78, 170, 504; Armenians in, 360; Asia and, 500; China and, 544; cities of, 131–34; in cold war, 335; culture of, 61–62; energy used by, 51–52; European region and, 241–42, 282, 285, 298; farming in, 137–40; free enterprise system in, 126–28; hostages in Iran from, 80, 408; Japan and, 501, 531–32; Latin America and, 216–19, 222, 227–29, 234; Middle East and, 370, 406–8; multiculturalism in, 5–6; natural resources of, 120–23; oil in, 399; Pacific islands and, 557, 574; Saudi Arabia and, 422; South Africa and, 472; sub-Sahara Africa and, 458, 463, 474; Vietnam War and, 483; in World War II, 303. *See also* Northern America
Untouchables (India), 508
Upper Canada, 103, 104
Ural Mountains, 240, 323, 347
Urals region, 351
Uranium, 53, 122, 144, 299, 350, 428, 456, 466, 571
Urbanization, 108, 194, 445–46
Uruguay, 182, 192, 195, 205, 210
USSR. *See* Soviet Union
Utah, 92, 120, 139
Uzbek (language), 345

Uzbekistan, 319, 341, 345
Uzbeks, 321

V

Valencia (Spain), 299
Valleys, 486, 487
Vancouver (Canada), 86, 109, 145
Vanuatu, 574, 579
Vargha, Janos, 302
Vatican City (Rome, Italy), 241
Vavilov, Nikolay, 358
Vegetables, 139, 140, 151, 153, 206, 223, 249, 272, 273, 292, 299, 530
Vegetation, 37, 38; climate and, 41–45
Veld, 470
Venezuela, 52, 120, 171, 176, 188, 193, 204, 208–10, 216
Verala, Maria, 119
Verrazano, Giovanni da, 102
Vertical climate, 38, 45, 97, 181, 204, 222, 250
Vetos, 115, 281
Victoria, Lake, 433
Vienna Convention for the Protection of the Ozone Layer, 50
Vietnam, 80, 108, 335, 482, 483, 501, 506, 523, 526, 547–50
Vietnamese, 483
Vietnam War, 335, 483, 501–2
Vikings, 101
Vindhya Mountains, 535
Virginia, 102, 138
Vistula River, 310
Vital Triangle, 267, 351
Vladimir I (prince, Kiev), 364
Volcanoes, 26–27, 29, 487–88, 548, 575
Volga River, 324, 351
Volta River, 457
Von, Uong, 528
Vo Quy, 528

W

Wake Island, 557, 574
Wales, 290, 292
Walesa, Lech, 312
Wallace, Catherine, 577
Warsaw Pact, 334
Washington (D.C.), 115
Washington (state), 122, 134, 139, 140, 145
Watches, 521, 531
Water, 69, 121, 139, 391, 402–3, 505, 514, 525–26, 560, 570–71, 575, 578; climate and, 37; on earth's surface, 27, 30–31; as energy source, 53–54
Water buffalo, 390, 513, 517, 536
Waterclocks, 497
Waterfalls, 121, 122, 144
Waterpower, 144–46, 209, 254, 265, 299, 350, 457, 531, 571, 572
Waterways, 547
Weather, 34. *See also* Climate
Weathering, 29–30, 32
Wegener, Alfred, 27–28
Werikhe, Michael, 469
West Africa, 456–57
West Bank, 417
Western Europe, 52, 241, 265–67, 277–78, 285, 571–74

Western Hemisphere, 11
Western Samoa, 574, 579
West Germany, 68; reunification of, 303–5
West Indies, 107, 182, 199, 204
West Virginia, 121, 156
Wet seasons, 43
Whales, 101, 556
Wheat, 87, 132, 137–40, 151, 152, 157, 178, 205, 223, 272, 273, 277, 292, 299, 347, 348, 390, 391, 466, 518–19, 530, 537, 570, 571
Wind energy, 54
Winds, 491–92, 535, 549, 560
Winnipeg (Canada), 109
Wisconsin, 131, 137, 138
Women: in China, 542; in Russia, 342; in Saudi Arabia, 421; in sub-Sahara Africa, 444, 445, 449, 455, 469
Wood, 91, 97, 109, 121, 133, 155, 203, 442, 531
Wood blocks, 497
Wool, 293, 299, 347, 570–72
World Bank, 458
World Court, 162
World Health Organization (WHO), 525
World War I, 163, 291, 303, 334
World War II, 163, 234, 280, 291, 296, 303, 328, 461, 483, 501, 550, 557, 578–79
Writing, 379, 497
Wyoming, 121, 139, 156

X

Xinjiang (China), 541
Xi River, 487, 541
Xizang (China), 541

Y

Yams, 203, 449, 466, 475, 575
Yanbu, 421
Yangon (Myanmar), 506, 549
Yangzi River, 487, 496, 541
Yellow River, 487, 496, 541
Yeltsin, Boris, 336, 339–40, 356
Yenisei River, 324
Yerevan (Armenia), 360, 361
Yew trees, 236
Yokohama (Japan), 530
Yoruba, 474
Yucatán Peninsula (Mexico), 204
Yugoslavia, 241, 245, 260, 261, 287, 309, 310, 312, 334
Yukon Territory (Canada), 114
Yung Lo, 57
Yurts, 5

Z

Zagros Mountains, 374
Zaire, 456, 457, 462, 463, 467
Zaire (Congo) River, 432, 436, 491
Zambezi River, 432
Zambia, 429, 456, 457
Zero, 497
Zimbabwe, 441, 456, 457, 461, 463–64
Zinc, 87, 120, 144, 205, 571
Zionists, 416
Zoroastrians, 536

Photo Acknowledgments

INTRO UNIT

Page 2: © Leslie Wong/Leo de Wys. 3: (top) © J. Messersschmidt/Leo de Wys. 3:(bottom) FPG. 4: (top) © Jessie R. Blackburn/FPG; (bottom) © Martin Rodgers/ FPG. 5: © Jose Azel/Woodfin, Camp & Associates. 6: Exxon. 9,10:© Steve Vidler/ Leo de Wys. 12,13: FPG.

UNIT 1

18: Shostal Associates. 27, 34: John D. Cunningham. 31: (top) Wide World Photos, Inc., (bottom) ©Steve Vidler/ Leo de Wys. 32: © Lee Kuhn/ FPG. 36,45: United Nations. 38: © Gary Braasch/Woodfin, Camp & Associates. 40: J.Swietlik/Travel Arctic. 41: © J. Abraham/Leo de Wys. 44 (both): John D. Cunningham. 45: Ontario Ministry of Agriculture and Food. 46: Sask Travel. 51: © Steve Northup/Black Star. 52: © Stephen Smolar. 54: (top) Courtesy of Union Carbide (bottom) NASA.

UNIT 2

58-59: © Alon Reininger/Contact/Woodfin Camp. 60 (top): Courtesy Maryknoll Missioners. 60 (middle): John D. Cunningham. 60 (bottom): Courtesy Maryknoll Missioners. 61: Gerry Cranham/Photo Researchers. 62: Lester Sebel. 65: Pam Hasegawa/Taurus Photos. 66 (left): K. Collidge/Taurus Photos. 66 (right): United Nations. 68: Tadanori Saito/Photo Researchers. 73: Robert Manst. 74 (left): 1978 Bernard Pierre Wolff/Photo Researchers. 74 (right): V. Rastelli/Woodfin Camp. 75 (both): J. Brignolo/Texaco. 78: Gamma Liaison. 79: Lester Sebel. 80: United Nations.

UNIT 3

84-85: George Hunter/Shostal Associates. 86: Ontario Ministry of Tourism and Recreation. 87 (top): General Motors Canada. 87 (bottom): Sask Travel. 92 (both): American Airlines. 93. National Film Board of Canada. 96: Travel Arctic. 97: Wernher Krutein/ Liaison International...98: John D. Cunningham. 101: American Museum of Natural History. 102: American Airlines. 108: Laird/Leo de Wys. 109: Canadian Consulate General. 114: Ontario Ministry of Tourism and Recreation. 115: John D. Cunningham. 120, 122: Union Pacific Corporation. 126: Everett C. Johnson/ Leo de Wys. 127: Danilo Boschung/Leo de Wys. 131, 133, 137, 138, 139, 140: John D. Cunningham. 144: Rio Algom LImited. 145: New Brunswick Department of Tourism. 146: Courtesy of Alcan Aluminum. 147: Ontario Ministry of Tourism and Recreation. 150: Eric Kroll/Taurus Photos. 151: Sask Travel. 152: Government of Quebec Ministry of Agriculture. 156: © Theodore Vogel/Photo Researchers, 157: Ontario Ministry of Tourism and Recreation. 162: Arthur Mina. 163: Wide World:

UNIT 4

168-169: Four By Five. 170: Joseph Brignolo/Texaco. 171: Courtesy Maryknoll Missioners/Hunt. 175: S. Vidler/Leo de Wys. 176: Loren McIntyre/Woodfin Camp. 181: John D. Cunningham. 182: United Nations. 183: John D. Cunningham. 186: Arthur Laxer. 187: © Helen Cruickshank/Photo Researchers. 188: Coronet Instructional Media. 192: United Nations. 193: Joseph Brignolo/Texaco. 194: Courtesy Maryknoll Missioners/Wheater. 195: Commonwealth of Puerto Rico. 199: S. Vidler/Leo de Wys. 200 (both): Courtesy of Maryknoll Missioners/ Roa, Wheater. 201: Courtesy of Maryknoll Missioners/Wheater. 202: S. Vicler/Leo de Wys. 203: © 1977 Victor Englebert/Photo Researchers. 204: Courtesy Maryknoll Missioners/Roa. 205 (top): Joseph Brignolo/Texaco. 205 (bottom): John D. Cunningham. 208: Lavine/Leo de Wys. 209: Boutin/Leo de Wys. 210: © Dirck Halstead/Leo de Wys. 212: © 1973 Phil Lucas/Leo de Wys. 213 (top): N. Graham/Leo de Wys. 213 (bottom): © 1982 Claus Meyer/Black Star. 214: Van Phillips/Leo de Wys. 216: U.P.I. 217: Courtesy of Maryknoll Missioners/P.J. Casey. 218: U.P.I. 222: John D. Cunningham. 223: Courtesy of Maryknoll Missioners. 224: © Gianfranco Gorgoni/Leo de Wys. 227: © David Burnett/Leo de Wys. 228, 229: Commonwealth of Puerto Rico. 232: Messerschidt/Leo de Wys. 233: Joseph Brignolo/Texaco.

UNIT 5

238-239: The Photo Source. 241: John D. Cunningham. 244: H. Armstrong Roberts. 245: Swiss National Tourist Office. 246, 249: Lester Sebel. 250: S. Vidler/Leo de Wys. 253, 254, 255 (both): The Granger Collection. 259: Summer Productions/Taurus ©. 260: Inter Nationes. 261: The Swedish Institute. 265: Lester Sebel. 266: German Information Center. 267: United Nations. 271: Beryl Goldberg. 273: Lester Sebel. 274: H. Armstrong Roberts. 275: German Information Center/Bundesregierung,

510: Coronet Instructional Media. 513 (top): Trans World Airlines. 513 (bottom): Coronet Instructional Media. 514 (top): Brian Brake/Photo Researchers. 514 (bottom): Coronet Instructional Media. 515: United Nations. 516: Joseph F Viesti. 517 (both): Coronet Instructional Media. 518 (top): H. Armstrong Roberts. 518 (bottom): Standard Oil Company of New Jersey. 519: Sekai Bunka Photo. 520: S. Vidler/Leo de Wys. 521 (top): Coronet Instructional Media. 521 (bottom): Japan Tourist Association. 522 (top): Coronet Instructional Media. 522 (bottom), 523: United Nations. 525 (top): © 1971 Bernard Pierre Wolff/Photo Researchers. 525 (bottom): Coronet Instructional Media. 526 (both): United Nations. 528: Gamma Liaison/Richard Tomkins. 529 (top): © Paolo Koch/Photo Researchers. 529 (bottom), 530, 531: Sekai Bunka Photo. 535: Coronet Instructional Media. 536 (top): Bettmann. 536 (bottom): United Nations. 537: Government of India Tourist Office. 538: Air India. 541: U.P.I. 542: © 1980 Nik Wheeler/Black Star. 542 (bottom): U.P.I. 544: © 1972 Tom Davenport/Photo Researchers. 547: © Rick Smolan/Leo de Wys. 548: © 1975 Bernard Pierre Wolff/Photo Researchers. 549 (both): © Paolo Koch/Photo Researchers.

UNIT 10

554-555: The Photo Source. 556: Coronet Instruc- tional Media. 557, 560, 561: Australian News and Information Bureau. 565: Click. 566 (top): © 1980 Thomas Hopker/Woodfin Camp. 566 (bottom): Australian News and Information Bureau. 569: Robin Smith/Shostal Associates. 570: Photo Researchers. 571: Shostal Associates. 572: © 1978 Earl Dibble/Photo Researchers. 574 (top): © Thomas Nebbia/Woodfin Camp. 574 (bottom): David Moore/Black Star. 575 (left): United Nations. 575 (right): Coronet Instructional Media. 578: Jack Fields/Photo Researchers. 579 (left): United Nations. 579 (right): Jack Fields/Photo Researchers. 581: Index Stock.

Unit Openers

Intro Unit: © Gary Faber/ Image Bank
Unit 1: Photo Researchers
Unit 2: © Steve Vidler/ Leo de Wys
Unit 3: © David R. Frazier/ Photo Researchers
Unit 4: © M. Bertinetti/ Photo Researchers
Unit 5: © Wide World Photos, Inc.
Unit 6: Novosti/Sovfoto
Unit 7: © William Strode/ Gamma Liaison
Unit 8: © Robert Caputo/ Stock Boston
Unit 9: Westlight
Unit 10: © Douglas Peebles/Westlight